TRAGEDIES
& POEMS

WILLIAM SHAKESPEARE

———o———

Edited by

PETER ALEXANDER

*Regius Professor of English Language
and Literature, University of Glasgow.
With an Introduction, a Preface to each
play, a Glossary and an Index of
Characters in the plays.*

COLLINS
LONDON AND GLASGOW

GENERAL EDITOR: G. F. MAINE

THE COMPLETE WORKS OF SHAKESPEARE are available in
Collins Classics in four volumes: VOL I. *Comedies*, VOL. II
Histories, VOL. III *Tragedies*, VOL. IV *Tragedies and Poems*.
The text is that of the *Tudor Shakespeare*, edited by Professor
Peter Alexander

This edition first published 1958
Latest reprint 1975

CONTENTS

THE FOLIO TEXTS

THOSE who wish to see Shakespeare and his works in their historical setting will not neglect the evidence provided by the references his contemporaries make to the man and his plays. Among these references the Preliminary matter to the First Folio edition of the plays, given to the public by his colleagues in 1623, must be regarded as specially important. These references stand in a context that must be allowed for: the men who wrote the dedication to the Earls of Pembroke and Montgomery and the address "To the great Variety of Readers" were actors who had long been associated with the dramatist; Ben Jonson and the scholars who contributed the lines in praise of Shakespeare's genius were naturally admirers and students of his work. We are, therefore, hearing what may be regarded as a partial judgment. There is however a tone in their pronouncements that speaks for their sincerity; and the close connection of some of the contributors with the man himself, as well as the literary and scholarly standing of others, entitles them to a careful and candid hearing.

The dedication "To the most noble and incomparable paire of brethren" is written in a style no longer fashionable, but when Heminge and Condell refer to their dead friend they do so in terms that there is still no excuse of misunderstanding; they have collected his plays they tell us,

> without ambition either of selfe-profit, or fame: onely to keepe the memory of so worthy a Friend, & Fellow alive, as was our *Shakespeare*.

Heminge and Condell had worked with Shakespeare for some twenty or so years; they were actors but also managers of the company's business, and they must have been as intimate with the dramatist as they were with the productions they had taken part in and helped to put on the stage. Shakespeare's popularity with London playgoers had contributed largely to the success of the company and the happy financial position of the individual sharers. Heminge and Condell had reason to remember with gratitude this part of Shakespeare's contribution to their association; that their feeling towards him went far beyond such considerations is, however, attested by Ben Jonson himself. In his *Discoveries* Ben Jonson, in a passage to be quoted later, tells us he honoured Shakespeare's memory "on this side idolatry as much as any"; the context makes it clear that the idolators were Shakespeare's friends, the actors. Of the wholehearted admiration these friends felt for the man and his genius there can be no question.

In their address "To the great Variety of Readers" Heminge and Condell mention a feature of Shakespeare's technique in the very terms that provoked Jonson's observation; for they say of the author,

> Who, as he was a happie imitator of Nature, was a most gentle expresser of it. His mind and hand went together: And what he thought, he uttered with that easinesse, that wee have scarce received from him a blot in his papers.

7

Jonson expressed his disapproval of this item in the actors' praise when he wrote :

> I remember the players have often mentioned it as an honour to Shakespeare, that in his writing (whatsoever he penned) he never blotted out a line. My answer hath been, " Would he had blotted a thousand " which they thought a malevolent speech. I had not told posterity this but for their ignorance who chose that circumstance to commend their friend by wherein he most faulted ; and to justify mine own candour, for I loved the man, and do honour his memory on this side idolatry as much as any. He was, indeed, honest, and of an open and free nature ; had an excellent phantasy, brave notions, and gentle expressions, wherein he flowed with that facility that sometimes it was necessary he should be stopped.

Some critics have suggested that it was Ben Jonson who wrote the dedication and the address to the readers on behalf of the actors, actually inserting in the address, to please the actors, the praise of Shakespeare's facility that he so much disapproved of. Such a suggestion seems out of keeping with Jonson's temper and not to be squared with his own comment on the actors' words.

How exactly we are to interpret the statement about Shakespeare's " easiness " in composition may be a matter of some difficulty ; as is the precise meaning we are to take from the words of Heminge and Condell about the authority of their publication and its relation to the previous versions of a number of the plays in quarto. What recent investigation of the latter problem makes clear is that they spoke in perfect good faith, though without the scholarly knowledge of the difficulties that stood between them and the perfect realisation of their good intentions. However, therefore, we may understand their account of Shakespeare's readiness in composition, we must regard it as the testimony of those who must have seen Shakespeare at work, though not necessarily in the hours when he was withdrawn not merely from the world but even from his immediate associates.

Ben Jonson made his contribution to the First Folio with the lines " To the memory of my beloved, The Author, Mr. William Shakespeare : and what he hath left us." It might be said that there is a contradiction between the lines in this famous poem where Ben Jonson says,

> Yet must I not give Nature all : Thy Art,
>> My gentle *Shakespeare*, must enjoy a part.
> For though the *Poets* matter, Nature be,
>> His Art doth give the fashion. And, that he,
> Who casts to write a living line, must sweat,
>> (such as thine are) and strike the second heat
> Upon the *Muses* anvile : turne the same,
>> (And himselfe with it) that he thinkes to frame ;
> Or for the lawrell, he may gaine a scorne,
>> For a good *Poet's* made, as well as borne.
> And such wert thou.

and his remark, as recorded by Drummond of Hawthornden, " That Shakespeare wanted Arte ". To suppose, however, that Jonson was saying in the intimacy of conversation what the demands of convention prevented his observing in public, is to misunderstand the senses in which the Elizabethans understood the meaning of " Art ". The Artist was often thought of as a learned man, and this learning was associated by Jonson himself, at times, with a knowledge and imitation of classical authors and their conventions. That Shakespeare, unlike Jonson, was not sedulous in this form of imitation Jonson did not fail to notice in his printed pages ; he was however too great a critic not to recognise the limitations of such a definition of Art, and in the creative hour in which he celebrated his friend's genius he saw the meaning of Art in a truer light, and in the same lines qualified the notion that Shakespeare was a ready improviser by reminding us of the profound meditation and sustained labour that such works as Shakespeare had written must have demanded.

To Ben Jonson's poem the editors added contributions from the Universities of Oxford and Cambridge. Leonard Digges, who contributed the verses " To the memory of the deceased Author, Maister W. Shakespeare ", was an Oxford scholar ; he was the stepson of Thomas Russell whom Shakespeare made the overseer of his will. Leonard Digges and his elder brother Sir Dudley Digges must have known Shakespeare, as Dr. Hotson has shown, on familiar terms. Digges was a friend of James Mabbe, a fellow of Magdalen College, who contributed the lines that follow those by Digges and stand over the initials I. M. The Cambridge contribution came from Hugh Holland, a fellow of Trinity College.

The Preliminary matter to the First Folio is therefore a set of contributions of the first importance as historical and critical documents ; like most documents they must be interpreted in their context and with the tact that such evidence, if it is to be properly understood, calls for. No one who wishes to erect his own idea of Shakespeare on a sound and trustworthy basis can afford to neglect them.

To their text the editors prefixed the preliminary matter here reproduced. Opposite the engraved portrait of Shakespeare which stood as frontispiece—now known as the Droeshout engraving after the name of the engraver—they placed Ben Jonson's lines *To the Reader*. Then follow their dedicatory epistle, the address " To the great Variety of Readers ", and the tributes from Ben Jonson and other.

Their " Catalogue " does not mention *Troilus and Cressida*, for they were able to include this play, in a kind of no man's land, between the Histories and the Tragedies, only at the last moment and after the settlement of a dispute with the publishers who had issued the Quarto version in 1609. Heminge and Condell originally intended to place *Troilus and Cressida* among the Tragedies immediately after *Romeo and Juliet*.

THE FIRST FOLIO

TO THE READER

This Figure, that thou here seest put,
　　It was for gentle Shakespeare cut;
Wherein the Grauer had a strife
　　with Nature, to out-doo the life:
O, could he but haue drawne his wit
　　As well in brasse, as he hath hit
His face; the Print would then surpasse
　　All, that vvas euer vvrit in brasse.
But, since he cannot, Reader, looke
　　Not on his Picture, but his Booke.

B. I.

TO THE MOST NOBLE AND INCOMPARABLE PAIRE OF BRETHREN WILLIAM, EARLE OF PEMBROKE, &C., LORD CHAMBERLAINE TO THE KINGS MOST EXCELLENT MAIESTY, AND PHILIP, EARLE OF MONTGOMERY, &C., GENTLEMAN OF HIS MAIESTIES BED-CHAMBER; BOTH KNIGHTS OF THE MOST NOBLE ORDER OF THE GARTER, AND OUR SINGULAR GOOD LORDS.

Right Honourable,

WHILST we studie to be thankful in our particular, for the many fauors we haue receiued from your L.L. we are falne vpon the ill fortune, to mingle two the most diuerse things than can bee, feare, and rashnesse; rashnesse in the enterprize, and feare of the successe. For, when we valew the places your H.H. sustaine, we cannot but know their dignity greater, then to descend to the reading of these trifles: and, while we name them trifles, we haue depriu'd our selues of the defence of our Dedication. But since your L.L. haue beene pleas'd to thinke these trifles some-thing, heeretofore; and haue prosequuted both them, and their Author liuing, with so much fauour: we hope, that (they out-liuing him, and he not hauing the fate, common with some, to be exequutor to his owne writings) you will vse the like indulgence toward them, you haue done vnto their parent. There is a great difference, whether any Booke choose his Patrones, or finde them: This hath done both. For, so much were your L.L. likings of the seuerall parts, when they were acted, as before they were published, the Volume ask'd to be yours. We haue but collected them, and done an office to the dead, to procure his Orphanes, Guardians; without ambition either of selfe-profit, or fame: onely to keepe the memory of so worthy a Friend, & Fellow aliue, as was our *Shakespeare*, by humble offer of his playes, to your most noble patronage. Wherein, as we haue justly obserued, no man to come neere your L.L. but with a kind of religious addresse; it hath bin the height of our care, who are the Presenters, to make the present worthy of your H.H. by the perfection. But, there we must also craue our abilities to be considerd, my Lords. We cannot go beyond our owne powers. Country hands reach foorth milke, creame, fruites, or what they haue: and many Nations (we haue heard) that had not gummes & incense, obtained their requests with a leauened Cake. It was no fault to approch their Gods, by what meanes they could: And the most, though meanest, of things are made more precious, when they are dedicated to Temples. In that name therefore, we most humbly consecrate to your H.H. these remaines of your seruant *Shakespeare;* that what delight is in them, may be euer your L.L. the reputation his, & the faults ours, if any be committed, by a payre so carefull to shew their gratitude both to the liuing, and the dead, as is

Your Lordshippes most bounden,

IOHN HEMINGE.
HENRY CONDELL.

TO
THE GREAT VARIETY
OF READERS

FROM the most able, to him that can but spell : There you are
number'd. We had rather you were weighd. Especially, when
the fate of all Bookes depends vpon your capacities : and not of your
heads alone, but of your purses. Well ! it is now publique, & you wil
stand for your priuiledges wee know : to read, and censure. Do so,
but buy it first. That doth best commend a Booke, the Stationer saies.
Then, how odde soeuer your braines be, or your wisedomes, make
your licence the same, and spare not. Iudge your sixe-pen'orth, your
shillings worth, your fiue shillings worth at a time, or higher, so you
rise to the iust rates, and welcome. But, what euer you do, Buy.
Censure will not driue a Trade, or make the Iacke go. And though
you be a Magistrate of wit, and sit on the Stage at *Black-Friers*, or the
Cock-pit, to arraigne Playes dailie, know, these Playes haue had their
triall alreadie, and stood out all Appeales ; and do now come forth
quitted rather by a Decree of Court, then any purchas'd Letters of
commendation.

It had bene a thing, we confesse, worthie to haue bene wished, that
the Author himselfe had liu'd to haue set forth, and ouerseen his owne
writings ; But since it hath bin ordain'd otherwise, and he by death
departed from that right, we pray you do not envie his Friends, the
office of their care, and paine, to haue collected & publish'd them ; and
so to haue publish'd them, as where (before) you were abus'd with
diuerse stolne, and surreptitious copies, maimed, and deformed by the
frauds and stealthes of iniurious imposters, that expos'd them : euen
those, are now offer'd to your view cur'd, and perfect of their limbes ;
and all the rest, absolute in their numbers, as he conceiued them.
Who, as he was a happie imitator of Nature, was a most gentle ex-
presser of it. His mind and hand went together : And what he
thought, he vttered with that easinesse, that wee haue scarse receiued
from him a blot in his papers. But it is not our prouince, who onely
gather his works, and giue them you, to praise him. It is yours that
reade him. And here we hope, to your diuers capacities, you will finde
enough, both to draw, and hold you : for his wit can no more lie hid,
then it could be lost. Reade him, therefore ; and againe, and againe :
And if then you doe not like him, surely you are in some manifest
danger, not to vnderstand him. And so we leaue you to other of his
Friends, whom if you need, can bee your guides : if you neede them
not, you can leade your selues, and others. And such Readers we
wish him.

IOHN HEMINGE.
HENRIE CONDELL.

TO THE MEMORY OF MY BELOUED, THE AVTHOR

MR. WILLIAM SHAKESPEARE:

AND WHAT HE HATH LEFT VS.

To draw no enuy (*Shakespeare*) on thy name,
  Am I thus ample to thy Booke, and Fame :
While I confesse thy writings to be such,
  As neither *Man*, nor *Muse*, can praise too much.
'Tis true, and all mens suffrage. But these wayes
  Were not the paths I meant vnto thy praise :
For seeliest Ignorance on these may light,
  Which, when it sounds at best, but eccho's right ;
Or blinde Affection, which doth ne're aduance
  The truth, but gropes, and vrgeth all by chance ;
Or crafty Malice, might pretend this praise,
  And thinke to ruine, where it seem'd to raise.
These are, as some infamous Baud, or Whore,
  Should praise a Matron. What could hurt her more ?
But thou art proofe against them, and indeed
  Aboue th' ill fortune of them, or the need.
I, therefore will begin. Soule of the Age !
  The applause ! delight ! the wonder of our Stage !
My *Shakespeare*, rise ; I will not lodge thee by
  Chaucer, or *Spenser*, or bid *Beaumont* lye
A little further, to make thee a roome :
  Thou art a Moniment, without a tombe,
And art aliue still, while thy Booke doth liue,
  And we haue wits to read, and praise to giue.
That I not mixe thee so, my braine excuses ;
  I meane with great, but disproportion'd *Muses* :
For, if I thought my judgement were of yeeres,
  I should commit thee surely with thy peeres,
And tell, how farre thou didst our *Lily* out-shine,
  Or sporting *Kid*, or *Marlowes* mighty line.
And though thou hadst small *Latine*, and lesse *Greeke*,
  From thence to honour thee, I would not seeke
For names ; but call forth thund'ring *Æschilus*,
  Euripides, and *Sophocles* to vs,
Paccuuius, *Accius*, him of *Cordoua* dead,
  To life againe, to heare thy Buskin tread,
And shake a Stage : Or, when thy Sockes were on,
  Leaue thee alone, for the comparison
Of all, that insolent *Greece*, or haughtie *Rome*
  sent forth, or since did from their ashes come.
Triumph, my *Britaine*, thou hast one to showe,
  To whom all Scenes of *Europe* homage owe.
He was not of an age, but for all time !
  And all the *Muses* still were in their prime,
When like *Apollo* he came forth to warme
  Our eares, or like a *Mercury* to charme !

Nature her selfe was proud of his designes,
  And ioy'd to weare the dressing of his lines !
Which were so richly spun, and wouen so fit,
  As, since, she will vouchsafe no other Wit.
The merry *Greeke*, tart *Aristophanes*,
  Neat *Terence*, witty *Plautus*, now not please ;
But antiquated, and deserted lye
  As they were not of Natures family.
Yet must I not giue Nature all : Thy Art,
  My gentle *Shakespeare*, must enioy a part.
For though the *Poets* matter, Nature be,
  His Art doth giue the fashion.   And, that he,
Who casts to write a liuing line, must sweat,
  (such as thine are) and strike the second heat
Vpon the *Muses* anuile : turne the same,
  (And himselfe with it) that he thinkes to frame ;
Or for the lawrell, he may gaine a scorne,
  For a good *Poet's* made, as well as borne.
And such wert thou.   Looke how the fathers face
  Liues in his issue, euen so, the race
Of *Shakespeares* minde, and manners brightly shines
  In his well torned, and true-filed lines :
In each of which, he seemes to shake a Lance,
  As brandish't at the eyes of Ignorance.
Sweet Swan of *Auon* ! what a sight it were
  To see thee in our waters yet appeare,
And make those flights vpon the bankes of *Thames*,
  That so did take *Eliza*, and our *Iames* !
But stay, I see thee in the *Hemisphere*
  Aduanc'd, and made a Constellation there !
Shine forth, thou Starre of *Poets*, and with rage,
  Or influence, chide, or cheere the drooping Stage ;
Which, since thy flight from hence, hath mourn'd like night,
  And despaires day, but for thy Volumes light.

BEN : IONSON.

VPON THE LINES AND LIFE

OF THE FAMOUS SCENICKE POET,

MASTER WILLIAM SHAKESPEARE

Those hands, which you so clapt, go now, and wring
You *Britaines* braue ; for done are *Shakespeares* dayes :
His dayes are done, that made the dainty Playes,
Which made the Globe of heau'n and earth to ring.
Dry'de is that veine, dry'd is the *Thespian* Spring,
Turn'd all to teares, and *Phœbus* clouds his rayes :
That corp's, that coffin now besticke those bayes,
Which crown'd him *Poet* first, then *Poets* King.
If *Tragedies* might any *Prologue* haue,
All those he made, would scarse make one to this :
Where *Fame*, now that he gone is to the graue
(Deaths publique tyring-house) the *Nuncius* is.
For though his line of life went soone about,
The life yet of his lines shall neuer out.

HVGH HOLLAND.

TO THE MEMORIE OF THE DECEASED AUTHOUR

MAISTER W. SHAKESPEARE.

SHAKE-SPEARE, at length thy pious fellowes giue
The world thy Workes : thy Workes, by which, out-liue
Thy Tombe, thy name must : when that stone is rent,
And Time dissolues thy *Stratford* Moniment,
Here we aliue shall view thee still.   This Booke,
When Brasse and Marble fade, shall make thee looke
Fresh to all Ages : when Posteritie
Shall loath what's new, thinke all is prodegie
That is not *Shake-speares* ; eu'ry Line, each Verse
Here shall reuiue, redeeme thee from thy Herse.
Nor Fire, nor cankring Age, as *Naso* said,
Of his, thy wit-fraught Booke shall once inuade.
Nor shall I e're beleeue, or thinke thee dead
(Though mist) vntill our bankrout Stage be sped
(Impossible) with some new straine t' out-do
Passions of *Iuliet*, and her *Romeo* ;
Or till I heare a Scene more nobly take,
Then when thy half-Sword parlying *Romans* spake.
Till these, till any of thy Volumes rest
Shall with more fire, more feeling be exprest,
Be sure, our *Shake-speare*, thou canst neuer dye,
But crown'd with Lawrell, liue eternally.

L. DIGGES.

TO THE MEMORIE OF

M. W. *SHAKE-SPEARE*

WEE wondred (*Shake-speare*) that thou went'st so soone
From the Worlds-Stage, to the Graues-Tyring-roome.
Wee thought thee dead, but this thy printed worth,
Tels thy Spectators, that thou went'st but forth
To enter with applause. An Actors Art,
Can dye, and liue, to acte a second part.
That's but an *Exit* of Mortalitie ;
This, a Re-entrance to a Plaudite.

I. M.

THE WORKES OF WILLIAM SHAKESPEARE,
CONTAINING ALL HIS COMEDIES, HISTORIES, AND TRAGEDIES:
TRUELY SET FORTH, ACCORDING TO THEIR FIRST ORIGINALL.

THE NAMES OF THE PRINCIPALL ACTORS IN ALL THESE PLAYES.

William Shakespeare.	Samuel Gilburne.
Richard Burbadge.	Robert Armin.
John Hemmings.	William Ostler.
Augustine Phillips.	Nathan Field.
William Kempt.	John Underwood.
Thomas Poope.	Nicholas Tooley.
George Bryan.	William Ecclestone.
Henry Condell.	Joseph Taylor.
William Slye.	Robert Benfield.
Richard Cowly.	Robert Goughe.
John Lowine.	Richard Robinson.
Samuell Crosse.	Iohn Shancke.
Alexander Cooke.	Iohn Rice.

THE FIRST FOLIO

A CATALOGVE

OF THE SEUERALL COMEDIES, HISTORIES, AND
TRAGEDIES CONTAINED IN THIS VOLUME.

COMEDIES.

The Tempest	*Folio* 1
The two Gentlemen of Verona	20
The Merry Wiues of Windsor	38
Measure for Measure	61
The Comedy of Errours	85
Much adoo about Nothing	101
Loues Labour lost	122
Midsommer Nights Dreame	145
The Merchant of Venice	163
As you Like it	185
The Taming of the Shrew	208
All is well, that Ends well	230
Twelfe-Night, or what you will	255
The Winters Tale	304

HISTORIES.

The Life and Death of King John	*Fol.* 1
The Life & death of Richard the second	23
The First part of King Henry the fourth	46
The Second part of K. Henry the fourth	74
The Life of King Henry the Fift	69
The First part of King Henry the Sixt	96
The Second part of King Hen. the Sixt	120
The Third part of King Henry the Sixt	147
The Life & Death of Richard the Third	173
The Life of King Henry the Eight	205

TRAGEDIES.

The Tragedy of Coriolanus	*Fol.* 1
Titus Andronicus	31
Romeo and Juliet	53
Timon of Athens	80
The Life and death of Julius Cæsar	109
The Tragedy of Macbeth	131
The Tragedy of Hamlet	152
King Lear	283
Othello, the Moore of Venice	310
Anthony and Cleopater	346
Cymbeline King of Britaine	369

17

THE SECOND FOLIO

In 1632 a second edition of the plays was called for. In this, the Second Folio, new tributes were included. The most important is by Milton, and is the first of his poems to be set out in print.

AN EPITAPH ON THE ADMIRABLE DRAMATICKE POET,

W. SHAKESPEARE.

What neede my *Shakespeare* for his honour'd Bones,
The labour of an Age, in piled stones
Or that his hallow'd Reliques should be hid
Under a starre-ypointing Pyramid ?
Dear Sonne of Memory, great Heire of *Fame*,
What needst thou such dull witnesse of thy Name ?
Thou in our wonder and astonishment
Hast built thy selfe a lasting Monument :
For whil'st to th' shame of slow-endevouring Art
Thy easie numbers flow, and that each part,
Hath from the leaves of thy unvalued Booke,
Those Delphicke Lines with deepe Impression tooke
Then thou our fancy of her selfe bereaving,
Dost make us Marble with too much conceiving,
And so Sepulcher'd in such pompe dost lie
That Kings for such a Tombe would wish to die.

This is how the lines appeared in the first issue of the Second Folio, and they should be compared with the version headed " On *Shakespeare*. 1630." in the 1645 edition of Milton's poems.

Almost as remarkable are the lines, also added to the Second Folio over the initials I. M. S.

ON WORTHY MASTER SHAKESPEARE
AND HIS POEMS

A Mind reflecting ages past, whose cleere
And equall surface can make things appeare
Distant a Thousand yeares, and represent
Them in their lively colours just extent.
To outrun hasty time, retrive the fates,
Rowle backe the heavens, blow ope the iron gates

Of death and Lethe, where (confused) lye
Great heapes of ruinous mortalitie.
In that deepe duskie dungeon to discerne
A royall Ghost from Churles ; By art to learne
The Physiognomie of shades, and give
Them suddaine birth, wondring how oft they live.
What story coldly tells, what Poets faine
At second hand, and picture without braine
Senselesse and soullesse showes. To give a Stage
(Ample and true with life) voyce, action, age,
As Plato's yeare and new Scene of the world
Them unto us, or us to them had hurld.
To raise our auncient Soveraignes from their herse
Make Kings his subjects, by exchanging verse
Enlive their pale trunkes, that the present age
Joyes in their joy, and trembles at their rage :
Yet so to temper passion, that our eares
Take pleasure in their paine ; And eyes in teares
Both weepe and smile ; fearefull at plots so sad,
Then, laughing at our feare ; abus'd, and glad
To be abus'd, affected with that truth
Which we perceive is false ; pleas'd in that ruth
At which we start ; and by elaborate play
Tortur'd and tickled ; by a crablike way
Time past made pastime, and in ugly sort
Disgorging up his ravaine for our sport—
——While the *Plebeian* Impe, from lofty throne,
Creates and rules a world, and workes upon
Mankind by secret engines ; Now to move
A chilling pitty, then a rigorous love :
To strike up and stroake down, both joy and ire ;
To steere th' affections ; and by heavenly fire
Mould us anew. Stolne from ourselves——
    This, and much more which cannot be exprest,
But by himselfe, his tongue and his owne brest,
Was *Shakespeares* freehold, which his cunning braine
Improv'd by favour of the ninefold traine.
The buskind Muse, the Commicke Queene, the graund
And lowder tone of Clio ; nimble hand,
And nimbler foote of the melodious paire,
The Silver voyced Lady ; the most faire
Calliope, whose speaking silence daunts.
And she whose prayse the heavenly body chants.
    These joyntly woo'd him, envying one another

(Obey'd by all as Spouse, but lov'd as brother)
And wrought a curious robe of sable grave
Fresh greene, and pleasant yellow, red most brave,
And constant blew, rich purple, guiltlesse white
The lowly Russet, and the Scarlet bright ;
Branch'd and embroydred like the painted Spring
Each leafe match'd with a flower, and each string
Of golden wire, each line of silke ; there run
Italian workes whose thred the Sisters spun ;
And there did sing, or seeme to sing, the choyce
Birdes of a forraine note and various voyce.
Here hangs a mossey rocke ; there playes a faire
But chiding fountaine purled : Not the ayre,
Nor cloudes nor thunder, but were living drawne,
Not out of common Tiffany or Lawne.
But fine materialls, which the Muses know
And onely know the countries where they grow.
  Now, when they could no longer him enjoy
In mortall garments pent ; death may destroy
They say his body, but his verse shall live
And more then nature takes, our hands shall give.
In a lesse volumne, but more strongly bound
Shakespeare shall breath and speake, with Laurell crown'd
Which never fades.   Fed with Ambrosian meate
In a well-lyned vesture rich and neate.
  So with this robe they cloath him, bid him weare it
For time shall never staine, nor envy teare it.

The friendly admirer of his
Endowments.

I. M. S.

Who I. M. S. may be is still a mystery ; but the tribute is a remarkable one, and a most important document in the history of Shakespearean criticism.

To complete the historical picture presented to us by the contributors to the First Folio, it is necessary to reproduce the following lines which were designed for a place in that publication, but rejected for reasons which we can still well understand.   They first appeared in a volume of 1640 which included among other items Shakespeare's sonnets rearranged and under somewhat fanciful headings.   The lines that follow are by Leonard Digges.

UPON MASTER WILLIAM SHAKESPEARE, THE DECEASED AUTHOUR, AND HIS POEMS.

Poets are borne not made, when I would prove
This truth, the glad rememberance I must love
Of never dying Shakespeare, who alone,
Is argument enough to make that one.
First, that he was a Poet none would doubt,
That heard th' applause of what he sees set out
Imprinted ; where thou hast (I will not say
Reader his Workes for to contrive a Play
To him twas none) the patterne of all wit,
Art without Art unparaleld as yet.
Next Nature onely helpt him, for looke thorow
This whole Booke, thou shalt find he doth not borrow,
One phrase from Greekes, nor Latines imitate,
Nor once from vulgar Languages Translate,
Nor Plagiari-like from others gleane,
Nor begges he from each witty friend a Scene
To peece his Acts with, all that he doth write,
Is pure his owne, plot, language exquisite,
But oh ! what praise more powerfull can we give
The dead, then that by him the Kings men live,
His Players, which should they but have shar'd the Fate,
All else expir'd within the short Termes date ;
How could the Globe have prospered, since through want
Of change, the Plaies and Poems had growne scant.
But happy Verse thou shalt be sung and heard,
When hungry quills shall be such honour bard.
Then vanish upstart Writers to each Stage,
You needy Poetasters of this Age,
Where *Shakespeare* liv'd or spake, Vermine forbeare,
Least with your froth you spot them, come not neere ;
But if you needs must write, if poverty
So pinch, that otherwise you starve and die
On Gods name may the Bull or Cockpit have
Your lame blancke Verse, to keepe you from the grave :
Or let new Fortunes younger brethren see,
What they can picke from your leane industry.
I doe not wonder when you offer at
Blacke-Friers, that you suffer : tis the fate
Of richer veines, prime judgements that have far'd
The worse, with this deceased man compar'd.
So have I seene, when Cesar would appeare,
And on the Stage at halfe-sword parley were,

21

Brutus and *Cassius* : oh how the Audience
Were ravish'd, with what wonder they went thence,
When some new day they would not brooke a line,
Of tedious (though well laboured) *Catiline* ;
Sejanus too was irkesome, they priz'de more
Honest *Iago*, or the jealous *Moore*.
And though the Fox and subtill *Alchimist*,
Long intermitted could not quite be mist,
Though these have sham'd all the Ancients, and might raise,
Their Authours merit with a crowne of Bayes.
Yet these sometimes, even at a friends desire
Acted, have scarce defrai'd the Seacoale fire
And doore-keepers : when let but *Falstaffe* come,
Hall, *Poines*, the rest you scarce shall have a roome
All is so pester'd : let but *Beatrice*
And *Benedicke* be seene, loe in a trice
The Cockpit Galleries, Boxes, all are full
To hear *Malvoglio*, that crosse garter'd Gull.
Briefe, there is nothing in his wit fraught Booke,
Whose sound we would not heare, on whose worth looke
Like old coynd gold, whose lines in every page,
Shall passe true currant to succeeding age.
But why doe I dead *Shakespeares* praise recite,
Some second *Shakespeare* must of *Shakespeare* write ;
For me tis needlesse, since an host of men,
Will pay to clap his praise, to free my Pen.

Digges must have penned these lines for the First Folio. They
contain however a comparison between the full houses that greeted
Shakespeare's plays and the smaller audiences drawn by Ben Jonson's.
As Ben Jonson was to be the main contributor to the prefatory matter
to the First Folio, Heminge and Condell would have to point out to
Digges the impropriety of including any such comparison in their
volume ; he doubtless agreed, and substituted the shorter set of
verses that now stands with Ben Jonson's . A happy chance, however,
has preserved the original version for us ; and affords us a glimpse of
the enthusiastic reception accorded some of Shakespeare's pieces,
and the impression the dramatist made not only on the general public
that frequented the theatre but on a scholarly member of Shakespeare's
audience.

It is impossible to discuss such questions as Shakespeare's personal
relations with his company, the publication of his plays, and the
attitude of contemporary audiences to his productions, without a
careful consideration of the Preliminaries to the First Folio.

PETER ALEXANDER

KING LEAR

SHAKESPEARE read the story of Lear and his daughters in several versions, among them that given by Spenser in Canto X of the Second Book of the *Faerie Queene*. There Guyon, having reached the house of Temperance where sober Alma dwells, and found in her library books dealing with the history of Britain, learns of the British rulers beginning with Brutus, the descendant of Aeneas, who first brought civilization to these parts, and ending with Gloriana the Faerie Queene herself. King Lear is the eleventh in this line. Of him Spenser says,

> Next him King Leyr in happie peace long raynd,
> But had no issue male him to succeed,
> But three faire daughters, which were well uptraind
> In all that seemed fitt for kingly seed :
> Mongst whom his realme he equally decreed
> To have divided. Tho, when feeble age
> Nigh to his utmost date he saw proceed,
> He cald his daughters, and with speeches sage
> Inquyrd, which of them most did love her parentage ?

Cordelia fails to pass the test ; the kingdom is parted between Gonorill and Regan ;

> But without dowre the wise Cordelia
> Was sent to Aggannip of Celtica.

The thankless daughters at last cast off their father who betakes himself to Cordelia. She raises an army and restores her father to the throne ; after his death she reigns long and honoured,

> Till that her sisters children, woxen strong,
> Through proud ambition against her rebeld,
> And overcommen kept in prison long,
> Till weary of that wretched life her selfe she hong.

Spenser's story with its unhappy ending is substantially that first told by Geoffrey of Monmouth about 1135 in his *Historia regum Britanniae*. This History of the Kings of Britain put Britain on a level with those countries that prided themselves on their Trojan ancestry ; and, though there were even among Geoffrey's contemporaries those who felt sceptical about his story, its success was overwhelming and critical comment was drowned in popular approval. Many versions of the story and of Lear's part in it lay between Geoffrey and Shakespeare, of which it will be sufficient to name in addition to Spenser's, the account in the *Mirror for Magistrates*, and in Holinshed's *Chronicles*, all known to Shakespeare. In these, as in Geoffrey of Monmouth, the story ends with Cordelia's suicide. Shakespeare's tragic ending is not, therefore, as some have supposed, the dramatist's device to give expression to his own despair and disillusionment, but only his own treatment of the original story; the misunderstanding of Shakespeare's treatment being due to the commentators' acquaintance with another play from the same source.

The old play, as it is generally called, entitled *The True Chronicle History of King Leir and his three daughters, Gonorill, Regan, and Cordella* was printed in 1605. Henslowe's Diary records a performance of a play called *Kinge Leare* as early as 6 April 1594. Against 14 May 1594 an entry stands in the Stationers' Register for a play of *Leire Kinge of England and his Three Daughters*, but no copy is known; and the later entry of 8 May 1605, which preceded the 1605 publication, is assumed to refer to the same work. This *King Leir* of 1605 and earlier omits the tragic conclusion completely and ends with the restoration of Leir by his daughter Cordella. The old play is one of the very few versions of Geoffrey's story that ends on this happy note; as Shakespeare was familiar with the story in its most widely known form he cannot be said to have added the tragic conclusion, for although he knew the old play he treats the source material in an entirely different key from that of *King Leir;* Shakespeare's conclusion is a development of his own conception of the familiar and unhappy tale.

To emphasize his reading of the story Shakespeare incorporated in his plot an episode from Sidney's *Arcadia*. Here too a father, the King of Paphlagonia, deceived by the son of a concubine, gives orders for the destruction of his legitimate son and heir. Leonatus the son escapes and after various wanderings returns to succour his father, by now blinded and driven out by the same villain who had plotted the death of the rightful heir. The dutiful and compassionate son with the help of friends regains the kingdom;

In which season the blind king (having in the chief cittie of his Realme, set the crowne upon his sonne *Leonatus* head) with many tears (both of joy and sorrow) setting forth to the whole people, his owne fault and his sonnes virtue, after he had kist him, and forst his sonne to accept honour of him (as of his newe-become subject) even in a moment died, as it should seeme: his hart broken with unkindnesse and affliction, stretched so far beyond his limits with this excesse of comfort, as it was able no longer to keep safe his roial spirits.

This is the note on which Shakespeare concludes the story of his own Lear and of Gloster; and he added the sub-plot to secure its proper amplification.

King Lear was performed at court on 26 December 1606; in the text are found the names of evil spirits taken from Samuel Harsnett's *Declaration of Egregious Popishe Impostures* published in 1603. These dates give the limits within which Shakespeare wrote the play as we now have it.

KING LEAR

DRAMATIS PERSONÆ

LEAR, *King of Britain.*
KING OF FRANCE.
DUKE OF BURGUNDY.
DUKE OF CORNWALL.
DUKE OF ALBANY.
EARL OF KENT.
EARL OF GLOUCESTER.
EDGAR, *son to Gloucester.*
EDMUND, *bastard son to Gloucester.*
CURAN, *a courtier.*
OLD MAN, *tenant to Gloucester.*
DOCTOR.

FOOL.
OSWALD, *steward to Goneril.*
A CAPTAIN, *employed by Edmund.*
GENTLEMAN *attendant on Cordelia.*
A HERALD.
SERVANTS *to Cornwall.*
GONERIL,
REGAN, } *daughters to Lear.*
CORDELIA,

KNIGHTS *attending on Lear,* OFFI-
CERS, MESSENGERS, SOLDIERS,
and ATTENDANTS.

THE SCENE : *Britain.*

ACT ONE

SCENE I. *King Lear's palace.*

Enter KENT, GLOUCESTER, *and* EDMUND.

KENT. I thought the King had more affected the Duke of Albany
than Cornwall.

GLO. It did always seem so to us ; but now, in the division of the
kingdom, it appears not which of the Dukes he values most ;
for equalities are so weigh'd that curiosity in neither can make
choice of either's moiety.   6

KENT. Is not this your son, my lord ?

GLO. His breeding, sir, hath been at my charge. I have so often
blush'd to acknowledge him that now I am braz'd to't.

KENT. I cannot conceive you.

GLO. Sir, this young fellow's mother could ; whereupon she grew
round-womb'd, and had indeed, sir, a son for her cradle ere she
had a husband for her bed. Do you smell a fault ?   15

KENT. I cannot wish the fault undone, the issue of it being so proper.

GLO. But I have a son, sir, by order of law, some year elder than this,
who yet is no dearer in my account. Though this knave came
something saucily to the world before he was sent for, yet was his
mother fair ; there was good sport at his making, and the whoreson
must be acknowledged.—Do you know this noble gentleman,
Edmund ?

EDM. No, my lord.   25

GLO. My Lord of Kent. Remember him hereafter as my honourable
friend.

EDM. My services to your lordship.

KENT. I must love you, and sue to know you better.

25

EDM. Sir, I shall study deserving.   30
GLO. He hath been out nine years, and away he shall again. [*Sennet.*]
    The King is coming.

Enter ONE *bearing a coronet ; then* LEAR, *then the* DUKES OF ALBANY
    and CORNWALL, *next* GONERIL, REGAN, CORDELIA, *with* FOLLOWERS.

LEAR. Attend the Lords of France and Burgundy, Gloucester.
GLO. I shall, my liege.   [*Exeunt* GLOUCESTER *and* EDMUND.
LEAR. Meantime we shall express our darker purpose.   35
    Give me the map there.   Know that we have divided
    In three our kingdom ; and 'tis our fast intent
    To shake all cares and business from our age,
    Conferring them on younger strengths, while we
    Unburden'd crawl toward death.   Our son of Cornwall,   40
    And you, our no less loving son of Albany,
    We have this hour a constant will to publish
    Our daughters' several dowers, that future strife
    May be prevented now.   The Princes, France and Burgundy,
    Great rivals in our youngest daughter's love,   45
    Long in our court have made their amorous sojourn,
    And here are to be answer'd.   Tell me, my daughters—
    Since now we will divest us both of rule,
    Interest of territory, cares of state—
    Which of you shall we say doth love us most ?   50
    That we our largest bounty may extend
    Where nature doth with merit challenge.   Goneril,
    Our eldest-born, speak first.
GON. Sir, I love you more than word can wield the matter ;
    Dearer than eyesight, space, and liberty ;   55
    Beyond what can be valued, rich or rare ;
    No less than life, with grace, health, beauty, honour ;
    As much as child e'er lov'd, or father found ;
    A love that makes breath poor and speech unable :
    Beyond all manner of so much I love you.   60
COR. [*Aside.*]   What shall Cordelia speak ?   Love, and be silent.
LEAR. Of all these bounds, even from this line to this,
    With shadowy forests and with champains rich'd,
    With plenteous rivers and wide-skirted meads,
    We make thee lady : to thine and Albany's issues   65
    Be this perpetual.—What says our second daughter,
    Our dearest Regan, wife of Cornwall ?   Speak.
REG. I am made of that self metal as my sister,
    And prize me at her worth.   In my true heart
    I find she names my very deed of love ;   70
    Only she comes too short, that I profess
    Myself an enemy to all other joys
    Which the most precious square of sense possesses,
    And find I am alone felicitate
    In your dear Highness' love.
COR. [*Aside.*]   Then poor Cordelia !   75
    And yet not so ; since I am sure my love's
    More ponderous than my tongue.
LEAR. To thee and thine hereditary ever
    Remain this ample third of our fair kingdom ;

No less in space, validity, and pleasure,   80
Than that conferr'd on Goneril.—Now, our joy,
Although our last and least ; to whose young love
The vines of France and milk of Burgundy
Strive to be interess'd ; what can you say to draw
A third more opulent than your sisters ? Speak.   85

COR. Nothing, my lord.

LEAR. Nothing !

COR. Nothing.

LEAR. Nothing will come of nothing. Speak again.

COR. Unhappy that I am, I cannot heave   90
My heart into my mouth. I love your Majesty
According to my bond ; no more nor less.

LEAR. How, how, Cordelia ! Mend your speech a little,
Lest you may mar your fortunes.

COR.   Good my lord,
You have begot me, bred me, lov'd me ; I   95
Return those duties back as are right fit,
Obey you, love you, and most honour you.
Why have my sisters husbands, if they say
They love you all ? Haply, when I shall wed,
That lord whose hand must take my plight shall carry   100
Half my love with him, half my care and duty.
Sure I shall never marry like my sisters,
To love my father all.

LEAR. But goes thy heart with this ?

COR.   Ay, my good lord.

LEAR. So young and so untender ?   105

COR. So young, my lord, and true.

LEAR. Let it be so ! Thy truth, then, be thy dower !
For, by the sacred radiance of the sun,
The mysteries of Hecat and the night ;
By all the operation of the orbs   110
From whom we do exist and cease to be ;
Here I disclaim all my paternal care,
Propinquity and property of blood,
And as a stranger to my heart and me
Hold thee from this for ever. The barbarous Scythian,   115
Or he that makes his generation messes
To gorge his appetite, shall to my bosom
Be as well neighbour'd, pitied, and reliev'd,
As thou my sometime daughter.

KENT.   Good my liege—

LEAR. Peace, Kent !   120
Come not between the dragon and his wrath.
I lov'd her most, and thought to set my rest
On her kind nursery. [To CORDELIA.] Hence, and avoid my sight!—
So be my grave my peace as here I give
Her father's heart from her ! Call France— Who stirs ?   125
Call Burgundy. Cornwall and Albany,
With my two daughters' dowers digest this third.
Let pride, which she calls plainness, marry her.
I do invest you jointly with my power,
Pre-eminence, and all the large effects   130

                                                              27

That troop with majesty. Ourself, by monthly course,
With reservation of an hundred knights,
By you to be sustain'd, shall our abode
Make with you by due turn. Only we shall retain
The name, and all th' addition to a king: 135
The sway, revenue, execution of the rest,
Beloved sons, be yours; which to confirm,
This coronet part between you.

KENT.   Royal Lear,
Whom I have ever honour'd as my king,
Lov'd as my father, as my master follow'd, 140
As my great patron thought on in my prayers—

LEAR. The bow is bent and drawn; make from the shaft.

KENT. Let it fall rather, though the fork invade
The region of my heart. Be Kent unmannerly
When Lear is mad. What wouldst thou do, old man? 145
Think'st thou that duty shall have dread to speak
When power to flattery bows? To plainness honour's bound
When majesty falls to folly. Reserve thy state;
And in thy best consideration check
This hideous rashness. Answer my life my judgment: 150
Thy youngest daughter does not love thee least;
Nor are those empty-hearted whose low sounds
Reverb no hollowness.

LEAR.   Kent, on my life, no more!

KENT. My life I never held but as a pawn
To wage against thine enemies; nor fear to lose it, 155
Thy safety being motive.

LEAR.   Out of my sight!

KENT. See better, Lear; and let me still remain
The true blank of thine eye.

LEAR. Now by Apollo—

KENT.   Now, by Apollo, King,
Thou swear'st thy gods in vain.

LEAR.   O, vassal! miscreant! 160
[Laying his hand on his sword.

ALB. and CORN. Dear sir, forbear.

KENT. Do;
Kill thy physician, and the fee bestow
Upon the foul disease. Revoke thy gift,
Or, whilst I can vent clamour from my throat, 165
I'll tell thee thou dost evil.

LEAR.   Hear me, recreant;
On thine allegiance, hear me.
That thou hast sought to make us break our vows—
Which we durst never yet—and with strain'd pride
To come betwixt our sentence and our power— 170
Which nor our nature nor our place can bear;
Our potency made good, take thy reward.
Five days we do allot thee for provision
To shield thee from disasters of the world,
And on the sixth to turn thy hated back 175
Upon our kingdom; if, on the tenth day following,
Thy banish'd trunk be found in our dominions,

    The moment is thy death.   Away! by Jupiter,
    This shall not be revok'd.
KENT. Fare thee well, King.   Sith thus thou wilt appear,   180
    Freedom lives hence, and banishment is here.
    [*To* CORDELIA.]   The gods to their dear shelter take thee, maid,
    That justly think'st, and hast most rightly said!
    [*To* REGAN *and* GONERIL.]   And your large speeches may your
        deeds approve,
    That good effects may spring from words of love!   185
    Thus Kent, O princes, bids you all adieu;
    He'll shape his old course in a country new.   [*Exit.*

Flourish.   Re-enter GLOUCESTER, *with* FRANCE, BURGUNDY, *and*
                            ATTENDANTS.

GLO. Here's France and Burgundy, my noble lord.
LEAR. My Lord of Burgundy,
    We first address toward you, who with this king   190
    Hath rivall'd for our daughter.   What in the least
    Will you require in present dower with her,
    Or cease your quest of love?
BUR.   Most royal Majesty,
    I crave no more than hath your Highness offer'd,
    Nor will you tender less.
LEAR.   Right noble Burgundy,   195
    When she was dear to us, we did hold her so;
    But now her price is fallen.   Sir, there she stands:
    If aught within that little seeming substance,
    Or all of it, with our displeasure piec'd,
    And nothing more, may fitly like your Grace,   200
    She's there, and she is yours.
BUR.   I know no answer.
LEAR. Will you, with those infirmities she owes,
    Unfriended, new-adopted to our hate,
    Dower'd with our curse, and stranger'd with our oath,
    Take her or leave her?
BUR.   Pardon me, royal sir;   205
    Election makes not up in such conditions.
LEAR. Then leave her, sir; for, by the pow'r that made me,
    I tell you all her wealth. [*To* FRANCE.]   For you, great King
    I would not from your love make such a stray
    To match you where I hate; therefore beseech you   210
    T' avert your liking a more worthier way,
    Than on a wretch whom nature is asham'd
    Almost t' acknowledge hers.
FRANCE.   This is most strange,
    That she, whom even but now was your best object,
    The argument of your praise, balm of your age,   215
    The best, the dearest, should in this trice of time
    Commit a thing so monstrous to dismantle
    So many folds of favour.   Sure her offence
    Must be of such unnatural degree
    That monsters it, or your fore-vouch'd affection   220
    Fall into taint—which to believe of her
    Must be a faith that reason without miracle

                                                    29

    Should never plant in me.

COR.   I yet beseech your Majesty—
  If for I want that glib and oily art
  To speak and purpose not, since what I well intend   225
  I'll do't before I speak—that you make known
  It is no vicious blot, murder, or foulness,
  No unchaste action or dishonoured step,
  That hath depriv'd me of your grace and favour ;
  But even for want of that for which I am richer—   230
  A still-soliciting eye, and such a tongue
  That I am glad I have not, though not to have it
  Hath lost me in your liking.

LEAR.   Better thou
  Hadst not been born than not t' have pleas'd me better.

FRANCE. Is it but this ? A tardiness in nature,   235
  Which often leaves the history unspoke
  That it intends to do ! My Lord of Burgundy,
  What say you to the lady ? Love's not love
  When it is mingled with regards that stands
  Aloof from th' entire point. Will you have her ?   240
  She is herself a dowry.

BUR.   Royal king,
  Give but that portion which yourself propos'd,
  And here I take Cordelia by the hand,
  Duchess of Burgundy.

LEAR. Nothing ! I have sworn ; I am firm.   245

BUR. I am sorry, then, you have so lost a father
  That you must lose a husband.

COR.   Peace be with Burgundy !
  Since that respects of fortune are his love
  I shall not be his wife.

FRANCE. Fairest Cordelia, that art most rich, being poor ;   250
  Most choice, forsaken ; and most lov'd, despis'd !
  Thee and thy virtues here I seize upon,
  Be it lawful I take up what's cast away.
  Gods, gods ! 'tis strange that from their cold'st neglect
  My love should kindle to inflam'd respect.   255
  Thy dow'rless daughter, King, thrown to my chance,
  Is queen of us, of ours, and our fair France.
  Not all the dukes of wat'rish Burgundy
  Can buy this unpriz'd precious maid of me.
  Bid them farewell, Cordelia, though unkind ;   260
  Thou losest here, a better where to find.

LEAR. Thou hast her, France ; let her be thine ; for we
  Have no such daughter, nor shall ever see
  That face of hers again. [To CORDELIA.] Therefore be gone
  Without our grace, our love, our benison.   265
  Come, noble Burgundy.   [Flourish. Exeunt LEAR, BURGUNDY,
                      CORNWALL, ALBANY, GLOUCESTER,
                      and ATTENDANTS.

FRANCE. Bid farewell to your sisters.

COR. The jewels of our father, with wash'd eyes
  Cordelia leaves you. I know you what you are ;

And, like a sister, am most loath to call   270
Your faults as they are named.   Love well our father.
To your professed bosoms I commit him ;
But yet, alas, stood I within his grace,
I would prefer him to a better place.
So, farewell to you both.   275
REG. Prescribe not us our duty.
GON.   Let your study
Be to content your lord, who hath receiv'd you
At fortune's alms.   You have obedience scanted,
And well are worth the want that you have wanted.
COR. Time shall unfold what plighted cunning hides,   280
Who covers faults, at last with shame derides.
Well may you prosper !
FRANCE.   Come, my fair Cordelia.
                              [Exeunt FRANCE and CORDELIA.
GON. Sister, it is not little I have to say of what most nearly appertains
to us both.   I think our father will hence to-night.
REG. That's most certain, and with you ; next month with us.
GON. You see how full of changes his age is ; the observation we
have made of it hath not been little.   He always lov'd our sister
most ; and with what poor judgment he hath now cast her off
appears too grossly.   291
REG. 'Tis the infirmity of his age ; yet he hath ever but slenderly
known himself.
GON. The best and soundest of his time hath been but rash ; then
must we look from his age to receive not alone the imperfections
of long-engraffed condition, but therewithal the unruly wayward-
ness that infirm and choleric years bring with them.
REG. Such unconstant starts are we like to have from him as this of
Kent's banishment.   300
GON. There is further compliment of leave-taking between France
and him.   Pray you, let us hit together ; if our father carry
authority with such disposition as he bears, this last surrender of
his will but offend us.
REG. We shall further think of it.
GON. We must do something, and i' th' heat.   [Exeunt.

                    SCENE II.   Gloucester's castle.

                    Enter EDMUND with a letter.

EDM. Thou, Nature, art my goddess ; to thy law
My services are bound.   Wherefore should I
Stand in the plague of custom, and permit
The curiosity of nations to deprive me,
For that I am some twelve or fourteen moonshines   5
Lag of a brother ? Why bastard ? Wherefore base ?
When my dimensions are as well compact,
My mind as generous, and my shape as true,
As honest madam's issue ? Why brand they us
With base ? with baseness ? bastardy ? base, base ?   10
Who, in the lusty stealth of nature, take

More composition and fierce quality
Than doth, within a dull, stale, tired bed,
Go to th' creating a whole tribe of fops
Got 'tween asleep and wake ? Well then,   15
Legitimate Edgar, I must have your land.
Our father's love is to the bastard Edmund
As to th' legitimate. Fine word ' legitimate '
Well, my legitimate, if this letter speed,
And my invention thrive, Edmund the base   20
Shall top th' legitimate. I grow ; I prosper.
Now, gods, stand up for bastards.

Enter GLOUCESTER.

GLO. Kent banish'd thus ! and France in choler parted !
  And the King gone to-night ! Prescrib'd his pow'r !
  Confin'd to exhibition ! All this done   25
  Upon the gad ! Edmund, how now ! What news ?
EDM. So please your lordship, none.   [*Putting up the letter.*
GLO. Why so earnestly seek you to put up that letter ?
EDM. I know no news, my lord.
GLO. What paper were you reading ?   30
EDM. Nothing, my lord.
GLO. No ? What needed then that terrible dispatch of it into your
  pocket ? The quality of nothing hath not such need to hide
  itself. Let's see. Come, if it be nothing, I shall not need
  spectacles.   35
EDM. I beseech you, sir, pardon me. It is a letter from my brother
  that I have not all o'er-read ; and for so much as I have perus'd,
  I find it not fit for your o'er-looking.
GLO. Give me the letter, sir.
EDM. I shall offend either to detain or give it. The contents, as in
  part I understand them, are to blame.
GLO. Let's see, let's see.
EDM. I hope, for my brother's justification, he wrote this but as an
  essay or taste of my virtue.   44
GLO. [*Reads.*] ' This policy and reverence of age makes the world
  bitter to the best of our times ; keeps our fortunes from us till
  our oldness cannot relish them. I begin to find an idle and fond
  bondage in the oppression of aged tyranny, who sways, not as it
  hath power, but as it is suffer'd. Come to me, that of this I may
  speak more. If our father would sleep till I wak'd him, you
  should enjoy half his revenue for ever, and live the beloved of
  your brother.
                     Edgar.'
  Hum—Conspiracy ! ' Sleep till I wak'd him, you should enjoy
  half his revenue.' My son Edgar ! Had he a hand to write this ?
  a heart and a brain to breed it in ? When came this to you ?
  Who brought it ?   55
EDM. It was not brought me, my lord ; there's the cunning of it.
  I found it thrown in at the casement of my closet.
GLO. You know the character to be your brother's ?
EDM. If the matter were good, my lord, I durst swear it were his ;
  but in respect of that, I would fain think it were not.
GLO. It is his.

EDM. It is his hand, my lord; but I hope his heart is not in the
contents.   65

GLO. Has he never before sounded you in this business?

EDM. Never, my lord; but I have heard him oft maintain it to be fit
that, sons at perfect age and fathers declin'd, the father should be
as ward to the son, and the son manage his revenue.   71

GLO. O villain, villain! His very opinion in the letter! Abhorred
villain! Unnatural, detested, brutish villain! Worse than
brutish! Go, sirrah, seek him; I'll apprehend him. Abom-
inable villain! Where is he?   75

EDM. I do not well know, my lord. If it shall please you to suspend
your indignation against my brother till you can derive from him
better testimony of his intent, you should run a certain course;
where, if you violently proceed against him, mistaking his purpose,
it would make a great gap in your own honour, and shake in
pieces the heart of his obedience. I dare pawn down my life for
him that he hath writ this to feel my affection to your honour,
and to no other pretence of danger.

GLO. Think you so?   85

EDM. If your honour judge it meet, I will place you where you shall
hear us confer of this, and by an auricular assurance have your
satisfaction; and that without any further delay than this very
evening.

GLO. He cannot be such a monster.   90

EDM. Nor is not, sure.

GLO. To his father, that so tenderly and entirely loves him. Heaven
and earth! Edmund, seek him out; wind me into him, I pray
you. Frame the business after your own wisdom. I would
unstate myself to be in a due resolution.

EDM. I will seek him, sir, presently; convey the business as I shall
find means, and acquaint you withal.   98

GLO. These late eclipses in the sun and moon portend no good to us.
Though the wisdom of nature can reason it thus and thus, yet
nature finds itself scourg'd by the sequent effects: love cools,
friendship falls off, brothers divide; in cities, mutinies; in
countries, discord; in palaces, treason; and the bond crack'd
'twixt son and father. This villain of mine comes under the
prediction: there's son against father. The King falls from bias
of nature: there's father against child. We have seen the best
of our time: machinations, hollowness, treachery, and all ruinous
disorders, follow us disquietly to our graves. Find out this
villain, Edmund; it shall lose thee nothing; do it carefully.
And the noble and true-hearted Kent banish'd! His offence,
honesty! 'Tis strange.   [*Exit*.

EDM. This is the excellent foppery of the world, that, when we are
sick in fortune, often the surfeits of our own behaviour, we make
guilty of our disasters the sun, the moon, and stars; as if we were
villains on necessity; fools by heavenly compulsion; knaves,
thieves, and treachers, by spherical predominance; drunkards,
liars, and adulterers, by an enforc'd obedience of planetary
influence; and all that we are evil in, by a divine thrusting on—an
admirable evasion of whoremaster man, to lay his goatish disposition on the charge of a star! My father compounded with
my mother under the Dragon's tail, and my nativity was under

Ursa Major, so that it follows I am rough and lecherous. Fut, I should have been that I am, had the maidenliest star in the firmament twinkled on my bastardizing. Edgar! 127

Enter EDGAR.

Pat! He comes like the catastrophe of the old comedy. My cue is villainous melancholy, with a sigh like Tom o' Bedlam.— O, these eclipses do portend these divisions! fa, sol, la, mi.

EDG. How now, brother Edmund! What serious contemplation are you in?

EDM. I am thinking, brother, of a prediction I read this other day what should follow these eclipses. 135

EDG. Do you busy yourself with that?

EDM. I promise you, the effects he writes of succeed unhappily; as of unnaturalness between the child and the parent; death, dearth, dissolutions of ancient amities; divisions in state, menaces and maledictions against king and nobles; needless diffidences, banishment of friends, dissipation of cohorts, nuptial breaches, and I know not what.

EDG. How long have you been a sectary astronomical?

EDM. Come, come! When saw you my father last?

EDG. The night gone by. 145

EDM. Spake you with him?

EDG. Ay, two hours together.

EDM. Parted you in good terms? Found you no displeasure in him by word nor countenance?

EDG. None at all.

EDM. Bethink yourself wherein you may have offended him; and at my entreaty forbear his presence, until some little time hath qualified the heat of his displeasure, which at this instant so rageth in him that with the mischief of your person it would scarcely allay. 155

EDG. Some villain hath done me wrong.

EDM. That's my fear. I pray you have a continent forbearance till the speed of his rage goes slower; and, as I say, retire with me to my lodging, from whence I will fitly bring you to hear my lord speak. Pray ye go; there's my key. If you do stir abroad, go arm'd. 161

EDG. Arm'd, brother!

EDM. Brother, I advise you to the best. I am no honest man if there be any good meaning toward you. I have told you what I have seen and heard—but faintly; nothing like the image and horror of it. Pray you, away.

EDG. Shall I hear from you anon?

EDM. I do serve you in this business. [*Exit* EDGAR.

A credulous father! and a brother noble, 170
Whose nature is so far from doing harms
That he suspects none; on whose foolish honesty
My practices ride easy! I see the business.
Let me, if not by birth, have lands by wit:
All with me's meet that I can fashion fit. [*Exit.*

SCENE III.   *The Duke of Albany's palace.*

Enter GONERIL *and* OSWALD, *her steward.*

GON. Did my father strike my gentleman for chiding of his fool?
OSW. Ay, madam.
GON. By day and night, he wrongs me ; every hour
    He flashes into one gross crime or other
    That sets us all at odds.   I'll not endure it.
    His knights grow riotous, and himself upbraids us
    On every trifle.   When he returns from hunting,
    I will not speak with him ; say I am sick.
    If you come slack of former services,   10
    You shall do well ; the fault of it I'll answer.   [*Horns within.*
OSW. He's coming, madam ; I hear him.
GON. Put on what weary negligence you please,
    You and your fellows ; I'd have it come to question.
    If he distaste it, let him to my sister,   15
    Whose mind and mine, I know, in that are one,
    Not to be overrul'd.   Idle old man,
    That still would manage those authorities
    That he hath given away !   Now, by my life,
    Old fools are babes again, and must be us'd   20
    With checks as flatteries, when they are seen abus'd.
    Remember what I have said.
OSW.   Well, madam.
GON. And let his knights have colder looks among you ;
    What grows of it, no matter.   Advise your fellows so.
    I would breed from hence occasions, and I shall,   25
    That I may speak.   I'll write straight to my sister
    To hold my very course.   Prepare for dinner.   [*Exeunt.*

SCENE IV.   *A hall in Albany's palace.*

Enter KENT, *disguised.*

KENT. If but as well I other accents borrow
    That can my speech defuse, my good intent
    May carry through itself to that full issue
    For which I raz'd my likeness.   Now, banish'd Kent,
    If thou canst serve where thou dost stand condemn'd,   5
    So may it come thy master whom thou lov'st
    Shall find thee full of labours.

Horns within.   Enter LEAR, KNIGHTS, *and* ATTENDANTS.

LEAR. Let me not stay a jot for dinner ; go get it ready. [*Exit an*
    ATTENDANT.]   How now !   What art thou ?
KENT. A man, sir.
LEAR. What dost thou profess ?   What wouldst thou with us ?
KENT. I do profess to be no less than I seem, to serve him truly that
    will put me in trust, to love him that is honest, to converse with
    him that is wise and says little, to fear judgment, to fight when I
    cannot choose, and to eat no fish.   17
LEAR. What art thou ?
KENT. A very honest-hearted fellow, and as poor as the King.

LEAR. If thou be'st as poor for a subject as he's for a king, thou art
   poor enough.   What wouldst thou ?

KENT. Service.

LEAR. Who wouldst thou serve ?

KENT. You.

LEAR. Dost thou know me, fellow ?   26

KENT. No, sir ; but you have that in your countenance which I
   would fain call master.

LEAR. What's that ?

KENT. Authority.

LEAR. What services canst thou do ?   31

KENT. I can keep honest counsel, ride, run, mar a curious tale in
   telling it, and deliver a plain message bluntly.   That which ordinary
   men are fit for, I am qualified in ; and the best of me is diligence.

LEAR. How old art thou ?

KENT. Not so young, sir, to love a woman for singing, nor so old to
   dote on her for anything : I have years on my back forty-eight.

LEAR. Follow me ; thou shalt serve me.   If I like thee no worse
   after dinner, I will not part from thee yet.   Dinner, ho, dinner !
   Where's my knave ? my fool ?—Go you and call my fool hither.
                                          [Exit an ATTENDANT.

Enter OSWALD.

You, you, sirrah, where's my daughter ?   44

OSW. So please you—   [Exit.

LEAR. What says the fellow there ?   Call the clotpoll back. [Exit a
   KNIGHT.]   Where's my fool, ho ?   I think the world's asleep.

Re-enter KNIGHT.

How now !   Where's that mongrel ?

KNIGHT. He says, my lord, your daughter is not well.

LEAR. Why came not the slave back to me when I call'd him ?   52

KNIGHT. Sir, he answered me in the roundest manner he would not.

LEAR. He would not !

KNIGHT. My lord, I know not what the matter is ; but, to my judgment, your Highness is not entertain'd with that ceremonious
   affection as you were wont ; there's a great abatement of kindness
   appears as well in the general dependants as in the Duke himself
   also and your daughter.   61

LEAR. Ha ! say'st thou so ?

KNIGHT. I beseech you pardon me, my lord, if I be mistaken ; for my
   duty cannot be silent when I think your Highness wrong'd.

LEAR. Thou but rememb'rest me of mine own conception.   I have
   perceived a most faint neglect of late, which I have rather blamed
   as mine own jealous curiosity than as a very pretence and purpose
   of unkindness.   I will look further into't.   But where's my fool ?
   I have not seen him this two days.   71

KNIGHT. Since my young lady's going into France, sir, the fool hath
   much pined away.

LEAR. No more of that ; I have noted it well.   Go you and tell my
   daughter I would speak with her. [Exit an ATTENDANT.]   Go you,
   call hither my fool. [Exit another ATTENDANT.   76

Re-enter OSWALD.

O, you sir, you! Come you hither, sir. Who am I, sir?

OSW. My lady's father.

LEAR. 'My lady's father'! my lord's knave! you whoreson dog!
  you slave! you cur!   80

OSW. I am none of these, my lord; I beseech your pardon.

LEAR. Do you bandy looks with me, you rascal!   [*Striking him.*

OSW. I'll not be strucken, my lord.

KENT. Nor tripp'd neither, you base football player.
                                              [*Tripping up his heels.*

LEAR. I thank thee, fellow; thou serv'st me, and I'll love thee.

KENT. Come, sir, arise, away! I'll teach you differences. Away,
  away! If you will measure your lubber's length again, tarry;
  but away! Go to! Have you wisdom? So.
                                              [*Pushes Oswald out.*

LEAR. Now, my friendly knave, I thank thee; there's earnest of thy
  service.   [*Giving* KENT *money.*

Enter FOOL.

FOOL. Let me hire him too; here's my coxcomb.
                                     [*Offering* KENT *his cap.*

LEAR. How now, my pretty knave! How dost thou?

FOOL. Sirrah, you were best take my coxcomb.

KENT. Why, fool?   97

FOOL. Why? For taking one's part that's out of favour. Nay, an
  thou canst not smile as the wind sits, thou'lt catch cold shortly.
  There, take my coxcomb. Why, this fellow has banish'd two
  on's daughters, and did the third a blessing against his will; if
  thou follow him, thou must needs wear my coxcomb.—How now,
  nuncle! Would I had two coxcombs and two daughters!

LEAR. Why, my boy?   105

FOOL. If I gave them all my living, I'd keep my coxcombs myself.
  There's mine; beg another of thy daughters.

LEAR. Take heed, sirrah—the whip.

FOOL. Truth's a dog must to kennel; he must be whipp'd out, when
  Lady the brach may stand by th' fire and stink.   112

LEAR. A pestilent gall to me!

FOOL. Sirrah, I'll teach thee a speech.

LEAR. Do.

FOOL. Mark it, nuncle:

> Have more than thou showest,
> Speak less than thou knowest,
> Lend less than thou owest,
> Ride more than thou goest,   120
> Learn more than thou trowest,
> Set less than thou throwest;
> Leave thy drink and thy whore,
> And keep in-a-door,
> And thou shalt have more   125
> Than two tens to a score.

KENT. This is nothing, fool.

FOOL. Then 'tis like the breath of an unfee'd lawyer—you gave me
  nothing for't. Can you make no use of nothing, nuncle?

LEAR. Why, no, boy; nothing can be made out of nothing.

FOOL. [*To* KENT.] Prithee tell him, so much the rent of his land comes to ; he will not believe a fool.

LEAR. A bitter fool !   135

FOOL. Dost thou know the difference, my boy, between a bitter fool and a sweet one ?

LEAR. No, lad ; teach me.

FOOL.   That lord that counsell'd thee
                                        To give away thy land,   140
                                      Come place him here by me—
                                        Do thou for him stand.
                                      The sweet and bitter fool
                                        Will presently appear ;
                                      The one in motley here,   145
                                        The other found out there.

LEAR. Dost thou call me fool, boy ?

FOOL. All thy other titles thou hast given away ; that thou wast born with.

KENT. This is not altogether fool, my lord.   150

FOOL. No, faith, lords and great men will not let me ; if I had a monopoly out, they would have part on't. And ladies too—they will not let me have all the fool to myself; they'll be snatching. Nuncle, give me an egg, and I'll give thee two crowns.   155

LEAR. What two crowns shall they be ?

FOOL. Why, after I have cut the egg i' th' middle and eat up the meat, the two crowns of the egg. When thou clovest thy crown i' th' middle, and gav'st away both parts, thou bor'st thine ass on thy back o'er the dirt. Thou hadst little wit in thy bald crown when thou gav'st thy golden one away. If I speak like myself in this, let him be whipp'd that first finds it so.

Sings.]   Fools had ne'er less grace in a year ;
                                        For wise men are grown foppish,   165
                                      And know not how their wits to wear,
                                        Their manners are so apish.

LEAR. When were you wont to be so full of songs, sirrah ?

FOOL. I have us'd it, nuncle, e'er since thou mad'st thy daughters thy mothers ; for when thou gav'st them the rod, and put'st down thine own breeches

[*Sings.*]   Then they for sudden joy did weep,
                                        And I for sorrow sung,
                                      That such a king should play bo-peep   175
                                        And go the fools among.

Prithee, nuncle, keep a schoolmaster that can teach thy fool to lie. I would fain learn to lie.

LEAR. An you lie, sirrah, we'll have you whipp'd.   179

FOOL. I marvel what kin thou and thy daughters are. They'll have me whipp'd for speaking true : thou'lt have me whipp'd for lying ; and sometimes I am whipp'd for holding my peace. I had rather be any kind o' thing than a fool ; and yet I would not be thee, nuncle ; thou hast pared thy wit o' both sides, and left nothing i' th' middle. Here comes one o' th' parings.   186

Enter GONERIL.

LEAR. How now, daughter ! What makes that frontlet on ? You are too much of late i' th' frown.

FOOL. Thou wast a pretty fellow when thou hadst no need to care
for her frowning ; now thou art an O without a figure. I am
better than thou art now : I am a fool, thou art nothing. [*To*
GONERIL.] Yes, forsooth, I will hold my tongue ; so your face
bids me, though you say nothing. Mum, mum !   195
             He that keeps nor crust nor crumb,
             Weary of all, shall want some.
Pointing to LEAR.] That's a sheal'd peascod.
GON. Not only, sir, this your all-licens'd fool,
     But other of your insolent retinue   200
     Do hourly carp and quarrel, breaking forth
     In rank and not-to-be-endured riots. Sir,
     I had thought, by making this well known unto you,
     To have found a safe redress ; but now grow fearful,
     By what yourself too late have spoke and done,   205
     That you protect this course, and put it on
     By your allowance ; which if you should, the fault
     Would not scape censure, nor the redresses sleep,
     Which, in the tender of a wholesome weal,
     Might in their working do you that offence   210
     Which else were shame, that then necessity
     Will call discreet proceeding.
FOOL. For, you know, nuncle,
     The hedge-sparrow fed the cuckoo so long
     That it had it head bit off by it young.   215
     So, out went the candle, and we were left darkling.
LEAR. Are you our daughter ?
GON. I would you would make use of your good wisdom,
     Whereof I know you are fraught, and put away   220
     These dispositions which of late transport you
     From what you rightly are.
FOOL. May not an ass know when the cart draws the horse ? Whoop,
     Jug ! I love thee.
LEAR. Does any here know me ? This is not Lear.
     Does Lear walk thus ? speak thus ? Where are his eyes ?
     Either his notion weakens, or his discernings
     Are lethargied.—Ha ! waking ? 'Tis not so.—
     Who is it that can tell me who I am ?
FOOL. Lear's shadow.   230
LEAR. I would learn that ; for, by the marks of sovereignty, know-
     ledge, and reason, I should be false persuaded I had daughters.
FOOL. Which they will make an obedient father.
LEAR. Your name, fair gentlewoman ?   235
GON. This admiration, sir, is much o' th' savour
     Of other your new pranks. I do beseech you
     To understand my purposes aright.
     As you are old and reverend, should be wise.
     Here do you keep a hundred knights and squires ;   240
     Men so disorder'd, so debosh'd and bold,
     That this our court, infected with their manners,
     Shows like a riotous inn. Epicurism and lust
     Makes it more like a tavern or a brothel
     Than a grac'd palace. The shame itself doth speak   245

For instant remedy. Be then desir'd
By her that else will take the thing she begs
A little to disquantity your train;
And the remainders that shall still depend
To be such men as may besort your age,   250
Which know themselves and you.

LEAR.   Darkness and devils!
Saddle my horses; call my train together.
Degenerate bastard! I'll not trouble thee;
Yet have I left a daughter.

GON. You strike my people; and your disorder'd rabble   255
Make servants of their betters.

Enter ALBANY.

LEAR. Woe that too late repents!—O, sir, are you come?
Is it your will? Speak, sir.—Prepare my horses.
Ingratitude, thou marble-hearted fiend,
More hideous when thou show'st thee in a child   260
Than the sea-monster!

ALB.   Pray, sir, be patient.

LEAR. [*To* GONERIL.] Detested kite! thou liest:
My train are men of choice and rarest parts,
That all particulars of duty know;
And in the most exact regard support   265
The worships of their name.—O most small fault,
How ugly didst thou in Cordelia show!
Which, like an engine, wrench'd my frame of nature
From the fix'd place; drew from my heart all love
And added to the gall. O Lear, Lear, Lear!   270
Beat at this gate that let thy folly in   [*Striking his head.*
And thy dear judgment out! Go, go, my people.

[*Exeunt* KENT *and* KNIGHTS.

ALB. My lord, I am guiltless, as I am ignorant
Of what hath moved you.

LEAR.   It may be so, my lord.
Hear, Nature, hear; dear goddess, hear.   275
Suspend thy purpose, if thou didst intend
To make this creature fruitful.
Into her womb convey sterility;
Dry up in her the organs of increase;
And from her derogate body never spring   280
A babe to honour her! If she must teem,
Create her child of spleen, that it may live
And be a thwart disnatur'd torment to her.
Let it stamp wrinkles in her brow of youth,
With cadent tears fret channels in her cheeks,   285
Turn all her mother's pains and benefits
To laughter and contempt, that she may feel
How sharper than a serpent's tooth it is
To have a thankless child. Away, away!   [*Exit.*

ALB. Now, gods that we adore, whereof comes this?   290

GON. Never afflict yourself to know more of it;
But let his disposition have that scope
As dotage gives it.

Re-enter LEAR.

LEAR. What, fifty of my followers at a clap !
        Within a fortnight !

ALB.   What's the matter, sir ?   295

LEAR. I'll tell thee. [*To* GONERIL.]   Life and death !   I am asham'd
        That thou hast power to shake my manhood thus ;
        That these hot tears, which break from me perforce,
        Should make thee worth them.   Blasts and fogs upon thee !
        Th' untented woundings of a father's curse   300
        Pierce every sense about thee !—Old fond eyes,
        Beweep this cause again, I'll pluck ye out,
        And cast you, with the waters that you loose,
        To temper clay.   Ha !   Is't come to this ?
        Let it be so.   I have another daughter,   305
        Who, I am sure, is kind and comfortable.
        When she shall hear this of thee, with her nails
        She'll flay thy wolfish visage.   Thou shalt find
        That I'll resume the shape which thou dost think
        I have cast off for ever.   [*Exit* LEAR.

GON.   Do you mark that ?

ALB. I cannot be so partial, Goneril,
        To the great love I bear you—

GON. Pray you, content.—What, Oswald, ho !   314
[*To the* FOOL.] You, sir, more knave than fool, after your master.

FOOL. Nuncle Lear, nuncle Lear, tarry—take the fool with thee.
                A fox, when one has caught her,
                And such a daughter,
                Should sure to the slaughter,   320
                If my cap would buy a halter.
                So the fool follows after.   [*Exit.

GON. This man hath had good counsel.   A hundred knights !
        'Tis politic and safe to let him keep
        At point a hundred knights—yes, that on every dream   325
        Each buzz, each fancy, each complaint, dislike,
        He may enguard his dotage with their pow'rs,
        And hold our lives in mercy.   Oswald, I say !

ALB. Well, you may fear too far.

GON.   Safer than trust too far.
        Let me still take away the harms I fear,   330
        Not fear still to be taken.   I know his heart.
        What he hath utter'd I have writ my sister.
        If she sustain him and his hundred knights,
        When I have show'd th' unfitness—

Re-enter OSWALD.

                                   How now, Oswald !
        What, have you writ that letter to my sister ?   335

OSW. Ay, madam.

GON. Take you some company, and away to horse;
        Inform her full of my particular fear,
        And thereto add such reasons of your own
        As may compact it more.   Get you gone ;   340
        And hasten your return. [*Exit* OSWALD.]   No, no, my lord,

This milky gentleness and course of yours,
Though I condemn not, yet, under pardon,
You are much more ataxt for want of wisdom
Than prais'd for harmful mildness.   345
ALB. How far your eyes may pierce I cannot tell.
  Striving to better, oft we mar what's well.
GON. Nay, then—
ALB. Well, well ; th' event.   [*Exeunt.*

SCENE V. *Court before the Duke of Albany's palace.*

Enter LEAR, KENT, *and* FOOL.

LEAR. Go you before to Gloucester with these letters. Acquaint my
  daughter no further with anything you know than comes from
  her demand out of the letter. If your diligence be not speedy,
  I shall be there afore you.
KENT. I will not sleep, my lord, till I have delivered your letter. [*Exit.*
FOOL. If a man's brains were in's heels, were't not in danger of kibes ?
LEAR. Ay, boy.
FOOL. Then, I prithee, be merry ; thy wit shall not go slipshod.
LEAR. Ha, ha, ha !   12
FOOL. Shalt see thy other daughter will use thee kindly ; for though
  she's as like this as a crab's like an apple, yet I can tell what I can
  tell.
LEAR. What canst tell, boy ?
FOOL. She will taste as like this as a crab does to a crab. Thou canst
  tell why one's nose stands i' th' middle on's face ?
LEAR. No.   20
FOOL. Why to keep one's eyes of either side's nose, that what a man
  cannot smell out, he may spy into.
LEAR. I did her wrong.
FOOL. Canst tell how an oyster makes his shell ?
LEAR. No.
FOOL. Nor I neither ; but I can tell why a snail has a house.
LEAR. Why ?
FOOL. Why, to put's head in ; not to give it away to his daughters,
  and leave his horns without a case.   30
LEAR. I will forget my nature. So kind a father !—Be my horses
  ready ?
FOOL. Thy asses are gone about 'em. The reason why the seven
  stars are no moe than seven is a pretty reason.
LEAR. Because they are not eight ?
FOOL. Yes, indeed. Thou wouldst make a good fool.
LEAR. To take't again perforce ! Monster ingratitude !
FOOL. If thou wert my fool, nuncle, I'd have thee beaten for being
  old before thy time.
LEAR. How's that ?   40
FOOL. Thou shouldst not have been old till thou hadst been wise.
LEAR. O, let me not be mad, not mad, sweet heaven !
  Keep me in temper ; I would not be mad !

Enter GENTLEMAN.

How now ! are the horses ready ?
GENT. Ready, my lord.

LEAR. Come, boy.
FOOL. She that's a maid now, and laughs at my departure,   48
     Shall not be a maid long, unless things be cut shorter.   [*Exeunt.*

ACT TWO

SCENE I.   *A court-yard in the Earl of Gloucester's castle.*

Enter EDMUND *and* CURAN, *meeting.*

EDM. Save thee, Curan.
CUR. And you, sir. I have been with your father, and given him
     notice that the Duke of Cornwall and Regan his Duchess will be
     here with him this night.
EDM. How comes that ?   5
CUR. Nay, I know not. You have heard of the news abroad ; I mean
     the whisper'd one, for they are yet but ear-bussing arguments ?
EDM. Not I. Pray you, what are they ?
CUR. Have you heard of no likely wars toward 'twixt the Dukes of
     Cornwall and Albany ?   11
EDM. Not a word.
CUR. You may do, then, in time. Fare you well, sir.   [*Exit.*
EDM. The Duke be here to-night ? The better ! best !
     This weaves itself perforce into my business.   15
     My father hath set guard to take my brother ;
     And I have one thing, of a queasy question,
     Which I must act. Briefness and fortune work
     Brother, a word ! Descend. Brother, I say !

Enter EDGAR.

     My father watches. O sir, fly this place ;   20
     Intelligence is given where you are hid ;
     You have now the good advantage of the night.
     Have you not spoken 'gainst the Duke of Cornwall ?
     He's coming hither, now, i' th' night, i' th' haste,
     And Regan with him. Have you nothing said   25
     Upon his party 'gainst the Duke of Albany ?
     Advise yourself.
EDG.   I am sure on't, not a word.
EDM. I hear my father coming. Pardon me,
     In cunning I must draw my sword upon you.
     Draw ; seem to defend yourself ; now quit you well.—   30
     Yield ; come before my father. Light, ho, here !—
     Fly, brother.—Torches, torches !—So, farewell.   [*Exit* EDGAR.
     Some blood drawn on me would beget opinion   [*Wounds his arm.*
     Of my more fierce endeavour. I have seen drunkards
     Do more than this in sport.—Father, father !   35
     Stop, stop ! No help ?

Enter GLOUCESTER, *and* SERVANTS *with torches.*

GLO. Now, Edmund, where's the villain ?
EDM. Here stood he in the dark, his sharp sword out,
     Mumbling of wicked charms, conjuring the moon
     To stand's auspicious mistress.
GLO.   But where is he ?   40

EDM. Look, sir, I bleed.

GLO. Where is the villain, Edmund?

EDM. Fled this way, sir. When by no means he could—

GLO. Pursue him, ho! Go after. [*Exeunt* SERVANTS.]—By no means
what?

EDM. Persuade me to the murder of your lordship;
But that I told him the revenging gods   45
'Gainst parricides did all their thunders bend;
Spoke with how manifold and strong a bond
The child was bound to th' father. Sir, in fine,
Seeing how loathly opposite I stood
To his unnatural purpose, in fell motion,   50
With his prepared sword, he charges home
My unprovided body, latch'd mine arm;
But when he saw my best alarum'd spirits,
Bold in the quarrel's right, rous'd to th' encounter,
Or whether gasted by the noise I made,   55
Full suddenly he fled.

GLO. Let him fly far.
Not in this land shall he remain uncaught;
And found—dispatch. The noble Duke my master,
My worthy arch and patron, comes to-night;
By his authority I will proclaim it,   60
That he which finds him shall deserve our thanks,
Bringing the murderous coward to the stake;
He that conceals him, death.

EDM. When I dissuaded him from his intent,
And found him pight to do it, with curst speech 65
I threaten'd to discover him; he replied,
'Thou unpossessing bastard! dost thou think,
If I would stand against thee, would the reposure
Of any trust, virtue, or worth, in thee
Make thy words faith'd? No. What I should deny—
As this I would; ay, though thou didst produce   71
My very character—I'd turn it all
To thy suggestion, plot, and damned practice;
And thou must make a dullard of the world,
If they not thought the profits of my death   75
Were very pregnant and potential spurs
To make thee seek it'.

GLO. O strong and fast'ned villain!
Would he deny his letter?—I never got him. [*Tucket within.*
Hark, the Duke's trumpets! I know not why he comes.
All ports I'll bar; the villain shall not scape; 80
The Duke must grant me that. Besides, his picture
I will send far and near, that all the kingdom
May have due note of him; and of my land,
Loyal and natural boy, I'll work the means
To make thee capable.   85

Enter CORNWALL, REGAN, *and* ATTENDANTS.

CORN. How now, my noble friend! since I came hither,
Which I can call but now, I have heard strange news.

REG. If it be true, all vengeance comes too short

Which can pursue th' offender.   How dost, my lord ?
GLO. O, madam, my old heart is crack'd, it's crack'd !   90
REG. What, did my father's godson seek your life ?
  He whom my father nam'd ?   your Edgar ?
GLO. O lady, lady, shame would have it hid !
REG. Was he not companion with the riotous knights
  That tend upon my father ?   95
GLO. I know not, madam.   'Tis too bad, too bad.
EDM. Yes, madam, he was of that consort.
REG. No marvel, then, though he were ill affected.
  'Tis they have put him on the old man's death,
  To have th' expense and waste of his revenues.   100
  I have this present evening from my sister
  Been well inform'd of them ; and with such cautions
  That, if they come to sojourn at my house,
  I'll not be there.
CORN.   Nor I, assure thee, Regan.
  Edmund, I hear that you have shown your father   105
  A child-like office.
EDM.   It was my duty, sir.
GLO. He did bewray his practice, and receiv'd
  This hurt you see, striving to apprehend him.
CORN. Is he pursued ?
GLO.   Ay, my good lord.
CORN. If he be taken, he shall never more   110
  Be fear'd of doing harm.   Make your own purpose,
  How in my strength you please.   For you, Edmund,
  Whose virtue and obedience doth this instant
  So much commend itself, you shall be ours.
  Natures of such deep trust we shall much need ;   115
  You we first seize on.
EDM.   I shall serve you, sir,
  Truly, however else.
GLO.   For him I thank your Grace.
CORN. You know not why we came to visit you—
REG. Thus out of season, threading dark-ey'd night :
  Occasions, noble Gloucester, of some poise,   120
  Wherein we must have use of your advice.
  Our father he hath writ, so hath our sister,
  Of differences, which I best thought it fit
  To answer from our home ; the several messengers
  From hence attend dispatch.   Our good old friend,   125
  Lay comforts to your bosom, and bestow
  Your needful counsel to our businesses,
  Which craves the instant use.
GLO.   I serve you, madam.
  Your Graces are right welcome.   [*Exeunt.*

SCENE II.   *Before Gloucester's castle.*

Enter KENT *and* OSWALD *severally.*

OSW. Good dawning to thee, friend.   Art of this house ?
KENT. Ay.

osw. Where may we set our horses?
KENT. I' th' mire.
osw. Prithee, if thou lov'st me, tell me.   5
KENT. I love thee not.
osw. Why then, I care not for thee.
KENT. If I had thee in Lipsbury pinfold, I would make thee care for
    me.
osw. Why dost thou use me thus? I know thee not.   10
KENT. Fellow, I know thee.
osw. What dost thou know me for?
KENT. A knave, a rascal, an eater of broken meats; a base, proud,
    shallow, beggarly, three-suited, hundred-pound, filthy, worsted-
    stocking knave; a lily-liver'd, action-taking, whoreson, glass-
    gazing, superserviceable, finical rogue; one-trunk-inheriting
    slave; one that wouldst be a bawd in way of good service, and
    art nothing but the composition of a knave, beggar, coward,
    pander, and the son and heir of a mongrel bitch; one whom I
    will beat into clamorous whining, if thou deny'st the least syllable
    of thy addition.   22
osw. Why, what a monstrous fellow art thou, thus to rail on one
    that is neither known of thee nor knows thee?
KENT. What a brazen-fac'd varlet art thou, to deny thou knowest me!
    Is it two days since I tripp'd up thy heels and beat thee before
    the King? Draw, you rogue; for, though it be night, yet the moon
    shines; I'll make a sop o' th' moonshine of you; you whoreson
    cullionly barbermonger, draw.   [*Drawing his sword.*
osw. Away! I have nothing to do with thee.   31
KENT. Draw, you rascal. You come with letters against the King,
    and take Vanity the puppet's part against the royalty of her father.
    Draw, you rogue, or I'll so carbonado your shanks. Draw, you
    rascal; come your ways.
osw. Help, ho! murder! help.   36
KENT. Strike, you slave; stand, rogue, stand; you neat slave, strike.
                                                        [*Beating him.*
osw. Help, ho! murder! murder!

Enter EDMUND *with his rapier drawn,* GLOUCESTER, CORNWALL, REGAN,
                        and SERVANTS.

EDM. How now! What's the matter? Part!   40
KENT. With you, goodman boy, an you please. Come, I'll flesh ye;
    come on, young master.
GLO. Weapons! arms! What's the matter here?
CORN. Keep peace, upon your lives;
    He dies that strikes again. What is the matter?   45
REG. The messengers from our sister and the King.
CORN. What is your difference? Speak.
osw. I am scarce in breath, my lord.
KENT. No marvel, you have so bestirr'd your valour. You cowardly
    rascal, nature disclaims in thee: a tailor made thee.   51
CORN. Thou art a strange fellow. A tailor make a man?
KENT. Ay, a tailor, sir. A stone-cutter or a painter could not have
    made him so ill, though they had been but two years o' th' trade.
CORN. Speak yet, how grew your quarrel?

OSW. This ancient ruffian, sir, whose life I have spar'd at suit of his
    grey beard—   58
KENT. Thou whoreson zed ! thou unnecessary letter ! My lord, if
    you will give me leave, I will tread this unbolted villain into
    mortar, and daub the wall of a jakes with him.—Spare my grey
    beard, you wagtail ?   62
CORN. Peace, sirrah !
    You beastly knave, know you no reverence ?
KENT. Yes, sir ; but anger hath a privilege.   65
CORN. Why art thou angry ?
KENT. That such a slave as this should wear a sword,
    Who wears no honesty.   Such smiling rogues as these,
    Like rats, oft bite the holy cords a-twain
    Which are too intrinse t' unloose ; smooth every passion   70
    That in the natures of their lords rebel ;
    Bring oil to fire, snow to their colder moods ;
    Renege, affirm, and turn their halcyon beaks
    With every gale and vary of their masters,
    Knowing nought, like dogs, but following.   75
    A plague upon your epileptic visage !
    Smile you my speeches, as I were a fool ?
    Goose, if I had you upon Sarum plain,
    I'd drive ye cackling home to Camelot.
CORN. What, are thou mad, old fellow ?   80
GLO. How fell you out ?   Say that.
KENT. No contraries hold more antipathy
    Than I and such a knave.
CORN. Why dost thou call him knave ?   What is his fault ?
KENT. His countenance likes me not.   85
CORN. No more, perchance, does mine, nor his, nor hers.
KENT. Sir, 'tis my occupation to be plain :
    I have seen better faces in my time
    Than stands on any shoulder that I see
    Before me at this instant.
CORN.   This is some fellow   90
    Who, having been prais'd for bluntness, doth affect
    A saucy roughness, and constrains the garb
    Quite from his nature.   He cannot flatter, he,
    An honest mind and plain—he must speak truth.
    An they will take it, so ; if not, he's plain.   95
    These kind of knaves I know, which in this plainness
    Harbour more craft and more corrupter ends
    Than twenty silly ducking observants
    That stretch their duties nicely.
KENT. Sir, in good faith, in sincere verity,   100
    Under th' allowance of your great aspect,
    Whose influence, like the wreath of radiant fire
    On flickering Phœbus' front—
CORN.   What mean'st by this ?
KENT. To go out of my dialect, which you discommend so much.
    I know, sir, I am no flatterer. He that beguil'd you in a plain
    accent was a plain knave ; which, for my part, I will not be,
    though I should win your displeasure to entreat me to't.
CORN. What was th' offence you gave him ?

OSW.   I never gave him any.   110
      It pleas'd the King his master very late
      To strike at me, upon his misconstruction ;
      When he, compact, and flattering his displeasure,
      Tripp'd me behind ; being down, insulted, rail'd,
      And put upon him such a deal of man   115
      That worthied him, got praises of the King
      For him attempting who was self-subdu'd ;
      And in the fleshment of this dread exploit,
      Drew on me here again.
KENT. None of these rogues and cowards
      But Ajax is their fool.
CORN.   Fetch forth the stocks.   120
      You stubborn ancient knave, you reverend braggart,
      We'll teach you.
KENT.   Sir, I am too old to learn.
      Call not your stocks for me ; I serve the King,
      On whose employment I was sent to you.
      You shall do small respect, show too bold malice   125
      Against the grace and person of my master,
      Stocking his messenger.
CORN. Fetch forth the stocks. As I have life and honour,
      There shall he sit till noon.
REG. Till noon ! Till night, my lord ; and all night too.   130
KENT. Why, madam, if I were your father's dog,
      You should not use me so.
REG.   Sir, being his knave, I will.
CORN. This is a fellow of the self-same colour
      Our sister speaks of. Come, bring away the stocks.
                                        [Stocks brought out.
GLO Let me beseech your Grace not to do so.   135
      His fault is much, and the good King his master
      Will check him for't ; your purpos'd low correction
      Is such as basest and contemned'st wretches
      For pilf'rings and most common trespasses
      Are punish'd with. The King must take it ill   140
      That he, so slightly valued in his messenger,
      Should have him thus restrained.
CORN.   I'll answer that.
REG. My sister may receive it much more worse
      To have her gentleman abus'd, assaulted,
      For following her affairs. Put in his legs.   145
                                      [Kent is put in the stocks.
      Come, my good lord, away.
                            [Exeunt all but GLOUCESTER and KENT.
GLO. I am sorry for thee, friend ; 'tis the Duke's pleasure
      Whose disposition, all the world well knows,
      Will not be rubb'd nor stopp'd. I'll entreat for thee.
KENT. Pray, do not sir. I have watch'd and travell'd hard ;   150
      Some time I shall sleep out, the rest I'll whistle.
      A good man's fortune may grow out at heels.
      Give you good morrow ;
GLO.   The Duke's to blame in this ;
      'Twill be ill taken.   [Exit.

48

KENT. Good King, that must approve the common saw,   155
  Thou out of heaven's benediction com'st
  To the warm sun!
  Approach, thou beacon to this under globe,
  That by thy comfortable beams I may
  Peruse this letter. Nothing almost sees miracles   160
  But misery. I know 'tis from Cordelia,
  Who hath most fortunately been inform'd
  Of my obscured course. [*Reads.*] ' —and shall find time
  From this enormous state—seeking to give
  Losses their remedies.' All weary and o'er-watch'd,   165
  Take vantage, heavy eyes, not to behold
  This shameful lodging.
  Fortune, good night; smile once more; turn thy wheel. [*He sleeps.*

SCENE III. *The open country.*

Enter EDGAR.

EDG. I heard myself proclaim'd,
  And by the happy hollow of a tree
  Escap'd the hunt. No port is free; no place
  That guard and most unusual vigilance
  Does not attend my taking. Whiles I may scape   5
  I will preserve myself; and am bethought
  To take the basest and most poorest shape
  That ever penury in contempt of man
  Brought near to beast. My face I'll grime with filth,
  Blanket my loins, elf all my hairs in knots,   10
  And with presented nakedness outface
  The winds and persecutions of the sky.
  The country gives me proof and precedent
  Of Bedlam beggars, who, with roaring voices,
  Strike in their numb'd and mortified bare arms   15
  Pins, wooden pricks, nails, sprigs of rosemary;
  And with this horrible object, from low farms,
  Poor pelting villages, sheep-cotes, and mills,
  Sometimes with lunatic bans, sometime with prayers,
  Enforce their charity. Poor Turlygod! poor Tom!   20
  That's something yet. Edgar I nothing am.   [*Exit.*

SCENE IV. *Before Gloucester's castle.*

Enter LEAR, FOOL *and* GENTLEMAN, *to* KENT *in the stocks.*

LEAR. 'Tis strange that they should so depart from home,
  And not send back my messenger.
GENT.   As I learn'd,
  The night before there was no purpose in them
  Of this remove.
KENT.   Hail to thee, noble master!
LEAR. Ha!   5
  Mak'st thou this shame thy pastime?
KENT.   No, my lord.
FOOL. Ha, ha! he wears cruel garters. Horses are tied by the heads,
  dogs and bears by th' neck, monkeys by th' loins, and men by

                                                                        49

th' legs. When a man's over-lusty at legs, then he wears wooden
netherstocks.   10

LEAR. What's he that hath so much thy place mistook
    To set thee here?

KENT.   It is both he and she,
    Your son and daughter.

LEAR. No.

KENT. Yes.   15

LEAR. No, I say.

KENT. I say, yea.

LEAR. No, no; they would not.

KENT. Yes, they have.

LEAR. By Jupiter, I swear, no.   20

KENT. By Juno, I swear, ay.

LEAR.   They durst not do't;
    They could not, would not do't; 'tis worse than murder
    To do upon respect such violent outrage.
    Resolve me with all modest haste which way
    Thou might'st deserve or they impose this usage,   25
    Coming from us.

KENT.   My lord, when at their home
    I did commend your Highness' letters to them
    Ere I was risen from the place that show'd
    My duty kneeling, came there a reeking post,
    Stew'd in his haste, half breathless, panting forth   30
    From Goneril his mistress salutations;
    Deliver'd letters, spite of intermission,
    Which presently they read; on whose contents
    They summon'd up their meiny, straight took horse,
    Commanded me to follow and attend   35
    The leisure of their answer, gave me cold looks;
    And meeting here the other messenger,
    Whose welcome I perceiv'd had poison'd mine,
    Being the very fellow which of late
    Display'd so saucily against your Highness,   40
    Having more man than wit about me, drew.
    He rais'd the house with loud and coward cries.
    Your son and daughter found this trespass worth
    The shame which here it suffers.

FOOL. Winter's not gone yet, if the wild geese fly that way.
                    Fathers that wear rags
                        Do make their children blind;
                    But fathers that bear bags
                        Shall see their children kind.   50
                    Fortune, that arrant whore,
                        Ne'er turns the key to th' poor.
    But, for all this, thou shalt have as many dolours for thy daughters
    as thou canst tell in a year.

LEAR. O, how this mother swells up toward my heart!   55
    Hysterica passio—down, thou climbing sorrow,
    Thy element's below. Where is this daughter?

KENT. With the earl, sir, here within.

LEAR.   Follow me not;
    Stay here.   [Exit.

GENT. Made you no more offence but what you speak of ?   60
KENT. None.
    How chance the King comes with so small a number ?
FOOL. An thou hadst been set i' th' stocks for that question, thou'dst
    well deserv'd it.
KENT. Why, fool ?   65
FOOL. We'll set thee to school to an ant, to teach thee there's no
    labouring i' th' winter. All that follow their noses are led by
    their eyes but blind men ; and there's not a nose among twenty
    but can smell him that's stinking. Let go thy hold when a
    great wheel runs down a hill, lest it break thy neck with following ;
    but the great one that goes upward, let him draw thee after.
    When a wise man gives thee better counsel, give me mine again.
    I would have none but knaves follow it, since a fool gives it.   75

        That sir which serves and seeks for gain,
           And follows but for form,
        Will pack when it begins to rain,
           And leave thee in the storm.
        But I will tarry ; the fool will stay   80
           And let the wise man fly.
        The knave turns fool that runs away ;
           The fool no knave, perdy.   85

KENT. Where learn'd you this, fool ?
FOOL. Not i' th' stocks, fool.

        Re-enter LEAR *and* GLOUCESTER.

LEAR. Deny to speak with me ! They are sick ! They are weary !
    They have travell'd all the night ! Mere fetches ;
    The images of revolt and flying off.
    Fetch me a better answer.
GLO.   My dear lord,
    You know the fiery quality of the Duke ;   90
    How unremovable and fix'd he is
    In his own course.
LEAR. Vengeance ! plague ! death ! confusion !
    Fiery ? What quality ? Why Gloucester, Gloucester,
    I'd speak with the Duke of Cornwall and his wife.   95
GLO. Well, my good lord, I have inform'd them so.
LEAR. Inform'd them ! Dost thou understand me, man ?
GLO. Ay, my good lord.
LEAR. The King would speak with Cornwall ; the dear father
    Would with his daughter speak ; commands their service.   100
    Are they inform'd of this ? My breath and blood !
    Fiery ? the fiery Duke ? Tell the hot Duke that—
    No, but not yet. May be he is not well.
    Infirmity doth still neglect all office
    Whereto our health is bound ; we are not ourselves   105
    When nature, being oppress'd, commands the mind
    To suffer with the body. I'll forbear ;
    And am fallen out with my more headier will
    To take the indispos'd and sickly fit
    For the sound man. Death on my state ! Wherefore   110
    Should he sit here ? This act persuades me

That this remotion of the Duke and her
Is practice only.   Give me my servant forth.
Go tell the Duke and's wife I'd speak with them—
Now, presently.   Bid them come forth and hear me,   115
Or at their chamber door I'll beat the drum
Till it cry sleep to death.

GLO. I would have all well betwixt you.   [*Exit.*

LEAR. O me, my heart, my rising heart! But, down.

FOOL. Cry to it, nuncle, as the cockney did to the eels when she put
'em i' th' paste alive; she knapp'd 'em o' th' coxcombs with a
stick, and cried ' Down, wantons, down '. 'Twas her brother
that, in pure kindness to his horse, butter'd his hay.   124

Enter CORNWALL, REGAN, GLOUCESTER, *and* SERVANTS.

LEAR. Good morrow to you both.

CORN.   Hail to your Grace !

[KENT *here set at liberty.*

REG. I am glad to see your Highness.

LEAR. Regan, I think you are; I know what reason
I have to think so.   If thou shouldst not be glad,
I would divorce me from thy mother's tomb,
Sepulchring an adultress. [*To* KENT.] O, are you free?   130
Some other time for that.—Beloved Regan,
Thy sister's naught.   O Regan, she hath tied
Sharp-tooth'd unkindness, like a vulture, here.

[*Points to his heart.*

I can scarce speak to thee; thou'lt not believe
With how deprav'd a quality—O Regan!   135

REG. I pray you, sir, take patience.   I have hope
You less know how to value her desert
Than she to scant her duty.

LEAR.   Say, how is that?

REG. I cannot think my sister in the least
Would fail her obligation.   If, sir, perchance   140
She have restrain'd the riots of your followers,
'Tis on such ground, and to such wholesome end,
As clears her from all blame.

LEAR. My curses on her!

REG.   O, sir, you are old;
Nature in you stands on the very verge   145
Of her confine.   You should be rul'd and led
By some discretion that discerns your state
Better than you yourself.   Therefore I pray you
That to our sister you do make return;
Say you have wrong'd her, sir.

LEAR.   Ask her forgiveness?   150
Do you but mark how this becomes the house:
' Dear daughter, I confess that I am old;   [*Kneeling.*
Age is unnecessary; on my knees I beg
That you'll vouchsafe me raiment, bed, and food '.

REG. Good sir, no more; these are unsightly tricks.   155
Return you to my sister.

LEAR. [*Rising.*]   Never, Regan.
She hath abated me of half my train;

Look'd black upon me ; struck me with her tongue,
Most serpent-like, upon the very heart.
All the stor'd vengeances of heaven fall   160
On her ingrateful top ! Strike her young bones,
You taking airs, with lameness.

CORN.   Fie, sir, fie !

LEAR. You nimble lightnings, dart your blinding flames
    Into her scornful eyes. Infect her beauty,
    You fen-suck'd fogs, drawn by the pow'rful sun   165
    To fall and blast her pride.

REG.   O the blest gods !
    So will you wish on me when the rash mood is on.

LEAR. No, Regan, thou shalt never have my curse :
    Thy tender-hefted nature shall not give   170
    Thee o'er to harshness. Her eyes are fierce, but thine
    Do comfort and not burn. 'Tis not in thee
    To grudge my pleasures, to cut off my train,
    To bandy hasty words, to scant my sizes,
    And, in conclusion, to oppose the bolt   175
    Against my coming in ; thou better know'st
    The offices of nature, bond of childhood,
    Effects of courtesy, dues of gratitude ;
    Thy half o' th' kingdom hast thou not forgot,
    Wherein I thee endow'd.

REG.   Good sir, to th' purpose.   180

LEAR. Who put my man i' th' stocks ?   [Tucket within.

CORN.   What trumpet's that ?

REG. I know't—my sister's. This approves her letter,
    That she would soon be here.

Enter OSWALD.

                              Is your lady come ?

LEAR. This is a slave whose easy-borrow'd pride
    Dwells in the fickle grace of her he follows.   185
    Out, varlet, from my sight !

CORN.   What means your Grace ?

Enter GONERIL.

LEAR. Who stock'd my servant ? Regan, I have good hope
    Thou didst not know on't.—Who comes here ? O heavens,
    If you do love old men, if your sweet sway
    Allow obedience, if you yourselves are old,   190
    Make it your cause ; send down, and take my part.
    [*To* GONERIL.] Art not asham'd to look upon this beard ?—
    O Regan, will you take her by the hand ?

GON. Why not by th' hand, sir ? How have I offended ?
    All's not offence that indiscretion finds,   195
    And dotage terms so.

LEAR.   O sides, you are too tough !
    Will you yet hold ?—How came my man i' th' stocks ?

CORN. I set him there, sir ; but his own disorders
    Deserv'd much less advancement.

LEAR.   You ! did you ?

REG. I pray you, father, being weak, seem so.   200

If, till the expiration of your month,
You will return and sojourn with my sister,
Dismissing half your train, come then to me.
I am now from home, and out of that provision
Which shall be needful for your entertainment.   205
LEAR. Return to her, and fifty men dismiss'd ?
No, rather I abjure all roofs, and choose
To wage against the enmity o' th' air,
To be a comrade with the wolf and owl—
Necessity's sharp pinch !   Return with her ?   210
Why, the hot-blooded France, that dowerless took
Our youngest born—I could as well be brought
To knee this throne, and, squire-like, pension beg
To keep base life afoot.   Return with her ?
Persuade me rather to be slave and sumpter   215
To this detested groom.   [*Pointing to* OSWALD.
GON.   At your choice, sir.
LEAR. I prithee, daughter, do not make me mad.
I will not trouble thee, my child ; farewell.
We'll no more meet, no more see one another.
But yet thou art my flesh, my blood, my daughter ;   220
Or rather a disease that's in my flesh,
Which I must needs call mine ; thou art a boil,
A plague-sore, or embossed carbuncle
In my corrupted blood.   But I'll not chide thee ;
Let shame come when it will, I do not call it ;   225
I do not bid the Thunder-bearer shoot,
Nor tell tales of thee to high-judging Jove.
Mend when thou canst ; be better at thy leisure ;
I can be patient ; I can stay with Regan,
I and my hundred knights.
REG.   Not altogether so.   230
I look'd not for you yet, nor am provided
For your fit welcome.   Give ear, sir, to my sister ;
For those that mingle reason with your passion
Must be content to think you old, and so—
But she knows what she does.
LEAR.   Is this well spoken ?   235
REG. I dare avouch it, sir.   What, fifty followers ?
Is it not well ?   What should you need of more ?
Yea, or so many, sith that both charge and danger
Speak 'gainst so great a number ?   How in one house
Should many people under two commands   240
Hold amity ?   'Tis hard ; almost impossible.
GON. Why might not you, my lord, receive attendance
From those that she calls servants, or from mine ?
REG. Why not, my lord ?   If then they chanc'd to slack ye,
We could control them.   If you will come to me—   245
For now I spy a danger—I entreat you
To bring but five and twenty.   To no more
Will I give place or notice.
LEAR. I gave you all.
REG.   And in good time you gave it.
LEAR. Made you my guardians, my depositaries ;   250

But kept a reservation to be followed
With such a number. What, must I come to you
With five and twenty, Regan ? Said you so ?
REG. And speak't again, my lord. No more with me.
LEAR. Those wicked creatures yet do look well-favour'd   255
    When others are more wicked ; not being the worst
    Stands in some rank of praise. [*To* GONERIL.] I'll go with thee.
    Thy fifty yet doth double five and twenty,
    And thou art twice her love.
GON.   Hear me, my lord :
    What need you five and twenty, ten, or five,   260
    To follow in a house where twice so many
    Have a command to tend you ?
REG.   What need one ?
LEAR. O, reason not the need ! Our basest beggars
    Are in the poorest thing superfluous.
    Allow not nature more than nature needs,   265
    Man's life is cheap as beast's. Thou art a lady ;
    If only to go warm were gorgeous,
    Why, nature needs not what thou gorgeous wear'st,
    Which scarcely keeps thee warm. But, for true need—
    You heavens, give me that patience, patience I need.   270
    You see me here, you gods, a poor old man,
    As full of grief as age ; wretched in both.
    If it be you that stirs these daughters' hearts
    Against their father, fool me not so much
    To bear it tamely ; touch me with noble anger,   275
    And let not women's weapons, water-drops,
    Stain my man's cheeks ! No, you unnatural hags,
    I will have such revenges on you both
    That all the world shall—I will do such things—
    What they are yet I know not ; but they shall be   280
    The terrors of the earth. You think I'll weep.
    No, I'll not weep.   [*Storm and tempest.*
    I have full cause of weeping ; but this heart
    Shall break into a hundred thousand flaws
    Or ere I'll weep. O fool, I shall go mad !   285
            [*Exeunt* LEAR, GLOUCESTER, KENT, *and* FOOL.
CORN. Let us withdraw ; 'twill be a storm.
REG. This house is little : the old man and's people
    Cannot be well bestow'd.
GON. 'Tis his own blame ; hath put himself from rest,
    And must needs taste his folly.   290
REG. For his particular, I'll receive him gladly,
    But not one follower.
GON.   So am I purpos'd.
    Where is my Lord of Gloucester ?
CORN. Followed the old man forth.

Re-enter GLOUCESTER.

                He is return'd.
GLO. The King is in high rage.
CORN.   Whither is he going ?   295
GLO. He calls to horse ; but will I know not whither.

CORN. 'Tis best to give him way ; he leads himself.
GON. My lord, entreat him by no means to stay.
GLO. Alack, the night comes on, and the high winds
  Do sorely ruffle ; for many miles about   300
  There's scarce a bush.
REG.   O sir, to wilful men
  The injuries that they themselves procure
  Must be their schoolmasters. Shut up your doors.
  He is attended with a desperate train ;
  And what they may incense him to, being apt   305
  To have his ear abus'd, wisdom bids fear.
CORN. Shut up your doors, my lord ; 'tis a wild night.
  My Regan counsels well. Come out o' th' storm.   [*Exeunt.*

ACT THREE

SCENE I. *A heath.*

Storm still. Enter KENT *and a* GENTLEMAN, *severally.*

KENT. Who's there, besides foul weather ?
GENT. One minded like the weather, most unquietly.
KENT. I know you. Where's the King ?
GENT. Contending with the fretful elements ;
  Bids the wind blow the earth into the sea,   5
  Or swell the curled waters 'bove the main,
  That things might change or cease ; tears his white hair,
  Which the impetuous blasts, with eyeless rage,
  Catch in their fury, and make nothing of ;
  Strives in his little world of man to outscorn   10
  The to-and-fro conflicting wind and rain.
  This night, wherein the cub-drawn bear would couch,
  The lion and the belly-pinched wolf
  Keep their fur dry, unbonneted he runs,
  And bids what will take all.
KENT.   But who is with him ?   15
GENT. None but the fool ; who labours to out-jest
  His heart-struck injuries.
KENT.   Sir, I do know you,
  And dare, upon the warrant of my note,
  Commend a dear thing to you. There is division,
  Although as yet the face of it be cover'd   20
  With mutual cunning, 'twixt Albany and Cornwall;
  Who have—as who have not that their great stars
  Thron'd and set high ?—servants, who seem no less,
  Which are to France the spies and speculations
  Intelligent of our state. What hath been seen,   25
  Either in snuffs and packings of the Dukes ;
  Or the hard rein which both of them hath borne
  Against the old kind King ; or something deeper,
  Whereof perchance these are but furnishings—
  But true it is from France there comes a power   30
  Into this scatter'd kingdom, who already,
  Wise in our negligence, have secret feet
  In some of our best ports, and are at point
  To show their open banner. Now to you :

If on my credit you dare build so far   35
To make your speed to Dover, you shall find
Some that will thank you making just report
Of how unnatural and bemadding sorrow
The King hath cause to plain.
I am a gentleman of blood and breeding ;   40
And from some knowledge and assurance offer
This office to you.
KENT. I will talk further with you.
GENT.   No, do not.
For confirmation that I am much more
Than my out-wall, open this purse and take   45
What it contains. If you shall see Cordelia,
As fear not but you shall, show her this ring ;
And she will tell you who your fellow is
That yet you do not know. Fie on this storm !
I will go seek the King.
GENT. Give me your hand. Have you no more to say ?   50
KENT. Few words, but, to effect, more than all yet ;
That when we have found the King—in which your pain
That way, I'll this—he that first lights on him
Holla the other.   [*Exeunt severally.*

SCENE II. *Another part of the heath.*

Storm still. Enter LEAR *and* FOOL.

LEAR. Blow, winds, and crack your cheeks ; rage, blow.
You cataracts and hurricanoes, spout
Till you have drench'd our steeples, drown'd the cocks.
You sulph'rous and thought-executing fires,
Vaunt-couriers of oak-cleaving thunderbolts,   5
Singe my white head. And thou, all-shaking thunder
Strike flat the thick rotundity o' th' world ;
Crack nature's moulds, all germens spill at once,
That makes ingrateful man.   9
FOOL. O nuncle, court holy water in a dry house is better than this
rain-water out o' door. Good nuncle, in ; ask thy daughters'
blessing. Here's a night pities neither wise men nor fools.
LEAR. Rumble thy bellyful. Spit, fire ; spout, rain.
Nor rain, wind, thunder, fire, are my daughters.   15
I tax not you, you elements, with unkindness ;
I never gave you kingdom, call'd you children ;
You owe me no subscription. Then let fall
Your horrible pleasure. Here I stand, your slave,
A poor, infirm, weak and despis'd old man ;   20
But yet I call you servile ministers
That will with two pernicious daughters join
Your high-engender'd battles 'gainst a head
So old and white as this. O, ho ! 'tis foul !   24
FOOL. He that has a house to put's head in has a good head-piece.

The cod-piece that will house
Before the head has any,
The head and he shall louse ;
So beggars marry many.   30

57

                    The man that makes his toe
                      What he his heart should make
                    Shall of a corn cry woe,
                      And turn his sleep to wake.

For there was never yet fair woman but she made mouths in a
glass.   36

Enter KENT.

LEAR. No, I will be the pattern of all patience ;
    I will say nothing.
KENT. Who's there ?
FOOL. Marry, here's grace and a cod-piece ; that's a wise man and a
    fool.   41
KENT. Alas, sir, are you here ?   Things that love night
    Love not such nights as these ; the wrathful skies
    Gallow the very wanderers of the dark
    And make them keep their caves.   Since I was man   45
    Such sheets of fire, such bursts of horrid thunder,
    Such groans of roaring wind and rain, I never
    Remember to have heard.   Man's nature cannot carry
    Th' affliction nor the fear.
LEAR.   Let the great gods,
    That keep this dreadful pudder o'er our heads,   50
    Find out their enemies now.   Tremble, thou wretch,
    That hast within thee undivulged crimes
    Unwhipp'd of justice.   Hide thee, thou bloody hand ;
    Thou perjur'd, and thou simular man of virtue
    That art incestuous ; caitiff, to pieces shake,   55
    That under covert and convenient seeming
    Hast practis'd on man's life.   Close pent-up guilts,
    Rive your concealing continents, and cry
    These dreadful summoners grace.   I am a man
    More sinn'd against than sinning.
KENT.   Alack, bare-headed ! 60
    Gracious my lord, hard by here is a hovel ;
    Some friendship will it lend you 'gainst the tempest.
    Repose you there, while I to this hard house—
    More harder than the stones whereof 'tis rais'd ;
    Which even but now, demanding after you,   65
    Denied me to come in—return, and force
    Their scanted courtesy.
LEAR.   My wits begin to turn.
    Come on, my boy.   How dost, my boy ?   Art cold ?
    I am cold myself.   Where is this straw, my fellow ?
    The art of our necessities is strange   70
    That can make vile things precious.   Come, your hovel.
    Poor fool and knave, I have one part in my heart
    That's sorry yet for thee.
FOOL. [*Sings.*]
                    He that has and a little tiny wit
                      With heigh-ho, the wind and the rain—   75
                    Must make content with his fortunes fit,
                      Though the rain it raineth every day.

LEAR. True, my good boy. Come, bring us to this hovel.

[*Exeunt* LEAR *and* KENT.

FOOL. This is a brave night to cool a courtezan. I'll speak a prophecy
    ere I go.   80
        When priests are more in word than matter ;
        When brewers mar their malt with water ;
        When nobles are their tailors' tutors ;
        No heretics burn'd, but wenches' suitors ;
        When every case in law is right ;   85
        No squire in debt, nor no poor knight ;
        When slanders do not live in tongues ;
        Nor cutpurses come not to throngs ;
        When usurers tell their gold i' th' field ;
        And bawds and whores do churches build—   90
        Then shall the realm of Albion
        Come to great confusion.
        Then comes the time, who lives to see't,
        That going shall be us'd with feet.
    This prophecy Merlin shall make, for I live before his time. [*Exit.*

SCENE III. *Gloucester's castle.*

Enter GLOUCESTER *and* EDMUND.

GLO. Alack, alack, Edmund, I like not this unnatural dealing. When
    I desired their leave that I might pity him, they took from me
    the use of mine own house, charg'd me, on pain of perpetual
    displeasure, neither to speak of him, entreat for him, or any way
    sustain him.   6
EDM. Most savage and unnatural !
GLO. Go to ; say you nothing. There is division between the Dukes ;
    and a worse matter than that. I have received a letter this night—
    'tis dangerous to be spoken ; I have lock'd the letter in my closet.
    These injuries the King now bears will be revenged home ; there
    is part of a power already footed. We must incline to the King.
    I will look him, and privily relieve him. Go you and maintain
    talk with the Duke, that my charity be not of him perceived ;
    if he ask for me, I am ill, and gone to bed. If I die for it, as no
    less is threatened me, the King my old master must be relieved.
    There is strange things toward, Edmund ; pray you be careful.

[*Exit.*

EDM. This courtesy forbid thee shall the Duke   21
    Instantly know, and of that letter too.
    This seems a fair deserving, and must draw me
    That which my father loses—no less than all.
    The younger rises, when the old doth fall.   [*Exit.*

SCENE IV. *Before a hovel on the heath.*

Storm still. Enter LEAR, KENT, *and* FOOL.

KENT. Here is the place, my lord ; good my lord, enter.
    The tyranny of the open night's too rough
    For nature to endure.
LEAR.   Let me alone.
KENT. Good my lord, enter here.

LEAR.   Wilt break my heart?
KENT. I had rather break mine own. Good my lord, enter.   5
LEAR. Thou think'st 'tis much that this contentious storm
    Invades us to the skin; so 'tis to thee,
    But where the greater malady is fix'd,
    The lesser is scarce felt. Thou'dst shun a bear;
    But if thy flight lay toward the roaring sea,   10
    Thou'dst meet the bear i' th' mouth. When the mind's free
    The body's delicate; this tempest in my mind
    Doth from my senses take all feeling else,
    Save what beats there. Filial ingratitude!
    Is it not as this mouth should tear this hand   15
    For lifting food to't? But I will punish home.
    No, I will weep no more. In such a night,
    To shut me out! Pour on; I will endure.
    In such a night as this! O Regan, Goneril!
    Your old kind father, whose frank heart gave all!   20
    O, that way madness lies; let me shun that;
    No more of that.
KENT.   Good my lord, enter here.
LEAR. Prithee go in thyself; seek thine own ease.
    This tempest will not give me leave to ponder
    On things would hurt me more. But I'll go in.   25
    [*To the* FOOL.] In, boy; go first.—You houseless poverty—
    Nay, get thee in. I'll pray, and then I'll sleep.   [*Exit* FOOL.
    Poor naked wretches, wheresoe'er you are,
    That bide the pelting of this pitiless storm,
    How shall your houseless heads and unfed sides,   30
    Your loop'd and window'd raggedness, defend you
    From seasons such as these? O, I have ta'en
    Too little care of this! Take physic, pomp;
    Expose thyself to feel what wretches feel,
    That thou mayst shake the superflux to them,   35
    And show the heavens more just.
EDG. [*Within.*] Fathom and half, fathom and half! Poor Tom!

Enter FOOL *from the hovel.*

FOOL. Come not in here, nuncle, here's a spirit. Help me, help me!
KENT. Give me thy hand. Who's there?   41
FOOL. A spirit, a spirit. He says his name's poor Tom.
KENT. What art thou that dost grumble there i' th' straw?
    Come forth.

Enter EDGAR, *disguised as a madman.*

EDG. Away! the foul fiend follows me.
    Through the sharp hawthorn blows the cold wind
    Humh! go to thy cold bed and warm thee.   47
LEAR. Didst thou give all to thy daughters? And art thou come to
    this?
EDG. Who gives anything to poor Tom? whom the foul fiend hath
    led through fire and through flame, through ford and whirlpool,
    o'er bog and quagmire; that hath laid knives under his pillow
    and halters in his pew, set ratsbane by his porridge; made him
    proud of heart, to ride on a bay trotting-horse over four-inched

bridges, to course his own shadow for a traitor. Bless thy five
wits ! Tom's a-cold. O, do de, do de, do de. Bless thee from
whirlwinds, starblasting, and taking ! Do poor Tom some
charity, whom the foul fiend vexes. There could I have him
now—and there—and there again—and there.   [*Storm still.*

LEAR. What, has his daughters brought him to this pass ?   63
  Could'st thou save nothing ? Would'st thou give 'em all ?

FOOL. Nay, he reserv'd a blanket, else we had been all sham'd.

LEAR. Now all the plagues that in the pendulous air
  Hang fated o'er men's faults light on thy daughters !

KENT. He hath no daughters, sir.

LEAR. Death, traitor ! Nothing could have subdu'd nature
  To such a lowness but his unkind daughters.   70
  Is it the fashion that discarded fathers
  Should have thus little mercy on their flesh ?
  Judicious punishment ! 'twas this flesh begot
  Those pelican daughters.

EDG. Pillicock sat on Pillicock-hill.   75
  Alow, alow, loo, loo !

FOOL. This cold night will turn us all to fools and madmen.

EDG. Take heed o' th' foul fiend ; obey thy parents ; keep thy words
  justly ; swear not ; commit not with man's sworn spouse ; set
  not thy sweet heart on proud array. Tom's a-cold.   82

LEAR. What hast thou been ?

EDG. A serving-man, proud in heart and mind ; that curl'd my hair ;
  wore gloves in my cap ; serv'd the lust of my mistress' heart,
  and did the act of darkness with her ; swore as many oaths as I
  spake words, and broke them in the sweet face of heaven ; one
  that slept in the contriving of lust, and wak'd to do it. Wine
  lov'd I deeply, dice dearly ; and in woman out-paramour'd the
  Turk. False of heart, light of ear, bloody of hand ; hog in sloth,
  fox in stealth, wolf in greediness, dog in madness, lion in prey.
  Let not the creaking of shoes nor the rustling of silks betray thy
  poor heart to woman. Keep thy foot out of brothels, thy hand
  out of plackets, thy pen from lenders' books, and defy the foul
  fiend.   96
  Still through the hawthorn blows the cold wind.
  Says suum, mun, nonny.
  Dolphin my boy, boy, sessa ! let him trot by.   [*Storm still.*

LEAR. Why, thou wert better in a grave than to answer with thy
  uncover'd body this extremity of the skies. Is man no more
  than this ? Consider him well. Thou ow'st the worm no silk,
  the beast no hide, the sheep no wool, the cat no perfume. Ha !
  here's three on's are sophisticated ! Thou art the thing itself :
  unaccommodated man is no more but such a poor, bare, forked
  animal as thou art. Off, off, you lendings ! Come, unbutton
  here.   [*Tearing off his clothes.*

Enter GLOUCESTER *with a torch.*

FOOL. Prithee, nuncle, be contented ; 'tis a naughty night to swim in.
  Now a little fire in a wild field were like an old lecher's heart—
  a small spark, all the rest on's body cold. Look, here comes a
  walking fire.   112

EDG. This is the foul fiend Flibbertigibbet ; he begins at curfew,

and walks till the first cock ; he gives the web and the pin, squenes
the eye, and makes the hare-lip ; mildews the white wheat, and
hurts the poor creature of earth.   117

> Swithold footed thrice the 'old ;
> He met the nightmare and her ninefold;
> Bid her alight   120
> And her troth plight,
> And aroint thee, witch, aroint thee !

KENT. How fares your Grace ?
LEAR. What's he ?
KENT. Who's there ?   What is't you seek ?
GLO. What are you there ?   Your names ?   126
EDG. Poor Tom ; that eats the swimming frog, the toad, the tadpole,
the wall-newt, and the water ; that in the fury of his heart, when
the foul fiend rages, eats cowdung for sallets, swallows the old rat
and the ditch-dog, drinks the green mantle of the standing pool ;
who is whipp'd from tithing to tithing, and stock-punish'd,
and imprison'd ; who hath had three suits to his back, six shirts
to his body—

> Horse to ride, and weapon to wear ;
> But mice and rats, and such small deer,   135
> Have been Tom's food for seven long year.

Beware my follower.   Peace, Smulkin ; peace, thou fiend !
GLO. What, hath your Grace no better company ?
EDG. The prince of darkness is a gentleman ; Modo he's call'd, and
Mahu.   140
GLO. Our flesh and blood, my lord, is grown so vile
That it doth hate what gets it.
EDG. Poor Tom's a-cold.
GLO. Go in with me : my duty cannot suffer
T' obey in all your daughters' hard commands.   145
Though their injunction be to bar my doors,
And let this tyrannous night take hold upon you,
Yet have I ventur'd to come seek you out,
And bring you where both fire and food is ready.
LEAR. First let me talk with this philosopher.   150
What is the cause of thunder ?
KENT. Good my lord, take his offer ; go into th' house.
LEAR. I'll talk a word with this same learned Theban.
What is your study ?
EDG. How to prevent the fiend and to kill vermin.   155
LEAR. Let me ask you one word in private.
KENT. Importune him once more to go, my lord ;
His wits begin t' unsettle.   [Storm still.
GLO.   Canst thou blame him ?
His daughters seek his death.   Ah, that good Kent !—
He said it would be thus—poor, banish'd man !   160
Thou sayest the King grows mad ; I'll tell thee, friend,
I am almost mad myself.   I had a son,
Now outlaw'd from my blood ; he sought my life
But lately, very late.   I lov'd him, friend—
No father his son dearer.   True to tell thee,   165
The grief hath craz'd my wits.   What a night's this !
I do beseech your Grace—

LEAR.   O, cry you mercy, sir.
  Noble philosopher, your company.
EDG. Tom's a-cold.
GLO. In, fellow, there, into th' hovel; keep thee warm.   170
LEAR. Come, let's in all.
KENT.   This way, my lord.
LEAR.   With him:
  I will keep still with my philosopher.
KENT. Good my lord, soothe him; let him take the fellow.
GLO. Take him you on.
KENT. Sirrah, come on; go along with us.   175
LEAR. Come, good Athenian.
GLO. No words, no words! Hush.
EDG.   Child Rowland to the dark tower came,
                His word was still ' Fie, foh, and fum,
                I smell the blood of a British man '.   [Exeunt.

SCENE V. *Gloucester's castle.*

Enter CORNWALL *and* EDMUND.

CORN. I will have my revenge ere I depart his house.
EDM. How, my lord, I may be censured, that nature thus gives way
  to loyalty, something fears me to think of.
CORN. I now perceive it was not altogether your brother's evil
  disposition made him seek his death; but a provoking merit,
  set a-work by a reprovable badness in himself.   7
EDM. How malicious is my fortune, that I must repent to be just!
  This is the letter he spoke of, which approves him an intelligent
  party to the advantages of France. O heavens! that this treason
  were not, or not I the detector!   12
CORN. Go with me to the Duchess.
EDM. If the matter of this paper be certain, you have mighty business
  in hand.
CORN. True or false, it hath made thee Earl of Gloucester. Seek out
  where thy father is, that he may be ready for our apprehension.
EDM. [*Aside.*] If I find him comforting the King, it will stuff his
  suspicion more fully.—I will persever in my course of loyalty,
  though the conflict be sore between that and my blood.   22
CORN. I will lay trust upon thee; and thou shalt find a dearer father
  in my love.   [*Exeunt.*

SCENE VI. *An outhouse of Gloucester's castle.*

Enter KENT *and* GLOUCESTER.

GLO. Here is better than the open air; take it thankfully. I will piece
  out the comfort with what addition I can. I will not be long
  from you.
KENT. All the pow'r of his wits have given way to his impatience.
  The gods reward your kindness!   [*Exit* GLOUCESTER.

Enter LEAR, EDGAR, *and* FOOL.

EDG. Frateretto calls me, and tells me Nero is an angler in the lake
  of darkness. Pray, innocent, and beware the foul fiend.

                                                                   63

FOOL. Prithee, nuncle, tell me whether a madman be a gentleman
    or a yeoman?   10

LEAR. A king, a king!

FOOL. No; he's a yeoman that has a gentleman to his son; for he's
    a mad yeoman that sees his son a gentleman before him.

LEAR. To have a thousand with red burning spits   15
    Come hizzing in upon 'em—

EDG. The foul fiend bites my back.

FOOL. He's mad that trusts in the tameness of a wolf, a horse's
    health, a boy's love, or a whore's oath.

LEAR. It shall be done; I will arraign them straight.
    [*To* EDGAR.]   Come, sit thou here, most learned justicer.   21
    [*To the* FOOL.]   Thou, sapient sir, sit here.—Now, you she-foxes!

EDG. Look where he stands and glares!
    Want'st thou eyes at trial, madam?
               Come o'er the bourn, Bessy, to me.   25

FOOL.   Her boat hath a leak,
               And she must not speak,
               Why she dares not come over to thee.

EDG. The foul fiend haunts poor Tom in the voice of a nightingale.
    Hoppedance cries in Tom's belly for two white herring. Croak
    not, black angel; I have no food for thee.   32

KENT. How do you, sir? Stand you not so amaz'd.
    Will you lie down and rest upon the cushions?

LEAR. I'll see their trial first. Bring in their evidence.
    [*To* EDGAR.]   Thou robed man of justice, take thy place.   36
    [*To the* FOOL.]   And thou, his yoke-fellow of equity,
    Bench by his side. [*To* KENT.]   You are o' th' commission,
    Sit you too.   40

EDG. Let us deal justly.
               Sleepest or wakest thou, jolly shepherd?
               Thy sheep be in the corn;
               And for one blast of thy minikin mouth,
               Thy sheep shall take no harm.
    Pur! the cat is grey.   45

LEAR. Arraign her first; 'tis Goneril. I here take my oath before
    this honourable assembly she kick'd the poor King her father.

FOOL. Come hither, mistress. Is your name Goneril?

LEAR. She cannot deny it.   50

FOOL. Cry you mercy, I took you for a joint-stool.

LEAR. And here's another, whose warp'd looks proclaim
    What store her heart is made on. Stop her there!
    Arms, arms, sword, fire! Corruption in the place!
    False justicer, why hast thou let her scape?   55

EDG. Bless thy five wits!

KENT. O pity! Sir, where is the patience now
    That you so oft have boasted to retain?

EDG. [*Aside.*]   My tears begin to take his part so much
    They mar my counterfeiting.   60

LEAR. The little dogs and all,
    Tray, Blanch, and Sweetheart, see, they bark at me.

EDG. Tom will throw his head at them.
    Avaunt, you curs!

> Be thy mouth or black or white,   65
> Tooth that poisons if it bite;
> Mastiff, greyhound, mongrel grim,
> Hound or spaniel, brach or lym,
> Or bobtail tike or trundle-tail—
> Tom will make him weep and wail;   70
> For, with throwing thus my head,
> Dogs leapt the hatch, and all are fled.

Do, de, de, de. Sessa! Come, march to wakes and fairs and
market towns. Poor Tom, thy horn is dry.   74

LEAR. Then let them anatomize Regan; see what breeds about her
heart. Is there any cause in nature that make these hard hearts?
[*To* EDGAR.] You, sir, I entertain for one of my hundred; only
I do not like the fashion of your garments. You will say they are
Persian, but let them be chang'd.   80

KENT. Now, good my lord, lie here and rest awhile.

LEAR. Make no noise, make no noise; draw the curtains. So, so.
We'll go to supper i' th' morning.

FOOL. And I'll go to bed at noon.   85

Re-enter GLOUCESTER.

GLO. Come hither, friend. Where is the King my master?

KENT. Here sir; but trouble him not—his wits are gone.

GLO Good friend, I prithee, take him in thy arms;
I have o'erheard a plot of death upon him.
There is a litter ready; lay him in't   90
And drive toward Dover, friend, where thou shalt meet
Both welcome and protection. Take up thy master;
If thou shouldst dally half an hour, his life,
With thine, and all that offer to defend him,
Stand in assured loss. Take up, take up;   95
And follow me, that will to some provision
Give thee quick conduct.

KENT.   Oppressed nature sleeps.
This rest might yet have balm'd thy broken sinews,
Which, if convenience will not allow,
Stand in hard cure. [*To the* FOOL.] Come, help to bear thy master;
Thou must not stay behind.

GLO.   Come, come, away. [*Exeunt all but* EDGAR.

EDG. When we our betters see bearing our woes,
We scarcely think our miseries our foes.
Who alone suffers suffers most i' th' mind,
Leaving free things and happy shows behind;   105
But then the mind much sufferance doth o'erskip
When grief hath mates, and bearing fellowship.
How light and portable my pain seems now,
When that which makes me bend makes the King bow—
He childed as I father'd! Tom, away!   110
Mark the high noises; and thyself bewray,
When false opinion, whose wrong thoughts defile thee,
In thy just proof repeals and reconciles thee.
What will hap more to-night, safe scape the King!
Lurk, lurk.   [*Exit.*

3   65

SCENE VII. *Gloucester's castle.*

Enter CORNWALL, REGAN, GONERIL, EDMUND, *and* SERVANTS.

CORN. [*To* GONERIL.] Post speedily to my lord your husband ; show
   him this letter. The army of France is landed.—Seek out the
   traitor Gloucester.   [*Exeunt some of the* SERVANTS.
REG. Hang him instantly.
GON. Pluck out his eyes.   5
CORN. Leave him to my displeasure. Edmund, keep you our sister
   company. The revenges we are bound to take upon your
   traitorous father are not fit for your beholding. Advise the Duke,
   where you are going, to a most festinate preparation ; we are
   bound to the like. Our posts shall be swift and intelligent
   betwixt us. Farewell, dear sister ; farewell, my Lord of
   Gloucester.   12

Enter OSWALD.

How now ! where's the King ?
OSW. My Lord of Gloucester hath convey'd him hence.
   Some five or six and thirty of his knights,   15
   Hot questrists after him, met him at gate ;
   Who, with some other of the lord's dependants,
   Are gone with him toward Dover, where they boast
   To have well-armed friends.
CORN.   Get horses for your mistress.
GON. Farewell, sweet lord, and sister.   20
CORN. Edmund, farewell. [*Exeunt* GONERIL, EDMUND, *and* OSWALD.
                    Go seek the traitor Gloucester,
   Pinion him like a thief, bring him before us.
                                        [*Exeunt other* SERVANTS.
   Though well we may not pass upon his life
   Without the form of justice, yet our power
   Shall do a court'sy to our wrath, which men   25
   May blame, but not control.

Enter GLOUCESTER, *brought in by* two *or* three.

                            Who's there ? the traitor ?
REG. Ingrateful fox ! 'tis he.
CORN. Bind fast his corky arms.
GLO. What means your Graces ? Good my friends, consider
   You are my guests ; do me no foul play, friends.   30
CORN. Bind him, I say.   [SERVANTS *bind him.*
REG.   Hard, hard. O filthy traitor !
GLO. Unmerciful lady as you are, I'm none.
CORN. To this chair bind him. Villain, thou shalt find—
                                        [REGAN *plucks his beard.*
GLO. By the kind gods, 'tis most ignobly done
   To pluck me by the beard.   35
REG. So white, and such a traitor !
GLO.   Naughty lady,
   These hairs which thou dost ravish from my chin
   Will quicken and accuse thee. I am your host.
   With robbers' hands my hospitable favours

You should not ruffle thus. What will you do ?   40
CORN. Come, sir, what letters had you late from France ?
REG. Be simple-answer'd, for we know the truth.
CORN. And what confederacy have you with the traitors
    Late footed in the kingdom ?
REG. To whose hands you have sent the lunatic King :   45
    Speak.
GLO. I have a letter guessingly set down,
    Which came from one that's of a neutral heart,
    And not from one oppos'd.
CORN.   Cunning.
REG.   And false.
CORN. Where hast thou sent the King ?
GLO.   To Dover.   50
REG. Wherefore to Dover ? Wast thou not charg'd at peril—
CORN. Wherefore to Dover ? Let him first answer that.
GLO. I am tied to the stake, and I must stand the course.
REG. Wherefore to Dover ?
GLO. Because I would not see thy cruel nails   55
    Pluck out his poor old eyes ; nor thy fierce sister
    In his anointed flesh rash boarish fangs.
    The sea, with such a storm as his bare head
    In hell-black night endur'd, would have buoy'd up
    And quench'd the stelled fires.   60
    Yet, poor old heart, he holp the heavens to rain.
    If wolves had at thy gate howl'd that dern time,
    Thou shouldst have said ' Good porter, turn the key '.
    All cruels else subscribe, but I shall see
    The winged vengeance overtake such children.   65
CORN. See't shalt thou never. Fellows, hold the chair.
    Upon these eyes of thine I'll set my foot.
GLO. He that will think to live till he be old,
    Give me some help !—O cruel ! O you gods !
REG. One side will mock another ; th' other too.   70
CORN. If you see vengeance—
I SERV.   Hold your hand, my lord.
    I have serv'd you ever since I was a child ;
    But better service have I never done you,
    Than now to bid you hold.
REG.   How now, you dog !
I SERV. If you did wear a beard upon your chin   75
    I'd shake it on this quarrel. What do you mean ?
CORN. My villain !   [*They draw and fight.*
I SERV. Nay, then come on, and take the chance of anger.
                      [CORNWALL *is wounded.*
REG. Give me thy sword. A peasant stand up thus !
      [*She takes a sword and stabs him from behind.*
I SERV. O, I am slain ! My lord, you have one eye left   80
    To see some mischief on him. O !   [*Dies.*
CORN. Lest it see more, prevent it. Out vile jelly !
    Where is thy lustre now ?
GLO. All dark and comfortless ! Where's my son Edmund ?
    Edmund, enkindle all the sparks of nature   85
    To quit this horrid act.

REG.   Out, treacherous villain!
    Thou call'st on him that hates thee.   It was he
    That made the overture of thy treasons to us;
    Who is too good to pity thee.
GLO. O my follies!   Then Edgar was abus'd.   90
    Kind gods, forgive me that, and prosper him.
REG. Go thrust him out at gates and let him smell
    His way to Dover.   [GLOUCESTER *led out.*
                How is't my lord?   How look you?
CORN. I have receiv'd a hurt.   Follow me, lady.
    Turn out that eyeless villain; throw this slave   95
    Upon the dunghill.   Regan, I bleed apace.
    Untimely comes this hurt.   Give me your arm.
                    [*Exit* CORNWALL, *led by* REGAN.
2 SERV. I'll never care what wickedness I do,
    If this man come to good.
3 SERV.   If she live long,
    And in the end meet the old course of death,   100
    Women will all turn monsters.
2 SERV. Let's follow the old Earl and get the Bedlam
    To lead him where he would.   His roguish madness
    Allows itself to anything.
3 SERV. Go thou.   I'll fetch some flax and whites of eggs   105
    To apply to his bleeding face.   Now heaven help him!   [*Exeunt.*

ACT FOUR

SCENE I.   *The Heath.*

Enter EDGAR.

EDG. Yet better thus and known to be contemn'd,
    Than still contemn'd and flatter'd.   To be worst,
    The lowest and most dejected thing of fortune,
    Stands still in esperance, lives not in fear.
    The lamentable change is from the best;   5
    The worst returns to laughter.   Welcome, then,
    Thou unsubstantial air that I embrace!
    The wretch that thou hast blown unto the worst
    Owes nothing to thy blasts.

Enter GLOUCESTER, *led by an* OLD MAN.

                But who comes here?
    My father, poorly led?   World, world, O world!   10
    But that thy strange mutations make us hate thee,
    Life would not yield to age.
OLD MAN. O my good lord, I have been your tenant, and your father's
    tenant, these fourscore years.
GLO. Away, get thee away; good friend, be gone.   15
    Thy comforts can do me no good at all;
    Thee they may hurt.
OLD MAN. You cannot see your way.
GLO. I have no way, and therefore want no eyes;
    I stumbled when I saw: full oft 'tis seen   20
    Our means secure us, and our mere defects

Prove our commodities.   O dear son Edgar,
The food of thy abused father's wrath !
Might I but live to see thee in my touch,
I'd say I had eyes again !

LD MAN. How now !   Who's there ?   25

OG. [*Aside.*]   O gods !   Who is't can say ' I am at the worst ' ?
I am worse than e'er I was.

LD MAN. 'Tis poor mad Tom.

OG. [*Aside.*]   And worse I may be yet.   The worst is not
So long as we can say ' This is the worst '.

LD MAN. Fellow, where goest ?

LO.   Is it a beggar-man ?   30

LD MAN. Madman and beggar too.

LO. He has some reason, else he could not beg.
I' th' last night's storm I such a fellow saw ;
Which made me think a man a worm.   My son
Came then into my mind ; and yet my mind   35
Was then scarce friends with him.   I have heard more since.
As flies to wanton boys are we to th' gods—
They kill us for their sport.

OG. [*Aside.*]   How should this be ?
Bad is the trade that must play fool to sorrow,
Ang'ring itself and others.—Bless thee, master !   40

LO. Is that the naked fellow ?

LD MAN.   Ay, my lord.

LO. Then, prithee, get thee away.   If for my sake
Thou wilt o'ertake us hence a mile or twain
I' th' way toward Dover, do it for ancient love ;
And bring some covering for this naked soul,   45
Which I'll entreat to lead me.

LD MAN.   Alack, sir, he is mad.

LO. 'Tis the times' plague when madmen lead the blind.
Do as I bid thee, or rather do thy pleasure ;
Above the rest, be gone.

LD MAN. I'll bring him the best 'parel that I have,   50
Come on't what will.   [*Exit.*

LO. Sirrah, naked fellow !

OG. Poor Tom's a-cold. [*Aside.*] I cannot daub it further.

LO. Come hither, fellow.

OG. [*Aside.*] And yet I must.—Bless thy sweet eyes, they bleed. 55

LO. Know'st thou the way to Dover ?

OG. Both stile and gate, horse-way and footpath.   Poor Tom hath
been scar'd out of his good wits.   Bless thee, good man's son,
from the foul fiend !   Five fiends have been in poor Tom at once :
of lust, as Obidicut ;   Hobbididence, prince of dumbness ;   Mahu,
of stealing ;   Modo, of murder ;   Flibbertigibbet, of mopping and
mowing, who since possesses chambermaids and waiting-women.
So, bless thee, master !

LO. Here, take this purse, thou whom the heavens' plagues   65
Have humbled to all strokes.   That I am wretched
Makes thee the happier.   Heavens, deal so still !
Let the superfluous and lust-dieted man
That slaves your ordinance, that will not see
Because he does not feel, feel your power quickly ;   70

So distribution should undo excess,
And each man have enough. Dost thou know Dover?

EDG. Ay, master.

GLO. There is a cliff whose high and bending head
Looks fearfully in the confined deep :
Bring me but to the very brim of it
And I'll repair the misery thou dost bear
With something rich about me. From that place
I shall no leading need.

EDG.   Give me thy arm ;
Poor Tom shall lead thee.   [*Exeu*

SCENE II. *Before the Duke of Albany's palace.*

Enter GONERIL *and* EDMUND.

GON. Welcome, my lord. I marvel our mild husband
Not met us on the way.

Enter OSWALD.

                                   Now, where's your master?

OSW. Madam, within, but never man so chang'd.
I told him of the army that was landed ;
He smil'd at it. I told him you were coming ;
His answer was 'The worse'. Of Gloucester's treachery,
And of the loyal service of his son,
When I inform'd him, then he call'd me sot,
And told me I had turn'd the wrong side out.
What most he should dislike seems pleasant to him ;
What like, offensive.

GON. [*To* EDMUND.] Then shall you go no further.
It is the cowish terror of his spirit
That dares not undertake ; he'll not feel wrongs
Which tie him to an answer. Our wishes on the way
May prove effects. Back, Edmund, to my brother ;
Hasten his musters and conduct his pow'rs.
I must change arms at home, and give the distaff
Into my husband's hands. This trusty servant
Shall pass between us. Ere long you are like to hear,
If you dare venture in your own behalf,
A mistress's command. Wear this ; spare speech.
                                              [*Giving a favou*

Decline your head ; this kiss, if it durst speak,
Would stretch thy spirits up into the air.
Conceive, and fare thee well.

EDM. Yours in the ranks of death.

GON.   My most dear Gloucester. [*Exit* EDMUN

O, the difference of man and man !
To thee a woman's services are due.
My fool usurps my body.

OSW.   Madam, here comes my lord.   [*Ex*

Enter ALBANY.

GON. I have been worth the whistle.

ALB.   O Goneril !

You are not worth the dust which the rude wind   30
Blows in your face. I fear your disposition :
That nature which contemns it origin
Cannot be border'd certain in itself ;
She that herself will sliver and disbranch
From her material sap perforce must wither   35
And come to deadly use.

ON. No more ; the text is foolish.

LB. Wisdom and goodness to the vile seem vile ;
Filths savour but themselves. What have you done ?
Tigers, not daughters, what have you perform'd ?   40
A father, and a gracious aged man,
Whose reverence even the head-lugg'd bear would lick,
Most barbarous, most degenerate, have you madded.
Could my good brother suffer you to do it ?
A man, a Prince, by him so benefited !   45
If that the heavens do not their visible spirits
Send quickly down to tame these vile offences,
It will come
Humanity must perforce prey on itself,
Like monsters of the deep.

ON.   Milk-liver'd man !   50
That bear'st a cheek for blows, a head for wrongs ;
Who hast not in thy brows an eye discerning
Thine honour from thy suffering ; that not know'st
Fools do those villains pity who are punish'd
Ere they have done their mischief. Where's thy drum ? 55
France spreads his banners in our noiseless land,
With plumed helm thy state begins to threat,
Whil'st thou, a moral fool, sits still, and cries
' Alack, why does he so ? '

LB.   See thyself, devil !
Proper deformity shows not in the fiend   60
So horrid as in woman.

ON.   O vain fool !

LB. Thou changed and self-cover'd thing, for shame !
Be-monster not thy feature. Were't my fitness
To let these hands obey my blood,
They are apt enough to dislocate and tear   65
Thy flesh and bones. Howe'er thou art a fiend,
A woman's shape doth shield thee.

ON. Marry, your manhood—mew !

Enter a MESSENGER.

LB. What news ?

ESS. O, my good lord, the Duke of Cornwall's dead,   70
Slain by his servant, going to put out
The other eye of Gloucester.

LB.   Gloucester's eyes !

ESS. A servant that he bred, thrill'd with remorse,
Oppos'd against the act, bending his sword
To his great master ; who, thereat enrag'd,   75
Flew on him, and amongst them fell'd him dead ;

But not without that harmful stroke which since
Hath pluck'd him after.

ALB.   This shows you are above,
You justicers, that these our nether crimes
So speedily can venge! But, O poor Gloucester!   8
Lost he his other eye?

MESS.   Both, both, my lord.
This letter, madam, craves a speedy answer;
'Tis from your sister.

GON. [*Aside.*] One way I like this well;
But being widow, and my Gloucester with her,
May all the building in my fancy pluck   8
Upon my hateful life. Another way
The news is not so tart.—I'll read, and answer.   [*Exit*

ALB. Where was his son, when they did take his eyes?

MESS. Come with my lady hither.

ALB.   He is not here.

MESS. No, my good lord; I met him back again.   9

ALB. Knows he the wickedness?

MESS. Ay, my good lord; 'twas he inform'd against him
And quit the house on purpose that their punishment
Might have the freer course.

ALB.   Gloucester, I live
To thank thee for the love thou show'dst the King,   9
And to revenge thine eyes. Come hither, friend:
Tell me what more thou know'st.   [*Exeunt*

SCENE III. *The French camp near Dover.*

Enter KENT *and a* GENTLEMEN.

KENT. Why the King of France is so suddenly gone back know you
no reason?

GENT. Something he left imperfect in the state, which since his
coming forth is thought of, which imports to the kingdom so
much fear and danger that his personal return was most required
and necessary.

KENT. Who hath he left behind him general?

GENT. The Marshal of France, Monsieur La Far.

KENT. Did your letters pierce the Queen to any demonstration of
grief?   1

GENT. Ay, sir; she took them, read them in my presence,
And now and then an ample tear trill'd down
Her delicate cheek. It seem'd she was a queen
Over her passion, who, most rebel-like,
Sought to be king o'er her.

KENT.   O, then it mov'd her.   1

GENT. Not to a rage; patience and sorrow strove
Who should express her goodliest. You have seen
Sunshine and rain at once: her smiles and tears
Were like a better way. Those happy smilets
That play'd on her ripe lip seem'd not to know   2
What guests were in her eyes, which parted thence
As pearls from diamonds dropp'd. In brief,

Sorrow would be a rarity most beloved
If all could so become it.
KENT.   Made she no verbal question?
GENT. Faith, once or twice she heav'd the name of father   26
Pantingly forth, as if it press'd her heart;
Cried 'Sisters! sisters! Shame of ladies! Sisters!
Kent! father! sisters! What i' th' storm? i' th' night?
Let pity not be believ'd!' There she shook
The holy water from her heavenly eyes,   30
And clamour moisten'd; then away she started
To deal with grief alone.
KENT.   It is the stars,
The stars above us, govern our conditions,
Else one self mate and make could not beget
Such different issues. You spoke not with her since?   35
GENT. No.
KENT. Was this before the King return'd?
GENT.   No, since.
KENT. Well, sir, the poor distressed Lear's i' th' town;
Who sometime in his better tune remembers
What we are come about, and by no means   40
Will yield to see his daughter.
GENT.   Why, good sir?
KENT. A sovereign shame so elbows him; his own unkindness,
That stripp'd her from his benediction, turn'd her
To foreign casualties, gave her dear rights
To his dog-hearted daughters—these things sting   45
His mind so venomously that burning shame
Detains him from Cordelia.
GENT.   Alack, poor gentleman!
KENT. Of Albany's and Cornwall's powers you heard not?
GENT. 'Tis so; they are afoot.
KENT. Well, sir, I'll bring you to our master Lear,   50
And leave you to attend him. Some dear cause
Will in concealment wrap me up awhile;
When I am known aright, you shall not grieve
Lending me this acquaintance. I pray you go
Along with me.   [Exeunt.

SCENE IV. *The French camp. A tent.*

Enter with drum and colours, CORDELIA, DOCTOR, *and* SOLDIERS.

COR. Alack, 'tis he! Why, he was met even now
As mad as the vex'd sea, singing aloud,
Crown'd with rank fumiter and furrow weeds,
With hardocks, hemlock, nettles, cuckoo-flow'rs,
Darnel, and all the idle weeds that grow   5
In our sustaining corn. A century send forth;
Search every acre in the high-grown field,
And bring him to our eye.   [Exit an Officer.
                         What can man's wisdom,
In the restoring his bereaved sense?
He that helps him, take all my outward worth.   10
DOCT. There is means, madam.

73

Our foster-nurse of nature is repose,
The which he lacks ; that to provoke in him
Are many simples operative, whose power
Will close the eye of anguish.

COR.   All blest secrets,   15
All you unpublish'd virtues of the earth,
Spring with my tears ; be aidant and remediate,
In the good man's distress. Seek, seek for him ;
Lest his ungovern'd rage dissolve the life
That wants the means to lead it.

Enter a MESSENGER.

MESS.   News, madam :
The British pow'rs are marching hitherward.   21
COR. 'Tis known before ; our preparation stands
In expectation of them. O dear father !
It is thy business that I go about ;
Therefore great France   25
My mourning and importun'd tears hath pitied.
No blown ambition doth our arms incite,
But love, dear love, and our ag'd father's right.
Soon may I hear and see him !   [*Exeunt.*

SCENE V. *Gloucester's castle.*

Enter REGAN *and* OSWALD.

REG. But are my brother's pow'rs set forth ?
OSW.   Ay madam.
REG. Himself in person there ?
OSW.   Madam, with much ado.
Your sister is the better soldier.
REG. Lord Edmund spake not with your lord at home ?
OSW. No, madam.   5
REG. What might import my sister's letter to him ?
OSW. I know not, lady.
REG. Faith, he is posted hence on serious matter.
It was great ignorance, Gloucester's eyes being out,
To let him live ; where he arrives he moves   10
All hearts against us. Edmund, I think, is gone
In pity of his misery, to dispatch
His nighted life ; moreover, to descry
The strength o' th' enemy.
OSW. I must needs after him, madam, with my letter.   15
REG. Our troops set forth to-morrow : stay with us ;
The ways are dangerous.
OSW.   I may not, madam :
My lady charg'd my duty in this business.
REG. Why should she write to Edmund ? Might not you
Transport her purposes by word ? Belike   20
Some things—I know not what. I'll love thee much—
Let me unseal the letter.
OSW.   Madam, I had rather—
REG. I know your lady does not love her husband ;
I am sure of that ; and at her late being here

74

She gave strange œillades and most speaking looks   25
To noble Edmund. I know you are of her bosom.
OSW. I, madam?
REG. I speak in understanding; y'are, I know't.
Therefore I do advise you take this note.
My lord is dead; Edmund and I have talk'd;   30
And more convenient is he for my hand
Than for your lady's. You may gather more.
If you do find him, pray you give him this;
And when your mistress hears thus much from you,
I pray desire her call her wisdom to her.   35
So fare you well.
If you do chance to hear of that blind traitor,
Preferment falls on him that cuts him off.
OSW. Would I could meet him, madam! I should show
What party I do follow.
REG.   Fare thee well.   [*Exeunt.*

SCENE VI. *The country near Dover.*

Enter GLOUCESTER, *and* EDGAR *dressed like a peasant.*

GLO. When shall I come to th' top of that same hill?
EDG. You do climb up it now; look how we labour.
GLO. Methinks the ground is even.
EDG.   Horrible steep.
Hark, do you hear the sea?
GLO.   No, truly.
EDG. Why then, your other senses grow mperfect   5
By your eyes' anguish.
GLO.   So may it be indeed.
Methinks thy voice is alter'd, and thou speak'st
In better phrase and matter than thou didst.
EDG. Y'are much deceiv'd: in nothing am I chang'd
But in my garments.
GLO.   Methinks y'are better spoken.   10
EDG. Come on, sir; here's the place. Stand still. How fearful
And dizzy 'tis to cast one's eyes so low!
The crows and choughs that wing the midway air
Show scarce so gross as beetles. Half-way down
Hangs one that gathers samphire—dreadful trade!   15
Methinks he seems no bigger than his head.
The fishermen that walk upon the beach
Appear like mice; and yond tall anchoring bark
Diminish'd to her cock; her cock, a buoy
Almost too small for sight. The murmuring surge   20
That on th' unnumb'red idle pebble chafes
Cannot be heard so high. I'll look no more;
Lest my brain turn, and the deficient sight
Topple down headlong.
GLO.   Set me where you stand.
EDG. Give me your hand. You are now within a foot   25
Of th' extreme verge. For all beneath the moon
Would I not leap upright.
GLO.   Let go my hand.

75

Here, friend, 's another purse ; in it a jewel
Well worth a poor man's taking. Fairies and gods
Prosper it with thee ! Go thou further off ;   30
Bid me farewell, and let me hear thee going.
EDG. Now fare ye well, good sir.
GLO.   With all my heart.
EDG. Why I do trifle thus with his despair
Is done to cure it.
GLO. [*Kneeling.*]   O you mighty gods !
This world I do renounce, and in your sights   35
Shake patiently my great affliction off.
If I could bear it longer, and not fall
To quarrel with your great opposeless wills,
My snuff and loathed part of nature should
Burn itself out. If Edgar live, O, bless him !   40
[*Rising.*] Now, fellow, fare thee well.
EDG.   Gone, sir ; farewell,
                [GLOUCESTER *casts himself down.*
And yet I know not how conceit may rob
The treasury of life, when life itself
Yields to the theft. Had he been where he thought,
By this had thought been past.—Alive or dead ?   45
Ho, you sir ! friend ! Hear you, sir ! Speak !—
Thus might he pass indeed. Yet he revives—
What are you, sir ?
GLO.   Away, and let me die.
EDG. Hadst thou been aught but gossamer, feathers, air,
So many fathom down precipitating,   50
Thou'dst shiver'd like an egg ; but thou dost breathe,
Hast heavy substance, bleed'st not, speak'st, art sound.
Ten masts at each make not the altitude
Which thou hast perpendicularly fell.
Thy life's a miracle. Speak yet again.   55
GLO. But have I fall'n, or no ?
EDG. From the dread summit of this chalky bourn.
Look up a-height ; the shrill-gorg'd lark so far
Cannot be seen or heard. Do but look up.
GLO. Alack, I have no eyes.   60
Is wretchedness depriv'd that benefit,
To end itself by death ? 'Twas yet some comfort,
When misery could beguile the tyrant's rage
And frustrate his proud will.
EDG.   Give me your arm.
Up—so. How is't ? Feel you your legs ? You stand.   65
GLO. Too well, too well.
EDG.   This is above all strangeness.
Upon the crown o' th' cliff what thing was that
Which parted from you ?
GLO.   A poor unfortunate beggar.
EDG. As I stood here below, methought his eyes
Were two full moons ; he had a thousand noses,   70
Horns whelk'd and waved like the enridged sea.
It was some fiend ; therefore, thou happy father,
Think that the clearest gods, who make them honours

Of men's impossibilities, have preserved thee.
GLO. I do remember now.   Henceforth I'll bear   75
Affliction till it do cry out itself
' Enough, enough ' and die.   That thing you speak of
I took it for a man ; often 'twould say,
' The fiend, the fiend '.   He led me to that place.
EDG. Bear free and patient thoughts.

Enter LEAR, *fantastically dressed with weeds.*

But who comes here ?   80
The safer sense will ne'er accommodate
His master thus.
LEAR. No, they cannot touch me for coining ; I am the King himself.
EDG. O thou side-piercing sight !   85
LEAR. Nature's above art in that respect.   There's your press-money.
That fellow handles his bow like a crow-keeper ; draw me a
clothier's yard.   Look, look, a mouse !   Peace, peace ; this piece
of toasted cheese will do't.   There's my gauntlet ; I'll prove it
on a giant.   Bring up the brown bills.   O, well flown, bird !
i' the clout, i' the clout—hewgh !   Give the word.   92
EDG. Sweet marjoram.
LEAR. Pass.
GLO. I know that voice.   95
LEAR. Ha ! Goneril, with a white beard !   They flatter'd me like a
dog, and told me I had white hairs in my beard ere the black ones
were there.   To say ' ay ' and ' no ' to everything that I said !
' Ay ' and ' no ' too was no good divinity.   When the rain came
to wet me once, and the wind to make me chatter ; when the
thunder would not peace at my bidding ; there I found 'em,
there I smelt 'em out.   Go to, they are not men o' their words.
They told me I was everything ; 'tis a lie—I am not ague-proof.
GLO. The trick of that voice I do well remember.   106
Is't not the King ?
LEAR.   Ay, every inch a king.
When I do stare, see how the subject quakes.
I pardon that man's life.   What was thy cause ?
Adultery ?   110
Thou shalt not die.   Die for adultery ?   No.
The wren goes to't, and the small gilded fly
Does lecher in my sight.
Let copulation thrive ; for Gloucester's bastard son
Was kinder to his father than my daughters   115
Got 'tween the lawful sheets.
To't, luxury, pell-mell, for I lack soldiers.
Behold yond simp'ring dame
Whose face between her forks presages snow,
That minces virtue and does shake the head   120
To hear of pleasure's name—
The fitchew nor the soiled horse goes to't
With a more riotous appetite.
Down from the waist they are centaurs,   125
Though women all above ;
But to the girdle do the gods inherit,
Beneath is all the fiends' ;

77

There's hell, there's darkness, there is the sulphurous pit—
Burning, scalding, stench, consumption.
Fie, fie, fie! pah, pah! Give me an ounce of civet, good
  apothecary, to sweeten my imagination. There's money for thee.

GLO. O, let me kiss that hand!   13

LEAR. Let me wipe it first ; it smells of mortality.

GLO. O ruin'd piece of nature! This great world
Shall so wear out to nought. Dost thou know me?

LEAR. I remember thine eyes well enough. Dost thou squiny at me?
No, do thy worst, blind Cupid ; I'll not love. Read thou this
challenge ; mark but the penning of it.

GLO. Were all thy letters suns, I could not see one.   14

EDG. [Aside.] I would not take this from report. It is,
And my heart breaks at it.

LEAR. Read.

GLO. What, with the case of eyes?   14

LEAR. O, ho, are you there with me? No eyes in your head nor no
money in your purse? Your eyes are in a heavy case, your purse
in a light ; yet you see how this world goes.

GLO. I see it feelingly.   14

LEAR. What, art mad? A man may see how this world goes with no
eyes. Look with thine ears. See how yond justice rails upon
yond simple thief. Hark, in thine ear : change places and, handy
dandy, which is the justice, which is the thief? Thou hast seen
a farmer's dog bark at a beggar?   15

GLO. Ay, sir.

LEAR. And the creature run from the cur?
There thou mightst behold the great image of authority : a dog's
  obey'd in office.
Thou rascal beadle, hold thy bloody hand.   16
Why dost thou lash that whore? Strip thy own back ;
Thou hotly lusts to use her in that kind
For which thou whip'st her. The usurer hangs the cozener.
Through tatter'd clothes small vices do appear ;
Robes and furr'd gowns hide all. Plate sin with gold,   16
And the strong lance of justice hurtless breaks ;
Arm it in rags, a pigmy's straw does pierce it.
None does offend, none—I say none ; I'll able 'em.
Take that of me, my friend, who have the power
To seal th' accuser's lips. Get thee glass eyes,   17
And, like a scurvy politician, seem
To see the things thou dost not. Now, now, now, now!
Pull off my boots. Harder, harder—so.

EDG. O, matter and impertinency mix'd!
Reason in madness!

LEAR. If thou wilt weep my fortunes, take my eyes.
I know thee well enough ; thy name is Gloucester.
Thou must be patient ; we came crying hither.
Thou know'st the first time that we smell the air   18
We wawl and cry. I will preach to thee. Mark.

GLO. Alack, alack the day!

LEAR. When we are born, we cry that we are come
To this great stage of fools. This a good block!
It were a delicate stratagem to shoe   18

78

A troop of horse with felt; I'll put't in proof;
And when I have stol'n upon these son-in-laws,
Then kill, kill, kill, kill, kill, kill!

Enter a GENTLEMAN, *with* ATTENDANTS.

ENT. O, here he is: lay hand upon him.—Sir,
   Your most dear daughter—   190
EAR. No rescue? What, a prisoner? I am even
   The natural fool of fortune. Use me well;
   You shall have ransom. Let me have surgeons;
   I am cut to th' brains.
ENT.   You shall have any thing.
EAR. No seconds? All myself?   195
   Why, this would make a man a man of salt,
   To use his eyes for garden water-pots,
   Ay, and laying Autumn's dust.
ENT.   Good sir—
EAR. I will die bravely, like a smug bridegroom. What!   200
   I will be jovial. Come, come; I am a king,
   My masters, know you that.
ENT. You are a royal one, and we obey you.
EAR. Then there's life in't. Nay, an you get it, you shall get it by
   running. Sa, sa, sa, sa.   [*Exit running;* ATTENDANTS *follow.*
ENT. A sight most pitiful in the meanest wretch,
   Past speaking of in a king! Thou hast one daughter
   Who redeems nature from the general curse
   Which twain have brought her to.
DG.   Hail, gentle sir.
ENT. Sir, speed you; what's your will?   210
DG. Do you hear aught, sir, of a battle toward?
ENT. Most sure and vulgar; every one hears that
   Which can distinguish sound.
DG.   But, by your favour,
   How near's the other army?
ENT. Near and on speedy foot; the main descry   215
   Stands on the hourly thought.
DG.   I thank you, sir; that's all.
ENT. Though that the Queen on special cause is here,
   Her army is mov'd on.
DG.   I thank you, sir.   [*Exit* GENTLEMAN.
LO. You ever-gentle gods, take my breath from me;
   Let not my worser spirit tempt me again   220
   To die before you please.
DG.   Well pray you, father.
LO. Now, good sir, what are you?
DG. A most poor man, made tame to fortune's blows,
   Who, by the art of known and feeling sorrows,
   Am pregnant to good pity. Give me your hand;   225
   I'll lead you to some biding.
LO.   Hearty thanks;
   The bounty and the benison of heaven
   To boot, and boot!

Enter OSWALD.

79

osw. A proclaim'd prize! Most happy!
    That eyeless head of thine was first fram'd flesh
    To raise my fortunes. Thou old unhappy traitor,   23(
    Briefly thyself remember. The sword is out
    That must destroy thee.
GLO.   Now let thy friendly hand
    Put strength enough to't.   [EDGAR *interposes*
osw.   Wherefore, bold peasant,
    Dar'st thou support a publish'd traitor? Hence;
    Lest that th' infection of his fortune take   23!
    Like hold on thee. Let go his arm.
EDG. Chill not let go, zir, without vurther 'casion.
osw. Let go, slave, or thou diest.
EDG. Good gentleman, go your gait, and let poor volk pass. An
    chud ha' bin zwagger'd out of my life, 'twould not ha' bin zo long
    as 'tis by a vortnight. Nay, come not near th' old man; keep
    out, che vor ye, or Ice try whether your costard or my ballow
    be the harder. Chill be plain with you.
osw. Out, dunghill!   24.
EDG. Chill pick your teeth, zir. Come; no matter vor your foins.
                                [*They fight*
osw. Slave, thou hast slain me. Villain, take my purse;
    If ever thou wilt thrive, bury my body,
    And give the letters which thou find'st about me   25(
    To Edmund Earl of Gloucester. Seek him out
    Upon the English party. O, untimely death!
    Death!
                                 [*He dies*
EDG. I know thee well; a serviceable villain,
    As duteous to the vices of thy mistress   25!
    As badness would desire.
GLO.   What, is he dead?
EDG. Sit you down, father; rest you.
    Let's see these pockets; the letters that he speaks of
    May be my friends. He's dead; I am only sorry
    He had no other death's-man. Let us see.   26(
    Leave, gentle wax; and, manners, blame us not:
    To know our enemies' minds we'd rip their hearts;
    Their papers is more lawful.

[*Reads.*] 'Let our reciprocal vows be rememb'red. You have many
    opportunities to cut him off; if your will want not, time and place
    will be fruitfully offer'd. There is nothing done if he return the
    conqueror; then am I the prisoner, and his bed my gaol; from
    the loathed warmth whereof deliver me, and supply the place for
    your labour.
        Your (wife, so I would say) affectionate servant, Goneril.'

O indistinguish'd space of woman's will!   27)
A plot upon her virtuous husband's life;
And the exchange my brother! Here, in the sands
Thee I'll rake up, the post unsanctified
Of murderous lechers; and in the mature time   27!
With this ungracious paper strike the sight
Of the death-practis'd duke. For him 'tis well
That of thy death and business I can tell.

GLO. The King is mad; how stiff is my vile sense,
    That I stand up, and have ingenious feeling   280
    Of my huge sorrows! Better I were distract;
    So should my thoughts be sever'd from my griefs,
    And woes by wrong imaginations lose
    The knowledge of themselves.   [*Drum afar off.*
EDG.   Give me your hand.
    Far off methinks I hear the beaten drum.   285
    Come, father, I'll bestow you with a friend.   [*Exeunt.*

SCENE VII. *A tent in the French camp.*

Music. Enter CORDELIA, KENT, DOCTOR, *and* GENTLEMAN.

COR. O thou good Kent, how shall I live and work
    To match thy goodness? My life will be too short,
    And every measure fail me.
KENT. To be acknowledg'd, madam, is o'erpaid.
    All my reports go with the modest truth;   5
    Nor more nor clipp'd, but so.
COR.   Be better suited.
    These weeds are memories of those worser hours;
    I prithee put them off.
KENT.   Pardon, dear madam;
    Yet to be known shortens my made intent:
    My boon I make it that you know me not   10
    Till time and I think meet.
COR. Then be't so, my good lord. [*To the* DOCTOR.] How does the
    King?
DOCT. Madam, sleeps still.
COR. O you kind gods,
    Cure this great breach in his abused nature!   15
    Th' untun'd and jarring senses, O, wind up
    Of this child-changed father!
DOCT.   So please your Majesty
    That we may wake the King; he hath slept long.
COR. Be govern'd by your knowledge, and proceed
    I' th' sway of your own will. [*To the* GENTLEMAN.] Is he array'd?
GENT. Ay, madam; in the heaviness of sleep   21
    We put fresh garments on him.
DOCT. Be by, good madam, when we do awake him;
    I doubt not of his temperance.
COR.   Very well.
DOCT. Please you, draw near. Louder the music there!   25

    He draws the curtains and discovers LEAR *asleep in bed.*

COR. O my dear father! Restoration hang
    Thy medicine on my lips, and let this kiss
    Repair those violent harms that my two sisters
    Have in thy reverence made.
KENT.   Kind and dear princess
COR. Had you not been their father, these white flakes   30
    Did challenge pity of them. Was this a face
    To be oppos'd against the warring winds?

To stand against the deep dread bolted thunder ?
In the most terrible and nimble stroke
Of quick cross lightning ? to watch—poor perdu !— 35
With this thin helm ? Mine enemy's dog,
Though he had bit me, should have stood that night
Against my fire ; and wast thou fain, poor father,
To hovel thee with swine and rogues forlorn,
In short and musty straw ? Alack, alack ! 40
'Tis wonder that thy life and wits at once
Had not concluded all.—He wakes ; speak to him.
DOCT. Madam, do you ; 'tis fittest.
COR. How does my royal lord ? How fares your Majesty ?
LEAR. You do me wrong to take me out o' th' grave. 45
    Thou art a soul in bliss ; but I am bound
    Upon a wheel of fire, that mine own tears
    Do scald like molten lead.
COR.   Sir, do you know me ?
LEAR. You are a spirit, I know. Where did you die ?
COR. Still, still far wide ! 50
DOCT. He's scarce awake ; let him alone awhile.
LEAR. Where have I been ? Where am I ? Fair daylight ?
    I am mightily abus'd. I should e'en die with pity
    To see another thus. I know not what to say.
    I will not swear these are my hands. Let's see. 55
    I feel this pin prick. Would I were assur'd
    Of my condition !
COR.   O, look upon me, sir,
    And hold your hands in benediction o'er me.
    No, sir, you must not kneel.
LEAR.   Pray, do not mock me :
    I am a very foolish fond old man, 60
    Fourscore and upward, not an hour more nor less ;
    And, to deal plainly,
    I fear I am not in my perfect mind.
    Methinks I should know you, and know this man ;
    Yet I am doubtful ; for I am mainly ignorant 65
    What place this is ; and all the skill I have
    Remembers not these garments ; nor I know not
    Where I did lodge last night. Do not laugh at me ;
    For, as I am a man, I think this lady
    To be my child Cordelia.
COR.   And so I am, I am. 70
LEAR. Be your tears wet ? Yes, faith. I pray weep not ;
    If you have poison for me I will drink it.
    I know you do not love me ; for your sisters
    Have, as I do remember, done me wrong :
    You have some cause, they have not.
COR.   No cause, no cause. 75
LEAR. Am I in France ?
KENT.   In your own kingdom, sir.
LEAR. Do not abuse me.
DOCT. Be comforted, good madam. The great rage,
    You see, is kill'd in him ; and yet it is danger
    To make him even o'er the time he has lost. 80

82

Desire him to go in ; trouble him no more
Till further settling.
COR. Will't please your Highness walk ?
LEAR.   You must bear with me.
Pray you now, forget and forgive ; I am old and foolish.   85
[*Exeunt all but* KENT *and* GENTLEMAN.
GENT. Holds it true, sir, that the Duke of Cornwall was so slain ?
KENT. Most certain, sir.
GENT. Who is conductor of his people ?
KENT. As 'tis said, the bastard son of Gloucester.   90
GENT. They say Edgar, his banish'd son, is with the Earl of Kent in
Germany.
KENT. Report is changeable. 'Tis time to look about ; the powers
of the kingdom approach apace.
GENT. The arbitrement is like to be bloody. Fare you well, sir. [*Exit.*
KENT. My point and period will be throughly wrought,   97
Or well or ill, as this day's battle's fought.   [*Exit.*

ACT FIVE

SCENE I. *The British camp near Dover.*

Enter, with drum and colours, EDMUND, REGAN, GENTLEMAN, *and*
SOLDIERS.

EDM. Know of the Duke if his last purpose hold,
Or whether since he is advis'd by aught
To change the course. He's full of alteration
And self-reproving—bring his constant pleasure. [*Exit an* OFFICER.
REG. Our sister's man is certainly miscarried.   5
EDM. 'Tis to be doubted, madam.
REG.   Now, sweet lord,
You know the goodness I intend upon you.
Tell me—but truly—but then speak the truth—
Do you not love my sister ?
EDM.   In honour'd love.
REG. But have you never found my brother's way   10
To the forfended place ?
EDM.   That thought abuses you.
REG. I am doubtful that you have been conjunct
And bosom'd with her, as far as we call hers.
EDM. No, by mine honour, madam.
REG. I never shall endure her. Dear my lord,   15
Be not familiar with her.
EDM.   Fear me not.
She and the Duke her husband !

Enter, with drum and colours, ALBANY, GONERIL, *and* SOLDIERS.

GON. [*Aside.*] I had rather lose the battle than that sister
Should loosen him and me.
ALB. Our very loving sister, well be-met.   20
Sir, this I heard : the King is come to his daughter
With others whom the rigour of our state
Forc'd to cry out. Where I could not be honest
I never yet was valiant. For this business,

   It touches us as France invades our land,   25
   Not bolds the King, with others whom, I fear,
   Most just and heavy causes make oppose.
EDM. Sir, you speak nobly.
REG.   Why is this reason'd?
GON. Combine together 'gainst the enemy;
   For these domestic-door particulars   30
   Are not the question here.
ALB.   Let's then determine
   With th' ancient of war on our proceeding.
EDM. I shall attend you presently at your tent.
REG. Sister, you'll go with us?
GON. No.   35
REG. 'Tis most convenient; pray you go with us.
GON. [Aside.] O, ho, I know the riddle.—I will go.

As they are going out, enter EDGAR, *disguised.*

EDG. If e'er your Grace had speech with man so poor,
   Hear me one word.
ALB.   I'll overtake you.—Speak.
                   [*Exeunt all but* ALBANY *and* EDGAR.
EDG. Before you fight the battle, ope this letter.   40
   If you have victory, let the trumpet sound
   For him that brought it; wretched though I seem
   I can produce a champion that will prove
   What is avouched there. If you miscarry,
   Your business of the world hath so an end,   45
   And machination ceases. Fortune love you!
ALB. Stay till I have read the letter.
EDG.   I was forbid it.
   When time shall serve, let but the herald cry,
   And I'll appear again.
ALB. Why, fare thee well. I will o'erlook thy paper. [*Exit* EDGAR.

Re-enter EDMUND.

EDM. The enemy's in view; draw up your powers.   51
   Here is the guess of their true strength and forces
   By diligent discovery; but your haste
   Is now urg'd on you.
ALB.   We will greet the time.   [*Exit.*
EDM. To both these sisters have I sworn my love;   55
   Each jealous of the other, as the stung
   Are of the adder. Which of them shall I take?
   Both? one? or neither? Neither can be enjoy'd,
   If both remain alive: to take the widow,
   Exasperates, makes mad her sister Goneril;   60
   And hardly shall I carry out my side,
   Her husband being alive. Now then, we'll use
   His countenance for the battle; which being done,
   Let her who would be rid of him devise
   His speedy taking off. As for the mercy   65
   Which he intends to Lear and to Cordelia—
   The battle done, and they within our power,

Shall never see his pardon ; for my state
Stands on me to defend, not to debate.   [*Exit.*

SCENE II. *A field between the two camps.*

Alarum within.   Enter, with drum and colours, the POWERS OF FRANCE
over the stage, CORDELIA *with her* FATHER *in her hand, and exeunt.*

Enter EDGAR *and* GLOUCESTER.

EDG. Here, father, take the shadow of this tree
For your good host ; pray that the right may thrive.
If ever I return to you again
I'll bring you comfort.

GLO.   Grace go with you, sir !   [*Exit* EDGAR.

Alarum and retreat within.   Re-enter EDGAR.

EDG. Away, old man ; give me thy hand ; away !   5
King Lear hath lost, he and his daughter ta'en.
Give me thy hand ; come on.

GLO. No further, sir ; a man may rot even here.

EDG. What, in ill thoughts again ?   Men must endure
Their going hence, even as their coming hither :   10
Ripeness is all.   Come on.

GLO.   And that's true too.   [*Exeunt.*

SCENE III. *The British camp near Dover.*

Enter, in conquest, with drum and colours, EDMUND ; LEAR *and* CORDELIA
prisoners ; SOLDIERS, CAPTAIN.

EDM. Some officers take them away.   Good guard,
Until their greater pleasures first be known
That are to censure them.

COR.   We are not the first
Who with best meaning have incurr'd the worst.
For thee, oppressed King, am I cast down ;   5
Myself could else out-frown false Fortune's frown.
Shall we not see these daughters and these sisters ?

LEAR. No, no, no, no !   Come, let's away to prison.
We two alone will sing like birds i' th' cage ;
When thou dost ask me blessing, I'll kneel down   10
And ask of thee forgiveness ; so we'll live,
And pray, and sing, and tell old tales, and laugh
At gilded butterflies, and hear poor rogues
Talk of court news ; and we'll talk with them too—
Who loses and who wins ; who's in, who's out—   15
And take upon 's the mystery of things
As if we were God's spies ; and we'll wear out
In a wall'd prison packs and sects of great ones
That ebb and flow by th' moon.

EDM.   Take them away.

LEAR. Upon such sacrifices, my Cordelia,   20
The gods themselves throw incense.   Have I caught thee ?
He that parts us shall bring a brand from heaven

And fire us hence like foxes. Wipe thine eyes ;
The good years shall devour them, flesh and fell,
Ere they shall make us weep. We'll see 'em starv'd first.   25
Come.   [*Exeunt* LEAR *and* CORDELIA, *guarded*.

EDM. Come hither, Captain ; hark.
[*Giving a paper*.] Take thou this note ; go follow them to prison.
One step I have advanc'd thee ; if thou dost
As this instructs thee, thou dost make thy way   30
To noble fortunes. Know thou this, that men
Are as the time is ; to be tender-minded
Does not become a sword. Thy great employment
Will not bear question ; either say thou'lt do't,
Or thrive by other means.

CAPT.   I'll do't, my lord.   35

EDM. About it ; and write happy when th' hast done.
Mark—I say, instantly ; and carry it so
As I have set it down.

CAPT. I cannot draw a cart nor eat dried oats ;
If it be man's work, I'll do't.   [*Exit*.

Flourish. Enter ALBANY, GONERIL, REGAN, *and* SOLDIERS.

ALB. Sir, you have show'd to-day your valiant strain,
And fortune led you well. You have the captives
Who were the opposites of this day's strife ;
I do require them of you, so to use them
As we shall find their merits and our safety   45
May equally determine.

EDM.   Sir, I thought it fit
To send the old and miserable king
To some retention and appointed guard ;
Whose age has charms in it, whose title more,
To pluck the common bosom on his side,   50
And turn our impress'd lances in our eyes
Which do command them. With him I sent the Queen
My reason all the same ; and they are ready
To-morrow, or at further space, t' appear
Where you shall hold your session. At this time   55
We sweat and bleed ; the friend hath lost his friend
And the best quarrels, in the heat, are curs'd
By those that feel their sharpness.
The question of Cordelia and her father
Requires a fitter place.

ALB.   Sir, by your patience,   60
I hold you but a subject of this war,
Not as a brother.

REG.   That's as we list to grace him.
Methinks our pleasure might have been demanded
Ere you had spoke so far. He led our powers,
Bore the commission of my place and person,   65
The which immediacy may well stand up
And call itself your brother.

GON.   Not so hot.
In his own grace he doth exalt himself,
More than in your addition.

REG.   In my rights,
  By me invested, he compeers the best.   70
ALB. That were the most, if he should husband you.
REG. Jesters do oft prove prophets.
GON.   Holla, holla !
  That eye that told you so look'd but asquint.
REG. Lady, I am not well ; else I should answer
  From a full-flowing stomach.   General,   75
  Take thou my soldiers, prisoners, patrimony ;
  Dispose of them, of me ; the walls is thine.
  Witness the world that I create thee here
  My lord and master.
GON.   Mean you to enjoy him ?
ALB. The let-alone lies not in your good will.   80
EDM. Nor in thine, lord.
ALB.   Half-blooded fellow, yes.
REG. [To EDMUND.] Let the drum strike, and prove my title thine.
ALB. Stay yet ; hear reason.   Edmund, I arrest thee
  On capital treason ; and, in thy attaint,   [Pointing to GONERIL.
  This gilded serpent.   For your claim, fair sister,   85
  I bar it in the interest of my wife ;
  'Tis she is sub-contracted to this lord,
  And I, her husband, contradict your banns.
  If you will marry, make your loves to me—
  My lady is bespoke.
GON.   An interlude !   90
ALB. Thou art arm'd, Gloster.   Let the trumpet sound.
  If none appear to prove upon thy person
  Thy heinous, manifest, and many treasons,
  There is my pledge ;   [Throwing down a glove.
                I'll make it on thy heart,
  Ere I taste bread, thou art in nothing less   95
  Than I have here proclaim'd thee.
REG.   Sick, O, sick !
GON. [Aside.] If not, I'll ne'er trust medicine.
EDM. There's my exchange. [Throwing down a glove.] What in the
  world he is
  That names me traitor, villain-like he lies.
  Call by thy trumpet : he that dares approach,   100
  On him, on you, who not, I will maintain
  My truth and honour firmly.
ALB. A herald, ho !
EDM.   A herald, ho, a herald !
ALB. Trust to thy single virtue ; for thy soldiers,
  All levied in my name, have in my name   105
  Took their discharge.
REG.   My sickness grows upon me.
ALB. She is not well ; convey her to my tent.   [Exit REGAN, led.

Enter a HERALD.

  Come hither, herald.   Let the trumpet sound,
  And read out this.
HERALD. [Reads.] 'If any man of quality or degree within the lists
  of the army will maintain upon Edmund, supposed Earl of

Gloucester, that he is a manifold traitor, let him appear by the
third sound of the trumpet.   He is bold in his defence.'
Sound, trumpet.   [1 Trumpet.
HERALD. Again !   [2 Trumpet.
HERALD. Again !   [3 Trumpet.
                                        [Trumpet answers within.

Enter EDGAR, *armed, at the third sound, a trumpet before him.*

ALB. Ask him his purposes, why he appears
Upon this call o' th' trumpet.
HERALD.   What are you ?
Your name, your quality, and why you answer   120
This present summons ?
EDG.   Know, my name is lost,
By treason's tooth bare-gnawn and canker-bit ;
Yet am I noble as the adversary
I come to cope.
ALB.   Which is that adversary ?
EDG. What's he that speaks for Edmund Earl of Gloucester ?   125
EDM. Himself.   What say'st thou to him ?
EDG.   Draw thy sword,
That, if my speech offend a noble heart,
Thy arm may do thee justice ; here is mine.
Behold, it is the privilege of mine honours,
My oath, and my profession.   I protest—   130
Maugre thy strength, youth, place, and eminence,
Despite thy victor sword and fire-new fortune,
Thy valour and thy heart—thou art a traitor ;
False to thy gods, thy brother, and thy father ;
Conspirant 'gainst this high illustrious prince ;   135
And, from th' extremest upward of thy head
To the descent and dust below thy foot,
A most toad-spotted traitor.   Say thou ' No ',
This sword, this arm, and my best spirits, are bent
To prove upon thy heart, whereto I speak,   140
Thou liest.
EDM.   In wisdom I should ask thy name ;
But, since thy outside looks so fair and warlike,
And that thy tongue some say of breeding breathes,
What safe and nicely I might well delay
By rule of knighthood, I disdain and spurn.   145
Back do I toss these treasons to thy head ;
With the hell-hated lie o'erwhelm thy heart ;
Which—for they yet glance by and scarcely bruise—
This sword of mine shall give them instant way
Where they shall rest for ever.   Trumpets, speak.   150
                    [*Alarums.   They fight.   EDMUND falls.*
ALB. Save him, save him !
GON.   This is practice, Gloucester.
By th' law of war thou wast not bound to answer
An unknown opposite ; thou art not vanquish'd,
But cozen'd and beguil'd.
ALB.   Shut your mouth, dame,
Or with this paper shall I stopple it.   Hold, sir.   155

Thou worse than any name, read thine own evil.
No tearing, lady; I perceive you know it.
GON. Say, if I do—the laws are mine, not thine.
Who can arraign me for't?
ALB.   Most monstrous! O   159
Know'st thou this paper?
GON.   Ask me not what I know.   [*Exit.*
ALB. Go after her. She's desperate; govern her. [*Exit an* OFFICER.
EDM. What you have charg'd me with, that have I done,
And more, much more; the time will bring it out.
'Tis past, and so am I. But what art thou
That hast this fortune on me? If thou'rt noble,   165
I do forgive thee.
EDG.   Let's exchange charity.
I am no less in blood than thou art, Edmund;
If more, the more th' hast wrong'd me.
My name is Edgar, and thy father's son.
The gods are just, and of our pleasant vices   170
Make instruments to plague us:
The dark and vicious place where thee he got
Cost him his eyes.
EDM.   Th' hast spoken right, 'tis true;
The wheel is come full circle; I am here.
ALB. Methought thy very gait did prophesy   175
A royal nobleness. I must embrace thee.
Let sorrow split my heart if ever I
Did hate thee or thy father!
EDG.   Worthy prince,
I know't.
ALB.   Where have you hid yourself?
How have you known the miseries of your father?   180
EDG. By nursing them, my lord. List a brief tale;
And when 'tis told, O that my heart would burst!
The bloody proclamation to escape
That follow'd me so near—O our lives' sweetness,
That we the pain of death would hourly die   185
Rather than die at once!—taught me to shift
Into a madman's rags, t' assume a semblance
That very dogs disdain'd; and in this habit
Met I my father with his bleeding rings,
Their precious stones new lost; became his guide,   190
Led him, begg'd for him, sav'd him from despair;
Never—O fault!—reveal'd myself unto him
Until some half-hour past, when I was arm'd;
Not sure, though hoping, of this good success,
I ask'd his blessing, and from first to last   195
Told him my pilgrimage. But his flaw'd heart—
Alack, too weak the conflict to support!—
'Twixt two extremes of passion, joy and grief,
Burst smilingly.
EDM. This speech of yours hath mov'd me,
And shall perchance do good; but speak you on;   200
You look as you had something more to say.
ALB. If there be more, more woeful, hold it in;

For I am almost ready to dissolve,
Hearing of this.

EDG.   This would have seem'd a period
To such as love not sorrow; but another,   205
To amplify too much, would make much more,
And top extremity.
Whilst I was big in clamour, came there in a man
Who, having seen me in my worst estate,
Shunn'd my abhorr'd society; but then, finding   210
Who 'twas that so endur'd, with his strong arms
He fastened on my neck and bellowed out
As he'd burst heaven; threw him on my father;
Told the most piteous tale of Lear and him
That ever ear receiv'd; which in recounting   215
His grief grew puissant, and the strings of life
Began to crack. Twice then the trumpets sounded
And there I left him tranc'd.

ALB.   But who was this?

EDG. Kent, sir, the banish'd Kent, who in disguise
Follow'd his enemy king, and did him service   220
Improper for a slave.

Enter a GENTLEMAN *with a bloody knife.*

GENT. Help, help, O, help!

EDG.   What kind of help?

ALB.   Speak, man.

EDG. What means this bloody knife?

GENT.   'Tis hot, it smokes;
It came even from the heart of—O, she's dead!

ALB. Who dead? Speak, man.   225

GENT. Your lady, sir, your lady! and her sister
By her is poison'd; she confesses it.

EDM. I was contracted to them both. All three
Now marry in an instant.

EDG.   Here comes Kent.

Enter KENT.

ALB. Produce the bodies, be they alive or dead. [*Exit* GENTLEMAN.
This judgment of the heavens, that makes us tremble,   231
Touches us not with pity. O, is this he?
The time will not allow the compliment
Which very manners urges.

KENT.   I am come
To bid my king and master aye good night.   235
Is he not here?

ALB.   Great thing of us forgot!
Speak, Edmund, where's the King? and where's Cordelia?
                    [*The bodies of* GONERIL *and* REGAN *are brought in.*
See'st thou this object, Kent?

KENT. Alack, why thus?

EDM.   Yet Edmund was belov'd.
The one the other poison'd for my sake,   240
And after slew herself.

ALB. Even so. Cover their faces.

90

EDM. I pant for life.   Some good I mean to do,
    Despite of mine own nature.   Quickly send—
    Be brief in it—to th' castle ; for my writ   245
    Is on the life of Lear and on Cordelia.
    Nay, send in time.
ALB.   Run, run, O, run !
EDG. To who, my lord ?   Who has the office ?   Send
    Thy token of reprieve.
EDM. Well thought on.   Take my sword ;   250
    Give it the Captain.
ALB.   Haste thee, for thy life.   [*Exit* EDGAR.
EDM. He hath commission from thy wife and me
    To hang Cordelia in the prison, and
    To lay the blame upon her own despair,
    That she fordid herself.   255
ALB. The gods defend her !   Bear him hence awhile.

                                     [EDMUND *is borne off.*

Enter LEAR, *with* CORDELIA *dead in his arms ;* EDGAR, CAPTAIN, *and*
                      OTHERS *following.*

LEAR. Howl, howl, howl, howl !   O, you are men of stones
    Had I your tongues and eyes, I'd use them so
    That heaven's vault should crack.   She's gone for ever.
    I know when one is dead and when one lives ;   260
    She's dead as earth.   Lend me a looking-glass ;
    If that her breath will mist or stain the stone,
    Why, then she lives.
KENT.   Is this the promis'd end ?
EDG. Or image of that horror ?
ALB.   Fall and cease !
LEAR. This feather stirs ; she lives.   If it be so,   265
    It is a chance which does redeem all sorrows
    That ever I have felt.
KENT.   O my good master !   [*Kneeling.*
LEAR. Prithee away.
EDG.   'Tis noble Kent, your friend.
LEAR. A plague upon you, murderers, traitors all !
    I might have sav'd her ; now she's gone for ever.   270
    Cordelia, Cordelia ! stay a little.   Ha !
    What is't thou say'st ? Her voice was ever soft,
    Gentle, and low—an excellent thing in woman.
    I kill'd the slave that was a-hanging thee.
CAPT. 'Tis true, my lords, he did.
LEAR.   Did I not, fellow ?   275
    I have seen the day, with my good biting falchion,
    I would have made them skip : I am old now,
    And these same crosses spoil me.   Who are you ?
    Mine eyes are not o' th' best.   I'll tell you straight.
KENT. If fortune brag of two she lov'd and hated,   280
    One of them we behold.
LEAR. This is a dull sight.   Are you not Kent ?
KENT.   The same—
    Your servant Kent.   Where is your servant Caius ?
LEAR. He's a good fellow, I can tell you that ;

                                                              91

He'll strike, and quickly too.   He's dead and rotten.   285
KENT. No, my good lord ;   I am the very man—
LEAR. I'll see that straight.
KENT. That from your first of difference and decay
    Have follow'd your sad steps.
LEAR.   You are welcome hither.
KENT. Nor no man else !   All's cheerless, dark, and deadly.   290
    Your eldest daughters have fordone themselves
    And desperately are dead.
LEAR.   Ay, so I think.
ALB. He knows not what he says ;   and vain is it
    That we present us to him.
EDG.   Very bootless.

Enter a MESSENGER.

MESS. Edmund is dead, my lord.
ALB.   That's but a trifle here.   295
    You lords and noble friends, know our intent.
    What comfort to this great decay may come
    Shall be applied.   For us, we will resign
    During the life of this old Majesty,
    To him our absolute power. [*To* EDGAR *and* KENT.]   You to your
        rights ;   300
    With boot, and such addition as your honours
    Have more than merited.   All friends shall taste
    The wages of their virtue, and all foes
    The cup of their deservings.   O, see, see !
LEAR. And my poor fool is hang'd !   No, no, no life   305
    Why should a dog, a horse, a rat have life,
    And thou no breath at all ?   Thou'lt come no more,
    Never, never, never, never, never.
    Pray you undo this button.   Thank you, sir.
    Do you see this ?   Look on her.   Look, her lips.   310
    Look there, look there !   [*He dies.*
EDG.   He faints.   My lord, my lord !
KENT. Break, heart ;   I prithee break.
EDG.   Look up, my lord.
KENT. Vex not his ghost.   O, let him pass !   He hates him
    That would upon the rack of this tough world
    Stretch him out longer.
EDG.   He is gone indeed.   315
KENT. The wonder is he hath endur'd so long :
    He but usurp'd his life.
ALB. Bear them from hence.   Our present business
    Is general woe. [*To* KENT *and* EDGAR.]   Friends of my soul, you
        twain
    Rule in this realm and the gor'd state sustain.   320
KENT. I have a journey, sir, shortly to go.
    My master calls me ;   I must not say no.
EDG. The weight of this sad time we must obey ;
    Speak what we feel, not what we ought to say.
    The oldest hath borne most ;   we that are young   325
    Shall never see so much nor live so long.

                         [*Exeunt with a dead march.*

OTHELLO

How Shakespeare hit upon the name Othello no one knows; for so far it has not been discovered in any document or printed work. Its very sound however carries with it something of the sense in which Shakespeare wished us to see the heroic character of the man.

In the Italian story, which Shakespeare found in Cinthio's *Hecatommithi* and from which he took the raw material for his plot, the only character given a name is Disdemona, her husband being always referred to as the Moor. How Cinthio envisaged his Moor is not clear, for only at one place does the Italian tell us of his colour: where the Ensign enforces his assertions that Disdemona loves the Captain by saying, ' your blackness already displeases her '. Shakespeare would have had to be more definite than this, since he was presenting his Moor on the stage; but in spite of the many references to Othello's colour and features commentators still argue about Shakespeare's intention.

There are two Moors in earlier plays by Shakespeare, Aaron in *Titus Andronicus* and the Prince of Morocco in *Merchant of Venice*. The first, Aaron, seems to have been presented on the stage as a negro, for apart from such references as that to his ' fleece of woolly hair ', we have in the Peacham drawing [*Shakespeare Survey*, 1948] what is perhaps an early illustration of how he figured on the stage; if so, he was clearly made up as a negro. E. K. Chambers, who was one of the first to emphasize the importance of this drawing, went so far as to say that this drawing should ' inform students of *Othello* as well as of *Titus*, that to the Elizabethan mind a Moor was not tawny but dead black '. He had, in his enthusiasm for his discovery, forgotten the stage direction in the first quarto (1600) of the *Merchant of Venice*, ' Enter *Morochus* a tawnie Moore all in white '. This is among other things a costume direction; it indicates the kind of robes to be worn by the Prince and his entourage; it also shows that the writer understood perfectly the difference between the black and the tawny Moor. As Dowden pointed out this distinction was accepted generally in the days of King James; ' For they make the river Senega to divide and bound the Moors, so that on the south side they are black, on the other only tawny '. The distinction must have been equally familiar to the Elizabethans, as a recent acquisition by the Shakespeare Institute at Stratford-upon-Avon makes evident.

On 8 August 1600 there arrived at Dover an embassy from Muley Hamet, King of Barbary, headed by Abd el-Ouahed. The ambassador and his party remained in England for some six months, attracting a good deal of comment and causing not a little embarrassment in official circles. The story of their stay is told, and the portrait painted of the ambassador in 1600 illustrated, in *Shakespeare Survey*, 1958. As Mr. Bernard Harris says there: ' Through all the ambiguity of terminology and stage tradition the portrait of the Moorish ambassador reminds us of the common acquaintance of the Elizabethans with real, as distinct from fictional, Moors '. The hand that penned the stage direction about the ' tawny Moore ' belonged to someone who was aware of the distinction between real and fictional Moors.

The embassy, though it accomplished little, helped to expedite the exchange of prisoners between England and Barbary, for an order followed by the Privy Council deporting 'negars and blacka-moores'; many of these Moorish captives must have been tawny. Elizabethan terminology may be ambiguous but it is obvious that the educated public could distinguish quite clearly between a berber and a negro.

The portrait of the Moorish Ambassador and the story of his embassy, when added to the evidence provided by the stage direction from *Merchant of Venice*, while they do not settle for us the particular choice of make-up Shakespeare decided on for his Othello, show that the question about his race is still an open one.

For answering this question Mr. Bernard Harris provides two suggestions. Emphasizing the deep difference between the Londoners and their visitors he says : ' To Elizabethan Londoners the appearance and conduct of the Moors was a spectacle and an outrage '. To present Othello as a Moor rather than a negro would not then have destroyed for Londoners the sense of incompatibility that Shakespeare required as one element in the attitude of a contemporary audience to the marriage of the Moor and the Venetian lady. So imperfect were the sympathies between the Londoners and the Moors that Mr. Bernard Harris adds : ' Cinthio's is not the whole tale after all ; the fundamental dramatic contrast of racial difference is Shakespeare's first departure from his source '. But this contrast was the very point of Cinthio's story, as Professor Dover Wilson has emphasized by drawing attention to Cinthio's introductory discourse to the tales ; for the story Shakespeare drew on was to illustrate the dangers of a marriage between those of different race and with a different manner of life. These, however, were the very circumstances that Shakespeare saw would provide the ideal foundation for a drama that would show how these differences so far from being impediments to the marriage of true minds were elements whose fusion would demonstrate the great triumph of love. This triumph Shakespeare shows us in Desdemona's dying words and in the manner of Othello's death. Shakespeare does not allow the attitude adopted by Cinthio's Disdemona, who regards her unhappiness as a warning against a marriage such as hers, to point the moral of Desdemona's fate ; for her marriage is one that conquers all that the wickedness of the world and the ignorance of man can do against it.

Shakespeare arranges his time scheme so that we see both the monstrous nature of the slander to which Desdemona is subjected and the peculiarity of the circumstances that gave it plausibility. In art the impression is the fact and Shakespeare has enforced the impression with a dramatic tact that matches his imaginative understanding.

OTHELLO

DRAMATIS PERSONÆ

DUKE OF VENICE
BRABANTIO, *a Senator, father to Desdemona.*
OTHER SENATORS.
GRATIANO, *brother to Brabantio,* } *two noble*
LODOVICO, *kinsman to Brabantio,* } *Venetians.*
OTHELLO, *the Moor, in the service of Venice.*
CASSIO, *his honourable Lieutenant.*
IAGO, *his Ancient, a villain.*
RODERIGO, *a gull'd Venetian gentleman.*

MONTANO, *Governor of Cyprus, before Othello.*
CLOWN, *servant to Othello.*

DESDEMONA, *daughter to Brabantio, and wife to Othello.*
EMILIA, *wife to Iago.*
BIANCA, *a courtezan, in love with Cassio.*
GENTLEMEN OF CYPRUS, SAILORS, OFFICERS, MESSENGERS, MUSICIANS, HERALD, ATTENDANTS, &c.

THE SCENE : *Venice ; Cyprus.*

ACT ONE

SCENE I. *Venice. A street.*

Enter RODERIGO *and* IAGO.

ROD. Tush, never tell me ; I take it much unkindly
 That you, Iago, who has had my purse
 As if the strings were thine, shouldst know of this.
IAGO. 'Sblood, but you will not hear me.
 If ever I did dream of such a matter,   5
 Abhor me.
ROD. Thou told'st me thou didst hold him in thy hate.
IAGO. Despise me if I do not. Three great ones of the city,
 In personal suit to make me his lieutenant,
 Off-capp'd to him ; and, by the faith of man,   10
 I know my price, I am worth no worse a place.
 But he, as loving his own pride and purposes,
 Evades them with a bombast circumstance
 Horribly stuff'd with epithets of war ;
 And, in conclusion,   15
 Nonsuits my mediators ; ' For, certes,' says he
 ' I have already chose my officer '.
 And what was he ?
 Forsooth, a great arithmetician,
 One Michael Cassio, a Florentine,   20
 A fellow almost damn'd in a fair wife,
 That never set a squadron in the field,
 Nor the division of a battle knows
 More than a spinster ; unless the bookish theoric,
 Wherein the toged consuls can propose   25
 As masterly as he—mere prattle, without practice,

Is all his soldiership. But he, sir, had the election;
And I, of whom his eyes had seen the proof
At Rhodes, at Cyprus, and on other grounds,
Christian and heathen, must be be-lee'd and calm'd   30
By debitor and creditor—this counter-caster,
He, in good time, must be his lieutenant be,
And I, God bless the mark! his Moorship's ancient.

ROD. By heaven, I rather would have been his hangman!   35

IAGO. Why, there's no remedy; 'tis the curse of service:
Preferment goes by letter and affection,
Not by the old gradation, where each second
Stood heir to the first. Now, sir, be judge yoursel
Whether I in any just term am affin'd
To love the Moor.

ROD.   I would not follow him, then.   40

IAGO. O, sir, content you.
I follow him to serve my turn upon him:
We cannot all be masters, nor all masters
Cannot be truly follow'd. You shall mark
Many a duteous and knee-crooking knave   45
That, doting on his own obsequious bondage,
Wears out his time, much like his master's ass,
For nought but provender; and when he's old, cashier'd.
Whip me such honest knaves. Others there are
Who, trimm'd in forms and visages of duty,   50
Keep yet their hearts attending on themselves;
And, throwing but shows of service on their lords,
Do well thrive by 'em and, when they have lin'd their coats,
Do themselves homage—these fellows have some soul;
And such a one do I profess myself.   55
For, sir,
It is as sure as you are Roderigo,
Were I the Moor, I would not be Iago.
In following him I follow but myself—
Heaven is my judge, not I for love and duty,   60
But seeming so for my peculiar end.
For when my outward action doth demonstrate
The native act and figure of my heart
In compliment extern, 'tis not long after
But I will wear my heart upon my sleeve   65
For daws to peck at: I am not what I am.

ROD. What a full fortune does the thick-lips owe,
If he can carry't thus!

IAGO.   Call up her father.
Rouse him, make after him, poison his delight,
Proclaim him in the streets; incense her kinsmen,   70
And, though he in a fertile climate dwell,
Plague him with flies; though that his joy be joy,
Yet throw such changes of vexation on't
As it may lose some colour.

ROD. Here is her father's house. I'll call aloud.   75

IAGO. Do, with like timorous accent and dire yell
As when, by night and negligence, the fire
Is spied in populous cities.

ROD. What, ho, Brabantio! Signior Brabantio, ho!

IAGO. Awake! What, ho, Brabantio! Thieves, thieves, thieves!
    Look to your house, your daughter, and your bags.   81
    Thieves! thieves!

            BRABANTIO *appears above at a window.*

BRA. What is the reason of this terrible summons?
    What is the matter there?

ROD. Signior, is all your family within?   85

IAGO. Are your doors lock'd?

BRA.   Why, wherefore ask you this?

IAGO. Zounds, sir, you're robb'd; for shame, put on your gown;
    Your heart is burst; you have lost half your soul.
    Even now, now, very now, an old black ram
    Is tupping your white ewe. Arise, arise;   90
    Awake the snorting citizens with the bell,
    Or else the devil will make a grandsire of you.
    Arise, I say.

BRA.   What, have you lost your wits?

ROD. Most reverend signior, do you know my voice?

BRA. Not I; what are you?   95

ROD. My name is Roderigo.

BRA.   The worser welcome!
    I have charg'd thee not to haunt about my doors;
    In honest plainness thou hast heard me say
    My daughter is not for thee; and now, in madness,
    Being full of supper and distempering draughts,   100
    Upon malicious bravery dost thou come
    To start my quiet.

ROD. Sir, sir, sir—

BRA.   But thou must needs be sure
    My spirit and my place have in their power
    To make this bitter to thee.

ROD.   Patience, good sir.   105

BRA. What tell'st thou me of robbing? This is Venice
    My house is not a grange.

ROD.   Most grave Brabantio,
    In simple and pure soul I come to you.   108

IAGO. Zounds, sir, you are one of those that will not serve God if
    the devil bid you. Because we come to do you service, and you
    think we are ruffians, you'll have your daughter cover'd with a
    Barbary horse; you'll have your nephews neigh to you; you'll
    have coursers for cousins and gennets for germans.

BRA. What profane wretch art thou?   115

IAGO. I am one, sir, that comes to tell you your daughter and the
    Moor are now making the beast with two backs.

BRA. Thou art a villain.

IAGO.   You are—a Senator.

BRA. This thou shalt answer; I know thee, Roderigo.   120

ROD. Sir, I will answer anything. But I beseech you,
    If't be your pleasure and most wise consent—
    As partly I find it is—that your fair daughter,
    At this odd-even and dull watch o' th' night,
    Transported with no worse nor better guard   125

4

But with a knave of common hire, a gondolier,
To the gross clasps of a lascivious Moor—
If this be known to you, and your allowance,
We then have done you bold and saucy wrongs ;
But if you know not this, my manners tell me   130
We have your wrong rebuke. Do not believe
That, from the sense of all civility,
I thus would play and trifle with your reverence.
Your daughter, if you have not given her leave,
I say again, hath made a gross revolt ;   135
Tying her duty, beauty, wit, and fortunes,
In an extravagant and wheeling stranger
Of here and everywhere.   Straight satisfy yourself.
If she be in her chamber or your house,
Let loose on me the justice of the state   140
For thus deluding you.

BRA. Strike on the tinder, ho !
Give me a taper ; call up all my people.
This accident is not unlike my dream.
Belief of it oppresses me already.
Light, I say ; light !   [*Exit from above.*

IAGO.   Farewell ; for I must leave you.   145
It seems not meet nor wholesome to my place
To be producted—as if I stay I shall—
Against the Moor ; for I do know the state,
However this may gall him with some check,
Cannot with safety cast him ; for he's embark'd   150
With such loud reason to the Cyprus wars,
Which even now stands in act, that, for their souls,
Another of his fathom they have none
To lead their business ; in which regard,
Though I do hate him as I do hell pains,   155
Yet, for necessity of present life,
I must show out a flag and sign of love,
Which is indeed but sign.   That you shall surely find him,
Lead to the Sagittary the raised search ;
And there will I be with him. So, farewell.   [*Exit.*

Enter below, BRABANTIO, *in his night gown, and* SERVANTS *with torches*

BRA. It is too true an evil. Gone she is ;
And what's to come of my despised time
Is nought but bitterness.   Now, Roderigo,
Where didst thou see her ?—O unhappy girl !—
With the Moor, say'st thou ?—Who would be a father ?— 165
How didst thou know 'twas she ?—O, thou deceivest me
Past thought !—What said she to you ?—Get moe tapers ;
Raise all my kindred.—Are they married think you ?

ROD. Truly, I think they are.

BRA. O heaven ! How got she out ? O treason of the blood ! 170
Fathers, from hence trust not your daughters' minds
By what you see them act. Is there not charms
By which the property of youth and maidhood
May be abus'd ? Have you not read, Roderigo,
Of some such thing ?

OD.   Yes, sir, I have indeed.   175
RA. Call up my brother.—O that you had had her !—
    Some one way, some another.—Do you know
    Where we may apprehend her and the Moor ?
OD. I think I can discover him, if you please
    To get good guard, and go along with me.   180
RA. Pray lead me on. At every house I'll call ;
    I may command at most.—Get weapons, ho !
    And raise some special officers of night.—
    On, good Roderigo ; I'll deserve your pains.   [*Exeunt.*

SCENE II. *Venice. Another street.*

Enter OTHELLO, IAGO, *and* ATTENDANTS *with torches.*

AGO. Though in the trade of war I have slain men,
    Yet do I hold it very stuff o' th' conscience
    To do no contriv'd murder. I lack iniquity
    Sometime to do me service. Nine or ten times
    I had thought to have yerk'd him here under the ribs.   5
TH. 'Tis better as it is.
AGO.   Nay, but he prated,
    And spoke such scurvy and provoking terms
    Against your honour
    That, with the little godliness I have,
    I did full hard forbear him. But I pray, sir,   10
    Are you fast married ? For be assur'd of this,
    That the magnifico is much beloved,
    And hath in his effect a voice potential
    As double as the Duke's. He will divorce you,
    Or put upon you what restraint and grievance   15
    That law, with all his might to enforce it on,
    Will give him cable.
TH.   Let him do his spite.
    My services which I have done the signiory
    Shall out-tongue his complaints. 'Tis yet to know—
    Which, when I know that boasting is an honour,   20
    I shall promulgate—I fetch my life and being
    From men of royal siege ; and my demerits
    May speak unbonneted to as proud a fortune
    As this that I have reach'd. For know, Iago,
    But that I love the gentle Desdemona,   25
    I would not my unhoused free condition
    Put into circumscription and confine
    For the seas' worth.

Enter CASSIO *and* OFFICERS *with torches.*

                    But look what lights come yonder.
AGO. Those are the raised father and his friends.
    You were best go in.
TH.   Not I ; I must be found.   30
    My parts, my title, and my perfect soul
    Shall manifest me rightly. Is it they ?
AGO. By Janus, I think no.
TH. The servants of the Duke and my lieutenant—

The goodness of the night upon you, friends ! 35
What is the news ?

CAS.   The Duke does greet you, General ;
And he requires your haste-post-haste appearance
Even on the instant.

OTH.   What is the matter, think you ?

CAS. Something from Cyprus, as I may divine.
It is a business of some heat : the galleys 40
Have sent a dozen sequent messengers
This very night at one another's heels ;
And many of the consuls, rais'd and met,
Are at the Duke's already. You have been hotly call'd for ;
When, being not at your lodging to be found, 45
The Senate hath sent about three several quests
To search you out.

OTH.   'Tis well I am found by you.
I will but spend a word here in the house,
And go with you.   [*Exit.*

CAS.   Ancient, what makes he here ?

IAGO. Faith, he to-night hath boarded a land carrack. 50
If it prove lawful prize, he's made for ever.

CAS. I do not understand.

IAGO.   He's married.

CAS.   To who ?

Re-enter OTHELLO.

IAGO. Marry, to—Come, Captain, will you go ?

OTH.   Have with you.

Enter BRABANTO, RODERIGIO, *and* OFFICERS *with torches and weapons*

CAS. Here comes another troop to seek for you.

IAGO. It is Brabantio. General, be advis'd ; 55
He comes to bad intent.

OTH.   Holla ! stand there.

ROD. Signior, it is the Moor.

BRA.   Down with him, thief.
                    [*They draw on both sides.*

IAGO. You, Roderigo ; come, sir, I am for you.

OTH. Keep up your bright swords, for the dew will rust them.
Good signior, you shall more command with years 60
Than with your weapons.

BRA. O thou foul thief, where hast thou stow'd my daughter ?
Damn'd as thou art, thou hast enchanted her ;
For I'll refer me to all things of sense,
If she in chains of magic were not bound, 65
Whether a maid so tender, fair, and happy,
So opposite to marriage that she shunn'd
The wealthy curled darlings of our nation,
Would ever have, to incur a general mock,
Run from her guardage to the sooty bosom 70
Of such a thing as thou—to fear, not to delight.
Judge me the world, if 'tis not gross in sense
That thou hast practis'd on her with foul charms,
Abus'd her delicate youth with drugs or minerals

That weakens motion. I'll have't disputed on ;   75
'Tis probable, and palpable to thinking.
I therefore apprehend and do attach thee
For an abuser of the world, a practiser
Of arts inhibited and out of warrant.
Lay hold upon him. If he do resist,   80
Subdue him at his peril.

OTH.   Hold your hands,
Both you of my inclining and the rest.
Were it my cue to fight, I should have known it
Without a prompter. Where will you that I go
To answer this your charge ?

BRA.   To prison ; till fit time   85
Of law and course of direct session
Call thee to answer.

OTH.   What if I do obey ?
How may the Duke be therewith satisfied,
Whose messengers are here about my side,
Upon some present business of the state,   90
To bring me to him.

OFF.   'Tis true, most worthy signior ;
The Duke's in council ; and your noble self,
I am sure, is sent for.

BRA.   How ! The Duke in council !
In this time of the night ! Bring him away.
Mine's not an idle cause. The Duke himself,   95
Or any of my brothers of the state,
Cannot but feel this wrong as 'twere their own ;
For if such actions may have passage free,
Bond-slaves and pagans shall our statesmen be.   [*Exeunt.*

SCENE III. *Venice. A council-chamber.*

Enter DUKE *and* SENATORS, *set at a table with lights ; and* ATTENDANTS.

DUKE. There is no composition in these news
That gives them credit.

1 SEN.   Indeed, they are disproportion'd ;
My letters say a hundred and seven galleys.

DUKE. And mine a hundred and forty.

2 SEN.   And mine two hundred.
But though they jump not on a just account—   5
As in these cases, where the aim reports,
'Tis oft with difference—yet do they all confirm
A Turkish fleet, and bearing up to Cyprus.

DUKE. Nay, it is possible enough to judgment.
I do not so secure me in the error   10
But the main article I do approve
In fearful sense.

SAILOR. [*Within.*] What, ho ! what, ho ! what, ho !

Enter SAILOR.

OFFICER. A messenger from the galleys.

DUKE.   Now, what's the business ?

SAIL. The Turkish preparation makes for Rhodes ;
　　So was I bid report here to the state   1
　　By Signior Angelo.
DUKE. How say you by this change ?
I SEN.   This cannot be,
　　By no assay of reason. 'Tis a pageant
　　To keep us in false gaze. When we consider
　　The importancy of Cyprus to the Turk,   20
　　And let ourselves again but understand
　　That as it more concerns the Turk than Rhodes,
　　So may he with more facile question bear it,
　　For that it stands not in such warlike brace,
　　But altogether lacks th' abilities   2
　　That Rhodes is dress'd in—if we make thought of this,
　　We must not think the Turk is so unskilful
　　To leave that latest which concerns him first,
　　Neglecting an attempt of ease and gain
　　To wake and wage a danger profitless.   30
DUKE. Nay, in all confidence, he's not for Rhodes.
OFFICER. Here is more news.

Enter a MESSENGER.

MESS. The Ottomites, reverend and gracious,
　　Steering with due course toward the isle of Rhodes,
　　Have there injointed them with an after fleet.   3
I SEN. Ay, so I thought. How many, as you guess ?
MESS. Of thirty sail ; and now they do restem
　　Their backward course, bearing with frank appearance
　　Their purposes toward Cyprus. Signior Montano,
　　Your trusty and most valiant servitor,   40
　　With his free duty recommends you thus,
　　And prays you to believe him.
DUKE. 'Tis certain, then, for Cyprus.
　　Marcus Lucchese, is not he in town ?
I SEN. He's now in Florence.   4
DUKE. Write from us : wish him post-post-haste dispatch.

Enter BRABANTIO, OTHELLO, IAGO, RODERIGO, *and* OFFICERS.

I SEN. Here comes Brabantio and the valiant Moor.
DUKE. Valiant Othello, we must straight employ you
　　Against the general enemy Ottoman.
　　[*To* BRABANTIO.] I did not see you ; welcome, gentle signior ;
　　We lack'd your counsel and your help to-night.   5
BRA. So did I yours. Good your Grace, pardon me :
　　Neither my place, nor aught I heard of business,
　　Hath rais'd me from my bed ; nor doth the general care
　　Take hold on me ; for my particular grief   5
　　Is of so flood-gate and o'erbearing nature
　　That it englutts and swallows other sorrows,
　　And it is still itself.
DUKE.   Why, what's the matter ?
BRA. My daughter ! O, my daughter !
ALL.   Dead ?
BRA.   Ay, to me.

She is abus'd, stol'n from me, and corrupted,
By spells and medicines bought of mountebanks ;
For nature so preposterously to err,
Being not deficient, blind, or lame of sense,
Sans witchcraft could not.

DUKE.   Whoe'er he be that in this foul proceeding   65
Hath thus beguil'd your daughter of herself,
And you of her, the bloody book of law
You shall yourself read in the bitter letter
After your own sense ; yea, though our proper son
Stood in your action.

BRA.   Humbly I thank your Grace.   70
Here is the man—this Moor whom now, it seems,
Your special mandate for the state affairs
Hath hither brought.

ALL.   We are very sorry for't.

DUKE. [To OTHELLO.] What, in your own part, can you say to this ?

BRA. Nothing, but this is so.   75

OTH. Most potent, grave, and reverend signiors,
My very noble and approv'd good masters :
That I have ta'en away this old man's daughter,
It is most true ; true, I have married her—
The very head and front of my offending   80
Hath this extent, no more. Rude am I in my speech,
And little blest with the soft phrase of peace ;
For since these arms of mine had seven years' pith,
Till now some nine moons wasted, they have us'd
Their dearest action in the tented field ;   85
And little of this great world can I speak
More than pertains to feats of broil and battle ;
And therefore little shall I grace my cause
In speaking for myself. Yet, by your gracious patience,
I will a round unvarnish'd tale deliver   90
Of my whole course of love—what drugs, what charms,
What conjuration, and what mighty magic,
For such proceedings am I charg'd withal,
I won his daughter.

BRA.   A maiden never bold,
Of spirit so still and quiet that her motion   95
Blush'd at herself ; and she—in spite of nature,
Of years, of country, credit, every thing—
To fall in love with what she fear'd to look on !
It is a judgment maim'd and most imperfect
That will confess perfection so could err   100
Against all rules of nature, and must be driven
To find out practices of cunning hell,
Why this should be. I therefore vouch again
That with some mixtures powerful o'er the blood,
Or with some dram conjur'd to this effect,   105
He wrought upon her.

DUKE.   To vouch this is no proof—
Without more wider and more overt test
Than these thin habits and poor likelihoods
Of modern seeming do prefer against him.

1 SEN. But, Othello, speak.   110
　　　Did you by indirect and forced courses
　　　Subdue and poison this young maid's affections?
　　　Or came it by request, and such fair question
　　　As soul to soul affordeth?
OTH.   I do beseech you,
　　　Send for the lady to the Sagittary,   115
　　　And let her speak of me before her father.
　　　If you do find me foul in her report,
　　　The trust, the office, I do hold of you
　　　Not only take away, but let your sentence
　　　Even fall upon my life.
DUKE.   Fetch Desdemona hither.   120
OTH. Ancient, conduct them; you best know the place.

　　　　　　　　　　　　　[Exeunt IAGO and ATTENDANTS

　　　And, till she come, as faithful as to heaven
　　　I do confess the vices of my blood,
　　　So justly to your grave ears I'll present
　　　How I did thrive in this fair lady's love,   125
　　　And she in mine.
DUKE. Say it, Othello.
OTH. Her father lov'd me, oft invited me;
　　　Still questioned me the story of my life
　　　From year to year—the battles, sieges, fortunes,   130
　　　That I have pass'd.
　　　I ran it through, even from my boyish days
　　　To th' very moment that he bade me tell it;
　　　Wherein I spake of most disastrous chances,
　　　Of moving accidents by flood and field;   135
　　　Of hairbreadth scapes i' th' imminent deadly breach;
　　　Of being taken by the insolent foe
　　　And sold to slavery; of my redemption thence,
　　　And portance in my travel's history;
　　　Wherein of antres vast and deserts idle,   140
　　　Rough quarries, rocks, and hills whose heads touch heaven,
　　　It was my hint to speak—such was the process;
　　　And of the Cannibals that each other eat,
　　　The Anthropophagi, and men whose heads
　　　Do grow beneath their shoulders. This to hear   145
　　　Would Desdemona seriously incline;
　　　But still the house affairs would draw her thence;
　　　Which ever as she could with haste dispatch,
　　　She'd come again, and with a greedy ear
　　　Devour up my discourse. Which I observing,   150
　　　Took once a pliant hour, and found good means
　　　To draw from her a prayer of earnest heart
　　　That I would all my pilgrimage dilate,
　　　Whereof by parcels she had something heard,
　　　But not intentively. I did consent,   155
　　　And often did beguile her of her tears,
　　　When I did speak of some distressful stroke
　　　That my youth suffered. My story being done,
　　　She gave me for my pains a world of sighs;
　　　She swore, in faith, 'twas strange, 'twas passing strange;   160

'Twas pitiful, 'twas wondrous pitiful.
She wish'd she had not heard it; yet she wish'd
That heaven had made her such a man. She thank'd me;
And bade me, if I had a friend that lov'd her,
I should but teach him how to tell my story,   165
And that would woo her. Upon this hint I spake;
She lov'd me for the dangers I had pass'd;
And I lov'd her that she did pity them.
This only is the witchcraft I have us'd.
Here comes the lady; let her witness it.   170

Enter DESDEMONA, IAGO, *and* ATTENDANTS.

DUKE. I think this tale would win my daughter too.
    Good Brabantio,
    Take up this mangled matter at the best.
    Men do their broken weapons rather use
    Than their bare hands.

BRA.   I pray you hear her speak.   175
    If she confess that she was half the wooer,
    Destruction on my head if my bad blame
    Light on the man! Come hither, gentle mistress.
    Do you perceive in all this noble company
    Where most you owe obedience?

DES.   My noble father,   180
    I do perceive here a divided duty:
    To you I am bound for life and education;
    My life and education both do learn me
    How to respect you; you are the lord of duty—
    I am hitherto your daughter; but here's my husband,   185
    And so much duty as my mother show'd
    To you, preferring you before her father,
    So much I challenge that I may profess
    Due to the Moor, my lord.

BRA.   God bu'y, I ha done.
    Please it your Grace, on to the state affairs—   190
    I had rather to adopt a child than get it.
    Come hither, Moor:
    I here do give thee that with all my heart
    Which, but thou hast already, with all my heart
    I would keep from thee. For your sake, jewel,   195
    I am glad at soul I have no other child;
    For thy escape would teach me tyranny,
    To hang clogs on them. I have done, by lord.

DUKE. Let me speak like yourself, and lay a sentence
    Which, as a grise or step, may help these lovers   200
    Into your favour.
    When remedies are past, the griefs are ended
    By seeing the worst, which late on hopes depended.
    To mourn a mischief that is past and gone
    Is the next way to draw new mischief on.   205
    What cannot be preserv'd when fortune takes,
    Patience her injury a mockery makes.
    The robb'd that smiles steals something from the thief;
    He robs himself that spends a bootless grief.

BRA. So let the Turk of Cyprus us beguile :   210
 We lose it not so long as we can smile.
 He bears the sentence well that nothing bears
 But the free comfort which from thence he hears ;
 But he bears both the sentence and the sorrow
 That to pay grief must of poor patience borrow.   215
 These sentences, to sugar or to gall,
 Being strong on both sides, are equivocal.
 But words are words : I never yet did hear
 That the bruis'd heart was pierced through the ear.
 I humbly beseech you proceed to th' affairs of state.   220
DUKE. The Turk with a most mighty preparation makes for Cyprus.
 Othello, the fortitude of the place is best known to you ; and
 though we have there a substitute of most allowed sufficiency,
 yet opinion, a sovereign mistress of effects, throws a more safer
 voice on you. You must therefore be content to slubber the
 gloss of your new fortunes with this more stubborn and boisterous
 expedition.
OTH. The tyrant custom, most grave senators,
 Hath made the flinty and steel couch of war   230
 My thrice-driven bed of down. I do agnize
 A natural and prompt alacrity
 I find in hardness ; and would undertake
 This present wars against the Ottomites.
 Most humbly, therefore, bending to your state,   235
 I crave fit disposition for my wife ;
 Due reference of place and exhibition ;
 With such accommodation and besort
 As levels with her breeding.
DUKE.   If you please,
 Be't at her father's.
BRA.   I'll not have it so.   240
OTH. Nor I.
DES.   Nor I. I would not there reside,
 To put my father in impatient thoughts
 By being in his eye. Most gracious Duke,
 To my unfolding lend your prosperous ear,
 And let me find a charter in your voice   245
 T' assist my simpleness.
DUKE. What would you, Desdemona ?
DES. That I did love the Moor to live with him,
 My downright violence and storm of fortunes
 May trumpet to the world. My heart's subdu'd   250
 Even to the very quality of my lord :
 I saw Othello's visage in his mind ;
 And to his honours and his valiant parts
 Did I my soul and fortunes consecrate.
 So that, dear lords, if I be left behind,   255
 A moth of peace, and he go to the war,
 The rites for why I love him are bereft me,
 And I a heavy interim shall support
 By his dear absence. Let me go with him.
OTH. Let her have your voice.   260
 Vouch with me, heaven, I therefore beg it not

To please the palate of my appetite ;
Nor to comply with heat—the young affects
In me defunct—and proper satisfaction ;
But to be free and bounteous to her mind.   265
And heaven defend your good souls that you think
I will your serious and great business scant
For she is with me.   No, when light-wing'd toys
Of feather'd Cupid seel with wanton dullness
My speculative and offic'd instruments,   270
That my disports corrupt and taint my business,
Let huswives make a skillet of my helm,
And all indign and base adversities
Make head against my estimation !

DUKE. Be it as you shall privately determine,   275
  Either for her stay or going.   Th' affair cries haste,
  And speed must answer it.   You must away to-night.

DES. To-night, my lord !

DUKE.   This night.

OTH.   With all my heart.

DUKE. At nine i' th' morning here we'll meet again.
  Othello, leave some officer behind,   280
  And he shall our commission bring to you ;
  With such things else of quality and respect
  As doth import you.

OTH.   So please your Grace, my ancient ;
  A man he is of honesty and trust.
  To his conveyance I assign my wife,   285
  With what else needful your good Grace shall think
  To be sent after me.

DUKE.   Let it be so.
  Good night to every one.   [*To* BRABANTIO.] And, noble signior,
  If virtue no delighted beauty lack,
  Your son-in-law is far more fair than black.   290

I SEN. Adieu, brave Moor ; use Desdemona well.

BRA. Look to her, Moor, if thou hast eyes to see :
  She has deceiv'd her father, and may thee.
                    [*Exeunt* DUKE, SENATORS, OFFICERS, *&c.*

OTH. My life upon her faith !—Honest Iago,
  My Desdemona must I leave to thee.   295
  I prithee let thy wife attend on her ;
  And bring them after in the best advantage.
  Come, Desdemona, I have but an hour
  Of love, of worldly matter and direction,
  To spend with thee.   We must obey the time.   300
                    [*Exeunt* OTHELLO *and* DESDEMONA.

ROD. Iago !

IAGO. What say'st thou, noble heart ?

ROD. What will I do, thinkest thou ?

IAGO. Why, go to bed and sleep.

ROD. I will incontinently drown myself.   305

IAGO. Well, if thou dost, I shall never love thee after it.   Why, thou
  silly gentleman !

ROD. It is silliness to live when to live is torment ; and then have we
  a prescription to die when death is our physician.

IAGO. O villainous! I ha look'd upon the world for four times seven years; and since I could distinguish betwixt a benefit and an injury, I never found a man that knew how to love himself. Ere I would say I would drown myself for the love of a guinea-hen, I would change my humanity with a baboon.   316

ROD. What should I do? I confess it is my shame to be so fond, but it is not in my virtue to amend it.

IAGO. Virtue? A fig! 'Tis in ourselves that we are thus or thus. Our bodies are our gardens to the which our wills are gardeners; so that if we will plant nettles or sow lettuce, set hyssop and weed up thyme, supply it with one gender of herbs or distract it with many, either to have it sterile with idleness or manur'd with industry—why, the power and corrigible authority of this lies in our wills. If the balance of our lives had not one scale of reason to poise another of sensuality, the blood and baseness of our natures would conduct us to most preposterous conclusions. But we have reason to cool our raging motions, our carnal stings, our unbitted lusts; whereof I take this that you call love to be a sect or scion.

ROD. It cannot be.   332

IAGO. It is merely a lust of the blood and a permission of the will. Come, be a man. Drown thyself? Drown cats and blind puppies! I have profess'd me thy friend, and I confess me knit to thy deserving with cables of perdurable toughness. I could never better stead thee than now. Put money in thy purse; follow thou the wars; defeat thy favour with an usurp'd beard. I say, put money in thy purse. It cannot be long that Desdemona should continue her love to the Moor—put money in thy purse—nor he his to her: it was a violent commencement in her, and thou shalt see an answerable sequestration—put but money in thy purse. These Moors are changeable in their wills—fill thy purse with money. The food that to him now is as luscious as locusts shall be to him shortly as acerbe as the coloquintida. She must change for youth; when she is sated with his body, she will find the error of her choice. Therefore put money in thy purse. If thou wilt needs damn thyself, do it a more delicate way than drowning. Make all the money thou canst. If sanctimony and a frail vow betwixt an erring barbarian and a super-subtle Venetian be not too hard for my wits and all the tribe of hell, thou shalt enjoy her; therefore make money. A pox a drowning thyself! 'Tis clean out of the way. Seek thou rather to be hang'd in compassing thy joy than to be drown'd and go without her.   358

ROD. Wilt thou be fast to my hopes, if I depend on the issue?

IAGO. Thou art sure of me—go make money. I have told thee often, and I retell thee again and again I hate the Moor. My cause is hearted: thine hath no less reason. Let us be conjunctive in our revenge against him. If thou canst cuckold him, thou dost thyself a pleasure, me a sport. There are many events in the womb of time which will be delivered. Traverse; go; provide thy money. We will have more of this to-morrow. Adieu.   369

ROD. Where shall we meet i' th' morning?

IAGO. At my lodging.

ROD. I'll be with thee betimes.

IAGO. Go to ; farewell. Do you hear, Roderigo?
ROD. What say you ?
IAGO. No more of drowning, do you hear ?   375
ROD. I am chang'd.
IAGO. Go to ; farewell. Put money enough in your purse.
ROD. I'll sell all my land.   [*Exit* RODERIGO.
IAGO. Thus do I ever make my fool my purse ;
    For I mine own gain'd knowledge should profane
    If I would time expend with such a snipe
    But for my sport and profit. I hate the Moor ;   380
    And it is thought abroad that 'twixt my sheets
    'Has done my office. I know not if't be true ;
    Yet I, for mere suspicion in that kind,
    Will do as if for surety. He holds me well ;
    The better shall my purpose work on him.   385
    Cassio's a proper man. Let me see now :
    To get his place, and to plume up my will
    In double knavery. How, how ? Let's see :
    After some time to abuse Othello's ear
    That he is too familiar with his wife.   390
    He hath a person and a smooth dispose
    To be suspected—fram'd to make women false.
    The Moor is of a free and open nature
    That thinks men honest that but seem to be so ;
    And will as tenderly be led by th' nose   395
    As asses are.
    I ha't—it is engender'd. Hell and night
    Must bring this monstrous birth to the world's light.   [*Exit.*

ACT TWO

SCENE I. *Cyprus. A sea-port.*

Enter MONTANO, *Governor of Cyprus, with two other* GENTLEMEN.

MON. What from the cape can you discern at sea ?
1 GENT. Nothing at all ; it is a high-wrought flood.
    I cannot 'twixt the heaven and the main
    Descry a sail.
MON. Methinks the wind hath spoke aloud at land ;   5
    A fuller blast ne'er shook our battlements.
    If it ha ruffian'd so upon the sea,
    What ribs of oak, when mountains melt on them,
    Can hold the mortise ? What shall we hear of this ?
2 GENT. A segregation of the Turkish fleet.   10
    For do but stand upon the banning shore,
    The chidden billow seems to pelt the clouds ;
    The wind-shak'd surge, with high and monstrous mane,
    Seems to cast water on the burning Bear,
    And quench the guards of th' ever-fired pole.   15
    I never did like molestation view
    On the enchafed flood.
MON.   If that the Turkish fleet
    Be not enshelter'd and embay'd, they are drown'd :
    It is impossible they bear it out.

Enter a third GENTLEMAN.

3 GENT. News, lads ! Your wars are done.   20
    The desperate tempest hath so bang'd the Turk
    That their designment halts. A noble ship of Venice
    Hath seen a grievous wreck and sufferance
    On most'part of their fleet.
MON. How ! Is this true ?
3 GENT.   The ship is here put in,   25
    A Veronesa ; Michael Cassio,
    Lieutenant to the warlike Moor Othello,
    Is come ashore : the Moor himself at sea,
    And is in full commission here for Cyprus.
MON. I am glad on't ; 'tis a worthy governor.   30
3 GENT. But this same Cassio, though he speak of comfort
    Touching the Turkish loss, yet he looks sadly
    And prays the Moor be safe ; for they were parted
    With foul and violent tempest.
MON.   Pray heaven he be ;
    For I have serv'd him, and the man commands   35
    Like a full soldier. Let's to the sea-side, ho !
    As well to see the vessel that's come in
    As to throw out our eyes for brave Othello,
    Even till we make the main and th' aerial blue
    An indistinct regard.
3 GENT.   Come, let's do so ;   40
    For every minute is expectancy
    Of more arrivance.

Enter CASSIO.

CAS. Thanks you, the valiant of this war-like isle,
    That so approve the Moor. O, let the heavens
    Give him defence against their elements,   45
    For I have lost him on a dangerous sea !
MON. Is he well shipp'd ?
CAS. His bark is stoutly timber'd, and his pilot
    Of very expert and approv'd allowance ;
    Therefore my hopes, not surfeited to death,   50
    Stand in bold cure.   [*Within :* A sail, a sail, a sail !

Enter a MESSENGER.

CAS. What noise ?
MESS. The town is empty ; on the brow o' th' sea
    Stand ranks of people, and they cry ' A sail !'
CAS. My hopes do shape him for the Governor.   [*A shot.*
2 GENT. They do discharge the shot of courtesy :
    Our friend at least.
CAS.   I pray you, sir, go forth,
    And give us truth who 'tis that is arriv'd.
2 GENT. I shall.   [*Exit.*
MON. But, good Lieutenant, is your general wiv'd ?   60
CAS. Most fortunately : he hath achiev'd a maid
    That paragons description and wild fame ;
    One that excels the quirks of blazoning pens,

And in th' essential vesture of creation
Does tire the ingener.

Re-enter second GENTLEMAN.

                              Now, who has put in ?   65
2 GENT. 'Tis one Iago, ancient to the General.
CAS. 'Has had most favourable and happy speed.
    Tempests themselves, high seas, and howling winds,
    The gutter'd rocks, and congregated sands,
    Traitors ensteep'd to enclog the guiltless keel,   70
    As having sense of beauty, do omit
    Their mortal natures, letting go safely by
    The divine Desdemona.
MON.   What is she ?
CAS. She that I spake of—our great Captain's Captain,
    Left in the conduct of the bold Iago ;   75
    Whose footing here anticipates our thoughts
    A se'nnight's speed. Great Jove, Othello guard,
    And swell his sail with thine own powerful breath,
    That he may bless this bay with his tall ship,
    Make love's quick pants in Desdemona's arms,   80
    Give renew'd fire to our extincted spirits,
    And bring all Cyprus comfort !

Enter DESDEMONA, IAGO, EMILIA, RODERIGO, *and* ATTENDANTS.

                                    O, behold,
    The riches of the ship is come ashore !
    Ye men of Cyprus, let her have your knees.
    Hail to thee, lady ! and the grace of heaven,   85
    Before, behind thee, and on every hand,
    Enwheel thee round !
DES.   I thank you, valiant Cassio.
    What tidings can you tell me of my lord ?
CAS. He is not yet arriv'd ; nor know I aught
    But that he's well, and will be shortly here.   90
DES. O, but I fear ! How lost you company ?
CAS. The great contention of the sea and skies
    Parted our fellowship.   [*Within :* A sail, a sail !
                        But hark—' A sail !'   [*A shot.*
2 GENT. They give their greeting to the citadel :
    This likewise is a friend.
CAS.   So speaks this voice.
    See for the news.   [*Exit* GENTLEMAN.
    Good ancient, you are welcome. [*To* EMILIA.] Welcome, mistress.
    Let it not gall your patience, good Iago,   97
    That I extend my manners ; 'tis my breeding
    That gives me this bold show of courtesy.   [*Kissing her.*
IAGO. Sir, would she give you so much of her lips
    As of her tongue she oft bestows on me,   101
    You'd have enough.
DES. Alas, she has no speech !
IAGO.   I know too much
    I find it aye when I ha list to sleep.

                                                                  111

Marry, before your ladyship, I grant,   105
She puts her tongue a little in her heart
And chides with thinking.

EMIL.   You ha little cause to say so.

IAGO. Come on, come on; you are pictures out a-doors, bells in
your parlours, wildcats in your kitchens, saints in your injuries,
devils being offended, players in your huswifery, and huswives in
your beds.

DES. O, fie upon thee, slanderer!

IAGO. Nay, it is true, or else I am a Turk:
You rise to play, and go to bed to work.   115

EMIL. You shall not write my praise.

IAGO.   No, let me not.

DES. What wouldst write of me if thou shouldst praise me?

IAGO. O gentle lady, do not put me to't;
For I am nothing if not critical.

DES. Come on, assay.—There's one gone to the harbour?   120

IAGO. Ay, madam.

DES. I am not merry; but I do beguile
The thing I am by seeming otherwise.
Come, how wouldst thou praise me?

IAGO. I am about it; but, indeed, my invention comes from my pate
as birdlime does from frieze—it plucks out brains and all. But
my Muse labours, and thus she is deliver'd:
If she be fair and wise—fairness and wit,
The one's for use, the other useth it.   130

DES. Well prais'd. How if she be black and witty?

IAGO. If she be black, and thereto have a wit,
She'll find a white that shall her blackness hit.

DES. Worse and worse!

EMIL. How if fair and foolish?   135

IAGO. She never yet was foolish that was fair;
For even her folly help'd her to an heir.

DES. These are old fond paradoxes to make fools laugh i' th' alehouse.
What miserable praise hast thou for her that's foul and foolish?

IAGO. There's none so foul, and foolish thereunto,
But does foul pranks which fair and wise ones do.

DES. O heavy ignorance! that praises the worst best. But what
praise couldst thou bestow on a deserving woman indeed—one
that, in the authority of her merits, did justly put on the vouch
of very malice itself?   146

IAGO. She that was ever fair, and never proud;
Had tongue at will, and yet was never loud;
Never lack'd gold, and yet went never gay;
Fled from her wish, and yet said 'Now I may';   150
She that, being ang'red, her revenge being nigh,
Bade her wrong stay and her displeasure fly;
She that in wisdom never was so frail
To change the cod's head for the salmon's tail;
She that could think, and ne'er disclose her mind;   155
See suitors following, and not look behind:
She was a wight, if ever such wight were—

DES. To do what?

IAGO. To suckle fools and chronicle small beer.

DES. O most lame and impotent conclusion ! Do not learn of him,
　　Emilia, though he be thy husband. How say you, Cassio ? Is he
　　not a most profane and liberal counsellor ?   163
CAS. He speaks home, madam. You may relish him more in the
　　soldier than in the scholar.
IAGO. [*Aside.*] He takes her by the palm. Ay, well said, whisper.
　　With as little a web as this will I ensnare as great a fly as Cassio.
　　Ay, smile upon her, do ; I will gyve thee in thine own courtship.
　　You say true ; 'tis so, indeed. If such tricks as these strip you
　　out of your lieutenantry, it had been better you had not kiss'd
　　your three fingers so oft, which now again you are most apt to play
　　the sir in. Very good ; well kissed ! and excellent courtesy !
　　'Tis so indeed. Yet again your fingers to your lips ? Would they
　　were clyster-pipes for your sake !   [*Trumpet within.*
　　The Moor ! I know his trumpet.   176
CAS.   'Tis truly so.
DES. Let's meet him, and receive him.
CAS.   Lo, where he comes !

                     Enter OTHELLO *and* ATTENDANTS.

OTH. O my fair warrior !
DES.   My dear Othello !   180
OTH. It gives me wonder great as my content
　　To see you here before me. O my soul's joy !
　　If after every tempest come such calms,
　　May the winds blow till they have waken'd death,
　　And let the labouring bark climb hills of seas   185
　　Olympus-high and duck again as low
　　As hell's from heaven. If it were now to die,
　　'Twere now to be most happy ; for I fear
　　My soul hath her content so absolute
　　That not another comfort like to this   190
　　Succeeds in unknown fate.
DES.   The heavens forbid
　　But that our loves and comforts should increase
　　Even as our days do grow !
OTH.   Amen to that, sweet powers !
　　I cannot speak enough of this content ;
　　It stops me here ; it is too much of joy.   195
　　And this, and this, the greatest discords be   [*They kiss.*
　　That e'er our hearts shall make !
IAGO. [*Aside.*]   O, you are well tun'd now !
　　But I'll set down the pegs that make this music,
　　As honest as I am.
OTH.   Come, let us to the castle.
　　News, friends : our wars are done ; the Turks are drown'd.
　　How do our old acquaintance of the isle ?   201
　　Honey, you shall be well desir'd in Cyprus ;
　　I have found great love amongst them. O my sweet,
　　I prattle out of fashion, and I dote
　　In mine own comforts. I prithee, good Iago.   205
　　Go to the bay, and disembark my coffers ;
　　Bring thou the Master to the Citadel ;
　　He is a good one, and his worthiness

Does challenge much respect.   Come, Desdemona,
Once more well met at Cyprus.   210
                                    [*Exeunt all but* IAGO *and* RODERIGO.
IAGO. [*To one leaving.*] Do thou meet me presently at the harbour.
[*To* RODERIGO.] Come hither.   If thou be'st valiant—as they say
base men being in love have then a nobility in their natures
more than is native to them—list me.   The Lieutenant to-night
watches on the court of guard.   First, I must tell thee this :
Desdemona is directly in love with him.
ROD. With him !   Why, 'tis not possible.   217
IAGO. Lay thy finger thus, and let thy soul be instructed.   Mark
me with what violence she first lov'd the Moor, but for bragging
and telling her fantastical lies.   To love him still for prating ?—
let not thy discreet heart think it.   Her eye must be fed ; and what
delight shall she have to look on the devil ?   When the blood is
made dull with the act of sport, there should be—again to inflame
it, and to give satiety a fresh appetite—loveliness in favour,
sympathy in years, manners, and beauties—all which the Moor
is defective in.   Now for want of these requir'd conveniences,
her delicate tenderness will find itself abus'd, begin to heave
the gorge, disrelish and abhor the Moor ;   very nature will instruct
her in it, and compel her to some second choice.   Now, sir, this
granted—as it is a most pregnant and unforc'd position—who
stands so eminent in the degree of this fortune as Cassio does ?
A knave very voluble ;   no further conscionable than in putting
on the mere form of civil and humane seeming, for the better
compassing of his salt and most hidden loose affection ?   Why,
none ;   why, none.   A slipper and subtle knave ;   a finder-out of
occasion ;   that has an eye can stamp and counterfeit advantages,
though true advantage never present itself ;   a devilish knave !
Besides, the knave is handsome, young, and hath all those requisites
in him that folly and green minds look after ;   a pestilent complete
knave, and the woman hath found him already.   244
ROD. I cannot believe that in her ;   she's full of most blest condition.
IAGO. Blest fig's end !   The wine she drinks is made of grapes.   If she
had been blest, she would never have lov'd the Moor.   Blest
pudding !   Didst thou not see her paddle with the palm of his
hand ?   Didst not mark that ?   250
ROD. Yes, that I did ;   but that was but courtesy.
IAGO. Lechery, by this hand ;   an index and obscure prologue to the
history of lust and foul thoughts.   They met so near with their
lips that their breaths embrac'd together.   Villainous thoughts,
Roderigo !   When these mutualities so marshal the way, hard
at hand comes the master and main exercise, th' incorporate
conclusion.   Pish !   But, sir, be you rul'd by me ;   I have brought
you from Venice.   Watch you to-night ;   for your command, I'll
lay't upon you.   Cassio knows you not ;   I'll not be far from you.
Do you find some occasion to anger Cassio, either by speaking too
loud, or tainting his discipline, or from what other course you please,
which the time shall more favourably minister.
ROD. Well.   265
IAGO. Sir, he's rash, and very sudden in choler, and haply with his
truncheon may strike at you ;   provoke him that he may ;   for
even out of that will I cause these of Cyprus to mutiny, whose

qualification shall come into no true taste again but by the dis-
planting of Cassio. So shall you have a shorter journey to your
desires by the means I shall then have to prefer them; and the
impediment most profitably remov'd, without the which there
were no expectation of our prosperity.   274

ROD. I will do this, if you can bring it to any opportunity.

IAGO. I warrant thee. Meet me by and by at the citadel. I must
fetch his necessaries ashore. Farewell.

ROD. Adieu.   [*Exit.*

IAGO. That Cassio loves her, I do well believe it;   280
That she loves him, 'tis apt and of great credit.
The Moor, howbeit that I endure him not,
Is of a constant, loving, noble nature;
And I dare think he'll prove to Desdemona
A most dear husband. Now I do love her too;   285
Not out of absolute lust, though peradventure
I stand accountant for as great a sin,
But partly led to diet my revenge,
For that I do suspect the lustful Moor
Hath leap'd into my seat; the thought whereof   290
Doth like a poisonous mineral gnaw my inwards;
And nothing can nor shall content my soul
Till I am even'd with him, wife for wife;
Or failing so, yet that I put the Moor
At least into a jealousy so strong   295
That judgment cannot cure. Which thing to do,
If this poor trash of Venice, whom I trash
For his quick hunting, stand the putting on,
I'll have our Michael Cassio on the hip,
Abuse him to the Moor in the rank garb—   300
For I fear Cassio with my night-cap too;
Make the Moor thank me, love me, and reward me,
For making him egregiously an ass,
And practising upon his peace and quiet
Even to madness. 'Tis here, but yet confus'd: 305
Knavery's plain face is never seen till us'd.   [*Exit.*

SCENE II. *Cyprus. A street.*

Enter Othello's HERALD *with a proclamation;* PEOPLE *following.*

HER. It is Othello's pleasure, our noble and valiant general, that,
upon certain tidings now arriv'd, importing the mere perdition
of the Turkish fleet, every man put himself into triumph; some
to dance, some to make bonfires, each man to what sport and
revels his addiction leads him; for, besides these beneficial news,
it is the celebration of his nuptial. So much was his pleasure
should be proclaimed. All offices are open; and there is full
liberty of feasting from this present hour of five till the bell have
told eleven. Heaven bless the isle of Cyprus and our noble
general Othello!   [*Exeunt.*

SCENE III. *Cyprus. The citadel.*

Enter OTHELLO, DESDEMONA, CASSIO, *and* ATTENDANTS.

OTH. Good Michael, look you to the guard to-night.
　　Let's teach ourselves that honourable stop,
　　Not to outsport discretion.
CAS.　　　　Iago hath direction what to do ;
　　But, notwithstanding, with my personal eye
　　Will I look to't.   5
OTH.　　　　Iago is most honest.
　　Michael, good night. To-morrow with your earliest
　　Let me have speech with you. [*To* DESDEMONA.] Come, my dear
　　　　love,
　　The purchase made, the fruits are to ensue ;
　　That profit's yet to come 'twixt me and you.—   10
　　Good night.　　[*Exeunt* OTHELLO, DESDEMONA, *and* ATTENDANTS.

Enter IAGO.

CAS. Welcome, Iago ; we must to the watch.
IAGO. Not this hour, Lieutenant ; 'tis not yet ten a clock. Our general
　　cast us thus early for the love of his Desdemona ; who let us not
　　therefore blame. He hath not yet made wanton the night with
　　her ; and she is sport for Jove.   17
CAS. She is a most exquisite lady.
IAGO. And, I'll warrant her, full of game.
CAS. Indeed, she is a most fresh and delicate creature.
IAGO. What an eye she has ! Methinks it sounds a parley to pro-
　　vocation.
CAS. An inviting eye ; and yet methinks right modest.
IAGO. And when she speaks, is it not an alarm to love ?
CAS. She is indeed perfection.   25
IAGO. Well, happiness to their sheets ! Come, Lieutenant, I have a
　　stoup of wine ; and here without are a brace of Cyprus gallants
　　that would fain have a measure to the health of the black Othello.
CAS. Not to-night, good Iago. I have very poor and unhappy brains
　　for drinking ; I could well wish courtesy would invent some other
　　custom of entertainment.   32
IAGO. O, they are our friends—but one cup ; I'll drink for you.
CAS. I have drunk but one cup to-night, and that was craftily qualified
　　too, and behold what innovation it makes here. I am unfortunate
　　in the infirmity, and dare not task my weakness with any more.
IAGO. What, man ! 'Tis a night of revels. The gallants desire it.
CAS. Where are they ?
IAGO. Here at the door ; I pray you call them in.
CAS. I'll do't ; but it dislikes me.   [*Exit.*
IAGO. If I can fasten but one cup upon him,
　　With that which he hath drunk to-night already,   45
　　He'll be as full of quarrel and offence
　　As my young mistress' dog. Now my sick fool Roderigo,
　　Whom love hath turn'd almost the wrong side outward,
　　To Desdemona hath to-night carous'd
　　Potations pottle deep ; and he's to watch.   50

Three else of Cyprus—noble swelling spirits,
That hold their honours in a wary distance,
The very elements of this warlike isle—
Have I to-night fluster'd with flowing cups,
And they watch too. Now, 'mongst this flock of drunkards   55
Am I to put our Cassio in some action
That may offend the isle—but here they come.

Re-enter CASSIO *with* MONTANO, *and* GENTLEMAN, *followed by* SERVANT
with wine.

If consequence do but approve my dream,
My boat sails freely, both with wind and stream.
CAS. Fore God, they have given me a rouse already.
MON. Good faith, a little one ; not past a pint, as I am a soldier.
IAGO. Some wine, ho !
     [*Sings.*]   And let me the canakin clink, clink
                           And let me the canakin clink.   65
                              A soldier's a man;
                              O, man's life's but a span ;
                           Why, then, let a soldier drink—
Some wine, boys.
CAS. Fore God, an excellent song !   70
IAGO. I learn'd it in England, where indeed they are most potent in
     potting : your Dane, your German, and your swag-bellied
     Hollander—Drink, ho !—are nothing to your English.
CAS. Is your Englishman so expert in his drinking ?
IAGO. Why, he drinks you with facility your Dane dead drunk ; he
     sweats not to overthrow your Almain ; he gives your Hollander a
     vomit ere the next pottle can be fill'd.   78
CAS. To the health of our General !
MON. I am for it, Lieutenant ; and I'll do you justice.
IAGO. O sweet England !   [*Sings.*
                     King Stephen was and a worthy peer,
                        His breeches cost him but a crown ;
                     He held 'em sixpence all too dear,
                        With that he call'd the tailor lown.   85
                     He was a wight of high renown,
                        And thou art but of low degree.
                     'Tis pride that pulls the country down ;
                        Then take thy auld cloak about thee—
Some wine, ho !   90
CAS. Fore God, this is a more exquisite song than the other.
IAGO. Will you hear't again ?
CAS. No ; for I hold him to be unworthy of his place that does those
     things. Well, God's above all ; and there be souls must be saved,
     and there be souls must not be saved.   96
IAGO. It's true, good Lieutenant.
CAS. For mine own part—no offence to the General, nor any man of
     quality—I hope to be saved.
IAGO. And so do I too, Lieutenant.   100
CAS. Ay, but, by your leave, not before me ; the Lieutenant is to be
     saved before the Ancient. Let's have no more of this ; let's to our
     affairs. God forgive us our sins. Gentlemen, let's look to our
     business. Do not think, gentlemen, I am drunk. This is my

ancient ; this is my right hand, and this is my left hand. I am not drunk now ; I can stand well enough, and I speak well enough.

ALL. Excellent well.   108

CAS. Why, very well, then. You must not think, then, that I am drunk.   [*Exit.*

MON. To the platform, masters ; come, let's set the watch.

IAGO. You see this fellow that is gone before :
   He is a soldier fit to stand by Cæsar
   And give direction ; and do but see his vice   115
   'Tis to his virtue a just equinox,
   The one as long as th' other. 'Tis pity of him.
   I fear the trust Othello puts him in,
   On some odd time of his infirmity,
   Will shake this island.

MON.   But is he often thus ?   120

IAGO. 'Tis evermore the prologue to his sleep :
   He'll watch the horologe a double set,
   If drink rock not his cradle.

MON.   It were well
   The General were put in mind of it.
   Perhaps he sees it not, or his good nature   125
   Prizes the virtue that appears in Cassio,
   And looks not on his evils. Is not this true ?

                             Enter RODERIGO.

IAGO. [*Aside to him.*] How, now, Roderigo !
   I pray you, after the Lieutenant ; go.   [*Exit* RODERIGO.

MON. And 'tis great pity that the noble Moor   130
   Should hazard such a place as his own second
   With one of an ingraft infirmity :
   It were an honest action to say
   So to the Moor.

IAGO.   Not I, for this fair island ;
   I do love Cassio well ; and would do much   135
   To cure him of this evil.   [*Within :* Help, help !
                   But hark, what noise ?

             Re-enter CASSIO, *driving in* RODERIGO.

CAS. Zounds, you rogue, you rascal !

MON. What's the matter, Lieutenant ?

CAS. A knave teach me my duty ! But I'll beat the knave into a twiggen bottle.   140

ROD. Beat me !

CAS. Dost thou prate, rogue ?   [*Strikes him.*

MON. Nay, good Lieutenant ; I pray you, sir, hold your hand.

CAS. Let me go, sir, or I'll knock you o'er the mazard.

MON. Come, come, you're drunk.

CAS. Drunk !   [*They fight.*

IAGO. [*Aside to* RODERIGO.] Away, I say !
   Go out and cry a mutiny !   [*Exit* RODERIGO.
   Nay, good Lieutenant. God's will, gentlemen !   150
   Help, ho !—Lieutenant—sir—Montano—sir—
   Help, masters ! Here's a goodly watch indeed !   [*A bell rung.*
   Who's that which rings the bell ? Diablo, ho !

The town will rise. God's will, Lieutenant, hold.
You'll be asham'd for ever.

Re-enter OTHELLO *and* GENTLEMAN, *with weapons.*

OTH. What is the matter here ?
MON. Zounds, I bleed still ; I am hurt to the death—He dies.
OTH. Hold, for your lives !
IAGO. Hold, ho ! Lieutenant—sir—Montano—gentlemen—
    Have you forgot all sense of place and duty ?
    Hold ! The General speaks to you ; hold, hold, for shame !   159
OTH. Why, how now, ho ! From whence ariseth this ?
    Are we turn'd Turks, and to ourselves do that
    Which Heaven hath forbid the Ottomites ?
    For Christian shame, put by this barbarous brawl.
    He that stirs next to carve for his own rage   165
    Holds his soul light : he dies upon his motion.
    Silence that dreadful bell ; it frights the isle
    From her propriety. What's the matter, masters ?
    Honest Iago, that looks dead with grieving,
    Speak. Who began this ? On thy love, I charge thee.   170
IAGO. I do not know. Friends all but now, even now,
    In quarter, and in terms, like bride and groom
    Divesting them for bed ; and then, but now,
    As if some planet had unwitted men,
    Swords out, and tilting one at other's breast   175
    In opposition bloody. I cannot speak
    Any beginning to this peevish odds ;
    And would in action glorious I had lost
    These legs that brought me to a part of it !
OTH. How comes it, Michael, you are thus forgot ?   180
CAS. I pray you, pardon me ; I cannot speak .
OTH. Worthy Montano, you were wont be civil ;
    The gravity and stillness of your youth
    The world hath noted, and your name is great
    In mouths of wisest censure—what's the matter   185
    That you unlace your reputation thus,
    And spend your rich opinion for the name
    Of a night-brawler ? Give me answer to't.
MON. Worthy Othello, I am hurt to danger ;
    Your officer Iago can inform you,   190
    While I spare speech, which something now offends me,
    Of all that I do know ; nor know I aught
    By me that's said or done amiss this night,
    Unless self-charity be sometimes a vice,
    And to defend ourselves it be a sin   195
    When violence assails us.
OTH.   Now, by heaven,
    My blood begins my safer guides to rule ;
    And passion, having my best judgment collied,
    Assays to lead the way. Zounds if I stir
    Or do but lift this arm, the best of you   200
    Shall sink in my rebuke. Give me to know
    How this foul rout began, who set it on ;
    And he that is approv'd in this offence,

Though he had twinn'd with me, both at a birth,
Shall lose me. What! in a town of war,   205
Yet wild, the people's hearts brim full of fear,
To manage private and domestic quarrel,
In night, and on the court and guard of safety!
'Tis monstrous. Iago, who began't?

MON. If partially affin'd, or leagu'd in office,   210
Thou dost deliver more or less than truth,
Thou art no soldier.

IAGO.   Touch me not so near;
I had rather ha this tongue cut from my mouth
Than it should do offence to Michael Cassio;
Yet, I persuade myself, to speak the truth   215
Shall nothing wrong him. This it is, General.
Montano and myself being in speech,
There comes a fellow crying out for help,
And Cassio following him with determin'd sword
To execute upon him. Sir, this gentleman   220
Steps in to Cassio and entreats his pause;
Myself the crying fellow did pursue,
Lest by his clamour, as it so fell out,
The town might fall in fright; he, swift of foot,
Outran my purpose, and I return'd the rather   225
For that I heard the clink and fall of swords,
And Cassio high in oath; which till to-night
I ne'er might see before. When I came back,
For this was brief, I found them close together
At blow and thrust, even as again they were   230
When you yourself did part them.
More of this matter can I not report;
But men are men; the best sometimes forget.
Though Cassio did some little wrong to him,
As men in rage strike those that wish them best,   235
Yet surely Cassio, I believe, receiv'd
From him that fled some strange indignity
Which patience could not pass.

OTH.   I know, Iago,
Thy honesty and love doth mince this matter,
Making it light to Cassio. Cassio, I love thee;   240
But never more be officer of mine.

Re-enter DESDEMONA, *attended.*

Look if my gentle love be not rais'd up.
I'll make thee an example.

DES. What is the matter, dear?

OTH.   All's well now, sweeting;
Come away to bed. [*To* MONTANO.] Sir, for your hurts,
Myself will be your surgeon. Lead him off. [MONTANO *is led off.*
Iago, look with care about the town,
And silence those whom this vile brawl distracted.
Come, Desdemona; 'tis the soldiers' life
To have their balmy slumbers wak'd with strife.   250
                    [*Exeunt all but* IAGO *and* CASSIO.

IAGO. What, are you hurt, Lieutenant?

120

CAS. Ay, past all surgery.

IAGO. Marry, God forbid !

CAS. Reputation, reputation, reputation ! O, I have lost my reputation!
I have lost the immortal part of myself, and what remains is bestial.
My reputation, Iago, my reputation !   257

IAGO. As I am an honest man, I had thought you had receiv'd some
bodily wound ; there is more sense in that than in reputation.
Reputation is an idle and most false imposition ; oft got without
merit, and lost without deserving. You have lost no reputation
at all, unless you repute yourself such a loser. What, man !
there are more ways to recover the General again ; you are but
now cast in his mood, a punishment more in policy than in malice ;
even so as one would beat his offenceless dog to affright an imperious lion. Sue to him again, and he's yours.   267

CAS. I will rather sue to be despis'd than to deceive so good a commander with so slight, so drunken, and so indiscreet an officer.
Drunk ! And speak parrot ! And squabble, swagger, swear !
And discourse fustian with one's own shadow ! O thou invisible
spirit of wine, if thou hast no name to be known by, let us call thee
devil !

IAGO. What was he that you follow'd with your sword ? What had he
done to you ?   276

CAS. I know not.

IAGO. Is't possible ?

CAS. I remember a mass of things, but nothing distinctly ; a quarrel,
but nothing wherefore. O God, that men should put an enemy
in their mouths to steal away their brains ! That we should with
joy, pleasance, revel and applause, transform ourselves into
beasts !   283

IAGO. Why, but you are now well enough. How come you thus
recovered ?

CAS. It hath pleas'd the devil drunkenness to give place to the devil
wrath. One unperfectness shows me another, to make me frankly
despise myself.

IAGO. Come, you are too severe a moraller. As the time, the place,
and the condition of this country stands, I could heartily wish
this had not so befall'n ; but since it is as it is, mend it for your
own good.   292

CAS. I will ask him for my place again : he shall tell me I am a
drunkard. Had I as many mouths as Hydra, such an answer
would stop them all. To be now a sensible man, by and by a
fool, and presently a beast ! O strange ! Every inordinate cup
is unblest, and the ingredience is a devil.

IAGO. Come, come, good wine is a good familiar creature if it be
well us'd ; exclaim no more against it. And, good Lieutenant,
I think you think I love you.   301

CAS. I have well approv'd it, sir. I drunk !

IAGO. You or any man living may be drunk at a time, man. I'll
tell you what you shall do. Our General's wife is now the General
—I may say so in this respect, for that he hath devoted and given
up himself to the contemplation, mark, and denotement, of her
parts and graces—confess yourself freely to her ; importune her
help to put you in your place again : she is of so free, so kind,
so apt, so blessed a disposition, she holds it a vice in her goodness

not to do more than she is requested. This broken joint between
you and her husband entreat her to splinter; and, my fortunes
against any lay worth naming, this crack of your love shall grow
stronger than it was before.   315

CAS. You advise me well.

IAGO. I protest, in the sincerity of love and honest kindness.

CAS. I think it freely; and betimes in the morning I will beseech the
virtuous Desdemona to undertake for me. I am desperate of my
fortunes if they check me here.

IAGO. You are in the right. Good night, Lieutenant; I must to the
watch.

CAS. Good night, honest Iago.   [*Exit.*

IAGO. And what's he, then, that says I play the villain?   325
When this advice is free I give and honest,
Probal to thinking, and indeed the course
To win the Moor again? For 'tis most easy
The inclining Desdemona to subdue
In any honest suit: she's fram'd as fruitful   330
As the free elements. And then for her
To win the Moor—were't to renounce his baptism
All seals and symbols of redeemed sin—
His soul is so enfetter'd to her love
That she may make, unmake, do what she list,   335
Even as her appetite shall play the god
With his weak function. How am I, then, a villain
To counsel Cassio to this parallel course,
Directly to his good? Divinity of hell!
When devils will their blackest sins put on,   340
They do suggest at first with heavenly shows,
As I do now; for whiles this honest fool
Plies Desdemona to repair his fortunes,
And she for him pleads strongly to the Moor,
I'll pour this pestilence into his ear—   345
That she repeals him for her body's lust;
And by how much she strives to do him good
She shall undo her credit with the Moor.
So will I turn her virtue into pitch;
And out of her own goodness make the net   350
That shall enmesh them all.

Enter RODERIGO.

How now, Roderigo!

ROD. I do follow here in the chase, not like a hound that hunts, but
one that fills up the cry. My money is almost spent; I have
been to-night exceedingly well cudgell'd; and I think the issue
will be—I shall have so much experience for my pains as that
comes to; and so, with no money at all, and a little more wit,
return again to Venice.   357

IAGO. How poor are they that have not patience!
What wound did ever heal but by degrees?
Thou know'st we work by wit, and not by witchcraft   360
And wit depends on dilatory time.
Does't not go well? Cassio hath beaten thee,
And thou, by that small hurt, hast cashier'd Cassio.

Though other things grow fair against the sun,
Yet fruits that blossom first will first be ripe.   365
Content thyself awhile.   By th' mass, 'tis morning !
Pleasure and action make the hours seem short.
Retire thee ; go where thou art billeted.
Away, I say ; thou shalt know more hereafter.   369
Nay, get thee gone.   [*Exit* RODERIGO.
           Two things are to be done :
My wife must move for Cassio to her mistress ;
I'll set her on ;
Myself awhile to draw the Moor apart
And bring him jump when he may Cassio find
Soliciting his wife.   Ay, that's the way ;   375
Dull not device by coldness and delay.   [*Exit.*

ACT THREE

SCENE I. *Cyprus.   Before the citadel.*

Enter CASSIO, *with* MUSICIANS.

CAS. Masters, play here ; I will content your pains.
    Something that's brief ; and bid ' Good morrow, General '.
                          [*Music.*

Enter CLOWN.

CLO. Why masters, ha your instruments been in Naples, that they
    speak i' th' nose thus ?
1 MUS. How, sir, how ?   5
CLO. Are these, I pray, call'd wind instruments ?
1 MUS. Ay, marry, are they, sir.
CLO. O, thereby hangs a tail.
1 MUS. Whereby hangs a tale, sir ?   9
CLO. Marry, sir, by many a wind instrument that I know.   But,
    masters, here's money for you ; and the General so likes your
    music that he desires you, of all loves, to make no more noise
    with it.
1 MUS. Well, sir, we will not.   14
CLO. If you have any music that may not be heard, to't again ; but,
    as they say, to hear music the General does not greatly care.
1 MUS. We have none such, sir.
CLO. Then put up your pipes in your bag, for I'll away. Go ; vanish
    into air ; away.   [*Exeunt* MUSICIANS.
CAS. Dost thou hear, my honest friend ?
CLO. No, I hear not your honest friend ; I hear you.   22
CAS. Prithee keep up thy quillets.   There's a poor piece of gold for
    thee.   If the gentlewoman that attends the General's wife be
    stirring, tell her there's one Cassio entreats her a little favour of
    speech.   Wilt thou do this ?
CLO. She is stirring, sir ; if she will stir hither, I shall seem to notify
    unto her.
CAS. Do, good my friend.   [*Exit* CLOWN

Enter IAGO.

            In happy time, Iago.
IAGO. You have not been abed, then ?   30

CAS. Why, no ; the day had broke before we parted.
    I have made bold, Iago,
    To send in to your wife : my suit to her
    Is that she will to virtuous Desdemona
    Procure me some access.
IAGO.   I'll send her to you presently;   35
    And I'll devise a mean to draw the Moor
    Out of the way, that your converse and business
    May be more free.
CAS. I humbly thank you for't. [Exit IAGO.] I never knew
    A Florentine more kind and honest.   40

Enter EMILIA.

EMIL. Good morrow, good Lieutenant. I am sorry
    For your displeasure ; but all will sure be well.
    The General and his wife are talking of it ;
    And she speaks for you stoutly : the Moor replies
    That he you hurt is of great fame in Cyprus   45
    And great affinity, and that in wholesome wisdom
    He might not but refuse you ; but he protests he loves you
    And needs no other suitor but his likings
    To take the safest occasion by the front
    To bring you in again.
CAS.   Yet, I beseech you,   50
    If you think fit, or that it may be done,
    Give me advantage of some brief discourse
    With Desdemona alone.
EMIL.   Pray you come in.
    I will bestow you where you shall have time
    To speak your bosom freely.
CAS.   I am much bound to you. [*Exeunt.*

SCENE II. *Cyprus. The citadel.*

Enter OTHELLO, IAGO, *and* GENTLEMEN.

OTH. These letters give, Iago, to the pilot ;
    And by him do my duties to the Senate.
    That done, I will be walking on the works ;
    Repair there to me.
IAGO.   Well, my good lord, I'll do't.
OTH. This fortification, gentlemen—shall we see't ?   5
GENT. We'll wait upon your lordship.   [*Exeunt.*

SCENE III. *Cyprus. The garden of the citadel.*

Enter DESDEMONA, CASSIO, *and* EMILIA.

DES. Be thou assur'd, good Cassio, I will do
    All my abilities in thy behalf.
EMIL. Good madam, do. I warrant it grieves my husband
    As if the case were his.
DES. O, that's an honest fellow. Do not doubt, Cassio,
    But I will have my lord and you again   5
    As friendly as you were.

CAS.   Bounteous madam,
  Whatever shall become of Michael Cassio,
  He's never any thing but your true servant.
DES. I know't—I thank you. You do love my lord ;   10
  You have known him long ; and be you well assur'd
  He shall in strangeness stand no farther off
  Than in a politic distance.
CAS.   Ay, but, lady,
  That policy may either last so long,
  Or feed upon such nice and waterish diet,   15
  Or breed itself so out of circumstances,
  That, I being absent, and my place supplied,
  My general will forget my love and service.
DES. Do not doubt that ; before Emilia here
  I give thee warrant of thy place. Assure thee,   20
  If I do vow a friendship, I'll perform it
  To the last article. My lord shall never rest ;
  I'll watch him tame, and talk him out of patience
  His bed shall seem a school, his board a shrift ;
  I'll intermingle everything he does   25
  With Cassio's suit. Therefore be merry, Cassio ;
  For thy solicitor shall rather die
  Than give thy cause away.

            Enter OTHELLO *and* IAGO.

EMIL. Madam, here comes my lord.
CAS. Madam, I'll take my leave.   30
DES. Why, stay, and hear me speak.
CAS. Madam, not now. I am very ill at ease,
  Unfit for mine own purposes.
DES. Well, do your discretion.   [*Exit* CASSIO.
IAGO. Ha ! I like not that.
OTH.   What dost thou say ?
IAGO. Nothing, my lord ; or if—I know not what.
OTH. Was not that Cassio parted from my wife ?
IAGO. Cassio, my lord ! No, sure, I cannot think it,
  That he would sneak away so guilty-like,   40
  Seeing your coming.
OTH.   I do believe 'twas he.
DES. How now, my lord !
  I have been talking with a suitor here,
  A man that languishes in your displeasure.
OTH. Who is't you mean ?   45
DES. Why, your lieutenant, Cassio. Good my lord,
  If I have any grace or power to move you,
  His present reconciliation take ;
  For if he be not one that truly loves you,
  That errs in ignorance, and not in cunning,   50
  I have no judgment in an honest face.
  I prithee call him back.
OTH.   Went he hence now ?
DES. Yes, faith ; so humbled
  That he hath left part of his grief with me
  To suffer with him. Good love, call him back.   55

                                                          125

OTH. Not now, sweet Desdemona ; some other time.
DES. But shall't be shortly ?
OTH.   The sooner, sweet, for you.
DES. Shall't be to-night at supper ?
OTH.   No, not to-night.
DES. To-morrow dinner, then ?
OTH.   I shall not dine at home ;
I meet the captains at the citadel.   60
DES. Why, then, to-morrow night, or Tuesday morn,
On Tuesday noon or night, on Wednesday morn.
I prithee name the time ; but let it not
Exceed three days. I'faith, he's penitent ;
And yet his trespass, in our common reason—   65
Save that, they say, the wars must make example
Out of her best—is not almost a fault
T' incur a private check. When shall he come ?
Tell me, Othello—I wonder in my soul
What you would ask me that I should deny,   70
Or stand so mamm'ring on. What ! Michael Cassio,
That came a-wooing with you, and so many a time,
When I have spoke of you dispraisingly,
Hath ta'en your part—to have so much to do
To bring him in ! By'r Lady, I could do much—   75
OTH. Prithee, no more ; let him come when he will ;
I will deny thee nothing.
DES.   Why, this is not a boon ;
'Tis as I should entreat you wear your gloves,
Or feed on nourishing dishes, or keep you warm,
Or sue to you to do a peculiar profit   80
To your own person. Nay, when I have a suit
Wherein I mean to touch your love indeed,
It shall be full of poise and difficult weight,
And fearful to be granted.
OTH.   I will deny thee nothing.
Whereon I do beseech thee grant me this,   85
To leave me but a little to myself.
DES. Shall I deny you ? No ; farewell, my lord.
OTH. Farewell, my Desdemona. I'll come to thee straight.
DES. Emilia, come.—Be as your fancies teach you ;
Whate'er you be, I am obedient.   90
                    [*Exeunt* DESDEMONA *and* EMILIA.
OTH. Excellent wretch ! Perdition catch my soul
But I do love thee ; and when I love thee not
Chaos is come again.
IAGO. My noble lord !
OTH.   What dost thou say, Iago ?
IAGO. Did Michael Cassio, when you woo'd my lady,   95
Know of your love ?
OTH. He did, from first to last. Why dost thou ask ?
IAGO. But for a satisfaction of my thought—
No further harm.
OTH.   Why of thy thought, Iago ?
IAGO. I did not think he had been acquainted with her.   100
OTH. O, yes ; and went between us very often.

IAGO. Indeed !
OTH. Indeed ? Ay, indeed. Discern'st thou aught in that ?
  Is he not honest ?
IAGO. Honest, my lord ?
OTH. Honest ? Ay, honest.
IAGO.   My lord, for aught I know.
OTH. What dost thou think ?
IAGO.   Think, my lord ?
OTH. Think, my lord ! By heaven, he echoes me,   110
  As if there were some monster in his thought
  Too hideous to be shown. Thou dost mean something :
  I heard thee say but now thou lik'st not that,
  When Cassio left my wife. What didst not like ?
  And when I told thee he was of my counsel   115
  In my whole course of wooing, thou criedst ' Indeed ! '
  And didst contract and purse thy brow together,
  As if thou then hadst shut up in thy brain
  Some horrible conceit. If thou dost love me,
  Show me thy thought.   120
IAGO. My lord, you know I love you.
OTH.   I think thou dost ;
  And for I know thou art full of love and honesty,
  And weigh'st thy words before thou giv'st them breath,
  Therefore these stops of thine affright me the more ;
  For such things in a false disloyal knave   125
  Are tricks of custom ; but in a man that's just
  They are close delations, working from the heart
  That passion cannot rule.
IAGO.   For Michael Cassio,
  I dare presume I think that he is honest.
OTH. I think so too.
IAGO.   Men should be that they seem ;   130
  Or those that be not, would they might seem none !
OTH. Certain, men should be what they seem.
IAGO. Why then, I think Cassio's an honest man.
OTH. Nay, yet there's more in this.
  I prithee speak to me as to thy thinkings,   135
  As thou dost ruminate ; and give thy worst of thoughts
  The worst of words.
IAGO.   Good my lord, pardon me.
  Though I am bound to every act of duty,
  I am not bound to that all slaves are free to—
  Utter my thoughts. Why, say they are vile and false, 140
  As where's that palace whereinto foul things
  Sometimes intrude not ? Who has that breast so pure
  But some uncleanly apprehensions
  Keep leets and law-days, and in sessions sit
  With meditations lawful ?   145
OTH. Thou dost conspire against thy friend, Iago,
  If thou but think'st him wrong'd, and mak'st his ear
  A stranger to thy thoughts.
IAGO.   I do beseech you,
  Though I perchance am vicious in my guess,
  As, I confess, it is my nature's plague   150

To spy into abuses, and oft my jealousy
Shapes faults that are not—that your wisdom
From one that so imperfectly conjects,
Would take no notice ; nor build yourself a trouble
Out of his scattering and unsure observance.   155
It were not for your quiet nor your good,
Nor for my manhood, honesty, or wisdom,
To let you know my thoughts.
OTH. Zounds ! What dost thou mean ?
IAGO. Good name in man and woman, dear my lord,
Is the immediate jewel of their souls :   160
Who steals my purse steals trash ; 'tis something, nothing
'Twas mine, 'tis his, and has been slave to thousands ;
But he that filches from me my good name
Robs me of that which not enriches him
And makes me poor indeed.   165
OTH. By heaven, I'll know thy thoughts.
IAGO. You cannot, if my heart were in your hand ;
Nor shall not, whilst 'tis in my custody.
OTH. Ha !
IAGO. O, beware, my lord, of jealousy ;
It is the green-ey'd monster which doth mock   170
The meat it feeds on. That cuckold lives in bliss
Who, certain of his fate, loves not his wronger ;
But, O, what damned minutes tells he o'er
Who dotes, yet doubts, suspects, yet strongly loves !
OTH. O misery !   175
IAGO. Poor and content is rich, and rich enough ;
But riches fineless is as poor as winter
To him that ever fears he shall be poor.
Good God, the souls of all my tribe defend
From jealousy !
OTH.   Why, why is this ?   180
Think'st thou I'd make a life of jealousy,
To follow still the changes of the moon
With fresh suspicions ? No ; to be once in doubt
Is once to be resolv'd. Exchange me for a goat
When I shall turn the business of my soul   185
To such exsufflicate and blown surmises
Matching thy inference. 'Tis not to make me jealous
To say my wife is fair, feeds well, loves company,
Is free of speech, sings, plays, and dances well ;
Where virtue is, these are more virtuous.   190
Nor from mine own weak merits will I draw
The smallest fear or doubt of her revolt ;
For she had eyes, and chose me. No, Iago ;
I'll see before I doubt ; when I doubt, prove ;
And, on the proof, there is no more but this—   195
Away at once with love or jealousy !
IAGO. I am glad of this ; for now I shall have reason
To show the love and duty that I bear you
With franker spirit. Therefore, as I am bound,
Receive it from me. I speak not yet of proof.   200
Look to your wife ; observe her well with Cassio ;

Wear your eyes thus, not jealous nor secure.
I would not have your free and noble nature
Out of self-bounty be abus'd ; look to't.
I know our country disposition well :   205
In Venice they do let God see the pranks
They dare not show their husbands ; their best conscience
Is not to leave't undone, but keep't unknown.

OTH. Dost thou say so ?

IAGO. She did deceive her father, marrying you ;   210
And when she seem'd to shake and fear your looks,
She lov'd them most.

OTH.   And so she did.

IAGO.   Why, go to then !
She that, so young, could give out such a seeming,
To seel her father's eyes up close as oak—
He thought 'twas witchcraft. But I am much to blame   215
I humbly do beseech you of your pardon
For too much loving you.

OTH.   I am bound to thee for ever.

IAGO. I see this hath a little dash'd your spirits.

OTH. Not a jot, not a jot.

IAGO.   I'faith, I fear it has.
I hope you will consider what is spoke   220
Comes from my love ; but I do see you are mov'd.
I am to pray you not to strain my speech
To grosser issues nor to larger reach
Than to suspicion.

OTH. I will not.

IAGO.   Should you do so, my lord,   225
My speech should fall into such vile success
Which my thoughts aim'd not. Cassio's my worthy friend—
My lord, I see you are mov'd.

OTH.   No, not much mov'd.
I do not think but Desdemona's honest.

IAGO. Long live she so ! and long live you to think so !   230

OTH. And yet, how nature erring from itself—

IAGO. Ay, there's the point : as—to be bold with you—
Not to affect many proposed matches
Of her own clime, complexion, and degree,
Whereto we see in all things nature tends—   235
Foh ! one may smell in such a will most rank,
Foul disproportion, thoughts unnatural.
But pardon me—I do not in position
Distinctly speak of her ; though I may fear
Her will, recoiling to her better judgment,   240
May fall to match you with her country forms,
And happily repent.

OTH.   Farewell, farewell.
If more thou dost perceive, let me know more ;
Set on thy wife to observe. Leave me, Iago.

IAGO. My lord, I take my leave.   [Going.

OTH. Why did I marry ? This honest creature doubtless
Sees and knows more—much more than he unfolds.

IAGO. [Returning.] My lord, I would I might entreat your honour

To scan this thing no further ; leave it to time.
Although 'tis fit that Cassio have his place,   2
For, sure, he fills it up with great ability,
Yet if you please to hold him off awhile,
You shall by that perceive him and his means.
Note if your lady strain his entertainment
With any strong or vehement importunity ;   2
Much will be seen in that. In the mean time
Let me be thought too busy in my fears—
As worthy cause I have to fear I am—
And hold her free, I do beseech your honour.
OTH. Fear not my government.   2
IAGO. I once more take my leave.   [Ex
OTH. This fellow's of exceeding honesty,
And knows all qualities, with a learned spirit,
Of human dealing. If I do prove her haggard,
Though that her jesses were my dear heart-strings,   2
I'd whistle her off and let her down the wind
To prey at fortune. Haply, for I am black
And have not those soft parts of conversation
That chamberers have, or for I am declin'd
Into the vale of years—yet that's not much—   2
She's gone ; I am abus'd ; and my relief
Must be to loathe her. O curse of marriage,
That we can call these delicate creatures ours,
And not their appetites ! I had rather be a toad,
And live upon the vapour of a dungeon,   2
Than keep a corner in the thing I love
For others' uses. Yet 'tis the plague of great ones;
Prerogativ'd are they less than the base ;
'Tis destiny unshunnable, like death :
Even then this forked plague is fated to us   2
When we do quicken. Look where she comes.

Re-enter DESDEMONA *and* EMILIA.

If she be false, O, then heaven mocks itself !
I'll not believe it.
DES.   How now, my dear Othello ?
Your dinner, and the generous islanders
By you invited, do attend your presence.   2
OTH. I am to blame.
DES.   Why do you speak so faintly ?
Are you not well ?
OTH. I have a pain upon my forehead here.
DES. Faith, that's with watching ; 'twill away again.
Let me but bind it hard, within this hour
It will be well. [*He puts the handkerchief from him, and she drops*   2
OTH.   Your napkin is too little.
Let it alone. Come, I'll go in with you.
DES. I am very sorry that you are not well.
                              [*Exeunt* OTHELLO *and* DESDEMON
EMIL. I am glad I have found this napkin.
This was her first remembrance from the Moor.   2
My wayward husband hath a hundred times

Woo'd me to steal it ; but she so loves the token—
For he conjur'd her she should ever keep it—
That she reserves it evermore about her
To kiss and talk to. I'll ha the work ta'en out,   300
And give't Iago. What he'll do with it
Heaven knows, not I ;
I nothing but to please his fantasy.

Re-enter IAGO.

IAGO. How now ! What do you here alone ?
EMIL. Do not you chide ; I have a thing for you.   305
IAGO. You have a thing for me ?
    It is a common thing !
EMIL. Ha !
IAGO. To have a foolish wife.
EMIL. O, is that all ? What will you give me now
    For that same handkerchief ?
IAGO.   What handkerchief ?   310
EMIL. What handkerchief !
    Why that the Moor first gave to Desdemona ;
    That which so often you did bid me steal.
IAGO. Hast stole it from her ?
EMIL. No, faith ; she let it drop by negligence,   315
    And to the advantage, I, being here, took't up.
    Look, here it is.
IAGO.   A good wench ! Give it me.
EMIL. What will you do with't, that you have been so earnest
    To have me filch it ?
IAGO.   Why, what's that to you ?   [*Snatching it.*
EMIL. If it be not for some purpose of import,   320
    Give me't again. Poor lady, she'll run mad
    When she shall lack it.
IAGO. Be not acknown on't ; I have use for it.
    Go, leave me.   [*Exit* EMILIA.
    I will in Cassio's lodging lose this napkin,   325
    And let him find it. Trifles light as air
    Are to the jealous confirmations strong
    As proofs of holy writ ; this may do something.
    The Moor already changes with my poison.
    Dangerous conceits are in their natures poisons   330
    Which at the first are scarce found to distaste
    But, with a little act upon the blood,
    Burn like the mines of sulphur.

Re-enter OTHELLO.

                            I did say so.
    Look where he comes ! Not poppy, nor mandragora,
    Nor all the drowsy syrups of the world,   335
    Shall ever medicine thee to that sweet sleep
    Which thou owed'st yesterday.
OTH.   Ha ! ha ! false to me, to me ?
IAGO. Why, how now, General ? No more of that.
OTH, Avaunt ! be gone ! Thou hast set me on the rack.

I swear 'tis better to be much abus'd 34
Than but to know 't a little.
IAGO.   How now, my lord !
OTH. What sense had I in her stol'n hours of lust ?
I saw 't not, thought it not, it harm'd not me.
I slept the next night well, fed well, was free and merry ;
I found not Cassio's kisses on her lips.
He that is robb'd, not wanting what is stol'n, 34
Let him not know't, and he's not robb'd at all.
IAGO. I am sorry to hear this.
OTH. I had been happy if the general camp,
Pioneers and all, had tasted her sweet body,
So I had nothing known. O, now for ever 35
Farewell the tranquil mind ! farewell content !
Farewell the plumed troops, and the big wars
That makes ambition virtue ! O, farewell !
Farewell the neighing steed and the shrill trump,
The spirit-stirring drum, th' ear-piercing fife, 35
The royal banner, and all quality,
Pride, pomp, and circumstance, of glorious war !
And O ye mortal engines whose rude throats
Th' immortal Jove's dread clamours counterfeit, 36
Farewell ! Othello's occupation's gone.
IAGO. Is't possible, my lord ?
OTH. Villain, be sure thou prove my love a whore—
                                [Taking him by the throa
Be sure of it ; give me the ocular proof ;
Or, by the worth of man's eternal soul, 36
Thou hadst been better have been born a dog
Than answer my wak'd wrath.
IAGO.   Is't come to this ?
OTH. Make me to see't ; or, at the least, so prove it
That the probation bear no hinge nor loop
To hang a doubt on ; or woe upon thy life ! 37
IAGO. My noble lord—
OTH. If thou dost slander her and torture me,
Never pray more ; abandon all remorse ;
On horror's head horrors accumulate ;
Do deeds to make heaven weep, all earth amaz'd ; 37
For nothing canst thou to damnation add
Greater than that.
IAGO.   O grace ! O heaven forgive me !
Are you a man ? Have you a soul or sense ?—
God buy you ; take mine office. O wretched fool,
That liv'st to make thine honesty a vice ! 38
O monstrous world ! Take note, take note, O world,
To be direct and honest is not safe.
I thank you for this profit ; and from hence
I'll love no friend, sith love breeds such offence.
OTH. Nay, stay. Thou shouldst be honest. 38
IAGO. I should be wise ; for honesty's a fool,
And loses that it works for.
OTH.   By the world,
I think my wife be honest, and think she is not ;

132

I think that thou art just, and think thou art not.
I'll have some proof. Her name, that was as fresh   390
As Dian's visage, is now begrim'd and black
As mine own face. If there be cords or knives,
Poison, or fire, or suffocating streams,
I'll not endure it. Would I were satisfied !

IAGO. I see, sir, you are eaten up with passion ;   395
  I do repent me that I put it to you.
  You would be satisfied ?

OTH.   Would ! Nay, and I will.

IAGO. And may ; but how—how satisfied, my lord ?
  Would you, the supervisor, grossly gape on—
  Behold her topp'd ?

OTH.   Death and damnation ! O !   400

IAGO. It were a tedious difficulty, I think,
  To bring them to that prospect. Damn them, then,
  If ever mortal eyes do see them bolster
  More than their own ! What then ? How then ?
  What shall I say ? Where's satisfaction ?   405
  It is impossible you should see this,
  Were they as prime as goats, as hot as monkeys,
  As salt as wolves in pride, and fools as gross
  As ignorance made drunk. But yet, I say,
  If imputation and strong circumstances   410
  Which lead directly to the door of truth
  Will give you satisfaction, you might have't.

OTH. Give me a living reason she's disloyal.

IAGO. I do not like the office ;
  But, sith I am enter'd in this cause so far,   415
  Prick'd to't by foolish honesty and love,
  I will go on. I lay with Cassio lately,
  And, being troubled with a raging tooth,
  I could not sleep.
  There are a kind of men so loose of soul   420
  That in their sleeps will mutter their affairs :
  One of this kind is Cassio.
  In sleep I heard him say ' Sweet Desdemona,
  Let us be wary, let us hide our loves ',
  And then, sir, would he gripe and wring my hand,   425
  Cry ' O sweet creature ! ' then kiss me hard,
  As if he pluck'd up kisses by the roots,
  That grew upon my lips—then laid his leg
  Over my thigh—and sigh'd, and kiss'd, and then
  Cried ' Cursed fate that gave thee to the Moor ! '   430

OTH. O monstrous ! monstrous !

IAGO.   Nay, this was but his dream.

OTH. But this denoted a foregone conclusion.

IAGO. 'Tis a shrewd doubt, though it be but a dream,
  And this may help to thicken other proofs
  That do demonstrate thinly.

OTH. I'll tear her all to pieces.   435

IAGO. Nay, but be wise ; yet we see nothing done ;
  She may be honest yet. Tell me but this :
  Have you not sometimes seen a handkerchief

Spotted with strawberries in your wife's hand ?

OTH. I gave her such a one ; 'twas my first gift.   44

IAGO. I know not that ; but such a handkerchief—
I am sure it was your wife's—did I to-day
See Cassio wipe his beard with.

OTH.   If it be that—

IAGO. If it be that, or any that was hers,
It speaks against her with the other proofs.   44

OTH. O that the slave had forty thousand lives !
One is too poor, too weak for my revenge.
Now do I see 'tis true. Look here, Iago—
All my fond love thus do I blow to heaven.
'Tis gone.   45

Arise, black vengeance, from the hollow hell.
Yield up, O love, thy crown and hearted throne
To tyrannous hate ! Swell, bosom, with thy fraught,
For 'tis of aspics' tongues.

IAGO.   Yet be content.

OTH. O, blood, blood, blood !   45

IAGO. Patience, I say ; your mind perhaps may change.

OTH. Never, Iago. Like to the Pontic sea,
Whose icy current and compulsive course
Ne'er feels retiring ebb, but keeps due on
To the Propontic and the Hellespont ;   46

Even so my bloody thoughts, with violent pace,
Shall ne'er look back, ne'er ebb to humble love,
Till that a capable and wide revenge
Swallow them up. [He kneels.] Now, by yond marble heaven,
In the due reverence of a sacred vow   46

I here engage my words.

IAGO. [Kneeling.] Do not rise yet.
Witness, you ever-burning lights above,
You elements that clip us round about,
Witness that here Iago doth give up
The execution of his wit, hands, heart,   47

To wrong'd Othello's service ! Let him command,
And to obey shall be in me remorse,
What bloody business ever.   [They rise

OTH.   I greet thy love,
Not with vain thanks, but with acceptance bounteous,
And will upon the instant put thee to't.   47

Within these three days let me hear thee say
That Cassio's not alive.

IAGO.   My friend is dead ;
'Tis done at your request. But let her live.

OTH. Damn her, lewd minx ! O, damn her, damn her !
Come, go with me apart ; I will withdraw   48

To furnish me with some swift means of death
For the fair devil. Now art thou my lieutenant.

IAGO. I am your own for ever.   [Exeunt

SCENE IV. *Cyprus. Before the citadel.*

Enter DESDEMONA, EMILIA, *and* CLOWN.

DES. Do you know, sirrah, where the Lieutenant Cassio lies?

CLO. I dare not say he lies anywhere.

DES. Why, man?

CLO. He's a soldier; and for one to say a soldier lies, 'tis stabbing.

DES. Go to. Where lodges he?

CLO. To tell you where he lodges is to tell you where I lie.

DES. Can anything be made of this?

CLO. I know not where he lodges; and for me to devise a lodging, and say he lies here or he lies there, were to lie in mine own throat.

DES. Can you inquire him out, and be edified by report?

CLO. I will catechize the world for him; that is, make questions, and by them answer.   15

DES. Seek him; bid him come hither: tell him I have mov'd my lord on his behalf, and hope all will be well.

CLO. To do this is within the compass of man's wit; and therefore I will attempt the doing it.   [*Exit.*

DES. Where should I lose the handkerchief, Emilia?

MIL. I know not, madam.   21

DES. Believe me, I had rather lose my purse
Full of crusadoes; and but my noble Moor
Is true of mind, and made of no such baseness
As jealous creatures are, it were enough   25
To put him to ill thinking.

MIL.   Is he not jealous?

DES. Who, he? I think the sun where he was born
Drew all such humours from him.

Enter OTHELLO.

MIL.   Look where he comes.

DES. I will not leave him now till Cassio
Be call'd to him. How is't with you, my lord?   30

OTH. Well, my good lady. [*Aside.*] O, hardness to dissemble!—
How do you, Desdemona?

DES.   Well, my good lord.

OTH. Give me your hand. This hand is moist, my lady.

DES. It yet hath felt no age nor known no sorrow.

OTH. This argues fruitfulness and liberal heart: 35
Hot, hot, and moist. This hand of yours requires
A sequester from liberty, fasting and prayer,
Much castigation, exercise devout;
For here's a young and sweating devil here
That commonly rebels. 'Tis a good hand,   40
A frank one.

DES.   You may indeed say so;
For 'twas that hand that gave away my heart.

OTH. A liberal hand. The hearts of old gave hands;
But our new heraldry is hands, not hearts.

DES. I cannot speak of this. Come now, your promise.   45

OTH. What promise, chuck?

DES. I have sent to bid Cassio come speak with you.
OTH. I have a salt and sorry rheum offends me ;
　　Lend me thy handkerchief.
DES.　　　　　　　　　　　　　Here, my lord.   5
OTH. That which I gave you.
DES.　　　　　　　　　I have it not about me.
OTH. Not ?
DES.　　　　No, faith, my lord.
OTH. That's a fault.　That handkerchief   5
　　Did an Egyptian to my mother give.
　　She was a charmer, and could almost read
　　The thoughts of people ; she told her, while she kept it,
　　'Twould make her amiable, and subdue my father
　　Entirely to her love ; but if she lost it,   6
　　Or made a gift of it, my father's eye
　　Should hold her loathely, and his spirits should hunt
　　After new fancies.　She, dying, gave it me,
　　And bid me, when my fate would have me wive,
　　To give it her.　I did so ; and take heed on't ;   6
　　Make it a darling like your precious eye ;
　　To lose't or give't away were such perdition
　　As nothing else could match.
DES.　　　　　　　　　　　Is't possible ?
OTH. 'Tis true.　There's magic in the web of it.
　　A sibyl that had numb'red in the world   7
　　The sun to course two hundred compasses
　　In her prophetic fury sew'd the work ;
　　The worms were hallowed that did breed the silk ;
　　And it was dy'd in mummy which the skilful
　　Conserv'd of maidens' hearts.
DES.　　　　　　　　　　I'faith !　Is't true ?   7
OTH. Most veritable ; therefore look to't well.
DES. Then would to God that I had never seen't !
OTH. Ha !　Wherefore ?
DES. Why do you speak so startingly and rash ?
OTH. Is't lost ?　Is't gone ?　Speak.　Is't out o' th' way ?   8
DES. Heaven bless us !
OTH. Say you ?
DES. It is not lost ; but what an if it were ?
OTH. How !
DES. I say it is not lost.
OTH.　　　　　　　　Fetch't, let me see't.
DES. Why, so I can, sir, but I will not now.
　　This is a trick to put me from my suit :
　　Pray you let Cassio be receiv'd again.
OTH. Fetch me the handkerchief : my mind misgives.   9
DES. Come, come ;
　　You'll never meet a more sufficient man.
OTH. The handkerchief !
DES.　　　　　　　I pray talk me of Cassio.
OTH. The handkerchief !
DES.　　　　　　　　A man that all his time
　　Hath founded his good fortunes on your love,   9
　　Shar'd dangers with you—

H.   The handkerchief!

s. I'faith, you are to blame.

H. Zounds!   [*Exit* OTHELLO.

IL. Is not this man jealous?

s. I ne'er saw this before.
  Sure there's some wonder in this handkerchief;
  I am most unhappy in the loss of it.

IL. 'Tis not a year or two shows us a man.
  They are all but stomachs, and we all but food;   105
  They eat us hungerly, and when they are full,
  They belch us.

Enter CASSIO *and* IAGO.

  Look you, Cassio and my husband.

30. There is no other way; 'tis she must do 't.
  And, lo, the happiness! Go and importune her.

s. How now, good Cassio, what's the news with you?   110

s. Madam, my former suit. I do beseech you
  That by your virtuous means I may again
  Exist, and be a member of his love
  Whom I, with all the office of my heart,
  Entirely honour. I would not be delay'd.   115
  If my offence be of such mortal kind
  That nor my service past, nor present sorrows,
  Nor purpos'd merit in futurity,
  Can ransom me into his love again,
  But to know so must be my benefit;   120
  So shall I clothe me in a forc'd content,
  And shut myself up in some other course,
  To fortune's alms.

s.   Alas, thrice-gentle Cassio!
  My advocation is not now in tune;
  My lord is not my lord; nor should I know him,   125
  Were he in favour as in humour alter'd.
  So help me every spirit sanctified,
  As I have spoken for you all my best,
  And stood within the blank of his displeasure
  For my free speech! you must awhile be patient.   130
  What I can do I will; and more I will
  Than for myself I dare; let that suffice you.

30. Is my lord angry?

IL.   He went hence but now,
  And certainly in strange unquietness.

30. Can he be angry? I have seen the cannon   135
  When it hath blown his ranks into the air,
  And, like the devil, from his very arm
  Puff'd his own brother—and is he angry?
  Something of moment, then. I will go meet him.
  There's matter in't indeed, if he be angry.   140

s. I prithee do so.   [*Exit* IAGO.
                     Something sure of state
  Either from Venice, or some unhatch'd practice
  Made demonstrable here in Cyprus to him,
  Hath puddled his clear spirit; and in such cases

                                                         137

Men's natures wrangle with inferior things,
Though great ones are their object. 'Tis even so ;
For let our finger ache, and it endues
Our other healthful members even to a sense
Of pain. Nay, we must think, men are not gods,
Nor of them look for such observancy
As fits the bridal. Beshrew me much, Emilia,
I was—unhandsome warrior as I am—
Arraigning his unkindness with my soul ;
But now I find I had suborn'd the witness,
And he's indicted falsely.

EMIL. Pray heaven it be state matters, as you think,
And no conception nor no jealous toy
Concerning you.

DES. Alas the day, I never gave him cause !

EMIL. But jealous souls will not be answer'd so ;
They are not ever jealous for the cause,
But jealous for they are jealous. 'Tis a monster
Begot upon it self, born on it self.

DES. Heaven keep that monster from Othello's mind !

EMIL. Lady, amen.

DES. I will go seek him. Cassio, walk hereabout.
If I do find him fit, I'll move your suit,
And seek to effect it to my uttermost.

CAS. I humbly thank your ladyship.

            [Exeunt DESDEMONA *and* EMILIA.

             Enter BIANCA.

BIAN. Save you, friend Cassio !

CAS.   What make you from home ?
How is it with you, my most fair Bianca ?
I' faith, sweet love, I was coming to your house.

BIAN. And I was going to your lodging, Cassio.
What, keep a week away ? seven days and nights ?
Eightscore eight hours ? and lovers' absent hours,
More tedious than the dial eight score times ?
O weary reckoning !

CAS.   Pardon me, Bianca.
I have this while with leaden thoughts been press'd ;
But I shall in a more continuate time
Strike off this score of absence. Sweet Bianca,

            [Giving her DESDEMONA'S *handkerchi*

Take me this work out.

BIAN.   O Cassio, whence came this ?
This is some token from a newer friend :
To the felt absence now I feel a cause.
Is't come to this ? Well, well.

CAS.   Go to, woman !
Throw your vile guesses in the devil's teeth,
From whence you have them. You are jealous now
That this is from some mistress, some remembrance.
No, by my faith, Bianca.

BIAN.   Why, whose is it ?

CAS. I know not neither ; I found it in my chamber.

I like the work well ; ere it be demanded—   190
As like enough it will—I would have it copied.
Take it, and do't ; and leave me for this time.
BIAN. Leave you ! Wherefore ?
CAS. I do attend here on the General ;
And think it no addition, nor my wish,   195
To have him see me woman'd.
BIAN.   Why, I pray you ?
CAS. Not that I love you not.
BIAN.   But that you do not love me.
I pray you bring me on the way a little ;
And say if I shall see you soon at night.
CAS. 'Tis but a little way that I can bring you,   200
For I attend here ; but I'll see you soon.
BIAN. 'Tis very good ; I must be circumstanc'd.   [Exeunt.

ACT FOUR

Scene I. *Cyprus. Before the citadel.*

Enter OTHELLO *and* IAGO.

IAGO. Will you think so ?
OTH.   Think so, Iago ?
IAGO.   What,
To kiss in private ?
OTH.   An unauthoriz'd kiss.
IAGO. Or to be naked with her friend abed
An hour or more, not meaning any harm ?
OTH. Naked abed, Iago, and not mean harm !   5
It is hypocrisy against the devil.
They that mean virtuously and yet do so,
The devil their virtue tempts, and they tempt heaven.
IAGO. So they do nothing, 'tis a venial slip ;
But if I give my wife a handkerchief—   10
OTH. What then ?
IAGO. Why, then 'tis hers, my lord ; and, being hers,
She may, I think, bestow't on any man.
OTH. She is protectress of her honour too :
May she give that ?   15
IAGO. Her honour is an essence that's not seen ;
They have it very oft that have it not.
But, for the handkerchief—
OTH. By heaven, I would most gladly have forgot it.
Thou said'st—O, it comes o'er my memory   20
As doth the raven o'er the infected house,
Boding to all—he had my handkerchief.
IAGO. Ay, what of that ?
OTH.   That's not so good now.
IAGO.   What
If I had said I had seen him do you wrong ?
Or heard him say—as knaves be such abroad,   25
Who having, by their own importunate suit,
Or voluntary dotage of some mistress,

139

Convinced or supplied them, cannot choose
But they must blab—
OTH.   Hath he said anything?
IAGO. He hath, my lord; but be you well assur'd,
No more than he'll unswear.
OTH.   What hath he said?
IAGO. Faith, that he did—I know not what he did.
OTH. What? what?
IAGO. Lie—
OTH.   With her?
IAGO.   With her, on her; what you will.
OTH. Lie with her—lie on her? We say lie on her when they beli
her. Lie with her. Zounds, that's fulsome. Handkerchief-
confessions—handkerchief! To confess, and be hang'd for h
labour—first, to be hang'd, and then to confess. I tremble a
it. Nature would not invest herself in such shadowing passio
without some instruction. It is not words that shakes me thus-
pish!—noses, ears, and lips. Is't possible? Confess! Han
kerchief! O devil!   [Falls in a tranc
IAGO. Work on,
My medicine, work. Thus credulous fools are caught;
And many worthy and chaste dames even thus,
All guiltless, meet reproach. What, ho! my lord!
My lord, I say! Othello!

Enter CASSIO.

How now, Cassio!
CAS. What's the matter?
IAGO. My lord is fall'n into an epilepsy.
This is his second fit; he had one yesterday.
CAS. Rub him about the temples.
IAGO.   No, forbear.
The lethargy must have his quiet course;
If not, he foams at mouth, and by and by
Breaks out to savage madness. Look, he stirs.
Do you withdraw yourself a little while;
He will recover straight; when he is gone,
I would on great occasion speak with you.   [*Exit* CASSI
How is it, General? Have you not hurt your head?
OTH. Dost thou mock me?
IAGO.   I mock you? No, by heaven!
Would you would bear your fortune like a man!
OTH. A horned man's a monster and a beast.
IAGO. There's many a beast then in a populous city,
And many a civil monster.
OTH. Did he confess it?
IAGO.   Good sir, be a man;
Think every bearded fellow that's but yok'd
May draw with you; there's millions now alive
That nightly lie in those unproper beds
Which they dare swear peculiar: your case is better.
O, 'tis the spite of hell, the fiend's arch-mock,
To lip a wanton in a secure couch,
And to suppose her chaste! No, let me know;

140

And knowing what I am, I know what she shall be.

OTH. O, thou art wise; 'tis certain.

IAGO.   Stand you awhile apart.
Confine yourself but in a patient list.   75
Whilst you were here o'erwhelmed with your grief—
A passion most unsuiting such a man—
Cassio came hither; I shifted him away,
And laid good 'scuse upon your ecstasy;
Bade him anon return, and here speak with me; 80
The which he promis'd. Do but encave yourself,
And mark the fleers, the gibes, and notable scorns,
That dwell in every region of his face;
For I will make him tell the tale anew—
Where, how, how oft, how long ago, and when,   85
He hath, and is again to cope your wife.
I say, but mark his gesture. Marry, patience;
Or I shall say you are all in all in spleen,
And nothing of a man.

OTH.   Dost thou hear, Iago?
I will be found most cunning in my patience;   90
But—dost thou hear?—most bloody.

IAGO.   That's not amiss;
But yet keep time in all. Will you withdraw?

                                        [OTHELLO *withdraws.*

Now will I question Cassio of Bianca,
A huswife that by selling her desires
Buys herself bread and clothes; it is a creature 95
That dotes on Cassio, as 'tis the strumpet's plague
To beguile many and be beguil'd by one.
He, when he hears of her, cannot restrain
From the excess of laughter.

                        Re-enter CASSIO.

                        Here he comes.
As he shall smile Othello shall go mad;   100
And his unbookish jealousy must construe
Poor Cassio's smiles, gestures, and light behaviours,
Quite in the wrong. How do you now, Lieutenant?

CAS. The worser that you give me the addition
Whose want even kills me.   105

IAGO. Ply Desdemona well, and you are sure on't.
Now, if this suit lay in Bianca's dower,
How quickly should you speed!

CAS.   Alas, poor caitiff!

OTH. Look how he laughs already!

IAGO. I never knew a woman love man so.   110

CAS. Alas, poor rogue! I think, i' faith, she loves me.

OTH. Now he denies it faintly, and laughs it out.

IAGO. Do you hear, Cassio?

OTH.   Now he importunes him
To tell it o'er. Go to; well said, well said.

IAGO. She gives it out that you shall marry her. 115
Do you intend it?

CAS. Ha, ha, ha!

                                                141

OTH. Do you triumph, Roman ? Do you triumph ?

CAS. I marry her ! What, a customer ! I prithee bear some chari
to my wit ; do not think it so unwholesome. Ha, ha, ha !

OTH. So, so, so—they laugh that wins.

IAGO. Faith, the cry goes that you marry her.

CAS. Prithee say true.

IAGO. I am a very villain else.   1

OTH. Ha you scor'd me ? Well.

CAS. This is the monkey's own giving out : she is persuaded I w
marry her, out of her own love and flattery, not out of my promis

OTH. Iago beckons me ; now he begins the story.

CAS. She was here even now ; she haunts me in every place. I wa
t'other day talking on the sea-bank with certain Venetians, an
thither comes the bauble—by this hand, she falls me thus abov
my neck.   13

OTH. Crying ' O dear Cassio ! ' as it were : his gesture imports it.

CAS. So hangs, and lolls, and weeps upon me ; so hales, and pulls m
Ha, ha, ha !

OTH. Now he tells how she pluck'd him to my chamber. O, I se
that nose of yours, but not that dog I shall throw't to.   14

CAS. Well, I must leave her company.

Enter BIANCA.

IAGO. Before me ! Look where she comes.

CAS. 'Tis such another fitchew ! marry, a perfum'd one. What d
you mean by this haunting of me ?   14

BIAN. Let the devil and his dam haunt you. What did you mean b
that same handkerchief you gave me even now ? I was a fir
fool to take it. I must take out the whole work—a likely piece
work that you should find it in your chamber and know not wh
left it there ! This is some minx's token, and I must take ou
the work ? There—give it your hobby-horse. Wheresoever yo
had it, I'll take out no work on't.

CAS. How now, my sweet Bianca ! how now ! how now !

OTH. By heaven, that should be my handkerchief !   1

BIAN. An you'll come to supper to-night, you may ; an you will no
come when you are next prepar'd for.   [*Exi*

IAGO. After her, after her.

CAS. Faith, I must ; she'll rail i' th' street else.

IAGO. Will you sup there ?   1

CAS. Faith, I intend so.

IAGO. Well, I may chance to see you ; for I would very fain speak wi
you.

CAS. Prithee come ; will you ?

IAGO. Go to ; say no more.   [*Exit* CASSI

OTH. [*Coming forward.*] How shall I murder him, Iago ?

IAGO. Did you perceive how he laugh'd at his vice ?

OTH. O Iago !

IAGO. And did you see the handkerchief ?

OTH. Was that mine ?   1

IAGO. Yours, by this hand. And to see how he prizes the foolis
woman your wife ! She gave it him, and he hath giv'n it h
whore.

OTH. I would have him nine years a-killing. A fine woman! a fair
    woman! a sweet woman!   175

IAGO. Nay, you must forget that.

OTH. Ay, let her rot, and perish, and be damn'd to-night; for she
    shall not live. No, my heart is turn'd to stone; I strike it, and
    it hurts my hand. O, the world hath not a sweeter creature;
    she might lie by an emperor's side and command him tasks. 181

IAGO. Nay, that's not your way.

OTH. Hang her! I do but say what she is: so delicate with her
    needle, an admirable musician—O, she will sing the savageness
    out of a bear!—of so high and plenteous wit and invention. 186

IAGO. She's the worse for all this.

OTH. O, a thousand, a thousand times—and then of so gentle a
    condition.

IAGO. Ay, too gentle.   190

OTH. Nay, that's certain. But yet the pity of it, Iago! O, Iago, the
    pity of it, Iago!

IAGO. If you be so fond over her iniquity, give her patent to offend;
    for, if it touch not you, it comes near nobody.   195

OTH. I will chop her into messes. Cuckold me!

IAGO. O, 'tis foul in her.

OTH. With mine officer!

IAGO. That's fouler.   199

OTH. Get me some poison, Iago—this night. I'll not expostulate with
    her, lest her body and beauty unprovide my mind again—this
    night, Iago.

IAGO. Do it not with poison; strangle her in her bed, even the bed
    she hath contaminated.   204

OTH. Good, good; the justice of it pleases; very good.

IAGO. And for Cassio—let me be his undertaker. You shall hear
    more by midnight.

OTH. Excellent good.   [*A trumpet.*
               What trumpet is that same?   208

IAGO. I warrant, something from Venice.

Enter LODOVICO, DESDEMONA, *and* ATTENDANTS.

'Tis Lodovico—this comes from the Duke.
    See, your wife's with him.

LOD. God save thee, worthy General!

OTH.   With all my heart, sir.

LOD. The Duke and Senators of Venice greet you.
                                [*Gives him a packet.*

OTH. I kiss the instrument of their pleasures.
                           [*Opens the packet and reads.*

DES. And what's the news, good cousin Lodovico?

IAGO. I am very glad to see you, signior;   215
    Welcome to Cyprus.

LOD. I thank you. How does Lieutenant Cassio?

IAGO.   Lives, sir.

DES. Cousin, there's fall'n between him and my lord
    An unkind breach; but you shall make all well.   220

OTH. Are you sure of that?

DES. My lord?

OTH. [*Reads.*] ' This fail you not to do as you will '—
LOD. He did not call ; he's busy in the paper.
    Is there division 'twixt thy lord and Cassio ?   229
DES. A most unhappy one. I would do much
    T' atone them, for the love I bear to Cassio.
OTH. Fire and brimstone !
DES. My lord ?
OTH. Are you wise ?
DES. What, is he angry ?
LOD.   May be the letter mov'd him ;   231
    For, as I think, they do command him home,
    Deputing Cassio in his government.
DES. By my troth, I am glad on't.
OTH.   Indeed!
DES.   My lord ?
OTH. I am glad to see you mad.
DES.   Why, sweet Othello ?   235
OTH. Devil !   [*Striking her.*
DES. I have not deserv'd this.
LOD. My lord, this would not be believ'd in Venice,
    Though I should swear I saw't. 'Tis very much.
    Make her amends ; she weeps.
OTH.   O devil, devil !   240
    If that the earth could teem with woman's tears,
    Each drop she falls would prove a crocodile.
    Out of my sight !
DES.   I will not stay to offend you.   [*Going.*
LOD. Truly, an obedient lady.
    I do beseech your lordship, call her back.
OTH. Mistress !   245
DES. My lord ?
OTH. What would you with her, sir ?
LOD.   Who, I, my lord ?
OTH. Ay ; you did wish that I would make her turn.
    Sir, she can turn, and turn, and yet go on,   250
    And turn again ; and she can weep, sir, weep ;
    And she's obedient, as you say, obedient,
    Very obedient.—Proceed you in your tears.—
    Concerning this, sir,—O, well-painted passion !—
    I am commanded home.—Get you away ;   255
    I'll send for you anon.—Sir, I obey the mandate,
    And will return to Venice.—Hence, avaunt !
                         [*Exit* DESDEMONA
    Cassio shall have my place. And, sir, to-night,
    I do entreat that we may sup together.
    You are welcome, sir, to Cyprus.—Goats and monkeys !   [*Exit*
LOD. Is this the noble Moor whom our full Senate   261
    Call all in all sufficient ? Is this the nature
    Whom passion could not shake, whose solid virtue
    The shot of accident nor dart of chance
    Could neither graze nor pierce ?
IAGO.   He is much chang'd.   265
LOD. Are his wits safe ? Is he not light of brain ?
IAGO. He's that he is. I may not breathe my censure.

What he might be, if what he might he is not,
I would to heaven he were!

LOD.   What, strike his wife!

IAGO. Faith, that was not so well; yet would I knew   270
That stroke would prove the worst!

LOD.   Is it his use?
Or did the letters work upon his blood,
And new-create this fault?

IAGO.   Alas, alas!
It is not honesty in me to speak
What I have seen and known. You shall observe him;   275
And his own courses will denote him so
That I may save my speech. Do but go after,
And mark how he continues.

LOD. I am sorry that I am deceiv'd in him.   [*Exeunt*.

SCENE II. *Cyprus.   The citadel.*

Enter OTHELLO *and* EMILIA.

OTH. You have seen nothing, then?

EMIL. Nor ever heard, nor ever did suspect.

OTH. Yes, you have seen Cassio and she together.

EMIL. But then I saw no harm, and then I heard
Each syllable that breath made up between them.   5

OTH. What, did they never whisper?

EMIL.   Never, my lord.

OTH. Nor send you out o' th' way?

EMIL. Never.

OTH. To fetch her fan, her gloves, her mask, nor nothing?

EMIL. Never, my lord.   10

OTH. That's strange.

EMIL. I durst, my lord, to wager she is honest,
Lay down my soul at stake. If you think other,
Remove your thought—it doth abuse your bosom.
If any wretch have put this in your head,   15
Let heaven requite it with the serpent's curse;
For if she be not honest, chaste, and true,
There's no man happy; the purest of their wives
Is foul as slander.

OTH.   Bid her come hither. Go.   [*Exit* EMILIA.
She says enough; yet she's a simple bawd   20
That cannot say as much. This is a subtle whore,
A closet-lock-and-key of villainous secrets;
And yet she'll kneel and pray; I have seen her do 't.

Re-enter EMILIA *with* DESDEMONA.

DES. My lord, what is your will?

OTH. Pray you chuck, come hither.

DES. What is your pleasure?

OTH. Let me see your eyes; look in my face.

DES. What horrible fancy's this?

OTH. [*To* EMILIA.] Some of your function, mistress:
Leave procreants alone, and shut the door;

145

Cough, or cry hem, if any body come.   29
Your mystery, your mystery ; nay, dispatch.   [*Exit* EMILIA.
DES. Upon my knees, what doth your speech import ?
    I understand a fury in your words,
    But not the words.
OTH. Why, what art thou ?
DES. Your wife, my lord ; your true and loyal wife.   35
OTH. Come, swear it, damn thyself ; lest, being like one of heaven,
    the devils themselves should fear to seize thee ; therefore be
    double-damn'd—swear thou art honest.
DES. Heaven doth truly know it.
OTH. Heaven truly knows that thou art false as hell.
DES. To whom, my lord ? With whom ? How am I false ?
OTH. Ah, Desdemona ! away ! away ! away !
DES. Alas the heavy day ! Why do you weep ?
    Am I the motive of these tears, my lord ?
    If haply you my father do suspect
    An instrument of this your calling back,   45
    Lay not your blame on me ; if you have lost him,
    Why, I have lost him too.
OTH.   Had it pleas'd heaven
    To try me with affliction ; had they rain'd
    All kind of sores and shames on my bare head,   50
    Steep'd me in poverty to the very lips,
    Given to captivity me and my utmost hopes,
    I should have found in some place of my soul
    A drop of patience ; but, alas, to make me
    The fixed figure for the time of scorn   55
    To point his slow unmoving finger at !—O, O !
    Yet could I bear that too ; well, very well ;
    But there, where I have garner'd up my heart,
    Where either I must live or bear no life,
    The fountain from the which my current runs,   60
    Or else dries up—to be discarded thence !
    Or keep it as a cistern for foul toads
    To knot and gender in ! Turn thy complexion there,
    Patience, thou young and rose-lipp'd cherubin—
    Ay, here, look grim as hell.   65
DES. I hope my noble lord esteems me honest.
OTH. O, ay ; as summer flies are in the shambles,
    That quicken even with blowing. O thou weed
    Who art so lovely fair and smell'st so sweet
    That the sense aches at thee !
    Would thou had'st never been born !   70
DES. Alas, what ignorant sin have I committed ?
OTH. Was this fair paper, this most goodly book,
    Made to write ' whore ' upon ? What committed !
    Committed ! O thou public commoner !
    I should make very forges of my cheeks   75
    That would to cinders burn up modesty,
    Did I but speak thy deeds. What committed !
    Heaven stops the nose at it, and the moon winks ;
    The bawdy wind, that kisses all it meets,
    Is hush'd within the hollow mine of earth   80

And will not hear it. What committed!
Impudent strumpet!
DES.   By heaven, you do me wrong.
OTH. Are not you a strumpet?
DES.   No, as I am a Christian.
If to preserve this vessel for my lord
From any other foul unlawful touch   85
Be not to be a strumpet, I am none.
OTH. What, not a whore?
DES.   No, as I shall be sav'd.
OTH. Is't possible?
DES. O, heaven forgive us!
OTH.   I cry you mercy, then.
I took you for that cunning whore of Venice   90
That married with Othello.—You, mistress,
That have the office opposite to Saint Peter
And keeps the gate of hell!

Re-enter EMILIA

                    You, you, ay you!
We ha done our course; there's money for your pains.
I pray you turn the key, and keep our counsel.   [*Exit.*
EMIL. Alas, what does this gentleman conceive?   96
How do you, madam? How do you, my good lady?
DES. Faith, half asleep.
EMIL. Good madam, what's the matter with my lord?
DES. With who?   100
EMIL. Why, with my lord, madam.
DES. Who is thy lord?
EMIL.   He that is yours, sweet lady.
DES. I have none. Do not talk to me, Emilia;
I cannot weep, nor answers have I none
But what should go by water. Prithee, to-night   105
Lay on my bed my wedding sheets—remember;
And call thy husband hither.
EMIL. Here's a change indeed!   [*Exit.*
DES. 'Tis meet I should be us'd so, very meet.
How have I been behav'd, that he might stick
The small'st opinion on my great'st abuse?   110

Re-enter EMILIA *with* IAGO.

IAGO. What is your pleasure, madam? How is't with you?
DES. I cannot tell. Those that do teach young babes
Do it with gentle means and easy tasks.
He might have chid me so; for, in good faith,
I am a child to chiding.
IAGO. What is the matter, lady?   115
EMIL. Alas, Iago, my lord hath so bewhor'd her,
Thrown such despite and heavy terms upon her
That true hearts cannot bear it.
DES. Am I that name, Iago?
IAGO.   What name, fair lady?
DES. Such as she says my lord did say I was.   120
EMIL. He call'd her whore. A beggar in his drink

147

Could not have laid such terms upon his callat.
IAGO. Why did he so?
DES. I do not know; I am sure I am none such.
IAGO. Do not weep, do not weep. Alas, the day!   125
EMIL. Hath she forsook so many noble matches,
    Her father, and her country, and her friends,
    To be call'd whore? Would it not make one weep?
DES. It is my wretched fortune.
IAGO.   Beshrew him for't!
    How comes this trick upon him?
DES.   Nay, heaven doth know   130
EMIL. I will be hang'd if some eternal villain,
    Some busy and insinuating rogue,
    Some cogging, cozening slave, to get some office,
    Have not devis'd this slander; I'll be hang'd else.
IAGO. Fie, there is no such man; it is impossible.   135
DES. If any such there be, heaven pardon him!
EMIL. A halter pardon him! and hell gnaw his bones!
    Why should he call her whore? Who keeps her company
    What place, what time, what form, what likelihood?
    The Moor's abus'd by some outrageous knave,   140
    Some base notorious knave, some scurvy fellow.
    O heaven, that such companions thou'dst unfold,
    And put in every honest hand a whip
    To lash the rascals naked through the world
    Even from the east to the west!
IAGO.   Speak within door.   145
EMIL. O, fie upon them! Some such squire he was
    That turn'd your wit the seamy side without
    And made you to suspect me with the Moor.
IAGO. You are a fool; go to.
DES.   O God! Iago,
    What shall I do to win my lord again?   150
    Good friend, go to him; for, by this light of heaven,
    I know not how I lost him. Here I kneel.
    If e'er my will did trespass 'gainst his love,
    Either in discourse of thought or actual deed,
    Or that mine eyes, mine ears, or any sense,   155
    Delighted them in any other form,
    Or that I do not yet, and ever did,
    And ever will—though he do shake me off
    To beggarly divorcement—love him dearly,
    Comfort forswear me! Unkindness may do much;   160
    And his unkindness may defeat my life,
    But never taint my love. I cannot say 'whore';
    It does abhor me now I speak the word;
    To do the act that might the addition earn,
    Not the world's mass of vanity could make me.   165
IAGO. I pray you be content; 'tis but his humour.
    The business of the state does him offence,
    And he does chide with you.
DES. If 'twere no other!
IAGO.   It is but so, I warrant.

                                                    [Trumpets within.

148

Hark how these instruments summon you to supper.   170
The messengers of Venice stay the meat.
Go in, and weep not; all things shall be well.

[*Exeunt* DESDEMONA *and* EMILIA.

Enter RODERIGO.

How now, Roderigo!

ROD. I do not find that thou deal'st justly with me.

IAGO. What in the contrary?   175

ROD. Every day thou daff'st me with some device, Iago; and rather,
as it seems to me now, keep'st from me all conveniency than
suppliest me with the least advantage of hope. I will, indeed, no
longer endure it; nor am I yet persuaded to put up in peace
what already I have foolishly suffer'd.   181

IAGO. Will you hear me, Roderigo?

ROD. Faith, I have heard too much; for your words and performances
are no kin together.

IAGO. You charge me most unjustly.   185

ROD. With nought but truth. I have wasted myself out of my means.
The jewels you have had from me to deliver to Desdemona would
half have corrupted a votarist. You have told me she hath receiv'd
them, and return'd me expectations and comforts of sudden respect
and acquaintance; but I find none.   191

IAGO. Well; go to; very well.

ROD. Very well! go to! I cannot go to, man, nor 'tis not very well;
by this hand, I say 'tis very scurvy, and begin to find myself fopt
in it.   195

IAGO. Very well.

ROD. I tell you 'tis not very well. I will make myself known to
Desdemona. If she will return me my jewels, I will give over
my suit and repent my unlawful solicitation; if not, assure yourself
I will seek satisfaction of you.

IAGO. You have said now.   201

ROD. Ay, and said nothing but what I protest intendment of doing.

IAGO. Why, now I see there's mettle in thee; and even from this
instant do build on thee a better opinion than ever before. Give
me thy hand, Roderigo. Thou hast taken against me a most just
exception; but yet, I protest, I have dealt most directly in thy
affair.

ROD. It hath not appear'd.   209

IAGO. I grant, indeed, it hath not appear'd; and your suspicion is not
without wit and judgment. But, Roderigo, if thou hast that in
thee indeed, which I have greater reason to believe now than
ever—I mean purpose, courage, and valour—this night show
it; if thou the next night following enjoy not Desdemona, take
me from this world with treachery, and devise engines for
my life.   216

ROD. Well, what is it? Is it within reason and compass?

IAGO. Sir, there is especial commission come from Venice to depute
Cassio in Othello's place.   220

ROD. Is that true? Why, then Othello and Desdemona return again
to Venice.

IAGO. O, no; he goes into Mauritania, and taketh away with him the
fair Desdemona, unless his abode be linger'd here by some

accident; wherein none can be so determinate as the removing
of Cassio.   226

ROD. How do you mean removing of him?

IAGO. Why, by making him uncapable of Othello's place—knocking
out his brains.

ROD. And that you would have me to do?   230

IAGO. Ay, an if you dare do yourself a profit and right. He sups to-
night with a harlotry, and thither will I go to him—he knows not
yet of his honourable fortune. If you will watch his going thence,
which I will fashion to fall out between twelve and one, you may
take him at your pleasure. I will be near to second your attempt,
and he shall fall between us. Come, stand not amaz'd at it, but
go along with me; I will show you such a necessity in his death
that you shall think yourself bound to put it on him. It is now
high supper-time, and the night grows to waste. About it.   241

ROD. I will hear further reason for this.

IAGO. And you shall be satisfied.   [*Exeunt.*

SCENE III. *Cyprus. The citadel.*

Enter OTHELLO, DESDEMONA, LODOVICO, EMILIA, *and* ATTENDANTS.

LOD. I do beseech you, sir, trouble yourself no further.

OTH. O, pardon me; 'twill do me good to walk.

LOD. Madam, good night; I humbly thank your ladyship.

DES. Your honour is most welcome.

OTH. Will you walk, sir? O, Desdemona!

DES. My lord?

OTH. Get you to bed on th' instant; I will be return'd forthwith.
Dispatch your attendant there. Look 't be done.

DES. I will, my lord. [*Exeunt* OTHELLO, LODOVICO, *and* ATTENDANTS.

EMIL. How goes it now? He looks gentler than he did.   10

DES. He says he will return incontinent.
He hath commanded me to go to bed,
And bade me to dismiss you.

EMIL.   Dismiss me!

DES. It was his bidding; therefore, good Emilia,
Give me my nightly wearing, and adieu.   15
We must not now displease him.

EMIL. I would you had never seen him.

DES. So would not I: my love doth so approve him
That even his stubbornness, his checks, his frowns—
Prithee unpin me—have grace and favour in them.   20

EMIL. I have laid those sheets you bade me on the bed.

DES. All's one. Good faith, how foolish are our minds!
If I do die before thee, prithee shroud me
In one of these same sheets.

EMIL.   Come, come, you talk.

DES. My mother had a maid call'd Barbary: 25
She was in love; and he she lov'd prov'd mad,
And did forsake her. She had a song of 'willow';
An old thing 'twas, but it express'd her fortune,
And she died singing it. That song to-night
Will not go from my mind; I have much to do   30
But to go hang my head all at one side

    And sing it like poor Barbary. Prithee dispatch.
EMIL. Shall I go fetch your night-gown?
DES. No, unpin me here.
    This Lodovico is a proper man.
EMIL. A very handsome man.   35
DES. He speaks well.
EMIL. I know a lady in Venice would have walk'd barefoot to Palestine
    for a touch of his nether lip.
DES. [*Sings.*] The poor soul sat sighing by a sycamore tree,
          Sing all a green willow;   40
    Her hand on her bosom, her head on her knee.
          Sing willow, willow, willow.
    The fresh streams ran by her, and murmur'd her moans,
          Sing willow, willow, willow;
    Her salt tears fell from her and soft'ned the stones;   45
          Sing willow—
Lay by these—
                    willow, willow.—
Prithee, hie thee; he'll come anon.—
          Sing all a green willow must be my garland.
    Let nobody blame him; his scorn I approve—
Nay, that's not next. Hark! who is't that knocks?
EMIL. It is the wind.
DES. [*Sings.*] I call'd my love false love; but what said he then?
          Sing willow, willow, willow:
    If I court moe women, you'll couch with moe men—   55
So, get thee gone; good night. Mine eyes do itch;
    Doth that bode weeping?
EMIL.   'Tis neither here nor there.
DES. I have heard it said so. O, these men, these men!
    Dost thou in conscience think—tell me, Emilia—
    That there be women do abuse their husbands   60
    In such gross kind?
EMIL.   There be some such, no question.
DES. Wouldst thou do such a deed for all the world?
EMIL. Why, would not you?
DES.   No, by this heavenly light!
EMIL. Nor I neither by this heavenly light; I might do't as well
    i' th' dark.
DES. Wouldst thou do such a deed for all the world?
EMIL. The world's a huge thing.
    It is a great price for a small vice.
DES. Good troth, I think thou wouldst not.
EMIL. By my troth, I think I should; and undo't when I had done it.
    Marry, I would not do such a thing for a joint-ring, nor for
    measures of lawn, nor for gowns, petticoats, nor caps, nor any
    petty exhibition; but for all the whole world—ud's pity, who
    would not make her husband a cuckold to make him a monarch?
    I should venture purgatory for't.   75
DES. Beshrew me, if I would do such a wrong for the whole world.
EMIL. Why, the wrong is but a wrong i' th' world; and having the
    world for your labour, 'tis a wrong in your own world, and you
    might quickly make it right.

DES. I do not think there is any such woman.   81
EMIL. Yes, a dozen; and as many to th' vantage as would store the
    world they play'd for.
    But I do think it is their husbands' faults
    If wives do fall. Say that they slack their duties,   85
    And pour our treasures into foreign laps;
    Or else break out in peevish jealousies,
    Throwing restraint upon us; or say they strike us,
    Or scant our former having in despite;
    Why, we have galls; and though we have some grace,   90
    Yet have we some revenge. Let husbands know
    Their wives have sense like them; they see and smell,
    And have their palates both for sweet and sour
    As husbands have. What is it that they do
    When they change us for others? Is it sport?   95
    I think it is. And doth affection breed it?
    I think it doth. Is't frailty that thus errs?
    It is so too. And have not we affections,
    Desires for sport, and frailty, as men have?
    Then let them use us well; else let them know   100
    The ills we do their ills instruct us so.
DES. Good night, good night. God me such uses send,
    Not to pick bad from bad, but by bad mend!   [Exeunt.

ACT FIVE

SCENE I. *Cyprus. A street.*

Enter IAGO *and* RODERIGO.

IAGO. Here, stand behind this bulk; straight will he come.
    Wear thy good rapier bare, and put it home.
    Quick, quick; fear nothing; I'll be at thy elbow.
    It makes us or it mars us; think on that,
    And fix most firm thy resolution.   5
ROD. Be near at hand; I may miscarry in't.
IAGO. Here, at thy hand. Be bold, and take thy stand. [Withdraws.
ROD. I have no great devotion to the deed;
    And yet he hath given me satisfying reasons—
    'Tis but a man gone. Forth, my sword; he dies.   10
IAGO. I have rubb'd this young quat almost to the sense,
    And he grows angry. Now, whether he kill Cassio
    Or Cassio him, or each do kill the other,
    Every way makes my gain. Live Roderigo,
    He calls me to a restitution large   15
    Of gold and jewels that I bobb'd from him
    As gifts to Desdemona;
    It must not be. If Cassio do remain,
    He hath a daily beauty in his life
    That makes me ugly; and besides, the Moor   20
    May unfold me to him; there stand I in much peril.
    No, he must die. Be 't so. I hear him coming.

Enter CASSIO.

ROD. I know his gait, 'tis he. Villain, thou diest !
                                          [*Thrusts at* CASSIO.
CAS. That thrust had been mine enemy indeed
    But that my coat is better than thou know'st.   25
    I will make proof of thine. [*Draws, and wounds* ROGERIGO.
ROD.   O, I am slain !
        [IAGO *stabs* CASSIO *from behind in the leg, and exit.*
CAS. I am maim'd for ever. Help, ho ! murder ! murder !   [*Falls.*

Enter OTHELLO *at a distance.*

OTH. The voice of Cassio. Iago keeps his word.
ROD. O, villain that I am !
OTH.   It is even so.
CAS. O, help, ho ! light ! a surgeon !   30
OTH. 'Tis he. O brave Iago, honest and just,
    That hast such noble sense of thy friend's wrong !
    Thou teachest me—minion, your dear lies dead,
    And your unblest fate hies. Strumpet, I come.
    Forth of my heart those charms, thine eyes, are blotted; 35
    Thy bed, lust-stain'd, shall with lust's blood be spotted. [*Exit.*

Enter LODOVICO *and* GRATIANO *at a distance.*

CAS. What, ho ! No watch ? No passage ? Murder ! murder !
GRA. 'Tis some mischance ; the voice is very direful.
CAS. O, help !
LOD.   Hark !   40
ROD. O wretched villain !
LOD. Two or three groan. 'Tis heavy night ;
    These may be counterfeits; let's think't unsafe
    To come in to the cry without more help.
ROD. Nobody come ? Then shall I bleed to death.   45

Re-enter IAGO *with a light.*

LOD. Hark !
GRA. Here's one comes in his shirt, with light and weapons.
IAGO. Who's there ? Whose noise is this that cries on murder ?
LOD. We do not know.
IAGO.   Did not you hear a cry ?
CAS. Here, here ! For heaven's sake, help me !
IAGO.   What's the matter ? 50
GRA. This is Othello's ancient, as I take it.
LOD. The same indeed ; a very valiant fellow.
IAGO. What are you here that cry so grievously ?
CAS. Iago ? O, I am spoil'd, undone by villains !
    Give me some help.   55
IAGO. O me, Lieutenant ! What villains have done this ?
CAS. I think that one of them is hereabout,
    And cannot make away.
IAGO.   O treacherous villains !—
    [*To* LODOVICO *and* GRATIANO.] What are you there ? Come in, and
    give some help.
ROD. O, help me there !   60

                                                          153

CAS. That's one of them.

IAGO. O murd'rous slave ! O villain !   [Stabs RODERIGO.

ROD. O damn'd Iago ! O inhuman dog !

IAGO. Kill men i' th' dark ! Where be these bloody thieves ?
　　How silent is this town ! Ho ! murder ! murder !
　　What may you be ? Are you of good or evil ?   65

LOD. As you shall prove us, praise us.

IAGO. Signior Lodovico ?

LOD. He, sir.

IAGO. I cry you mercy. Here's Cassio hurt by villains.

GRA. Cassio !   70

IAGO. How is't, brother ?

CAS. My leg is cut in two.

IAGO.   Marry, heaven forbid !
　　Light, gentlemen. I'll bind it with my shirt.

Enter BIANCA.

BIAN. What is the matter, ho ? Who is't that cried ?

IAGO. Who is't that cried !   75

BIAN. O my dear Cassio !
　　My sweet Cassio ! O Cassio, Cassio, Cassio !

IAGO. O notable strumpet ! Cassio, may you suspect
　　Who they should be that have thus mangled you ?

CAS. No.   80

GRA. I am sorry to find you thus ; I have been to seek you.

IAGO. Lend me a garter. So.
　　O, for a chair, to bear him easily hence !

BIAN. Alas, he faints ! O Cassio, Cassio, Cassio !

IAGO. Gentlemen all, I do suspect this trash   85
　　To be a party in this injury.
　　Patience awhile, good Cassio. Come, come ;
　　Lend me a light. Know we this face or no ?
　　Alas, my friend and my dear countryman
　　Roderigo ? No—yes, sure ; O heaven ! Roderigo.   90

GRA. What, of Venice ?

IAGO. Even he, sir ; did you know him ?

GRA.   Know him ! Ay.

IAGO. Signior Gratiano ? I cry your gentle pardon ;
　　These bloody accidents must excuse my manners,
　　That so neglected you.

GRA.   I am glad to see you.   95

IAGO. How do you, Cassio ?—O, a chair, a chair !

GRA. Roderigo !

IAGO. He, he, 'tis he. [*A chair brought in.*] O, that's well said ; the
　　chair.
　　Some good man bear him carefully from hence ;
　　I'll fetch the General's surgeon. [*To* BIANCA.] For you, mistress, 100
　　Save you your labour.—He that lies slain here, Cassio,
　　Was my dear friend. What malice was between you ?

CAS. None in the world ; nor do I know the man.

IAGO. [*To* BIANCA.] What, look you pale ?—O, bear him out o' th' air.
　　　　　　　　　　　　　　　　　[CASSIO *and* RODERIGO *are borne off.*
　　Stay you, good gentlemen.—Look you pale, mistress ?—   105
　　Do you perceive the gastness of her eye ?—

Nay, an you stare, we shall hear more anon.—
Behold her well; I pray you look upon her.
Do you see, gentlemen? Nay, guiltiness will speak
Though tongues were out of use.   110

Enter EMILIA.

EMIL. 'Las, what's the matter? What's the matter, husband?
IAGO. Cassio hath here been set on in the dark
By Roderigo and fellows that are 'scap'd.
He's almost slain, and Roderigo quite dead.
EMIL. Alas, good gentleman! Alas, good Cassio!   115
IAGO. This is the fruits of whoring. Prithee, Emilia,
Go know of Cassio where he supp'd to-night.—
What, do you shake at that?
BIAN. He supp'd at my house; but I therefore shake not.
IAGO. O, did he so? I charge you go with me.   120
EMIL. Fie, fie upon thee, strumpet!
BIAN. I am no strumpet, but of life as honest
As you that thus abuse me.
EMIL.   As I! Foh! Fie upon thee!
IAGO. Kind gentlemen, let's go see poor Cassio dress'd.—
Come, mistress, you must tell's another tale.   125
Emilia, run you to the citadel,
And tell my lord and lady what hath happ'd.
Will you go on afore? [*Aside.*] This is the night
That either makes me or fordoes me quite.   [*Exeunt.*

SCENE II. *Cyprus. The citadel.*

DESDEMONA *in her bed. Enter* OTHELLO *with a light.*

OTH. It is the cause, it is the cause, my soul—
Let me not name it to you, you chaste stars—
It is the cause. Yet I'll not shed her blood,
Nor scar that whiter skin of hers than snow,
And smooth as monumental alabaster.   5
Yet she must die, else she'll betray more men.
Put out the light, and then put out the light.
If I quench thee, thou flaming minister,
I can again thy former light restore,
Should I repent me; but once put out thy light,   10
Thou cunning'st pattern of excelling nature,
I know not where is that Promethean heat
That can thy light relume. When I have pluck'd thy rose,
I cannot give it vital growth again;
It needs must wither. I'll smell thee on the tree.   [*Kissing her.*
O balmy breath, that dost almost persuade
Justice to break her sword! One more, one more.
Be thus when thou art dead, and I will kill thee,
And love thee after. One more, and that's the last:
So sweet was ne'er so fatal. I must weep,   20
But they are cruel tears. This sorrow's heavenly;
It strikes where it doth love. She wakes.
DES. Who's there? Othello?
OTH.   Ay, Desdemona.

DES. Will you come to bed, my lord?
OTH. Have you pray'd to-night, Desdemona?   25
DES. Ay, my lord.
OTH. If you bethink yourself of any crime
    Unreconcil'd as yet to heaven and grace,
    Solicit for it straight.
DES.   Alack, my lord,
    What may you mean by that?   30
OTH. Well, do it, and be brief; I will walk by.
    I would not kill thy unprepared spirit;
    No, heaven forfend!—I would not kill thy soul.
DES. Talk you of killing?
OTH.   Ay, I do.
DES.   Then heaven
    Have mercy on me!
OTH.   Amen, with all my heart!
DES. If you say so, I hope you will not kill me.
OTH. Humh!
DES. And yet I fear you; for you're fatal then   40
    When your eyes roll so. Why I should fear I know not,
    Since guiltiness I know not; but yet I feel I fear.
OTH. Think on thy sins.
DES.   They are loves I bear to you.
OTH. Ay, and for that thou diest.
DES. That death's unnatural that kills for loving.   45
    Alas, why gnaw you so your nether lip?
    Some bloody passion shakes your very frame.
    These are portents; but yet I hope, I hope,
    They do not point on me.
OTH. Peace, and be still.
DES.   I will so. What's the matter?   50
OTH. That handkerchief which I so lov'd and gave thee
    Thou gav'st to Cassio.
DES.   No, by my life and soul!
    Send for the man and ask him.
OTH.   Sweet soul, take heed,
    Take heed of perjury; thou art on thy death-bed.
DES. Ay, but not yet to die.
OTH.   Yes, presently.   55
    Therefore confess thee freely of thy sin;
    For to deny each article with oath
    Cannot remove nor choke the strong conception
    That I do groan withal. Thou art to die.
DES. Then, Lord have mercy on me!
OTH.   I say, amen.   60
DES. And have you mercy too! I never did
    Offend you in my life; never lov'd Cassio
    But with such general warranty of heaven
    As I might love. I never gave him token.
OTH. By heaven, I saw my handkerchief in's hand.   65
    O perjur'd woman! thou dost stone my heart,
    And mak'st me call what I intend to do
    A murder, which I thought a sacrifice.
    I saw the handkerchief.

DES.   He found it, then ;
  I never gave it him. Send for him hither ;   70
  Let him confess a truth.

OTH.   He hath confess'd.

DES. What, my lord ?

OTH.   That he hath—ud's death !—us'd thee.

DES. How ? unlawfully ?

OTH.   Ay.

DES. He will not say so.

OTH.   No, his mouth is stopp'd ;   75
  Honest Iago hath ta'en order for't.

DES. O, my fear interprets ! What, is he dead ?

OTH. Had all his hairs been lives, my great revenge
  Had stomach for them all.

DES. Alas, he is betray'd, and I undone !   80

OTH. Out, strumpet ! Weep'st thou for him to my face ?

DES. O, banish me, my lord, but kill me not !

OTH. Down, strumpet.

DES. Kill me to-morrow ; let me live to-night.

OTH. Nay, an you strive—   85

D ES. But half an hour !

OTH.   Being done, there is no pause.

DES. But while I say one prayer !

OTH.   It is too late.   [Smothers her.

DES. O Lord, Lord, Lord !

EMIL. [Within.] My lord, my lord ! what, ho ! my lord, my lord !

OTH. What voice is this ? Not dead ? not yet quite dead ?
  I that am cruel am yet merciful ;
  I would not have thee linger in thy pain.   90
  So, so.

EMIL. [Within.] What, ho ! my lord, my lord !

OTH.   Who's there ?

EMIL. [Within.] O, good my lord, I'd speak a word with you !

OTH. Yes—'tis Emilia—by and by. She's dead.
  'Tis like she comes to speak of Cassio's death ;
  The noise was high. Ha ! no more moving ?   95
  Still as the grave. Shall she come in ? Were't good ?
  I think she stirs again. No. What's the best ?
  If she come in she'll sure speak to my wife.
  My wife ! my wife ! what wife ? I have no wife.   100
  O insupportable ! O heavy hour !
  Methinks it should be now a huge eclipse
  Of sun and moon, and that th' affrighted globe
  Did yawn at alteration.

EMIL. [Within.] I do beseech you that I may speak with you. O good
  my lord !   105

OTH. I had forgot thee : O, come in, Emilia.
  Soft, by and by. Let me the curtains draw.
  Where art thou ?   [Unlocks the door.

Enter EMILIA.

            What's the matter with thee now ?

EMIL. O, my good lord, yonder's foul murders done !

OTH. What, now ?   110

EMIL. But now, my lord.
OTH. It is the very error of the moon ;
　　She comes more nearer earth than she was wont,
　　And makes men mad.
EMIL. Cassio, my lord, hath kill'd a young Venetian   115
　　Call'd Roderigo.
OTH.　　　　　　　Roderigo kill'd!
　　And Cassio kill'd !
EMIL.　　　　　　No, Cassio is not kill'd.
OTH. Not Cassio kill'd ! Then murder's out of tune,
　　And sweet revenge grows harsh.
DES. O, falsely, falsely murder'd !
EMIL.　　　　　　　　　O Lord, what cry is that ?   120
OTH. That ! what ?
EMIL. Out and alas ! that was my lady's voice.
　　Help ! help, ho ! help ! O lady, speak again !
　　Sweet Desdemona ! O sweet mistress, speak !
DES. A guiltless death I die.   125
EMIL. O, who hath done this deed ?
DES. Nobody. I myself. Farewell.
　　Commend me to my kind lord. O, farewell !   [*She dies.*
OTH. Why, how should she be murd'red ?
EMIL.　　　　　　　　　Alas, who knows ?
OTH. You heard her say herself it was not I.   130
EMIL. She said so. I must needs report a truth.
OTH. She's like a liar gone to burning hell :
　　'Twas I that kill'd her.
EMIL.　　　　　　O, the more angel she,
　　And you the blacker devil !
OTH. She turn'd to folly, and she was a whore.   135
EMIL. Thou dost belie her, and thou art a devil.
OTH. She was false as water.
EMIL.　　　　　　Thou art rash as fire to say
　　That she was false. O, she was heavenly true !
OTH. Cassio did top her ; ask thy husband else.
　　O, I were damn'd beneath all depth in hell   140
　　But that I did proceed upon just grounds
　　To this extremity. Thy husband knew it all.
EMIL. My husband !
OTH. Thy husband.
EMIL. That she was false to wedlock ?   145
OTH. Ay, with Cassio. Nay, had she been true,
　　If heaven would make me such another world
　　Of one entire and perfect chrysolite,
　　I'd not have sold her for it.
EMIL. My husband !
OTH. Ay, 'twas he that told me on her first.   150
　　An honest man he is, and hates the slime
　　That sticks on filthy deeds.
EMIL. My husband !
OTH. What needs this iterance, woman ? I say thy husband.
EMIL. O mistress, villainy hath made mocks with love
　　My husband say that she was false !
OTH.　　　　　　　　He, woman ;   155

I say thy husband ; dost understand the word ?
My friend, thy husband—honest, honest Iago.

EMIL. If he say so, may his pernicious soul
    Rot half a grain a day !   He lies to th' heart.
    She was too fond of her most filthy bargain.   160

OTH.   Ha !

EMIL. Do thy worst :
    This deed of thine is no more worthy heaven
    Than thou wast worthy her.

OTH.   Peace, you were best.

EMIL. Thou hast not half that power to do me harm   165
    As I have to be hurt.   O gull !   O dolt !
    As ignorant as dirt !   Thou hast done a deed—
    I care not for thy sword ;   I'll make thee known,
    Though I lost twenty lives.   Help ! help, ho ! help !
    The Moor hath kill'd my mistress !   Murder ! murder !   170

Enter MONTANO, GRATIANO, IAGO, *and* OTHERS.

MON. What is the matter ?   How now, General !

EMIL. O, are you come, Iago ?   You have done well,
    That men must lay their murders on your neck.

GRA. What is the matter ?

EMIL. Disprove this villain, if thou be'st a man :   175
    He says thou told'st him that his wife was false.
    I know thou didst not ;   thou'rt not such a villain.
    Speak, for my heart is full.

IAGO. I told him what I thought, and told no more
    Than what he found himself was apt and true.   180

EMIL. But did you ever tell him she was false ?

IAGO. I did.

EMIL. You told a lie—an odious, damned lie.
    Upon my soul, a lie—a wicked lie.
    She false with Cassio !   Did you say with Cassio ?   185

IAGO. With Cassio, mistress.   Go to, charm your tongue.

EMIL. I will not charm my tongue ;   I am bound to speak.
    My mistress here lies murdered in her bed.

ALL. O heavens forfend !

EMIL. And your reports have set the murder on.   190

OTH. Nay, stare not, masters : it is true, indeed.

GRA. 'Tis a strange truth.

MON. O monstrous act !

EMIL.   Villainy, villainy, villainy !
    I think upon't.   I think—I smell't.   O villainy !
    I thought so then.   I'll kill myself for grief.   195
    O villainy, villainy !

IAGO. What, are you mad ?   I charge you get you home.

EMIL. Good gentlemen, let me have leave to speak.
    'Tis proper I obey him, but not now.
    Perchance, Iago, I will ne'er go home.   200

OTH. O ! O ! O !   [*Falls on the bed.*

EMIL.   Nay, lay thee down and roar ;
    For thou hast kill'd the sweetest innocent
    That e'er did lift up eye.

OTH. [*Rising*.]   O, she was foul !
       I scarce did know you, uncle. There lies your niece,
       Whose breath indeed these hands have newly stopp'd.   205
       I know this act shows horrible and grim.
GRA. Poor Desdemona ! I am glad thy father's dead.
       Thy match was mortal to him, and pure grief
       Shore his old thread atwain. Did he live now,
       This sight would make him do a desperate turn,   210
       Yea, curse his better angel from his side,
       And fall to reprobance.
OTH.   'Tis pitiful ; but yet Iago knows
       That she with Cassio hath the act of shame
       A thousand times committed ; Cassio confess'd it ;   215
       And she did gratify his amorous works
       With that recognizance and pledge of love
       Which I first gave her ; I saw it in his hand.
       It was a handkerchief, an antique token
       My father gave my mother.   220
EMIL. O God ! O heavenly God !
IAGO. Zounds, hold your peace.
EMIL.   'Twill out, 'twill out. I, peace !
       No, I will speak as liberal as the north.
       Let heaven and men and devils, let them all,
       All, all, cry shame against me, yet I'll speak.   225
IAGO. Be wise, and get you home.
EMIL.   I will not. [IAGO *offers to stab his wife.*
GRA. Fie ! your sword upon a woman ?
EMIL. O thou dull Moor ! That handkerchief thou speak'st of
       I found by fortune, and did give my husband ;
       For often with a solemn earnestness—   230
       More than indeed belong'd to such a trifle—
       He begg'd of me to steal it.
IAGO.   Villainous whore !
EMIL. She give it Cassio ! No, alas, I found it,
       And I did give't my husband.
IAGO.   Filth, thou liest.
EMIL. By heaven, I do not, I do not, gentlemen.   235
       O murderous coxcomb ! What should such a fool
       Do with so good a wife ?   [*The Moor runs at* IAGO ; MONTANO
                 and OTHERS *disarm the Moor.* IAGO *kills his wife and escapes.*
OTH. Are there no stones in heaven but what serves for the thunder ?
       Precious villain !
GRA. The woman falls ; sure he hath kill'd his wife.
EMIL. Ay, ay. O, lay me by my mistress' side.   240
GRA. He's gone, but his wife's kill'd.
MON. 'Tis a notorious villain. Take you this weapon,
       Which I have here recover'd from the Moor.
       Come, guard the door without ; let him not pass,
       But kill him rather. I'll after that same villain,   245
       For 'tis a damned slave.

                              [*Exeunt* MONTANO, GRATIANO, *and* OTHERS.

OTH. I am not valiant neither—
       But every puny whipster gets my sword.

But why should honour outlive honesty?
Let it go all.
MIL. What did thy song bode, lady?
　Hark, canst thou hear me? I will play the swan,　　　250
　And die in music. [*Sings.*] Willow, willow, willow.—
　Moor, she was chaste; she lov'd thee, cruel Moor;
　So come my soul to bliss, as I speak true;
　So speaking as I think, alas, I die.　　　　　　　[*She dies.*
TH. I have another weapon in this chamber;　　　　　255
　It was a sword of Spain, the ice-brook's temper.
　O, here it is. Uncle, I must come forth.
RA. [*Within.*] If thou attempt it, it will cost thee dear;
　Thou hast no weapon, and perforce must suffer.
TH. Look in upon me, then, and speak with me,　　　260
　Or, naked as I am, I will assault thee.

　　　　　　　　Re-enter GRATIANO.

RA. What is the matter?
TH.　　　　　　　　Behold, I have a weapon;
　A better never did itself sustain
　Upon a soldier's thigh. I have seen the day
　That with this little arm and this good sword　　　265
　I have made my way through more impediments
　Than twenty times your stop. But, O vain boast!
　Who can control his fate? 'Tis not so now.
　Be not afraid though you do see me weapon'd;
　Here is my journey's end, here is my butt,　　　　270
　And very sea-mark of my utmost sail.
　Do you go back dismay'd? 'Tis a lost fear;
　Man but a rush against Othello's breast,
　And he retires. Where should Othello go?
　Now, how dost thou look now? O ill-starr'd wench　275
　Pale as thy smock! When we shall meet at compt,
　This look of thine will hurl my soul from heaven,
　And fiends will snatch at it. Cold, cold, my girl!
　Even like thy chastity. O cursed, cursed slave!
　Whip me, ye devils,　　　　　　　　　　　　　　280
　Fom the possession of this heavenly sight.
　Blow me about in winds, roast me in sulphur,
　Wash me in steep-down gulfs of liquid fire.
　O Desdemona! Dead! Desdemona! Dead! O! O!

nter LODOVICO, MONTANO, CASSIO *carried in a chair, and* OFFICERS,
　　　　　　　　　　　with IAGO *prisoner.*

oD. Where is this rash and most unfortunate man?　　286
TH. That's he that was Othello—here I am.
oD. Where is that viper? Bring the villain forth.
TH. I look down towards his feet—but that's a fable.
　If that thou be'st a devil, I cannot kill thee.　[*Wounds* IAGO.
oD. Wrench his sword from him.
GO. I bleed, sir; but not kill'd.
TH. I am not sorry neither: I'd have thee live;
　For, in my sense, 'tis happiness to die.
oD. O thou Othello, that was once so good,

6　　　　　　　　　　　　　　　　　　　　　　161

Fall'n in the practice of a damned slave, 2
What shall be said to thee ?
OTH.   Why, any thing :
An honourable murderer, if you will ;
For nought I did in hate, but all in honour.
LOD. This wretch hath part confess'd his villainy.
Did you and he consent in Cassio's death ? 3
OTH. Ay.
CAS. Dear General, I never gave you cause.
OTH. I do believe it, and I ask your pardon.
Will you, I pray, demand that demi-devil
Why he hath thus ensnar'd my soul and body ? 3
IAGO. Demand me nothing. What you know, you know
From this time forth I never will speak word.
LOD. What, not to pray ?
GRA.   Torments will ope your lips
OTH. Well, thou dost best.
LOD. Sir, you shall understand what hath befall'n, 3
Which, as I think, you know not. Here is a letter
Found in the pocket of the slain Roderigo ;
And here another : the one of them imports
The death of Cassio to be undertook
By Roderi o. 3
OTH. O villain !
CAS.   Most heathenish and most gross !
LOD. Now here's another discontented paper,
Found in his pocket too ; and this, it seems,
Roderigo meant t' have sent this damned villain ;
But that, belike, Iago in the nick 3
Came in and satisfied him.
OTH.   O thou pernicious caitiff !
How came you, Cassio, by that handkerchief
That was my wife's ?
CAS.   I found it in my chamber ;
And he himself confess'd it even now
That there he dropp'd it for a special purpose 3
Which wrought to his desire.
OTH.   O fool ! fool ! fool !
CAS. There is besides in Roderigo's letter,
How he upbraids Iago that he made him
Brave me upon the watch ; whereon it came
That I was cast ; and even but now he spake, 3
After long seeming dead, Iago hurt him,
Iago set him on.
LOD. You must forsake this room and go with us.
Your power and your command is taken off,
And Cassio rules in Cyprus. For this slave, 3
If there be any cunning cruelty
That can torment him much and hold him long,
It shall be his. You shall close prisoner rest
Till that the nature of your fault be known
To the Venetian state. Come, bring away. 3
OTH. Soft you ; a word or two before you go.
I have done the state some service, and they know't—

No more of that. I pray you, in your letters,
When you shall these unlucky deeds relate,
Speak of me as I am ; nothing extenuate,   345
Nor set down aught in malice.   Then must you speak
Of one that lov'd not wisely, but too well ;
Of one not easily jealous, but, being wrought,
Perplexed in the extreme ; of one whose hand,
Like the base Indian, threw a pearl away   350
Richer than all his tribe ; of one whose subdu'd eyes,
Albeit unused to the melting mood,
Drops tears as fast as the Arabian trees
Their med'cinable gum. Set you down this :
And say besides that in Aleppo once,   355
Where a malignant and a turban'd Turk
Beat a Venetian and traduc'd the state,
I took by th' throat the circumcised dog,
And smote him—thus.   [He stabs himself.
OD. O bloody period !
RA.   All that is spoke is marr'd.   360
TH. I kiss'd thee ere I kill'd thee. No way but this—
   Killing my self, to die upon a kiss.   [Falls on the bed and dies.
AS. This did I fear, but thought he had no weapon ;
   For he was great of heart.
OD. [To IAGO.]   O Spartan dog,
More fell than anguish, hunger, or the sea !   365
Look on the tragic loading of this bed.
This is thy work.—The object poisons sight ;
Let it be hid. Gratiano, keep the house,
And seize upon the fortunes of the Moor,
For they succeed on you. To you, Lord Governor   370
Remains the censure of this hellish villain ;
The time, the place, the torture—O, enforce it
Myself will straight aboard ; and to the state
This heavy act with heavy heart relate.   [Exeunt.

ANTONY AND CLEOPATRA

THIS is the play which most clearly shows how the critic mus[t] insist that Shakespeare's stage-craft be judged not by the materia[l] demands of the modern stage that aims at realism of setting an[d] place but by the conditions governing the treatment of Shakespeare['] unlocalized stage. A play with some forty-two scenes, some of them running only to two, four, or six lines, with regular changes of place cannot be produced in its original form in a style that aims at th[e] realistic representation of background. Yet the play reads withou[t] our losing our sense of the continuity of the action; now we are i[n] Egypt, now in Rome, but the relation of scene to scene is never i[n] doubt. Granville-Barker has very cleverly emphasized this aspect o[f] the plotting by two quotations from Dr. Johnson. Johnson recognize[d] the continuity of interest when he said :

> This play keeps curiosity always busy, and the passions alway[s] interested. The continual hurry of the action, the variety o[f] incidents, and the quick succession of one personage to another call the mind forward without intermission from the first Act t[o] the last.

Yet, as Granville-Barker notes, having praised the sustained interes[t] of the piece Johnson thinks of the way he imagines a play shoul[d] be put together to satisfy a scholarly scrutiny and concludes,

> The events, of which the principals are described according t[o] history, are produced without any art of connection or care o[f] disposition.

Shakespeare, it would seem, had flung together some episodes from the story of Antony, and by a happy chance they so fitted togethe[r] that the mind passes without intermission from one to the other[.] Those who fancy chance is so accommodating should, as one criti[c] has said, try their own luck at this game in the hope they may pul[l] from fortune's wheel so interesting and sustained a plot.

The continuity that Johnson emphasizes was lost on the stage o[f] his day as it must be on any realistic stage. Shakespeare took n[o] care to dispose things to fit such a stage; the art of connecton demanded by that stage was different in form at least from tha[t] required at the Globe in Shakespeare's day. Unfortunately th[e] belief that the world is getting better and better has persuaded som[e] to believe that Shakespeare's stage must be inferior to that of yester-day, and that this inferiority helps to explain the clumsiness of such a play as *Antony and Cleopatra* and the impossibility of adapting i[t] as a whole to the picture stage. It is allowed that the Greek theatr[e] has its right to its own peculiarities, for it is protected by the distance the language places between it and modern comprehension; th[e] Age of Elizabeth and James, however, seems to come very close t[o] us especially in a modernized text, and one is apt to forget that th[e] Acts and Scenes of such an edition do not correspond precisely t[o] what the Acts and Scenes of a modern piece stand for. Putting aside Act-division in Shakespeare for the moment, we may say that within the Act there was no break between scene and scene. Shakespeare'[s] stage allowed of the same fluidity that is found in reading. Characters come and go without any shifting of scenery; what they say shows us where they are or how what they speak and do is related to what has gone before. The spectator's interest is carried on from episode to episode just as in reading, for what we are interested in is how events translate themselves in terms of the characters' emotions and purposes; we do not need to see the battle at Actium, for what happened there and its consequences for the actors are brought home to us by the words of those who are watching it. In their fears and horror is mirrored for us the defeat of Antony.

The conflict in Johnson's thoughts about the play has been echoed by many commentators. Dowden felt that *Antony and Cleopatra* could not be said to be well constructed, yet after explaining why his judgment seems reasonable he concludes, ' None the less the final impression is one of unity—and that impression is ineffaceable '. It is difficult to see what more one can ask from a play than this unity and power of impression; and this quarrel with a masterpiece that achieves its end by means we disapprove of is seen as a failure of our historical sense once we relate the play to ' the theatre of its activity '.

It has been pointed out by Bradley and others that the first half of *Antony and Cleopatra* is, compared with *Julius Cæsar* or *Macbeth*, superficially lacking in drama. The opening conversation between the Roman officers is not followed as in *Julius Cæsar* by any public commotion; we have no fighting as in *Romeo and Juliet* or *Coriolanus*, only conversations between various parties and what may seem courtly or imperial junketings. Yet Shakespeare creates a sense of opposition and tension that is none the less powerful and ominous because to the casual eye the surface of affairs seems to run smoothly and well. At the very moment when Menas thinks Antony and Octavius are ' for ever knit together ' Enobarbus can say ' the band that seems to tie their friendship together will be the very strangler of their amity '. Rome and Egypt stand for two different and indeed opposite views of life. The tension shows in the opening scene in the conversation of the soldiers and the feelings attending the departure of Antony to the West; and, in the Roman scenes that follow, Shakespeare, although he establishes for us Antony's competence and power when he cares to assume the part of the Roman soldier and politician, reveals the side to which Antony's inclinations draw him. Antony does not bear himself as one broken down by debauchery and incapable of anything more than lechery in idleness; he turns to Cleopatra not in his decay but at the very time when he has vindicated his position as one of the rulers of the world. Yet so clearly has Shakespeare established the incompatibility of the two ways of life that Actium seems the inevitable sequel to the smooth but deadly drift of Antony's inclinations.

The duel between Antony and Octavius repeats in a more spacious theatre that between Richard and Bolingbroke. Richard throws away a kingdom, while Antony squanders an empire, and as Antony has the capacity for rule and affairs that Richard had not, the Roman's conduct might be judged the more heinous, especially when such an aggravation as his liaison with Cleopatra is put in the balance. Yet two considerations throw out the parallel between Richard and

Antony. Richard is a king of England and it is not merely wh
he does but its effect as well that interests the dramatist and t
spectators; Richard has a task against which he cannot altogeth
escape measurement. No such national feelings obscure or dist
the sense of what Antony is; and now Cleopatra need not be cit
against him. Rather she becomes a witness to his pre-eminence, a
the more remarkable she is in herself the more convincing her tes
mony. Unlike the English king Antony had a positive rather than
negative attitude to the circumstances in which he found himse
He chose one way in preference to another, although capable of eith
part. His choice makes clear to us the man he was and that with
his faults he had the greatness without which there could have be
no tragedy.

DRAMATIS PERSONÆ.

MARK ANTONY,
OCTAVIUS CÆSAR,   } Triumvirs.
M. AEMILIUS LEPIDUS,
SEXTUS POMPEIUS.

DOMITIUS ENOBARBUS,
VENTIDIUS,
EROS,
SCARUS,   } friends to
DERCETAS,   Antony.
DEMETRIUS,
PHILO,

MÆCENAS,
AGRIPPA,
DOLABELLA,
PROCULEIUS,   } friends to Cæsar.
THYREUS,
GALLUS,

MENAS,
MENECRATES,   } friends to Pompey.
VARRIUS,

TAURUS, *Lieutenant-General to Cæsar.*

CANIDIUS, *Lieutenant-General to Antony.*

SILIUS, *an Officer in Ventidius's army.*

EUPHRONIUS, *an ambassador from Antony to Cæsar.*

ALEXAS,
MARDIAN,   } *attendants on*
SELEUCUS,   *Cleopatra.*
DIOMEDES,

A SOOTHSAYER.
A CLOWN.

CLEOPATRA, *Queen of Egypt.*

OCTAVIA, *sister to Cæsar and wife to Antony.*

CHARMIAN, } *ladies attending on*
IRAS,   *Cleopatra.*

OFFICERS, SOLDIERS, MESSENGERS *and* ATTENDANTS.

THE SCENE : *The Roman Empire.*

ACT ONE

SCENE I. *Alexandria. Cleopatra's palace.*

Enter DEMETRIUS *and* PHILO.

PHI. Nay, but this dotage of our general's
O'erflows the measure. Those his goodly eyes,
That o'er the files and musters of the war
Have glow'd like plated Mars, now bend, now turn,
The office and devotion of their view   5
Upon a tawny front. His captain's heart,
Which in the scuffles of great fights hath burst
The buckles on his breast, reneges all temper,
And is become the bellows and the fan
To cool a gipsy's lust.

Flourish. Enter ANTONY, CLEOPATRA, *her* LADIES, *the* TRAIN,
with EUNUCHS *fanning her.*

            Look where they come !   10
Take but good note, and you shall see in him

167

The triple pillar of the world transform'd
Into a strumpet's fool.   Behold and see.

CLEO. If it be love indeed, tell me how much.

ANT. There's beggary in the love that can be reckon'd.   1$

CLEO. I'll set a bourn how far to be belov'd.

ANT. Then must thou needs find out new heaven, new earth.

Enter a MESSENGER.

MESS. News, my good lord, from Rome.

ANT.   Grates me the sum.

CLEO. Nay, hear them, Antony.
Fulvia perchance is angry ; or who knows   20
If the scarce-bearded Cæsar have not sent
His pow'rful mandate to you : ' Do this or this ;
Take in that kingdom and enfranchise that ;
Perform't, or else we damn thee '.

ANT.   How, my love ?

CLEO. Perchance ? Nay, and most like,   2$
You must not stay here longer ; your dismission
Is come from Cæsar ; therefore hear it, Antony.
Where's Fulvia's process ? Cæsar's I would say ? Both ?
Call in the messengers.   As I am Egypt's Queen,
Thou blushest, Antony, and that blood of thine   3$
Is Cæsar's homager.   Else so thy cheek pays shame
When shrill-tongu'd Fulvia scolds.   The messengers !

ANT. Let Rome in Tiber melt, and the wide arch
Of the rang'd empire fall !   Here is my space.
Kingdoms are clay ; our dungy earth alike   3$
Feeds beast as man.   The nobleness of life
Is to do thus [*embracing*], when such a mutual pair
And such a twain can do't, in which I bind,
On pain of punishment, the world to weet
We stand up peerless.

CLEO.   Excellent falsehood !   4$
Why did he marry Fulvia, and not love her ?
I'll seem the fool I am not.   Antony
Will be himself.

ANT.   But stirr'd by Cleopatra.
Now for the love of Love and her soft hours,
Let's not confound the time with conference harsh ;   4$
There's not a minute of our lives should stretch
Without some pleasure now.   What sport to-night ?

CLEO. Hear the ambassadors.

ANT.   Fie, wrangling queen !
Whom everything becomes—to chide, to laugh,
To weep ; whose every passion fully strives   5$
To make itself in thee fair and admir'd.
No messenger but thine, and all alone
To-night we'll wander through the streets and note
The qualities of people.   Come, my queen ;
Last night you did desire it.   Speak not to us.   5$
                        [*Exeunt* ANTONY *and* CLEOPATRA, *with the* TRAIN

DEM. Is Cæsar with Antonius priz'd so slight ?

PHI. Sir, sometimes when he is not Antony,

He comes too short of that great property
Which still should go with Antony.

M.   I am full sorry
That he approves the common liar, who   60
Thus speaks of him at Rome ; but I will hope
Of better deeds to-morrow. Rest you happy !   [*Exeunt.*

SCENE II. *Alexandria. Cleopatra's palace.*

Enter CHARMIAN, IRAS, ALEXAS, *and a* SOOTHSAYER.

AR. Lord Alexas, sweet Alexas, most anything Alexas, almost
most absolute Alexas, where's the soothsayer that you prais'd so
to th' Queen ? O that I knew this husband, which you say
must charge his horns with garlands !

EX. Soothsayer !

OTH. Your will ?

AR. Is this the man ? Is't you, sir, that know things ?

OTH. In nature's infinite book of secrecy
A little I can read.

EX.   Show him your hand.   10

Enter ENOBARBUS.

O. Bring in the banquet quickly ; wine enough
Cleopatra's health to drink.

AR. Good, sir, give me good fortune.

OTH. I make not, but foresee.

AR. Pray, then, foresee me one.   15

OTH. You shall be yet far fairer than you are.

AR. He means in flesh.

AS. No, you shall paint when you are old.

AR. Wrinkles forbid !

EX. Vex not his prescience ; be attentive.   20

AR. Hush !

OTH. You shall be more beloving than beloved.

AR. I had rather heat my liver with drinking.

EX. Nay, hear him.   24

AR. Good now, some excellent fortune ! Let me be married to
three kings in a forenoon, and widow them all. Let me have a
child at fifty, to whom Herod of Jewry may do homage. Find me
to marry me with Octavius Cæsar, and companion me with my
mistress.

OTH. You shall outlive the lady whom you serve.   30

AR. O, excellent ! I love long life better than figs.

OTH. You have seen and prov'd a fairer former fortune
Than that which is to approach.

AR. Then belike my children shall have no names. Prithee, how
many boys and wenches must I have ?   35

OTH. If every of your wishes had a womb,
And fertile every wish, a million.

AR. Out, fool ! I forgive thee for a witch.

EX. You think none but your sheets are privy to your wishes.

AR. Nay, come, tell Iras hers.

EX. We'll know all our fortunes.

ENO. Mine, and most of our fortunes, to-night, shall be—drunk t
   bed.   4

IRAS. There's a palm presages chastity, if nothing else.

CHAR. E'en as the o'erflowing Nilus presageth famine.

IRAS. Go, you wild bedfellow, you cannot soothsay.

CHAR. Nay, if an oily palm be not a fruitful prognostication, I canno
   scratch mine ear.   Prithee, tell her but a worky-day fortune.   5

SOOTH. Your fortunes are alike.

IRAS. But how, but how ? Give me particulars.

SOOTH. I have said.

IRAS. Am I not an inch of fortune better than she ?

CHAR. Well, if you were but an inch of fortune better than I, wher
   would you choose it ?   5

IRAS. Not in my husband's nose.

CHAR. Our worser thoughts heavens mend ! Alexas—come, hi
   fortune, his fortune ! O, let him marry a woman that cannot go
   sweet Isis, I beseech thee ! And let her die too, and give him
   worse ! And let worse follow worse, till the worst of all follov
   him laughing to his grave, fiftyfold a cuckold ! Good Isis, hea
   me this prayer, though thou deny me a matter of more weight
   good Isis, I beseech thee !   6

IRAS. Amen.   Dear goddess, hear that prayer of the people ! Fo
   as it is a heartbreaking to see a handsome man loose-wiv'd, so i
   is a deadly sorrow to behold a foul knave uncuckolded.   Therefor
   dear Isis, keep decorum, and fortune him accordingly !

CHAR. Amen.   7

ALEX. Lo now, if it lay in their hands to make me a cuckold, the
   would make themselves whores but they'ld do't !

Enter CLEOPATRA.

ENO. Hush ! Here comes Antony.

CHAR.   Not he ; the Queen.

CLEO. Saw you my lord ?

ENO.   No, lady.

CLEO. Was he not here ?

CHAR.   No, madam.

CLEO. He was dispos'd to mirth ; but on the sudden
   A Roman thought hath struck him.   Enobarbus !   8

ENO. Madam ?

CLEO. Seek him, and bring him hither.   Where's Alexas ?

ALEX. Here, at your service.   My lord approaches.

Enter ANTONY, *with a* MESSENGER *and* ATTENDANTS.

CLEO. We will not look upon him.   Go with us.
                     [*Exeunt* CLEOPATRA, ENOBARBUS, *and the res*

MESS. Fulvia thy wife first came into the field.   8

ANT. Against my brother Lucius ?

MESS. Ay.
   But soon that war had end, and the time's state
   Made friends of them, jointing their force 'gainst Cæsar,
   Whose better issue in the war from Italy   9
   Upon the first encounter drave them.

ANT.   Well, what worst ?

MESS. The nature of bad news infects the teller.

ANT. When it concerns the fool or coward.   On !
    Things that are past are done with me.   'Tis thus :
    Who tells me true, though in his tale lie death,   95
    I hear him as he flatter'd.
MESS.   Labienus—
    This is stiff news—hath with his Parthian force
    Extended Asia from Euphrates,
    His conquering banner shook from Syria
    To Lydia and to Ionia,   100
    Whilst—
ANT.   Antony, thou wouldst say.
MESS.   O, my lord !
ANT. Speak to me home ; mince not the general tongue ;
    Name Cleopatra as she is call'd in Rome.
    Rail thou in Fulvia's phrase, and taunt my faults
    With such full licence as both truth and malice   105
    Have power to utter.   O, then we bring forth weeds
    When our quick minds lie still, and our ills told us
    Is as our earing.   Fare thee well awhile.
MESS. At your noble pleasure.   [*Exit.*
ANT. From Sicyon, ho, the news ! Speak there !   110
1 ATT. The man from Sicyon—is there such an one ?
2 ATT. He stays upon your will.
ANT.   Let him appear.
    These strong Egyptian fetters I must break,
    Or lose myself in dotage.

        Enter another MESSENGER *with a letter.*

              What are you ?
2 MESS. Fulvia thy wife is dead.
ANT.   Where died she ?   115
2 MESS. In Sicyon.
    Her length of sickness, with what else more serious
    Importeth thee to know, this bears.   [*Gives the letter.*
ANT.   Forbear me.
                   [*Exit* MESSENGER.
    There's a great spirit gone ! Thus did I desire it.
    What our contempts doth often hurl from us   120
    We wish it ours again ; the present pleasure,
    By revolution low'ring, does become
    The opposite of itself.   She's good, being gone ;
    The hand could pluck her back that shov'd her on.
    I must from this enchanting queen break off.   125
    Ten thousand harms, more than the ills I know,
    My idleness doth hatch.   How now, Enobarbus !

            Re-enter ENOBARBUS.

ENO. What's your pleasure, sir ?
ANT. I must with haste from hence.
ENO. Why, then we kill all our women. We see how mortal an
    unkindness is to them ; if they suffer our departure, death's the
    word.   132
ANT. I must be gone.

ENO. Under a compelling occasion, let women die. It were pity to
cast them away for nothing, though between them and a great
cause they should be esteemed nothing. Cleopatra, catching but
the least noise of this, dies instantly; I have seen her die twenty
times upon far poorer moment. I do think there is mettle in
death, which commits some loving act upon her, she hath such
a celerity in dying.

ANT. She is cunning past man's thought.   14

ENO. Alack, sir, no! Her passions are made of nothing but the
finest part of pure love. We cannot call her winds and waters
sighs and tears; they are greater storms and tempests than
almanacs can report. This cannot be cunning in her; if it be
she makes a show'r of rain as well as Jove.

ANT. Would I had never seen her!   14'

ENO. O sir, you had then left unseen a wonderful piece of work
which not to have been blest withal would have discredited your
travel.   15'

ANT. Fulvia is dead.

ENO. Sir?

ANT. Fulvia is dead.

ENO. Fulvia?

ANT. Dead.   15

ENO. Why, sir, give the gods a thankful sacrifice. When it pleaseth
their deities to take the wife of a man from him, it shows to man
the tailors of the earth; comforting therein that when old robes
are worn out there are members to make new. If there were no
more women but Fulvia, then had you indeed a cut, and the case
to be lamented. This grief is crown'd with consolation: your
old smock brings forth a new petticoat; and indeed the tears live
in an onion that should water this sorrow.

ANT. The business she hath broached in the state   16
Cannot endure my absence.

ENO. And the business you have broach'd here cannot be without
you; especially that of Cleopatra's, which wholly depends on
your abode.

ANT. No more light answers. Let our officers   17
Have notice what we purpose. I shall break
The cause of our expedience to the Queen,
And get her leave to part. For not alone
The death of Fulvia, with more urgent touches,
Do strongly speak to us; but the letters too   17
Of many our contriving friends in Rome
Petition us at home. Sextus Pompeius
Hath given the dare to Cæsar, and commands
The empire of the sea; our slippery people,
Whose love is never link'd to the deserver   18
Till his deserts are past, begin to throw
Pompey the Great and all his dignities
Upon his son; who, high in name and power,
Higher than both in blood and life, stands up
For the main soldier; whose quality, going on,   18
The sides o' th' world may danger. Much is breeding
Which, like the courser's hair, hath yet but life
And not a serpent's poison. Say our pleasure,

172

To such whose place is under us, requires
Our quick remove from hence.   190
NO.   I shall do't.   [*Exeunt.*

SCENE III.   *Alexandria.   Cleopatra's palace.*

Enter CLEOPATRA, CHARMIAN, IRAS, *and* ALEXAS.

LEO. Where is he?
HAR.   I did not see him since.
LEO. See where he is, who's with him, what he does.
   I did not send you.   If you find him sad,
   Say I am dancing;   if in mirth, report
   That I am sudden sick.   Quick, and return.   [*Exit* ALEXAS.
HAR. Madam, methinks, if you did love him dearly,
   You do not hold the method to enforce
   The like from him.
LEO.   What should I do I do not?
HAR. In each thing give him way;   cross him in nothing.
LEO. Thou teachest like a fool—the way to lose him.   10
HAR. Tempt him not so too far;   I wish, forbear;
   In time we hate that which we often fear.

Enter ANTONY.

   But here comes Antony.
LEO.   I am sick and sullen.
NT. I am sorry to give breathing to my purpose—
LEO. Help me away, dear Charmian;   I shall fall.   15
   It cannot be thus long;   the sides of nature
   Will not sustain it.
NT.   Now, my dearest queen—
LEO. Pray you, stand farther from me.
NT.   What's the matter?
LEO. I know by that same eye there's some good news.
   What says the married woman?   You may go.   20
   Would she had never given you leave to come!
   Let her not say 'tis I that keep you here—
   I have no power upon you;   hers you are.
NT. The gods best know—
LEO.   O, never was there queen
   So mightily betray'd!   Yet at the first   25
   I saw the treasons planted.
NT.   Cleopatra—
LEO. Why should I think you can be mine and true,
   Though you in swearing shake the throned gods,
   Who have been false to Fulvia?   Riotous madness,
   To be entangled with those mouth-made vows,   30
   Which break themselves in swearing!
NT.   Most sweet queen—
LEO. Nay, pray you seek no colour for your going,
   But bid farewell, and go.   When you sued staying,
   Then was the time for words.   No going then!
   Eternity was in our lips and eyes,   35
   Bliss in our brows' bent, none our parts so poor
   But was a race of heaven.   They are so still,

                                                                173

Or thou, the greatest soldier of the world,
Art turn'd the greatest liar.

ANT.   How now, lady!

CLEO. I would I had thy inches.   Thou shouldst know   4
There were a heart in Egypt.

ANT.   Hear me, Queen :
The strong necessity of time commands
Our services awhile ; but my full heart
Remains in use with you.   Our Italy
Shines o'er with civil swords : Sextus Pompeius   4
Makes his approaches to the port of Rome ;
Equality of two domestic powers
Breed scrupulous faction ; the hated, grown to strength,
Are newly grown to love.   The condemn'd Pompey,
Rich in his father's honour, creeps apace   5
Into the hearts of such as have not thrived
Upon the present state, whose numbers threaten ;
And quietness, grown sick of rest, would purge
By any desperate change.   My more particular,
And that which most with you should safe my going,   5
Is Fulvia's death.

CLEO. Though age from folly could not give me freedom,
It does from childishness.   Can Fulvia die ?

ANT. She's dead, my Queen.
Look here, and at thy sovereign leisure read
The garboils she awak'd.   At the last, best.   6
See when and where she died.

CLEO.   O most false love !
Where be the sacred vials thou shouldst fill
With sorrowful water ?   Now I see, I see,
In Fulvia's death how mine receiv'd shall be.   6

ANT. Quarrel no more, but be prepar'd to know
The purposes I bear ; which are, or cease,
As you shall give th' advice.   By the fire
That quickens Nilus' slime, I go from hence
Thy soldier, servant, making peace or war   7
As thou affects.

CLEO.   Cut my lace, Charmian, come
But let it be ; I am quickly ill and well—
So Antony loves.

ANT.   My precious queen, forbear,
And give true evidence to his love, which stands
An honourable trial.

CLEO.   So Fulvia told me.   7
I prithee turn aside and weep for her ;
Then bid adieu to me, and say the tears
Belong to Egypt.   Good now, play one scene
Of excellent dissembling, and let it look
Like perfect honour.

ANT.   You'll heat my blood ; no more.   8

CLEO. You can do better yet ; but this is meetly.

ANT. Now, by my sword—

CLEO.   And target.   Still he mends ;
But this is not the best.   Look, prithee, Charmian,

How this Herculean Roman does become
The carriage of his chafe.   85
ANT. I'll leave you, lady.
CLEO.   Courteous lord, one word.
Sir, you and I must part—but that's not it.
Sir, you and I have lov'd—but there's not it.
That you know well.   Something it is I would—
O, my oblivion is a very Antony,   90
And I am all forgotten !
ANT.   But that your royalty
Holds idleness your subject, I should take you
For idleness itself.
CLEO.   'Tis sweating labour
To bear such idleness so near the heart
As Cleopatra this.   But, sir, forgive me ;   95
Since my becomings kill me when they do not
Eye well to you.   Your honour calls you hence ;
Therefore be deaf to my unpitied folly,
And all the gods go with you !   Upon your sword
Sit laurel victory, and smooth success   100
Be strew'd before your feet !
ANT.   Let us go.   Come.
Our separation so abides and flies
That thou, residing here, goes yet with me,
And I, hence fleeting, here remain with thee.
Away !   [Exeunt.

SCENE IV.   Rome.   Cæsar's house.

Enter OCTAVIUS CÆSAR, reading a letter ; LEPIDUS, and their TRAIN.

ÆS. You may see, Lepidus, and henceforth know,
It is not Cæsar's natural vice to hate
Our great competitor.   From Alexandria
This is the news : he fishes, drinks, and wastes
The lamps of night in revel ; is not more manlike   5
Than Cleopatra, nor the queen of Ptolemy
More womanly than he ; hardly gave audience, or
Vouchsaf'd to think he had partners.   You shall find there
A man who is the abstract of all faults
That all men follow.
LEP.   I must not think there are   10
Evils enow to darken all his goodness.
His faults, in him, seem as the spots of heaven,
More fiery by night's blackness ; hereditary
Rather than purchas'd ; what he cannot change
Than what he chooses.   15
ÆS. You are too indulgent.   Let's grant it is not
Amiss to tumble on the bed of Ptolemy,
To give a kingdom for a mirth, to sit
And keep the turn of tippling with a slave,
To reel the streets at noon, and stand the buffet   20
With knaves that smell of sweat.   Say this becomes him—
As his composure must be rare indeed
Whom these things cannot blemish—yet must Antony

No way excuse his foils when we do bear
So great weight in his lightness.   If he fill'd   25
His vacancy with his voluptuousness,
Full surfeits and the dryness of his bones
Call on him for't ! But to confound such time
That drums him from his sport and speaks as loud
As his own state and ours—'tis to be chid   30
As we rate boys who, being mature in knowledge,
Pawn their experience to their present pleasure,
And so rebel to judgment.

Enter a MESSENGER.

LEP.   Here's more news.
MESS. Thy biddings have been done ; and every hour,
Most noble Cæsar, shalt thou have report   35
How 'tis abroad.   Pompey is strong at sea,
And it appears he is belov'd of those
That only have fear'd Cæsar.   To the ports
The discontents repair, and men's reports
Give him much wrong'd.
CÆS.   I should have known no less.   40
It hath been taught us from the primal state
That he which is was wish'd until he were ;
And the ebb'd man, ne'er lov'd till ne'er worth love,
Comes dear'd by being lack'd.   This common body,
Like to a vagabond flag upon the stream,   45
Goes to and back, lackeying the varying tide,
To rot itself with motion.
MESS.   Cæsar, I bring thee word
Menecrates and Menas, famous pirates,
Make the sea serve them, which they ear and wound
With keels of every kind.   Many hot inroads   50
They make in Italy ; the borders maritime
Lack blood to think on't, and flush youth revolt.
No vessel can peep forth but 'tis as soon
Taken as seen ; for Pompey's name strikes more
Than could his war resisted.
CÆS.   Antony,   55
Leave thy lascivious wassails.   When thou once
Was beaten from Modena, where thou slew'st
Hirtius and Pansa, consuls, at thy heel
Did famine follow ; whom thou fought'st against,
Though daintily brought up, with patience more   60
Than savages could suffer.   Thou didst drink
The stale of horses and the gilded puddle
Which beasts would cough at.   Thy palate then did deign
The roughest berry on the rudest hedge ;
Yea, like the stag when snow the pasture sheets,   65
The barks of trees thou brows'd.   On the Alps
It is reported thou didst eat strange flesh,
Which some did die to look on.   And all this—
It wounds thine honour that I speak it now—
Was borne so like a soldier that thy cheek   70
So much as lank'd not.

LEP. 'Tis pity of him.
CÆS.   Let his shames quickly
    Drive him to Rome. 'Tis time we twain
    Did show ourselves i' th' field ; and to that end
    Assemble we immediate council. Pompey   75
    Thrives in our idleness.
LEP.   To-morrow, Cæsar,
    I shall be furnish'd to inform you rightly
    Both what by sea and land I can be able
    To front this present time.
CÆS.   Till which encounter
    It is my business too. Farewell.   80
LEP. Farewell, my lord. What you shall know meantime
    Of stirs abroad, I shall beseech you, sir,
    To let me be partaker.
CÆS.   Doubt not, sir ;
    I knew it for my bond.   *Exeunt.*

SCENE V. *Alexandria. Cleopatra's palace.*

Enter CLEOPATRA, CHARMIAN, IRAS, *and* MARDIAN.

CLEO. Charmian !
CHAR. Madam ?
CLEO. Ha, ha !
    Give me to drink mandragora.
CHAR.   Why, madam ?
CLEO. That I might sleep out this great gap of time   5
    My Antony is away.
CHAR.   You think of him too much.
CLEO. O, 'tis treason !
CHAR.   Madam, I trust, not so.
CLEO. Thou, eunuch Mardian !
MAR. What's your Highness' pleasure ?
CLEO. Not now to hear thee sing ; I take no pleasure
    In aught an eunuch has. 'Tis well for thee   10
    That, being unseminar'd, thy freer thoughts
    May not fly forth of Egypt. Hast thou affections ?
MAR. Yes, gracious madam.
CLEO. Indeed ?
MAR. Not in deed, madam ; for I can do nothing   15
    But what indeed is honest to be done.
    Yet have I fierce affections, and think
    What Venus did with Mars.
CLEO.   O Charmian,
    Where think'st thou he is now ? Stands he or sits he ?
    Or does he walk ? or is he on his horse ?   20
    O happy horse, to bear the weight of Antony !
    Do bravely, horse ; for wot'st thou whom thou mov'st ?
    The demi-Atlas of this earth, the arm
    And burgonet of men. He's speaking now,
    Or murmuring ' Where's my serpent of old Nile ? '   25
    For so he calls me. Now I feed myself
    With most delicious poison. Think on me,
    That am with Phœbus' amorous pinches black,

And wrinkled deep in time ? Broad-fronted Cæsar,
When thou wast here above the ground, I was   30
A morsel for a monarch ; and great Pompey
Would stand and make his eyes grow in my brow ;
There would he anchor his aspect and die
With looking on his life.

Enter ALEXAS.

ALEX. Sovereign of Egypt, hail !
CLEO. How much unlike art thou Mark Antony !   35
    Yet, coming from him, that great med'cine hath
    With his tinct gilded thee.
    How goes it with my brave Mark Antony ?
ALEX. Last thing he did, dear Queen,
    He kiss'd—the last of many doubled kisses—   40
    This orient pearl.   His speech sticks in my heart.
CLEO. Mine ear must pluck it thence.
ALEX.   ' Good friend,' quoth he
    ' Say the firm Roman to great Egypt sends
    This treasure of an oyster ; at whose foot,
    To mend the petty present, I will piece   45
    Her opulent throne with kingdoms.   All the East,
    Say thou, shall call her mistress.'   So he nodded,
    And soberly did mount an arm-gaunt steed,
    Who neigh'd so high that what I would have spoke
    Was beastly dumb'd by him.
CLEO.   What, was he sad or merry ?   50
ALEX. Like to the time o' th' year between the extremes
    Of hot and cold ; he was nor sad nor merry.
CLEO. O well-divided disposition ! Note him,
    Note him, good Charmian ; 'tis the man ; but note him !
    He was not sad, for he would shine on those   55
    That make their looks by his ; he was not merry,
    Which seem'd to tell them his remembrance lay
    In Egypt with his joy ; but between both.
    O heavenly mingle ! Be'st thou sad or merry,
    The violence of either thee becomes,   60
    So does it no man else.   Met'st thou my posts ?
ALEX. Ay, madam, twenty several messengers.
    Why do you send so thick ?
CLEO.   Who's born that day
    When I forget to send to Antony
    Shall die a beggar.   Ink and paper, Charmian.   65
    Welcome, my good Alexas.   Did I, Charmian,
    Ever love Cæsar so ?
CHAR.   O that brave Cæsar !
CLEO. Be chok'd with such another emphasis !
    Say ' the brave Antony '.
CHAR.   The valiant Cæsar !
CLEO. By Isis, I will give thee bloody teeth   70
    If thou with Cæsar paragon again
    My man of men.
CHAR.   By your most gracious pardon,
    I sing but after you.

CLEO.   My salad days,
    When I was green in judgment, cold in blood,
    To say as I said then.   But come, away!   75
    Get me ink and paper.
    He shall have every day a several greeting,
    Or I'll unpeople Egypt.

                                                    [*Exeunt.*

ACT TWO

SCENE I. *Messina. Pompey's House.*
Enter POMPEY, MENECRATES *and* MENAS, *in warlike manner.*

POM. If the great gods be just, they shall assist
    The deeds of justest men.
MENE.   Know, worthy Pompey,
    That what they do delay they not deny.
POM. Whiles we are suitors to their throne, decays
    The thing we sue for.
MENE.   We, ignorant of ourselves,   5
    Beg often our own harms, which the wise pow'rs
    Deny us for our good; so find we profit
    By losing of our prayers.
POM.   I shall do well.
    The people love me, and the sea is mine;
    My powers are crescent, and my auguring hope   10
    Says it will come to th' full.   Mark Antony
    In Egypt sits at dinner, and will make
    No wars without doors.   Cæsar gets money where
    He loses hearts.   Lepidus flatters both,
    Of both is flatter'd; but he neither loves,   15
    Nor either cares for him.
MEN.   Cæsar and Lepidus
    Are in the field.   A mighty strength they carry.
POM. Where have you this? 'Tis false.
MEN.   From Silvius, sir.
POM. He dreams.   I know they are in Rome together,
    Looking for Antony.   But all the charms of love,   20
    Salt Cleopatra, soften thy wan'd lip!
    Let witchcraft join with beauty, lust with both;
    Tie up the libertine in a field of feasts,
    Keep his brain fuming.   Epicurean cooks
    Sharpen with cloyless sauce his appetite,   25
    That sleep and feeding may prorogue his honour
    Even till a Lethe'd dullness—

                            Enter VARRIUS.

                            How now, Varrius!
VAR. This is most certain that I shall deliver:
    Mark Antony is every hour in Rome
    Expected.   Since he went from Egypt 'tis   30
    A space for farther travel.
POM.   I could have given less matter
    A better ear.   Menas, I did not think

                                                              179

This amorous surfeiter would have donn'd his helm
For such a petty war ; his soldiership
Is twice the other twain.   But let us rear   35
The higher our opinion, that our stirring
Can from the lap of Egypt's widow pluck
The ne'er-lust-wearied Antony.

MEN.   I cannot hope
Cæsar and Antony shall well greet together.
His wife that's dead did trespasses to Cæsar ;   40
His brother warr'd upon him ; although, I think,
Not mov'd by Antony.

POM.   I know not, Menas,
How lesser enmities may give way to greater.
Were't not that we stand up against them all,
'Twere pregnant they should square between themselves ;   45
For they have entertained cause enough
To draw their swords.   But how the fear of us
May cement their divisions, and bind up
The petty difference we yet not know.
Be't as our gods will have't !   It only stands   50
Our lives upon to use our strongest hands.
Come, Menas.   [*Exeunt.*

SCENE II.   *Rome.   The house of Lepidus.*

Enter ENOBARBUS *and* LEPIDUS.

LEP. Good Enobarbus, 'tis a worthy deed,
And shall become you well, to entreat your captain
To soft and gentle speech.

ENO.   I shall entreat him
To answer like himself.   If Cæsar move him,
Let Antony look over Cæsar's head   5
And speak as loud as Mars.   By Jupiter,
Were I the wearer of Antonius' beard,
I would not shave't to-day.

LEP.   'Tis not a time
For private stomaching.

ENO.   Every time
Serves for the matter that is then born in't.   10
LEP. But small to greater matters must give way.
ENO. Not if the small come first.

LEP.   Your speech is passion
But pray you stir no embers up.   Here comes
The noble Antony.

Enter ANTONY *and* VENTIDIUS.

ENO.   And yonder, Cæsar.

Enter CÆSAR, MÆCENAS, *and* AGRIPPA.

ANT. If we compose well here, to Parthia.   15
Hark, Ventidius.
CÆS. I do not know, Mæcenas.   Ask Agrippa.
LEP. Noble friends,
That which combin'd us was most great, and let not

A leaner action rend us.   What's amiss,
May it be gently heard.   When we debate   20
Our trivial difference loud, we do commit
Murder in healing wounds.   Then, noble partners,
The rather for I earnestly beseech,
Touch you the sourest points with sweetest terms,
Nor curstness grow to th' matter.

ANT.   'Tis spoken well.   25
Were we before our armies, and to fight,
I should do thus.   [Flourish.

CÆS. Welcome to Rome.

ANT. Thank you.

CÆS. Sit.

ANT. Sit, sir.

CÆS. Nay, then.   [They sit.

ANT. I learn you take things ill which are not so,
Or being, concern you not.

CÆS.   I must be laugh'd at
If, or for nothing or a little, I   35
Should say myself offended, and with you
Chiefly i' the world ; more laugh'd at that I should
Once name you derogately when to sound your name
It not concern'd me.

ANT.   My being in Egypt, Cæsar,
What was't to you ?   40

CÆS. No more than my residing here at Rome
Might be to you in Egypt.   Yet, if you there
Did practise on my state, your being in Egypt
Might be my question.

ANT.   How intend you—practis'd ?

CÆS.   You may be pleas'd to catch at mine intent 45
By what did here befall me.   Your wife and brother
Made wars upon me, and their contestation
Was theme for you ; you were the word of war.

ANT. You do mistake your business ; my brother never
Did urge me in his act.   I did inquire it,   50
And have my learning from some true reports
That drew their swords with you.   Did he not rather
Discredit my authority with yours,
And make the wars alike against my stomach,
Having alike your cause ? Of this my letters   55
Before did satisfy you.   If you'll patch a quarrel,
As matter whole you have not to make it with,
It must not be with this.

CÆS.   You praise yourself
By laying defects of judgment to me ; but
You patch'd up your excuses.

ANT.   Not so, not so ;   60
I know you could not lack, I am certain on't,
Very necessity of this thought, that I,
Your partner in the cause 'gainst which he fought,
Could not with graceful eyes attend those wars
Which fronted mine own peace.   As for my wife,   65
I would you had her spirit in such another !

The third o' th' world is yours, which with a snaffle
You may pace easy, but not such a wife.

ENO. Would we had all such wives, that the men might go to wars with
the women !   70

ANT. So much uncurbable, her garboils, Cæsar,
Made out of her impatience—which not wanted
Shrewdness of policy too—I grieving grant
Did you too much disquiet.   For that you must
But say I could not help it.

CÆS.   I wrote to you   75
When rioting in Alexandria ; you
Did pocket up my letters, and with taunts
Did gibe my missive out of audience.

ANT.   Sir,
He fell upon me ere admitted.   Then
Three kings I had newly feasted, and did want   80
Of what I was i' th' morning ; but next day
I told him of myself, which was as much
As to have ask'd him pardon.   Let this fellow
Be nothing of our strife ; if we contend,
Out of our question wipe him.

CÆS.   You have broken   85
The article of your oath, which you shall never
Have tongue to charge me with.

LEP.   Soft, Cæsar !

ANT.   No ;
Lepidus, let him speak.
The honour is sacred which he talks on now,
Supposing that I lack'd it.   But on, Cæsar :   90
The article of my oath—

CÆS. To lend me arms and aid when I requir'd them,
The which you both denied.

ANT.   Neglected, rather ;
And then when poisoned hours had bound me up
From mine own knowledge.   As nearly as I may,   95
I'll play the penitent to you ; but mine honesty
Shall not make poor my greatness, nor my power
Work without it.   Truth is, that Fulvia,
To have me out of Egypt, made wars here ;
For which myself, the ignorant motive, do   100
So far ask pardon as befits mine honour
To stoop in such a case.

LEP.   'Tis noble spoken.

MÆC. If it might please you to enforce no further
The griefs between ye—to forget them quite
Were to remember that the present need   105
Speaks to atone you.

LEP.   Worthily spoken, Mæcenas.

ENO. Or, if you borrow one another's love for the instant, you
may, when you hear no more words of Pompey, return it again.
You shall have time to wrangle in when you have nothing else
to do.

ANT. Thou art a soldier only.   Speak no more.   111

ENO. That truth should be silent I had almost forgot.

ANT. You wrong this presence; therefore speak no more.
ENO. Go to, then—your considerate stone!
CÆS. I do not much dislike the matter, but   115
  The manner of his speech; for't cannot be
  We shall remain in friendship, our conditions
  So diff'ring in their acts.   Yet if I knew
  What hoop should hold us stanch, from edge to edge
  O' th' world, I would pursue it.   119
AGR. Give me leave, Cæsar.
CÆS.   Speak, Agrippa.
AGR. Thou hast a sister by the mother's side,
  Admir'd Octavia.   Great Mark Antony
  Is now a widower.
CÆS.   Say not so, Agrippa.
  If Cleopatra heard you, your reproof   125
  Were well deserv'd of rashness.
ANT. I am not married, Cæsar.   Let me hear
  Agrippa further speak.
AGR. To hold you in perpetual amity,
  To make you brothers, and to knit your hearts   130
  With an unslipping knot, take Antony
  Octavia to his wife; whose beauty claims
  No worse a husband than the best of men;
  Whose virtue and whose general graces speak
  That which none else can utter.   By this marriage   135
  All little jealousies, which now seem great,
  And all great fears, which now import their dangers,
  Would then be nothing.   Truths would be tales,
  Where now half tales be truths.   Her love to both
  Would each to other, and all loves to both,   140
  Draw after her.   Pardon what I have spoke;
  For 'tis a studied, not a present thought,
  By duty ruminated.
ANT.   Will Cæsar speak?
CÆS. Not till he hears how Antony is touch'd
  With what is spoke already.
ANT.   What power is in Agrippa,   145
  If I would say 'Agrippa, be it so',
  To make this good?
CÆS.   The power of Cæsar, and
  His power unto Octavia.
ANT.   May I never
  To this good purpose, that so fairly shows,
  Dream of impediment!   Let me have thy hand.   150
  Further this act of grace; and from this hour
  The heart of brothers govern in our loves
  And sway our great designs!
CÆS.   There is my hand.
  A sister I bequeath you, whom no brother
  Did ever love so dearly.   Let her live   155
  To join our kingdoms and our hearts; and never
  Fly off our loves again!
LEP.   Happily, amen!
ANT. I did not think to draw my sword 'gainst Pompey;

For he hath laid strange courtesies and great
Of late upon me.   I must thank him only,   160
Lest my remembrance suffer ill report ;
At heel of that, defy him.

LEP.   Time calls upon's.
Of us must Pompey presently be sought,
Or else he seeks out us.

ANT.   Where lies he ?   164

CÆS. About the Mount Misenum.

ANT. What is his strength by land ?

CÆS. Great and increasing ; but by sea
He is an absolute master.

ANT   So is the fame.
Would we had spoke together !   Haste we for it.
Yet, ere we put ourselves in arms, dispatch we
The business we have talk'd of.

CÆS.   With most gladness ;   170
And do invite you to my sister's view,
Whither straight I'll lead you.

ANT.   Let us, Lepidus,
Not lack your company.

LEP.   Noble Antony,
Not sickness should detain me.

            [*Flourish. Exeunt all but* ENOBARBUS, AGRIPPA, MÆCENAS.

MÆC. Welcome from Egypt, sir.   175

ENO. Half the heart of Cæsar, worthy Mæcenas !   My honourable
    friend, Agrippa !

AGR. Good Enobarbus !

MÆC. We have cause to be glad that matters are so well digested.
    You stay'd well by't in Egypt.   180

ENO. Ay, sir ; we did sleep day out of countenance and made the night
    light with drinking.

MÆC. Eight wild boars roasted whole at a breakfast, and but twelve
    persons there.   Is this true ?

ENO. This was but as a fly by an eagle.   We had much more mon-
    strous matter of feast, which worthily deserved noting.

MÆC. She's a most triumphant lady, if report be square to her.

ENO. When she first met Mark Antony she purs'd up his heart, upon
    the river of Cydnus.   191

AGR. There she appear'd indeed !   Or my reporter devis'd well for her.

ENO. I will tell you.
    The barge she sat in, like a burnish'd throne,   195
    Burn'd on the water.   The poop was beaten gold ;
    Purple the sails, and so perfumed that
    The winds were love-sick with them ; the oars were silver,
    Which to the tune of flutes kept stroke, and made
    The water which they beat to follow faster,   200
    As amorous of their strokes.   For her own person,
    It beggar'd all description.   She did lie
    In her pavilion, cloth-of-gold, of tissue,
    O'erpicturing that Venus where we see
    The fancy out-work nature.   On each side her   205
    Stood pretty dimpled boys, like smiling Cupids,
    With divers-colour'd fans, whose wind did seem

To glow the delicate cheeks which they did cool,
And what they undid did.

AGR.   O, rare for Antony!

ENO. Her gentlewomen, like the Nereides,   210
So many mermaids, tended her i' th' eyes,
And made their bends adornings.   At the helm
A seeming mermaid steers.   The silken tackle
Swell with the touches of those flower-soft hands
That yarely frame the office.   From the barge   215
A strange invisible perfume hits the sense
Of the adjacent wharfs.   The city cast
Her people out upon her; and Antony,
Enthron'd i' th' market-place, did sit alone,
Whistling to th' air; which, but for vacancy,   220
Had gone to gaze on Cleopatra too,
And made a gap in nature.

AGR.   Rare Egyptian!

ENO. Upon her landing, Antony sent to her,
Invited her to supper.   She replied
It should be better he became her guest;   225
Which she entreated.   Our courteous Antony,
Whom ne'er the word of 'No' woman heard speak,
Being barber'd ten times o'er, goes to the feast,
And for his ordinary pays his heart
For what his eyes eat only.

AGR.   Royal wench!   230
She made great Cæsar lay his sword to bed.
He ploughed her, and she cropp'd.

ENO.   I saw her once
Hop forty paces through the public street;
And, having lost her breath, she spoke, and panted,
That she did make defect perfection,   235
And, breathless, pow'r breathe forth.

MÆC. Now Antony must leave her utterly.

ENO. Never!   He will not.
Age cannot wither her, nor custom stale
Her infinite variety.   Other women cloy   240
The appetites they feed, but she makes hungry
Where most she satisfies; for vilest things
Become themselves in her, that the holy priests
Bless her when she is riggish.

MÆC. If beauty, wisdom, modesty, can settle   245
The heart of Antony, Octavia is
A blessed lottery to him.

AGR.   Let us go.
Good Enobarbus, make yourself my guest
Whilst you abide here.

ENO. Humbly, sir, I thank you.   [Exeunt.

SCENE III.   Rome.   Cæsar's house.

Enter ANTONY, CÆSAR, OCTAVIA between them.

ANT. The world and my great office will sometimes
Divide me from your bosom.

OCTA.   All which time
Before the gods my knee shall bow my prayers
To them for you.
ANT.   Good night, sir. My Octavia,
Read not my blemishes in the world's report.   5
I have not kept my square ; but that to come
Shall all be done by th' rule. Good night, dear lady.
OCTA. Good night, sir.
CÆS. Good night.   [*Exeunt* CÆSAR *and* OCTAVIA.

          Enter SOOTHSAYER.

ANT. Now, sirrah, you do wish yourself in Egypt ?   10
SOOTH. Would I had never come from thence, nor you thither !
ANT. If you can—your reason.
SOOTH. I see it in my motion, have it not in my tongue ; but yet hie
    you to Egypt again.   15
ANT. Say to me,
Whose fortunes shall rise higher, Cæsar's or mine ?
SOOTH. Cæsar's.
Therefore, O Antony, stay not by his side.
Thy dæmon, that thy spirit which keeps thee, is   20
Noble, courageous, high, unmatchable,
Where Cæsar's is not ; but near him thy angel
Becomes a fear, as being o'erpow'r'd. Therefore
Make space enough between you.
ANT.   Speak this no more.
SOOTH. To none but thee ; no more but when to thee.   25
If thou dost play with him at any game,
Thou art sure to lose ; and of that natural luck
He beats thee 'gainst the odds. Thy lustre thickens
When he shines by. I say again, thy spirit
Is all afraid to govern thee near him ;   30
But, he away, 'tis noble.
ANT.   Get thee gone.
Say to Ventidius I would speak with him.   [*Exit* SOOTHSAYER.
He shall to Parthia.—Be it art or hap,
He hath spoken true. The very dice obey him ;
And in our sports my better cunning faints   35
Under his chance. If we draw lots, he speeds ;
His cocks do win the battle still of mine,
When it is all to nought, and his quails ever
Beat mine, inhoop'd, at odds. I will to Egypt ;
And though I make this marriage for my peace,   40
I' th' East my pleasure lies.

          Enter VENTIDIUS.

          O, come, Ventidius,
You must to Parthia. Your commission's ready ;
Follow me and receive't.   [*Exeunt.*

SCENE IV. *Rome. A street.*

Enter LEPIDUS, MÆCENAS, and AGRIPPA.

LEP. Trouble yourselves no further.   Pray you hasten
  Your generals after.
AGR.   Sir, Mark Antony
  Will e'en but kiss Octavia, and we'll follow.
LEP. Till I shall see you in your soldier's dress,
  Which will become you both, farewell.
MÆC.   We shall,   5
  As I conceive the journey, be at th' Mount
  Before you, Lepidus.
LEP.   Your way is shorter ;
  My purposes do draw me much about.
  You'll win two days upon me.
BOTH.   Sir, good success !
LEP. Farewell.
                                              [*Exeunt.*

SCENE V. *Alexandria. Cleopatra's palace.*

Enter CLEOPATRA, CHARMIAN, IRAS, and ALEXAS.

CLEO. Give me some music—music, moody food
  Of us that trade in love.
ALL.   The music, ho !

Enter MARDIAN the EUNUCH.

CLEO. Let it alone ! Let's to billiards.   Come, Charmian.
CHAR. My arm is sore ; best play with Mardian.
CLEO. As well a woman with an eunuch play'd   5
  As with a woman.   Come, you'll play with me, sir ?
MAR. As well as I can, madam.
CLEO. And when good will is show'd, though't come too short,
  The actor may plead pardon.   I'll none now.
  Give me mine angle—we'll to th' river.   There,   10
  My music playing far off, I will betray
  Tawny-finn'd fishes ; my bended hook shall pierce
  Their slimy jaws ; and as I draw them up
  I'll think them every one an Antony,
  And say ' Ah ha ! Y'are caught '.
CHAR.   'Twas merry when   15
  You wager'd on your angling ; when your diver
  Did hang a salt fish on his hook, which he
  With fervency drew up.
CLEO.   That time ? O times
  I laugh'd him out of patience ; and that night
  I laugh'd him into patience ; and next morn,   20
  Ere the ninth hour, I drunk him to his bed,
  Then put my tires and mantles on him, whilst
  I wore his sword Philippan.

Enter a MESSENGER.

                    O ! from Italy ?
  Ram thou thy fruitful tidings in mine ears,

That long time have been barren.
MESS.   Madam, madam—   25
CLEO. Antony's dead ! If thou say so, villain,
    Thou kill'st thy mistress ; but well and free,
    If thou so yield him, there is gold, and here
    My bluest veins to kiss—a hand that kings
    Have lipp'd, and trembled kissing.   30
MESS. First, madam, he is well.
CLEO.   Why, there's more gold.
    But, sirrah, mark, we use
    To say the dead are well.   Bring it to that,
    The gold I give thee will I melt and pour
    Down thy ill-uttering throat.   35
MESS. Good madam, hear me.
CLEO.   Well, go to, I will.
    But there's no goodness in thy face.   If Antony
    Be free and healthful—why so tart a favour
    To trumpet such good tidings ? If not well,
    Thou shouldst come like a Fury crown'd with snakes,   40
    Not like a formal man.
MESS.   Will't please you hear me ?
CLEO. I have a mind to strike thee ere thou speak'st.
    Yet, if thou say Antony lives, is well,
    Or friends with Cæsar, or not captive to him,
    I'll set thee in a shower of gold, and hail   45
    Rich pearls upon thee.
MESS.   Madam, he's well.
CLEO.   Well said.
MESS. And friends with Cæsar.
CLEO.   Th'art an honest man.
MESS. Cæsar and he are greater friends than ever.
CLEO. Make thee a fortune from me.
MESS.   But yet, madam—
CLEO. I do not like ' but yet '.   It does allay   50
    The good precedence ; fie upon ' but yet ' !
    ' But yet ' is as a gaoler to bring forth
    Some monstrous malefactor.   Prithee, friend,
    Pour out the pack of matter to mine ear,
    The good and bad together.   He's friends with Cæsar ;   55
    In state of health, thou say'st ; and, thou say'st, free.
MESS. Free, madam ! No ; I made no such report.
    He's bound unto Octavia.
CLEO.   For what good turn ?
MESS. For the best turn i' th' bed.
CLEO.   I am pale, Charmian.
MESS. Madam, he's married to Octavia.   60
CLEO. The most infectious pestilence upon thee ! [Strikes him down.
MESS. Good madam, patience.
CLEO.   What say you ? Hence, [Strikes him.
    Horrible villain ! or I'll spurn thine eyes
    Like balls before me ; I'll unhair thy head ;
                                    [She hales him up and down.
    Thou shalt be whipp'd with wire and stew'd in brine,   65
    Smarting in ling'ring pickle.

MESS.   Gracious madam,
  I that do bring the news made not the match.
CLEO. Say 'tis not so, a province I will give thee,
  And make thy fortunes proud. The blow thou hadst
  Shall make thy peace for moving me to rage ;   70
  And I will boot thee with what gift beside
  Thy modesty can beg.
MESS.   He's married, madam.
CLEO. Rogue, thou hast liv'd too long.   [*Draws a knife.*
MESS.   Nay, then I'll run.
  What mean you, madam ? I have made no fault.   [*Exit.*
CHAR. Good madam, keep yourself within yourself :   75
  The man is innocent.
CLEO. Some innocents scape not the thunderbolt.
  Melt Egypt into Nile ! and kindly creatures
  Turn all to serpents ! Call the slave again.
  Though I am mad, I will not bite him.   Call !   80
CHAR. He is afear'd to come.
CLEO.   I will not hurt him.
  These hands do lack nobility, that they strike
  A meaner than myself ; since I myself
  Have given myself the cause.

Enter the MESSENGER *again.*

                 Come hither, sir.
  Though it be honest, it is never good   85
  To bring bad news. Give to a gracious message
  An host of tongues ; but let ill tidings tell
  Themselves when they be felt.
MESS.   I have done my duty.
CLEO. Is he married ?
  I cannot hate thee worser than I do   90
  If thou again say ' Yes '.
MESS.   He's married, madam.
CLEO. The gods confound thee ! Dost thou hold there still ?
MESS. Should I lie, madam ?
CLEO.   O, I would thou didst,
  So half my Egypt were submerg'd and made
  A cistern for scal'd snakes ! Go, get thee hence.   95
  Hadst thou Narcissus in thy face, to me
  Thou wouldst appear most ugly. He is married ?
MESS. I crave your Highness' pardon.
CLEO.   He is married ?
MESS. Take no offence that I would not offend you ;
  To punish me for what you make me do   100
  Seems much unequal. He's married to Octavia.
CLEO. O, that his fault should make a knave of thee
  That art not what th'art sure of ! Get thee hence.
  The merchandise which thou hast brought from Rome
  Are all too dear for me. Lie they upon thy hand,   105
  And be undone by 'em !   [*Exit* MESSENGER.
CHAR.   Good your Highness, patience.
CLEO. In praising Antony I have disprais'd Cæsar.
CHAR. Many times, madam.

CLEO. I am paid for't now. Lead me from hence,
I faint. O Iras, Charmian ! 'Tis no matter.   110
Go to the fellow, good Alexas ; bid him
Report the feature of Octavia, her years,
Her inclination ; let him not leave out
The colour of her hair. Bring me word quickly. [*Exit* ALEXAS.
Let him for ever go—let him not, Charmian—   115
Though he be painted one way like a Gorgon,
The other way's a Mars.   [*To* MARDIAN.
Bid you Alexas
Bring me word how tall she is.—Pity me, Charmian,
But do not speak to me. Lead me to my chamber. [*Exeunt.*

SCENE VI. *Near Misenum.*

Flourish. Enter POMPEY *and* MENAS *at one door, with drum and
trumpet ; at another,* CÆSAR, ANTONY, LEPIDUS, ENOBARBUS, MÆCENAS,
   AGRIPPA, *with* SOLDIERS *marching.*

POM. Your hostages I have, so have you mine ;
And we shall talk before we fight.
CÆS.   Most meet
That first we come to words ; and therefore have we
Our written purposes before us sent ;
Which if thou hast considered, let us know   5
If 'twill tie up thy discontented sword
And carry back to Sicily much tall youth
That else must perish here.
POM.   To you all three,
The senators alone of this great world,
Chief factors for the gods : I do not know   10
Wherefore my father should revengers want,
Having a son and friends, since Julius Cæsar,
Who at Philippi the good Brutus ghosted,
There saw you labouring for him. What was't
That mov'd pale Cassius to conspire ? and what   15
Made the all-honour'd honest Roman, Brutus,
With the arm'd rest, courtiers of beauteous freedom,
To drench the Capitol, but that they would
Have one man but a man ? And that is it
Hath made me rig my navy, at whose burden   20
The anger'd ocean foams ; with which I meant
To scourge th' ingratitude that despiteful Rome
Cast on my noble father.
CÆS.   Take your time.
ANT. Thou canst not fear us, Pompey, with thy sails ;
We'll speak with thee at sea ; at land thou know'st   25
How much we do o'er-count thee.
POM.   At land, indeed,
Thou dost o'er-count me of my father's house.
But since the cuckoo builds not for himself,
Remain in't as thou mayst.
LEP.   Be pleas'd to tell us—
For this is from the present—how you take   30
The offers we have sent you.

CÆS.   There's the point.
ANT. Which do not be entreated to, but weigh
    What it is worth embrac'd.
CÆS.   And what may follow,
    To try a larger fortune.
POM.   You have made me offer
    Of Sicily, Sardinia ; and I must   35
    Rid all the sea of pirates ; then to send
    Measures of wheat to Rome ; this 'greed upon,
    To part with unhack'd edges and bear back
    Our targes undinted.
ALL.   That's our offer.
POM.   Know, then,
    I came before you here a man prepar'd   40
    To take this offer ; but Mark Antony
    Put me to some impatience. Though I lose
    The praise of it by telling, you must know,
    When Cæsar and your brother were at blows,
    Your mother came to Sicily and did find   45
    Her welcome friendly.
ANT.   I have heard it, Pompey,
    And am well studied for a liberal thanks
    Which I do owe you.
POM.   Let me have your hand.
    I did not think, sir, to have met you here.
ANT. The beds i' th' East are soft ; and thanks to you,   50
    That call'd me timelier than my purpose hither ;
    For I gave gained by't.
CÆS.   Since I saw you last
    There is a change upon you.
POM.   Well, I know not
    What counts harsh fortune casts upon my face ;
    But in my bosom shall she never come   55
    To make my heart her vassal.
LEP.   Well met here.
POM. I hope so, Lepidus. Thus we are agreed.
    I crave our composition may be written,
    And seal'd between us.
CÆS.   That's the next to do.
POM. We'll feast each other ere we part, and let's   60
    Draw lots who shall begin.
ANT.   That will I, Pompey.
POM. No, Antony, take the lot ;
    But, first or last, your fine Egyptian cookery
    Shall have the fame. I have heard that Julius Cæsar
    Grew fat with feasting there.
ANT.   You have heard much.   65
POM. I have fair meanings, sir.
ANT.   And fair words to them.
POM. Then so much have I heard ;
    And I have heard Apollodorus carried—
ENO. No more of that ! He did so.
POM.   What, I pray you ?
ENO. A certain queen to Cæsar in a mattress.   70

POM. I know thee now.   How far'st thou, soldier ?

ENO.   Well ;
    And well am like to do, for I perceive
    Four feasts are toward.

POM.   Let me shake thy hand.
    I never hated thee ; I have seen thee fight,
    When I have envied thy behaviour.

ENO.   Sir,   75
    I never lov'd you much ; but I ha' prais'd ye
    When you have well deserv'd ten times as much
    As I have said you did.

POM.   Enjoy thy plainness ;
    It nothing ill becomes thee.
    Aboard my galley I invite you all.   80
    Will you lead, lords ?

ALL. Show's the way, sir.

POM.   Come.
              [*Exeunt all but* ENOBARBUS *and* MENAS.

MEN. [*Aside.*] Thy father, Pompey, would ne'er have made this
    treaty.—
    You and I have known, sir.

ENO. At sea, I think.

MEN. We have, sir.   85

ENO. You have done well by water.

MEN. And you by land.

ENO. I will praise any man that will praise me ; though it cannot be
    denied what I have done by land.

MEN. Nor what I have done by water.   90

ENO. Yes, something you can deny for your own safety : you have
    been a great thief by sea.

MEN. And you by land.

ENO. There I deny my land service.   But give me your hand, Menas ;
    if our eyes had authority, here they might take two thieves kissing.

MEN. All men's faces are true, whatsome'er their hands are.   97

ENO. But there is never a fair woman has a true face.

MEN. No slander : they steal hearts.

ENO. We came hither to fight with you.   100

MEN. For my part, I am sorry it is turn'd to a drinking.   Pompey
    doth this day laugh away his fortune.

ENO. If he do, sure he cannot weep't back again.

MEN. Y'have said, sir.   We look'd not for Mark Antony here.   Pray
    you, is he married to Cleopatra ?   105

ENO. Cæsar's sister is call'd Octavia.

MEN. True, sir ; she was the wife of Caius Marcellus.

ENO. But she is now the wife of Marcus Antonius.

MEN. Pray ye, sir ?

ENO. 'Tis true.

MEN. Then is Cæsar and he for ever knit together.   111

ENO. If I were bound to divine of this unity, I would not prophesy so.

MEN. I think the policy of that purpose made more in the marriage
    than the love of the parties.

ENO. I think so too.   But you shall find the band that seems to tie
    their friendship together will be the very strangler of their amity :
    Octavia is of a holy, cold, and still conversation.   119

IEN. Who would not have his wife so?

NO. Not he that himself is not so; which is Mark Antony. He will to his Egyptian dish again; then shall the sighs of Octavia blow the fire up in Cæsar, and, as I said before, that which is the strength of their amity shall prove the immediate author of their variance. Antony will use his affection where it is; he married but his occasion here.　　　　　127

IEN. And thus it may be. Come, sir, will you aboard? I have a health for you.

NO. I shall take it, sir. We have us'd our throats in Egypt.

IEN. Come, let's away.　　　　　[Exeunt.

SCENE VII. On board Pompey's galley, off Misenum.

Music plays. Enter two or three SERVANTS with a banquet.

SERV. Here they'll be, man. Some o' their plants are ill-rooted already; the least wind i' th' world will blow them down.

SERV. Lepidus is high-colour'd.

SERV. They have made him drink alms-drink.　　　　　5

SERV. As they pinch one another by the disposition, he cries out 'No more!'; reconciles them to his entreaty and himself to th' drink.

SERV. But it raises the greater war between him and his discretion.

SERV. Why, this it is to have a name in great men's fellowship. I had as lief have a reed that will do me no service as a partizan I could not heave.　　　　　13

SERV. To be call'd into a huge sphere, and not to be seen to move in't, are the holes where eyes should be, which pitifully disaster the cheeks.　　　　　16

A sennet sounded. Enter CÆSAR, ANTONY, LEPIDUS, POMPEY, AGRIPPA, MÆCENAS, ENOBARBUS, MENAS, with other CAPTAINS.

NT. [To CÆSAR.] Thus do they, sir: they take the flow o' th' Nile
　　By certain scales i' th' pyramid; they know
　　By th' height, the lowness, or the mean, if dearth
　　Or foison follow. The higher Nilus swells　　　　　20
　　The more it promises; as it ebbs, the seedsman
　　Upon the slime and ooze scatters his grain,
　　And shortly comes to harvest.

EP. Y'have strange serpents there.

NT. Ay, Lepidus.　　　　　25

EP. Your serpent of Egypt is bred now of your mud by the operation of your sun; so is your crocodile.

NT. They are so.

OM. Sit—and some wine! A health to Lepidus!

EP. I am not so well as I should be, but I'll ne'er out.

NO. Not till you have slept. I fear me you'll be in till then.

EP. Nay, certainly, I have heard the Ptolemies' pyramises are very goodly things. Without contradiction I have heard that.　　　　　35

KEN. [Aside to POMPEY.] Pompey, a word.

OM. [Aside to MENAS.] Say in mine ear; what is't?

KEN. [Aside to POMPEY.] Forsake thy seat, I do beseech thee, Captain,
　　And hear me speak a word.

POM. [*Whispers in's ear.*] Forbear me till anon—
This wine for Lepidus!
LEP. What manner o' thing is your crocodile?   4
ANT. It is shap'd, sir, like itself, and it is as broad as it hath breadth
it is just so high as it is, and moves with it own organs. It live
by that which nourisheth it, and the elements once out of it, i
transmigrates.
LEP. What colour is it of?   4
ANT. Of it own colour too.
LEP. 'Tis a strange serpent.
ANT. 'Tis so. And the tears of it are wet.
CÆS. Will this description satisfy him?
ANT. With the health that Pompey gives him, else he is a very epicure.
POM. [*Aside to* MENAS.] Go, hang, sir, hang! Tell me of that
Away!
Do as I bid you.—Where's this cup I call'd for?
MEN. [*Aside to* POMPEY.] If for the sake of merit thou wilt hear me
Rise from thy stool.   5
POM. [*Aside to* MENAS.] I think th'art mad. [*Rises and walks aside.*
The matter?
MEN. I have ever held my cap off to thy fortunes.
POM. Thou hast serv'd me with much faith. What's else to say?—
Be jolly lords.
ANT.   These quicksands, Lepidus,
Keep off them, for you sink.
MEN. Wilt thou be lord of all the world?
POM.   What say'st thou?   6
MEN. Wilt thou be lord of the whole world? That's twice.
POM. How should that be?
MEN.   But entertain it,
And though thou think me poor, I am the man
Will give thee all the world.
POM.   Hast thou drunk well?
MEN. No, Pompey, I have kept me from the cup.   6
Thou art, if thou dar'st be, the earthly Jove;
Whate'er the ocean pales or sky inclips
Is thine, if thou wilt ha't.
POM.   Show me which way.
MEN. These three world-sharers, these competitors,
Are in thy vessel. Let me cut the cable: 7
And when we are put off, fall to their throats.
All there is thine.
POM. Ah, this thou shouldst have done,
And not have spoke on't. In me 'tis villainy:
In thee't had been good service. Thou must know
'Tis not my profit that does lead mine honour: 7
Mine honour, it. Repent that e'er thy tongue
Hath so betray'd thine act. Being done unknown,
I should have found it afterwards well done,
But must condemn it now. Desist, and drink.
MEN. [*Aside.*] For this,   8
I'll never follow thy pall'd fortunes more.
Who seeks, and will not take when once 'tis offer'd,
Shall never find it more.

POM. This health to Lepidus !
ANT. Bear him ashore. I'll pledge it for him, Pompey.
ENO. Here's to thee, Menas !
MEN.   Enobarbus, welcome !   85
POM. Fill till the cup be hid.
ENO. There's a strong fellow, Menas.
                    [*Pointing to the Servant who carries off* LEPIDUS.
MEN. Why ?
ENO. 'A bears the third part of the world, man ; see'st not ?
MEN. The third part, then, is drunk. Would it were all,   90
    That it might go on wheels !
ENO. Drink thou ; increase the reels.
MEN. Come.
POM. This is not yet an Alexandrian feast.
ANT. It ripens towards it. Strike the vessels, ho !   95
    Here's to Cæsar !
CÆS.   I could well forbear 't.
    It's monstrous labour when I wash my brain
    And it grows fouler.
ANT.   Be a child o' th' time.
CÆS. Possess it, I'll make answer.
    But I had rather fast from all four days   100
    Than drink so much in one.
ENO. [*To* ANTONY.] Ha, my brave emperor !
    Shall we dance now the Egyptian Bacchanals
    And celebrate our drink ?
POM.   Let's ha't, good soldier.
ANT. Come, let's all take hands,
    Till that the conquering wine hath steep'd our sense   105
    In soft and delicate Lethe.
ENO.   All take hands.
    Make battery to our ears with the loud music,
    The while I'll place you ; then the boy shall sing ;
    The holding every man shall bear as loud
    As his strong sides can volley.   110
                    [*Music plays.* ENOBARBUS *places them hand in hand.*

                    The Song.
            Come, thou monarch of the vine,
            Plumpy Bacchus with pink eyne !
            In thy fats our cares be drown'd,
            With thy grapes our hairs be crown'd.
            Cup us till the world go round,   115
            Cup us till the world go round !

CÆS. What would you more ? Pompey, good night. Good brother.
    Let me request you off ; our graver business
    Frowns at this levity. Gentle lords, let's part ;
    You see we have burnt our cheeks. Strong Enobarb   120
    Is weaker than the wine, and mine own tongue
    Splits what it speaks. The wild disguise hath almost
    Antick'd us all. What needs more words ? Good night.
    Good Antony, your hand.
POM.   I'll try you on the shore.
ANT. And shall, sir. Give's your hand.

                                                             195

POM.   O Antony,   12?
  You have my father's house—but what? We are friends.
  Come, down into the boat.
ENO.   Take heed you fall not.
                    [Exeunt all but ENOBARBUS and MENAS.
  Menas, I'll not on shore.
MEN.   No, to my cabin.
  These drums! these trumpets, flutes! what!
  Let Neptune hear we bid a loud farewell   130
  To these great fellows. Sound and be hang'd, sound out!
                    [Sound a flourish, with drums.
ENO. Hoo! says 'a. There's my cap.
MEN. Hoo! Noble Captain, come.   [Exeunt

ACT THREE

SCENE I. A plain in Syria.

Enter VENTIDIUS, *as it were in triumph, with* SILIUS *and other* ROMANS
OFFICERS and SOLDIERS; *the dead body of* PACORUS *borne before him*

VEN. Now, darting Parthia, art thou struck, and now
  Pleas'd fortune does of Marcus Crassus' death
  Make me revenger. Bear the King's son's body
  Before our army. Thy Pacorus, Orodes,
  Pays this for Marcus Crassus.
SIL.   Noble Ventidius,   5
  Whilst yet with Parthian blood thy sword is warm
  The fugitive Parthians follow; spur through Media,
  Mesopotamia, and the shelters whither
  The routed fly. So thy grand captain, Antony,
  Shall set thee on triumphant chariots and   10
  Put garlands on thy head.
VEN.   O Silius, Silius,
  I have done enough. A lower place, note well,
  May make too great an act; for learn this, Silius:
  Better to leave undone than by our deed
  Acquire too high a fame when him we serve's away.   15
  Cæsar and Antony have ever won
  More in their officer, than person. Sossius,
  One of my place in Syria, his lieutenant,
  For quick accumulation of renown,
  Which he achiev'd by th' minute, lost his favour.   20
  Who does i' th' wars more than his captain can
  Becomes his captain's captain; and ambition,
  The soldier's virtue, rather makes choice of loss
  Than gain which darkens him.
  I could do more to do Antonius good,   25
  But 'twould offend him; and in his offence
  Should my performance perish.
SIL.   Thou hast, Ventidius, that
  Without the which a soldier and his sword
  Grants scarce distinction. Thou wilt write to Antony?
VEN. I'll humbly signify what in his name,   30
  That magical word of war, we have effected;

196

How, with his banners, and his well-paid ranks,
The ne'er-yet-beaten horse of Parthia
We have jaded out o' th' field.

SIL.   Where is he now?

VEN. He purposeth to Athens; whither, with what haste   35
The weight we must convey with's will permit,
We shall appear before him.—On, there; pass along.   [*Exeunt.*

SCENE II. *Rome. Cæsar's house.*

Enter AGRIPPA *at one door,* ENOBARBUS *at another.*

AGR. What, are the brothers parted?

ENO. They have dispatch'd with Pompey; he is gone;
The other three are sealing. Octavia weeps
To part from Rome; Cæsar is sad; and Lepidus,
Since Pompey's feast, as Menas says, is troubled   5
With the green sickness.

AGR.   'Tis a noble Lepidus.

ENO. A very fine one. O, how he loves Cæsar!

AGR. Nay, but how dearly he adores Mark Antony!

ENO. Cæsar? Why he's the Jupiter of men.

AGR. What's Antony? The god of Jupiter.   10

ENO. Spake you of Cæsar? How! the nonpareil!

AGR. O, Antony! O thou Arabian bird!

ENO. Would you praise Cæsar, say 'Cæsar'—go no further.

AGR. Indeed, he plied them both with excellent praises.

ENO. But he loves Cæsar best. Yet he loves Antony.   15
Hoo! hearts, tongues, figures, scribes, bards, poets, cannot
Think, speak, cast, write, sing, number—hoo!—
His love to Antony. But as for Cæsar,
Kneel down, kneel down, and wonder.

AGR.   Both he loves.

ENO. They are his shards, and he their beetle. [*Trumpets within.*]
So—
This is to horse. Adieu, noble Agrippa.

AGR. Good fortune, worthy soldier, and farewell.

Enter CÆSAR, ANTONY, LEPIDUS, *and* OCTAVIA.

ANT. No further, sir.

CÆS. You take from me a great part of myself;
Use me well in't. Sister, prove such a wife   25
As my thoughts make thee, and as my farthest band
Shall pass on thy approof. Most noble Antony,
Let not the piece of virtue which is set
Betwixt us as the cement of our love
To keep it builded be the ram to batter   30
The fortress of it; for better might we
Have lov'd without this mean, if on both parts
This be not cherish'd.

ANT.   Make me not offended
In your distrust.

CÆS.   I have said.

ANT.   You shall not find,
Though you be therein curious, the least cause   35

For what you seem to fear. So the gods keep you,
And make the hearts of Romans serve your ends !
We will here part.

CÆS. Farewell, my dearest sister, fare thee well.
The elements be kind to thee and make   40
Thy spirits all of comfort ! Fare thee well.

OCTA. My noble brother !

ANT. The April's in her eyes. It is love's spring,
And these the showers to bring it on. Be cheerful.

OCTA. Sir, look well to my husband's house ; and—

CÆS.   What,   46
Octavia ?

OCTA. I'll tell you in your ear.

ANT. Her tongue will not obey her heart, nor can
Her heart inform her tongue—the swan's down feather,
That stands upon the swell at the full of tide,
And neither way inclines.   50

ENO. [Aside to AGRIPPA.] Will Cæsar weep ?

AGR. [Aside to ENOBARBUS.] He has a cloud in's face.

ENO. [Aside to AGRIPPA.] He were the worse for that, were he a
horse ;
So is he, being a man.

AGR. [Aside to ENOBARBUS.] Why, Enobarbus,
When Antony found Julius Cæsar dead,
He cried almost to roaring ; and he wept   55
When at Philippi he found Brutus slain.

ENO. [Aside to AGRIPPA.] That year, indeed, he was troubled with
rheum ;
What willingly he did confound he wail'd,
Believe't—till I weep too.

CÆS. No, sweet Octavia,
You shall hear from me still ; the time shall not   60
Out-go my thinking on you.

ANT.   Come, sir, come ;
I'll wrestle with you in my strength of love.
Look here I have you ; thus I let you go,
And give you to the gods.

CÆS.   Adieu ; be happy !

LEP. Let all the number of the stars give light   65
To thy fair way !

CÆS. Farewell, farewell !   [Kisses OCTAVIA.

ANT. Farewell !   [Trumpets sound. Exeunt.

SCENE III. Alexandria. Cleopatra's palace.

Enter CLEOPATRA, CHARMIAN, IRAS, and ALEXAS.

CLEO. Where is the fellow ?

ALEX.   Half afeard to come.

CLEO. Go to, go to.

Enter the MESSENGER as before.

Come hither, sir.

ALEX.   Good Majesty,

Herod of Jewry dare not look upon you
But when you are well pleas'd.

CLEO.   That Herod's head
I'll have.   But how, when Antony is gone,   5
Through whom I might command it ?   Come thou near.

MESS. Most gracious Majesty !

CLEO. Didst thou behold Octavia ?

MESS.   Ay, dread Queen.

CLEO. Where ?

MESS.   Madam, in Rome
I look'd her in the face, and saw her led
Between her brother and Mark Antony.   10

CLEO. Is she as tall as me ?

MESS.   She is not, madam.

CLEO. Didst hear her speak ? Is she shrill-tongu'd or low ?

MESS. Madam, I heard her speak : she is low voic'd.

CLEO. That's not so good.   He cannot like her long.

CHAR. Like her ? O Isis ! 'tis impossible.   15

CLEO. I think so, Charmian.   Dull of tongue and dwarfish !
What majesty is in her gait ? Remember,
If e'er thou look'dst on majesty.

MESS.   She creeps.
Her motion and her station are as one ;
She shows a body rather than a life,   20
A statue than a breather.

CLEO.   Is this certain ?

MESS. Or I have no observance.

CHAR.   Three in Egypt
Cannot make better note.

CLEO.   He's very knowing ;
I do perceive't.   There's nothing in her yet.
The fellow has good judgment.

CHAR.   Excellent.   25

CLEO. Guess at her years, I prithee.

MESS.   Madam,
She was a widow.

CLEO.   Widow ? Charmian, hark !

MESS. And I do think she's thirty.

CLEO. Bear'st thou her face in mind ? Is't long or round ?

MESS. Round even to faultiness.   30

CLEO. For the most part, too, they are foolish that are so.
Her hair, what colour ?

MESS. Brown, madam ; and her forehead
As low as she would wish it.

CLEO.   There's gold for thee.
Thou must not take my former sharpness ill.
I will employ thee back again ; I find thee   35
Most fit for business.   Go make thee ready ;
Our letters are prepar'd.   [Exit MESSENGER.

CHAR.   A proper man.

CLEO. Indeed, he is so.   I repent me much
That so I harried him.   Why, methinks, by him,
This creature's no such thing.

CHAR.   Nothing, madam.   40
CLEO. The man hath seen some majesty, and should know.
CHAR. Hath he seen majesty ? Isis else defend,
      And serving you so long !
CLEO. I have one thing more to ask him yet, good Charmian.
      But 'tis no matter ; thou shalt bring him to me   45
      Where I will write. All may be well enough.
CHAR. I warrant you, madam.   [*Exeunt.*

SCENE IV. *Athens. Antony's house.*

Enter ANTONY *and* OCTAVIA.

ANT. Nay, nay, Octavia, not only that—
      That were excusable, that and thousands more
      Of semblable import—but he hath wag'd
      New wars 'gainst Pompey ; made his will, and read it
      To public ear ;   5
      Spoke scantly of me ; when perforce he could not
      But pay me terms of honour, cold and sickly
      He vented them, most narrow measure lent me ;
      When the best hint was given him, he not took't,
      Or did it from his teeth.
OCTA.   O my good lord,   10
      Believe not all ; or if you must believe,
      Stomach not all. A more unhappy lady,
      If this division chance, ne'er stood between,
      Praying for both parts.
      The good gods will mock me presently   15
      When I shall pray ' O, bless my lord and husband ! '
      Undo that prayer by crying out as loud
      ' O, bless my brother ! ' Husband win, win brother,
      Prays, and destroys the prayer ; no mid-way
      'Twixt these extremes at all.
ANT.   Gentle Octavia,   20
      Let your best love draw to that point which seeks
      Best to preserve it. If I lose mine honour,
      I lose myself ; better I were not yours
      Than yours so branchless. But, as you requested,
      Yourself shall go between's. The meantime, lady,   25
      I'll raise the preparation of a war
      Shall stain your brother. Make your soonest haste ;
      So your desires are yours.
OCTA.   Thanks to my lord.
      The Jove of power make me, most weak, most weak,
      Your reconciler ! Wars 'twixt you twain would be   30
      As if the world should cleave, and that slain men
      Should solder up the rift.
ANT. When it appears to you where this begins,
      Turn your displeasure that way, for our faults
      Can never be so equal that your love   35
      Can equally move with them. Provide your going ;
      Choose your own company, and command what cost
      Your heart has mind to.   [*Exeunt.*

SCENE V. *Athens. Antony's house.*

Enter ENOBARBUS *and* EROS, *meeting.*

ENO. How now, friend Eros !

EROS. There's strange news come, sir.

ENO. What, man ?

EROS. Cæsar and Lepidus have made wars upon Pompey.

ENO. This is old.   What is the success ?

EROS. Cæsar, having made use of him in the wars 'gainst Pompey,
   presently denied him rivality, would not let him partake in the
   glory of the action ; and not resting here, accuses him of letters
   he had formerly wrote to Pompey ; upon his own appeal, seizes
   him.   So the poor third is up, till death enlarge his confine.   12

ENO. Then, world, thou hast a pair of chaps—no more ;
   And throw between them all the food thou hast,
   They'll grind the one the other.   Where's Antony ?   15

EROS. He's walking in the garden—thus, and spurns
   The rush that lies before him ; cries ' Fool Lepidus ! '
   And threats the throat of that his officer
   That murd'red Pompey.

ENO.   Our great navy's rigg'd.

EROS. For Italy and Cæsar.   More, Domitius :   20
   My lord desires you presently ; my news
   I might have told hereafter.

ENO.   'Twill be naught ;
   But let it be.   Bring me to Antony.

EROS. Come, sir.   ]*Exeunt.*

SCENE VI. *Rome. Cæsar's house.*

Enter CÆSAR, AGRIPPA, *and* MÆCENAS.

CÆS. Contemning Rome, he has done all this and more
   In Alexandria.   Here's the manner of 't :
   I' th' market-place, on a tribunal silver'd,
   Cleopatra and himself in chairs of gold
   Were publicly enthron'd ; at the feet sat   5
   Cæsarion, whom they call my father's son,
   And all the unlawful issue that their lust
   Since then hath made between them.   Unto her
   He gave the stablishment of Egypt ; made her
   Of lower Syria, Cyprus, Lydia,   10
   Absolute queen.

MÆC.   This in the public eye ?

CÆS. I' th' common show-place, where they exercise.
   His sons he there proclaim'd the kings of kings :
   Great Media, Parthia, and Armenia,
   He gave to Alexander ;. to Ptolemy he assign'd   15
   Syria, Cilicia, and Phœnicia.   She
   In th' habiliments of the goddess Isis
   That day appear'd ; and oft before gave audience,
   As 'tis reported, so.

MÆC.   Let Rome be thus
   Inform'd.

AGR.   Who, queasy with his insolence   2(
  Already, will their good thoughts call from him.
CÆS. The people knows it, and have now receiv'd
  His accusations.
AGR.   Who does he accuse ?
CÆS. Cæsar ; and that, having in Sicily
  Sextus Pompeius spoil'd, we had not rated him   25
  His part o' th' isle.   Then does he say he lent me
  Some shipping, unrestor'd.   Lastly, he frets
  That Lepidus of the triumvirate
  Should be depos'd ; and, being, that we detain
  All his revenue.
AGR.   Sir, this should be answer'd.   3(
CÆS. 'Tis done already, and the messenger gone.
  I have told him Lepidus was grown too cruel,
  That he his high authority abus'd,
  And did deserve his change.   For what I have conquer'd
  I grant him part ; but then, in his Armenia   35
  And other of his conquer'd kingdoms, I
  Demand the like.
MÆC.   He'll never yield to that.
CÆS. Nor must not then be yielded to in this.

Enter OCTAVIA, *with her* TRAIN.

OCTA. Hail, Cæsar, and my lord ! hail, most dear Cæsar !
CÆS. That ever I should call thee cast-away !   4(
OCTA. You have not call'd me so, nor have you cause.
CÆS. Why have you stol'n upon us thus ? You come not
  Like Cæsar's sister.   The wife of Antony
  Should have an army for an usher, and
  The neighs of horse to tell of her approach   45
  Long ere she did appear.   The trees by th' way
  Should have borne men, and expectation fainted,
  Longing for what it had not.   Nay, the dust
  Should have ascended to the roof of heaven,
  Rais'd by your populous troops.   But you are come   5(
  A market-maid to Rome, and have prevented
  The ostentation of our love, which left unshown
  Is often left unlov'd.   We should have met you
  By sea and land, supplying every stage
  With an augmented greeting.
OCTA.   Good my ord,   55
  To come thus was I not constrain'd, but did it
  On my free will.   My lord, Mark Antony,
  Hearing that you prepar'd for war, acquainted
  My grieved ear withal ; whereon I begg'd
  His pardon for return.
CÆS.   Which soon he granted,   6(
  Being an obstruct 'tween his lust and him.
OCTA. Do not say so, my lord.
CÆS.   I have eyes upon him,
  And his affairs come to me on the wind.
  Where is he now ?
OCTA.   My lord, in Athens.

CÆS. No, my most wronged sister : Cleopatra　　　　　　　65
　　Hath nodded him to her.　He hath given his empire
　　Up to a whore, who now are levying
　　The kings o' th' earth for war.　He hath assembled
　　Bocchus, the king of Libya ; Archelaus
　　Of Cappadocia ; Philadelphos, king　　　　　　　　　70
　　Of Paphlagonia ; the Thracian king, Adallas ;
　　King Manchus of Arabia ; King of Pont ;
　　Herod of Jewry ; Mithridates, king
　　Of Comagene ; Polemon and Amyntas,
　　The kings of Mede and Lycaonia, with a　　　　　　75
　　More larger list of sceptres.
OCTA.　　　　　　　　　　　　Ay me most wretched,
　　That have my heart parted betwixt two friends,
　　That does afflict each other !
CÆS.　　　　　　　　　　　　Welcome hither.
　　Your letters did withhold our breaking forth,
　　Till we perceiv'd both how you were wrong led　　　80
　　And we in negligent danger.　Cheer your heart ;
　　Be you not troubled with the time, which drives
　　O'er your content these strong necessities,
　　But let determin'd things to destiny
　　Hold unbewail'd their way.　Welcome to Rome ;　　85
　　Nothing more dear to me.　You are abus'd
　　Beyond the mark of thought, and the high gods,
　　To do you justice, make their ministers
　　Of us and those that love you.　Best of comfort,
　　And ever welcome to us.
AGR.　　　　　　　　　　　　Welcome, lady.　　　　90
MÆC. Welcome, dear madam.
　　Each heart in Rome does love and pity you ;
　　Only th' adulterous Antony, most large
　　In his abominations, turns you off,
　　And gives his potent regiment to a trull　　　　　95
　　That noises it against us.
OCTA.　　　　　　　　　Is it so, sir ?
CÆS. Most certain.　Sister ; welcome.　Pray you
　　Be ever known to patience.　My dear'st sister !　　[Exeunt.

　　　　SCENE VII.　Antony's camp near Actium.

　　　　　　Enter CLEOPATRA and ENOBARBUS.

CLEO. I will be even with thee, doubt it not.
ENO. But why, why, why ?
CLEO. Thou hast forspoke my being in these wars,
　　And say'st it is not fit.
ENO.　　　　　　　Well, is it, is it ?
CLEO. Is't not denounc'd against us ? Why should not we　　5
　　Be there in person ?
ENO. [Aside.]　　　　　　Well, I could reply :
　　If we should serve with horse and mares together
　　The horse were merely lost ; the mares would bear
　　A soldier and his horse.

　　　　　　　　　　　　　　　　　　　　　　　203

CLEO.   What is't you say?
ENO. Your presence needs must puzzle Antony;   1
   Take from his heart, take from his brain, from 's time,
   What should not then be spar'd. He is already
   Traduc'd for levity; and 'tis said in Rome
   That Photinus an eunuch and your maids
   Manage this war.
CLEO.   Sink Rome, and their tongues rot   1
   That speak against us! A charge we bear i' th' war,
   And, as the president of my kingdom, will
   Appear there for a man. Speak not against it;
   I will not stay behind.

Enter ANTONY *and* CANIDIUS.

ENO.   Nay, I have done.
   Here comes the Emperor.
ANT.   Is it not strange, Canidius,   2
   That from Tarentum and Brundusium
   He could so quickly cut the Ionian sea,
   And take in Toryne?—You have heard on't, sweet?
CLEO. Celerity is never more admir'd
   Than by the negligent.
ANT.   A good rebuke,   2
   Which might have well becom'd the best of men
   To taunt at slackness. Canidius, we
   Will fight with him by sea.
CLEO.   By sea! What else?
CAN. Why will my lord do so?
ANT. For that he dares us to't.
ENO. So hath my lord dar'd him to single fight.   3
CAN. Ay, and to wage this battle at Pharsalia,
   Where Cæsar fought with Pompey. But these offers,
   Which serve not for his vantage, he shakes off;
   And so should you.
ENO. Your ships are not well mann'd;
   Your mariners are muleteers, reapers, people
   Ingross'd by swift impress. In Cæsar's fleet   3
   Are those that often have 'gainst Pompey fought;
   Their ships are yare; yours heavy. No disgrace
   Shall fall you for refusing him at sea,
   Being prepar'd for land.
ANT.   By sea, by sea.   4
ENO. Most worthy sir, you therein throw away
   The absolute soldiership you have by land;
   Distract your army, which doth most consist
   Of war-mark'd footmen; leave unexecuted
   Your own renowned knowledge; quite forgo   4
   The way which promises assurance; and
   Give up yourself merely to chance and hazard
   From firm security.
ANT.   I'll fight at sea.
CLEO. I have sixty sails, Cæsar none better.
ANT. Our overplus of shipping will we burn,   5
   And, with the rest full-mann'd, from th' head of Actium

Beat th' approaching Cæsar.   But if we fail,
We then can do't at land.

Enter a MESSENGER.

                          Thy business?
MESS. The news is true, my lord : he is descried ;
    Cæsar has taken Toryne.   55
ANT. Can he be there in person ? 'Tis impossible—
    Strange that his power should be.   Canidius,
    Our nineteen legions thou shalt hold by land,
    And our twelve thousand horse.   We'll to our ship.
    Away, my Thetis !

Enter a SOLDIER.

                          How now, worthy soldier ?   60
SOLD. O noble Emperor, do not fight by sea ;
    Trust not to rotten planks.   Do you misdoubt
    This sword and these my wounds ? Let th' Egyptians
    And the Phœnicians go a-ducking ; we
    Have us'd to conquer standing on the earth   65
    And fighting foot to foot.
ANT.   Well, well—away.
        [*Exeunt* ANTONY, CLEOPATRA, *and* ENOBARBUS.
SOLD. By Hercules, I think I am i' th' right.
CAN. Soldier, thou art ; but his whole action grows
    Not in the power on't.   So our leader's led,
    And we are women's men.
SOLD.   You keep by land   70
    The legions and the horse whole, do you not ?
CAN. Marcus Octavius, Marcus Justeius,
    Publicola, and Cælius are for sea ;
    But we keep whole by land.   This speed of Cæsar's
    Carries beyond belief.
SOLD.   While he was yet in Rome,   75
    His power went out in such distractions as
    Beguil'd all spies.
CAN.   Who's his lieutenant, hear you ?
SOLD. They say one Taurus.
CAN.   Well I know the man.

Enter a MESSENGER.

MESS. The Emperor calls Canidius.
CAN. With news the time's with labour and throes forth   80
    Each minute some.   [*Exeunt.*

SCENE VIII.   *A plain near Actium.*

Enter CÆSAR, *with his* ARMY, *marching.*

CÆS. Taurus !
TAUR. My lord ?
CÆS. Strike not by land ; keep whole ; provoke not battle
    Till we have done at sea.   Do not exceed
    The prescript of this scroll.   Our fortune lies
    Upon this jump.   [*Exeunt.*

SCENE IX.   *Another part of the plain.*

Enter ANTONY *and* ENOBARBUS.

ANT. Set we our squadrons on yond side o' th' hill,
  In eye of Cæsar's battle ; from which place
  We may the number of the ships behold,
  And so proceed accordingly.

                                          [*Exeunt*

SCENE X.   *Another part of the plain.*

CANIDIUS *marcheth with his land* ARMY *one way over the stage, and*
  TAURUS, *the Lieutenant of Cæsar, the other way.   After their
  going in is heard the noise of a sea-fight.*

Alarum.   Enter ENOBARBUS.

ENO. Naught, naught, all naught ! I can behold no longer.
  Th' Antoniad, the Egyptian admiral,
  With all their sixty, fly and turn the rudder.
  To see't mine eyes are blasted.

Enter SCARUS.

SCAR.   Gods and goddesses,
  All the whole synod of them !
ENO.   What's thy passion ?   5
SCAR. The greater cantle of the world is lost
  With very ignorance ; we have kiss'd away
  Kingdoms and provinces.
ENO.   How appears the fight ?
SCAR. On our side like the token'd pestilence,
  Where death is sure.   Yon ribaudred nag of Egypt—   10
  Whom leprosy o'ertake !—i' th' midst o' th' fight,
  When vantage like a pair of twins appear'd,
  Both as the same, or rather ours the elder—
  The breese upon her, like a cow in June—   14
  Hoists sails and flies.
ENO.   That I beheld ;
  Mine eyes did sicken at the sight and could not
  Endure a further view.
SCAR.   She once being loof'd,
  The noble ruin of her magic, Antony,
  Claps on his sea-wing, and, like a doting mallard,   20
  Leaving the fight in height, flies after her.
  I never saw an action of such shame ;
  Experience, manhood, honour, ne'er before
  Did violate so itself.
ENO.   Alack, alack !

Enter CANIDIUS.

CAN. Our fortune on the sea is out of breath,   25
  And sinks most lamentably.   Had our general
  Been what he knew himself, it had gone well.
  O, he has given example for our flight
  Most grossly by his own !

ENO.   Ay, are you thereabouts ?
  Why then, good night indeed.   30
CAN. Toward Peloponnesus are they fled.
SCAR. 'Tis easy to't ; and there I will attend
  What further comes.
CAN.   To Cæsar will I render
  My legions and my horse ; six kings already
  Show me the way of yielding.
ENO.   I'll yet follow   35
  The wounded chance of Antony, though my reason
  Sits in the wind against me.   [*Exeunt.*

SCENE XI. *Alexandria. Cleopatra's palace.*

Enter ANTONY *with* ATTENDANTS.

ANT. Hark ! the land bids me tread no more upon't ;
  It is asham'd to bear me. Friends, come hither.
  I am so lated in the world that I
  Have lost my way for ever. I have a ship
  Laden with gold ; take that ; divide it. Fly,   5
  And make your peace with Cæsar.
ALL.   Fly ? Not we !
ANT. I have fled myself, and have instructed cowards
  To run and show their shoulders. Friends, be gone ;
  I have myself resolv'd upon a course
  Which has no need of you ; be gone.   10
  My treasure's in the harbour, take it. O,
  I follow'd that I blush to look upon.
  My very hairs do mutiny ; for the white
  Reprove the brown for rashness, and they them
  For fear and doting. Friends, be gone ; you shall   15
  Have letters from me to some friends that will
  Sweep your way for you. Pray you look not sad,
  Nor make replies of loathness ; take the hint
  Which my despair proclaims. Let that be left
  Which leaves itself. To the sea-side straight way.   20
  I will possess you of that ship and treasure.
  Leave me, I pray, a little ; pray you now ;
  Nay, do so, for indeed I have lost command.
  Therefore I pray you. I'll see you by and by.   [*Sits down.*

Enter CLEOPATRA, *led by* CHARMIAN *and* IRAS, EROS *following.*

EROS. Nay, gentle madam, to him ! Comfort him.   25
IRAS. Do, most dear Queen.
CHAR. Do ? Why, what else ?
CLEO. Let me sit down. O Juno !
ANT. No, no, no, no, no.
EROS. See you here, sir ?   30
ANT. O, fie, fie, fie !
CHAR. Madam !
IRAS. Madam, O good Empress !
EROS. Sir, sir !
ANT. Yes, my lord, yes. He at Philippi kept   35
  His sword e'en like a dancer, while I struck
  The lean and wrinkled Cassius ; and 'twas I

                                                                  207

That the mad Brutus ended; he alone
Dealt on lieutenantry, and no practice had
In the brave squares of war.   Yet now—no matter.   40
CLEO. Ah, stand by !
EROS. The Queen, my lord, the Queen !
IRAS. Go to him, madam, speak to him.
He is unqualitied with very shame.
CLEO. Well then, sustain me.   O !   45
EROS. Most noble sir, arise ; the Queen approaches.
Her head's declin'd, and death will seize her but
Your comfort makes the rescue.
ANT. I have offended reputation—
A most unnoble swerving.
EROS.   Sir, the Queen.   50
ANT. O, whither hast thou led me, Egypt ?   See
How I convey my shame out of thine eyes
By looking back what I have left behind
'Stroy'd in dishonour.
CLEO.   O my lord, my lord,
Forgive my fearful sails !   I little thought   55
You would have followed.
ANT.   Egypt, thou knew'st too well
My heart was to thy rudder tied by th' strings,
And thou shouldst tow me after.   O'er my spirit
Thy full supremacy thou knew'st, and that
Thy beck might from the bidding of the gods   60
Command me.
CLEO.   O, my pardon !
ANT.   Now I must
To the young man send humble treaties, dodge
And palter in the shifts of lowness, who
With half the bulk o' th' world play'd as I pleas'd,
Making and marring fortunes.   You did know   65
How much you were my conqueror, and that
My sword, made weak by my affection, would
Obey it on all cause.
CLEO.   Pardon, pardon !
ANT. Fall not a tear, I say ; one of them rates
All that is won and lost.   Give me a kiss ;   70
Even this repays me.
We sent our schoolmaster ; is 'a come back ?
Love, I am full of lead.   Some wine,
Within there, and our viands !   Fortune knows
We scorn her most when most she offers blows.   [Exeunt

SCENE XII.   Cæsar's camp in Egypt.

Enter CÆSAR, AGRIPPA, DOLABELLA, THYREUS, with OTHERS.

CÆS. Let him appear that's come from Antony.
Know you him ?
DOL.   Cæsar, 'tis his schoolmaster :
An argument that he is pluck'd, when hither
He sends so poor a pinion of his wing,

208

Which had superfluous kings for messengers   5
Not many moons gone by.

Enter EUPHRONIUS, *Ambassador from* ANTONY.

CÆS.   Approach, and speak.
EUP. Such as I am, I come from Antony.
 I was of late as petty to his ends
 As is the morn-dew on the myrtle leaf
 To his grand sea.
CÆS.   Be't so.   Declare thine office.   10
EUP. Lord of his fortunes he salutes thee, and
 Requires to live in Egypt; which not granted,
 He lessens his requests and to thee sues
 To let him breathe between the heavens and earth,
 A private man in Athens.   This for him.   15
 Next, Cleopatra does confess thy greatness,
 Submits her to thy might, and of thee craves
 The circle of the Ptolemies for her heirs,
 Now hazarded to thy grace.
CÆS.   For Antony,
 I have no ears to his request.   The Queen   20
 Of audience nor desire shall fail, so she
 From Egypt drive her all-disgraced friend,
 Or take his life there.   This if she perform,
 She shall not sue unheard.   So to them both.
EUP. Fortune pursue thee !
CÆS.   Bring him through the bands.   25
            [Exit EUPHRONIUS.
 [*To* THYREUS.]   To try thy eloquence, now 'tis time.   Dispatch;
 From Antony win Cleopatra.   Promise,
 And in our name, what she requires; add more,
 From thine invention, offers.   Women are not
 In their best fortunes strong; but want will perjure   30
 The ne'er-touch'd vestal.   Try thy cunning, Thyreus;
 Make thine own edict for thy pains, which we
 Will answer as a law.
THYR.   Cæsar, I go.
CÆS. Observe how Antony becomes his flaw,
 And what thou think'st his very action speaks   35
 In every power that moves.
THYR.   Cæsar, I shall.   [*Exeunt.*

SCENE XIII.   *Alexandria.   Cleopatra's palace.*

Enter CLEOPATRA, ENOBARBUS, CHARMIAN, *and* IRAS.

CLEO. What shall we do, Enobarbus ?
ENO.   Think, and die.
CLEO. Is Antony or we in fault for this ?
ENO. Antony only, that would make his will
 Lord of his reason.   What though you fled
 From that great face of war, whose several ranges
 Frighted each other ?   Why should he follow ?   5
 The itch of his affection should not then
 Have nick'd his captainship, at such a point,

When half to half the world oppos'd, he being
The mered question. 'Twas a shame no less   10
Than was his loss, to course your flying flags
And leave his navy gazing.
CLEO.   Prithee, peace.

Enter EUPHRONIUS, *the Ambassador ; with* ANTONY.

ANT. Is that his answer ?
EUP. Ay, my lord.
ANT. The Queen shall then have courtesy, so she   15
   Will yield us up.
EUP.   He says so.
ANT.   Let her know't.
   To the boy Cæsar send this grizzled head,
   And he will fill thy wishes to the brim
   With principalities.
CLEO.   That head, my lord ?
ANT. To him again. Tell him he wears the rose   20
   Of youth upon him ; from which the world should note
   Something particular. His coin, ships, legions,
   May be a coward's whose ministers would prevail
   Under the service of a child as soon
   As i' th' command of Cæsar. I dare him therefore   25
   To lay his gay comparisons apart,
   And answer me declin'd, sword against sword,
   Ourselves alone. I'll write it. Follow me.
                        [*Exeunt* ANTONY *and* EUPHRONIUS.
ENO. [*Aside.*] Yes, like enough high-battled Cæsar will
   Unstate his happiness, and be stag'd to th' show   30
   Against a sworder ! I see men's judgments are
   A parcel of their fortunes, and things outward
   Do draw the inward quality after them,
   To suffer all alike. That he should dream,
   Knowing all measures, the full Cæsar will   35
   Answer his emptiness ! Cæsar, thou hast subdu'd
   His judgment too.

Enter a SERVANT.

SERV. A messenger from Cæsar.
CLEO. What, no more ceremony ? See, my women !
   Against the blown rose may they stop their nose
   That kneel'd unto the buds. Admit him, sir. [*Exit* SERVANT.
ENO. [*Aside.*] Mine honesty and I begin to square.   41
   The loyalty well held to fools does make
   Our faith mere folly. Yet he that can endure
   To follow with allegiance a fall'n lord
   Does conquer him that did his master conquer,   45
   And earns a place i' th' story.

Enter THYREUS.

CLEO. Cæsar's will ?
THYR.   Hear it apart.
CLEO. None but friends : say boldly.
THYR. So, haply, are they friends to Antony.

ENO. He needs as many, sir, as Cæsar has,
  Or needs not us. If Cæsar please, our master   50
  Will leap to be his friend. For us, you know
  Whose he is we are, and that is Cæsar's.

THYR.   So.
  Thus then, thou most renown'd : Cæsar entreats
  Not to consider in what case thou stand'st
  Further than he is Cæsar.

CLEO.   Go on. Right royal !   55

THYR. He knows that you embrace not Antony
  As you did love, but as you fear'd him.

CLEO.   O !

THYR. The scars upon your honour, therefore, he
  Does pity, as constrained blemishes,
  Not as deserv'd.

CLEO.   He is a god, and knows   60
  What is most right. Mine honour was not yielded,
  But conquer'd merely.

ENO. [Aside.]   To be sure of that,
  I will ask Antony. Sir, sir, thou art so leaky
  That we must leave thee to thy sinking, for
  Thy dearest quit thee.   [Exit.

THYR.   Shall I say to Cæsar   65
  What you require of him ? For he partly begs
  To be desir'd to give. It much would please him
  That of his fortunes you should make a staff
  To lean upon. But it would warm his spirits
  To hear from me you had left Antony,   70
  And put yourself under his shroud,
  The universal landlord.

CLEO.   What's your name ?

THYR. My name is Thyreus.

CLEO.   Most kind messenger,
  Say to great Cæsar this : in deputation
  I kiss his conqu'ring hand. Tell him I am prompt   75
  To lay my crown at 's feet, and there to kneel.
  Tell him from his all-obeying breath I hear
  The doom of Egypt.

THYR.   'Tis your noblest course.
  Wisdom and fortune combating together,
  If that the former dare but what it can,   80
  No chance may shake it. Give me grace to lay
  My duty on your hand.

CLEO.   Your Cæsar's father oft,
  When he hath mus'd of taking kingdoms in,
  Bestow'd his lips on that unworthy place,
  As it rain'd kisses.

      Re-enter ANTONY *and* ENOBARBUS.

ANT. Favours, by Jove that thunders !   85
  What art thou, fellow ?

THYR.   One that but performs
  The bidding of the fullest man, and worthiest
  To have command obey'd.

ENO. [*Aside*.]   You will be whipt.
ANT. Approach there.—Ah, you kite !—Now, gods and devils !
    Authority melts from me.   Of late, when I cried ' Ho ! '   90
    Like boys unto a muss, kings would start forth
    And cry ' Your will ? '   Have you no ears ?   I am
    Antony yet.

                    Enter SERVANTS.

                Take hence this Jack and whip him.
ENO. 'Tis better playing with a lion's whelp
    Than with an old one dying.
ANT.   Moon and stars !   95
    Whip him.   Were't twenty of the greatest tributaries
    That do acknowledge Cæsar, should I find them
    So saucy with the hand of she here—what's her name
    Since she was Cleopatra ?   Whip him, fellows,
    Till like a boy you see him cringe his face,   100
    And whine aloud for mercy.   Take him hence.
THYR. Mark Antony—
ANT.   Tug him away.   Being whipt,
    Bring him again : the Jack of Cæsar's shall
    Bear us an errand to him.   [*Exeunt* SERVANTS *with* THYREUS.
    You were half blasted ere I knew you.   Ha !   105
    Have I my pillow left unpress'd in Rome,
    Forborne the getting of a lawful race,
    And by a gem of women, to be abus'd
    By one that looks on feeders ?
CLEO.   Good my lord—   110
ANT. You have been a boggler ever.
    But when we in our viciousness grow hard—
    O misery on't !—the wise gods seel our eyes,
    In our own filth drop our clear judgments, make us
    Adore our errors, laugh at's while we strut
    To our confusion.
CLEO.   O' is't come to this ?   115
ANT. I found you as a morsel cold upon
    Dead Cæsar's trencher.   Nay, you were a fragment
    Of Cneius Pompey's, besides what hotter hours,
    Unregist'red in vulgar fame, you have
    Luxuriously pick'd out ; for I am sure,   120
    Though you can guess what temperance should be,
    You know not what it is.
CLEO.   Wherefore is this ?
ANT. To let a fellow that will take rewards,
    And say ' God quit you ! ' be familiar with
    My playfellow, your hand, this kingly seal   125
    And plighter of high hearts !   O that I were
    Upon the hill of Basan to outroar
    The horned herd !   For I have savage cause,
    And to proclaim it civilly were like
    A halter'd neck which does the hangman thank   130
    For being yare about him.

                Re-enter a SERVANT *with* THYREUS.
                    Is he whipt ?

SERV. Soundly, my lord.

ANT.   Cried he ? and begg'd 'a pardon ?

SERV. He did ask favour.

ANT. If that thy father live, let him repent
Thou wast not made his daughter ; and be thou sorry   135
To follow Cæsar in his triumph, since
Thou hast been whipt for following him.   Henceforth
The white hand of a lady fever thee !
Shake thou to look on't.   Get thee back to Cæsar ;
Tell him thy entertainment ; look thou say   140
He makes me angry with him ; for he seems
Proud and disdainful, harping on what I am,
Not what he knew I was.   He makes me angry ;
And at this time most easy 'tis to do't,
When my good stars, that were my former guides,   145
Have empty left their orbs and shot their fires
Into th' abysm of hell.   If he mislike
My speech and what is done, tell him he has
Hipparchus, my enfranched bondman, whom
He may at pleasure whip or hang or torture,   150
As he shall like, to quit me.   Urge it thou.
Hence with thy stripes, be gone.   [*Exit* THYREUS.

CLEO. Have you done yet ?

ANT.   Alack, our terrene moon
Is now eclips'd, and it portends alone
The fall of Antony.

CLEO.   I must stay his time.   155

ANT. To flatter Cæsar, would you mingle eyes
With one that ties his points ?

CLEO.   Not know me yet ?

ANT. Cold-hearted toward me ?

CLEO.   Ah, dear, if I be so,
From my cold heart let heaven engender hail,
And poison it in the source, and the first stone   160
Drop in my neck ; as it determines, so
Dissolve my life ! The next Cæsarion smite !
Till by degrees the memory of my womb,
Together with my brave Egyptians all,
By the discandying of this pelleted storm,   165
Lie graveless, till the flies and gnats of Nile
Have buried them for prey.

ANT.   I am satisfied.
Cæsar sits down in Alexandria, where
I will oppose his fate.   Our force by land
Hath nobly held ; our sever'd navy too   170
Have knit again, and fleet, threat'ning most sea-like.
Where hast thou been, my heart ? Dost thou hear, lady ?
If from the field I shall return once more
To kiss these lips, I will appear in blood.
I and my sword will earn our chronicle.   175
There's hope in't yet.

CLEO.   That's my brave lord !

ANT. I will be treble-sinew'd, hearted, breath'd,
And fight maliciously.   For when mine hours

213

Were nice and lucky, men did ransom lives   180
Of me for jests ; but now I'll set my teeth,
And send to darkness all that stop me.   Come,
Let's have one other gaudy night.   Call to me
All my sad captains ; fill our bowls once more ;
Let's mock the midnight bell.

CLEO.   It is my birthday.   185
I had thought t'have held it poor ; but since my lord
Is Antony again, I will be Cleopatra.

ANT. We will yet do well.

CLEO. Call all his noble captains to my lord.

ANT. Do so, we'll speak to them ; and to-night I'll force   190
The wine peep through their scars.   Come on, my queen,
There's sap in't yet.   The next time I do fight
I'll make death love me ; for I will contend
Even with his pestilent scythe.   [*Exeunt all but* ENOBARBUS.

ENO. Now he'll outstare the lightning.   To be furious   195
Is to be frighted out of fear, and in that mood
The dove will peck the estridge ; and I see still
A diminution in our captain's brain
Restores his heart.   When valour preys on reason,
It eats the sword it fights with.   I will seek   200
Some way to leave him.   [*Exit.*

ACT FOUR

SCENE I. *Cæsar's camp before Alexandria.*

Enter CÆSAR, AGRIPPA, *and* MÆCENAS, *with his* ARMY ; CÆSAR
reading a letter.

CÆS. He calls me boy, and chides as he had power
To beat me out of Egypt.   My messenger
He hath whipt with rods ; dares me to personal combat,
Cæsar to Antony.   Let the old ruffian know
I have many other ways to die, meantime   5
Laugh at his challenge.

MÆC.   Cæsar must think
When one so great begins to rage, he's hunted
Even to falling.   Give him no breath, but now
Make boot of his distraction.   Never anger
Made good guard for itself.

CÆS.   Let our best heads   10
Know that to-morrow the last of many battles
We mean to fight.   Within our files there are
Of those that serv'd Mark Antony but late
Enough to fetch him in.   See it done ;
And feast the army ; we have store to do't,   15
And they have earn'd the waste.   Poor Antony !   [*Exeunt.*

SCENE II. *Alexandria. Cleopatra's palace.*

Enter ANTONY, CLEOPATRA, ENOBARBUS, CHARMIAN, IRAS, ALEXAS, *with* OTHERS.

ANT. He will not fight with me, Domitius ?
ENO.   No.
ANT. Why should he not ?
ENO. He thinks, being twenty times of better fortune,
   He is twenty men to one.
ANT.   To-morrow, soldier,
   By sea and land I'll fight. Or I will live,   5
   Or bathe my dying honour in the blood
   Shall make it live again. Woo't thou fight well ?
ENO. I'll strike, and cry ' Take all '.
ANT.   Well said ; come on.
   Call forth my household servants ; let's to-night
   Be bounteous at our meal.

Enter three or four SERVITORS.

                             Give me thy hand,   10
   Thou has been rightly honest. So hast thou ;
   Thou, and thou, and thou. You have serv'd me well,
   And kings have been your fellows.
CLEO. [*Aside to* ENOBARBUS.] What means this ?
ENO. [*Aside to* CLEOPATRA.] 'Tis one of those odd tricks which sorrow shoots
   Out of the mind.
ANT.   And thou art honest too.   15
   I wish I could be made so many men,
   And all of you clapp'd up together in
   An Antony, that I might do you service
   So good as you have done.
SERV.   The gods forbid !
ANT. Well, my good fellows, wait on me to-night.   20
   Scant not my cups, and make as much of me
   As when mine empire was your fellow too,
   And suffer'd my command.
CLEO. [*Aside to* ENOBARBUS.] What does he mean ?
ENO. [*Aside to* CLEOPATRA.] To make his followers weep.
ANT.   Tend me to-night ;
   May be it is the period of your duty.   25
   Haply you shall not see me more ; or if,
   A mangled shadow. Perchance to-morrow
   You'll serve another master. I look on you
   As one that takes his leave. Mine honest friends,
   I turn you not away ; but, like a master   30
   Married to your good service, stay till death.
   Tend me to-night two hours, I ask no more,
   And the gods yield you for't !
ENO.   What mean you, sir,
   To give them this discomfort ? Look, they weep ;
   And I, an ass, am onion-ey'd. For shame !   30
   Transform us not to women.

ANT.   Ho, ho, ho!
Now the witch take me if I meant it thus!
Grace grow where those drops fall! My hearty friends,
You take me in too dolorous a sense;
For I spake to you for your comfort, did desire you   40
To burn this night with torches. Know, my hearts
I hope well of to-morrow, and will lead you
Where rather I'll expect victorious life
Than death and honour. Let's to supper, come,
And drown consideration.   [*Exeunt.*

SCENE III. *Alexandria. Before Cleopatra's palace.*

Enter a COMPANY OF SOLDIERS.

1 SOLD. Brother, good night. To-morrow is the day.
2 SOLD. It will determine one way. Fare you well.
  Heard you of nothing strange about the streets?
1 SOLD. Nothing. What news?
2 SOLD. Belike 'tis but a rumour. Good night to you.
1 SOLD. Well, sir, good night.

They meet other SOLDIERS.

2 SOLD. Soldiers, have careful watch.
1 SOLD. And you. Good night, good night.
        [*The two companies separate and place themselves in every
                                    corner of the stage.*

2 SOLD. Here we. And if to-morrow
  Our navy thrive, I have an absolute hope   10
  Our landmen will stand up.
3 SOLD.   'Tis a brave army,
  And full of purpose.
        [*Music of the Hautboys is under the stage.*

2 SOLD.   Peace, what noise?
3 SOLD.   List, list!
2 SOLD. Hark!
3 SOLD.   Music i' th' air.
4 SOLD.   Under the earth.
3 SOLD. It signs well, does it not?
4 SOLD.   No.
3 SOLD.   Peace, I say!
  What should this mean?   15
2 SOLD. 'Tis the god Hercules, whom Antony lov'd,
  Now leaves him.
3 SOLD. Walk; let's see if other watchmen
  Do hear what we do.
2 SOLD.   How now, masters!
SOLDIERS. [*Speaking together.*]   How now!
  How now! Do you hear this?
1 SOLD.   Ay; is't not strange?
3 SOLD. Do you hear, masters? Do you hear?
1 SOLD. Follow the noise so far as we have quarter;
  Let's see how it will give off.
SOLDIERS. Content. 'Tis strange.   [*Exeunt.*

SCENE IV. *Alexandria. Cleopatra's palace.*

Enter ANTONY *and* CLEOPATRA, CHARMIAN, IRAS, *with* OTHERS.

ANT. Eros ! mine armour, Eros !
CLEO.   Sleep a little.
ANT. No, my chuck.   Eros ! Come, mine armour, Eros !

Enter EROS *with armour.*

Come, good fellow, put mine iron on.
If fortune be not ours to-day, it is
Because we brave her.   Come.
CLEO.   Nay, I'll help too.   5
What's this for ?
ANT.   Ah, let be, let be ! Thou art
The armourer of my heart.   False, false ; this, this.
CLEO. Sooth, la, I'll help.   Thus it must be.
ANT.   Well, well ;
We shall thrive now.   Seest thou, my good fellow ?
Go put on thy defences.
EROS.   Briefly, sir.   10
CLEO. Is not this buckled well ?
ANT.   Rarely, rarely !
He that unbuckles this, till we do please
To daff't for our repose, shall hear a storm.
Thou fumblest, Eros, and my queen's a squire
More tight at this than thou.   Dispatch.   O love,   15
That thou couldst see my wars to-day, and knew'st
The royal occupation !   Thou shouldst see
A workman in't.

Enter an armed SOLDIER.

                    Good-morrow to thee.   Welcome.
Thou look'st like him that knows a warlike charge.
To business that we love we rise betime,   20
And go to't with delight.
SOLD.   A thousand, sir,
Early though't be, have on their riveted trim,
And at the port expect you.
                              [*Shout.   Flourish of trumpets within.*

Enter CAPTAINS *and* SOLDIERS.

CAPT. The morn is fair.   Good morrow, General.
ALL. Good morrow, General.
ANT.   'Tis well blown, lads.   25
This morning, like the spirit of a youth
That means to be of note, begins betimes.
So, so.   Come, give me that.   This way.   Well said.
Fare thee well, dame, whate'er becomes of me.
This is a soldier's kiss.   Rebukeable,   30
And worthy shameful check it were, to stand
On more mechanic compliment ; I'll leave thee
Now like a man of steel.   You that will fight,
Follow me close ; I'll bring you to't.   Adieu.

                [*Exeunt* ANTONY, EROS, CAPTAINS *and* SOLDIERS.

CHAR. Please you retire to your chamber ?

CLEO.   Lead me.   35
    He goes forth gallantly.   That he and Cæsar might
    Determine this great war in single fight !
    Then, Antony—but now.   Well, on.   [*Exeunt.*

SCENE V. *Alexandria. Antony's camp.*

Trumpets sound. Enter ANTONY *and* EROS, *a* SOLDIER
meeting them.

SOLD. The gods make this a happy day to Antony !

ANT. Would thou and those thy scars had once prevail'd
    To make me fight at land !

SOLD.   Hadst thou done so
    The kings that have revolted, and the soldier
    That has this morning left thee, would have still   5
    Followed thy heels.

ANT.   Who's gone this morning ?

SOLD.   Who ?
    One ever near thee.   Call for Enobarbus,
    He shall not hear thee ; or from Cæsar's camp
    Say ' I am none of thine '.

ANT.   What say'st thou ?

SOLD.   Sir,
    He is with Cæsar.

EROS.   Sir, his chests and treasure   10
    He has not with him.

ANT.   Is he gone ?

SOLD.   Most certain.

ANT. Go, Eros, send his treasure after ; do it ;
    Detain no jot, I charge thee.   Write to him—
    I will subscribe—gentle adieus and greetings ;
    Say that I wish he never find more cause   15
    To change a master.   O, my fortunes have
    Corrupted honest men !   Dispatch.   Enobarbus !   [*Exeunt.*

SCENE VI. *Alexandria. Cæsar's camp.*

Flourish. Enter AGRIPPA, CÆSAR, *with* DOLABELLA *and*
ENOBARBUS.

CÆS. Go forth, Agrippa, and begin the fight.
    Our will is Antony be took alive ;
    Make it so known.

AGR.   Cæsar, I shall.   [*Exit.*

CÆS. The time of universal peace is near.   5
    Prove this a prosp'rous day, the three-nook'd world
    Shall bear the olive freely.

Enter a MESSENGER.

MESS.   Antony
    Is come into the field.

CÆS.   Go charge Agrippa
    Plant those that have revolted in the vant,

That Antony may seem to spend his fury   10
Upon himself.   [*Exeunt all but* ENOBARBUS.
ENO. Alexas did revolt and went to Jewry on
    Affairs of Antony ; there did dissuade
    Great Herod to incline himself to Cæsar
    And leave his master Antony.   For this pains   15
    Cæsar hath hang'd him.   Canidius and the rest
    That fell away have entertainment, but
    No honourable trust.   I have done ill,
    Of which I do accuse myself so sorely
    That I will joy no more.

                Enter a SOLDIER *of Cæsar's.*

SOLD.   Enobarbus, Antony   20
    Hath after thee sent all thy treasure, with
    His bounty overplus.   The messenger
    Came on my guard, and at thy tent is now
    Unloading of his mules.
ENO.   I give it you.
SOLD. Mock not, Enobarbus.   25
    I tell you true.   Best you saf'd the bringer
    Out of the host.   I must attend mine office,
    Or would have done't myself.   Your emperor
    Continues still a Jove.   [*Exit.*
ENO. I am alone the villain of the earth,   30
    And feel I am so most.   O Antony,
    Thou mine of bounty, how wouldst thou have paid
    My better service, when my turpitude
    Thou dost so crown with gold !   This blows my heart.
    If swift thought break it not, a swifter mean   35
    Shall outstrike thought ; but thought will do't, I feel.
    I fight against thee ?   No !   I will go seek
    Some ditch wherein to die ; the foul'st best fits
    My latter part of life.   [*Exit.*

        SCENE VII.   *Field of battle between the camps.*

        Alarum.   Drums and trumpets.   Enter AGRIPPA
                         and OTHERS.

AGR. Retire.   We have engag'd ourselves too far.
    Cæsar himself has work, and our oppression
    Exceeds what we expected.   [*Exeunt.*

        Alarums.   Enter ANTONY, *and* SCARUS *wounded.*

SCAR. O my brave Emperor, this is fought indeed !
    Had we done so at first, we had droven them home   5
    With clouts about their heads.
ANT.   Thou bleed'st apace.
SCAR. I had a wound here that was like a T,
    But now 'tis made an H.
ANT.   They do retire.
SCAR. We'll beat 'em into bench-holes.   I have yet
    Room for six scotches more.

Enter EROS.

EROS. They are beaten, sir, and our advantage serves
 For a fair victory.

SCAR.   Let us score their backs
 And snatch 'em up, as we take hares, behind.
 'Tis sport to maul a runner.

ANT.   I will reward thee
 Once for thy sprightly comfort, and tenfold   15
 For thy good valour. Come thee on.

SCAR. I'll halt after.   [*Exeunt.*

SCENE VIII. *Under the walls of Alexandria.*

Alarum. Enter ANTONY, *again in a march ;* SCARUS *with*
OTHERS.

ANT. We have beat him to his camp. Run one before
 And let the Queen know of our gests. To-morrow,
 Before the sun shall see's, we'll spill the blood
 That has to-day escap'd. I thank you all ;
 For doughty-handed are you, and have fought   5
 Not as you serv'd the cause, but as't had been
 Each man's like mine ; you have shown all Hectors.
 Enter the city, clip your wives, your friends,
 Tell them your feats ; whilst they with joyful tears
 Wash the congealment from your wounds and kiss 10
 The honour'd gashes whole.

Enter CLEOPATRA, *attended.*

    [*To* SCARUS.] Give me thy hand —
 To this great fairy I'll commend thy acts,
 Make her thanks bless thee. O thou day o' th' world,
 Chain mine arm'd neck. Leap thou, attire and all,
 Through proof of harness to my heart, and there   15
 Ride on the pants triumphing.

CLEO.   Lord of lords !
 O infinite virtue, com'st thou smiling from
 The world's great snare uncaught ?

ANT.   Mine nightingale, 19
 We have beat them to their beds. What, girl ! though grey
 Do something mingle with our younger brown, yet ha' we
 A brain that nourishes our nerves, and can
 Get goal for goal of youth. Behold this man ;
 Commend unto his lips thy favouring hand—
 Kiss it, my warrior—he hath fought to-day
 As if a god in hate of mankind had   25
 Destroyed in such a shape.

CLEO.   I'll give thee, friend,
 An armour all of gold ; it was a king's.

ANT. He has deserv'd it, were it carbuncled
 Like holy Phœbus' car. Give me thy hand.
 Through Alexandria make a jolly march ;   30
 Bear our hack'd targets like the men that owe them.

Had our great palace the capacity
To camp this host, we all would sup together,
And drink carouses to the next day's fate,
Which promises royal peril.   Trumpeters,   35
With brazen din blast you the city's ear ;
Make mingle with our rattling tabourines,
That heaven and earth may strike their sounds together
Applauding our approach.   [*Exeunt.*

SCENE IX.   *Cæsar's camp.*

Enter a CENTURION *and his* COMPANY ; ENOBARBUS *follows.*

CENT. If we be not reliev'd within this hour,
    We must return to th' court of guard.   The night
    Is shiny, and they say we shall embattle
    By th' second hour i' th' morn.
1 WATCH.   This last day was
    A shrewd one to's.
ENO. O, bear me witness, night—   5
2 WATCH. What man is this ?
1 WATCH.   Stand close and list him.
ENO. Be witness to me, O thou blessed moon,
    When men revolted shall upon record
    Bear hateful memory, poor Enobarbus did
    Before thy face repent !
CENT.   Enobarbus ?
2 WATCH.   Peace !   10
    Hark further.
ENO. O sovereign mistress of true melancholy,
    The poisonous damp of night disponge upon me,
    That life, a very rebel to my will,
    May hang no longer on me.   Throw my heart   15
    Against the flint and hardness of my fault,
    Which, being dried with grief, will break to powder,
    And finish all foul thoughts.   O Antony,
    Nobler than my revolt is infamous,
    Forgive me in thine own particular,
    But let the world rank me in register   20
    A master-leaver and a fugitive !
    O Antony ! O Antony !   *Dies.*
1 WATCH. Let's speak to him.
CENT. Let's hear him, for the things he speaks
    May concern Cæsar.
2 WATCH.   Let's do so.   But he sleeps.   25
CENT. Swoons rather ; for so bad a prayer as his
    Was never yet for sleep.
1 WATCH.   Go we to him.
2 WATCH. Awake, sir, awake ; speak to us.
1 WATCH. Hear you, sir ?
CENT. The hand of death hath raught him.
    [*Drums afar off.*]   Hark ! the drums
    Demurely wake the sleepers.   Let us bear him   30
    To th' court of guard ; he is of note.   Our hour
    Is fully out.

2 WATCH.   Come on, then ;
    He may recover yet.   [*Exeunt with the body.*

SCENE X. *Between the two camps.*

Enter ANTONY *and* SCARUS, *with their* ARMY.

ANT. Their preparation is to-day by sea ;
    We please them not by land.
SCAR.   For both, my lord.
ANT. I would they'd fight i' th' fire or i' th' air ;
    We'd fight there too. But this it is, our foot
    Upon the hills adjoining to the city   5
    Shall stay with us—Order for sea is given ;
    They have put forth the haven—
    Where their appointment we may best discover
    And look on their endeavour.   [*Exeunt.*

SCENE XI. *Between the camps.*

Enter CÆSAR *and his* ARMY.

CÆS. But being charg'd, we will be still by land,
    Which, as I take't, we shall ; for his best force
    Is forth to man his galleys. To the vales,
    And hold our best advantage.   [*Exeunt.*

SCENE XII. *A hill near Alexandria.*

Enter ANTONY *and* SCARUS.

ANT. Yet they are not join'd. Where yond pine does stand
    I shall discover all. I'll bring thee word
    Straight how 'tis like to go.   [*Exit.*
SCAR.   Swallows have built
    In Cleopatra's sails their nests. The augurers
    Say they know not, they cannot tell ; look grimly,   5
    And dare not speak their knowledge. Antony
    Is valiant and dejected ; and by starts
    His fretted fortunes give him hope and fear
    Of what he has and has not.
                  [*Alarum afar off, as at a sea-fight.*

Re-enter ANTONY.

ANT.   All is lost !
    This foul Egyptian hath betrayed me   10
    My fleet hath yielded to the foe, and yonder
    They cast their caps up and carouse together
    Like friends long lost. Triple-turn'd whore ! 'tis thou
    Hast sold me to this novice ; and my heart
    Makes only wars on thee. Bid them all fly ;   15
    For when I am reveng'd upon my charm,
    I have done all. Bid them all fly ; begone. [*Exit* SCARUS.
    O sun, thy uprise shall I see no more !
    Fortune and Antony part here ; even here
    Do we shake hands. All come to this ? The hearts   20
    That spaniel'd me at heels, to whom I gave

Their wishes, do discandy, melt their sweets
On blossoming Cæsar; and this pine is bark'd
That overtopp'd them all.   Betray'd I am.
O this false soul of Egypt! this grave charm—   25
Whose eye beck'd forth my wars and call'd them home,
Whose bosom was my crownet, my chief end—
Like a right gypsy hath at fast and loose
Beguil'd me to the very heart of loss.
What, Eros, Eros!

Enter CLEOPATRA.

       Ah, thou spell! Avaunt!   30
CLEO. Why is my lord enrag'd against his love?
ANT. Vanish, or I shall give thee thy deserving
And blemish Cæsar's triumph.   Let him take thee
And hoist thee up to the shouting plebeians;
Follow his chariot, like the greatest spot   35
Of all thy sex; most monster-like, be shown
For poor'st diminutives, for doits, and let
Patient Octavia plough thy visage up
With her prepared nails.   [*Exit* CLEOPATRA.
      'Tis well th'art gone,
If it be well to live; but better 'twere   40
Thou fell'st into my fury, for one death
Might have prevented many. Eros, ho!
The shirt of Nessus is upon me; teach me,
Alcides, thou mine ancestor, thy rage;
Let me lodge Lichas on the horns o' th' moon,   45
And with those hands that grasp'd the heaviest club
Subdue my worthiest self. The witch shall die.
To the young Roman boy she hath sold me, and I fall
Under this plot. She dies for't. Eros, ho!
            [*Exit.*

SCENE XIII. *Alexandria. Cleopatra's palace.*

Enter CLEOPATRA, CHARMIAN, IRAS, *and* MARDIAN.

CLEO. Help me, my women. O, he is more mad
Than Telamon for his shield; the boar of Thessaly
Was never so emboss'd.
CHAR.   To th' monument!
There lock yourself, and send him word you are dead.
The soul and body rive not more in parting
Than greatness going off.   5
CLEO.   To th' monument!
Mardian, go tell him I have slain myself;
Say that the last I spoke was 'Antony'
And word it, prithee, piteously. Hence, Mardian,
And bring me how he takes my death. To th' monument!
            [*Exeunt.*

SCENE XIV. *Cleopatra's palace.*

Enter ANTONY *and* EROS.

ANT. Eros, thou yet behold'st me?

EROS.   Ay, noble lord.
ANT. Sometime we see a cloud that's dragonish;
    A vapour sometime like a bear or lion,
    A tower'd citadel, a pendent rock,
    A forked mountain, or blue promontory   5
    With trees upon't that nod unto the world
    And mock our eyes with air.   Thou hast seen these signs;
    They are black vesper's pageants.
EROS.   Ay, my lord.
ANT. That which is now a horse, even with a thought
    The rack dislimns, and makes it indistinct,   10
    As water is in water.
EROS.   It does, my lord.
ANT. My good knave Eros, now thy captain is
    Even such a body.   Here I am Antony;
    Yet cannot hold this visible shape, my knave.
    I made these wars for Egypt;   and the Queen—   15
    Whose heart I thought I had, for she had mine,
    Which, whilst it was mine, had annex'd unto't
    A million moe, now lost—she, Eros, has
    Pack'd cards with Cæsar, and false-play'd my glory
    Unto an enemy's triumph.   20
    Nay, weep not, gentle Eros;   there is left us
    Ourselves to end ourselves.

                    Enter MARDIAN.

                        O, thy vile lady!
    She has robb'd me of my sword.
MAR.   No, Antony;
    My mistress lov'd thee, and her fortunes mingled
    With thine entirely.
ANT.   Hence, saucy eunuch;   peace!   25
    She hath betray'd me, and shall die the death.
MAR. Death of one person can be paid but once,
    And that she has discharg'd.   What thou wouldst do
    Is done unto thy hand.   The last she spake
    Was 'Antony!   most noble Antony!'   30
    Then in the midst a tearing groan did break
    The name of Antony;   it was divided
    Between her heart and lips.   She rend'red life,
    Thy name so buried in her.
ANT.   Dead then?
MAR.   Dead.
ANT. Unarm, Eros;   the long day's task is done,   35
    And we must sleep.   That thou depart'st hence safe
    Does pay thy labour richly.   Go.   [*Exit* MARDIAN.
                        Off, pluck off!
    The sevenfold shield of Ajax cannot keep
    The battery from my heart.   O, cleave, my sides!
    Heart, once be stronger than thy continent,   40
    Crack thy frail case.   Apace, Eros, apace.—
    No more a soldier.   Bruised pieces, go;
    You have been nobly borne.—From me awhile.   [*Exit* EROS.
    I will o'ertake thee, Cleopatra, and

Weep for my pardon. So it must be, for now   45
All length is torture. Since the torch is out.
Lie down, and stray no farther. Now all labour
Mars what it does ; yea, very force entangles
Itself with strength. Seal then, and all is done.
Eros !—I come, my queen.—Eros !—Stay for me ;   50
Where souls do couch on flowers, we'll hand in hand,
And with our sprightly port make the ghosts gaze.
Dido and her Æneas shall want troops,
And all the haunt be ours.—Come, Eros, Eros !

Re-enter EROS.

EROS. What would my lord ?

ANT.   Since Cleopatra died,   55
I have liv'd in such dishonour that the gods
Detest my baseness. I, that with my sword
Quarter'd the world, and o'er green Neptune's back
With ships made cities, condemn myself to lack
The courage of a woman ; less noble mind   60
Than she which by her death our Cæsar tells
' I am conqueror of myself.' Thou art sworn, Eros,
That, when the exigent should come—which now
Is come indeed—when I should see behind me
Th' inevitable prosecution of   65
Disgrace and horror, that, on my command,
Thou then wouldst kill me. Do't ; the time is come.
Thou strik'st not me ; 'tis Cæsar thou defeat'st.
Put colour in thy cheek.

EROS.   The gods withhold me !
Shall I do that which all the Parthian darts,   70
Though enemy, lost aim and could not ?

ANT.   Eros,
Wouldst thou be window'd in great Rome and see
Thy master thus with pleach'd arms, bending down
His corrigible neck, his face subdu'd
To penetrative shame, whilst the wheel'd seat   75
Of fortunate Cæsar, drawn before him, branded
His baseness that ensued ?

EROS.   I would not see't.

ANT. Come, then ; for with a wound I must be cur'd.
Draw that thy honest sword, which thou hast worn
Most useful for thy country.

EROS.   O, sir, pardon me !   80

ANT. When I did make thee free, swor'st thou not then
To do this when I bade thee ? Do it at once,
Or thy precedent services are all
But accidents unpurpos'd. Draw, and come.

EROS. Turn from me then that noble countenance,   85
Wherein the worship of the whole world lies.

ANT. Lo thee !   [*Turning from him.*

EROS. My sword is drawn.

ANT.   Then let it do at once
The thing why thou hast drawn it.

EROS.   My dear master,

8

My captain and my emperor, let me say,   9(
Before I strike this bloody stroke, farewell.
ANT. 'Tis said, man ; and farewell.
EROS. Farewell, great chief. Shall I strike now ?
ANT.   Now, Eros.
EROS. Why, there then ! Thus do I escape the sorrow
Of Antony's death.   [*Kills himself*
ANT.   Thrice nobler than myself !   9!
Thou teachest me, O valiant Eros, what
I should, and thou couldst not. My queen and Eros
Have, by their brave instruction, got upon me
A nobleness in record. But I will be
A bridegroom in my death, and run into't   10(
As to a lover's bed. Come, then ; and, Eros,
Thy master dies thy scholar. To do thus   [*Falling on his sword*
I learn'd of thee. How ? not dead ? not dead ?—
The guard, ho ! O, dispatch me !

Enter DERCETAS *and a* GUARD.

I GUARD.   What's the noise ?
ANT. I have done my work ill, friends. O, make an end   10!
Of what I have begun.
2 GUARD.   The star is fall'n.
I GUARD. And time is at his period.
ALL.   Alas, and woe !
ANT. Let him that loves me, strike me dead.
I GUARD. Not I.
2 GUARD. Nor I.
3 GUARD. Nor any one.   [*Exeunt* GUARD
DER. Thy death and fortunes bid thy followers fly.   11)
This sword but shown to Cæsar, with this tidings,
Shall enter me with him.

Enter DIOMEDES.

DIO. Where's Antony ?
DER.   There, Diomed, there.
DIO.   Lives he ?
Wilt thou not answer, man ?   [*Exit* DERCETAS
ANT. Art thou there, Diomed ? Draw thy sword and give me   11(
Sufficing strokes for death.
DIO.   Most absolute lord,
My mistress Cleopatra sent me to thee.
ANT. When did she send thee ?
DIO.   Now, my lord.
ANT.   Where is she ?
DIO. Lock'd in her monument. She had a prophesying fear   12(
Of what hath come to pass ; for when she saw—
Which never shall be found—you did suspect
She had dispos'd with Cæsar, and that your rage
Would not be purg'd, she sent you word she was dead ;
But fearing since how it might work, hath sent   12)
Me to proclaim the truth ; and I am come,
I dread, too late.
ANT. Too late, good Diomed. Call my guard, I prithee.

DIO. What, ho! the Emperor's guard! The guard, what ho!
  Come, your lord calls!   130

        Enter four or five of the GUARD of ANTONY.

ANT. Bear me, good friends, where Cleopatra bides;
  'Tis the last service that I shall command you.
GUARD. Woe, woe are we, sir, you may not live to wear
  All your true followers out.
ALL.   Most heavy day!
ANT. Nay, good my fellows, do not please sharp fate   135
  To grace it with your sorrows. Bid that welcome
  Which comes to punish us, and we punish it,
  Seeming to bear it lightly. Take me up.
  I have led you oft; carry me now, good friends,
  And have my thanks for all.   [*Exeunt, bearing ANTONY.*

        SCENE XV. *Alexandria. A monument.*

Enter CLEOPATRA and her MAIDS aloft, with CHARMIAN and IRAS.

CLEO. O Charmian, I will never go from hence!
CHAR. Be comforted, dear madam.
CLEO.   No, I will not.
  All strange and terrible events are welcome,
  But comforts we despise; our size of sorrow,
  Proportion'd to our cause, must be as great   5
  As that which makes it.

        Enter DIOMEDES, below.

                      How now! Is he dead?
DIO. His death's upon him, but not dead.
  Look out o' th' other side your monument;
  His guard have brought him thither.

        Enter, below, ANTONY, borne by the GUARD.

CLEO.   O sun,
  Burn the great sphere thou mov'st in! Darkling stand   10
  The varying shore o' th' world. O Antony,
  Antony, Antony! Help, Charmian; help, Iras, help;
  Help, friends below! Let's draw him hither.
ANT.   Peace!
  Not Cæsar's valour hath o'erthrown Antony,
  But Antony's hath triumph'd on itself.   15
CLEO. So it should be, that none but Antony
  Should conquer Antony; but woe 'tis so!
ANT. I am dying, Egypt, dying; only
  I here importune death awhile, until
  Of many thousand kisses the poor last   20
  I lay upon thy lips.
CLEO.   I dare not, dear.
  Dear my lord, pardon! I dare not,
  Lest I be taken. Not th' imperious show
  Of the full-fortun'd Cæsar ever shall
  Be brooch'd with me. If knife, drugs, serpents, have   25
  Edge, sting, or operation, I am safe.

Your wife Octavia, with her modest eyes
And still conclusion, shall acquire no honour
Demuring upon me.   But come, come, Antony—
Help me, my women—we must draw thee up ;   3
Assist, good friends.

ANT.   O, quick, or I am gone.

CLEO. Here's sport indeed ! How heavy weighs my lord !
Our strength is all gone into heaviness ;
That makes the weight.   Had I great Juno's power,
The strong-wing'd Mercury should fetch thee up,   3
And set thee by Jove's side.   Yet come a little.
Wishers were ever fools.   O come, come, come,
                    [*They heave* ANTONY *aloft to* CLEOPATRA.
And welcome, welcome ! Die where thou hast liv'd.
Quicken with kissing.   Had my lips that power,
Thus would I wear them out.

ALL.   A heavy sight !   4

ANT. I am dying, Egypt, dying.
Give me some wine, and let me speak a little.

CLEO. No, let me speak ; and let me rail so high
That the false huswife Fortune break her wheel,
Provok'd by my offence.

ANT.   One word, sweet queen :   4
Of Cæsar seek your honour, with your safety.   O !

CLEO. They do not go together.

ANT.   Gentle, hear me :
None about Cæsar trust but Proculeius.

CLEO. My resolution and my hands I'll trust ;
None about Cæsar.   5

ANT. The miserable change now at my end
Lament nor sorrow at ; but please your thoughts
In feeding them with those my former fortunes
Wherein I liv'd the greatest prince o' th' world,
The noblest ; and do now not basely die,   5
Not cowardly put off my helmet to
My countryman—a Roman by a Roman
Valiantly vanquish'd.   Now my spirit is going
I can no more.

CLEO.   Noblest of men, woo't die ?
Hast thou no care of me ? Shall I abide   6
In this dull world, which in thy absence is
No better than a sty ? O, see, my women,   [ANTONY *dies*
The crown o' th' earth doth melt.   My lord !
O, wither'd is the garland of the war,
The soldier's pole is fall'n ! Young boys and girls   6
Are level now with men.   The odds is gone,
And there is nothing left remarkable
Beneath the visiting moon.   [*Swoons*

CHAR. O, quietness, lady !

IRAS. She's dead too, our sovereign.

CHAR. Lady !

IRAS. Madam !

CHAR. O madam, madam, madam !

IRAS. Royal Egypt, Empress !   7

HAR. Peace, peace, Iras !
LEO. No more but e'en a woman, and commanded
  By such poor passion as the maid that milks
  And does the meanest chares.   It were for me   75
  To throw my sceptre at the injurious gods ;
  To tell them that this world did equal theirs
  Till they had stol'n our jewel.   All's but nought ;
  Patience is sottish, and impatience does
  Become a dog that's mad.   Then is it sin   80
  To rush into the secret house of death
  Ere death dare come to us ?   How do you, women ?
  What, what ! good cheer ! Why, how now, Charmian
  My noble girls ! Ah, women, women, look,
  Our lamp is spent, it's out ! Good sirs, take heart.   85
  We'll bury him ; and then, what's brave, what's noble,
  Let's do it after the high Roman fashion,
  And make death proud to take us.   Come, away ;
  This case of that huge spirit now is cold.
  Ah, women, women ! Come ; we have no friend   90
  But resolution and the briefest end.
                [Exeunt ; those above bearing off Antony's body.

                            ACT FIVE

          SCENE I.   Alexandria.   Cæsar's camp.

  Enter CÆSAR, AGRIPPA, DOLABELLA, MÆCENAS, GALLUS, PROCULEIUS,
                  and OTHERS, his Council of War.

ES. Go to him, Dolabella, bid him yield ;
  Being so frustrate, tell him he mocks
  The pauses that he makes.
DOL.   Cæsar, I shall.   [Exit.

        Enter DERCETAS with the sword of ANTONY.

ES. Wherefore is that ? And what art thou that dar'st
  Appear thus to us ?
ER.   I am call'd Dercetas ;   5
  Mark Antony I serv'd, who best was worthy
  Best to be serv'd.   Whilst he stood up and spoke,
  He was my master, and I wore my life
  To spend upon his haters.   If thou please
  To take me to thee, as I was to him   10
  I'll be to Cæsar ; if thou pleasest not,
  I yield thee up my life.
ES.   What is't thou say'st ?
ER. I say, O Cæsar, Antony is dead.
ES. The breaking of so great a thing should make
  A greater crack.   The round world   15
  Should have shook lions into civil streets,
  And citizens to their dens.   The death of Antony
  Is not a single doom ; in the name lay
  A moiety of the world.
R.   He is dead, Cæsar,
  Not by a public minister of justice,   20

                                                                   229

Nor by a hired knife ; but that self hand
Which writ his honour in the acts it did
Hath, with the courage which the heart did lend it,
Splitted the heart.   This is his sword ;
I robb'd his wound of it ; behold it stain'd
With his most noble blood.

CÆS.   Look you sad, friends ?
The gods rebuke me, but it is tidings
To wash the eyes of kings.

AGR.   And strange it is
That nature must compel us to lament
Our most persisted deeds.

MÆC.   His taints and honours
Wag'd equal with him.

AGR.   A rarer spirit never
Did steer humanity.   But you gods will give us
Some faults to make us men.   Cæsar is touch'd.

MÆC. When such a spacious mirror's set before him,
He needs must see himself.

CÆS.   O Antony,
I have follow'd thee to this ! But we do lance
Diseases in our bodies.   I must perforce
Have shown to thee such a declining day
Or look on thine ; we could not stall together
In the whole world.   But yet let me lament,
With tears as sovereign as the blood of hearts,
That thou, my brother, my competitor
In top of all design, my mate in empire,
Friend and companion in the front of war,
The arm of mine own body, and the heart
Where mine his thoughts did kindle—that our stars,
Unreconciliable, should divide
Our equalness to this.   Hear me, good friends—

Enter an EGYPTIAN.

But I will tell you at some meeter season.
The business of this man looks out of him ;
We'll hear him what he says.   Whence are you ?

EGYPT. A poor Egyptian, yet the Queen, my mistress,
Confin'd in all she has, her monument,
Of thy intents desires instruction,
That she preparedly may frame herself
To th' way she's forc'd to.

CÆS.   Bid her have good heart.
She soon shall know of us, by some of ours,
How honourable and how kindly we
Determine for her ; for Cæsar cannot learn
To be ungentle.

EGYPT.   So the gods preserve thee !   [E

CÆS. Come hither, Proculeius.   Go and say
We purpose her no shame.   Give her what comforts
The quality of her passion shall require,
Lest, in her greatness, by some mortal stroke
She do defeat us ; for her life in Rome

Would be eternal in our triumph.   Go,
And with your speediest bring us what she says,
And how you find her.

PRO.   Cæsar, I shall.   [Exit.
CÆS. Gallus, go you along.   [Exit GALLUS.
                    Where's Dolabella,
To second Proculeius ?
ALL. Dolabella !   70
CÆS. Let him alone, for I remember now
How he's employ'd ; he shall in time be ready.
Go with me to my tent, where you shall see
How hardly I was drawn into this war,
How calm and gentle I proceeded still   75
In all my writings.   Go with me, and see
What I can show in this.   [Exeunt.

SCENE II.   Alexandria.   The monument.

Enter CLEOPATRA, CHARMIAN, IRAS, and MARDIAN.

CLEO. My desolation does begin to make
A better life.   'Tis paltry to be Cæsar :
Not being Fortune, he's but Fortune's knave,
A minister of her will ; and it is great
To do that thing that ends all other deeds,   5
Which shackles accidents and bolts up change,
Which sleeps, and never palates more the dug,
The beggar's nurse and Cæsar's.

Enter, to the gates of the monument, PROCULEIUS, GALLUS,
and SOLDIERS.

PRO. Cæsar sends greeting to the Queen of Egypt,
And bids thee study on what fair demands   10
Thou mean'st to have him grant thee.
CLEO.   What's thy name ?
PRO. My name is Proculeius.
CLEO.   Antony
Did tell me of you, bade me trust you ; but
I do not greatly care to be deceiv'd,
That have no use for trusting.   If your master   15
Would have a queen his beggar, you must tell him
That majesty, to keep decorum, must
No less beg than a kingdom.   If he please
To give me conquer'd Egypt for my son,
He gives me so much of mine own as I   20
Will kneel to him with thanks.
PRO.   Be of good cheer ;
Y'are fall'n into a princely hand ; fear nothing.
Make your full reference freely to my lord,
Who is so full of grace that it flows over
On all that need.   Let me report to him   25
Your sweet dependency, and you shall find
A conqueror that will pray in aid for kindness
Where he for grace is kneel'd to.
CLEO.   Pray you tell him

231

I am his fortune's vassal and I send him
The greatness he has got.   I hourly learn   30
A doctrine of obedience, and would gladly
Look him i' th' face.
PRO.   This I'll report, dear lady.
Have comfort, for I know your plight is pitied
Of him that caus'd it.
GAL. You see how easily she may be surpris'd.   35

[*Here* PROCULEIUS *and two of the* GUARD *ascend the monument by a
ladder placed against a window, and come behind* CLEOPATRA. *Some
of the* GUARD *unbar and open the gates.*

Guard her till Cæsar come.   [*Exit*
IRAS. Royal Queen !
CHAR. O Cleopatra ! thou art taken, Queen !
CLEO. Quick, quick, good hands.   [*Drawing a dagger*
PRO.   Hold, worthy lady, hold,
                    [*Disarms her.*
Do not yourself such wrong, who are in this   40
Reliev'd, but not betray'd.
CLEO.   What, of death too,
That rids our dogs of languish ?
PRO.   Cleopatra,
Do not abuse my master's bounty by
Th' undoing of yourself.   Let the world see
His nobleness well acted, which your death   45
Will never let come forth.
CLEO.   Where art thou, death ?
Come hither, come ! Come, come, and take a queen
Worth many babes and beggars !
PRO.   O, temperance, lady !
CLEO. Sir, I will eat no meat ; I'll not drink, sir ;
If idle talk will once be necessary,   50
I'll not sleep neither.   This mortal house I'll ruin,
Do Cæsar what he can.   Know, sir, that I
Will not wait pinion'd at your master's court,
Nor once be chastis'd with the sober eye
Of dull Octavia.   Shall they hoist me up,   55
And show me to the shouting varletry
Of censuring Rome ? Rather a ditch in Egypt
Be gentle grave unto me ! Rather on Nilus' mud
Lay me stark-nak'd, and let the water-flies
Blow me into abhorring ! Rather make   60
My country's high pyramides my gibbet,
And hang me up in chains !
PRO.   You do extend
These thoughts of horror further than you shall
Find cause in Cæsar.

Enter DOLABELLA.

DOL. Proculeius,
What thou hast done thy master Cæsar knows,   65
And he hath sent for thee.   For the Queen,
I'll take her to my guard.

PRO.   So, Dolabella,
    It shall content me best.   Be gentle to her.
    [*To* CLEOPATRA.] To Cæsar I will speak what you shall please,
    If you'll employ me to him.
CLEO.   Say I would die.   70
                                    [*Exeunt* PROCULEIUS *and* SOLDIERS.
DOL. Most noble Empress, you have heard of me?
CLEO. I cannot tell.
DOL.   Assuredly you know me.
CLEO. No matter, sir, what I have heard or known.
    You laugh when boys or women tell their dreams;
    Is't not your trick?
DOL.   I understand not, madam.   75
CLEO. I dreamt there was an Emperor Antony—
    O, such another sleep, that I might see
    But such another man!
DOL.   If it might please ye—
CLEO. His face was as the heav'ns, and therein stuck
    A sun and moon, which kept their course and lighted   80
    The little O, the earth.
DOL.   Most sovereign creature—
CLEO. His legs bestrid the ocean; his rear'd arm
    Crested the world.   His voice was propertied
    As all the tuned spheres, and that to friends;
    But when he meant to quail and shake the orb,   85
    He was as rattling thunder.   For his bounty,
    There was no winter in't; an autumn 'twas
    That grew the more by reaping.   His delights
    Were dolphin-like: they show'd his back above
    The element they liv'd in.   In his livery   90
    Walk'd crowns and crownets; realms and islands were
    As plates dropp'd from his pocket.
DOL.   Cleopatra—
CLEO. Think you there was or might be such a man
    As this I dreamt of?
DOL.   Gentle madam, no.
CLEO. You lie, up to the hearing of the gods.   95
    But if there be nor ever were one such,
    It's past the size of dreaming.   Nature wants stuff
    To vie strange forms with fancy; yet t' imagine
    An Antony were nature's piece 'gainst fancy,
    Condemning shadows quite.
DOL.   Hear me, good madam.   100
    Your loss is, as yourself, great; and you bear it
    As answering to the weight.   Would I might never
    O'ertake pursu'd success, but I do feel,
    By the rebound of yours, a grief that smites
    My very heart at root.
CLEO.   I thank you, sir.   105
    Know you what Cæsar means to do with me?
DOL. I am loath to tell you what I would you knew.
CLEO. Nay, pray you, sir.
DOL.   Though he be honourable—
CLEO. He'll lead me, then, in triumph?

DOL. Madam, he will.   I know't.   [*Flourish.*
WITHIN.   Make way there—Cæsar !

Enter CÆSAR ; GALLUS, PROCULEIUS, MÆCENAS, SELEUCUS, *and
others of his* TRAIN.

CÆS. Which is the Queen of Egypt ?
DOL. It is the Emperor, madam.   [CLEOPATRA *kneels.*
CÆS. Arise, you shall not kneel.
  I pray you, rise ; rise, Egypt.
CLEO.   Sir, the gods
  Will have it thus ; my master and my lord   115
  I must obey.
CÆS.   Take to you no hard thoughts.
  The record of what injuries you did us,
  Though written in our flesh, we shall remember
  As things but done by chance.
CLEO.   Sole sir o' th' world,
  I cannot project mine own cause so well   120
  To make it clear, but do confess I have
  Been laden with like frailties which before
  Have often sham'd our sex.
CÆS.   Cleopatra, know
  We will extenuate rather than enforce.
  If you apply yourself to our intents—   125
  Which towards you are most gentle—you shall find
  A benefit in this change ; but if you seek
  To lay on me a cruelty by taking
  Antony's course, you shall bereave yourself
  Of my good purposes, and put your children   130
  To that destruction which I'll guard them from,
  If thereon you rely.   I'll take my leave.
CLEO. And may, through all the world.   'Tis yours, and we,
  Your scutcheons and your signs of conquest, shall
  Hang in what place you please.   Here, my good lord. 135
CÆS. You shall advise me in all for Cleopatra.
CLEO. This is the brief of money, plate, and jewels,
  I am possess'd of.   'Tis exactly valued,
  Not petty things admitted.   Where's Seleucus ?
SEL. Here, madam.   140
CLEO. This is my treasurer ; let him speak, my lord,
  Upon his peril, that I have reserv'd
  To myself nothing.   Speak the truth, Seleucus.
SEL. Madam,
  I had rather seal my lips than to my peril   145
  Speak that which is not.
CLEO.   What have I kept back ?
SEL. Enough to purchase what you have made known.
CÆS. Nay, blush not, Cleopatra ; I approve
  Your wisdom in the deed.
CLEO.   See, Cæsar ! O, behold,
  How pomp is followed !   Mine will now be yours ;   150
  And, should we shift estates, yours would be mine.
  The ingratitude of this Seleucus does
  Even make me wild.   O slave, of no more trust

Than love that's hir'd ! What, goest thou back ? Thou shalt
Go back, I warrant thee ; but I'll catch thine eyes　　　155
Though they had wings.　Slave, soulless villain, dog !
O rarely base !

CÆS.　　　　　　Good Queen, let us entreat you.

CLEO. O Cæsar, what a wounding shame is this,
That thou vouchsafing here to visit me,
Doing the honour of thy lordliness　　　　　160
To one so meek, that mine own servant should
Parcel the sum of my disgraces by
Addition of his envy ! Say, good Cæsar,
That I some lady trifles have reserv'd,
Immoment toys, things of such dignity　　　　165
As we greet modern friends withal ; and say
Some nobler token I have kept apart
For Livia and Octavia, to induce
Their mediation—must I be unfolded
With one that I have bred ? The gods ! It smites me　　170
Beneath the fall I have.　[*To* SELEUCUS.]　Prithee go hence ;
Or I shall show the cinders of my spirits
Through th' ashes of my chance.　Wert thou a man,
Thou wouldst have mercy on me.

CÆS.　　　　　　Forbear, Seleucus. [*Exit* SELEUCUS.

CLEO. Be it known that we, the greatest, are misthought　　175
For things that others do ; and when we fall
We answer others' merits in our name,
Are therefore to be pitied.

CÆS.　　　　　　Cleopatra,
Not what you have reserv'd, nor what acknowledg'd,
Put we i' th' roll of conquest. Still be't yours,　　　180
Bestow it at your pleasure ; and believe
Cæsar's no merchant, to make prize with you
Of things that merchants sold. Therefore be cheer'd ;
Make not your thoughts your prisons. No, dear Queen ;
For we intend so to dispose you as　　　　　185
Yourself shall give us counsel. Feed and sleep.
Our care and pity is so much upon you
That we remain your friend ; and so, adieu.

CLEO. My master and my lord !

CÆS.　　　　　　Not so, Adieu.
　　　　　　　[*Flourish.　Exeunt* CÆSAR *and his* TRAIN.

CLEO. He words me, girls, he words me, that I should not　　190
Be noble to myself. But hark thee, Charmian !
　　　　　　　　　　[*Whispers* CHARMIAN.

IRAS. Finish, good lady ; the bright day is done,
And we are for the dark.

CLEO.　　　　　　Hie thee again.
I have spoke already, and it is provided ;
Go put it to the haste.

CHAR.　　　　　　Madam, I will.　　　195

　　　　　Re-enter DOLABELLA.

DOL. Where's the Queen ?

CHAR.　　　　　　Behold, sir.　　　　[*Exit.*

CLEO.   Dolabella!

DOL. Madam, as thereto sworn by your command,
Which my love makes religion to obey,
I tell you this : Cæsar through Syria
Intends his journey, and within three days   200
You with your children will he send before.
Make your best use of this ; I have perform'd
Your pleasure and my promise.

CLEO.   Dolabella,
I shall remain your debtor.

DOL.   I your servant.
Adieu, good Queen ; I must attend on Cæsar.   205

CLEO. Farewell, and thanks.   [*Exit* DOLABELLA.
                         Now, Iras, what think'st thou ?
Thou an Egyptian puppet shall be shown
In Rome as well as I. Mechanic slaves,
With greasy aprons, rules, and hammers, shall
Uplift us to the view ; in their thick breaths,   210
Rank of gross diet, shall we be enclouded,
And forc'd to drink their vapour.

IRAS.   The gods forbid !

CLEO. Nay, 'tis most certain, Iras. Saucy lictors
Will catch at us like strumpets, and scald rhymers
Ballad us out o' tune ; the quick comedians   215
Extemporally will stage us, and present
Our Alexandrian revels ; Antony
Shall be brought drunken forth, and I shall see
Some squeaking Cleopatra boy my greatness
I' th' posture of a whore.

IRAS.   O the good gods !   220

CLEO. Nay, that's certain.

IRAS. I'll never see't, for I am sure mine nails
Are stronger than mine eyes.

CLEO.   Why, that's the way
To fool their preparation and to conquer
Their most absurd intents.

                    Enter CHARMIAN.

                         Now, Charmian !   225
Show me, my women, like a queen. Go fetch
My best attires. I am again for Cydnus,
To meet Mark Antony. Sirrah, Iras, go.
Now, noble Charmian, we'll dispatch indeed ;
And when thou hast done this chare, I'll give thee leave   230
To play till doomsday. Bring our crown and all.
                              [*Exit* IRAS. *A noise within.*
Wherefore's this noise ?

                    Enter a GUARDSMAN.

GUARD.   Here is a rural fellow
That will not be denied your Highness' presence.
He brings you figs.

CLEO. Let him come in.   [*Exit* GUARDSMAN.
                         What poor an instrument   235

May do a noble deed ! He brings me liberty.
My resolution's plac'd, and I have nothing
Of woman in me. Now from head to foot
I am marble-constant ; now the fleeting moon
No planet is of mine.

Re-enter GUARDSMAN *and* CLOWN, *with a basket.*

GUARD. This is the man.
CLEO.   Avoid, and leave him.   [*Exit* GUARDSMAN
Hast thou the pretty worm of Nilus there
That kills and pains not ?   242
CLOWN. Truly, I have him. But I would not be the party that
    should desire you to touch him, for his biting is immortal ; those
    that do die of it do seldom or never recover.
CLEO. Remember'st thou any that have died on't ?
CLOWN. Very many, men and women too. I heard of one of them no
    longer than yesterday : a very honest woman, but something
    given to lie, as a woman should not do but in the way of honesty ;
    how she died of the biting of it, what pain she felt—truly she
    makes a very good report o' th' worm. But he that will believe
    all that they say shall never be saved by half that they do. But
    this is most falliable, the worm's an odd worm.   256
CLEO. Get thee hence ; farewell.
CLOWN. I wish you all joy of the worm.   [*Sets down the basket.*
CLEO. Farewell.
CLOWN. You must think this, look you, that the worm will do his kind.
CLEO. Ay, ay ; farewell.
CLOWN. Look you, the worm is not to be trusted but in the keeping
    of wise people ; for indeed there is no goodness in the worm. 265
CLEO. Take thou no care ; it shall be heeded.
CLOWN. Very good. Give it nothing, I pray you, for it is not worth
    the feeding.
CLEO. Will it eat me ?   269
CLOWN. You must not think I am so simple but I know the devil
    himself will not eat a woman. I know that a woman is a dish for
    the gods, if the devil dress her not. But truly, these same whore-
    son devils do the gods great harm in their women, for in every
    ten that they make the devils mar five.   275
CLEO. Well, get thee gone ; farewell.
CLOWN. Yes, forsooth. I wish you joy o' th' worm.   [*Exit.*

Re-enter IRAS, *with a robe, crown, &c.*

CLEO. Give me my robe, put on my crown ; I have
    Immortal longings in me. Now no more
    The juice of Egypt's grape shall moist this lip.   280
    Yare, yare, good Iras ; quick. Methinks I hear
    Antony call. I see him rouse himself
    To praise my noble act. I hear him mock
    The luck of Cæsar, which the gods give men
    To excuse their after wrath. Husband, I come.   285
    Now to that name my courage prove my title !
    I am fire and air ; my other elements
    I give to baser life. So, have you done ?
    Come then, and take the last warmth of my lips.

Farewell, kind Charmian.   Iras, long farewell.   290
          [*Kisses them.* IRAS *falls and dies.*
Have I the aspic in my lips ?   Dost fall ?
If thus thou and nature can so gently part,
The stroke of death is as a lover's pinch,
Which hurts and is desir'd.   Dost thou lie still ?
If thou vanishest, thou tell'st the world   295
It is not worth leave-taking.
CHAR. Dissolve, thick cloud, and rain, that I may say
 The gods themselves do weep.
CLEO.   This proves me base.
If she first meet the curled Antony,
He'll make demand of her, and spend that kiss   300
Which is my heaven to have.   Come, thou mortal wretch,
     [*To an asp, which she applies to her breast.*
With thy sharp teeth this knot intrinsicate
Of life at once untie.   Poor venomous fool,
Be angry and dispatch.   O couldst thou speak,
That I might hear thee call great Cæsar ass   305
Unpolicied !
CHAR.   O Eastern star !
CLEO.   Peace, peace !
Dost thou not see my baby at my breast
That sucks the nurse asleep ?
CHAR.   O, break ! O, break !
CLEO. As sweet as balm, as soft as air, as gentle—
O Antony !   Nay, I will take thee too :   310
     [*Applying another asp to her arm.*
What should I stay—   [*Dies.*
CHAR. In this vile world ? So, fare thee well.
Now boast thee, death, in thy possession lies
A lass unparallel'd.   Downy windows, close ;
And golden Phœbus never be beheld   315
Of eyes again so royal !   Your crown's awry ;
I'll mend it and then play—

     Enter the GUARD, *rushing in.*

1 GUARD. Where's the Queen ?
CHAR.   Speak softly, wake her not.
1 GUARD. Cæsar hath sent—
CHAR.   Too slow a messenger.   [*Applies an asp.*
O, come apace, dispatch.   I partly feel thee.   320
1 GUARD. Approach, ho !   All's not well : Cæsar's beguil'd.
2 GUARD. There's Dolabella sent from Cæsar ;   call him.
1 GUARD. What work is here !   Charmian, is this well done ?
CHAR. It is well done, and fitting for a princess
Descended of so many royal kings.   325
Ah, soldier !   [CHARMIAN *dies.*

     Re-enter DOLABELLA.

DOL. How goes it here ?
2 GUARD.   All dead.
DOL.   Cæsar, thy thoughts
Touch their effects in this.   Thyself art coming

To see perform'd the dreaded act which thou
So sought'st to hinder.   330
WITHIN.   A way there, a way for Cæsar !

Re-enter CÆSAR *and all his* TRAIN.

DOL. O sir, you are too sure an augurer :
That you did fear is done.
ÆS.   Bravest at the last,
She levell'd at our purposes, and being royal,
Took her own way.   The manner of their deaths ?
I do not see them bleed.
DOL.   Who was last with them ?   335
GUARD. A simple countryman that brought her figs.
This was his basket.
ÆS.   Poison'd then.
GUARD.   O Cæsar,
This Charmian liv'd but now ; she stood and spake
I found her trimming up the diadem
On her dead mistress.   Tremblingly she stood,   340
And on the sudden dropp'd.
ÆS.   O noble weakness !
If they had swallow'd poison 'twould appear
By external swelling ; but she looks like sleep,
As she would catch another Antony
In her strong toil of grace.
DOL.   Here on her breast   345
There is a vent of blood, and something blown ;
The like is on her arm.
GUARD. This is an aspic's trail ; and these fig-leaves
Have slime upon them, such as th' aspic leaves
Upon the caves of Nile.
ÆS.   Most probable   350
That so she died ; for her physician tells me
She hath pursu'd conclusions infinite
Of easy ways to die.   Take up her bed,
And bear her women from the monument.
She shall be buried by her Antony ;   355
No grave upon the earth shall clip in it
A pair so famous.   High events as these
Strike those that make them ; and their story is
No less in pity than his glory which
Brought them to be lamented.   Our army shall   360
In solemn show attend this funeral,
And then to Rome.   Come, Dolabella, see
High order in this great solemnity.   [*Exeunt.*

CYMBELINE

Cymbeline stands in the First Folio last among the tragedies, but in spite of this and the title that names it *The Tragedy of Cymbeline* it belongs to a group of plays that come in date of composition after the Tragedies and that may contain violent or unhappy deaths without, however, failing to provide for the characters with whom the spectators are most concerned a happy ending. The Queen and Cloten her son are both dead before the last act of *Cymbeline* closes, but this does not detract from the happiness of the others, for even the King himself may be excused for finding in the recovery of his lost sons and missing daughter a happiness that gives him no leisure to brood on the loss of a homicidal-minded spouse.

It is inevitable that comparisons between these later plays and the tragedies should raise a number of questions that can be answered in a reasonable way only by looking at Shakespeare's plays from a position that allows us to see them as episodes in his whole career as a dramatist. Why should Shakespeare, having shown in *Othello* his powers of construction and concentration, choose in *Cymbeline* so apparently rambling and episodic a manner of plotting? The suggestion that this change merely reflects a decline in his powers seems unlikely, if only because we cannot trace the progress of any such decay. His last tragedy, *Coriolanus*, does not lack firmness of outline or any of the old authority; his next works are in an entirely different vein. This change is clearly deliberate. Some critics have felt it necessary to provide some explanation other than a change of direction in the dramatist's interests, or at least to insist that this change of interest was consequent on physical and mental collapse. It is clear however that many of the features that distinguish *Cymbeline* from the tragedies are either deliberate or to be explained by a mental condition that would be quite incompatible with other aspects of the work. Shakespeare knew as well as we know, Granville-Barker points out, that in the Rome of Augustus no one could have found Frenchmen, Dutchmen, and Spaniards, discussing the rival merits of their mistresses, or the villain of the piece wagering ten thousand ducats. Shakespeare had already shown his audiences a very different picture of the Rome of Augustus. Neither *Julius Cæsar* nor *Coriolanus* offers an antiquarian's reconstruction of Rome, but what we have there is something quite different from Philario's supper party. Either the nervous breakdown we hear about from the commentators had razed from Shakespeare's mind his earlier reading in Plutarch and elsewhere, or Shakespeare was now engaged on a type of plot that not merely permitted but accommodated such unhistorical detail.

Shakespeare has put together features from many different sources. Into the story of Cymbeline, which he adapted from Holinshed, who tells of that king's relations with the Emperor Augustus, we find inserted an Italian tale of intrigue from the *Decameron*. Boccaccio tells how a Genoese merchant laid a wager on his wife's chastity, and, being persuaded that he has lost, gives orders for his wife's death. She escapes in man's attire and takes service with the Sultan, discovers and unmasks her calumniator, and is reconciled to her husband. As in Shakespeare, the villain is carried in a chest into the lady's bed-chamber, and in the night steals a girdle and other of her belongings as well as noting the mole on her left breast. His fate however is harder than Iachimo's, for the Sultan has him anointed with honey and left bound to a stake till he is eaten alive by wasps and hornets. The English version of the story, *Frederick of Jennen*, does not contain this detail which Shakespeare used not in *Cymbeline*, but in *The Winter's Tale*, as a comic stroke by Autolycus, in the threat to the clown at IV.iv :

> He has a son—who shall be flay'd alive ; then 'nointed
> over with honey, set on the head of a wasp's nest . . .

Shakespeare must therefore have used Boccaccio, whatever other versions he consulted, and this need cause no surprise as it is clear from *Othello* and elsewhere that he had recourse to Italian novelle for material.

In this intrigue part of his plot Shakespeare incorporates the familiar motif of the sleep that resembles death, a useful device that permits of the transition in the narrative required by the plot. Shakespeare in describing the stand made by Belarius, Guiderius, and Arviragus, in V.ii had recourse to the account in Holinshed of the exploit of a husbandman Hay and his two sons who secured for the Scots at the battle of Loncart with the Danes in A.D. 976 the victory in what looked like the face of defeat.

It was this amalgam of history and folk-motif, and bourgeois intrigue, that so taxed Dr. Johnson's sense of decorum that he declared,

> To remark the folly of the fiction, the absurdity of the conduct, the confusion of the names and manners of different times, and the impossibility of the events in any system of life, were to waste criticism upon unresisting imbecility, upon faults too evident for detection, and too gross for aggravation.

We cannot suppose that Shakespeare was unaware of the medley he had concocted, and that no system of life in the sense of a historical period could be cited to justify his liberties. That apart, however, there is little one can regard as out of place in a romantic adventure of this time. Sleeping-potions are part of the machinery of such a genre and bandits may live on the fringes of elegant society.

Johnson's criticism, however, has suggested to many commentators that the play is not wholly Shakespeare's. Some have gone very far in their assignments to other hands ; but by considering what a very judicious adherent to the general feeling that the play is not wholly by Shakespeare has to say on this topic we may realize the critical difficulties this view in its turn raises. ' A fair amount of the play —both of its design and execution—is pretty certainly not Shakespeare's ', summarizes Granville-Barker's impression. Yet when he comes to discuss the detail of the plot and the way the pieces dovetail together his analysis contradicts his general impression. With such various individuals or groups as the stolen princes, Iachimo, Posthumus, to work into the story Shakespeare cannot keep them all

continuously before us, nor does he wish to do so, for Imogen is the
real protagonist of the play ; she provides the continuity. To let
Posthumus slip from the current of the story and then to reintroduce
him again as in the play seems to Granville-Barker the surest evidence
of an alien hand, although the actual writing in this section is, he
admits, not un-Shakespearean. Yet Shakespeare in emphasizing the
repentance of Posthumus before he regains his lost happiness prepares him for the final discovery very much as he prepares Leontes
for the statue scene in *The Winter's Tale*. It cannot be claimed that
the treatment of these two penitents differs so markedly in style and
feeling that we must assign the passages to different hands.

The real difficulty that the introduction of hands other than
Shakespeare's into the discussion raises is best seen, however, when
Granville-Barker comes to analyse the last scene. As he admits,

> The finer phases of the play's construction are to be seen in the
> swift forwarding of the first part of the story, in the subtle com-
> position of Iachimo's three scenes . . . . and in the elaboration of
> the finale . . . . This last has not lacked praise.

and he quotes Barrett-Wendell's observations on the complexity and
fullness of the material to be resolved. It is difficult to believe that
the composer of this finale, who cannot have been anyone but Shakespeare, was piecing together fragments casually introduced by other
hands. There is a contrivance about it all that makes it difficult to
believe that what went before could come from any mind other than
that which so effectively ran them together at the conclusion.

CYMBELINE

DRAMATIS PERSONÆ

CYMBELINE, *King of Britain.*
CLOTEN, *son to the Queen by a former husband.*
POSTHUMUS LEONATUS, *a gentleman, husband to Imogen.*
BELARIUS, *a banished lord, disguised under the name of* MORGAN.

GUIDERIUS,
ARVIRAGUS, } *sons to Cymbeline, disguised under the names of* POLYDORE *and* CADWAL, *supposed sons to Belarius.*

PHILARIO, *friend to Posthumus*
IACHIMO, *friend to Philario,* } *Italians.*

A FRENCH GENTLEMAN, *friend to Philario.*

CAIUS LUCIUS, *General of the Roman Forces.*
A ROMAN CAPTAIN.
TWO BRITISH CAPTAINS.
PISANIO, *servant to Posthumus.*
CORNELIUS, *a physician.*
TWO LORDS *of Cymbeline's court.*
TWO GENTLEMEN *of the same.*
TWO GAOLERS.

QUEEN, *wife to Cymbeline.*
IMOGEN, *daughter to Cymbeline by a former queen.*
HELEN, *a lady attending on Imogen.*

APPARITIONS.
LORDS, LADIES, ROMAN SENATORS, TRIBUNES, a SOOTHSAYER, a DUTCH GENTLEMAN, a SPANISH GENTLEMAN, MUSICIANS, OFFICERS, CAPTAINS, SOLDIERS, MESSENGERS *and* ATTENDANTS.

THE SCENE : *Britain ; Italy.*

ACT ONE

SCENE I. *Britain. The garden of Cymbeline's palace.*

1 GENT. You do not meet a man but frowns ; our bloods
No more obey the heavens than our courtiers
Still seem as does the King's.

2 GENT.   But what's the matter ?

1 GENT. His daughter, and the heir of's kingdom, whom
He purpos'd to his wife's sole son—a widow   5
That late he married—hath referr'd herself
Unto a poor but worthy gentleman. She's wedded
Her husband banish'd ; she imprison'd. All
Is outward sorrow, though I think the King
Be touch'd at very heart.

2 GENT.   None but the King ?   10

1 GENT. He that hath lost her too. So is the Queen,
That most desir'd the match. But not a courtier,
Although they wear their faces to the bent
Of the King's looks, hath a heart that is not
Glad at the thing they scowl at.

2 GENT.   And why so ?   15
1 GENT. He that hath miss'd the Princess is a thing
      Too bad for bad report ; and he that hath her—
      I mean that married her, alack, good man !
      And therefore banish'd—is a creature such
      As, to seek through the regions of the earth   20
      For one his like, there would be something failing
      In him that should compare. I do not think
      So fair an outward and such stuff within
      Endows a man but he.
2 GENT.   You speak him far.
1 GENT. I do extend him, sir, within himself ;   25
      Crush him together rather than unfold
      His measure duly.
2 GENT.   What's his name and birth ?
1 GENT. I cannot delve him to the root ; his father
      Was call'd Sicilius, who did join his honour
      Against the Romans with Cassibelan,   30
      But had his titles by Tenantius, whom
      He serv'd with glory and admir'd success,
      So gain'd the sur-addition Leonatus ;
      And had, besides this gentleman in question,
      Two other sons, who, in the wars o' th' time,   35
      Died with their swords in hand ; for which their father
      Then old and fond of issue, took such sorrow
      That he quit being ; and his gentle lady,
      Big of this gentleman, our theme, deceas'd
      As he was born. The King he takes the babe   40
      To his protection, calls him Posthumus Leonatus,
      Breeds him and makes him of his bed-chamber,
      Puts to him all the learnings that his time
      Could make him the receiver of ; which he took,
      As we do air, fast as 'twas minist'red,   45
      And in's spring became a harvest, liv'd in court—
      Which rare it is to do—most prais'd, most lov'd,
      A sample to the youngest ; to th' more mature
      A glass that feated them ; and to the graver
      A child that guided dotards. To his mistress,   50
      For whom he now is banish'd—her own price
      Proclaims how she esteem'd him and his virtue ;
      By her election may be truly read
      What kind of man he is.
2 GENT.   I honour him
      Even out of your report. But pray you tell me,   55
      Is she sole child to th' King ?
1 GENT.   His only child.
      He had two sons—if this be worth your hearing,
      Mark it—the eldest of them at three years old,
      I' th' swathing clothes the other, from their nursery
      Were stol'n ; and to this hour no guess in knowledge 60
      Which way they went.
2 GENT. How long is this ago ?
1 GENT.   Some twenty years.
2 GENT. That a king's children should be so convey'd,
244

So slackly guarded, and the search so slow
That could not trace them!

1 GENT.   Howsoe'er 'tis strange,   65
  Or that the negligence may well be laugh'd at,
  Yet is it true, sir.

2 GENT.   I do well believe you.

1 GENT. We must forbear; here comes the gentleman,
  The Queen, and Princess.   [Exeunt.

Enter the QUEEN, POSTHUMUS, *and* IMOGEN.

QUEEN. No, be assur'd you shall not find me, daughter,   70
  After the slander of most stepmothers,
  Evil-ey'd unto you. You're my prisoner, but
  Your gaoler shall deliver you the keys
  That lock up your restraint. For you, Posthumus,
  So soon as I can win th' offended King,   75
  I will be known your advocate. Marry, yet
  The fire of rage is in him, and 'twere good
  You lean'd unto his sentence with what patience
  Your wisdom may inform you.

POST.   Please your Highness,
  I will from hence to-day.

QUEEN.   You know the peril.   80
  I'll fetch a turn about the garden, pitying
  The pangs of barr'd affections, though the King
  Hath charg'd you should not speak together.   [Exit.

IMO.   O
  Dissembling courtesy! How fine this tyrant
  Can tickle where she wounds! My dearest husband,   85
  I something fear my father's wrath, but nothing—
  Always reserv'd my holy duty—what
  His rage can do on me. You must be gone;
  And I shall here abide the hourly shot
  Of angry eyes, not comforted to live   90
  But that there is this jewel in the world
  That I may see again.

POST.   My queen! my mistress!
  O lady, weep no more, lest I give cause
  To be suspected of more tenderness
  Than doth become a man. I will remain   95
  The loyal'st husband that did e'er plight troth;
  My residence in Rome at one Philario's,
  Who to my father was a friend, to me
  Known but by letter; thither write, my queen,
  And with mine eyes I'll drink the words you send,   100
  Though ink be made of gall.

Re-enter QUEEN.

QUEEN.   Be brief, I pray you.
  If the King come, I shall incur I know not
  How much of his displeasure. [*Aside.*] Yet I'll move him
  To walk this way. I never do him wrong
  But he does buy my injuries, to be friends;   105
  Pays dear for my offences.   [*Exit.*

POST. Should we be taking leave
    As long a term as yet we have to live,
    The loathness to depart would grow. Adieu !
IMO. Nay, stay a little.
    Were you but riding forth to air yourself,   110
    Such parting were too petty. Look here, love :
    This diamond was my mother's ; take it, heart ;
    But keep it till you woo another wife,
    When Imogen is dead.
POST.   How, how ? Another ?
    You gentle gods, give me but this I have,   115
    And sear up my embracements from a next
    With bonds of death ! Remain, remain thou here [Puts on the ring.
    While sense can keep it on. And, sweetest, fairest,
    As I my poor self did exchange for you,
    To your so infinite loss, so in our trifles   120
    I still win of you. For my sake wear this ;
    It is a manacle of love ; I'll place it
    Upon this fairest prisoner.   [Puts a bracelet on her arm.
IMO.   O the gods !
    When shall we see again ?

Enter CYMBELINE *and* LORDS.

POST.   Alack, the King !
CYM. Thou basest thing, avoid ; hence from my sight   125
    If after this command thou fraught the court
    With thy unworthiness, thou diest. Away !
    Thou'rt poison to my blood.
POST.   The gods protect you,
    And bless the good remainders of the court !
    I am gone.   [Exit.
IMO.   There cannot be a pinch in death   130
    More sharp than this is.
CYM.   O disloyal thing,
    That shouldst repair my youth, thou heap'st
    A year's age on me !
IMO.   I beseech you, sir,
    Harm not yourself with your vexation.
    I am senseless of your wrath ; a touch more rare   135
    Subdues all pangs, all fears.
CYM.   Past grace ? obedience ?
IMO. Past hope, and in despair ; that way past grace.
CYM. That mightst have had the sole son of my queen !
IMO. O blessed that I might not ! I chose an eagle,
    And did avoid a puttock.   140
CYM. Thou took'st a beggar, wouldst have made my throne
    A seat for baseness.
IMO.   No ; I rather added
    A lustre to it.
CYM.   O thou vile one !
IMO.   Sir,
    It is your fault that I have lov'd Posthumus.
    You bred him as my playfellow, and he is   145
    A man worth any woman ; overbuys me

Almost the sum he pays.

CYM.   What, art thou mad?

IMO. Almost, sir.   Heaven restore me!   Would I were
A neat-herd's daughter, and my Leonatus
Our neighbour shepherd's son!

Re-enter QUEEN.

CYM.   Thou foolish thing!   150
[*To the* QUEEN.] They were again together.   You have done
Not after our command.   Away with her,
And pen her up.

QUEEN.   Beseech your patience.—Peace,
Dear lady daughter, peace!—Sweet sovereign,
Leave us to ourselves, and make yourself some comfort   155
Out of your best advice.

CYM.   Nay, let her languish
A drop of blood a day and, being aged,
Die of this folly.   [*Exit, with* LORDS.

Enter PISANIO.

QUEEN.   Fie! you must give way.
Here is your servant.   How now, sir!   What news?

PIS. My lord your son drew on my master.

QUEEN.   Ha!   160
No harm, I trust, is done?

PIS.   There might have been,
But that my master rather play'd than fought,
And had no help of anger; they were parted
By gentlemen at hand.

QUEEN.   I am very glad on't.

IMO. Your son's my father's friend; he takes his part   165
To draw upon an exile!   O brave sir!
I would they were in Afric both together;
Myself by with a needle, that I might prick
The goer-back.   Why came you from your master?

PIS. On his command.   He would not suffer me   170
To bring him to the haven; left these notes
Of what commands I should be subject to,
When't pleas'd you to employ me.

QUEEN.   This hath been
Your faithful servant.   I dare lay mine honour
He will remain so.

PIS.   I humbly thank your Highness.   175

QUEEN. Pray walk awhile.

IMO.   About some half-hour hence,
Pray you speak with me.   You shall at least
Go see my lord aboard.   For this time leave me.   [*Exeunt.*

SCENE II.   *Britain.   A public place.*

Enter CLOTEN *and two* LORDS.

I LORD. Sir, I would advise you to shift a shirt; the violence of
action hath made you reek as a sacrifice.   Where air comes out,

air comes in; there's none abroad so wholesome as that you vent.

CLO. If my shirt were bloody, then to shift it. Have I hurt him?

2 LORD. [*Aside.*] No, faith; not so much as his patience.

1 LORD. Hurt him! His body's a passable carcass if he be not hurt. It is a throughfare for steel if it be not hurt. 10

2 LORD. [*Aside.*] His steel was in debt; it went o' th' back side the town.

CLO. The villain would not stand me.

2 LORD. [*Aside.*] No; but he fled forward still, toward your face.

1 LORD. Stand you? You have land enough of your own; but he added to your having, gave you some ground.

2 LORD. [*Aside.*] As many inches as you have oceans. Puppies!

CLO. I would they had not come between us. 21

2 LORD. [*Aside.*] So would I, till you had measur'd how long a fool you were upon the ground.

CLO. And that she should love this fellow, and refuse me!

2 LORD. [*Aside.*] If it be a sin to make a true election, she is damn'd.

1 LORD. Sir, as I told you always, her beauty and her brain go not together; she's a good sign, but I have seen small reflection of her wit. 30

2 LORD. [*Aside.*] She shines not upon fools, lest the reflection should hurt her.

CLO. Come, I'll to my chamber. Would there had been some hurt done!

2 LORD. [*Aside.*] I wish not so; unless it had been the fall of an ass, which is no great hurt. 36

CLO. You'll go with us?

1 LORD. I'll attend your lordship.

CLO. Nay, come, let's go together.

2 LORD. Well, my lord. [*Exeunt.*

SCENE III. *Britain. Cymbeline's palace.*

Enter IMOGEN *and* PISANIO.

IMO. I would thou grew'st unto the shores o' th' haven,
And questioned'st every sail; if he should write,
And I not have it, 'twere a paper lost,
As offer'd mercy is. What was the last
That he spake to thee?

PIS.   It was: his queen, his queen! 5

IMO. Then wav'd his handkerchief?

PIS.   And kiss'd it, madam.

IMO. Senseless linen, happier therein than I!
And that was all?

PIS.   No, madam; for so long
As he could make me with his eye, or care
Distinguish him from others, he did keep
The deck, with glove, or hat, or handkerchief, 10
Still waving, as the fits and stirs of's mind
Could best express how slow his soul sail'd on,
How swift his ship.

IMO.   Thou shouldst have made him
As little as a crow, or less, ere left 15
To after-eye him.

248

PIS.   Madam, so I did.
IMO. I would have broke mine eyestrings, crack'd them but
     To look upon him, till the diminution
     Of space had pointed him sharp as my needle;
     Nay, followed him till he had melted from   20
     The smallness of a gnat to air, and then
     Have turn'd mine eye and wept. But, good Pisanio,
     When shall we hear from him?
PIS.   Be assur'd, madam,
     With his next vantage.
IMO. I did not take my leave of him, but had   25
     Most pretty things to say. Ere I could tell him
     How I would think on him at certain hours
     Such thoughts and such; or I could make him swear
     The shes of Italy should not betray
     Mine interest and his honour; or have charg'd him,   30
     At the sixth hour of morn, at noon, at midnight,
     T' encounter me with orisons, for then
     I am in heaven for him; or ere I could
     Give him that parting kiss which I had set
     Betwixt two charming words, comes in my father,   35
     And like the tyrannous breathing of the north
     Shakes all our buds from growing.

                           Enter a LADY.

LADY.   The Queen, madam,
     Desires your Highness' company.
IMO. Those things I bid you do, get them dispatch'd.
     I will attend the Queen.
PIS.   Madam, I shall.   [*Exeunt.*

             SCENE IV. *Rome. Philario's house.*

        Enter PHILARIO, IACHIMO, *a* FRENCHMAN, *a* DUTCHMAN, *and*
                           a SPANIARD.

IACH. Believe it, sir, I have seen him in Britain. He was then of a
     crescent note, expected to prove so worthy as since he hath been
     allowed the name of. But I could then have look'd on him
     without the help of admiration, though the catalogue of his
     endowments had been tabled by his side, and I to peruse him by
     items.
PHI. You speak of him when he was less furnish'd than now he is
     with that which makes him both without and within.   9
FRENCH. I have seen him in France; we had very many there could
     behold the sun with as firm eyes as he.
IACH. This matter of marrying his king's daughter, wherein he
     must be weighed rather by her value than his own, words him, I
     doubt not, a great deal from the matter.   15
FRENCH. And then his banishment.
IACH. Ay, and the approbation of those that weep this lamentable
     divorce under her colours are wonderfully to extend him, be it
     but to fortify her judgment, which else an easy battery might lay
     flat, for taking a beggar, without less quality. But how comes it
     he is to sojourn with you? How creeps acquaintance?   22

PHI. His father and I were soldiers together, to whom I have been often bound for no less than my life.

Enter POSTHUMUS.

Here comes the Briton. Let him be so entertained amongst you as suits with gentlemen of your knowing to a stranger of his quality. I beseech you all be better known to this gentleman, whom I commend to you as a noble friend of mine. How worthy he is I will leave to appear hereafter, rather than story him in his own hearing. 31

FRENCH. Sir, we have known together in Orleans.

POST. Since when I have been debtor to you for courtesies, which I will be ever to pay and yet pay still.

FRENCH. Sir, you o'errate my poor kindness. I was glad I did atone my countryman and you; it had been pity you should have been put together with so mortal a purpose as then each bore, upon importance of so slight and trivial a nature. 39

POST. By your pardon, sir. I was then a young traveller; rather shunn'd to go even with what I heard than in my every action to be guided by others' experiences; but upon my mended judgment—if I offend not to say it is mended—my quarrel was not altogether slight. 44

FRENCH. Faith, yes, to be put to the arbitrament of swords, and by such two that would by all likelihood have confounded one the other or have fall'n both.

IACH. Can we, with manners, ask what was the difference? 49

FRENCH. Safely, I think. 'Twas a contention in public, which may, without contradiction, suffer the report. It was much like an argument that fell out last night, where each of us fell in praise of our country mistresses; this gentleman at that time vouching—and upon warrant of bloody affirmation—his to be more fair, virtuous, wise, chaste, constant, qualified, and less attemptable, than any the rarest of our ladies in France. 57

IACH. That lady is not now living, or this gentleman's opinion, by this, worn out.

POST. She holds her virtue still, and I my mind.

IACH. You must not so far prefer her fore ours of Italy.

POST. Being so far provok'd as I was in France, I would abate her nothing, though I profess myself her adorer, not her friend. 65

IACH. As fair and as good—a kind of hand-in-hand comparison—had been something too fair and too good for any lady in Britain. If she went before others I have seen as that diamond of yours outlustres many I have beheld, I could not but believe she excelled many; but I have not seen the most precious diamond that is, nor you the lady.

POST. I prais'd her as I rated her. So do I my stone.

IACH. What do you esteem it at?

POST. More than the world enjoys. 75

IACH. Either your unparagon'd mistress is dead, or she's outpriz'd by a trifle.

POST. You are mistaken: the one may be sold or given, if there were wealth enough for the purchase or merit for the gift; the other is not a thing for sale, and only the gift of the gods.

IACH. Which the gods have given you?

POST. Which by their graces I will keep.   83
IACH. You may wear her in title yours; but you know strange fowl
     light upon neighbouring ponds. Your ring may be stol'n too.
     So your brace of unprizable estimations, the one is but frail and
     the other casual; a cunning thief, or a that-way-accomplish'd
     courtier, would hazard the winning both of first and last.
POST. Your Italy contains none so accomplish'd a courtier to con-
     vince the honour of my mistress, if in the holding or loss of that
     you term her frail. I do nothing doubt you have store of thieves;
     notwithstanding, I fear not my ring.
PHI. Let us leave here, gentlemen.   95
POST. Sir, with all my heart. This worthy signior, I thank him,
     makes no stranger of me; we are familiar at first.
IACH. With five times so much conversation I should get ground of
     your fair mistress; make her go back even to the yielding, had I
     admittance and opportunity to friend.   102
POST. No, no.
IACH. I dare thereupon pawn the moiety of my estate to your ring,
     which, in my opinion, o'ervalues it something. But I make my
     wager rather against your confidence than her reputation; and,
     to bar your offence herein too, I durst attempt it against any lady
     in the world.
POST. You are a great deal abus'd in too bold a persuasion, and I doubt
     not you sustain what y'are worthy of by your attempt.   111
IACH. What's that?
POST. A repulse; though your attempt, as you call it, deserve more—
     a punishment too.
PHI. Gentlemen, enough of this. It came in too suddenly; let it
     die as it was born, and I pray you be better acquainted.
IACH. Would I had put my estate and my neighbour's on th' appro-
     bation of what I have spoke!
POST. What lady would you choose to assail?   120
IACH. Yours, whom in constancy you think stands so safe. I will lay
     you ten thousand ducats to your ring that, commend me to the
     court where your lady is, with no more advantage than the
     opportunity of a second conference, and I will bring from thence
     that honour of hers which you imagine so reserv'd.
POST. I will wage against your gold gold to it. My ring I hold dear
     as my finger; 'tis part of it.
IACH. You are a friend, and therein the wiser. If you buy ladies'
     flesh at a million a dram, you cannot preserve it from tainting.
     But I see you have some religion in you, that you fear.   132
POST. This is but a custom in your tongue; you bear a graver
     purpose, I hope.
IACH. I am the master of my speeches, and would undergo what's
     spoken, I swear.
POST. Will you? I shall but lend my diamond till your return. Let
     there be covenants drawn between's. My mistress exceeds in
     goodness the hugeness of your unworthy thinking. I dare you
     to this match: here's my ring.   141
PHI. I will have it no lay.
IACH. By the gods, it is one. If I bring you no sufficient testimony
     that I have enjoy'd the dearest bodily part of your mistress, my
     ten thousand ducats are yours; so is your diamond too. If I

come off, and leave her in such honour as you have trust in, she
your jewel, this your jewel, and my gold are yours—provided I
have your commendation for my more free entertainment.   149
POST. I embrace these conditions; let us have articles betwixt us.
Only, thus far you shall answer: if you make your voyage upon
her, and give me directly to understand you have prevail'd, I am
no further your enemy—she is not worth our debate; if she
remain unseduc'd, you not making it appear otherwise, for your
ill opinion and th' assault you have made to her chastity you shall
answer me with your sword.   157
IACH. Your hand—a covenant! We will have these things set down
by lawful counsel, and straight away for Britain, lest the bargain
should catch cold and starve.   I will fetch my gold and have our
two wagers recorded.
POST. Agreed.   [Exeunt POSTHUMUS and IACHIMO.
FRENCH. Will this hold, think you?
PHI. Signior Iachimo will not from it.   Pray let us follow 'em.
                                                         [Exeunt.

SCENE V. Britain.   Cymbeline's palace.

Enter QUEEN, LADIES, and CORNELIUS.

QUEEN. Whiles yet the dew's on ground gather those flowers;
    Make haste; who has the note of them?
LADY.   I, madam.
QUEEN. Dispatch.   [Exeunt LADIES.
    Now, Master Doctor, have you brought those drugs?
COR. Pleaseth your Highness, ay.   Here they are, madam.   5
                                            [Presenting a box.
    But I beseech your Grace, without offence—
    My conscience bids me ask—wherefore you have
    Commanded of me these most poisonous compounds
    Which are the movers of a languishing death,
    But, though slow, deadly?
QUEEN.   I wonder, doctor,   10
    Thou ask'st me such a question.   Have I not been
    Thy pupil long?   Hast thou not learn'd me how
    To make perfumes? distil? preserve? yea, so
    That our great king himself doth woo me oft
    For my confections?   Having thus far proceeded—   15
    Unless thou think'st me devilish—is't not meet
    That I did amplify my judgment in
    Other conclusions?   I will try the forces
    Of these thy compounds on such creatures as
    We count not worth the hanging—but none human—   20
    To try the vigour of them, and apply
    Allayments to their act, and by them gather
    Their several virtues and effects.
COR.   Your Highness
    Shall from this practice but make hard your heart;
    Besides, the seeing these effects will be   25
    Both noisome and infectious.
QUEEN.   O, content thee.

Enter PISANIO.

[*Aside.*] Here comes a flattering rascal ; upon him
Will I first work. He's for his master,
And enemy to my son.—How now, Pisanio !
Doctor, your service for this time is ended ;   30
Take your own way.
COR. [*Aside.*]   I do suspect you, madam ;
But you shall do no harm.
QUEEN. [*To* PISANIO.]   Hark thee, a word.
COR. [*Aside.*] I do not like her. She doth think she has
Strange ling'ring poisons. I do know her spirit,
And will not trust one of her malice with   35
A drug of such damn'd nature. Those she has
Will stupefy and dull the sense awhile,
Which first perchance she'll prove on cats and dogs,
Then afterward up higher ; but there is
No danger in what show of death it makes,   40
More than the locking up the spirits a time,
To be more fresh, reviving. She is fool'd
With a most false effect ; and I the truer
So to be false with her.
QUEEN.   No further service, Doctor,   44
Until I send for thee.
COR.   I humbly take my leave.   [*Exit.*
QUEEN. Weeps she still, say'st thou ? Dost thou think in time
She will not quench, and let instructions enter
Where folly now possesses ? Do thou work.
When thou shalt bring me word she loves my son,
I'll tell thee on the instant thou art then   50
As great as is thy master ; greater, for
His fortunes all lie speechless, and his name
Is at last gasp. Return he cannot, nor
Continue where he is. To shift his being
Is to exchange one misery with another,   55
And every day that comes comes to decay
A day's work in him. What shalt thou expect
To be depender on a thing that leans,
Who cannot be new built, nor has no friends
So much as but to prop him ?

          [*The* QUEEN *drops the box.* PISANIO *takes it up.*
                   Thou tak'st up   60
Thou know'st not what ; but take it for thy labour.
It is a thing I made, which hath the King
Five times redeem'd from death. I do not know
What is more cordial. Nay, I prithee take it ;
It is an earnest of a further good   65
That I mean to thee. Tell thy mistress how
The case stands with her ; do't as from thyself.
Think what a chance thou changest on ; but think
Thou hast thy mistress still ; to boot, my son,
Who shall take notice of thee. I'll move the King   70
To any shape of thy preferment, such
As thou'lt desire ; and then myself, I chiefly,

That set thee on to this desert, am bound
To load thy merit richly.   Call my women.
Think on my words.   [*Exit* PISANIO.
     A sly and constant knave,   75
Not to be shak'd ; the agent for his master,
And the remembrancer of her to hold
The hand-fast to her lord.   I have given him that
Which, if he take, shall quite unpeople her
Of leigers for her sweet ; and which she after, 80
Except she bend her humour, shall be assur'd
To taste of too.

     Re-enter PISANIO *and* LADIES.

    So, so.   Well done, well done.
The violets, cowslips, and the primroses,
Bear to my closet.   Fare thee well, Pisanio ;
Think on my words.   [*Exeunt* QUEEN *and* LADIES.
PIS.   And shall do.   85
But when to my good lord I prove untrue
I'll choke myself—there's all I'll do for you.   [*Exit.*

   SCENE VI.   *Britain.   The palace.*

     Enter IMOGEN *alone.*

IMO. A father cruel and a step-dame false ;
A foolish suitor to a wedded lady
That hath her husband banish'd.   O, that husband !
My supreme crown of grief ! and those repeated
Vexations of it !   Had I been thief-stol'n,   5
As my two brothers, happy ! but most miserable
Is the desire that's glorious.   Blessed be those,
How mean soe'er, that have their honest wills,
Which seasons comfort.   Who may this be ?   Fie !

    Enter PISANIO *and* IACHIMO.

PIS. Madam, a noble gentleman of Rome   10
Comes from my lord with letters.
IACH.   Change you, madam ?
The worthy Leonatus is in safety,
And greets your Highness dearly.   [*Presents a letter.*
IMO.   Thanks, good sir.
You're kindly welcome.
IACH. [*Aside.*]   All of her that is out of door most rich ! 15
If she be furnish'd with a mind so rare,
She is alone th' Arabian bird, and I
Have lost the wager.   Boldness be my friend !
Arm me, audacity, from head to foot !
Or, like the Parthian, I shall flying fight ; 20
Rather, directly fly.
IMO. [*Reads.*]   ' He is one of the noblest note, to whose kindnesses,
I am most infinitely tied.   Reflect upon him accordingly, as you
value your trust.   LEONATUS.'
So far I read aloud ;   25
But even the very middle of my heart
Is warm'd by th' rest and takes it thankfully.

You are as welcome, worthy sir, as I
Have words to bid you ; and shall find it so
In all that I can do.

IACH.　　　　　　　　　Thanks, fairest lady.　　　　　　30
What, are men mad ? Hath nature given them eyes
To see this vaulted arch and the rich crop
Of sea and land, which can distinguish 'twixt
The fiery orbs above and the twinn'd stones
Upon the number'd beach, and can we not　　　　　35
Partition make with spectacles so precious
'Twixt fair and foul ?

IMO.　　　　　　　What makes your admiration ?

IACH. It cannot be i' th' eye, for apes and monkeys,
'Twixt two such shes, would chatter this way and
Contemn with mows the other ; nor i' th' judgment,　　40
For idiots in this case of favour would
Be wisely definite ; nor i' th' appetite ;
Sluttery, to such neat excellence oppos'd,
Should make desire vomit emptiness,
Not so allur'd to feed.　　　　　　　　　　　45

IMO. What is the matter, trow ?

IACH.　　　　　　　　The cloyed will—
That satiate yet unsatisfied desire, that tub
Both fill'd and running—ravening first the lamb,
Longs after for the garbage.

IMO.　　　　　　　　　What, dear sir,
Thus raps you ? Are you well ?　　　　　　　50

IACH. Thanks, madam ; well.—Beseech you, sir,
Desire my man's abode where I did leave him.
He's strange and peevish.

PIS.　　　　　　　I was going, sir,
To give him welcome.　　　　　　　　　　[Exit.

IMO. Continues well my lord ? His health beseech you ?　55

IACH. Well, madam.

IMO. Is he dispos'd to mirth ? I hope he is.

IACH. Exceeding pleasant ; none a stranger there
So merry and so gamesome. He is call'd
The Britain reveller.

IMO.　　　　　　　When he was here　　　　60
He did incline to sadness, and oft-times
Not knowing why.

ACH.　　　　　I never saw him sad.
There is a Frenchman his companion, one
An eminent monsieur that, it seems, much loves
A Gallian girl at home. He furnaces　　　　　65
The thick sighs from him ; whiles the jolly Briton—
Your lord, I mean—laughs from's free lungs, cries ' O,
Can my sides hold, to think that man—who knows
By history, report, or his own proof,
What woman is, yea, what she cannot choose　　　70
But must be—will's free hours languish for
Assured bondage ? '

IMO.　　　　　　Will my lord say so ?

ACH. Ay, madam, with his eyes in flood with laughter.

It is a recreation to be by
And hear him mock the Frenchman.   But heavens know
Some men are much to blame.
IMO.   Not he, I hope.   75
IACH. Not he ; but yet heaven's bounty towards him might
Be us'd more thankfully.   In himself, 'tis much ;
In you, which I account his, beyond all talents.
Whilst I am bound to wonder, I am bound   80
To pity too.
IMO.   What do you pity, sir ?
IACH. Two creatures heartily.
IMO.   Am I one, sir ?
You look on me : what wreck discern you in me
Deserves your pity ?
IACH.   Lamentable ! What,
To hide me from the radiant sun and solace   85
I' th' dungeon by a snuff ?
IMO.   I pray you, sir,
Deliver with more openness your answers
To my demands.   Why do you pity me ?
IACH. That others do,
I was about to say, enjoy your——But   90
It is an office of the gods to venge it,
Not mine to speak on't.
IMO.   You do seem to know
Something of me, or what concerns me ; pray you—
Since doubting things go ill often hurts more
Than to be sure they do ; for certainties   95
Either are past remedies, or, timely knowing,
The remedy then born—discover to me
What both you spur and stop.
IACH.   Had I this cheek
To bathe my lips upon ; this hand, whose touch,
Whose every touch, would force the feeler's soul   100
To th' oath of loyalty ; this object, which
Takes prisoner the wild motion of mine eye,
Fixing it only here ; should I, damn'd then,
Slaver with lips as common as the stairs
That mount the Capitol ; join gripes with hands   105
Made hard with hourly falsehood—falsehood as
With labour ; then by-peeping in an eye
Base and illustrious as the smoky light
That's fed with stinking tallow—it were fit
That all the plagues of hell should at one time   110
Encounter such revolt.
IMO.   My lord, I fear,
Has forgot Britain.
IACH.   And himself.   Not I
Inclin'd to this intelligence pronounce
The beggary of his change ; but 'tis your graces
That from my mutest conscience to my tongue   115
Charms this report out.
IMO.   Let me hear no more.
IACH. O dearest soul, your cause doth strike my heart

With pity that doth make me sick ! A lady
So fair, and fasten'd to an empery,
Would make the great'st king double, to be partner'd   120
With tomboys hir'd with that self exhibition
Which your own coffers yield ! with diseas'd ventures
That play with all infirmities for gold
Which rottenness can lend nature ! such boil'd stuff
As well might poison poison ! Be reveng'd ;   125
Or she that bore you was no queen, and you
Recoil from your great stock.

IMO.   Reveng'd ?
How should I be reveng'd ? If this be true—
As I have such a heart that both mine ears
Must not in haste abuse—if it be true,   130
How should I be reveng'd ?

IACH.   Should he make me
Live like Diana's priest betwixt cold sheets,
Whiles he is vaulting variable ramps,
In your despite, upon your purse ? Revenge it.
I dedicate myself to your sweet pleasure,   135
More noble than that runagate to your bed,
And will continue fast to your affection,
Still close as sure.

IMO.   What ho, Pisanio !

IACH. Let me my service tender on your lips.

IMO. Away ! I do condemn mine ears that have   140
So long attended thee. If thou wert honourable,
Thou wouldst have told this tale for virtue, not
For such an end thou seek'st, as base as strange.
Thou wrong'st a gentleman who is as far
From thy report as thou from honour ; and   145
Solicits here a lady that disdains
Thee and the devil alike.—What ho, Pisanio !—
The King my father shall be made acquainted
Of thy assault. If he shall think it fit
A saucy stranger in his court to mart   150
As in a Romish stew, and to expound
His beastly mind to us, he hath a court
He little cares for, and a daughter who
He not respects at all.—What ho, Pisanio !

IACH. O happy Leonatus ! I may say   155
The credit that thy lady hath of thee
Deserves thy trust, and thy most perfect goodness
Her assur'd credit. Blessed live you long,
A lady to the worthiest sir that ever
Country call'd his ! and you his mistress, only   160
For the most worthiest fit ! Give me your pardon.
I have spoke this to know if your affiance
Were deeply rooted, and shall make your lord
That which he is new o'er ; and he is one
The truest manner'd, such a holy witch   165
That he enchants societies into him,
Half all men's hearts are his.

IO.   You make amends.

9   257

IACH. He sits 'mongst men like a descended god:
   He hath a kind of honour sets him off
   More than a mortal seeming.   Be not angry,   17
   Most mighty Princess, that I have adventur'd
   To try your taking of a false report, which hath
   Honour'd with confirmation your great judgment
   In the election of a sir so rare,
   Which you know cannot err.   The love I bear him   17
   Made me to fan you thus; but the gods made you,
   Unlike all others, chaffless.   Pray your pardon.
IMO. All's well, sir; take my pow'r i' th' court for yours.
IACH. My humble thanks.   I had almost forgot
   T' entreat your Grace but in a small request,   18
   And yet of moment too, for it concerns
   Your lord; myself and other noble friends
   Are partners in the business.
IMO.   Pray what is't?
IACH. Some dozen Romans of us, and your lord—
   The best feather of our wing—have mingled sums   18
   To buy a present for the Emperor;
   Which I, the factor for the rest, have done
   In France.   'Tis plate of rare device, and jewels
   Of rich and exquisite form, their values great;
   And I am something curious, being strange,   19
   To have them in safe stowage.   May it please you
   To take them in protection?
IMO.   Willingly;
   And pawn mine honour for their safety.   Since
   My lord hath interest in them, I will keep them
   In my bedchamber.
IACH.   They are in a trunk,   19
   Attended by my men.   I will make bold
   To send them to you only for this night;
   I must aboard to-morrow.
IMO.   O, no, no.
IACH. Yes, I beseech you; or I shall short my word
   By length'ning my return.   From Gallia   20
   I cross'd the seas on purpose and on promise
   To see your Grace.
IMO.   I thank you for your pains.
   But not away to-morrow!
IACH.   O, I must, madam.
   Therefore I shall beseech you, if you please
   To greet your lord with writing, do't to-night.   20
   I have outstood my time, which is material
   To th' tender of our present.
IMO.   I will write.
   Send your trunk to me; it shall safe be kept
   And truly yielded you.   You're very welcome.   [Exeun

ACT TWO

SCENE I. *Britain. Before Cymbeline's palace.*

Enter CLOTEN *and the two* LORDS.

LO. Was there ever man had such luck! When I kiss'd the jack,
upon an up-cast to be hit away! I had a hundred pound on't;
and then a whoreson jackanapes must take me up for swearing,
as if I borrowed mine oaths of him, and might not spend them at
my pleasure.

LORD. What got he by that? You have broke his pate with your
bowl.

LORD. [*Aside.*] If his wit had been like him that broke it, it
would have run all out.

LO. When a gentleman is dispos'd to swear, it is not for any standers-
by to curtail his oaths. Ha?   11

LORD. No, my lord; [*Aside.*] nor crop the ears of them.

LO. Whoreson dog! I give him satisfaction? Would he had been
one of my rank!

LORD. [*Aside.*] To have smell'd like a fool.

LO. I am not vex'd more at anything in th' earth. A pox on't!
I had rather not be so noble as I am; they dare not fight with me,
because of the Queen my mother. Every jackslave hath his
bellyfull of fighting, and I must go up and down like a cock that
nobody can match.   21

LORD. [*Aside.*] You are cock and capon too; and you crow,
cock, with your comb on.

LO. Sayest thou?

LORD. It is not fit your lordship should undertake every companion that you give offence to.

OL. No, I know that; but it is fit I should commit offence to my
inferiors.

LORD. Ay, it is fit for your lordship only.

LO. Why, so I say.   30

LORD. Did you hear of a stranger that's come to court to-night?

LO. A stranger, and I not known on't?

LORD. [*Aside.*] He's a strange fellow himself, and knows it not.

LORD. There's an Italian come, and, 'tis thought, one of Leonatus'
friends.

LO. Leonatus? A banish'd rascal; and he's another, whatsoever
he be. Who told you of this stranger?

LORD. One of your lordship's pages.   40

LO. Is it fit I went to look upon him? Is there no derogation in't?

LORD. You cannot derogate, my lord.

LO. Not easily, I think.

LORD. [*Aside.*] You are a fool granted; therefore your issues,
being foolish, do not derogate.   46

LO. Come, I'll go see this Italian. What I have lost to-day at
bowls I'll win to-night of him. Come, go.

LORD. I'll attend your lordship.   [*Exeunt* CLOTEN *and* FIRST LORD.
That such a crafty devil as is his mother   50
Should yield the world this ass! A woman that

Bears all down with her brain ; and this her son
Cannot take two from twenty, for his heart,
And leave eighteen. Alas, poor princess,
Thou divine Imogen, what thou endur'st, 5
Betwixt a father by thy step-dame govern'd,
A mother hourly coining plots, a wooer
More hateful than the foul expulsion is
Of thy dear husband, than that horrid act
Of the divorce he'd make ! The heavens hold firm 6
The walls of thy dear honour, keep unshak'd
That temple, thy fair mind, that thou mayst stand
T' enjoy thy banish'd lord and this great land ! [Exi

SCENE II. *Britain. Imogen's bedchamber in Cymbeline's palace
a trunk in one corner.*

Enter IMOGEN *in her bed, and a* LADY *attending.*

IMO. Who's there ? My woman ? Helen ?
LADY. Please you, madam.
IMO. What hour is it ?
LADY. Almost midnight, madam.
IMO. I have read three hours then. Mine eyes are weak ;
Fold down the leaf where I have left. To bed.
Take not away the taper, leave it burning ;
And if thou canst awake by four o' th' clock,
I prithee call me. Sleep hath seiz'd me wholly. [*Exit* LADY
To your protection I commend me, gods.
From fairies and the tempters of the night
Guard me, beseech ye ! [*Sleeps.* IACHIMO *comes from the trunk*
IACH. The crickets sing, and man's o'er-labour'd sense 1
Repairs itself by rest. Our Tarquin thus
Did softly press the rushes ere he waken'd
The chastity he wounded. Cytherea,
How bravely thou becom'st thy bed ! fresh lily, 1
And whiter than the sheets ! That I might touch !
But kiss ; one kiss ! Rubies unparagon'd,
How dearly they do't ! 'Tis her breathing that
Perfumes the chamber thus. The flame o' th' taper
Bows toward her and would under-peep her lids 2
To see th' enclosed lights, now canopied
Under these windows white and azure, lac'd
With blue of heaven's own tinct. But my design
To note the chamber. I will write all down :
Such and such pictures ; there the window ; such 2
Th' adornment of her bed ; the arras, figures—
Why, such and such ; and the contents o' th' story.
Ah, but some natural notes about her body
Above ten thousand meaner movables
Would testify, t' enrich mine inventory. 3
O sleep, thou ape of death, lie dull upon her !
And be her sense but as a monument,
Thus in a chapel lying ! Come off, come off ;
[*Taking off her bracelet*

As slippery as the Gordian knot was hard !
'Tis mine ; and this will witness outwardly,   35
As strongly as the conscience does within,
To th' madding of her lord.   On her left breast
A mole cinque-spotted, like the crimson drops
I' th' bottom of a cowslip.   Here's a voucher
Stronger than ever law could make ; this secret   40
Will force him think I have pick'd the lock and ta'en
The treasure of her honour.   No more.   To what end ?
Why should I write this down that's riveted,
Screw'd to my memory ?   She hath been reading late
The tale of Tereus ; here the leaf's turn'd down   45
Where Philomel gave up.   I have enough.
To th' trunk again, and shut the spring of it.
Swift, swift, you dragons of the night, that dawning
May bare the raven's eye !   I lodge in fear ;
Though this a heavenly angel, hell is here.   [*Clock strikes.*
One, two, three.   Time, time !   [*Exit into the trunk.*

SCENE III. *Cymbeline's palace.   An ante-chamber adjoining
Imogen's apartments.*

Enter CLOTEN *and* LORDS.

I LORD. Your lordship is the most patient man in loss, the most
coldest that ever turn'd up ace.

CLO. It would make any man cold to lose.

I LORD. But not every man patient after the noble temper of your
lordship.   You are most hot and furious when you win.

CLO. Winning will put any man into courage.   If I could get this
foolish Imogen, I should have gold enough.   It's almost morning,
is't not ?

I LORD. Day, my lord.   10

CLO. I would this music would come.   I am advised to give her music
a mornings ; they say it will penetrate.

Enter MUSICIANS.

Come on, tune.   If you can penetrate her with your fingering,
so.   We'll try with tongue too.   If none will do, let her remain ;
but I'll never give o'er.   First, a very excellent good-conceited
thing ; after, a wonderful sweet air, with admirable rich words
to it—and then let her consider.   18

Song.

Hark, hark ! the lark at heaven's gate sings,
And Phœbus 'gins arise,   20
His steeds to water at those springs
On chalic'd flow'rs that lies ;
And winking Mary-buds begin
To ope their golden eyes.
With everything that pretty bin,   25
My lady sweet, arise ;
Arise, arise !

So, get you gone.   If this penetrate, I will consider your music
the better ; if it do not, it is a vice in her ears which horsehairs

and calves' guts, nor the voice of unpaved eunuch to boot, can
never amend.   [*Exeunt* MUSICIANS.

Enter CYMBELINE *and* QUEEN.

2 LORD. Here comes the King.
CLO. I am glad I was up so late, for that's the reason I was up so
    early. He cannot choose but take this service I have done
    fatherly.—Good morrow to your Majesty and to my graciovs
    mother.   36
CYM. Attend you here the door of our stern daughter ?
    Will she not forth ?
CLO. I have assail'd her with musics, but she vouchsafes no notice.
CYM. The exile of her minion is too new ;
    She hath not yet forgot him ; some more time
    Must wear the print of his remembrance out,
    And then she's yours.
QUEEN. You are most bound to th' King,
    Who lets go by no vantages that may   45
    Prefer you to his daughter. Frame yourself
    To orderly soliciting, and be friended
    With aptness of the season ; make denials
    Increase your services ; so seem as if
    You were inspir'd to do those duties which   50
    You tender to her ; that you in all obey her,
    Save when command to your dismission tends,
    And therein you are senseless.
CLO.   Senseless ? Not so.

Enter a MESSENGER.

MESS. So like you, sir, ambassadors from Rome ;
    The one is Caius Lucius.
CYM.   A worthy fellow,   55
    Albeit he comes on angry purpose now ;
    But that's no fault of his. We must receive him
    According to the honour of his sender ;
    And towards himself, his goodness forespent on us,
    We must extend our notice. Our dear son,   60
    When you have given good morning to your mistress,
    Attend the Queen and us ; we shall have need
    T' employ you towards this Roman. Come, our queen.
                                        [*Exeunt all but* CLOTEN.
CLO. If she be up, I'll speak with her ; if not,
    Let her lie still and dream. By your leave, ho !   [*Knocks.*
    I know her women are about her ; what   66
    If I do line one of their hands ? 'Tis gold
    Which buys admittance ; oft it doth—yea, and makes
    Diana's rangers false themselves, yield up
    Their deer to th' stand o' th' stealer ; and 'tis gold   70
    Which makes the true man kill'd and saves the thief ;
    Nay, sometime hangs both thief and true man. What
    Can it not do and undo ? I will make
    One of her women lawyer to me, for
    I yet not understand the case myself.   75
    By your leave.   [*Knocks.*

Enter a LADY.

LADY. Who's there that knocks?

CLO.   A gentleman.

LADY.   No more?

CLO. Yes, and a gentlewoman's son.

LADY.   That's more
    Than some whose tailors are as dear as yours
    Can justly boast of. What's your lordship's pleasure?   80

CLO. Your lady's person; is she ready?

LADY.   Ay,
    To keep her chamber.

CLO. There is gold for you; sell me your good report.

LADY. How? My good name? or to report of you
    What I shall think is good? The Princess!

Enter IMOGEN.

CLO. Good morrow, fairest sister. Your sweet hand.   [*Exit* LADY.

IMO. Good morrow, sir. You lay out too much pains
    For purchasing but trouble. The thanks I give
    Is telling you that I am poor of thanks,
    And scarce can spare them.

CLO.   Still I swear I love you.   90

IMO. If you but said so, 'twere as deep with me.
    If you swear still, your recompense is still
    That I regard it not.

CLO.   This is no answer.

IMO. But that you shall not say I yield, being silent,
    I would not speak. I pray you spare me. Faith,   95
    I shall unfold equal discourtesy
    To your best kindness; one of your great knowing
    Should learn, being taught, forbearance.

CLO. To leave you in your madness 'twere my sin;
    I will not.   100

IMO. Fools are not mad folks.

CLO. Do you call me fool?

IMO.   As I am mad, I do;
    If you'll be patient, I'll no more be mad;
    That cures us both. I am much sorry, sir,
    You put me to forget a lady's manners   105
    By being so verbal; and learn now, for all,
    That I, which know my heart, do here pronounce,
    By th' very truth of it, I care not for you,
    And am so near the lack of charity
    To accuse myself I hate you; which I had rather   110
    You felt than make't my boast.

CLO.   You sin against
    Obedience, which you owe your father. For
    The contract you pretend with that base wretch,
    One bred of alms and foster'd with cold dishes,
    With scraps o' th' court—it is no contract, none.   115
    And though it be allowed in meaner parties—
    Yet who than he more mean?—to knit their souls—
    On whom there is no more dependency

                                                            263

> But brats and beggary—in self-figur'd knot,
> Yet you are curb'd from that enlargement by   120
> The consequence o' th' crown, and must not foil
> The precious note of it with a base slave,
> A hilding for a livery, a squire's cloth,
> A pantler—not so eminent !
>
> IMO.   Profane fellow !
> Wert thou the son of Jupiter, and no more   125
> But what thou art besides, thou wert too base
> To be his groom.   Thou wert dignified enough,
> Even to the point of envy, if 'twere made
> Comparative for your virtues to be styl'd
> The under-hangman of his kingdom, and hated   130
> For being preferr'd so well.
>
> CLO.   The south fog rot him !
> IMO. He never can meet more mischance than come
> To be but nam'd of thee.   His mean'st garment
> That ever hath but clipp'd his body is dearer
> In my respect than all the hairs above thee,   135
> Were they all made such men.   How now, Pisanio !

Enter PISANIO.

> CLO. ' His garments ' ! Now the devil—
> IMO. To Dorothy my woman hie thee presently.
> CLO. ' His garment ' !
> IMO.   I am sprited with a fool ;
> Frighted, and ang'red worse.   Go bid my woman   140
> Search for a jewel that too casually
> Hath left mine arm.   It was thy master's ; shrew me,
> If I would lose it for a revenue
> Of any king's in Europe ! I do think
> I saw't this morning ; confident I am   145
> Last night 'twas on mine arm ; I kiss'd it.
> I hope it be not gone to tell my lord
> That I kiss aught but he.
>
> PIS.   'Twill not be lost.
> IMO. I hope so.   Go and search.   [*Exit* PISANIO.
> CLO.   You have abus'd me.
> ' His meanest garment ' !
> IMO.   Ay, I said so, sir.   150
> If you will make 't an action, call witness to 't.
> CLO. I will inform your father.
> IMO.   Your mother too.
> She's my good lady and will conceive, I hope,
> But the worst of me.   So I leave you, sir,
> To th' worst of discontent.   [*Exit.*
> CLO.   I'll be reveng'd.   155
> ' His mean'st garment ' ! Well.   [*Exit.*

SCENE IV.   *Rome.   Philario's house.*

Enter POSTHUMUS *and* PHILARIO.

> POST. Fear it not, sir ; I would I were so sure
> To win the King as I am bold her honour

Will remain hers.

PHI.   What means do you make to him ?

POST. Not any ; but abide the change of time,
  Quake in the present winter's state, and wish   5
  That warmer days would come. In these fear'd hopes
  I barely gratify your love ; they failing,
  I must die much your debtor.

PHI. Your very goodness and your company
  O'erpays all I can do. By this your king   10
  Hath heard of great Augustus. Caius Lucius
  Will do's commission throughly ; and I think
  He'll grant the tribute, send th' arrearages,
  Or look upon our Romans, whose remembrance
  Is yet fresh in their grief.

POST.   I do believe   15
  Statist though I am none, nor like to be,
  That this will prove a war ; and you shall hear
  The legions now in Gallia sooner landed
  In our not-fearing Britain than have tidings
  Of any penny tribute paid. Our countrymen   20
  Are men more order'd than when Julius Cæsar
  Smil'd at their lack of skill, but found their courage
  Worthy his frowning at. Their discipline,
  Now mingled with their courages, will make known
  To their approvers they are people such   25
  That mend upon the world.

Enter IACHIMO.

PHI.   See ! Iachimo !

POST. The swiftest harts have posted you by land,
  And winds of all the corners kiss'd your sails,
  To make your vessel nimble.

PHI.   Welcome, sir.

POST. I hope the briefness of your answer made   30
  The speediness of your return.

IACH.   Your lady
  Is one of the fairest that I have look'd upon.

POST. And therewithal the best ; or let her beauty
  Look through a casement to allure false hearts,
  And be false with them.

IACH.   Here are letters for you.   35

POST. Their tenour good, I trust.

IACH.   'Tis very like.

PHI. Was Caius Lucius in the Britain court
  When you were there ?

IACH.   He was expected then,
  But not approach'd.

POST.   All is well yet.
  Sparkles this stone as it was wont, or is't not   40
  Too dull for your good wearing ?

IACH.   If I have lost it,
  I should have lost the worth of it in gold.
  I'll make a journey twice as far t' enjoy
  A second night of such sweet shortness which

Was mine in Britain ; for the ring is won.   45
POST. The stone's too hard to come by.
IACH.   Not a whit,
Your lady being so easy.
POST.   Make not, sir,
Your loss your sport. I hope you know that we
Must not continue friends.
IACH.   Good sir, we must,
If you keep covenant. Had I not brought   50
The knowledge of your mistress home, I grant
We were to question farther ; but I now
Profess myself the winner of her honour,
Together with your ring ; and not the wronger
Of her or you, having proceeded but   55
By both your wills.
POST.   If you can make't apparent
That you have tasted her in bed, my hand
And ring is yours. If not, the foul opinion
You had of her pure honour gains or loses
Your sword or mine, or masterless leaves both   60
To who shall find them.
IACH.   Sir, my circumstances,
Being so near the truth as I will make them,
Must first induce you to believe—whose strength
I will confirm with oath ; which I doubt not
You'll give me leave to spare when you shall find   65
You need it not.
POST.   Proceed.
IACH.   First, her bedchamber,
Where I confess I slept not, but profess
Had that was well worth watching—it was hang'd
With tapestry of silk and silver ; the story,
Proud Cleopatra when she met her Roman   70
And Cydnus swell'd above the banks, or for
The press of boats or pride. A piece of work
So bravely done, so rich, that it did strive
In workmanship and value ; which I wonder'd
Could be so rarely and exactly wrought,   75
Since the true life on't was—
POST.   This is true ;
And this you might have heard of here, by me
Or by some other.
IACH.   More particulars
Must justify my knowledge.
POST.   So they must,
Or do your honour injury.
IACH.   The chimney   80
Is south the chamber, and the chimneypiece
Chaste Dian bathing. Never saw I figures
So likely to report themselves. The cutter
Was as another nature, dumb ; outwent her,
Motion and breath left out.
POST.   This is a thing   85
Which you might from relation likewise reap,

Being, as it is, much spoke of.
IACH.   The roof o' th' chamber
   With golden cherubins is fretted ; her andirons—
   I had forgot them—were two winking Cupids
   Of silver, each on one foot standing, nicely   90
   Depending on their brands.
POST.   This is her honour
   Let it be granted you have seen all this, and praise
   Be given to your remembrance ; the description
   Of what is in her chamber nothing saves
   The wager you have laid.
IACH.   Then, if you can, [*Shows the bracelet.*
   Be pale. I beg but leave to air this jewel. See !   95
   And now 'tis up again. It must be married
   To that your diamond ; I'll keep them.
POST.   Jove !
   Once more let me behold it. Is it that
   Which I left with her ?
IACH.   Sir—I thank her—that.   100
   She stripp'd it from her arm ; I see her yet ;
   Her pretty action did outsell her gift.
   And yet enrich'd it too. She gave it me, and said
   She priz'd it once.
POST.   May be she pluck'd it off
   To send it me.
IACH.   She writes so to you, doth she ?   105
POST. O, no, no, no ! 'tis true. Here, take this too ; [*Gives the ring.*
   It is a basilisk unto mine eye,
   Kills me to look on't. Let there be no honour
   Where there is beauty ; truth where semblance ; love
   Where there's another man. The vows of women   110
   Of no more bondage be to where they are made
   Than they are to their virtues, which is nothing.
   O, above measure false !
PHI.   Have patience, sir,
   And take your ring again ; 'tis not yet won.
   It may be probable she lost it, or   115
   Who knows if one her women, being corrupted
   Hath stol'n it from her ?
POST.   Very true ;
   And so I hope he came by't. Back my ring.
   Render to me some corporal sign about her,
   More evident than this ; for this was stol'n.   120
IACH. By Jupiter, I had it from her arm !
POST. Hark you, he swears ; by Jupiter he swears.
   'Tis true—nay, keep the ring, 'tis true. I am sure
   She would not lose it. Her attendants are
   All sworn and honourable—they induc'd to steal it !   125
   And by a stranger ! No, he hath enjoy'd her.
   The cognizance of her incontinency
   Is this : she hath bought the name of whore thus dearly.
   There, take thy hire ; and all the fiends of hell
   Divide themselves between you !
PHI.   Sir, be patient ;   130

This is not strong enough to be believ'd
Of one persuaded well of.

POST.   Never talk on't ;
She hath been colted by him.

IACH.   If you seek
For further satisfying, under her breast—
Worthy the pressing—lies a mole, right proud   135
Of that most delicate lodging. By my life,
I kiss'd it ; and it gave me present hunger
To feed again, though full. You do remember
This stain upon her ?

POST.   Ay, and it doth confirm
Another stain, as big as hell can hold,   140
Were there no more but it.

IACH.   Will you hear more ?

POST. Spare your arithmetic ; never count the turns.
Once, and a million !

IACH.   I'll be sworn—

POST.   No swearing.
If you will swear you have not done't, you lie ;
And I will kill thee if thou dost deny   145
Thou'st made me cuckold.

IACH.   I'll deny nothing.

POST. O that I had her here to tear her limb-meal !
I will go there and do't, i' th' court, before
Her father. I'll do something—   [Exit.

PHI.   Quite besides
The government of patience ! You have won.   150
Let's follow him and pervert the present wrath
Her hath against himself.

IACH.   With all my heart.   [Exeunt.

SCENE V. Rome. Another room in Philario's house.

Enter POSTHUMUS.

POST. Is there no way for men to be, but women
Must be half-workers ? We are all bastards,
And that most venerable man which I
Did call my father was I know not where
When I was stamp'd. Some coiner with his tools   5
Made me a counterfeit ; yet my mother seem'd
The Dian of that time. So doth my wife
The nonpareil of this. O, vengeance, vengeance !
Me of my lawful pleasure she restrain'd,
And pray'd me oft forbearance ; did it with   10
A pudency so rosy, the sweet view on't
Might well have warm'd old Saturn ; that I thought her
As chaste as unsunn'd snow. O, all the devils !
This yellow Iachimo in an hour—was't not ?
Or less !—at first ? Perchance he spoke not, but,   15
Like a full-acorn'd boar, a German one,
Cried ' O ! ' and mounted ; found no opposition
But what he look'd for should oppose and she
Should from encounter guard. Could I find out

The woman's part in me ! For there's no motion   20
That tends to vice in man but I affirm
It is the woman's part.   Be it lying, note it,
The woman's ; flattering, hers ; deceiving, hers ;
Lust and rank thoughts, hers, hers ; revenges, hers ;
Ambitions, covetings, change of prides, disdain,   25
Nice longing, slanders, mutability,
All faults that man may name, nay, that hell knows,
Why, hers, in part or all ; but rather all ;
For even to vice
They are not constant, but are changing still   30
One vice but of a minute old for one
Not half so old as that.   I'll write against them,
Detest them, curse them.   Yet 'tis greater skill
In a true hate to pray they have their will :
The very devils cannot plague them better.   [*Exit*.

ACT THREE

Scene I. *Britain.   A hall in Cymbeline's palace.*

Enter in state, CYMBELINE, QUEEN, CLOTEN, *and* LORDS *at one door, and
at another* CAIUS LUCIUS *and* ATTENDANTS.

CYM. Now say, what would Augustus Cæsar with us ?
LUC. When Julius Cæsar—whose remembrance yet
    Lives in men's eyes, and will to ears and tongues
    Be theme and hearing ever—was in this Britain,
    And conquer'd it, Cassibelan, thine uncle,   5
    Famous in Cæsar's praises no whit less
    Than in his feats deserving it, for him
    And his succession granted Rome a tribute,
    Yearly three thousand pounds, which by thee lately
    Is left untender'd.
QUEEN.   And, to kill the marvel,   10
    Shall be so ever.
CLO.   There be many Cæsars
    Ere such another Julius.   Britain is
    A world by itself, and we will nothing pay
    For wearing our own noses.
QUEEN.   That opportunity,
    Which then they had to take from 's, to resume   15
    We have again.   Remember, sir, my liege,
    The kings your ancestors, together with
    The natural bravery of your isle, which stands
    As Neptune's park, ribb'd and pal'd in
    With rocks unscalable and roaring waters,   20
    With sands that will not bear your enemies' boats
    But suck them up to th' top-mast.   A kind of conquest
    Cæsar made here ; but made not here his brag
    Of 'came, and saw, and overcame'.   With shame—
    The first that ever touch'd him—he was carried   25
    From off our coast, twice beaten ; and his shipping—
    Poor ignorant baubles !—on our terrible seas,
    Like egg-shells mov'd upon their surges, crack'd

As easily 'gainst our rocks ; for joy whereof
The fam'd Cassibelan, who was once at point—   30
O, giglot fortune !—to master Cæsar's sword,
Made Lud's Town with rejoicing fires bright
And Britons strut with courage.

CLO. Come, there's no more tribute to be paid. Our kingdom is
stronger than it was at that time ; and, as I said, there is no moe
such Cæsars. Other of them may have crook'd noses ; but to
owe such straight arms, none.   37

CYM. Son, let your mother end.

CLO. We have yet many among us can gripe as hard as Cassibelan.
I do not say I am one ; but I have a hand. Why tribute ? Why
should we pay tribute ? If Cæsar can hide the sun from us with a
blanket, or put the moon in his pocket, we will pay him tribute
for light ; else, sir, no more tribute, pray you now.   44

CYM. You must know,
Till the injurious Romans did extort
This tribute from us, we were free.   Cæsar's ambition—
Which swell'd so much that it did almost stretch
The sides o' th' world—against all colour here
Did put the yoke upon's ; which to shake off   50
Becomes a warlike people, whom we reckon
Ourselves to be.

CLO.   We do.

CYM.   Say then to Cæsar,
Our ancestor was that Mulmutius which
Ordain'd our laws—whose use the sword of Cæsar
Hath too much mangled ; whose repair and franchise   55
Shall, by the power we hold, be our good deed,
Though Rome be therefore angry.   Mulmutius made our laws,
Who was the first of Britain which did put
His brows within a golden crown, and call'd
Himself a king.

LUC.   I am sorry, Cymbeline,   60
That I am to pronounce Augustus Cæsar—
Cæsar, that hath moe kings his servants than
Thyself domestic officers—thine enemy.
Receive it from me, then : war and confusion
In Cæsar's name pronounce I 'gainst thee ; look   65
For fury not to be resisted. Thus defied,
I thank thee for myself.

CYM.   Thou art welcome, Caius.
Thy Cæsar knighted me ; my youth I spent
Much under him ; of him I gather'd honour,
Which he to seek of me again, perforce,   70
Behoves me keep at utterance.   I am perfect
That the Pannonians and Dalmatians for
Their liberties are now in arms, a precedent
Which not to read would show the Britons cold ;
So Cæsar shall not find them.

LUC.   Let proof speak.   75

CLO. His Majesty bids you welcome. Make pastime with us a day
or two, or longer. If you seek us afterwards in other terms,
you shall find us in our salt-water girdle. If you beat us out of

it, it is yours ; if you fall in the adventure, our crows shall fare
the better for you ; and there's an end.   81
LUC. So, sir.
CYM. I know your master's pleasure, and he mine ;
    All the remain is, welcome.   [*Exeunt.*

SCENE II. *Britain.   Another room in Cymbeline's palace.*

Enter PISANIO *reading of a letter.*

PIS. How ? of adultery ? Wherefore write you not
    What monsters her accuse ? Leonatus !
    O master, what a strange infection
    Is fall'n into thy ear ! What false Italian—
    As poisonous-tongu'd as handed—hath prevail'd   5
    On thy too ready hearing ? Disloyal ? No.
    She's punish'd for her truth, and undergoes,
    More goddess-like than wife-like, such assaults
    As would take in some virtue. O my master !
    Thy mind to her is now as low as were   10
    Thy fortunes. How ? that I should murder her ?
    Upon the love, and truth, and vows, which I
    Have made to thy command ? I, her ? Her blood ?
    If it be so to do good service, never
    Let me be counted serviceable. How look I   15
    That I should seem to lack humanity
    So much as this fact comes to ? [*Reads.*] ' Do't.   The letter
    That I have sent her, by her own command
    Shall give thee opportunity.' O damn'd paper,
    Black as the ink that's on thee ! Senseless bauble,   20
    Art thou a fedary for this act, and look'st
    So virgin-like without ? Lo here she comes.

Enter IMOGEN.

    I am ignorant in what I am commanded.
IMO. How now, Pisanio !
PIS. Madam, here is a letter from my lord.   25
IMO. Who ? thy lord ? That is my lord—Leonatus ?
    O, learn'd indeed were that astronomer
    That knew the stars as I his characters—
    He'd lay the future open. You good gods,
    Let what is here contain'd relish of love,   30
    Of my lord's health, of his content ; yet not
    That we two are asunder—let that grieve him !
    Some griefs are med'cinable ; that is one of them,
    For it doth physic love—of his content,
    All but in that. Good wax, thy leave. Blest be   35
    You bees that make these locks of counsel ! Lovers
    And men in dangerous bonds pray not alike ;
    Though forfeiters you cast in prison, yet
    You clasp young Cupid's tables. Good news, gods ! [*Reads.*
' Justice, and your father's wrath, should he take me in his
dominion, could not be so cruel to me as you, O the dearest of
creatures, would even renew me with your eyes. Take notice
that I am in Cambria, at Milford Haven. What your own love

271

will out of this advise you, follow.   So he wishes you all happiness
that remains loyal to his vow, and your increasing in love   45
                                        Leonatus Posthumus.'

O for a horse with wings !   Hear'st thou, Pisanio ?
He is at Milford Haven.   Read, and tell me
How far 'tis thither.   If one of mean affairs
May plod it in a week, why may not I   50
Glide thither in a day ? Then, true Pisanio—
Who long'st like me to see thy lord, who long'st—
O, let me 'bate !—but not like me, yet long'st,
But in a fainter kind—O, not like me,
For mine's beyond beyond !—say, and speak thick—   55
Love's counsellor should fill the bores of hearing
To th' smothering of the sense—how far it is
To this same blessed Milford.   And by th' way
Tell me how Wales was made so happy as
T' inherit such a haven.   But first of all,   60
How we may steal from hence ; and for the gap
That we shall make in time from our hence-going
And our return, to excuse.   But first, how get hence.
Why should excuse be born or ere begot ?
We'll talk of that hereafter.   Prithee speak,   65
How many score of miles may we well ride
'Twixt hour and hour ?

PIS.   One score 'twixt sun and sun,
        Madam, 's enough for you, and too much too.
IMO. Why, one that rode to's execution, man,
        Could never go so slow.   I have heard of riding wagers   70
        Where horses have been nimbler than the sands
        That run i' th' clock's behalf.   But this is fool'ry.
        Go bid my woman feign a sickness ;   say
        She'll make to her father ; and provide me presently
        A riding suit, no costlier than would fit   75
        A franklin's huswife.
PIS.   Madam, you're best consider.
IMO. I see before me, man.   Nor here, nor here,
        Nor what ensues, but have a fog in them
        That I cannot look through.   Away, I prithee ;
        Do as I bid thee.   There's no more to say ;   80
        Accessible is none but Milford way.   [Exeunt.

        SCENE III.   *Wales.   A mountainous country with a cave.*

        Enter from the cave BELARIUS, GUIDERIUS, *and* ARVIRAGUS.

BEL. A goodly day not to keep house with such
        Whose roof's as low as ours ! Stoop, boys ; this gate
        Instructs you how t' adore the heavens, and bows you
        To a morning's holy office.   The gates of monarchs
        Are arch'd so high that giants may jet through   5
        And keep their impious turbans on without
        Good morrow to the sun.   Hail, thou fair heaven !
        We house i' th' rock, yet use thee not so hardly
        As prouder livers do.

GUI.   Hail, heaven !
ARV.   Hail, heaven !
BEL. Now for our mountain sport. Up to yond hill,   10
      Your legs are young ; I'll tread these flats. Consider,
      When you above perceive me like a crow,
      That it is place which lessens and sets off ;
      And you may then revolve what tales I have told you
      Of courts, of princes, of the tricks in war.   15
      This service is not service so being done,
      But being so allow'd. To apprehend thus
      Draws us a profit from all things we see,
      And often to our comfort shall we find
      The sharded beetle in a safer hold   20
      Than is the full-wing'd eagle. O, this life
      Is nobler than attending for a check,
      Richer than doing nothing for a bribe,
      Prouder than rustling in unpaid-for silk :
      Such gain the cap of him that makes him fine,   25
      Yet keeps his book uncross'd. No life to ours !
GUI. Out of your proof you speak. We, poor unfledg'd,
      Have never wing'd from view o' th' nest, nor know not
      What air's from home. Haply this life is best,
      If quiet life be best ; sweeter to you   30
      That have a sharper known ; well corresponding
      With your stiff age. But unto us it is
      A cell of ignorance, travelling abed,
      A prison for a debtor that not dares
      To stride a limit.
ARV.   What should we speak of   35
      When we are old as you ? When we shall hear
      The rain and wind beat dark December, how,
      In this our pinching cave, shall we discourse
      The freezing hours away ? We have see nothing ;
      We are beastly : subtle as the fox for prey,   40
      Like warlike as the wolf for what we eat.
      Our valour is to chase what flies ; our cage
      We make a choir, as doth the prison'd bird,
      And sing our bondage freely.
BEL.   How you speak !
      Did you but know the city's usuries,   45
      And felt them knowingly—the art o' th' court,
      As hard to leave as keep, whose top to climb
      Is certain falling, or so slipp'ry that
      The fear's as bad as falling ; the toil o' th' war,
      A pain that only seems to seek out danger   50
      I' th' name of fame and honour, which dies i' th' search,
      And hath as oft a sland'rous epitaph
      As record of fair act ; nay, many times,
      Doth ill deserve by doing well ; what's worse—
      Must curtsy at the censure. O, boys, this story   55
      The world may read in me ; my body's mark'd
      With Roman swords, and my report was once
      First with the best of note. Cymbeline lov'd me ;
      And when a soldier was the theme, my name

                                                            273

Was not far off.   Then was I as a tree   60
Whose boughs did bend with fruit ; but in one night
A storm, or robbery, call it what you will,
Shook down my mellow hangings, nay, my leaves,
And left me bare to weather.
GUI.   Uncertain favour !
BEL. My fault being nothing—as I have told you oft—   65
But that two villains, whose false oaths prevail'd
Before my perfect honour, swore to Cymbeline
I was confederate with the Romans.   So
Follow'd my banishment, and this twenty years
This rock and these demesnes have been my world,   70
Where I have liv'd at honest freedom, paid
More pious debts to heaven than in all
The fore-end of my time.   But up to th' mountains !
This is not hunters' language.   He that strikes
The venison first shall be the lord o' th' feast ;   75
To him the other two shall minister ;
And we will fear no poison, which attends
In place of greater state.   I'll meet you in the valleys.
                         [*Exeunt* GUIDERIUS *and* ARVIRAGUS.
How hard it is to hide the sparks of nature !
These boys know little they are sons to th' King,   80
Nor Cymbeline dreams that they are alive.
They think they are mine ; and though train'd up thus meanly
I' th' cave wherein they bow, their thoughts do hit
The roofs of palaces, and nature prompts them
In simple and low things to prince it much   85
Beyond the trick of others.   This Polydore,
The heir of Cymbeline and Britain, who
The King his father call'd Guiderius—Jove !
When on my three-foot stool I sit and tell
The warlike feats I have done, his spirits fly out   90
Into my story ; say ' Thus mine enemy fell,
And thus I set my foot on's neck ' ; even then
The princely blood flows in his cheek, he sweats,
Strains his young nerves, and puts himself in posture
That acts my words.   The younger brother, Cadwal,   95
Once Arviragus, in as like a figure
Strikes life into my speech, and shows much more
His own conceiving.   Hark, the game is rous'd !
O Cymbeline, heaven and my conscience knows
Thou didst unjustly banish me ! Whereon,   100
At three and two years old, I stole these babes,
Thinking to bar thee of succession as
Thou refts me of my lands.   Euriphile,
Thou wast their nurse ; they took thee for their mother,
And every day do honour to her grave.   105
Myself, Belarius, that am Morgan call'd,
They take for natural father.   The game is up.
                                              [*Exit.*

SCENE IV. *Wales, near Milford Haven.*

Enter PISANIO *and* IMOGEN.

IMO. Thou told'st me, when we came from horse, the place
Was near at hand.   Ne'er long'd my mother so
To see me first as I have now.   Pisanio ! Man !
Where is Posthumus ? What is in thy mind
That makes thee stare thus ? Wherefore breaks that sigh   5
From th' inward of thee ? One but painted thus
Would be interpreted a thing perplex'd
Beyond self-explication.   Put thyself
Into a haviour of less fear, ere wildness
Vanquish my staider senses.   What's the matter ?   10
Why tender'st thou that paper to me with
A look untender ! If't be summer news,
Smile to't before ; if winterly, thou need'st
But keep that count'nance still.   My husband's hand ?
That drug-damn'd Italy hath out-craftied him,   15
And he's at some hard point.   Speak, man ; thy tongue
May take off some extremity, which to read
Would be even mortal to me.

PIS.   Please you read,
And you shall find me, wretched man, a thing
The most disdain'd of fortune.   20

IMO. [*Reads.*]   ' Thy mistress, Pisanio, hath play'd the strumpet in
my bed, the testimonies whereof lie bleeding in me. I speak
not out of weak surmises, but from proof as strong as my grief
and as certain as I expect my revenge.   That part thou, Pisanio,
must act for me, if thy faith be not tainted with the breach of hers.
Let thine own hands take away her life ; I shall give thee opportunity at Milford Haven ; she hath my letter for the purpose ;
where, if thou fear to strike, and to make me certain it is done,
thou art the pander to her dishonour, and equally to me disloyal.'

PIS. What shall I need to draw my sword ? The paper   30
Hath cut her throat already.   No, 'tis slander,
Whose edge is sharper than the sword, whose tongue
Outvenoms all the worms of Nile, whose breath
Rides on the posting winds and doth belie
All corners of the world.   Kings, queens, and states,   35
Maids, matrons, nay, the secrets of the grave,
This viperous slander enters.   What cheer, madam ?

MO. False to his bed ? What is it to be false ?
To lie in watch there, and to think on him ?
To weep twixt clock and clock ? If sleep charge nature,   40
To break it with a fearful dream of him,
And cry myself awake ? That's false to's bed,
Is it ?

PIS. Alas, good lady !

IMO. I false ! Thy conscience witness ! Iachimo,
Thou didst accuse him of incontinency ;   45
Thou then look'dst like a villain ; now, methinks,
Thy favour's good enough.   Some jay of Italy,
Whose mother was her painting, hath betray'd him.

Poor I am stale, a garment out of fashion,
And for I am richer than to hang by th' walls   50
I must be ripp'd.   To pieces with me ! O,
Men's vows are women's traitors ! All good seeming,
By thy revolt, O husband, shall be thought
Put on for villainy ; not born where't grows,
But worn a bait for ladies.

PIS.   Good madam, hear me.   55

IMO.   True honest men being heard, like false Æneas,
Were, in his time, thought false ; and Sinon's weeping
Did scandal many a holy tear, took pity
From most true wretchedness.   So thou, Posthumus,
Wilt lay the leaven on all proper men :   60
Goodly and gallant shall be false and perjur'd
From thy great fail.   Come, fellow, be thou honest ;
Do thou thy master's bidding ; when thou seest him,
A little witness my obedience.   Look !
I draw the sword myself ; take it, and hit   65
The innocent mansion of my love, my heart.
Fear not ; 'tis empty of all things but grief ;
Thy master is not there, who was indeed
The riches of it.   Do his bidding ; strike.
Thou mayst be valiant in a better cause,   70
But now thou seem'st a coward.

PIS.   Hence, vile instrument !
Thou shalt not damn my hand.

IMO.   Why, I must die ;
And if I do not by thy hand, thou art
No servant of thy master's.   Against self-slaughter
There is a prohibition so divine   75
That cravens my weak hand.   Come, here's my heart—
Something's afore't.   Soft, soft ! we'll no defence !—
Obedient as the scabbard.   What is here ?
The scriptures of the loyal Leonatus
All turn'd to heresy ? Away, away,   80
Corrupters of my faith ! you shall no more
Be stomachers to my heart.   Thus may poor fools
Believe false teachers ; though those that are betray'd
Do feel the treason sharply, yet the traitor
Stands in worse case of woe.   And thou, Posthumus,   85
That didst set up my disobedience 'gainst the King
My father, and make me put into contempt the suits
Of princely fellows, shalt hereafter find
It is no act of common passage but
A strain of rareness ; and I grieve myself
To think, when thou shalt be disedg'd by her
That now thou tirest on, how thy memory
Will then be pang'd by me.   Prithee dispatch.
The lamp entreats the butcher.   Where's thy knife ?   95
Thou art too slow to do thy master's bidding,
When I desire it too.

PIS.   O gracious lady,
Since I receiv'd command to do this business
I have not slept one wink.

IMO.   Do't, and to bed then.
PIS. I'll wake mine eyeballs first.
IMO.   Wherefore then   100
  Didst undertake it ? Why hast thou abus'd
  So many miles with a pretence ? This place ?
  Mine action and thine own ? our horses' labour ?
  The time inviting thee ? the perturb'd court,
  For my being absent ?—whereunto I never   105
  Purpose return. Why hast thou gone so far
  To be unbent when thou hast ta'en thy stand,
  Th' elected deer before thee ?
PIS.   But to win time
  To lose so bad employment, in the which
  I have consider'd of a course   Good lady,   110
  Hear me with patience.
IMO.   Talk thy tongue weary—speak.
  I have heard I am a strumpet, and mine ear,
  Therein false struck, can take no greater wound,
  Nor tent to bottom that. But speak.
PIS.   Then, madam,
  I thought you would not back again.
IMO.   Most like—   115
  Bringing me here to kill me.
PIS.   Not so, neither ;
  But if I were as wise as honest, then
  My purpose would prove well. It cannot be
  But that my master is abus'd. Some villain,
  Ay, and singular in his art, hath done you both   120
  This cursed injury.
IMO. Some Roman courtezan !
PIS.   No, on my life !
  I'll give but notice you are dead, and send him
  Some bloody sign of it, for 'tis commanded
  I should do so. You shall be miss'd at court,   125
  And that will well confirm it.
IMO.   Why, good fellow,
  What shall I do the while ? where bide ? how live ?
  Or in my life what comfort, when I am
  Dead to my husband ?
PIS.   If you'll back to th' court—
IMO. No court, no father, nor no more ado   130
  With that harsh, noble, simple nothing—
  That Cloten, whose love-suit hath been to me
  As fearful as a siege.
PIS.   If not at court,
  Then not in Britain must you bide.
IMO.   Where then ?
  Hath Britain all the sun that shines ? Day, night, 135
  Are they not but in Britain ? I' th' world's volume
  Our Britain seems as of it, but not in 't ;
  In a great pool a swan's nest. Prithee think
  There's livers out of Britain.
PIS.   I am most glad
  You think of other place. Th' ambassador,   140

Lucius the Roman, comes to Milford Haven
To-morrow. Now, if you could wear a mind
Dark as your fortune is, and but disguise
That which t' appear itself must not yet be
By self-danger, you should tread a course   145
Pretty and full of view ; yea, happily, near
The residence of Posthumus ; so nigh, at least,
That though his actions were not visible, yet
Report should render him hourly to your ear
As truly as he moves.

IMO.   O ! for such means,   150
Though peril to my modesty, not death on't,
I would adventure.

PIS.   Well then, here's the point:
You must forget to be a woman ; change
Command into obedience ; fear and niceness—
The handmaids of all women, or, more truly,   155
Woman it pretty self—into a waggish courage ;
Ready in gibes, quick-answer'd, saucy, and
As quarrelous as the weasel. Nay, you must
Forget that rarest treasure of your cheek,
Exposing it—but, O, the harder heart !   160
Alack, no remedy !—to the greedy touch
Of common-kissing Titan, and forget
Your laboursome and dainty trims wherein
You made great Juno angry.

IMO.   Nay, be brief ;
I see into thy end, and am almost   165
A man already.

PIS.   First, make yourself but like one.
Fore-thinking this, I have already fit—
'Tis in my cloak-bag—doublet, hat, hose, all
That answer to them. Would you, in their serving,
And with what imitation you can borrow   170
From youth of such a season, fore noble Lucius
Present yourself, desire his service, tell him
Wherein you're happy—which will make him know
If that his head have ear in music ; doubtless
With joy he will embrace you ; for he's honourable,   175
And, doubling that, most holy. Your means abroad—
You have me, rich ; and I will never fail
Beginning nor supplyment.

IMO.   Thou art all the comfort
The gods will diet me with. Prithee away !
There's more to be consider'd ; but we'll even   180
All that good time will give us. This attempt
I am soldier to, and will abide it with
A prince's courage. Away, I prithee.

PIS. Well, madam, we must take a short farewell,
Lest, being miss'd, I be suspected of   185
Your carriage from the court. My noble mistress,
Here is a box ; I had it from the Queen.
What's in't is precious. If you are sick at sea
Or stomach-qualm'd at land, a dram of this

Will drive away distemper. To some shade,   190
And fit you to your manhood. May the gods
Direct you to the best !
IMO.   Amen. I thank thee. [*Exeunt severally.*

SCENE V. *Britain. Cymbeline's palace.*

Enter CYMBELINE, QUEEN, CLOTEN, LUCIUS, *and* LORDS.

CYM. Thus far ; and so farewell.
LUC.   Thanks, royal sir.
My emperor hath wrote ; I must from hence,
And am right sorry that I must report ye
My master's enemy.
CYM.   Our subjects, sir,
Will not endure his yoke ; and for ourself   5
To show less sovereignty than they, must needs
Appear unkinglike.
LUC.   So, sir. I desire of you
A conduct overland to Milford Haven.
Madam, all joy befall your Grace, and you !
CYM. My lords, you are appointed for that office ;   10
The due of honour in no point omit.
So farewell, noble Lucius.
LUC.   Your hand, my lord.
CLO. Receive it friendly ; but from this time forth
I wear it as your enemy.
LUC.   Sir, the event
Is yet to name the winner. Fare you well.   15
CYM. Leave not the worthy Lucius, good my lords,
Till he have cross'd the Severn. Happiness !
                              [*Exeunt* LUCIUS *and* LORDS.
QUEEN. He goes hence frowning ; but it honours us
That we have given him cause.
CLO.   'Tis all the better ;
Your valiant Britons have their wishes in it.   20
CYM. Lucius hath wrote already to the Emperor
How it goes here. It fits us therefore ripely
Our chariots and our horsemen be in readiness.
The pow'rs that he already hath in Gallia
Will soon be drawn to head, from whence he moves   25
His war for Britain.
QUEEN.   'Tis not sleepy business,
But must be look'd to speedily and strongly.
CYM. Our expectation that it would be thus
Hath made us forward. But, my gentle queen,
Where is our daughter ? She hath not appear'd   30
Before the Roman, nor to us hath tender'd
The duty of the day. She looks us like
A thing more made of malice than of duty ;
We have noted it. Call her before us, for
We have been too slight in sufferance.   [*Exit a* MESSENGER.
QUEEN.   Royal sir,   35
Since the exile of Posthumus, most retir'd
Hath her life been ; the cure whereof, my lord,

'Tis time must do.   Beseech your Majesty,
Forbear sharp speeches to her ; she's a lady
So tender of rebukes that words are strokes,
And strokes death to her.   40

Re-enter MESSENGER.

CYM.   Where is she, sir ? How
Can her contempt be answer'd ?
MESS.   Please you, sir,
Her chambers are all lock'd, and there's no answer
That will be given to th' loud of noise we make.
QUEEN. My lord, when last I went to visit her,   45
She pray'd me to excuse her keeping close ;
Whereto constrain'd by her infirmity
She should that duty leave unpaid to you
Which daily she was bound to proffer.   This
She wish'd me to make known ; but our great court   50
Made me to blame in memory.
CYM.   Her doors lock'd ?
Not seen of late ? Grant, heaven's, that which I fear
Prove false !   [*Exit.*
QUEEN.   Son, I say, follow the King.
CLO. That man of hers, Pisanio, her old servant,   55
I have not seen these two days.
QUEEN.   Go, look after.   [*Exit* CLOTEN.
Pisanio, thou that stand'st so for Posthumus !
He hath a drug of mine.   I pray his absence
Proceed by swallowing that ; for he believes
It is a thing most precious.   But for her,   60
Where is she gone ? Haply despair hath seiz'd her ;
Or, wing'd with fervour of her love, she's flown
To her desir'd Posthumus.   Gone she is
To death or to dishonour, and my end
Can make good use of either.   She being down,   65
I have the placing of the British crown.

Re-enter CLOTEN.

How now, my son ?
CLO.   'Tis certain she is fled.
Go in and cheer the King.   He rages ; none
Dare come about him.
QUEEN.   All the better.   May
This night forestall him of the coming day !   [*Exit.*
CLO. I love and hate her ; for she's fair and royal, 71
And that she hath all courtly parts more exquisite
Than lady, ladies, woman.   From every one
The best she hath, and she, of all compounded,
Outsells them all.   I love her therefore ; but   75
Disdaining me and throwing favours on
The low Posthumus slanders so her judgment
That what's else rare is chok'd ; and in that point
I will conclude to hate her, nay, indeed,
To be reveng'd upon her.   For when fools   80
Shall—

Enter PISANIO.

      Who is here ? What, are you packing, sirrah ?
Come hither. Ah, you precious pander ! Villain,
Where is thy lady ? In a word, or else
Thou art straightway with the fiends.

PIS.   O good my lord !

CLO. Where is thy lady ? or, by Jupiter—   85
I will not ask again. Close villain,
I'll have this secret from thy heart, or rip
Thy heart to find it. Is she with Posthumus ?
From whose so many weights of baseness cannot
A dram of worth be drawn.

PIS.   Alas, my lord,   90
How can she be with him ? When was she miss'd ?
He is in Rome.

CLO.   Where is she, sir ? Come nearer.
No farther halting ! Satisfy me home
What is become of her.

PIS. O my all-worthy lord !

CLO.   All-worthy villain !   95
Discover where thy mistress is at once,
At the next word. No more of ' worthy lord ' !
Speak, or thy silence on the instant is
Thy condemnation and thy death.

PIS.   Then, sir,
This paper is the history of my knowledge   100
Touching her flight.   [*Presenting a letter.*

CLO.   Let's see't. I will pursue her
Even to Augustus' throne.

PIS. [*Aside.*]   Or this or perish.
She's far enough ; and what he learns by this
May prove his travel, not her danger.

CLO.   Humh !

PIS. [*Aside.*] I'll write to my lord she's dead. O Imogen,   105
Safe mayst thou wander, safe return again !

CLO. Sirrah, is this letter true ?

PIS. Sir, as I think.

CLO. It is Posthumus' hand ; I know't. Sirrah, if thou wouldst not
be a villain, but do me true service, undergo those employ-
ments wherein I should have cause to use thee with a serious
industry—that is, what villainy soe'er I bid thee do, to perform
it directly and truly—I would think thee an honest man ; thou
shouldst neither want my means for thy relief nor my voice for
thy preferment.   116

PIS. Well, my good lord.

CLO. Wilt thou serve me ? For since patiently and constantly thou
hast stuck to the bare fortune of that beggar Posthumus, thou
canst not, in the course of gratitude, but be a diligent follower of
mine. Wilt thou serve me ?

PIS. Sir, I will.

CLO. Give me thy hand ; here's my purse. Hast any of thy late
master's garments in thy possession ?   125

PIS. I have, my lord, at my lodging, the same suit he wore when he took leave of my lady and mistress.

CLO. The first service thou dost me, fetch that suit hither. Let it be thy first service ; go.   129

PIS. I shall, my lord.   [*Exit.*

CLO. Meet thee at Milford Haven ! I forgot to ask him one thing ; I'll remember 't anon. Even there, thou villain Posthumus, will I kill thee. I would these garments were come. She said upon a time—the bitterness of it I now belch from my heart—that she held the very garment of Posthumus in more respect than my noble and natural person, together with the adornment of my qualities. With that suit upon my back will I ravish her ; first kill him, and in her eyes. There shall she see my valour, which will then be a torment to her contempt. He on the ground, my speech of insultment ended on his dead body, and when my lust hath dined—which, as I say, to vex her I will execute in the clothes that she so prais'd—to the court I'll knock her back, foot her home again. She hath despis'd me rejoicingly, and I'll be merry in my revenge.   146

Re-enter PISANIO, *with the clothes.*

Be those the garments ?

PIS. Ay, my noble lord.

CLO. How long is 't since she went to Milford Haven ?

PIS. She can scarce be there yet.   150

CLO. Bring this apparel to my chamber ; that is the second thing that I have commanded thee. The third is that thou wilt be a voluntary mute to my design. Be but duteous and true, prefer-ment shall tender itself to thee. My revenge is now at Milford, would I had wings to follow it ! Come, and be true.   [*Exit.*

PIS. Thou bid'st me to my loss ; for true to thee   157
   Were to prove false, which I will never be,
   To him that is most true. To Milford go,
   And find not her whom thou pursuest. Flow, flow,   160
   You heavenly blessings, on her ! This fool's speed
   Be cross'd with slowness ! Labour be his meed !   [*Exit.*

SCENE VI. *Wales. Before the cave of Belarius.*

Enter IMOGEN *alone, in boy's clothes.*

IMO. I see a man's life is a tedious one.
   I have tir'd myself, and for two nights together
   Have made the ground my bed. I should be sick
   But that my resolution helps me. Milford,
   When from the mountain-top Pisanio show'd thee,   5
   Thou wast within a ken. O Jove ! I think
   Foundations fly the wretched ; such, I mean,
   Where they should be reliev'd. Two beggars told me
   I could not miss my way. Will poor folks lie,
   That have afflictions on them, knowing 'tis   10
   A punishment or trial ? Yes ; no wonder,
   When rich ones scarce tell true. To lapse in fulness
   Is sorer than to lie for need ; and falsehood
   Is worse in kings than beggars. My dear lord!

Thou art one o' th' false ones. Now I think on thee   15
My hunger's gone; but even before, I was
At point to sink for food. But what is this?
Here is a path to't; 'tis some savage hold.
I were best not call; I dare not call. Yet famine,
Ere clean it o'erthrow nature, makes it valiant.   20
Plenty and peace breeds cowards; hardness ever
Of hardiness is mother. Ho! who's here?
If anything that's civil, speak; if savage,
Take or lend. Ho! No answer? Then I'll enter.
Best draw my sword; and if mine enemy   25
But fear the sword, like me, he'll scarcely look on't.
Such a foe, good heavens!   [*Exit into the cave.*

Enter BELARIUS, GUIDERIUS, *and* ARVIRAGUS.

BEL. You, Polydore, have prov'd best woodman and
Are master of the feast. Cadwal and I
Will play the cook and servant; 'tis our match.   30
The sweat of industry would dry and die
But for the end it works to. Come, our stomachs
Will make what's homely savoury; weariness
Can snore upon the flint, when resty sloth
Finds the down pillow hard. Now, peace be here,   35
Poor house, that keep'st thyself!
GUI.   I am thoroughly weary.
ARV. I am weak with toil, yet strong in appetite.
GUI. There is cold meat i' th' cave; we'll browse on that
Whilst what we have kill'd be cook'd.
BEL. [*Looking into the cave.*]   Stay, come not in.
But that it eats our victuals, I should think   40
Here were a fairy.
GUI.   What's the matter, sir?
BEL. By Jupiter, an angel! or, if not,
An earthly paragon! Behold divineness
No elder than a boy!

Re-enter IMOGEN.

IMO. Good masters, harm me not.   45
Before I enter'd here I call'd, and thought
To have begg'd or bought what I have took. Good troth,
I have stol'n nought; nor would not though I had found
Gold strew'd i' th' floor. Here's money for my meat.
I would have left it on the board, so soon   50
As I had made my meal, and parted
With pray'rs for the provider.
GUI.   Money, youth?
ARV. All gold and silver rather turn to dirt,
As 'tis no better reckon'd but of those
Who worship dirty gods.
IMO.   I see you're angry.   55
Know, if you kill me for my fault, I should
Have died had I not made it.
BEL.   Whither bound?
IMO. To Milford Haven.

BEL. What's your name?
IMO. Fidele, sir. I have a kinsman who   60
Is bound for Italy; he embark'd at Milford;
To whom being going, almost spent with hunger,
I am fall'n in this offence.
BEL.   Prithee, fair youth,
Think us no churls, nor measure our good minds
By this rude place we live in. Well encounter'd!   65
'Tis almost night; you shall have better cheer
Ere you depart, and thanks to stay and eat it.
Boys, bid him welcome.
GUI.   Were you a woman, youth,
I should woo hard but be your groom. In honesty
I bid for you as I'd buy.
ARV.   I'll make't my comfort   70
He is a man. I'll love him as my brother;
And such a welcome as I'd give to him
After long absence, such is yours. Most welcome!
Be sprightly, for you fall 'mongst friends.
IMO.   'Mongst friends,
If brothers. [Aside.] Would it had been so that they   75
Had been my father's sons! Then had my prize
Been less, and so more equal ballasting
To thee, Posthumus.
BEL.   He wrings at some distress.
GUI. Would I could free't!
ARV.   Or I, whate'er it be,
What pain it cost, what danger! Gods!
BEL. [Whispering.]   Hark, boys.   80
IMO. [Aside.] Great men,
That had a court no bigger than this cave,
That did attend themselves, and had the virtue
Which their own conscience seal'd them, laying by
That nothing-gift of differing multitudes,   85
Could not out-peer these twain. Pardon me, gods!
I'd change my sex to be companion with them,
Since Leonatus' false.
BEL.   It shall be so.
Boys, we'll go dress our hunt. Fair youth, come in.
Discourse is heavy, fasting; when we have supp'd,   90
We'll mannerly demand thee of thy story,
So far as thou wilt speak it.
GUI.   Pray draw near.
ARV. The night to th' owl and morn to th' lark less welcome.
IMO. Thanks, sir.
ARV. I pray draw near.   [Exeunt.

SCENE VII. Rome. A public place.

Enter two ROMAN SENATORS and TRIBUNES.

1 SEN. This is the tenour of the Emperor's writ:
That since the common men are now in action
'Gainst the Pannonians and Dalmatians,
And that the legions now in Gallia are

Full weak to undertake our wars against   5
The fall'n-off Britons, that we do incite
The gentry to this business. He creates
Lucius proconsul; and to you, the tribunes,
For this immediate levy, he commands
His absolute commission. Long live Cæsar!   10

TRI. Is Lucius general of the forces?

2 SEN.   Ay.

TRI. Remaining now in Gallia?

1 SEN.   With those legions
Which I have spoke of, whereunto your levy
Must be supplyant. The words of your commission
Will tie you to the numbers and the time   15
Of their dispatch.

TRI.   We will discharge our duty.   [*Exeunt.*

ACT FOUR

SCENE I. *Wales. Near the cave of Belarius.*

Enter CLOTEN *alone.*

CLO. I am near to th' place where they should meet, if Pisanio have
mapp'd it truly. How fit his garments serve me! Why should
his mistress, who was made by him that made the tailor, not be
fit too? The rather—saving reverence of the word—for 'tis said
a woman's fitness comes by fits. Therein I must play the workman. I dare speak it to myself, for it is not vain-glory for a man
and his glass to confer in his own chamber—I mean, the lines of
my body are as well drawn as his; no less young, more strong,
not beneath him in fortunes, beyond him in the advantage of the
time, above him in birth, alike conversant in general services, and
more remarkable in single oppositions. Yet this imperceiverant
thing loves him in my despite. What mortality is! Posthumus,
thy head, which now is growing upon thy shoulders, shall within
this hour be off; thy mistress enforced; thy garments cut to
pieces before her face; and all this done, spurn her home to her
father, who may, haply, be a little angry for my so rough usage;
but my mother, having power of his testiness, shall turn all into
my commendations. My horse is tied up safe. Out, sword,
and to a sore purpose! Fortune, put them into my hand. This is
the very description of their meeting-place; and the fellow dares
not deceive me.   [*Exit.*

SCENE II. *Wales. Before the cave of* BELARIUS.

Enter, from the cave, BELARIUS, GUIDERIUS, ARVIRAGUS, *and* IMOGEN.

BEL. [*To* IMOGEN.] You are not well. Remain here in the cave;
We'll come to you after hunting.

ARV. [*To* IMOGEN.]   Brother, stay here.
Are we not brothers?

IMO.   So man and man should be;
But clay and clay differs in dignity,

Whose dust is both alike.   I am very sick.   5
GUI. Go you to hunting ; I'll abide with him.
IMO. So sick I am not, yet I am not well ;
    But not so citizen a wanton as
    To seem to die ere sick.   So please you, leave me ;
    Stick to your journal course.   The breach of custom   10
    Is breach of all.   I am ill, but your being by me
    Cannot amend me ; society is no comfort
    To one not sociable.   I am not very sick,
    Since I can reason of it.   Pray you trust me here.
    I'll rob none but myself ; and let me die,   15
    Stealing so poorly.
GUI.   I love thee ; I have spoke it.
    How much the quantity, the weight as much
    As I do love my father.
BEL.   What ? how ? how ?
ARV. If it be sin to say so, sir, I yoke me
    In my good brother's fault.   I know not why   20
    I love this youth, and I have heard you say
    Love's reason's without reason.   The bier at door,
    And a demand who is't shall die, I'd say
    ' My father, not this youth '.
BEL. [Aside.]   O noble strain !
    O worthiness of nature ! breed of greatness !   25
    Cowards father cowards and base things sire base.
    Nature hath meal and bran, contempt and grace.
    I'm not their father ; yet who this should be
    Doth miracle itself, lov'd before me.—
    'Tis the ninth hour o' th' morn.
ARV.   Brother, farewell.   30
IMO. I wish ye sport.
ARV.   Your health.   [To BELARIUS.] So please you, sir.
IMO. [Aside.]   These are kind creatures.   Gods, what lies I have
        heard !
    Our courtiers say all's savage but at court.
    Experience, O, thou disprov'st report !
    Th' imperious seas breed monsters ; for the dish,   35
    Poor tributary rivers as sweet fish.
    I am sick still ; heart-sick.   Pisanio,
    I'll now taste of thy drug.   [Swallows some.
GUI.   I could not stir him.
    He said he was gentle, but unfortunate ;
    Dishonestly afflicted, but yet honest.   40
ARV. Thus did he answer me ; yet said hereafter
    I might know more.
BEL.   To th' field, to th' field !
    We'll leave you for this time.   Go in and rest.
ARV. We'll not be long away.
BEL.   Pray be not sick,
    For you must be our huswife.
IMO.   Well, or ill,   45
    I am bound to you.
BEL.   And shalt be ever.
                                [Exit IMOGEN into the cave.

This youth, howe'er distress'd, appears he hath had
Good ancestors.

ARV.   How angel-like he sings!

GUI. But his neat cookery! He cut our roots in characters,
And sauc'd our broths as Juno had been sick,
And he her dieter.

ARV.   Nobly he yokes
A smiling with a sigh, as if the sigh
Was that it was for not being such a smile ;
The smile mocking the sigh that it would fly   55
From so divine a temple to commix
With winds that sailors rail at.

GUI.   I do note
That grief and patience, rooted in him both,
Mingle their spurs together.

ARV.   Grow patience !
And let the stinking elder, grief, untwine   60
His perishing root with the increasing vine !

BEL. It is great morning. Come, away ! Who's there ?

Enter CLOTEN.

CLO. I cannot find those runagates ; that villain
Hath mock'd me. I am faint.

BEL.   Those runagates ?
Means he not us ? I partly know him ; 'tis   65
Cloten, the son o' th' Queen. I fear some ambush.
I saw him not these many years, and yet
I know 'tis he. We are held as outlaws. Hence !

GUI. He is but one ; you and my brother search
What companies are near. Pray you away ;   70
Let me alone with him.   [*Exeunt* BELARIUS *and* ARVIRAGUS.

CLO.   Soft ! What are you
That fly me thus ? Some villain mountaineers ?
I have heard of such. What slave art thou ?

GUI.   A thing
More slavish did I ne'er than answering
'A slave' without a knock.

CLO.   Thou art a robber,   75
A law-breaker, a villain. Yield thee, thief.

GUI. To who ? To thee ? What art thou ? Have not I
An arm as big as thine, a heart as big ?
Thy words, I grant, are bigger, for I wear not
My dagger in my mouth. Say what thou art ;   80
Why I should yield to thee.

CLO.   Thou villain base,
Know'st me not by my clothes ?

GUI.   No, nor thy tailor, rascal,
Who is thy grandfather ; he made those clothes,
Which, as it seems, make thee.

CLO.   Thou precious varlet,
My tailor made them not.

GUI.   Hence, then, and thank   85
The man that gave them thee. Thou art some fool ;
I am loath to beat thee.

287

CLO.   Thou injurious thief,
  Hear but my name, and tremble.
GUI.   What's thy name?
CLO. Cloten, thou villain.
GUI. Cloten, thou double villain, be thy name,   90
  I cannot tremble at it.   Were it toad, or adder, spider,
  'Twould move me sooner.
CLO.   To thy further fear,
  Nay, to thy mere confusion, thou shalt know
  I am son to th' Queen.
GUI.   I'm sorry for't; not seeming
  So worthy as thy birth.
CLO.   Art not afeard?   95
GUI. Those that I reverence, those I fear—the wise:
  At fools I laugh, not fear them.
CLO.   Die the death.
  When I have slain thee with my proper hand,
  I'll follow those that even now fled hence,
  And on the gates of Lud's Town set your heads.   100
  Yield, rustic mountaineer.   [*Exeunt, fighting.*

Re-enter BELARIUS *and* ARVIRAGUS.

BEL. No company's abroad.
ARV. None in the world; you did mistake him, sure.
BEL. I cannot tell; long is it since I saw him,
  But time hath nothing blurr'd those lines of favour   105
  Which then he wore; the snatches in his voice,
  And burst of speaking, were as his.   I am absolute
  'Twas very Cloten.
ARV.   In this place we left them.
  I wish my brother make good time with him,
  You say he is so fell.
BEL.   Being scarce made up,   110
  I mean to man, he had not apprehension
  Or roaring terrors; for defect of judgment
  Is oft the cease of fear.

Re-enter GUIDERIUS *with* CLOTEN'S *head.*

               But, see, thy brother.
GUI. This Cloten was a fool, an empty purse;
  There was no money in't.   Not Hercules   115
  Could have knock'd out his brains, for he had none;
  Yet I not doing this, the fool had borne
  My head as I do his.
BEL.   What hast thou done?
GUI. I am perfect what: cut off one Cloten's head,
  Son to the Queen, after his own report;   120
  Who call'd me traitor, mountaineer, and swore
  With his own single hand he'd take us in,
  Displace our heads where—thank the gods!—they grow,
  And set them on Lud's Town.
BEL.   We are all undone.
GUI. Why, worthy father, what have we to lose   125
  But that he swore to take, our lives?   The law
288

Protects not us ; then why should we be tender
To let an arrogant piece of flesh threat us,
Play judge and executioner all himself,
For we do fear the law ? What company   130
Discover you abroad ?

EL.   No single soul
Can we set eye on, but in all safe reason
He must have some attendants.   Though his humour
Was nothing but mutation—ay, and that
From one bad thing to worse—not frenzy, not   135
Absolute madness could so far have rav'd,
To bring him here alone.   Although perhaps
It may be heard at court that such as we
Cave here, hunt here, are outlaws, and in time
May make some stronger head—the which he hearing,   140
As it is like him, might break out and swear
He'd fetch us in ; yet is't not probable
To come alone, either he so undertaking
Or they so suffering.   Then on good ground we fear,
If we do fear this body hath a tail   145
More perilous than the head.

RV.   Let ordinance
Come as the gods foresay it.   Howsoe'er,
My brother hath done well.

EL.   I had no mind
To hunt this day ; the boy Fidele's sickness
Did make my way long forth.

JI.   With his own sword,   150
Which he did wave against my throat, I have ta'en
His head from him.   I'll throw't into the creek
Behind our rock, and let it to the sea
And tell the fishes he's the Queen's son, Cloten.
That's all I reck.   [*Exit.*

EL.   I fear 'twill be reveng'd.   155
Would, Polydore, thou hadst not done't ! though valour
Becomes thee well enough.

RV.   Would I had done't,
So the revenge alone pursu'd me ! Polydore,
I love thee brotherly, but envy much
Thou hast robb'd me of this deed.   I would revenges,   160
That possible strength might meet, would seek us through,
And put us to our answer.

L.   Well, 'tis done.
We'll hunt no more to-day, nor seek for danger
Where there's no profit.   I prithee to our rock.
You and Fidele play the cooks ; I'll stay   165
Till hasty Polydore return, and bring him
To dinner presently.

V.   Poor sick Fidele !
I'll willingly to him ; to gain his colour
I'd let a parish of such Cloten's blood,
And praise myself for charity.   [*Exit.*

L.   O thou goddess,   170
Thou divine Nature, thou thyself thou blazon'st

10

289

In these two princely boys ! They are as gentle
As zephyrs blowing below the violet,
Not wagging his sweet head ; and yet as rough,
Their royal blood enchaf'd, as the rud'st wind   1⁷
That by the top doth take the mountain pine
And make him stoop to th' vale. 'Tis wonder
That an invisible instinct should frame them
To royalty unlearn'd, honour untaught,
Civility not seen from other, valour   18
That wildly grows in them, but yields a crop
As if it had been sow'd. Yet still it's strange
What Cloten's being here to us portends,
Or what his death will bring us.

Re-enter GUIDERIUS.

GUI.   Where's my brother ?
I have sent Cloten's clotpoll down the stream,   1⁸
In embassy to his mother ; his body's hostage
For his return.   [*Solemn musi*

BEL.   My ingenious instrument !
Hark, Polydore, it sounds. But what occasion
Hath Cadwal now to give it motion ? Hark !

GUI. Is he at home ?

BEL.   He went hence even now.   1⁹

GUI. What does he mean ? Since death of my dear'st mother
It did not speak before. All solemn things
Should answer solemn accidents. The matter ?
Triumphs for nothing and lamenting toys
Is jollity for apes and grief for boys.   1⁹
Is Cadwal mad ?

Re-enter ARVIRAGUS, *with* IMOGEN *as dead, bearing her in his arms.*

BEL.   Look, here he comes,
And brings the dire occasion in his arms
Of what we blame him for !

ARV.   The bird is dead
That we have made so much on. I had rather
Have skipp'd from sixteen years of age to sixty,   2⁰
To have turn'd my leaping time into a crutch,
Than have seen this.

GUI.   O sweetest, fairest lily !
My brother wears thee not the one half so well
As when thou grew'st thyself.

BEL.   O melancholy !
Who ever yet could sound thy bottom ? find   2⁰
The ooze to show what coast thy sluggish crare
Might'st easiliest harbour in ? Thou blessed thing !
Jove knows what man thou mightst have made ; but I,
Thou diedst, a most rare boy, of melancholy.
How found you him ?

ARV.   Stark, as you see ;   2
Thus smiling, as some fly had tickled slumber,
Not as death's dart, being laugh'd at ; his right cheek
Reposing on a cushion.

UI.   Where ?
RV.   O' th' floor ;
His arms thus leagu'd. I thought he slept, and put
My clouted brogues from off my feet, whose rudeness   215
Answer'd my steps too loud.
UI.   Why, he but sleeps.
If he be gone he'll make his grave a bed ;
With female fairies will his tomb be haunted,
And worms will not come to thee.
RV.   With fairest flowers,
Whilst summer lasts and I live here, Fidele,   220
I'll sweeten thy sad grave. Thou shalt not lack
The flower that's like thy face, pale primrose ; nor
The azur'd hare-bell, like thy veins ; no, nor
The leaf of eglantine, whom not to slander,
Out-sweet'ned not thy breath.   The ruddock would,   225
With charitable bill—O bill, sore shaming
Those rich-left heirs that let their fathers lie
Without a monument !—bring thee all· this ;
Yea, and furr'd moss besides, when flow'rs are none,
To winter-ground thy corse—
UI.   Prithee have done,   230
And do not play in wench-like words with that
Which is so serious. Let us bury him,
And not protract with admiration what
Is now due debt. To th' grave.
RV.   Say, where shall's lay him ?
UI. By good Euriphile, our mother.
RV.   Be't so ;
And let us, Polydore, though now our voices
Have got the mannish crack, sing him to th' ground,
As once to our mother ; use like note and words,
Save that Euriphile must be Fidele.
UI. Cadwal,   240
I cannot sing. I'll weep, and word it with thee ;
For notes of sorrow out of tune are worse
Than priests and fanes that lie.
RV.   We'll speak it, then.
EL. Great griefs, I see, med'cine the less, for Cloten
Is quite forgot. He was a queen's son, boys ;   245
And though he came our enemy, remember
He was paid for that. Though mean and mighty rotting
Together have one dust, yet reverence—
That angel of the world—doth make distinction
Of place 'tween high and low. Our foe was princely ;   250
And though you took his life, as being our foe,
Yet bury him as a prince.
UI.   Pray you fetch him hither.
Thersites' body is as good as Ajax ',
When neither are alive.
RV.   If you'll go fetch him,   254
We'll say our song the whilst. Brother, begin. [*Exit* BELARIUS.
UI. Nay, Cadwal, we must lay his head to th' East ;
My father hath a reason for't.

ARV.   'Tis true.
GUI. Come on, then, and remove him.
ARV.   So.   Begin.

                              Song.

GUI.   Fear no more the heat o' th' sun
                      Nor the furious winter's rages ;   26
                  Thou thy worldly task hast done,
                      Home art gone, and ta'en thy wages.
                  Golden lads and girls all must,
                  As chimney-sweepers, come to dust.

ARV.   Fear no more the frown o' th' great ;   26
                      Thou art past the tyrant's stroke.
                  Care no more to clothe and eat ;
                      To thee the reed is as the oak.
                  The sceptre, learning, physic, must
                  All follow this and come to dust.   27

GUI.   Fear no more the lightning flash,
ARV.   Nor th' all-dreaded thunder-stone ;
GUI.   Fear not slander, censure rash ;
ARV.   Thou hast finish'd joy and moan.
BOTH.   All lovers young, all lovers must   27
                  Consign to thee and come to dust.

GUI.   No exorciser harm thee !
ARV.   Nor no witchcraft charm thee !
GUI.   Ghost unlaid forbear thee !
ARV.   Nothing ill come near thee !   28
BOTH.   Quiet consummation have,
                  And renowned be thy grave !

            Re-enter BELARIUS *with the body of* CLOTEN.

GUI. We have done our obsequies.   Come, lay him down.
BEL. Here's a few flowers ; but 'bout midnight, more.
    The herbs that have on them cold dew o' th' night   28
    Are strewings fit'st for graves.   Upon their faces.
    You were as flow'rs, now wither'd.   Even so
    These herblets shall which we upon you strew.
    Come on, away.   Apart upon our knees.
    The ground that gave them first has them again.   29
    Their pleasures here are past, so is their pain.
                                        [*Exeunt all but* IMOGEN
IMO. [*Awaking.*]   Yes, sir, to Milford Haven.   Which is the way ?
    I thank you.   By yond bush ?   Pray, how far thither ?
    'Ods pittikins ! can it be six mile yet ?
    I have gone all night.   Faith, I'll lie down and sleep.   29
    But, soft ! no bedfellow.   O gods and goddesses !
                                        [*Seeing the body*
    These flow'rs are like the pleasures of the world ;
    This bloody man, the care on't.   I hope I dream ;
    For so I thought I was a cave-keeper,
    And cook to honest creatures.   But 'tis not so ;   30
    'Twas but a bolt of nothing, shot at nothing,

Which the brain makes of fumes. Our very eyes
Are sometimes, like our judgments, blind. Good faith,
I tremble still with fear ; but if there be
Yet left in heaven as small a drop of pity   305
As a wren's eye, fear'd gods, a part of it !
The dream's here still. Even when I wake it is
Without me, as within me ; not imagin'd, felt.
A headless man ? The garments of Posthumus ?
I know the shape of's leg ; this is his hand,   310
His foot Mercurial, his Martial thigh,
The brawns of Hercules ; but his Jovial face—
Murder in heaven ! How ! 'Tis gone. Pisanio,
All curses madded Hecuba gave the Greeks,
And mine to boot, be darted on thee ! Thou,   315
Conspir'd with that irregulous devil, Cloten,
Hath here cut off my lord. To write and read
Be henceforth treacherous ! Damn'd Pisanio
Hath with his forged letters—damn'd Pisanio—
From this most bravest vessel of the world   320
Struck the main-top. O Posthumus ! alas,
Where is thy head ? Where's that ? Ay me ! where's that ?
Pisanio might have kill'd thee at the heart,
And left this head on. How should this be ? Pisanio ?
'Tis he and Cloten ; malice and lucre in them   325
Have laid this woe here. O, 'tis pregnant, pregnant !
The drug he gave me, which he said was precious
And cordial to me, have I not found it
Murd'rous to th' senses ? That confirms it home.
This is Pisanio's deed, and Cloten. O !   330
Give colour to my pale cheek with thy blood,
That we the horrider may seem to those
Which chance to find us. O, my lord, my lord !
                                    [Falls fainting on the body.

        Enter LUCIUS, CAPTAINS, *and a* SOOTHSAYER.

CAP. To them the legions garrison'd in Gallia,
After your will, have cross'd the sea, attending   335
You here at Milford Haven ; with your ships,
They are in readiness.

LUC.   But what from Rome ?

CAP. The Senate hath stirr'd up the confiners
And gentlemen of Italy, most willing spirits,
That promise noble service ; and they come   340
Under the conduct of bold Iachimo,
Sienna's brother.

LUC.   When expect you them ?

CAP. With the next benefit o' th' wind.

LUC.   This forwardness
Makes our hopes fair. Command our present numbers
Be muster'd ; bid the captains look to't. Now, sir,   345
What have you dream'd of late of this war's purpose ?

SOOTH. Last night the very gods show'd me a vision—
I fast and pray'd for their intelligence—thus :
I saw Jove's bird, the Roman eagle, wing'd

                                                    293

From the spongy south to this part of the west,   350
There vanish'd in the sunbeams ; which portends,
Unless my sins abuse my divination,
Success to th' Roman host.

LUC.   Dream often so,
And never false.   Soft, ho ! what trunk is here
Without his top ?   The ruin speaks that sometime   355
It was a worthy building.   How ? a page ?
Or dead or sleeping on him ?   But dead, rather ;
For nature doth abhor to make his bed
With the defunct, or sleep upon the dead.
Let's see the boy's face.

CAP.   He's alive, my lord.   360

LUC. He'll then instruct us of this body.   Young one,
Inform us of thy fortunes ; for it seems
They crave to be demanded.   Who is this
Thou mak'st thy bloody pillow ?   Or who was he
That, otherwise than noble nature did,   365
Hath alter'd that good picture ?   What's thy interest
In this sad wreck ? How came't ? Who is't ? What art thou ?

IMO. I am nothing ; or if not,
Nothing to be were better.   This was my master,
A very valiant Briton and a good,   370
That here by mountaineers lies slain.   Alas !
There is no more such masters.   I may wander
From east to occident ; cry out for service ;
Try many, all good ; serve truly ; never
Find such another master.

LUC.   'Lack, good youth !   375
Thou mov'st no less with thy complaining than
Thy master in bleeding.   Say his name, good friend.

IMO. Richard du Champ. [*Aside.*]   If I do lie, and do
No harm by it, though the gods hear, I hope
They'll pardon it.—Say you, sir ?

LUC. Thy name ?

IMO. Fidele, sir.

LUC. Thou dost approve thyself the very same ;
Thy name well fits thy faith, thy faith thy name.
Wilt take thy chance with me ?   I will not say   385
Thou shalt be so well master'd ; but, be sure,
No less belov'd.   The Roman Emperor's letters,
Sent by a consul to me, should not sooner
Than thine own worth prefer thee.   Go with me.

IMO. I'll follow, sir.   But first, an't please the gods,   390
I'll hide my master from the flies, as deep
As these poor pickaxes can dig ; and when
With wild wood-leaves and weeds I ha' strew'd his grave,
And on it said a century of prayers,
Such as I can, twice o'er, I'll weep and sigh ;   395
And leaving so his service, follow you,
So please you entertain me.

LUC.   Ay, good youth ;
And rather father thee than master thee.
My friends,

294

The boy hath taught us manly duties ; let us   400
Find out the prettiest daisied plot we can,
And make him with our pikes and partisans
A grave. Come, arm him. Boy, he is preferr'd
By thee to us ; and he shall be interr'd
As soldiers can. Be cheerful ; wipe thine eyes.   405
Some falls are means the happier to arise.   [*Exeunt.*

SCENE III. *Britain. Cymbeline's palace.*

Enter CYMBELINE, LORDS, PISANIO, *and* ATTENDANTS.

CYM. Again ! and bring me word how 'tis with her.
                                               [*Exit an* ATTENDANT.
      A fever with the absence of her son ;
      A madness, of which her life's in danger. Heavens,
      How deeply you at once do touch me ! Imogen,
      The great part of my comfort, gone ; my queen   5
      Upon a desperate bed, and in a time
      When fearful wars point at me ; her son gone,
      So needful for this present. It strikes me past
      The hope of comfort. But for thee, fellow,
      Who needs must know of her departure and   10
      Dost seem so ignorant, we'll enforce it from thee
      By a sharp torture.
PIS.   Sir, my life is yours ;
      I humbly set it at your will ; but for my mistress,
      I nothing know where she remains, why gone,
      Nor when she purposes return. Beseech your Highness,   15
      Hold me your loyal servant.
LORD.   Good my liege,
      The day that she was missing he was here.
      I dare be bound he's true and shall perform
      All parts of his subjection loyally. For Cloten,
      There wants no diligence in seeking him,   20
      And will no doubt be found.
CYM.   The time is troublesome.
      [*To* PISANIO.] We'll slip you for a season ; but our jealousy
      Does yet depend.
LORD.   So please your Majesty,
      The Roman legions, all from Gallia drawn,
      Are landed on your coast, with a supply   25
      Of Roman gentlemen by the Senate sent.
CYM. Now for the counsel of my son and queen !
      I am amaz'd with matter.
LORD.   Good my liege,
      Your preparation can affront no less
      Than what you hear of. Come more, for more you're ready.   30
      The want is but to put those pow'rs in motion
      That long to move.
CYM.   I thank you. Let's withdraw,
      And meet the time as it seeks us. We fear not
      What can from Italy annoy us ; but
      We grieve at chances here. Away !   [*Exeunt all but* PISANIO.
PIS. I heard no letter from my master since

I wrote him Imogen was slain. 'Tis strange.
Nor hear I from my mistress, who did promise
To yield me often tidings.   Neither know I
What is betid to Cloten, but remain   40
Perplex'd in all.   The heavens still must work.
Wherein I am false I am honest ; not true, to be true.
These present wars shall find I love my country,
Even to the note o' th' King, or I'll fall in them.
All other doubts, by time let them be clear'd :   45
Fortune brings in some boats that are not steer'd.   [Exit.

SCENE IV. *Wales. Before the cave of Belarius.*

Enter BELARIUS, GUIDERIUS, *and* ARVIRAGUS.

GUI. The noise is round about us.
BEL.   Let us from it.
ARV. What pleasure, sir, find we in life, to lock it
    From action and adventure ?
GUI.   Nay, what hope
    Have we in hiding us ? This way the Romans
    Must or for Britons slay us, or receive us   5
    For barbarous and unnatural revolts
    During their use, and slay us after.
BEL.   Sons,
    We'll higher to the mountains ; there secure us.
    To the King's party there's no going.   Newness
    Of Cloten's death—we being not known, not muster'd   10
    Among the bands—may drive us to a render
    Where we have liv'd, and so extort from's that
    Which we have done, whose answer would be death,
    Drawn on with torture.
GUI.   This is, sir, a doubt
    In such a time nothing becoming you   15
    Nor satisfying us.
ARV.   It is not likely
    That when they hear the Roman horses neigh,
    Behold their quarter'd fires, have both their eyes
    And ears so cloy'd importantly as now,
    That they will waste their time upon our note,   20
    To know from whence we are.
BEL.   O, I am known
    Of many in the army.   Many years,
    Though Cloten then but young, you see, not wore him
    From my remembrance.   And, besides, the King
    Hath not deserv'd my service nor your loves,   25
    Who find in my exile the want of breeding,
    The certainty of this hard life ; aye hopeless
    To have the courtesy your cradle promis'd,
    But to be still hot summer's tanlings and
    The shrinking slaves of winter.
GUI.   Than be so,   30
    Better to cease to be.   Pray, sir, to th' army.
    I and my brother are not known ; yourself

So out of thought, and thereto so o'ergrown,
Cannot be questioned.

ARV.   By this sun that shines,
I'll thither.   What thing is't that I never   35
Did see man die!   scarce ever look'd on blood
But that of coward hares, hot goats, and venison!
Never bestrid a horse, save one that had
A rider like myself, who ne'er wore rowel
Nor iron on his heel!   I am asham'd   40
To look upon the holy sun, to have
The benefit of his blest beams, remaining
So long a poor unknown.

GUI.   By heavens, I'll go!
If you will bless me sir, and give me leave,
I'll take the better care; but if you will not,   45
The hazard therefore due fall on me by
The hands of Romans!

ARV.   So say I.   Amen.

BEL.   No reason I, since of your lives you set
So slight a valuation, should reserve
My crack'd one to more care.   Have with you, boys!   50
If in your country wars you chance to die,
That is my bed too, lads, and there I'll lie.
Lead, lead. [Aside.]   The time seems long; their blood thinks
     scorn
Till it fly out and show them princes born.   [Exeunt.

ACT FIVE

Scene I.   Britain.   The Roman camp.

Enter POSTHUMUS *alone, with a bloody handkerchief.*

POST.   Yea, bloody cloth, I'll keep thee; for I wish'd
Thou shouldst be colour'd thus.   You married ones,
If each of you should take this course, how many
Must murder wives much better than themselves
For wrying but a little!   O Pisanio!   5
Every good servant does not all commands;
No bond but to do just ones.   Gods! if you
Should have ta'en vengeance on my faults, I never
Had liv'd to put on this; so had you saved
The noble Imogen to repent, and struck   10
Me, wretch more worth your vengeance.   But alack,
You snatch some hence for little faults; that's love,
To have them fall no more.   You some permit
To second ills with ills, each elder worse,
And make them dread it, to the doer's thrift.   15
But Imogen is your own.   Do your best wills,
And make me blest to obey.   I am brought hither
Among th' Italian gentry, and to fight
Against my lady's kingdom.   'Tis enough
That, Britain, I have kill'd thy mistress; peace!   20
I'll give no wound to thee.   Therefore, good heavens,

Hear patiently my purpose. I'll disrobe me
Of these Italian weeds, and suit myself
As does a Britain peasant. So I'll fight
Against the part I come with ; so I'll die   2⁵
For thee, O Imogen, even for whom my life
Is every breath a death. And thus unknown,
Pitied nor hated, to the face of peril.
Myself I'll dedicate. Let me make men know
More valour in me than my habits show.   3⁰
Gods, put the strength o' th' Leonati in me !
To shame the guise o' th' world, I will begin
The fashion—less without and more within.   [*Exit*

SCENE II.   *Britain.   A field of battle between the British and Roma*
                                        camps.

Enter LUCIUS, IACHIMO, *and the* ROMAN ARMY *at one door, and th*
    BRITISH ARMY *at another,* LEONATUS POSTHUMUS *following like*
    poor soldier.   They march over and go out.   Alarums.   The
    enter again, in skirmish, IACHIMO *and* POSTHUMUS.   *He vanquishet*
    and disarmeth Iachimo, and then leaves him.

IACH. The heaviness and guilt within my bosom
    Takes off my manhood.   I have belied a lady,
    The Princess of this country, and the air on't
    Revengingly enfeebles me ; or could this carl,
    A very drudge of nature's, have subdu'd me
    In my profession ?   Knighthoods and honours borne
    As I wear mine are titles but of scorn.
    If that thy gentry, Britain, go before
    This lout as he exceeds our lords, the odds
    Is that we scarce are men, and you are gods.   [*Exi*

The battle continues ; the BRITONS *fly ;* CYMBELINE *is taken.   The*
    enter to his rescue BELARIUS, GUIDERIUS, *and* ARVIRAGUS.

BEL. Stand, stand ! We have th' advantage of the ground ;
    The lane is guarded ; nothing routs us but
    The villainy of our fears.
GUI. *and* ARV.   Stand, stand, and fight !

Re-enter POSTHUMUS, *and seconds the Britons ; they rescue* CYMBELIN
    and exeunt.   Then re-enter LUCIUS *and* IACHIMO, *with* IMOGEN.

LUC. Away, boy, from the troops, and save thyself ;
    For friends kill friends, and the disorder's such
    As war were hoodwink'd.
IACH.   'Tis their fresh supplies.
LUC. It is a day turn'd strangely.   Or betimes
    Let's reinforce or fly.   [*Exeun*

SCENE III.   *Another part of the field.*

Enter POSTHUMUS *and a Britain* LORD.

LORD. Cam'st thou from where they made the stand ?
POST.   I did :
    Though you, it seems, come from the fliers.

298

LORD.   I did.
POST. No blame be to you, sir, for all was lost,
    But that the heavens fought. The King himself
    Of his wings destitute, the army broken,   5
    And but the backs of Britons seen, all flying,
    Through a strait lane—the enemy, full-hearted,
    Lolling the tongue with slaught'ring, having work
    More plentiful than tools to do't, struck down
    Some mortally, some slightly touch'd, some falling   10
    Merely through fear, that the strait path was damm'd
    With dead men hurt behind, and cowards living
    To die with length'ned shame.
LORD.   Where was this lane?
POST. Close by the battle, ditch'd, and wall'd with turf,
    Which gave advantage to an ancient soldier—   15
    An honest one, I warrant, who deserv'd
    So long a breeding as his white beard came to,
    In doing this for's country. Athwart the lane
    He, with two striplings—lads more like to run
    The country base than to commit such slaughter;   20
    With faces fit for masks, or rather fairer
    Than those for preservation cas'd or shame—
    Made good the passage, cried to those that fled
    ' Our Britain's harts die flying, not our men.
    To darkness fleet souls that fly backwards! Stand;   25
    Or we are Romans and will give you that,
    Like beasts, which you shun beastly, and may save
    But to look back in frown. Stand, stand!' These three,
    Three thousand confident, in act as many—
    For three performers are the file when all   30
    The rest do nothing—with this word ' Stand, stand!'
    Accommodated by the place, more charming
    With their own nobleness, which could have turn'd
    A distaff to a lance, gilded pale looks,
    Part shame, part spirit renew'd; that some turn'd coward   35
    But by example—O, a sin in war
    Damn'd in the first beginners!—gan to look
    The way that they did and to grin like lions
    Upon the pikes o' th' hunters. Then began
    A stop i' th' chaser, a retire; anon   40
    A rout, confusion thick. Forthwith they fly,
    Chickens, the way which they stoop'd eagles; slaves,
    The strides they victors made; and now our cowards,
    Like fragments in hard voyages, became
    The life o' th' need. Having found the back-door open   45
    Of the unguarded hearts, heavens, how they wound!
    Some slain before, some dying, some their friends
    O'erborne i' th' former wave. Ten chas'd by one
    Are now each one the slaughterman of twenty.
    Those that would die or ere resist are grown   50
    The mortal bugs o' th' field.
LORD.   This was strange chance:
    A narrow lane, an old man, and two boys.
POST. Nay, do not wonder at it; you are made

                                                          299

Rather to wonder at the things you hear
Than to work any. Will you rhyme upon't,   55
And vent it for a mock'ry ? Here is one :
' Two boys, an old man (twice a boy), a lane,
Preserv'd the Britons, was the Romans' bane ' .
LORD. Nay, be not angry, sir.
POST.   'Lack, to what end ?
Who dares not stand his foe I'll be his friend ;   60
For if he'll do as he is made to do,
I know he'll quickly fly my friendship too.
You have put me into rhyme.
LORD.   Farewell ; you're angry. [Exit.
POST. Still going ? This is a lord ! O noble misery,
To be i' th' field and ask ' What news ? ' of me !   65
To-day how many would have given their honours
To have sav'd their carcasses ! took heel to do't,
And yet died too ! I, in mine own woe charm'd,
Could not find death where I did hear him groan,
Nor feel him where he struck. Being an ugly monster,   70
'Tis strange he hides him in fresh cups, soft beds,
Sweet words ; or hath moe ministers than we
That draw his knives i' th' war. Well, I will find him ;
For being now a favourer to the Briton,
No more a Briton, I have resum'd again   75
The part I came in. Fight I will no more,
But yield me to the veriest hind that shall
Once touch my shoulder. Great the slaughter is
Here made by th' Roman ; great the answer be
Britons must take. For me, my ransom's death ;   80
On either side I come to spend my breath,
Which neither here I'll keep nor bear again,
But end it by some means for Imogen.

Enter two BRITISH CAPTAINS *and* SOLDIERS.

1 CAP. Great Jupiter be prais'd ! Lucius is taken.
'Tis thought the old man and his sons were angels.   85
2 CAP. There was a fourth man, in a silly habit,
That gave th' affront with them.
1 CAP.   So 'tis reported ;
But none of 'em can be found. Stand ! who's there ?
POST. A Roman,
Who had not now been drooping here if seconds   90
Had answer'd him.
2 CAP.   Lay hands on him ; a dog !
A leg of Rome shall not return to tell
What crows have peck'd them here. He brags his service,
As if he were of note. Bring him to th' King.

Enter CYMBELINE, BELARIUS, GUIDERIUS, ARVIRAGUS, PISANIO, *and*
ROMAN CAPTIVES. *The Captains present* POSTHUMUS *to* CYMBELINE,
who delivers him over to a GAOLER. *Exeunt omnes.*

SCENE IV. *Britain. A prison.*

Enter POSTHUMUS *and two* GAOLERS.

1 GAOL. You shall not now be stol'n, you have locks upon you ;
    So graze as you find pasture.

2 GAOL.   Ay, or a stomach. [*Exeunt* GAOLRES.

POST. Most welcome, bondage ! for thou art a way,
    I think, to liberty. Yet am I better
    Than one that's sick o' th' gout, since he had rather   5
    Groan so in perpetuity than be cur'd
    By th' sure physician death, who is the key
    T' unbar these locks. My conscience, thou art fetter'd
    More than my shanks and wrists ; you good gods, give me
    The penitent instrument to pick that bolt,   10
    Then, free for ever ! Is't enough I am sorry ?
    So children temporal fathers do appease ;
    Gods are more full of mercy. Must I repent,
    I cannot do it better than in gyves,
    Desir'd more than constrain'd. To satisfy,   15
    If of my freedom 'tis the main part, take
    No stricter render of me than my all.
    I know you are more clement than vile men,
    Who of their broken debtors take a third,
    A sixth, a tenth, letting them thrive again   20
    On their abatement ; that's not my desire.
    For Imogen's dear life take mine ; and though
    'Tis not so dear, yet 'tis a life ; you coin'd it.
    'Tween man and man they weigh not every stamp ;
    Though light, take pieces for the figure's sake ;   25
    You rather mine, being yours. And so, great pow'rs,
    If you will take this audit, take this life,
    And cancel these cold bonds. O Imogen !
    I'll speak to thee in silence.   [*Sleeps.*

Solemn Music. Enter, as in an apparition, SICILIUS LEONATUS, *father
    to* POSTHUMUS, *an old man attired like a warrior ; leading in his
    hand an ancient matron, his* WIFE, *and mother to* POSTHUMUS, *with
    music before them. Then, after other music, follows the two young
    LEONATI, brothers to* POSTHUMUS, *with wounds, as they died in the
    wars. They circle* POSTHUMUS *round as he lies sleeping.*

SICI.   No more, thou thunder-master, show   30
              Thy spite on mortal flies.
          With Mars fall out, with Juno chide,
              That thy adulteries
                  Rates and revenges.
          Hath my poor boy done aught but well,   35
              Whose face I never saw ?
          I died whilst in the womb he stay'd
              Attending nature's law ;
          Whose father then, as men report
              Thou orphans' father art,
          Thou shouldst have been, and shielded him   40
              From this earth-vexing smart.

MOTHER.	Lucina lent not me her aid,	
	But took me in my throes,	
	That from me was Posthumus ripp'd,	45
	Came crying 'mongst his foes,	
	A thing of pity.	

SICI.	Great Nature like his ancestry	
	Moulded the stuff so fair	
	That he deserv'd the praise o' th' world	50
	As great Sicilius' heir.	

I BRO.	When once he was mature for man,	
	In Britain where was he	
	That could stand up his parallel,	
	Or fruitful object be	55
	In eye of Imogen, that best	
	Could deem his dignity ?	

MOTHER.	With marriage wherefore was he mock'd,	
	To be exil'd and thrown	
	From Leonati seat and cast	60
	From her his dearest one,	
	Sweet Imogen ?	

SICI.	Why did you suffer Iachimo,	
	Slight thing of Italy,	
	To taint his nobler heart and brain	65
	With needless jealousy,	
	And to become the geck and scorn	
	O' th' other's villainy ?	

2 BRO.	For this from stiller seats we came,	
	Our parents and us twain,	70
	That, striking in our country's cause,	
	Fell bravely and were slain,	
	Our fealty and Tenantius' right	
	With honour to maintain.	

I BRO.	Like hardiment Posthumus hath	75
	To Cymbeline perform'd.	
	Then, Jupiter, thou king of gods,	
	Why hast thou thus adjourn'd	
	The graces for his merits due,	
	Being all to dolours turn'd ?	80

SICI.	Thy crystal window ope ; look out ;	
	No longer exercise	
	Upon a valiant race thy harsh	
	And potent injuries.	

MOTHER.	Since, Jupiter, our son is good,	85
	Take off his miseries.	

SICI.	Peep through thy marble mansion. Help !	
	Or we poor ghosts will cry	
	To th' shining synod of the rest	
	Against thy deity.	90

BROTHERS.	Help, Jupiter ! or we appeal,	
	And from thy justice fly.	

JUPITER *descends in thunder and lightning, sitting upon an eagle. He*
throws a thunderbolt. The Ghosts fall on their knees.

JUP. No more, you petty spirits of region low,
       Offend our hearing; hush! How dare you ghosts
       Accuse the Thunderer whose bolt, you know,   95
       Sky-planted, batters all rebelling coasts?
       Poor shadows of Elysium, hence, and rest
       Upon your never-withering banks of flow'rs.
       Be not with mortal accidents opprest:
       No care of yours it is; you know 'tis ours.   100
       Whom best I love I cross; to make my gift,
       The more delay'd, delighted. Be content;
       Your low-laid son our godhead will uplift;
       His comforts thrive, his trials well are spent.
       Our Jovial star reign'd at his birth, and in   105
       Our temple was he married. Rise, and fade!
       He shall be lord of Lady Imogen,
       And happier much by his affliction made.
       This tablet lay upon his breast, wherein
       Our pleasure his full fortune doth confine;   110
       And so, away; no farther with your din
       Express impatience, lest you stir up mine.
       Mount, eagle, to my palace crystalline.   [*Ascends.*
SICI. He came in thunder; his celestial breath
       Was sulphurous to smell; the holy eagle   115
       Stoop'd, as to foot us. His ascension is
       More sweet than our blest fields. His royal bird
       Prunes the immortal wing, and cloys his beak,
       As when his god is pleas'd.
ALL.   Thanks, Jupiter!
SICI. The marble pavement closes, he is enter'd   120
       His radiant roof Away! and, to be blest,
       Let us with care perform his great behest.   [*Ghosts vanish.*
POST. [*Waking.*] Sleep, thou has been a grandsire and begot
       A father to me; and thou hast created
       A mother and two brothers. But, O scorn,   125
       Gone! They went hence so soon as they were born.
       And so I am awake. Poor wretches, that depend
       On greatness' favour, dream as I have done;
       Wake and find nothing. But, alas, I swerve;
       Many dream not to find, neither deserve,   130
       And yet are steep'd in favours; so am I,
       That have this golden chance, and know not why.
       What fairies haunt this ground? A book? O rare one!
       Be not, as is our fangled world, a garment
       Nobler than that it covers. Let thy effects   135
       So follow to be most unlike our courtiers,
       As good as promise.
[*Reads*] 'When as a lion's whelp shall, to himself unknown, without
    seeking find, and be embrac'd by a piece of tender air; and when
    from a stately cedar shall be lopp'd branches which, being dead
    many years, shall after revive, be jointed to the old stock, and

                                                                303

freshly grow ; then shall Posthumus end his miseries, Britain be
fortunate and flourish in peace and plenty.'
'Tis still a dream, or else such stuff as madmen
Tongue, and brain not ; either both or nothing,   145
Or senseless speaking, or a speaking such
As sense cannot untie.   Be what it is,
The action of my life is like it, which
I'll keep, if but for sympathy.

Re-enter GAOLER.

GAOL. Come, sir, are you ready for death ?   150
POST. Over-roasted rather ; ready long ago.
GAOL. Hanging is the word, sir ; if you be ready for that, you are
   well cook'd.
POST. So, if I prove a good repast to the spectators, the dish pays the
   shot.   155
GAOL. A heavy reckoning for you, sir.   But the comfort is, you shall
   be called to no more payments, fear no more tavern bills, which
   are often the sadness of parting, as the procuring of mirth.   You
   come in faint for want of meat, depart reeling with too much
   drink ; sorry that you have paid too much, and sorry that you are
   paid too much ; purse and brain both empty ; the brain the
   heavier for being too light, the purse too light, being drawn of
   heaviness.   O, of this contradiction you shall now be quit.   O,
   the charity of a penny cord !   It sums up thousands in a trice.
   You have no true debitor and creditor but it ; of what's past, is,
   and to come, the discharge.   Your neck, sir, is pen, book, and
   counters ; so the acquittance follows.
POST. I am merrier to die than thou art to live.   170
GAOL. Indeed, sir, he that sleeps feels not the toothache.   But a man
   that were to sleep your sleep, and a hangman to help him to bed,
   I think he would change places with his officer ; for look you, sir,
   you know not which way you shall go.   175
POST. Yes indeed do I, fellow.
GAOL. Your death has eyes in's head, then ; I have not seen him so
   pictur'd.   You must either be directed by some that take upon
   them to know, or to take upon yourself that which I am sure you
   do not know, or jump the after-inquiry on your own peril.   And
   how you shall speed in your journey's end, I think you'll never
   return to tell one.   183
POST. I tell thee, fellow, there are none want eyes to direct them the
   way I am going, but such as wink and will not use them.
GAOL. What an infinite mock is this, that a man should have the best
   use of eyes to see the way of blindness !   I am sure hanging's the
   way of winking.   189

Enter a MESSENGER.

MESS. Knock off his manacles ; bring your prisoner to the King.
POST. Thou bring'st good news : I am call'd to be made free.
GAOL. I'll be hang'd then.   194
POST. Thou shalt be then freer than a gaoler ; no bolts for the dead.
                              [*Exeunt* POSTHUMUS *and* MESSENGER.
GAOL. Unless a man would marry a gallows and beget young gibbets,

I never saw one so prone. Yet, on my conscience, there are
verier knaves desire to live, for all he be a Roman; and there be
some of them too that die against their wills; so should I, if I
were one. I would we were all of one mind, and one mind
good. O, there were desolation of gaolers and gallowses! I
speak against my present profit, but my wish hath a preferment
in't.   [*Exit.*

SCENE V. *Britain. Cymbeline's tent.*

Enter CYMBELINE, BELARIUS, GUIDERIUS, ARVIRAGUS, PISANIO, LORDS,
OFFICERS, *and* ATTENDANTS.

CYM. Stand by my side, you whom the gods have made
Preservers of my throne. Woe is my heart
That the poor soldier that so richly fought,
Whose rags sham'd gilded arms, whose naked breast
Stepp'd before targes of proof, cannot be found.   5
He shall be happy that can find him, if
Our grace can make him so.

BEL.   I never saw
Such noble fury in so poor a thing;
Such precious deeds in one that promis'd nought
But beggary and poor looks.

CYM.   No tidings of him?   10

PIS. He hath been search'd among the dead and living,
But no trace of him.

CYM.   To my grief, I am
The heir of his reward; [*To* BELARIUS, GUIDERIUS *and* ARVIRAGUS]
which I will add
To you, the liver, heart, and brain, of Britain,
By whom I grant she lives. 'Tis now the time   15
To ask of whence you are. Report it.

BEL.   Sir,
In Cambria are we born, and gentlemen;
Further to boast were neither true nor modest,
Unless I add we are honest.

CYM.   Bow your knees.
Arise my knights o' th' battle; I create you   20
Companions to our person, and will fit you
With dignities becoming your estates.

Enter CORNELIUS *and* LADIES.

There's business in these faces. Why so sadly
Greet you our victory? You look like Romans,
And not o' th' court of Britain.

COR.   Hail, great King!   25
To sour your happiness I must report
The Queen is dead.

CYM.   Who worse than a physician
Would this report become? But I consider
By med'cine life may be prolong'd, yet death
Will seize the doctor too. How ended she?   30

COR. With horror, madly dying, like her life;
Which, being cruel to the world, concluded

Most cruel to herself. What she confess'd
I will report, so please you ; these her women
Can trip me if I err, who with wet cheeks   3
Were present when she finish'd.

CYM.   Prithee say.

COR. First, she confess'd she never lov'd you ; only
Affected greatness got by you, not you ;
Married your royalty, was wife to your place ;
Abhorr'd your person.

CYM.   She alone knew this ;   4
And but she spoke it dying, I would not
Believe her lips in opening it. Proceed.

COR. Your daughter, whom she bore in hand to love
With such integrity, she did confess
Was as a scorpion to her sight ; whose life,   4
But that her flight prevented it, she had
Ta'en off by poison.

CYM.   O most delicate fiend !
Who is't can read a woman ? Is there more ?

COR. More, sir, and worse. She did confess she had
For you a mortal mineral, which, being took,   5
Should by the minute feed on life, and ling'ring,
By inches waste you.   In which time she purpos'd,
By watching, weeping, tendance, kissing, to
O'ercome you with her show ; and in time,
When she had fitted you with her craft, to work   5
Her son into th' adoption of the crown ;
But failing of her end by his strange absence,
Grew shameless-desperate, open'd, in despite
Of heaven and men, her purposes, repented
The evils she hatch'd were not effected ; so,   6
Despairing, died.

CYM.   Heard you all this, her women ?

LADY. We did, so please your Highness.

CYM.   Mine eyes
Were not in fault, for she was beautiful ;
Mine ears, that heard her flattery ; nor my heart
That thought her like her seeming. It had been vicious   6
To have mistrusted her ; yet, O my daughter !
That it was folly in me thou mayst say,
And prove it in thy feeling. Heaven mend all !

Enter LUCIUS, IACHIMO, *the* SOOTHSAYER, *and other* ROMAN PRISONERS
guarded ; POSTHUMUS *behind, and* IMOGEN.

Thou com'st not, Caius, now for tribute ; that
The Britons have raz'd out, though with the loss   7
Of many a bold one, whose kinsmen have made suit
That their good souls may be appeas'd with slaughter
Of you their captives, which ourself have granted ;
So think of your estate.

LUC. Consider, sir, the chance of war. The day   7
Was yours by accident ; had it gone with us,
We should not, when the blood was cool, have threaten'd
Our prisoners with the sword. But since the gods

Will have it thus, that nothing but our lives
May be call'd ransom, let it come. Sufficeth   80
A Roman with a Roman's heart can suffer.
Augustus lives to think on't ; and so much
For my peculiar care. This one thing only
I will entreat : my boy, a Briton born,
Let him be ransom'd. Never master had   85
A page so kind, so duteous, diligent,
So tender over his occasions, true,
So feat, so nurse-like ; let his virtue join
With my request, which I'll make bold your Highness
Cannot deny ; he hath done no Briton harm   90
Though he have serv'd a Roman. Save him, sir,
And spare no blood beside.
CYM.   I have surely seen him ;
His favour is familiar to me. Boy,
Thou hast look'd thyself into my grace,
And art mine own. I know not why, wherefore   95
To say 'Live, boy'. Ne'er thank thy master. Live ;
And ask of Cymbeline what boon thou wilt,
Fitting my bounty and thy state, I'll give it ;
Yea, though thou do demand a prisoner,
The noblest ta'en.
IMO.   I humbly thank your Highness.   100
LUC. I do not bid thee beg my life, good lad,
And yet I know thou wilt.
IMO.   No, no ! Alack,
There's other work in hand. I see a thing
Bitter to me as death ; your life, good master,
Must shuffle for itself.
LUC.   The boy disdains me,   105
He leaves me, scorns me. Briefly die their joys
That place them on the truth of girls and boys.
Why stands he so perplex'd ?
CYM.   What wouldst thou, boy ?
I love thee more and more ; think more and more
What's best to ask. Know'st him thou look'st on ? Speak, 110
Wilt have him live ? Is he thy kin ? thy friend ?
IMO. He is a Roman, no more kin to me
Than I to your Highness ; who, being born your vassal,
Am something nearer.
CYM.   Wherefore ey'st him so ?
IMO. I'll tell you, sir, in private, if you please   115
To give me hearing.
CYM.   Ay, with all my heart,
And lend my best attention. What's thy name ?
IMO. Fidele, sir.
CYM.   Thou'rt my good youth, my page ;
I'll be thy master. Walk with me ; speak freely.
                [CYMBELINE and IMOGEN converse apart.
BEL. Is not this boy reviv'd from death ?
ARV.   One sand another   120
Not more resembles—that sweet rosy lad
Who died and was Fidele. What think you ?

                                                    307

GUI. The same dead thing alive.
BEL. Peace, peace ! see further. He eyes us not ; forbear.
Creatures may be alike ; were't he, I am sure   125
He would have spoke to us.
GUI.   But we saw him dead.
BEL. Be silent ; let's see further.
PIS. [Aside.]   It is my mistress.
Since she is living, let the time run on
To good or bad.   [CYMBELINE and IMOGEN advance
CYM. Come, stand thou by our side ;   129
Make thy demand aloud. [To IACHIMO.] Sir, step you forth ;
Give answer to this boy, and do it freely,
Or, by our greatness and the grace of it,
Which is our honour, bitter torture shall
Winnow the truth from falsehood. On, speak to him.
IMO. My boon is that this gentleman may render   135
Of whom he had this ring.
POST. [Aside.]   What's that to him ?
CYM. That diamond upon your finger, say
How came it yours ?
IACH. Thou'lt torture me to leave unspoken that
Which to be spoke would torture thee.
CYM.   How ? me ?   140
IACH. I am glad to be constrain'd to utter that
Which torments me to conceal. By villainy
I got this ring ; 'twas Leonatus' jewel,
Whom thou didst banish ; and—which more may grieve thee,
As it doth me— a nobler sir ne'er liv'd   145
'Twixt sky and ground. Wilt thou hear more, my lord ?
CYM. All that belongs to this.
IACH.   That paragon, thy daughter,
For whom my heart drops blood and my false spirits
Quail to remember—Give me leave, I faint.
CYM. My daughter ? What of her ? Renew thy strength ; 150
I had rather thou shouldst live while nature will
Than die ere I hear more. Strive, man, and speak.
IACH. Upon a time—unhappy was the clock
That struck the hour !—it was in Rome—accurs'd
The mansion where !—'twas at a feast—O, would   155
Our viands had been poison'd, or at least
Those which I heav'd to head !—the good Posthumus—
What should I say ? he was too good to be
Where ill men were, and was the best of all
Amongst the rar'st of good ones—sitting sadly   160
Hearing us praise our loves of Italy
For beauty that made barren the swell'd boast
Of him that best could speak ; for feature, laming
The shrine of Venus or straight-pight Minerva,
Postures beyond brief nature ; for condition,   165
A shop of all the qualities that man
Loves woman for ; besides that hook of wiving,
Fairness which strikes the eye—
CYM.   I stand on fire.
Come to the matter.

308

IACH.   All too soon I shall,
    Unless thou wouldst grieve quickly. This Posthumus,   170
    Most like a noble lord in love and one
    That had a royal lover, took his hint ;
    And not dispraising whom we prais'd—therein
    He was as calm as virtue—he began
    His mistress' picture ; which by his tongue being made,   175
    And then a mind put in't, either our brags
    Were crack'd of kitchen trulls, or his description
    Prov'd us unspeaking sots.
CYM.   Nay, nay, to th' purpose.
IACH. Your daughter's chastity—there it begins.
    He spake of her as Dian had hot dreams   180
    And she alone were cold ; whereat I, wretch,
    Made scruple of his praise, and wager'd with him
    Pieces of gold 'gainst this which then he wore
    Upon his honour'd finger, to attain
    In suit the place of's bed, and win this ring   185
    By hers and mine adultery. He, true knight,
    No lesser of her honour confident
    Than I did truly find her, stakes this ring ;
    And would so, had it been a carbuncle
    Of Phœbus' wheel ; and might so safely, had it   190
    Been all the worth of's car. Away to Britain
    Post I in this design. Well may you, sir,
    Remember me at court, where I was taught
    Of your chaste daughter the wide difference
    'Twixt amorous and villainous. Being thus quench'd   195
    Of hope, not longing, mine Italian brain
    Gan in your duller Britain operate
    Most vilely ; for my vantage, excellent ;
    And, to be brief, my practice so prevail'd
    That I return'd with simular proof enough   200
    To make the noble Leonatus mad,
    By wounding his belief in her renown
    With tokens thus and thus ; averring notes
    Of chamber-hanging, pictures, this her bracelet—
    O cunning, how I got it !—nay, some marks   205
    Of secret on her person, that he could not
    But think her bond of chastity quite crack'd,
    I having ta'en the forfeit. Whereupon—
    Methinks I see him now—
POST. [Coming forward.]   Ay, so thou dost,
    Italian fiend ! Ay me, most credulous fool,   210
    Egregious murderer, thief, anything
    That's due to all the villains past, in being.
    To come ! O, give me cord, or knife, or poison,
    Some upright justicer ! Thou, King, send out
    For torturers ingenious. It is I   215
    That all th' abhorred things o' th' earth amend
    By being worse than they. I am Posthumus,
    That kill'd thy daughter ; villain-like, I lie—
    That caus'd a lesser villain than myself,
    A sacrilegious thief, to do't. The temple   220

Of virtue was she ; yea, and she herself.
Spit, and throw stones, cast mire upon me, set
The dogs o' th' street to bay me. Every villain
Be call'd Posthumus Leonatus, and
Be villainy less than 'twas !   O Imogen !   225
My queen, my life, my wife !   O Imogen,
Imogen, Imogen !

IMO.   Peace, my lord. Hear, hear !
POST. Shall's have a play of this ? Thou scornful page,
There lies thy part.   [*Strikes her. She falls.*
PIS.   O gentlemen, help !
Mine and your mistress !   O, my lord Posthumus !   230
You ne'er kill'd Imogen till now. Help, help !
Mine honour'd lady !
CYM.   Does the world go round ?
POST. How comes these staggers on me ?
PIS.   Wake, my mistress !
CYM. If this be so, the gods do mean to strike me
To death with mortal joy.
PIS.   How fares my mistress ?
IMO. O, get thee from my sight ;
Thou gav'st me poison. Dangerous fellow, hence !
Breathe not where princes are.
CYM.   The tune of Imogen !
PIS. Lady,
The gods throw stones of sulphur on me, if   240
That box I gave you was not thought by me
A precious thing !   I had it from the Queen.
CYM. New matter still ?
IMO.   It poison'd me.
COR.   O gods !
I left out one thing which the Queen confess'd,
Which must approve thee honest. ' If Pisanio   245
Have ' said she ' given his mistress that confection
Which I gave him for cordial, she is serv'd
As I would serve a rat.'
CYM.   What's this, Cornelius ?
COR. The Queen, sir, very oft importun'd me
To temper poisons for her ; still pretending   250
The satisfaction of her knowledge only
In killing creatures vile, as cats and dogs,
Of no esteem. I, dreading that her purpose
Was of more danger, did compound for her
A certain stuff, which, being ta'en would cease   255
The present pow'r of life, but in short time
All offices of nature should again
Do their due functions. Have you ta'en of it ?
IMO. Most like I did, for I was dead.
BEL.   My boys,
There was our error.
GUI.   This is sure Fidele.   260
IMO. Why did you throw your wedded lady from you ?
Think that you are upon a rock, and now
Throw me again.   [*Embracing him.*

POST.   Hang there like fruit, my soul,
　　Till the tree die !
CYM.   How now, my flesh ? my child ?
　　What, mak'st thou me a dullard in this act ?   265
　　Wilt thou not speak to me ?
IMO. [*Kneeling.*]   Your blessing, sir.
BEL. [*To* GUIDERIUS *and* ARVIRAGUS.]
　　Though you did love this youth, I blame ye not ;
　　You had a motive for't.
CYM.   My tears that fall
　　Prove holy water on thee ! Imogen,
　　Thy mother's dead.
IMO.   I am sorry for't, my lord.   270
CYM. O, she was naught, and long of her it was
　　That we meet here so strangely ; but her son
　　Is gone, we know not how nor where.
PIS.   My lord,
　　Now fear is from me, I'll speak troth. Lord Cloten,
　　Upon my lady's missing, came to me   275
　　With his sword drawn, foam'd at the mouth, and swore,
　　If I discover'd not which way she was gone,
　　It was my instant death. By accident
　　I had a feigned letter of my master's
　　Then in my pocket, which directed him   280
　　To seek her on the mountains near to Milford ;
　　Where, in a frenzy, in my master's garments,
　　Which he enforc'd from me, away he posts
　　With unchaste purpose, and with oath to violate
　　My lady's honour. What became of him   285
　　I further know not.
GUI.   Let me end the story :
　　I slew him there.
CYM.   Marry, the gods forfend !
　　I would not thy good deeds should from my lips
　　Pluck a hard sentence. Prithee, valiant youth,
　　Deny't again.
GUI.   I have spoke it, and I did it.   290
CYM. He was a prince.
GUI. A most incivil one. The wrongs he did me
　　Were nothing prince-like ; for he did provoke me
　　With language that would make me spurn the sea,
　　If it could so roar to me. I cut off's head,   295
　　And am right glad he is not standing here
　　To tell this tale of mine.
CYM.   I am sorry for thee.
　　By thine own tongue thou art condemn'd, and must
　　Endure our law. Thou'rt dead.
IMO.   That headless man
　　I thought had been my lord.
CYM.   Bind the offender,   300
　　And take him from our presence.
BEL.   Stay, sir King.
　　This man is better than the man he slew,
　　As well descended as thyself, and hath

311

More of thee merited than a band of Clotens
Had ever scar for. [*To the* GUARD.] Let his arms alone ;   305
They were not born for bondage.

CYM.   Why, old soldier,
Wilt thou undo the worth thou art unpaid for
By tasting of our wrath ? How of descent
As good as we ?

ARV.   In that he spake too far.

CYM. And thou shalt die for't.

BEL.   We will die all three ;   310
But I will prove that two on's are as good
As I have given out him. My sons, I must
For mine own part unfold a dangerous speech,
Though haply well for you.

ARV.   Your danger's ours.

GUI. And our good his.

BEL.   Have at it then by leave !   315
Thou hadst, great King, a subject who
Was call'd Belarius.

CYM.   What of him ? He is
A banish'd traitor.

BEL.   He it is that hath
Assum'd this age ; indeed a banish'd man ;
I know not how a traitor.

CYM.   Take him hence,
The whole world shall not save him.

BEL.   Not too hot.
First pay me for the nursing of thy sons,
And let it be confiscate all, so soon
As I have receiv'd it.

CYM.   Nursing of my sons ?

BEL. I am too blunt and saucy : here's my knee.   325
Ere I arise I will prefer my sons ;
Then spare not the old father. Mighty sir,
These two young gentlemen that call me father,
And think they are my sons, are none of mine ;
They are the issue of your loins, my liege,   330
And blood of your begetting.

CYM.   How ? my issue ?

BEL. So sure as you your father's. I, old Morgan,
Am that Belarius whom you sometime banish'd.
Your pleasure was my mere offence, my punishment
Itself, and all my treason ; that I suffer'd   335
Was all the harm I did. These gentle princes—
For such and so they are—these twenty years
Have I train'd up ; those arts they have as I
Could put into them. My breeding was, sir, as
Your Highness knows. Their nurse, Euriphile,   340
Whom for the theft I wedded, stole these children
Upon my banishment ; I mov'd her to't,
Having receiv'd the punishment before
For that which I did then. Beaten for loyalty
Excited me to treason. Their dear loss,   345
The more of you 'twas felt, the more it shap'd

Unto my end of stealing them. But, gracious sir,
Here are your sons again, and I must lose
Two of the sweet'st companions in the world.
The benediction of these covering heavens   350
Fall on their heads like dew ! for they are worthy
To inlay heaven with stars.

M.   Thou weep'st and speak'st.
The service that you three have done is more
Unlike than this thou tell'st. I lost my children.
If these be they, I know not how to wish   355
A pair of worthier sons.

L.   Be pleas'd awhile.
This gentleman, whom I call Polydore,
Most worthy prince, as yours, is true Guiderius ;
This gentleman, my Cadwal, Arviragus,
Your younger princely son ; he, sir, was lapp'd   360
In a most curious mantle, wrought by th' hand
Of his queen mother, which for more probation
I can with ease produce.

M.   Guiderius had
Upon his neck a mole, a sanguine star ;
It was a mark of wonder.

L.   This is he,   365
Who hath upon him still that natural stamp.
It was wise nature's end in the donation,
To be his evidence now.

M.   O, what am I ?
A mother to the birth of three ? Ne'er mother
Rejoic'd deliverance more. Blest pray you be,   370
That, after this strange starting from your orbs,
You may reign in them now ! O Imogen,
Thou hast lost by this a kingdom.

O.   No, my lord ;
I have got two worlds by't. O my gentle brothers,
Have we thus met ? O, never say hereafter   375
But I am truest speaker ! You call'd me brother,
When I was but your sister : I you brothers,
When we were so indeed.

M.   Did you e'er meet ?

V. Ay, my good lord.

I.   And at first meeting lov'd,
Continu'd so until we thought he died.   380

R. By the Queen's dram she swallow'd.

M.   O rare instinct !
When shall I hear all through ? This fierce abridgment
Hath to it circumstantial branches, which
Distinction should be rich in. Where ? how liv'd you ?
And when came you to serve our Roman captive ?   385
How parted with your brothers ? how first met them ?
Why fled you from the court ? and whither ? These,
And your three motives to the battle, with
I know not how much more, should be demanded,
And all the other by-dependances,   390
From chance to chance ; but nor the time nor place

313

Will serve our long interrogatories. See,
Posthumus anchors upon Imogen;
And she, like harmless lightning, throws her eye
On him, her brothers, me, her master, hitting   39
Each object with a joy; the counterchange
Is severally in all. Let's quit this ground,
And smoke the temple with our sacrifices.
[_To_ BELARIUS.] Thou art my brother; so we'll hold thee ever.

IMO. You are my father too, and did relieve me   40
  To see this gracious season.

CYM.   All o'erjoy'd
  Save these in bonds. Let them be joyful too,
  For they shall taste our comfort.

IMO.   My good master,
  I will yet do you service.

LUC.   Happy be you!

CYM. The forlorn soldier, that so nobly fought,   40
  He would have well becom'd this place and grac'd
  The thankings of a king.

POST.   I am, sir,
  The soldier that did company these three
  In poor beseeming; 'twas a fitment for
  The purpose I then follow'd. That I was he,   41
  Speak, Iachimo. I had you down, and might
  Have made you finish.

IACH. [_Kneeling._]   I am down again;
  But now my heavy conscience sinks my knee,
  As then your force did. Take that life, beseech you,
  Which I so often owe; but your ring first,   41
  And here the bracelet of the truest princess
  That ever swore her faith.

POST.   Kneel not to me.
  The pow'r that I have on you is to spare you;
  The malice towards you to forgive you. Live,
  And deal with others better.

CYM.   Nobly doom'd!   42
  We'll learn our freeness of a son-in-law;
  Pardon's the word to all.

ARV.   You holp us, sir,
  As you did mean indeed to be our brother;
  Joy'd are we that you are.

POST. Your servant, Princes. Good my lord of Rome,   42
  Call forth your soothsayer. As I slept, methought
  Great Jupiter, upon his eagle back'd,
  Appear'd to me, with other spritely shows
  Of mine own kindred. When I wak'd, I found
  This label on my bosom; whose containing   43
  Is so from sense in hardness that I can
  Make no collection of it. Let him show
  His skill in the construction.

LUC.   Philarmonus!

SOOTH. Here, my good lord.

LUC.   Read, and declare the meaning.   43

SOOTH. [_Reads._] ' When as a lion's whelp shall, to himself unknowı

without seeking find, and be embrac'd by a piece of tender air;
and when from a stately cedar shall be lopp'd branches which,
being dead many years, shall after revive, be jointed to the old
stock, and freshly grow; then shall Posthumus end his miseries,
Britain be fortunate and flourish in peace and plenty.'
Thou, Leonatus, art the lion's whelp;   441
The fit and apt construction of thy name,
Being Leo-natus, doth import so much,
[*To* CYMBELINE.] The piece of tender air, thy virtuous daughter,
Which we call 'mollis aer', and 'mollis aer'   445
We term it 'mulier'; which 'mulier' I divine
Is this most constant wife, who even now
Answering the letter of the oracle,
Unknown to you, unsought, were clipp'd about
With this most tender air.

CYM.   This hath some seeming.   450

SOOTH. The lofty cedar, royal Cymbeline,
Personates thee; and thy lopp'd branches point
Thy two sons forth, who, by Belarius stol'n,
For many years thought dead, are now reviv'd,
To the majestic cedar join'd, whose issue   455
Promises Britain peace and plenty.

CYM.   Well,
My peace we will begin. And, Caius Lucius,
Although the victor, we submit to Cæsar
And to the Roman empire, promising
To pay our wonted tribute, from the which   460
We were dissuaded by our wicked queen,
Whom heavens in justice, both on her and hers,
Have laid most heavy hand.

SOOTH. The fingers of the pow'rs above do tune
The harmony of this peace. The vision   465
Which I made known to Lucius ere the stroke
Of yet this scarce-cold battle, at this instant
Is full accomplish'd; for the Roman cagle,
From south to west on wing soaring aloft,
Lessen'd herself and in the beams o' th' sun   470
So vanish'd; which foreshow'd our princely eagle,
Th' imperial Cæsar, should again unite
His favour with the radiant Cymbeline,
Which shines here in the west.

CYM.   Laud we the gods;
And let our crooked smokes climb to their nostrils   475
From our bless'd altars. Publish we this peace
To all our subjects. Set we forward; let
A Roman and a British ensign wave
Friendly together. So through Lud's Town march;
And in the temple of great Jupiter   480
Our peace we'll ratify; seal it with feasts.
Set on there! Never was a war did cease,
Ere bloody hands were wash'd, with such a peace.   [*Exeunt.*

PERICLES

HEMINGE and Condell did not include *Pericles* in their collected edition of the plays. Only in the second issue of the Third Folio was it added to the others. Six others were added with it at that time: *The London Prodigal*, *The History of Thomas Lord Cromwell*, *Sir John Oldcastle*, *The Puritan Widow*, *A Yorkshire Tragedy*, *The Tragedy of Locrine*. None of these six has any claim to be Shakespeare's, so that *Pericles* comes into the Folio canon in bad company. Its merits are in certain places, however, so conspicuous that there can be little doubt that Shakespeare contributed a considerable part of the piece.

That Heminge and Condell omitted *Pericles* from the First Folio because it was only in part by Shakespeare is a conjecture supported by other external evidence about its printing. On 20 May 1608 the publisher Edward Blount entered *Pericles* and *Antony and Cleopatra* in the Stationers' Register as his copy. As Blount was the stationer to whom Heminge and Condell entrusted the sixteen plays for entry in the Stationers' Register immediately before their publication in the First Folio, there can hardly have been any difficulty in including *Pericles* had the editors so desired, for the right of publication was safely in the hands of Blount, their agent, thanks to his entry of 20 May. It is true that in spite of Blount's entry an edition, not sponsored by Blount, and with a very unsatisfactory text, appeared in quarto in 1609. This pirated version might be regarded as an obstacle to Blount's own printing of the piece, for the state of the law governing printing in Elizabethan and Jacobean times made such anomalies possible, were it not that Jaggard included it in the 1619 volume of plays he attributed to Shakespeare; as Jaggard was the printer of the First Folio, both the printer and his colleague the publisher Blount had such a claim on *Pericles* that its omission from the First Folio cannot be attributed to any difficulty about printing rights. Its omission was therefore in no way forced on the editors, and although the quarto edition attributed the piece to Shakespeare, Heminge and Condell would know the authorship of a play performed by their company, as *Pericles* was, and if they knew that Shakespeare had no more than a share, however extensive in it, this would explain their leaving it aside. Unfortunately when the stationers added it to the Third Folio in 1664 they had no good version at their disposal and merely reprinted a reprint of the faulty edition of 1609.

The assumption that *Pericles* was omitted from the First Folio because of its divided authorship is also supported by the very clear division of the play into two parts. The first two acts are on the whole poor stuff; while suddenly with the opening of the third act the voice of Shakespeare is unmistakable; from there to the end Shakespeare was clearly in charge. As the version of the play that has come down to us is a most imperfect one, it has been suggested that the differences between the first and second parts of the piece might be explained by the different quality not of the original text but of those who reported it. This, however, would not explain those differences between the parts that underlie the vocabulary and versification; and were this suggestion accepted and the play attributed wholly to Shakespeare, we should then be confronted with the difficulty of explaining its omission from the First Folio. The differences between the two parts are so obvious at different levels as to make the attribution of the play to two authors the simplest solution, and one that agrees entirely with the external evidence from publication.

That Shakespeare was responsible for the second part of the play finds confirmation not merely in the style and vocabulary but in the general tone and treatment of a theme he keeps handling and rehandling in his final period. Marina and her fortunes correspond to Perdita and Miranda and their loss or banishment and restoration. The theme had so strong a hold on his imagination that he was able to adapt what must be judged the not very promising story of *Pericles* to his purpose. *The Winter's Tale* may be said to contain a number of violent episodes, for it was no part of Shakespeare's plan to minimize the unpleasant features of the world in which his heroines had to find their happiness, but the Pericles story has some specially unpleasant features, as Chaucer had in earlier times protested. That the play is not wholly Shakespeare's allows us to conjecture that he did not himself turn of his own accord to the wonderfully popular, in spite of the features Chaucer comments on, story of the Prince of Tyre, but that examining in his professional capacity as the company's senior dramatist a play submitted for inspection or even perhaps a yet unfinished piece, he saw the advantage of grafting a conception of his own on to what was a pretty rude stock. The result was completely successful as a popular attraction. Numerous contemporary references attest its drawing power. One of the most interesting occurs in Ben Jonson's Ode beginning,

> Come leave the loathed stage
> And the more loathsome age;
> Where pride and impudence, in faction knit,
> Usurp the chair of wit!

This Ode he wrote after the failure of his comedy *The New Inn* in his own defence; asking himself what the age finds to its taste, Jonson continues,

> No doubt some mouldy tale,
> Like Pericles, and stale
> As the shrieve's crusts, and nasty as his fish—

Another tribute hard on the heels of its earlier production must be noticed. In 1608 George Wilkins published *The Painfull Adventures of Pericles Prince of Tyre* which he offers to the reader as 'The True History of the Play of *Pericles*' as acted by the King's men. It has been suggested that Wilkins was also the author of part of the play; yet his procedure in adapting the play to his prose version, as well as his manner, does not seem that of one as familiar with the original as its part author would be. The play draws on two main sources, Gower's version of the Apollonius of Tyre story in his *Confessio*

317

Amantis, and Laurence Twine's *Patterne of Paynfull Adventures*. Wilkins does not seem to know Gower at first hand, while he supplements freely from Twine.

It must be recognized that while the presence of Shakespeare's hand in a considerable part of the play seems beyond all question, we can only guess at the particular circumstances in which he contributed to such a piece, although the demands of the Jacobean theatre must often have prompted a ready and skilful pen to fill out or adjust some production to an acceptable shape. We have Jonson's word that a second pen had a good share in his *Sejanus;* we can only guess that the happy genius who helped Jonson out was Shakespeare, for the borrowed matter Jonson replaced later with his own. In *Pericles* we have an instance, doubtless, where Shakespeare transformed a piece ; but who the other author was, and the details generally of the collaboration, careful examination by scholars has so far failed to establish with certainty. What has been achieved, however by this study in the interpretation of the play is important and indeed decisive. Dryden could say

> *Shakespear's* own Muse her *Pericles* first bore
> The Prince of *Tyre* was elder than the *Moore*.

Later criticism has shown that *Pericles* though a far less closely knit drama comes after not before *Othello ;* yet at the same time the placing of *Pericles* with *The Winter's Tale*, *Cymbeline* and *The Tempest* emphasizes the peculiar nature of the interests Shakespeare now had in mind and assists in the interpretation without which neither *Pericles* nor its companions can be fairly judged.

PERICLES, PRINCE OF TYRE

DRAMATIS PERSONÆ

GOWER, *as Chorus.*
ANTIOCHUS, *King of Antioch.*
PERICLES, *Prince of Tyre.*
HELICANUS, } *two lords of Tyre.*
ESCANES,
SIMONIDES, *King of Pentapolis.*
CLEON, *Governor of Tharsus.*
LYSIMACHUS, *Governor of Mytilene.*
CERIMON, *a lord of Ephesus.*
THALIARD, *a lord of Antioch.*
PHILEMON, *servant to Cerimon.*
LEONINE, *servant to Dionyza.*
MARSHAL.

A PANDER.
BOULT, *his servant.*
THE DAUGHTER OF ANTIOCHUS.
DIONYZA, *wife to Cleon.*
THAISA, *daughter to Simonides.*
MARINA, *daughter to Pericles and Thaisa.*
LYCHORIDA, *nurse to Marina.*
A BAWD.
DIANA.
LORDS, LADIES, KNIGHTS, GENTLEMEN, SAILORS, PIRATES, FISHERMEN, *and* MESSENGERS.

THE SCENE : *Dispersedly in various countries.*

ACT ONE

Antioch. Before the palace.

Enter GOWER.

To sing a song that old was sung,
From ashes ancient Gower is come,
Assuming man's infirmities,
To glad your ear and please your eyes.
It hath been sung at festivals,   5
On ember-eves and holy-ales ;
And lords and ladies in their lives
Have read it for restoratives.
The purchase is to make men glorious ;
Et bonum quo antiquius, eo melius.   10
If you, born in those latter times,
When wit's more ripe, accept my rhymes,
And that to hear an old man sing
May to your wishes pleasure bring,
I life would wish, and that I might   15
Waste it for you, like taper-light.
This Antioch, then, Antiochus the Great
Built up, this city, for his chiefest seat ;
The fairest in all Syria—
I tell you what mine authors say.   20
This king unto him took a fere,
Who died and left a female heir,
So buxom, blithe, and full of face,
As heaven had lent her all his grace ;
With whom the father liking took,   25
And her to incest did provoke.

Bad child! Worse father! To entice his own
To evil should be done by none.
But custom what they did begin
Was with long use account no sin.   30
The beauty of this sinful dame
Made many princes thither frame
To seek her as a bed-fellow,
In marriage-pleasures play-fellow;
Which to prevent he made a law—   35
To keep her still, and men in awe—
That whoso ask'd her for his wife,
His riddle told not, lost his life.
So for her many a wight did die,
As yon grim looks do testify.   40
What now ensues to the judgment of your eye
I give, my cause who best can justify.   [*Exit.*

SCENE I. *Antioch. The palace.*

Enter ANTIOCHUS, PRINCE PERICLES, *and* FOLLOWERS.

ANT. Young Prince of Tyre, you have at large received
    The danger of the task you undertake.
PER. I have, Antiochus, and, with a soul
    Embold'ned with the glory of her praise,
    Think death no hazard in this enterprise.   5
ANT. Bring in our daughter, clothed like a bride   [*Music.*
    For the embracements even of Jove himself;
    At whose conception, till Lucina reigned,
    Nature this dowry gave to glad her presence:
    The senate-house of planets all did sit,   10
    To knit in her their best perfections.

Enter the DAUGHTER OF ANTIOCHUS.

PER. See where she comes, apparell'd like the spring,
    Graces her subjects, and her thoughts the king
    Of every virtue gives renown to men.
    Her face the book of praises, where is read   15
    Nothing but curious pleasures, as from thence
    Sorrow were ever raz'd, and testy wrath
    Could never be her mild companion.
    You gods that made me man, and sway in love,
    That have inflam'd desire in my breast   20
    To taste the fruit of yon celestial tree,
    Or die in the adventure, be my helps,
    As I am son and servant to your will,
    To compass such a boundless happiness!
ANT. Prince Pericles—   25
PER. That would be son to great Antiochus.
ANT. Before thee stands this fair Hesperides,
    With golden fruit, but dangerous to be touch'd;
    For death-like dragons here affright thee hard.
    Her face, like heaven, enticeth thee to view   30
    Her countless glory, which desert must gain;

And which, without desert, because thine eye
Presumes to reach, all the whole heap must die.
Yon sometimes famous princes, like thyself,
Drawn by report, advent'rous by desire,   35
Tell thee, with speechless tongues and semblance pale,
That, without covering, save yon field of stars,
Here they stand martyrs, slain in Cupid's wars;
And with dead cheeks advise thee to desist
For going on death's net, whom none resist.   40

PER. Antiochus, I thank thee, who hath taught
My frail mortality to know itself,
And by those fearful objects to prepare
This body, like to them, to what I must;
For death remembered should be like a mirror,   45
Who tells us life's but breath, to trust it error.
I'll make my will then, and, as sick men do,
Who know the world, see heaven, but, feeling woe,
Gripe not at earthly joys as erst they did;
So I bequeath a happy peace to you   50
And all good men, as every prince should do;
My riches to the earth from whence they came;
[To the PRINCESS.] But my unspotted fire of love to you.
Thus ready for the way of life or death,
I wait the sharpest blow, Antiochus.   55

ANT. Scorning advice, read the conclusion then:
Which read and not expounded, 'tis decreed,
As these before thee, thou thyself shalt bleed.

DAUGH. Of all 'say'd yet, mayst thou prove prosperous!
Of all 'say'd yet, I wish thee happiness!   60

PER. Like a bold champion I assume the lists,
Nor ask advice of any other thought
But faithfulness and courage.   [Reads.

The Riddle.
I am no viper, yet I feed
On mother's flesh which did me breed.   65
I sought a husband, in which labour
I found that kindness in a father.
He's father, son, and husband mild;
I mother, wife, and yet his child.
How they may be, and yet in two,   70
As you will live, resolve it you

[Aside]Sharp physic is the last.   But, O you powers
That give heaven countless eyes to view men's acts,
Why cloud they not their sights perpetually,
If this be true, which makes me pale to read it?   75
Fair glass of light, I lov'd you, and could still,
Were not this glorious casket stor'd with ill.
But I must tell you now my thoughts revolt;
For he's no man on whom perfections wait
That, knowing sin within, will touch the gate.   80
You are a fair viol, and your sense the strings;
Who, finger'd to make man his lawful music,

11

Would draw heaven down, and all the gods, to hearken
But, being play'd upon before your time,
Hell only danceth at so harsh a chime.   8
Good sooth, I care not for you.

ANT. Prince Pericles, touch not, upon thy life,
For that's an article within our law
As dangerous as the rest.   Your time's expir'd :
Either expound now, or receive your sentence.   90

PER. Great King,
Few love to hear the sins they love to act ;
'Twould braid yourself too near for me to tell it.
Who has a book of all that monarchs do,
He's more secure to keep it shut than shown ;   95
For vice repeated is like the wand'ring wind,
Blows dust in others' eyes, to spread itself ;
And yet the end of all is bought thus dear,
The breath is gone, and the sore eyes see clear
To stop the air would hurt them.   The blind mole casts   100
Copp'd hills towards heaven, to tell the earth is throng'd
By man's oppression, and the poor worm doth die for't.
Kings are earth's gods ; in vice their law's their will ;
And if Jove stray, who dares say Jove doth ill ?
It is enough you know ; and it is fit,   105
What being more known grows worse, to smother it.
All love the womb that their first being bred ;
Then give my tongue like leave to love my head.

ANT. [Aside.] Heaven, that I had thy head !   He has found the
   meaning.
But I will gloze with him.—Young Prince of Tyre,   110
Though by the tenour of our strict edict,
Your exposition misinterpreting,
We might proceed to cancel of your days ;
Yet hope, succeeding from so fair a tree
As your fair self, doth tune us otherwise.   115
Forty days longer we do respite you ;
If by which time our secret be undone,
This mercy shows we'll joy in such a son ;
And until then your entertain shall be
As doth befit our honour and your worth.   120
                                          [Exeunt all but PERICLES.

PER. How courtesy would seem to cover sin,
When what is done is like an hypocrite,
The which is good in nothing but in sight !
If it be true that I interpret false,
Then were it certain you were not so bad   125
As with foul incest to abuse your soul ;
Where now you're both a father and a son
By your untimely claspings with your child—
Which pleasure fits a husband, not a father—
And she an eater of her mother's flesh   130
By the defiling of her parent's bed ;
And both like serpents are, who, though they feed
On sweetest flowers, yet they poison breed.
Antioch, farewell ! for wisdom sees those men

Blush not in actions blacker than the night   135
Will shun no course to keep them from the light.
One sin I know another doth provoke :
Murder's as near to lust as flame to smoke.
Poison and treason are the hands of sin,
Ay, and the targets to put off the shame.   140
Then, lest my life be cropp'd to keep you clear,
By flight I'll shun the danger which I fear.   [*Exit.*

Re-enter ANTIOCHUS.

ANT. He hath found the meaning,
For which we mean to have his head.
He must not live to trumpet forth my infamy,   145
Nor tell the world Antiochus doth sin
In such a loathed manner ;
And therefore instantly this prince must die ;
For by his fall my honour must keep high.
Who attends us there ?   150

Enter THALIARD.

THAL. Doth your Highness call ?
ANT. Thaliard, you are of our chamber, and our mind partakes
Her private actions to your secrecy ;
And for your faithfulness we will advance you.   155
Thaliard, behold here's poison and here's gold ;
We hate the Prince of Tyre, and thou must kill him.
It fits thee not to ask the reason why,
Because we bid it.   Say, is it done ?
THAL.   My lord,
'Tis done.
ANT. Enough.   160

Enter a MESSENGER.

Let your breath cool yourself, telling your haste.
MESS. My lord, Prince Pericles is fled.   [*Exit.*
ANT. As thou wilt live, fly after ; and like an arrow shot from a well-
experienc'd archer hits the mark his eye doth level at, so thou
never return unless thou say Prince Pericles is dead.
THAL. My lord, if I can get him within my pistol's length I'll make
him sure enough.   So, farewell to your Highness.   170
ANT. Thaliard, adieu ! [*Exit* THALIARD.] Till Pericles be dead
My heart can lend no succour to my head.   [*Exit.*

SCENE II.   *Tyre.   The palace.*

Enter PERICLES *with his* LORDS.

PER. Let none disturb us.   [*Exeunt* LORDS.
Why should this change of thoughts,
The sad companion, dull-ey'd melancholy,
Be my so us'd a guest as not an hour
In the day's glorious walk, or peaceful night,
The tomb where grief should sleep, can breed me quiet ?   5
Here pleasures court mine eyes, and mine eyes shun them,
And danger, which I fear'd, is at Antioch,

323

Whose arm seems far too short to hit me here.
Yet neither pleasure's art can joy my spirits,
Nor yet the other's distance comfort me.   10
Then it is thus : the passions of the mind,
That have their first conception by misdread,
Have after-nourishment and life by care ;
And what was first but fear what might be done
Grows elder now, and cares it be not done.   15
And so with me. The great Antiochus—
'Gainst whom I am too little to contend,
Since he's so great can make his will his act—
Will think me speaking, though I swear to silence ;
Nor boots it me to say I honour him,   20
If he suspect I may dishonour him ;
And what may make him blush in being known,
He'll stop the course by which it might be known.
With hostile forces he'll o'erspread the land,
And with th' ostent of war will look so huge   25
Amazement shall drive courage from the state ;
Our men be vanquish'd ere they do resist,
And subjects punish'd that ne'er thought offence ;
Which care of them, not pity of myself—
Who am no more but as the tops of trees   30
Which fence the roots they grow by and defend them—
Makes both my body pine and soul to languish,
And punish that before that he would punish.

Enter HELICANUS *and all the* LORDS.

1 LORD. Joy and all comfort in your sacred breast !
2 LORD. And keep your mind till you return to us,   35
   Peaceful and comfortable !
HEL. Peace, peace, and give experience tongue.
   They do abuse the king that flatter him,
   For flattery is the bellows blows up sin ;
   The thing the which is flattered but a spark,   40
   To which that blast gives heat and stronger glowing ;
   Whereas reproof, obedient, and in order,
   Fits kings as they are men, for they may err.
   When Signior Sooth here does proclaim a peace,
   He flatters you, makes war upon your life.   45
   Prince, pardon me, or strike me if you please ;
   I cannot be much lower than my knees.   [*Kneels.*
PER. All leave us else ; but let your cares o'erlook
   What shipping and what lading's in our haven,
   And then return to us. [*Exeunt* LORDS.] Helicanus, thou   50
   Hast moved us. What seest thou in our looks ?
HEL. An angry brow, dread lord.
PER. If there be such a dart in princes' frowns,
   How durst thy tongue move anger to our face ?
HEL. How dare the plants look up to heaven, from whence   55
   They have their nourishment ?
PER.   Thou know'st I have power
   To take thy life from thee.
HEL. I have ground the axe myself ;

    Do but you strike the blow.

ER.   Rise, pr'ythee, rise.
  Sit down. Thou art no flatterer.   60
  I thank thee for't; and heaven forbid
  That kings should let their ears hear their faults chid!
  Fit counsellor and servant for a prince,
  Who by thy wisdom mak'st a prince thy servant,
  What wouldst thou have me do?

EL.   To bear with patience   65
  Such griefs as you yourself do lay upon yourself.

ER. Thou speak'st like a physician, Helicanus,
  That ministers a potion unto me
  That thou wouldst tremble to receive thyself.
  Attend me, then: I went to Antioch,   70
  Where, as thou know'st, against the face of death,
  I sought the purchase of a glorious beauty,
  From whence an issue I might propagate
  Are arms to princes and bring joys to subjects.
  Her face was to mine eye beyond all wonder;   75
  The rest—hark in thine ear—as black as incest;
  Which by my knowledge found, the sinful father
  Seem'd not to strike, but smooth. But thou know'st this,
  'Tis time to fear when tyrants seem to kiss.
  Which fear so grew in me I hither fled   80
  Under the covering of a careful night,
  Who seem'd my good protector; and, being here,
  Bethought me what was past, what might succeed.
  I knew him tyrannous; and tyrants' fears
  Decrease not, but grow faster than the years;   85
  And should he doubt it, as no doubt he doth,
  That I should open to the list'ning air
  How many worthy princes' bloods were shed
  To keep his bed of blackness unlaid ope,
  To lop that doubt, he'll fill this land with arms,   90
  And make pretence of wrong that I have done him;
  When all, for mine, if I may call offence,
  Must feel war's blow, who spares not innocence;
  Which love to all, of which thyself art one,
  Who now reprov'dst me for't—

EL.   Alas, sir!   95

ER. Drew sleep out of mine eyes, blood from my cheeks,
  Musings into my mind, with thousand doubts
  How I might stop this tempest ere it came;
  And, finding little comfort to relieve them,
  I thought it princely charity to grieve them.   100

EL. Well, my lord, since you have given me leave to speak,
  Freely will I speak. Antiochus you fear,
  And justly too, I think, you fear the tyrant,
  Who either by public war or private treason
  Will take away your life.   105
  Therefore, my lord, go travel for a while
  Till that his rage and anger be forgot,
  Or till the Destinies do cut his thread of life.
  Your rule direct to any; if to me,

Day serves not light more faithful than I'll be.   11
PER. I do not doubt thy faith;
    But should he wrong my liberties in my absence?
HEL. We'll mingle our bloods together in the earth,
    From whence we had our being and our birth.
PER. Tyre, I now look from thee then, and to Tharsus   11
    Intend my travel, where I'll hear from thee;
    And by whose letters I'll dispose myself.
    The care I had and have of subjects' good
    On thee I lay, whose wisdom's strength can bear it.
    I'll take thy word for faith, not ask thine oath: 12
    Who shuns not to break one will sure crack both.
    But in our orbs we'll live so round and safe
    That time of both this truth shall ne'er convince,
    Thou show'dst a subject's shine, I a true prince. [Exeunt.

SCENE III. *Tyre. The palace.*

Enter THALIARD.

THAL. So, this is Tyre, and this the court. Here must I kill Kin
    Pericles; and if I do it not, I am sure to be hang'd at home
    'Tis dangerous. Well, I perceive he was a wise fellow and ha
    good discretion that, being bid to ask what he would of the king
    desired he might know none of his secrets. Now do I see h
    had some reason for't; for if a king bid a man be a villain, he'
    bound by the indenture of his oath to be one. Husht! her
    comes the lords of Tyre.

Enter HELICANUS, ESCANES, *with other* LORDS.

HEL. You shall not need, my fellow peers of Tyre,   1
    Further to question me of your king's departure:
    His seal'd commission, left in trust with me,
    Does speak sufficiently he's gone to travel.
THAL. [*Aside.*] How! the king gone!
HEL. If further yet you will be satisfied   1
    Why, as it were unlicens'd of your loves,
    He would depart, I'll give some light unto you.
    Being at Antioch—
THAL. [*Aside.*] What from Antioch?
HEL. Royal Antiochus, on what cause I know not,
    Took some displeasure at him; at least he judg'd so;   2
    And doubting lest that he had err'd or sinn'd,
    To show his sorrow, he'd correct himself;
    So puts himself unto the shipman's toil,
    With whom each minute threatens life or death.
THAL. [*Aside.*] Well, I perceive   2
    I shall not be hang'd now although I would;
    But since he's gone, the King's seas must please
    He scap'd the land to perish at the seas.
    I'll present myself.—Peace to the Lords of Tyre!
HEL. Lord Thaliard from Antiochus is welcome.
THAL. From him I come   3
    With message unto princely Pericles;
    But since my landing I have understood

Your lord has betook himself to unknown travels,
Now message must return from whence it came.

L. We have no reason to desire it,   35
Commended not to our master, not to us;
Yet, ere you shall depart, this we desire—
As friends to Antioch, we may feast in Tyre.   [*Exeunt.*

SCENE IV. *Tharsus. The Governor's house.*

ter CLEON *the Governor of Tharsus, with* DIONYZA *his wife, and* OTHERS.

E. My Dionyza, shall we rest us here,
And by relating tales of others' griefs
See if 'twill teach us to forget our own?

o. That were to blow at fire in hope to quench it;
For who digs hills because they do aspire   5
Throws down one mountain to cast up a higher.
O my distressed lord, even such our griefs are!
Here they are but felt and seen with mischief's eyes,
But like to groves, being topp'd, they higher rise.

E. O Dionyza,   10
Who wanteth food, and will not say he wants it,
Or can conceal his hunger till he famish?
Our tongues and sorrows to sound deep
Our woes into the air; our eyes to weep?
Till tongues fetch breath that may proclaim them louder;   15
That, if heaven slumber while their creatures want,
They may awake their helps to comfort them.
I'll then discourse our woes, felt several years,
And, wanting breath to speak, help me with tears.

o. I'll do my best, sir.   20

E. This Tharsus, o'er which I have the government,
A city on whom plenty held full hand,
For Riches strew'd herself even in her streets;
Whose towers bore heads so high they kiss'd the clouds,
And strangers ne'er beheld but wond'red at;   25
Whose men and dames so jetted and adorn'd,
Like one another's glass to trim them by;
Their tables were stor'd full, to glad the sight,
And not so much to feed on as delight;
All poverty was scorn'd, and pride so great   30
The name of help grew odious to repeat.

o. O, 'tis too true!

E. But see what heaven can do! By this our change
These mouths who but of late earth, sea, and air,
Were all too little to content and please,   35
Although they gave their creatures in abundance,
As houses are defil'd for want of use,
They are now starv'd for want of exercise.
Those palates who, not yet two summers younger,
Must have inventions to delight the taste,   40
Would now be glad of bread, and beg for it.
Those mothers who to nouzle up their babes
Thought nought too curious are ready now
To eat those little darlings whom they lov'd.

So sharp are hunger's teeth that man and wife
Draw lots who first shall die to lengthen life.
Here stands a lord, and there a lady weeping;
Here many sink, yet those which see them fall
Have scarce strength left to give them burial.
Is not this true?

DIO. Our cheeks and hollow eyes do witness it.

CLE. O, let those cities that of Plenty's cup
And her prosperities so largely taste,
With their superfluous riots, hear these tears!
The misery of Tharsus may be theirs.

Enter a LORD.

LORD. Where's the Lord Governor?

CLE. Here.
Speak out thy sorrows which thou bring'st in haste,
For comfort is too far for us to expect.

LORD. We have descried, upon our neighbouring shore,
A portly sail of ships make hitherward.

CLE. I thought as much.
One sorrow never comes but brings an heir
That may succeed as his inheritor;
And so in ours: some neighbouring nation,
Taking advantage of our misery,
Hath stuff'd the hollow vessels with their power,
To beat us down, the which are down already;
And make a conquest of unhappy me,
Whereas no glory's got to overcome.

LORD. That's the least fear; for by the semblance
Of their white flags display'd, they bring us peace,
And come to us as favourers, not as foes.

CLE. Thou speak'st like him's untutor'd to repeat:
Who makes the fairest show means most deceit.
But bring they what they will and what they can,
What need we fear?
Our ground's the lowest, and we are halfway there.
Go tell their general we attend him here,
To know for what he comes, and whence he comes,
And what he craves.

LORD. I go, my lord. [*Ex*

CLE. Welcome is peace, if he on peace consist;
If wars, we are unable to resist.

Enter PERICLES, *with* ATTENDANTS.

PER. Lord Governor, for so we hear you are,
Let not our ships and number of our men
Be like a beacon fir'd t'amaze your eyes.
We have heard your miseries as far as Tyre,
And seen the desolation of your streets;
Nor come we to add sorrow to your tears,
But to relieve them of their heavy load;
And these our ships, you happily may think
Are like the Troyan horse war stuff'd within
With bloody veins, expecting overthrow,

Are stor'd with corn to make your needy bread,   95
And give them life whom hunger starv'd half dead.
ALL. The gods of Greece protect you !
And we'll pray for you.   [*They kneel.*
PER.   Arise, I pray you, rise
We do not look for reverence, but for love,
And harbourage for ourself, our ships, and men.   100
CLE. The which when any shall not gratify,
Or pay you with unthankfulness in thought,
Be it our wives, our children, or ourselves,
The curse of heaven and men succeed their evils !
Till when—the which I hope shall ne'er be seen—   105
Your Grace is welcome to our town and us.
PER. Which welcome we'll accept ; feast here awhile,
Until our stars that frown lend us a smile.   [*Exeunt.*

ACT TWO

Enter GOWER.

GOW. Here have you seen a mighty king
His child I wis to incest bring ;
A better prince and benign lord,
That will prove awful both in deed and word.
Be quiet then, as men should be,   5
Till he hath pass'd necessity.
I'll show you those in troubles reign,
Losing a mite, a mountain gain.
The good in conversation,
To whom I give my benison,   10
Is still at Tharsus, where each man
Thinks all is writ he spoken can ;
And, to remember what he does,
Build his statue to make him glorious.
But tidings to the contrary   15
Are brought your eyes. What need speak I ?

Dumb show.

Enter, at one door, PERICLES, *talking with* CLEON ; *all the* TRAIN *with them. Enter, at another door, a* GENTLEMAN *with a letter to* PERICLES ; PERICLES *shows the letter to* CLEON. PERICLES *gives the* MESSENGER *a reward, and knights him. Exit* PERICLES *at one door and* CLEON *at another.*

Good Helicane, that stay'd at home,
Not to eat honey like a drone
From others' labours ; for though he strive
To killen bad, keep good alive ;   20
And, to fulfil his prince' desire,
Sends word of all that haps in Tyre :
How Thaliard came full bent with sin
And had intent to murder him ;
And that in Tharsus was not best   25
Longer for him to make his rest.

He, doing so, put forth to seas,
Where when men been, there's seldom ease;
For now the wind begins to blow;
Thunder above and deeps below   30
Makes such unquiet that the ship
Should house him safe is wreck'd and split;
And he, good prince, having all lost,
By waves from coast to coast is toss'd.
All perishen of man, of pelf,   35
Ne aught escapen but himself;
Till fortune, tir'd with doing bad,
Threw him ashore, to give him glad.
And here he comes.   What shall be next,
Pardon old Gower—this longs the text.   [*Exit.*

SCENE I.   *Pentapolis.   An open place by the seaside.*

Enter PERICLES, *wet.*

PER. Yet cease your ire, you angry stars of heaven!
Wind, rain, and thunder, remember earthly man
Is but a substance that must yield to you;
And I, as fits my nature, do obey you.
Alas, the sea hath cast me on the rocks,   5
Wash'd me from shore to shore, and left me breath
Nothing to think on but ensuing death.
Let it suffice the greatness of your powers
To have bereft a prince of all his fortunes;
And having thrown him from your wat'ry grave,   10
Here to have death in peace is all he'll crave.

Enter three FISHERMEN.

1 FISH. What, ho, Pilch!
2 FISH. Ha, come and bring away the nets.
1 FISH. What, Patchbreech, I say!
3 FISH. What say you, master?   15
1 FISH. Look how thou stirr'st now.   Come away, or I'll fetch thee
with a wanion.
3 FISH. Faith, master, I am thinking of the poor men that were cast
away before us even now.   19
1 FISH. Alas, poor souls!   It grieved my heart to hear what pitiful
cries they made to us to help them, when, well-a-day, we could
scarce help ourselves.
3 FISH. Nay, master, said not I as much when I saw the porpas how
he bounc'd and tumbled?   They say they're half fish, half
flesh.   A plague on them!   They ne'er come but I look to be
wash'd.   Master, I marvel how the fishes live in the sea.   27
1 FISH. Why, as men do a-land—the great ones eat up the little ones.
I can compare our rich misers to nothing so fitly as to a whale:
'a plays and tumbles, driving the poor fry before him, and at last
devours them all at a mouthful.   Such whales have I heard on
a' th' land, who never leave gaping till they've swallow'd the
whole parish, church, steeple, bells, and all.
PER. [*Aside.*] A pretty moral.   35

FISH. But, master, if I had been the sexton, I would have been that
    day in the belfry.

FISH. Why, man?

FISH. Because he should have swallowed me too; and when I had
    been in his belly I would have kept such a jangling of the bells
    that he should never have left till he cast bells, steeple, church,
    and parish up again. But if the good King Simonides were of
    my mind—

ER. [*Aside.*] Simonides!   45

FISH. We would purge the land of these drones that rob the bee of
    her honey.

ER. [*Aside.*] How from the finny subject of the sea
    These fishers tell the infirmities of men,
    And from their wat'ry empire recollect   50
    All that may men approve or men detect!—
    Peace be at your labour, honest fishermen!

FISH. Honest—good fellow! What's that? If it be a day fits
    you, scratch't out of the calendar, and nobody look after it. 55

ER. May see the sea hath cast upon your coast—

FISH. What a drunken knave was the sea to cast thee in our way!

ER. A man whom both the waters and the wind
    In that vast tennis-court hath made the ball   60
    For them to play upon entreats you pity him;
    He asks of you that never us'd to beg.

FISH. No, friend, cannot you beg? Here's them in our country
    of Greece gets more with begging than we can do with working.

FISH. Canst thou catch any fishes, then?

ER. I never practis'd it.

FISH. Nay, then thou wilt starve, sure; for here's nothing to be
    got now-a-days unless thou canst fish for't.   70

ER. What I have been I have forgot to know;
    But what I am want teaches me to think on:
    A man throng'd up with cold; my veins are chill,
    And have no more of life than may suffice
    To give my tongue that heat to ask your help;   75
    Which if you shall refuse, when I am dead,
    For that I am a man, pray see me buried.

FISH. Die quoth-a? Now gods forbid't! And I have a gown here!
    Come, put it on; keep thee warm. Now, afore me, a handsome
    fellow! Come, thou shalt go home, and we'll have flesh for
    holidays, fish for fasting days, and moreo'er puddings and flap-
    jacks; and thou shalt be welcome.   83

ER. I thank you, sir.

FISH. Hark you, my friend; you said you could not beg.

ER. I did but crave.

FISH. But crave! Then I'll turn craver too, and so I shall scape
    whipping.

ER. Why, are all your beggars whipp'd, then?   90

FISH. O, not all, my friend, not all! For if all your beggars were
    whipp'd, I would wish no better office than to be beadle. But,
    master, I'll go draw up the net.   [*Exit with* THIRD FISHERMAN.

ER. [*Aside.*] How well this honest mirth becomes their labour! 94

FISH. Hark you, sir; do you know where ye are?

ER. Not well.

1 FISH. Why, I'll tell you : this is call'd Pentapolis, and our king th[e]
    good Simonides.
PER. The good Simonides, do you call him ?
1 FISH. Ay, sir ; and he deserves so to be call'd for his peaceabl[e]
    reign and good government.   10[3]
PER. He is a happy king, since he gains from his subjects the nam[e]
    of good by his government. How far is his court distant from
    this shore ?
1 FISH. Marry, sir, half a day's journey ; and I'll tell you, he hath a[?]
    fair daughter, and to-morrow is her birthday ; and there ar[e]
    princes and knights come from all parts of the world to joust
    and tourney for her love.
PER. Were my fortunes equal to my desires, I could wish to mak[e]
    one there.   110
1 FISH. O sir, things must be as they may ; and what a man canno[t]
    get he may lawfully deal for—his wife's soul.

    Re-enter SECOND *and* THIRD FISHERMEN, *drawing up a net.*

2 FISH. Help, master, help ! Here's a fish hangs in the net like a[?]
    poor man's right in the law ; 'twill hardly come out. Ha[?]
    Bots on't ! 'Tis come at last, and 'tis turn'd to a rusty armour[.]
PER. An armour, friends ! I pray you let me see it.
    Thanks, Fortune, yet, that after all my crosses
    Thou givest me somewhat to repair myself ;   120
    And though it was mine own, part of my heritage
    Which my dead father did bequeath to me,
    With this strict charge, even as he left his life :
    ' Keep it, my Pericles. It hath been a shield
    'Twixt me and death ; ' and pointed to this brace   125
    ' For that it sav'd me, keep it. In like necessity—
    The which the gods protect thee from !—may't defend thee ! '
    It kept where I kept, I so dearly lov'd it ;
    Till the rough seas, that spare not any man,
    Took it in rage, though calm'd have given't again—   130
    I thank thee for't. My shipwreck now's no ill,
    Since I have here my father's gift in his will.
1 FISH. What mean you, sir ?
PER. To beg of you, kind friends, this coat of worth
    For it was sometime target to a king ;   135
    I know it by this mark. He lov'd me dearly,
    And for his sake I wish the having of it ;
    And that you'd guide me to your sovereign's court,
    Where with it I may appear a gentleman ;
    And if that ever my low fortune's better,   140
    I'll pay your bounties ; till then rest your debtor.
1 FISH. Why, wilt thou tourney for the lady ?
PER. I'll show the virtue I have borne in arms.
1 FISH. Why, do'e take it, and the gods give thee good on't !   145
2 FISH. Ay, but hark you, my friend ; 'twas we that made up this
    garment through the rough seams of the waters ; there are certain
    condolements, certain vails. I hope, sir, if you thrive, you'll
    remember from whence you had them.   150
PER. Believe't, I will.
    By your furtherance I am cloth'd in steel ;

And spite of all the rupture of the sea
This jewel holds his building on my arm.
Unto thy value I will mount myself   155
Upon a courser whose delightful steps
Shall make the gazer joy to see him tread.
Only, my friend, I yet am unprovided
Of a pair of bases.   159
FISH. We'll sure provide. Thou shalt have my best gown to
make thee a pair ; and I'll bring thee to the court myself.
R. Then honour be but a goal to my will ;
This day I'll rise, or else add ill to ill.   [Exeunt.

ENE II.   Pentapolis.   A public way or platform leading to the lists.
   A pavilion by the side of it for the reception of the King, Princess,
   Lords, &c.

        Enter SIMONIDES, THAISA, LORDS, and ATTENDANTS.

1. Are the knights ready to begin the triumph ?
LORD. They are, my liege ;
   And stay your coming to present themselves.
1. Return them we are ready ; and our daughter here,
   In honour of whose birth these triumphs are,   5
   Sits here like beauty's child, whom nature gat
   For men to see, and seeing wonder at.   [Exit a LORD.
AI. It pleaseth you, my royal father, to express
   My commendations great, whose merit's less.
1. It's fit it should be so ; for princes are   10
   A model which heaven makes like to itself :
   As jewels lose their glory if neglected,
   So princes their renowns if not respected.
   'Tis now your honour, daughter, to entertain
   The labour of each knight in his device.   15
AI. Which, to preserve mine honour, I'll perform.

ter a KNIGHT ; he passes over, and his SQUIRE presents his shield to
                        the PRINCESS.

1. Who is the first that doth prefer himself ?
AI. A knight of Sparta, my renowned father ;
   And the device he bears upon his shield
   Is a black Ethiope reaching at the sun ;   20
   The word, ' Lux tua vita mihi '.
1. He loves you well that holds his life of you.

                The SECOND KNIGHT passes by.

Who is the second that presents himself ?
AI. A prince of Macedon, my royal father ;
   And the device he bears upon his shield   25
   Is an arm'd knight that's conquer'd by a lady ;
   The motto thus, in Spanish, ' Piu por dulzura que por fuerza '.

                The THIRD KNIGHT passes by.

1. And what's the third ?
AI.   The third of Antioch

                                                              333

And his device a wreath of chivalry ;
The word, ' Me pompæ provexit apex '.

The FOURTH KNIGHT *passes by.*

SIM. What is the fourth ?
THAI. A burning torch that's turned upside down
The word, ' Quod me alit, me extinguit '.
SIM. Which shows that beauty hath his power and will,
Which can as well inflame as it can kill.

The FIFTH KNIGHT *passes by.*

THAI. The fifth, an hand environed with clouds,
Holding out gold that's by the touchstone tried;
The motto thus, ' Sic spectanda fides '.

PERICLES *as* SIXTH KNIGHT *passes by.*

SIM. And what's the sixth and last, the which the knight himself
With such a graceful courtesy deliver'd ?
THAI. He seems to be a stranger ; but his present is
A withered branch, that's only green at top ;
The motto, ' In hac spe vivo '.
SIM. A pretty moral ;
From the dejected state wherein he is,
He hopes by you his fortunes yet may flourish.
1 LORD. He had need mean better than his outward show
Can any way speak in his just commend ;
For by his rusty outside he appears
To have practis'd more the whipstock than the lance.
2 LORD. He well may be a stranger, for he comes
To an honour'd triumph strangely furnished.
3 LORD. And on set purpose let his armour rust
Until this day, to scour it in the dust.
SIM. Opinion's but a fool, that makes us scan
The outward habit by the inward man.
But stay, the knights are coming.   We will withdraw
Into the gallery.   [*Exeur*
[*Great shouts within, and all cry* ' The mean knight

SCENE III.   *Pentapolis.   A hall of state.   A banquet prepared.*

Enter KING SIMONIDES, THAISA, LADIES, LORDS, KNIGHTS, *from tiltir
and* ATTENDANTS.

SIM. Knights !
To say you're welcome were superfluous.
To place upon the volume of your deeds,
As in a title-page, your worth in arms
Were more than you expect, or more than's fit,
Since every worth in show commends itself.
Prepare for mirth, for mirth becomes a feast ;
You are princes and my guests.
THAI. But you my knight and guest ;
To whom this wreath of victory I give,
And crown you king of this day's happiness.
PER. 'Tis more by fortune, lady, than my merit.

м. Call it by what you will, the day is yours ;
  And here I hope is none that envies it.
  In framing an artist, art hath thus decreed,   15
  To make some good, but others to exceed ;
  And you are her labour'd scholar.   Come, queen o' th' feast—
  For, daughter, so you are—here take your place.
  Marshal the rest as they deserve their grace.
NIGHTS. We are honour'd much by good Simonides.   20
м. Your presence glads our days.   Honour we love;
  For who hates honour hates the gods above.
ARSHAL. Sir, yonder is your place.
ER.   Some other is more fit.
 KNIGHT. Contend not, sir ; for we are gentlemen
  That neither in our hearts nor outward eyes   25
  Envy the great nor shall the low despise.
ER. You are right courteous knights.
м.   Sit, sir, sit.
  [*Aside.*] By Jove, I wonder, that is king of thoughts,
  These cates resist me, she but thought upon.
HAI. [*Aside.*] By Juno, that is queen of marriage,   30
  All viands that I eat do seem unsavoury,
  Wishing him my meat.—Sure he's a gallant gentleman.
м. He's but a country gentleman ;
  Has done no more than other knights have done ;
  Has broken a staff or so ; so let it pass.   35
HAI. [*Aside.*] To me he seems like diamond to glass.
ER. [*Aside.*] Yon king's to me like to my father's picture,
  Which tells me in that glory once he was ;
  Had princes sit like stars about his throne,
  And he the sun, for them to reverence ;   40
  None that beheld him but, like lesser lights,
  Did vail their crowns to his supremacy :
  Where now his son's like a glowworm in the night,
  The which hath fire in darkness, none in light.
  Whereby I see that Time's the king of men ;   45
  He's both their parent, and he is their grave,
  And gives them what he will, not what they crave.
м. What, are you merry, Knights ?
KNIGHT. Who can be other in this royal presence ?
м. Here, with a cup that's stor'd unto the brim—   50
  As you do love, fill to your mistress' lips—
  We drink this health to you.
NIGHTS.   We thank your Grace.
м. Yet pause awhile.
  Yon knight doth sit too melancholy,
  As if the entertainment in our court   55
  Had not a show might countervail his worth.
  Note it not you, Thaisa ?
HAI.   What is't
  To me, my father ?
M.   O, attend, my daughter :
  Princes, in this, should live like gods above,   60
  Who freely give to every one that comes
  To honour them ;

And princes not doing so are like to gnats,
Which make a sound, but kill'd are wond'red at.
Therefore to make his entertain more sweet,
Here, say we drink this standing-bowl of wine to him.

THAI. Alas, my father, it befits not me
Unto a stranger knight to be so bold :
He may my proffer take for an offence,
Since men take women's gifts for impudence.

SIM. How!
Do as I bid you, or you'll move me else.

THAI. [Aside.] Now, by the gods, he could not please me better.

SIM. And furthermore tell him we desire to know of him
Of whence he is, his name and parentage.

THAI. The King my father, sir, has drunk to you.

PER. I thank him.

THAI. Wishing it so much blood unto your life.

PER. I thank both him and you, and pledge him freely.

THAI. And further he desires to know of you
Of whence you are, your name and parentage.

PER. A gentleman of Tyre—my name, Pericles
My education been in arts and arms ;
Who, looking for adventures in the world,
Was by the rough seas reft of ships and men,
And after shipwreck driven upon this shore.

THAI. He thanks your Grace ; names himself Pericles,
A gentleman of Tyre,
Who only by misfortune of the seas,
Bereft of ships and men, cast on this shore.

SIM. Now, by the gods, I pity his misfortune,
And will awake him from his melancholy.
Come, gentlemen, we sit too long on trifles
And waste the time which looks for other revels.
Even in your armours, as you are address'd,
Will very well become a soldier's dance.
I will not have excuse, with saying this
Loud music is too harsh for ladies' heads,
Since they love men in arms as well as beds.   [They danc
So, this was well ask'd, 'twas so well perform'd.   1(
Come, sir ;
Here is a lady that wants breathing too ;
And I have heard you knights of Tyre
Are excellent in making ladies trip ;
And that their measures are as excellent.

PER. In those that practise them they are, my lord.   1(

SIM. O, that's as much as you would be denied
Of your fair courtesy. [The KNIGHTS and LADIES dance.] Unclasp
unclasp.
Thanks, gentlemen, to all ; all have done well,
[To PERICLES.] But you the best.—Pages and lights, to conduct
These knights unto their several lodgings !—Yours, sir,   1)
We have given order to be next our own.

PER. I am at your Grace's pleasure.

SIM. Princes, it is too late to talk of love,
And that's the mark I know you level at.

Therefore each one betake him to his rest;   115
To-morrow all for speeding do their best.   [*Exeunt.*

SCENE IV. *Tyre. The Governor's house.*

Enter HELICANUS *and* ESCANES.

HEL. No, Escanes; know this of me—
    Antiochus from incest liv'd not free;
    For which, the most high gods not minding longer
    To withhold the vengeance that they had in store,
    Due to this heinous capital offence,   5
    Even in the height and pride of all his glory,
    When he was seated in a chariot
    Of an inestimable value, and his daughter with him,
    A fire from heaven came and shrivell'd up
    Their bodies, even to loathing; for they so stunk   10
    That all those eyes ador'd them ere their fall
    Scorn now their hand should give them burial.
ESCA. 'Twas very strange.
HEL.   And yet but justice; for though
    This king were great, his greatness was no guard
    To bar heaven's shaft, but sin had his reward.   15
ESCA. 'Tis very true.

Enter two or three LORDS.

1 LORD. See, not a man in private conference
    Or council has respect with him but he.
2 LORD. It shall no longer grieve without reproot.
3 LORD. And curs'd be he that will not second it!   20
1 LORD. Follow me, then.   Lord Helicane, a word.
HEL. With me? and welcome.   Happy day, my lords.
1 LORD. Know that our griefs are risen to the top,
    And now at length they overflow their banks.
HEL. Your griefs! for what?   Wrong not your prince you love. 25
1 LORD. Wrong not yourself, then, noble Helicane;
    But if the prince do live, let us salute him,
    Or know what ground's made happy by his breath.
    If in the world he live, we'll seek him out;
    If in his grave he rest, we'll find him there;   30
    And be resolv'd he lives to govern us,
    Or, dead, give's cause to mourn his funeral,
    And leave us to our free election.
2 LORD. Whose death's indeed the strongest in our censure;
    And knowing this kingdom, if without a head,   35
    Like goodly buildings left without a roof,
    Soon fall to ruin, your noble self,
    That best know how to rule and how to reign,
    We thus submit unto—our sovereign.
ALL. Live, noble Helicane!   40
HEL. By honour's cause, forbear your suffrages.
    If that you love Prince Pericles, forbear.
    Take I your wish, I leap into the seas,
    Where's hourly trouble for a minute's ease.
    A twelvemonth longer let me entreat you   45

To forbear the absence of your king;
If in which time expir'd he not return,
I shall with aged patience bear your yoke.
But if I cannot win you to this love,
Go search like nobles, like noble subjects,   50
And in your search spend your adventurous worth;
Whom if you find, and win unto return,
You shall like diamonds sit about his crown.

1 LORD. To wisdom he's a fool that will not yield;
And since Lord Helicane enjoineth us,   55
We with our travels will endeavour it.

HEL. Then you love us, we you, and we'll clasp hands:
When peers thus knit, a kingdom ever stands.   [Exeunt.

SCENE V.   *Pentapolis.   The palace.*

Enter SIMONIDES, *reading of a letter, at one door.   The* KNIGHTS *meet
him.*

1 KNIGHT. Good morrow to the good Simonides.

SIM. Knights, from my daughter this I let you know,
That for this twelvemonth she'll not undertake
A married life.
Her reason to herself is only known,   5
Which from her by no means can I get.

2 KNIGHT. May we not get access to her, my lord?

SIM. Faith, by no means; she hath so strictly tied her
To her chamber that it is impossible.
One twelve moons more she'll wear Diana's livery.   10
This by the eye of Cynthia hath she vow'd,
And on her virgin honour will not break it.

3 KNIGHT. Loath to bid farewell, we take our leaves.
                                              [*Exeunt* KNIGHTS.

SIM. So,
They are well despatch'd.   Now to my daughter's letter.   15
She tells me here she'll wed the stranger knight,
Or never more to view nor day nor light.
'Tis well, mistress; your choice agrees with mine;
I like that well.   Nay, how absolute she's in't,
Not minding whether I dislike or no!   20
Well, I do commend her choice;
And will no longer have it be delay'd.
Soft! here he comes: I must dissemble it.

Enter PERICLES.

PER. All fortune to the good Simonides!

SIM. To you as much, sir!   I am beholding to you   25
For your sweet music this last night.   I do
Protest my ears were never better fed
With such delightful pleasing harmony.

PER. It is your Grace's pleasure to commend;
Not my desert.

SIM.   Sir, you are music's master.   30

PER. The worst of all her scholars, my good lord.

SIM. Let me ask you one thing:

338

    What do you think of my daughter, sir?
PER. A most virtuous princess.   35
SIM. And she is fair too, is she not?
PER. As a fair day in summer—wondrous fair.
SIM. Sir, my daughter thinks very well of you;
    Ay, so well that you must be her master,
    And she will be your scholar; therefore look to it.
PER. I am unworthy for her schoolmaster.   40
SIM. She thinks not so; peruse this writing else.
PER. [Aside.] What's here?
    A letter, that she loves the knight of Tyre.
    'Tis the king's subtlety to have my life.—
    O, seek not to entrap me, gracious lord,   45
    A stranger and distressed gentleman,
    That never aim'd so high to love your daughter,
    But bent all offices to honour her!
SIM. Thou hast bewitch'd my daughter, and thou art
    A villain.
PER.   By the gods, I have not.   50
    Never did thought of mine levy offence;
    Nor never did my actions yet commence
    A deed might gain her love or your displeasure.
SIM. Traitor, thou liest.
PER.   Traitor!
SIM.   Ay, traitor.
PER. Even in his throat—unless it be the King—   55
    That calls me traitor I return the lie.
SIM. [Aside.] Now, by the gods, I do applaud his courage.
PER. My actions are as noble as my thoughts,
    That never relish'd of a base descent.
    I came unto your court for honour's cause,   60
    And not to be a rebel to her state;
    And he that otherwise accounts of me,
    This sword shall prove he's honour's enemy.
SIM. No?
    Here comes my daughter, she can witness it.   65

Enter THAISA.

PER. Then, as you are as virtuous as fair,
    Resolve your angry father if my tongue
    Did e'er solicit, or my hand susbcribe
    To any syllable that made love to you.
THAI. Why, sir, say if you had,   70
    Who takes offence at that would make me glad?
SIM. Yea, mistress, are you so peremptory?
    [Aside.] I am glad on't with all my heart.—
    I'll tame you; I'll bring you in subjection.
    Will you, not having my consent,   75
    Bestow your love and your affections
    Upon a stranger?—[Aside.] who, for aught I know,
    May be, nor can I think the contrary,
    As great in blood as I myself.—
    Therefore, hear you, mistress: either frame   80
    Your will to mine—and you, sir, hear you,

       Either be rul'd by me—or I will make you—
       Man and wife.
       Nay, come, your hands and lips must seal it too;
       And being join'd, I'll thus your hopes destroy,   85
       And for further grief—God give you joy!
       What, are you both pleas'd?
THAI.   Yes, if you love me, sir.
PER. Even as my life my blood that fosters it.
SIM. What, are you both agreed?
BOTH. Yes, if't please your Majesty.   90
SIM. It pleaseth me so well that I will see you wed;
       And then, with what haste you can, get you to bed.   [*Exeunt.*

ACT THREE

Enter GOWER.

GOW. Now sleep yslaked hath the rout;
       No din but snores the house about,
       Made louder by the o'er-fed breast
       Of this most pompous marriage feast.
       The cat, with eyne of burning coal,   5
       Now couches fore the mouse's hole;
       And crickets sing at the oven's mouth,
       Aye the blither for their drouth.
       Hymen hath brought the bride to bed,
       Where, by the loss of maidenhead,   10
       A babe is moulded. Be attent,
       And time that is so briefly spent
       With your fine fancies quaintly eche.
       What's dumb in show I'll plain with speech.

Dumb Show.

Enter PERICLES *and* SIMONIDES *at one door, with* ATTENDANTS; *a* MESSENGER *meets them, kneels, and gives* PERICLES *a letter.* PERICLES *shows it* SIMONIDES; *the* LORDS *kneel to* PERICLES. *Then enter* THAISA, *with child, with* LYCHORIDA, *a nurse. The* KING *shows her the letter; she rejoices. She and* PERICLES *take leave of her father, and depart with* LYCHORIDA *and their* ATTENDANTS. *Then exeunt* SIMONIDES *and the* REST.

       By many a dern and painful perch   15
       Of Pericles the careful search,
       By the four opposing coigns
       Which the world together joins,
       Is made with all due diligence
       That horse and sail and high expense   20
       Can stead the quest. At last from Tyre—
       Fame answering the most strange inquire—
       To the court of King Simonides
       Are letters brought, the tenour these:
       Antiochus and his daughter dead,   25
       The men of Tyrus on the head
       Of Helicanus would set on
       The crown of Tyre, but he will none.

The mutiny he there hastes t' oppress ;
Says to 'em, if King Pericles   30
Come not home in twice six moons,
He, obedient to their dooms,
Will take the crown.   The sum of this,
Brought hither to Pentapolis,
Y-ravished the regions round,   35
And every one with claps can sound
' Our heir-apparent is a king ! '
Who dream'd, who thought of such a thing ?
Brief, he must hence depart to Tyre.
His queen with child makes her desire—   40
Which who shall cross ?—along to go.
Omit we all their dole and woe.
Lychorida, her nurse, she takes,
And so to sea.   Their vessel shakes
On Neptune's billow ; half the flood   45
Hath their keel cut : but fortune's mood
Varies again ; the grizzled north
Disgorges such a tempest forth
That, as a duck for life that dives,
So up and down the poor ship drives.   50
The lady shrieks, and, well-a-near,
Does fall in travail with her fear ;
And what ensues in this fell storm
Shall for itself itself perform.
I nill relate, action may   55
Conveniently the rest convey ;
Which might not what by me is told.
In your imagination hold
This stage the ship, upon whose deck
The sea-toss'd Pericles appears to speak.   [Exit.

SCENE I.   *Enter* PERICLES, *a-shipboard.*

PER. Thou god of this great vast, rebuke these surges,
Which wash both heaven and hell ; and thou that hast
Upon the winds command, bind them in brass,
Having call'd them from the deep ! O, still
Thy deaf'ning dreadful thunders ; gently quench   5
Thy nimble sulphurous flashes !—O, how, Lychorida,
How does my queen ?—Thou stormest venomously ;
Wilt thou spit all thyself ?   The seaman's whistle
Is as a whisper in the ears of death,
Unheard.—Lychorida !—Lucina, O   10
Divinest patroness, and midwife gentle
To those that cry by night, convey thy deity
Aboard our dancing boat ; make swift the pangs
Of my queen's travails !

Enter LYCHORIDA, *with an* INFANT.

Now, Lychorida !

LYC. Here is a thing too young for such a place,   15
Who, if it had conceit, would die, as I

Am like to do.   Take in your arms this piece
Of your dead queen.
PER.   How, how, Lychorida?
LYC. Patience, good sir; do not assist the storm.
Here's all that is left living of your queen—   20
A little daughter.   For the sake of it,
Be manly, and take comfort.
PER.   O you gods!
Why do you make us love your goodly gifts,
And snatch them straight away?   We here below
Recall not what we give, and therein may   25
Use honour with you.
LYC. Patience, good sir, even for this charge.
PER. Now, mild may be thy life!
For a more blusterous birth had never babe;
Quiet and gentle thy conditions! for
Thou art the rudeliest welcome to this world   30
That ever was prince's child.   Happy what follows
Thou hast as chiding a nativity
As fire, air, water, earth, and heaven, can make,
To herald thee from the womb.
Even at the first thy loss is more than can   35
Thy portage quit with all thou canst find here.
Now the good gods throw their best eyes upon't!

Enter two SAILORS.

1 SAIL. What courage, sir?   God save you!
PER. Courage enough: I do not fear the flaw;
It hath done to me the worst.   Yet, for the love   40
Of this poor infant, this fresh-new seafarer,
I would it would be quiet.
1 SAIL. Slack the bolins there.—Thou wilt not, wilt thou?   Blow,
and split thyself.
2 SAIL. But sea-room, an the brine and cloudy billow kiss the moon,
I care not.   46
1 SAIL. Sir, your queen must overboard: the sea works high, the
wind is loud, and will not lie till the ship be clear'd of the dead.
PER. That's your superstition.
1 SAIL. Pardon us, sir; with us at sea it hath been still observed,
and we are strong in custom.   Therefore briefly yield 'er; for
she must overboard straight.
PER. As you think meet.   Most wretched queen!
LYC. Here she lies, sir.   55
PER. A terrible childbed hast thou had, my dear;
No light, no fire.   Th' unfriendly elements
Forgot thee utterly; nor have I time
To give thee hallow'd to thy grave, but straight
Must cast thee, scarcely coffin'd, in the ooze;   60
Where, for a monument upon thy bones,
And aye-remaining lamps, the belching whale
And humming water must o'erwhelm thy corpse,
Lying with simple shells.   O Lychorida,
Bid Nestor bring me spices, ink and paper,   65
My casket and my jewels; and bid Nicander

Bring me the satin coffer.   Lay the babe
Upon the pillow.   Hie thee, whiles I say
A priestly farewell to her.   Suddenly, woman. [*Exit* LYCHORIDA.
2 SAIL. Sir, we have a chest beneath the hatches, caulk'd and bitumed
   ready.   71
PER. I thank thee.   Mariner, say what coast is this ?
2 SAIL. We are near Tharsus.
PER. Thither, gentle mariner,
   Alter thy course for Tyre.   When canst thou reach it ?   75
2 SAIL. By break of day, if the wind cease.
PER. O, make for Tharsus !
   There will I visit Cleon, for the babe
   Cannot hold out to Tyrus ; there I'll leave it
   At careful nursing.   Go thy ways, good mariner :   80
   I'll bring the body presently.   [*Exeunt.*

SCENE II.   *Ephesus.   Cerimon's house.*

Enter CERIMON, *with a* SERVANT, *and some* PERSONS *who have been
shipwrecked.*

CER. Philemon, ho !

Enter PHILEMON.

PHIL. Doth my lord call ?
CER. Get fire and meat for these poor men.
   'T'as been a turbulent and stormy night.
SERV. I have been in many ; but such a night as this,   5
   Till now, I ne'er endured.
CER. Your master will be dead ere you return ;
   There's nothing can be minist'red to nature
   That can recover him. [*To* PHILEMON.] Give this to the pothecary,
   And tell me how it works.   [*Exeunt all but* CERIMON.

Enter two GENTLEMEN.

1 GENT. Good morrow.   10
2 GENT. Good morrow to your lordship.
CER. Gentlemen, why do you stir so early ?
1 GENT. Sir,
   Our lodgings, standing bleak upon the sea,
   Shook as the earth did quake ;   15
   The very principals did seem to rend,
   And all to topple.   Pure surprise and fear
   Made me to quit the house.
2 GENT. That is the cause we trouble you so early ;
   'Tis not our husbandry.
CER.   O, you say well.   20
1 GENT. But I much marvel that your lordship, having
   Rich tire about you, should at these early hours
   Shake off the golden slumber of repose.
   'Tis most strange
   Nature should be so conversant with pain,   25
   Being thereto not compell'd.
CER.   I hold it ever
   Virtue and cunning were endowments greater

343

Than nobleness and riches : careless heirs
May the two latter darken and expend ;
But immortality attends the former,   30
Making a man a god.   'Tis known I ever
Have studied physic, through which secret art,
By turning o'er authorities, I have,
Together with my practice, made familiar
To me and to my aid the blest infusions   35
That dwell in vegetives, in metals, stones ;
And I can speak of the disturbances
That nature works, and of her cures ; which doth give me
A more content in course of true delight
Than to be thirsty after tottering honour,   40
Or tie my treasure up in silken bags,
To please the fool and death.

2 GENT.   Your honour has through Ephesus pour'd forth
Your charity, and hundreds call themselves
Your creatures, who by you have been restor'd :   45
And not your knowledge, your personal pain, but even
Your purse, still open, hath built Lord Cerimon
Such strong renown as time shall never raze.

Enter two or three SERVANTS *with a chest.*

1 SERV.   So, lift there.
CER.   What's that ?   50
1 SERV.   Sir, even now did the sea toss up upon our shore this chest.
'Tis of some wreck.
CER.   Set't down, let's look upon't.
2 GENT.   'Tis like a coffin, sir.
CER.   Whate'er it be,   55
'Tis wondrous heavy.   Wrench it open straight.
If the sea's stomach be o'ercharg'd with gold,
'Tis a good constraint of fortune it belches upon us.
2 GENT.   'Tis so, my lord.
CER.   How close 'tis caulk'd and bitumed !
Did the sea cast it up ?   61
1 SERV.   I never saw so huge a billow, sir, as toss'd it upon shore.
CER.   Wrench it open.   Soft !   It smells most sweetly in my sense.
2 GENT.   A delicate odour.
CER.   As ever hit my nostril.   So, up with it.
O you most potent gods !   What's here ?   A corse !
1 GENT.   Most strange !   67
CER.   Shrouded in cloth of state ; balm'd and entreasur'd with full
bags of spices.   A passport too.   Apollo, perfect me in the
characters !   [*Reads from a scroll.*

Here I give to understand—
If e'er this coffin drives a-land—
I, King Pericles, have lost   75
This queen, worth all our mundane cost.
Who finds her, give her burying ;
She was the daughter of a king.
Besides this treasure for a fee,
The gods requite his charity !   80

If thou livest, Pericles, thou hast a heart
That ever cracks for woe ! This chanc'd to-night.
2 GENT. Most likely, sir.
CER.   Nay, certainly to-night ;
For look how fresh she looks ! They were too rough
That threw her in the sea. Make a fire within.   85
Fetch hither all my boxes in my closet.   [*Exit a* SERVANT.
Death may usurp on nature many hours,
And yet the fire of life kindle again
The o'erpress'd spirits. I heard of an Egyptian
That had nine hours lien dead,   90
Who was by good appliance recovered.

Re-enter a SERVANT, *with boxes, napkins, and fire.*

Well said, well said ! The fire and cloths.
The rough and woeful music that we have,
Cause it to sound, beseech you.
The vial once more. How thou stirr'st, thou block !   95
The music there ! I pray you give her air.
Gentlemen,
This queen will live ; nature awakes ; a warmth
Breathes out of her. She hath not been entranc'd
Above five hours. See how she gins to blow   100
Into life's flower again !
1 GENT.   The heavens,
Through you, increase our wonder, and set up
Your fame for ever.
CER.   She is alive. Behold,
Her eyelids, cases to those heavenly jewels
Which Pericles hath lost, begin to part   105
Their fringes of bright gold ; the diamonds
Of a most praised water do appear,
To make the world twice rich. Live, and make
Us weep to hear your fate, fair creature,
Rare as you seem to be.   [*She moves.*
THAI. O dear Diana, where am I ?   110
Where's my lord ? What world is this ?
2 GENT. Is not this strange ?
1 GENT.   Most rare.
CER. Hush, my gentle neighbours !
Lend me your hands : to the next chamber bear her ;   115
Get linen. Now this matter must be look'd to,
For her relapse is mortal.
Come, come ; and Æsculapius guide us !
                              [*Exeunt, carrying her away.*

SCENE III. *Tharsus. Cleon's house.*

Enter PERICLES, CLEON, DIONYZA, *and* LYCHORIDA *with* MARINA *in her
arms.*

PER. Most honour'd Cleon, I must needs be gone ;
My twelve months are expir'd, and Tyrus stands
In a litigious peace. You and your lady

Take from my heart all thankfulness !   The gods
Make up the rest upon you !   5

CLE. Your shafts of fortune, though they hurt you mortally,
Yet glance full wand'ringly on us.

DIO.   O your sweet queen !
That the strict Fates had pleas'd you had brought her hither,
To have bless'd mine eyes with her !

PER.   We cannot but obey
The powers above us.   Could I rage and roar   10
As doth the sea she lies in, yet the end
Must be as 'tis.   My gentle babe Marina, whom,
For she was born at sea, I have nam'd so, here
I charge your charity withal, leaving her
The infant of your care ; beseeching you   15
To give her princely training, that she may
Be manner'd as she is born.

CLE. Fear not, my lord, but think
Your grace, that fed my country with your corn,
For which the people's prayers still fall upon you,
Must in your child be thought on.   If neglection   20
Should therein make me vile, the common body,
By you reliev'd, would force me to my duty.
But if to that my nature need a spur,
The gods revenge it upon me and mine
To the end of generation !   25

PER.   I believe you;
Your honour and your goodness teach me to't
Without your vows.   Till she be married, madam,
By bright Diana, whom we honour all,
Unscissor'd shall this hair of mine remain,
Though I show ill in't.   So I take my leave.   30
Good madam, make me blessed in your care
In bringing up my child.

DIO.   I have one myself,
Who shall not be more dear to my respect
Than yours, my lord.

PER.   Madam, my thanks and prayers.

CLE. We'll bring your Grace e'en to the edge o' th' shore,   35
Then give you up to the mask'd Neptune and
The gentlest winds of heaven.

PER.   I will embrace
Your offer.   Come, dearest madam.   O, no tears,
Lychorida, no tears.
Look to your little mistress, on whose grace   40
You may depend hereafter.   Come, my lord.   [Exeunt.

SCENE IV. Ephesus. Cerimon's house.

Enter CERIMON and THAISA.

CER. Madam, this letter, and some certain jewels,
Lay with you in your coffer ; which are
At your command.   Know you the character ?

THAI. It is my lord's.
That I was shipp'd at sea I well remember,   5

Even on my eaning time ; but whether there
Delivered, by the holy gods,
I cannot rightly say.   But since King Pericles,
My wedded lord, I ne'er shall see again,
A vestal livery will I take me to,   10
And never more have joy.

CER. Madam, if this you purpose as ye speak,
Diana's temple is not distant far,
Where you may abide till your date expire.
Moreover, if you please, a niece of mine
Shall there attend you.   15

THAI. My recompense is thanks, that's all ;
Yet my good will is great, though the gift small.   [*Exeunt.*

ACT FOUR

Enter GOWER.

GOW. Imagine Pericles arriv'd at Tyre,
Welcom'd and settled to his own desire.
His woeful queen we leave at Ephesus,
Unto Diana there a votaress.
Now to Marina bend your mind,   5
Whom our fast-growing scene must find
At Tharsus, and by Cleon train'd
In music, letters ; who hath gain'd
Of education all the grace,
Which makes her both the heart and place   10
Of general wonder.   But, alack,
That monster Envy, oft the wrack
Of earned praise, Marina's life
Seeks to take off by treason's knife.
And in this kind hath our Cleon   15
One daughter, and a wench full grown,
Even ripe for marriage-rite ; this maid
Hight Philoten ; and it is said
For certain in our story, she
Would ever with Marina be.   20
Be't when she weav'd the sleided silk
With fingers long, small, white as milk ;
Or when she would with sharp needle wound
The cambric, which she made more sound
By hurting it ; or when to th' lute   25
She sung, and made the night-bird mute,
That still records with moan ; or when
She would with rich and constant pen
Vail to her mistress Dian ; still
This Philoten contends in skill   30
With absolute Marina.   So
The dove of Paphos might with the crow
Vie feathers white.   Marina gets
All praises, which are paid as debts,
And not as given.   This so darks   35
In Philoten all graceful marks

347

That Cleon's wife, with envy rare,
A present murderer does prepare
For good Marina, that her daughter
Might stand peerless by this slaughter.   40
The sooner her vile thoughts to stead,
Lychorida, our nurse, is dead;
And cursed Dionyza hath
The pregnant instrument of wrath
Prest for this blow. The unborn event   45
I do commend to your content;
Only I carry winged time
Post on the lame feet of my rhyme;
Which never could I so convey
Unless your thoughts went on my way.   50
Dionyza does appear,
With Leonine, a murderer.   [*Exit.*

SCENE I. *Tharsus. An open place near the seashore.*

Enter DIONYZA *and* LEONINE.

DIO. Thy oath remember; thou hast sworn to do't.
'Tis but a blow, which never shall be known.
Thou canst not do a thing in the world so soon
To yield thee so much profit. Let not conscience,
Which is but cold, inflaming love in thy bosom,   5
Inflame too nicely; nor let pity, which
Even women have cast off, melt thee, but be
A soldier to thy purpose.
LEON. I will do't; but yet she is a goodly creature.
DIO. The fitter, then, the gods should have her.
Here she comes weeping for her only mistress' death.
Thou art resolv'd?   12
LEON. I am resolv'd.

Enter MARINA *with a basket of flowers.*

MAR. No, I will rob Tellus of her weed,
To strew thy green with flowers. The yellows, blues, 15
The purple violets, and marigolds,
Shall as a carpet hang upon thy grave
While summer days do last. Ay me! poor maid,
Born in a tempest, when my mother died,
This world to me is like a lasting storm,   20
Whirring me from my friends.
DIO. How now, Marina! Why do you keep alone?
How chance my daughter is not with you? Do not
Consume your blood with sorrowing; you have
A nurse of me. Lord, how your favour's chang'd   25
With this unprofitable woe! Come,
Give me your flowers. On the sea margent
Walk with Leonine; the air is quick there,
And it pierces and sharpens the stomach. Come,
Leonine, take her by the arm, walk with her.   30
MAR. No, I pray you;
I'll not bereave you of your servant.

DIO.   Come, come;
I love the king your father, and yourself,
With more than foreign heart. We every day   35
Expect him here. When he shall come, and find
Our paragon to all reports thus blasted,
He will repent the breadth of his great voyage;
Blame both my lord and me that we have taken
No care to your best courses. Go, I pray you,   40
Walk, and be cheerful once again; reserve
That excellent complexion which did steal
The eyes of young and old. Care not for me;
I can go home alone.

MAR.   Well, I will go;
But yet I have no desire to it.   45

DIO. Come, come, I know 'tis good for you.
Walk half an hour, Leonine, at the least.
Remember what I have said.

LEON.   I warrant you, madam.

DIO. I'll leave you, my sweet lady, for a while.
Pray walk softly; do not heat your blood.   50
What! I must have a care of you.

MAR.   My thanks, sweet madam.

                                        [Exit DIONYZA.

Is this wind westerly that blows?

LEON.   South-west.

MAR. When I was born the wind was north.

LEON.   Was't so?

MAR. My father, as nurse says, did never fear,
But cried 'Good seamen!' to the sailors, galling   55
His kingly hands hauling ropes;
And, clasping to the mast, endur'd a sea
That almost burst the deck.

LEON. When was this?

MAR. When I was born.   60
Never was waves nor wind more violent;
And from the ladder-tackle washes off
A canvas-climber. 'Ha!' says one 'wilt out?'
And with a dropping industry they skip
From stern to stern; the boatswain whistles, and   65
The master calls, and trebles their confusion.

LEON. Come, say your prayers.

MAR. What mean you?

LEON. If you require a little space for prayer,
I grant it. Pray; but be not tedious, for   70
The gods are quick of ear, and I am sworn
To do my work with haste.

MAR. Why will you kill me?

LEON. To satisfy my lady.

MAR. Why would she have me kill'd?
Now, as I can remember, by my troth,   75
I never did her hurt in all my life.
I never spake bad word, nor did ill turn
To any living creature. Believe me, la,
I never kill'd a mouse, nor hurt a fly;

                                                    349

I trod upon a worm against my will,   8c
But I wept for it.   How have I offended,
Wherein my death might yield her any profit,
Or my life imply her any danger ?

LEON. My commission
Is not to reason of the deed, but do't.   8￼

MAR. You will not do't for all the world, I hope.
You are well-favour'd, and your looks foreshow
You have a gentle heart.   I saw you lately
When you caught hurt in parting two that fought.
Good sooth, it show'd well in you.   Do so now :   9￼
Your lady seeks my life ; come you between,
And save poor me, the weaker.

LEON.   I am sworn,
And will dispatch.   [*Seizes her*

Enter PIRATES.

1 PIRATE. Hold, villain !   LEONINE *runs away*
2 PIRATE. A prize ! a prize !   9￼
3 PIRATE. Half part, mates, half part !
Come, let's have her aboard suddenly.
                                          [*Exeunt* PIRATES *with* MARINA

Re-enter LEONINE.

LEON. These roguing thieves serve the great pirate Valdes,
And they have seiz'd Marina.   Let her go ;
There's no hope she will return.   I'll swear she's dead   10￼
And thrown into the sea.   But I'll see further.
Perhaps they will but please themselves upon her,
Not carry her aboard.   If she remain,
Whom they have ravish'd must by me be slain.   [*Exi*

SCENE II. *Mytilene. A brothel.*

Enter PANDER, BAWD, *and* BOULT.

PAND. Boult !
BOULT. Sir ?
PAND. Search the market narrowly.   Mytilene is full of gallants
We lost too much money this mart by being too wenchless.
BAWD. We were never so much out of creatures.   We have but poo
three, and they can do no more than they can do ; and they wit
continual action are even as good as rotten.
PAND. Therefore let's have fresh ones, whate'er we pay for them
If there be not a conscience to be us'd in every trade, we shal
never prosper.
BAWD. Thou say'st true ; 'tis not our bringing up of poor bastards—
as, I think, I have brought up some eleven—   1
BOULT. Ay, to eleven ; and brought them down again.   But shall
search the market ?
BAWD. What else, man ?   The stuff we have, a strong wind wi￼
blow it to pieces, they are so pitifully sodden.
PAND. Thou sayest true ; they are too unwholesome, o' conscience
The poor Transylvanian is dead that lay with the little baggage

350

BOULT. Ay, she quickly poop'd him ; she made him roast meat for
worms. But I'll go search the market.   [*Exit.*

PAND. Three or four thousand chequins were as pretty a proportion
to live quietly, and so give over.

BAWD. Why to give over, I pray you ? Is it a shame to get when
we are old ?   28

PAND. O, our credit comes not in like the commodity, nor the commodity wages not with the danger ; therefore, if in our youths
we could pick up some pretty estate, 'twere not amiss to keep our
door hatch'd. Besides, the sore terms we stand upon with the
gods will be strong with us for giving o'er.

BAWD. Come, other sorts offend as well as we.   35

PAND. As well as we ! Ay, and better too ; we offend worse. Neither
is our profession any trade ; it's no calling. But here comes
Boult.

Re-enter BOULT, *with the* PIRATES *and* MARINA.

BOULT. [*To* MARINA.] Come your ways.—My masters, you say she's
a virgin ?   40

I PIRATE. O, sir, we doubt it not.

BOULT. Master, I have gone through for this piece you see. If you
like her, so ; if not, I have lost my earnest.

BAWD. Boult, has she any qualities ?   45

BOULT. She has a good face, speaks well, and has excellent good
clothes ; there's no further necessity of qualities can make her be
refus'd.

BAWD. What's her price, Boult ?

BOULT. I cannot be bated one doit of a thousand pieces.   51

PAND. Well, follow me, my masters ; you shall have your money
presently. Wife, take her in ; instruct her what she has to do,
that she may not be raw in her entertainment.

                                      [*Exeunt* PANDER *and* PIRATES.

BAWD. Boult, take you the marks of her—the colour of her hair,
complexion, height, her age, with warrant of her virginity ; and
cry ' He that will give most shall have her first '. Such a maidenhead were no cheap thing, if men were as they have been. Get
this done as I command you.   61

BOULT. Performance shall follow.   [*Exit.*

MAR. Alack that Leonine was so slack, so slow !
He should have struck, not spoke ; or that these pirates,
Not enough barbarous, had not o'erboard thrown me
For to seek my mother !   66

BAWD. Why lament you, pretty one ?

MAR. That I am pretty.

BAWD. Come, the gods have done their part in you.

MAR. I accuse them not.   70

BAWD. You are light into my hands, where you are like to live.

MAR. The more my fault
To scape his hands where I was like to die.

BAWD. Ay, and you shall live in pleasure.   75

MAR. No.

BAWD. Yes, indeed shall you, and taste gentlemen of all fashions.
You shall fare well ; you shall have the difference of all complex-
ions. What ! do you stop your ears ?

MAR. Are you a woman?

BAWD. What would you have me be, an I be not a woman?

MAR. An honest woman, or not a woman.   84

BAWD. Marry, whip thee, gosling! I think I shall have something
to do with you. Come, you're a young foolish sapling, and
must be bow'd as I would have you.

MAR. The gods defend me!   89

BAWD. If it please the gods to defend you by men, then men must
comfort you, men must feed you, men must stir you up. Boult's
return'd.

Re-enter BOULT.

Now, sir, hast thou cried her through the market?

BOULT. I have cried her almost to the number of her hairs; I have
drawn her picture with my voice.   9

BAWD. And I prithee tell me how dost thou find the inclination o
the people, especially of the younger sort?

BOULT. Faith, they listened to me as they would have hearkened to
their father's testament. There was a Spaniard's mouth so
wat'red that he went to bed to her very description.   10

BAWD. We shall have him here to-morrow with his best ruff on.

BOULT. To-night, to-night. But, mistress, do you know the French
knight that cowers i' th' hams?

BAWD. Who? Monsieur Veroles?

BOULT. Ay, he; he offered to cut a caper at the proclamation; bu
he made a groan at it, and swore he would see her to-morrow.

BAWD. Well, well; as for him, he brought his disease hither: her
he does but repair it. I know he will come in our shadow to
scatter his crowns in the sun.

BOULT. Well, if we had of every nation a traveller, we should lodg
them with this sign.   11

BAWD. [To MARINA.] Pray you, come hither awhile. You hav
fortunes coming upon you. Mark me: you must seem to d
that fearfully which you commit willingly; to despise profi
where you have most gain. To weep that you live as ye d
makes pity in your lovers; seldom but that pity begets you
good opinion, and that opinion a mere profit.   12

MAR. I understand you not.

BOULT. O, take her home, mistress, take her home. These blushe
of hers must be quench'd with some present practice.

BAWD. Thou sayest true, i' faith, so they must; for your bride goe
to that with shame which is her way to go with warrant.

BOULT. Faith, some do, and some do not. But, mistress, if I hav
bargain'd for the joint—   13

BAWD. Thou mayest cut a morsel off the spit.

BOULT. I may so.

BAWD. Who should deny it? Come, young one, I like the manne
of your garments well.   13

BOULT. Ay, by my faith, they shall not be chang'd yet.

BAWD. Boult, spend thou that in the town; report what a sojourne
we have; you'll lose nothing by custom. When nature fram'
this piece she meant thee a good turn; therefore say what
paragon she is, and thou hast the harvest out of thine own repor

BOULT. I warrant you, mistress, thunder shall not so awake the beds o

eels as my giving out her beauty stir up the lewdly inclined.
I'll bring home some to-night.   145
BAWD. Come your ways; follow me.
MAR. If fires be hot, knives sharp, or water deep,
    Untied I still my virgin knot will keep.
    Diana aid my purpose!   149
BAWD. What have we to do with Diana? Pray, you will you go
    with us?   [*Exeunt.*

SCENE III. *Tharsus. Cleon's house*

Enter CLEON *and* DIONYZA.

DIO. Why are you foolish? Can it be undone?
CLE. O Dionyza, such a piece of slaughter
    The sun and moon ne'er look'd upon!
DIO.   I think
    You'll turn a child again.
CLE. Were I chief lord of all this spacious world,   5
    I'd give it to undo the deed. O lady,
    Much less in blood than virtue, yet a princess
    To equal any single crown o' th' earth
    I' th' justice of compare! O villain Leonine!
    Whom thou hast pois'ned too.   10
    If thou hadst drunk to him, 't had been a kindness
    Becoming well thy fact. What canst thou say
    When noble Pericles shall demand his child?
DIO. That she is dead. Nurses are not the Fates,
    To foster it, nor ever to preserve.   15
    She died at night; I'll say so. Who can cross it?
    Unless you play the pious innocent,
    And for an honest attribute cry out
    ' She died by foul play '.
CLE.   O, go to. Well, well.
    Of all the faults beneath the heavens the gods   20
    Do like this worst.
DIO.   Be one of those that thinks
    The petty wrens of Tharsus will fly hence,
    And open this to Pericles. I do shame
    To think of what a noble strain you are,
    And of how coward a spirit.
CLE.   To such proceeding   25
    Who ever but his approbation added,
    Though not his prime consent, he did not flow
    From honourable sources.
DIO.   Be it so, then.
    Yet none does know, but you, how she came dead,
    Nor none can know, Leonine being gone.   30
    She did distain my child, and stood between
    Her and her fortunes. None would look on her,
    But cast their gazes on Marina's face;
    Whilst ours was blurted at, and held a mawkin,
    Not worth the time of day. It pierc'd me thorough;   35
    And though you call my course unnatural,
    You not your child well loving, yet I find

12

It greets me as an enterprise of kindness
Perform'd to your sole daughter.

CLE.   Heavens forgive it !

DIO. And as for Pericles,   40
What should he say ? We wept after her hearse,
And yet we mourn ; her monument
Is almost finish'd, and her epitaphs
In glittering golden characters express
A general praise to her, and care in us   45
At whose expense 'tis done.

CLE.   Thou art like the harpy,
Which, to betray, dost, with thine angel's face,
Seize with thine eagle's talons.

DIO. You are like one that superstitiously
Doth swear to the gods that winter kills the flies ;   50
But yet I know you'll do as I advise.   [*Exeunt.*

SCENE IV.   *Before Marina's monument at Tharsus.*

Enter GOWER.

GOW. Thus time we waste, and longest leagues make short ;
Sail seas in cockles, have an wish but for't ;
Making, to take our imagination,
From bourn to bourn, region to region.
By you being pardon'd, we commit no crime   5
To use one language in each several clime
Where our scenes seem to live.   I do beseech you
To learn of me, who stand i' th' gaps to teach you
The stages of our story.   Pericles
Is now again thwarting the wayward seas,   10
Attended on by many a lord and knight,
To see his daughter, all his life's delight.
Old Helicanus goes along.   Behind
Is left to govern it, you bear in mind,
Old Escanes, whom Helicanus late   15
Advanc'd in time to great and high estate.
Well-sailing ships and bounteous winds have brought
This king to Tharsus—think this pilot thought ;
So with his steerage shall your thoughts grow on—
To fetch his daughter home, who first is gone.   20
Like motes and shadows see them move awhile ;
Your ears unto your eyes I'll reconcile.

Dumb show.

Enter PERICLES, *at one door, with all his* TRAIN *:* CLEON *and* DIONYZA
at the other. CLEON *shows* PERICLES *the tomb of Marina, whereat*
PERICLES *makes lamentation, puts on sackcloth, and in a mighty*
passion departs.   Then exeunt CLEON *and* DIONYZA.

See how belief may suffer by foul show !
This borrowed passion stands for true old woe ;
And Pericles, in sorrow all devour'd,
With sighs shot through and biggest tears o'ershower'd,   25

Leaves Tharsus, and again embarks. He swears
Never to wash his face nor cut his hairs ;
He puts on sackcloth, and to sea. He bears
A tempest which his mortal vessel tears,   30
And yet he rides it out. Now please you wit
The epitaph is for Marina writ
By wicked Dionyza.

        [Reads the inscription on Marina's monument.
  'The fairest, sweetest, and best lies here,
  Who withered in her spring of year.   35
  She was of Tyrus the King's daughter,
  On whom foul death hath made this slaughter ;
  Marina was she call'd ; and at her birth,
  Thetis, being proud, swallowed some part o' th' earth
  Therefore the earth, fearing to be o'er-flowed,   40
  Hath Thetis' birth-child on the heavens bestowed ;
  Wherefore she does—and swears she'll never stint—
  Make raging battery upon shores of flint.'

No visor does become black villainy
So well as soft and tender flattery.   45
Let Pericles believe his daughter's dead,
And bear his courses to be ordered
By Lady Fortune ; while our scene must play
His daughter's woe and heavy well-a-day
In her unholy service. Patience, then,   50
And think you now are all in Mytilen.   *Exit.*

SCENE V. *Mytilene. A street before the brothel.*

Enter, from the brothel, two GENTLEMEN.

GENT. Did you ever hear the like ?

GENT. No, nor never shall do in such a place as this, she being
  once alive.

GENT. But to have divinity preach'd there ! Did you ever dream
  of such a thing ?   5

GENT. No, no. Come, I am for no more bawdy-houses. Shall's
  go hear the vestals sing ?

GENT. I'll do anything now that is virtuous ; but I am out of the
  road of rutting for ever.   *[Exeunt.*

SCENE VI. *Mytilene. A room in the brothel.*

Enter PANDER, BAWD, *and* BOULT.

AND. Well, I had rather than twice the worth of her she had ne'er
  come here.

AWD. Fie, fie, upon her ! She's able to freeze the god Priapus, and
  undo a whole generation. We must either get her ravished or
  be rid of her. When she should do for clients her fitment, and
  do me the kindness of our profession, she has me her quirks, her
  reasons, her master-reasons, her prayers, her knees ; that she
  would make a puritan of the devil, if he should cheapen a kiss
  of her.   10

BOULT. Faith, I must ravish her, or she'll disfurnish us of all our
    cavalleria and make our swearers priests.
PAND. Now the pox upon her green-sickness for me!
BAWD. Faith, there's no way to be rid on't but by the way to the pox.
    Here comes the Lord Lysimachus disguised.   16
BOULT. We should have both lord and lown, if the peevish baggage
    would but give way to customers.

Enter LYSIMACHUS.

LYS. How now!   How a dozen of virginities?
BAWD. Now, the gods to bless your Honour!   20
BOULT. I am glad to see your Honour in good health.
LYS. You may so; 'tis the better for you that your resorters stand
    upon sound legs.   How now!   Wholesome iniquity have you,
    that a man may deal withal and defy the surgeon?   25
BAWD. We have here one, sir, if she would—but there never came
    her like in Mytilene.
LYS. If she'd do the deed of darkness, thou wouldst say.
BAWD. Your Honour knows what 'tis to say well enough.
LYS. Well, call forth, call forth.
BOULT. For flesh and blood, sir, white and red, you shall see a rose;
    and she were a rose indeed, if she had but—   35
LYS. What, prithee?
BOULT. O, sir, I can be modest.
LYS. That dignifies the renown of a bawd no less than it gives a good
    report to a number to be chaste.   [*Exit* BOULT.
BAWD. Here comes that which grows to the stalk—never plucked yet,
    I can assure you.   41

Re-enter BOULT *with* MARINA.

    Is she not a fair creature?
LYS. Faith, she would serve after a long voyage at sea.   Well, there's
    for you.   Leave us.
BAWD. I beseech your Honour, give me leave: a word, and I'll have
    done presently.   46
LYS. I beseech you, do.
BAWD. [*Aside to* MARINA.] First, I would have you note this is an
    honourable man.
MAR. I desire to find him so, that I may worthily note him.
BAWD. Next, he's the governor of this country, and a man whom
    I am bound to.   53
MAR. If he govern the country, you are bound to him indeed; but
    how honourable he is in that I know not.
BAWD. Pray you, without any more virginal fencing, will you use
    him kindly?   He will line your apron with gold.
MAR. What he will do graciously I will thankfully receive.   60
LYS. Ha' you done?
BAWD. My lord, she's not pac'd yet; you must take some pains to
    work her to your manage.   Come, we will leave his Honour and
    her together.   Go thy ways.   [*Exeunt* BAWD, PANDER, *and* BOULT.
LYS. Now, pretty one, how long have you been at this trade?   66
MAR. What trade, sir?
LYS. Why, I cannot name't but I shall offend.
MAR. I cannot be offended with my trade.   Please you to name it.

YS. How long have you been of this profession?

MAR. E'er since I can remember.

YS. Did you go to't so young? Were you a gamester at five or at seven?

MAR. Earlier too, sir, if now I be one.   75

YS. Why, the house you dwell in proclaims you to be a creature of sale.

MAR. Do you know this house to be a place of such resort, and will come into't? I hear say you're of honourable parts, and are the governor of this place.   80

YS. Why, hath your principal made known unto you who I am?

MAR. Who is my principal?

YS. Why, your herb-woman; she that sets seeds and roots of shame and iniquity. O, you have heard something of my power, and so stand aloof for more serious wooing. But I protest to thee, pretty one, my authority shall not see thee, or else look friendly upon thee. Come, bring me to some private place. Come, come.

MAR. If you were born to honour, show it now;   91
     If put upon you, make the judgment good
     That thought you worthy of it.

YS. How's this? how's this? Some more; be sage.

MAR.   For me,
     That am a maid, though most ungentle fortune   95
     Have plac'd me in this sty, where, since I came,
     Diseases have been sold dearer than physic—
     That the gods
     Would set me free from this unhallowed place,
     Though they did change me to the meanest bird   100
     That flies i' th' purer air!

YS.   I did not think
     Thou couldst have spoke so well; ne'er dreamt thou couldst
     Had I brought hither a corrupted mind,
     Thy speech had altered it. Hold, here's gold for thee:
     Persever in that clear way thou goest,   105
     And the gods strengthen thee!

MAR. The good gods preserve you!

YS. For me, be you thoughten
     That I came with no ill intent; for to me
     The very doors and windows savour vilely.
     Fare thee well. Thou art a piece of virtue, and   110
     I doubt not but thy training hath been noble.
     Hold, here's more gold for thee.
     A curse upon him, die he like a thief,
     That robs thee of thy goodness! If thou dost
     Hear from me, it shall be for thy good.   115

Re-enter BOULT.

BOULT. I beseech your Honour, one piece for me.

YS. Avaunt, thou damned door keeper!
     Your house, but for this virgin that doth prop it,
     Would sink and overwhelm you. Away!   [*Exit.*

BOULT. How's this? We must take another course with you. If your peevish chastity, which is not worth a breakfast in the

cheapest country under the cope, shall undo a whole household,
let me be gelded like a spaniel.   Come your ways.

MAR. Whither would you have me ?   12

BOULT. I must have your maidenhead taken off, or the common
hangman shall execute it.   Come your ways.   We'll have no
more gentlemen driven away.   Come your ways, I say.

Re-enter BAWD.

BAWD. How now !   What's the matter ?   130

BOULT. Worse and worse, mistress ; she has here spoken holy words
to the Lord Lysimachus.

BAWD. O abominable !

BOULT. She makes our profession as it were to stink afore the face
of the gods.   13

BAWD. Marry, hang her up for ever !

BOULT. The nobleman would have dealt with her like a nobleman,
and she sent him away as cold as a snowball ; saying his prayers
too.

BAWD. Boult, take her away ; use her at thy pleasure.   Crack the
glass of her virginity, and make the rest malleable.

BOULT. An if she were a thornier piece of ground than she is, she
shall be ploughed.

MAR. Hark, hark, you gods !   14

BAWD. She conjures.   Away with her.   Would she had never come
within my doors !   Marry, hang you !   She's born to undo us.
Will you not go the way of womenkind ?   Marry, come up, my
dish of chastity with rosemary and bays !   [*Exit*

BOULT. Come, mistress ; come your ways with me.   15

MAR. Whither wilt thou have me ?

BOULT. To take from you the jewel you hold so dear.

MAR. Prithee tell me one thing first.

BOULT. Come now, your one thing.   15

MAR. What canst thou wish thine enemy to be ?

BOULT. Why, I could wish him to be my master, or, rather, my
mistress.

MAR. Neither of these are so bad as thou art,
Since they do better thee in their command.
Thou hold'st a place for which the pained'st fiend   16
Of hell would not in reputation change ;
Thou art the damned doorkeeper to every
Coistrel that comes inquiring for his Tib ;
To the choleric fisting of every rogue   16
Thy ear is liable ; thy food is such
As hath been belch'd on by infected lungs.

BOULT. What would you have me do ?   Go to the wars, would you,
where a man may serve seven years for the loss of a leg, and
have not money enough in the end to buy him a wooden one ?

MAR. Do anything but this thou doest.   Empty
Old receptacles, or common shores, of filth ;
Serve by indenture to the common hangman.
Any of these ways are yet better than this ;   17
For what thou professest, a baboon, could he speak,
Would own a name too dear.   That the gods
Would safely deliver me from this place !

Here, here's gold for thee.
If that thy master would gain by me,   180
Proclaim that I can sing, weave, sew, and dance,
With other virtues which I'll keep from boast ;
And I will undertake all these to teach.
I doubt not but this populous city will
Yield many scholars.   185

ULT. But can you teach all this you speak of ?

AR. Prove that I cannot, take me home again
And prostitute me to the basest groom
That doth frequent your house.

ULT. Well, I will see what I can do for thee. If I can place thee,
I will.   191

AR. But amongst honest women ?

ULT. Faith, my acquaintance lies little amongst them. But since
my master and mistress have bought you, there's no going but
by their consent. Therefore I will make them acquainted with
your purpose, and I doubt not but I shall find them tractable
enough. Come, I'll do for thee what I can ; come your ways.
                                                        [Exeunt.

ACT FIVE

Enter GOWER.

OW. Marina thus the brothel scapes and chances
Into an honest house, our story says.
She sings like one immortal, and she dances
As goddess-like to her admired lays ;
Deep clerks she dumbs ; and with her needle composes   5
Nature's own shape of bud, bird, branch, or berry,
That even her art sisters the natural roses ;
Her inkle, silk, twin with the rubied cherry ;
That pupils lacks she none of noble race,
Who pour their bounty on her ; and her gain   10
She gives the cursed bawd.   Here we her place ;
And to her father turn our thoughts again,
Where we left him on the sea.   We there him lost ;
Whence, driven before the winds, he is arriv'd
Here where his daughter dwells ; and on this coast   15
Suppose him now at anchor.   The city striv'd
God Neptune's annual feast to keep ; from whence
Lysimachus our Tyrian ship espies,
His banners sable, trimm'd with rich expense ;
And to him in his barge with fervour hies.   20
In your supposing once more put your sight.
Of heavy Pericles, think this his bark ;
Where what is done in action, more, if might,
Shall be discover'd ; please you sit and hark.   [Exit.

359

SCENE I. *On board Pericles' ship, off Mytilene. A pavilion on dec*
     with a curtain before it ; PERICLES *within it, reclining on a couch*
     A barge lying beside the Tyrian vessel.

Enter two SAILORS, *one belonging to the Tyrian vessel, the other to th*
                              barge ; to them HELICANUS.

TYR. SAIL. [*To the* SAILOR *of* MYTILENE.] Where is Lord Helicanus ?
     He can resolve you.
     O, here he is.
     Sir, there is a barge put off from Mytilene,
     And in it is Lysimachus the Governor,
     Who craves to come aboard.   What is your will ?
HEL. That he have his.   Call up some gentlemen.
TYR. SAIL. Ho, gentlemen ! my lord calls.

                    Enter two or three GENTLEMEN.

1 GENT. Doth your lordship call ?
HEL. Gentlemen, there is some of worth would come aboard ;
     I pray greet him fairly.
                    [*The* GENTLEMEN *and the two* SAILORS *descend,*
                                   and go on board the barg

Enter, from thence, LYSIMACHUS *and* LORDS, *with the* GENTLEM[E]
                         and the two SAILORS.

TYR. SAIL. Sir,
     This is the man that can, in aught you would,
     Resolve you.
LYS. Hail, reverend sir !   The gods preserve you !
HEL. And you, sir, to outlive the age I am,
     And die as I would do.
LYS.   You wish me well.
     Being on shore, honouring of Neptune's triumphs,
     Seeing this goodly vessel ride before us,
     I made to it, to know of whence you are.
HEL. First, what is your place ?
LYS.   I am the Governor
     Of this place you lie before.
HEL. Sir,
     Our vessel is of Tyre, in it the King ;
     A man who for this three months hath not spoken
     To any one, nor taken sustenance
     But to prorogue his grief.
LYS. Upon what ground is his distemperature ?
HEL. 'Twould be too tedious to repeat ;
     But the main grief springs from the loss
     Of a beloved daughter and a wife.
LYS. May we not see him ?
HEL. You may ;
     But bootless is your sight—he will not speak
     To any.
LYS. Yet let me obtain my wish.
HEL. Behold him.   [PERICLES *discovered.*]   This was a goodly pers[on]
     Till the disaster that, one mortal night,

    Drove him to this.

LYS. Sir King, all hail !   The gods preserve you !
    Hail, royal sir !

HEL. It is in vain ; he will not speak to you.   40

I LORD. Sir, we have a maid in Mytilene, I durst wager,
    Would win some words of him.

LYS.   'Tis well bethought.
    She, questionless, with her sweet harmony
    And other chosen attractions, would allure,   45
    And make a batt'ry through his deafen'd parts,
    Which now are midway stopp'd.
    She is all happy as the fairest of all,
    And, with her fellow maids, is now upon
    The leafy shelter that abuts against   50
    The island's side.

    [*He whispers* FIRST LORD, *who goes off in the barge of Lysimachus.*

HEL. Sure, all's effectless ; yet nothing we'll omit
    That bears recovery's name.   But, since your kindness
    We have stretch'd thus far, let us beseech you
    That for our gold we may provision have,   55
    Wherein we are not destitute for want,
    But weary for the staleness.

LYS.   O sir, a courtesy
    Which if we should deny, the most just gods
    For every graff would send a caterpillar,
    And so inflict our province.   Yet once more   60
    Let me entreat to know at large the cause
    Of your king's sorrow.

HEL. Sit, sir, I will recount it to you.
    But, see, I am prevented.

Re-enter, from the barge, FIRST LORD, *with* MARINA *and another* GIRL.

LYS.   O, here is
    The lady that I sent for.   Welcome, fair one !
    Is't not a goodly presence ?

HEL.   She's a gallant lady.   65

LYS. She's such a one that, were I well assur'd
    Came of gentle kind and noble stock,
    I'd wish no better choice, and think me rarely wed.
    Fair one, all goodness that consists in bounty
    Expect even here, where is a kingly patient.   70
    If that thy prosperous and artificial feat
    Can draw him but to answer thee in aught,
    Thy sacred physic shall receive such pay
    As thy desires can wish.

MAR.   Sir, I will use
    My utmost skill in his recovery,   75
    Provided
    That none but I and my companion maid
    Be suffered to come near him.

LYS.   Come, let us leave her ;
    And the gods make her prosperous !   [MARINA *sings.*

LYS. Mark'd he your music ?

MAR.   No, nor look'd on us.
LYS. See, she will speak to him.   80
MAR. Hail sir! my lord, lend ear.
PER. Hum, ha!
MAR. I am a maid,
    My lord, that ne'er before invited eyes,
    But have been gaz'd on like a comet.   She speaks,   85
    My lord, that, may be, hath endur'd a grief
    Might equal yours, if both were justly weigh'd.
    Though wayward fortune did malign my state,
    My derivation was from ancestors
    Who stood equivalent with mighty kings;   90
    But time hath rooted out my parentage,
    And to the world and awkward casualties
    Bound me in servitude.   [Aside.]   I will desist;
    But there is something glows upon my cheek,
    And whispers in mine ear 'Go not till he speak'.   95
PER. My fortunes—parentage—good parentage—
    To equal mine!—was it not thus?   What say you?
MAR. I said, my lord, if you did know my parentage
    You would not do me violence.
PER. I do think so.   Pray you turn your eyes upon me.   100
    You are like something that—What countrywoman?
    Here of these shores?
MAR.   No, nor of any shores.
    Yet I was mortally brought forth, and am
    No other than I appear.
PER. I am great with woe, and shall deliver weeping.   105
    My dearest wife was like this maid, and such a one
    My daughter might have been: my queen's square brows
    Her stature to an inch; as wand-like straight;
    As silver-voic'd; her eyes as jewel-like,
    And cas'd as richly; in pace another Juno;   110
    Who starves the ears she feeds, and makes them hungry
    The more she gives them speech.   Where do you live?
MAR. Where I am but a stranger.   From the deck
    You may discern the place.
PER.   Where were you bred?
    And how achiev'd you these endowments, which   115
    You make more rich to owe?
MAR. If I should tell my history, it would seem
    Like lies, disdain'd in the reporting.
PER.   Prithee speak.
    Falseness cannot come from thee; for thou lookest
    Modest as Justice, and thou seem'st a palace   120
    For the crown'd Truth to dwell in.   I will believe thee,
    And make my senses credit thy relation
    To points that seem impossible; for thou lookest
    Like one I lov'd indeed.   What were thy friends?
    Didst thou not say, when I did push thee back—   125
    Which was when I perceiv'd thee—that thou cam'st
    From good descending?
MAR.   So indeed I did.
PER. Report thy parentage.   I think thou said'st
362

Thou hadst been toss'd from wrong to injury,
And that thou thought'st thy griefs might equal mine,   130
If both were opened.

MAR.   Some such thing
I said, and said no more but what my thoughts
Did warrant me was likely.

PER.   Tell thy story;
If thine consider'd prove the thousand part
Of my endurance, thou art a man, and I   135
Have suffered like a girl.   Yet thou dost look
Like Patience gazing on kings' graves, and smiling
Extremity out of act.   What were thy friends?
How lost thou them?   Thy name, my most kind virgin?
Recount, I do beseech thee.   Come, sit by me.   140

MAR. My name is Marina.

PER.   O, I am mock'd,
And thou by some incensed god sent hither
To make the world to laugh at me.

MAR.   Patience, good sir,
Or here I'll cease.

PER. Nay, I'll be patient.
Thou little know'st how thou dost startle me   145
To call thyself Marina.

MAR. The name
Was given me by one that had some power,
My father, and a king.

PER.   How! a king's daughter?
And call'd Marina?

MAR. You said you would believe me;
But, not to be a troubler of your peace,   150
I will end here.

PER.   But are you flesh and blood?
Have you a working pulse, and are no fairy?
Motion!   Well; speak on.   Where were you born?
And wherefore call'd Marina?

MAR.   Call'd Marina
For I was born at sea.

PER.   At sea! what mother?   155

MAR. My mother was the daughter of a king;
Who died the minute I was born,
As my good nurse Lychorida hath oft
Delivered weeping.

PER.   O, stop there a little!
[*Aside.*] This is the rarest dream that e'er dull sleep   160
Did mock sad fools withal.   This cannot be:
My daughter's buried.—Well, where were you bred?
I'll hear you more, to th' bottom of your story,
And never interrupt you.

MAR. You scorn; believe me, 'twere best I did give o'er.   165

PER. I will believe you by the syllable
Of what you shall deliver.   Yet give me leave—
How came you in these parts? where were you bred?

MAR. The King my father did in Tharsus leave me;
Till cruel Cleon, with his wicked wife,   170

Did seek to murder me ; and having woo'd
A villain to attempt it, who having drawn to do't,
A crew of pirates came and rescued me ;
Brought me to Mytilene. But, good sir,
Whither will you have me ? Why do you weep ? It may be
You think me an impostor. No, good faith ;   176
I am the daughter to King Pericles,
If good King Pericles be.

PER. Ho, Helicanus !

HEL.   Calls my lord ?   180

PER. Thou art a grave and noble counsellor,
Most wise in general. Tell me, if thou canst,
What this maid is, or what is like to be,
That thus hath made me weep ?

HEL.   I know not ; but
Here is the regent, sir, of Mytilene   185
Speaks nobly of her.

LYS.   She never would tell
Her parentage ; being demanded that,
She would sit still and weep.

PER. O Helicanus, strike me, honour'd sir ;
Give me a gash, put me to present pain,   190
Lest this great sea of joys rushing upon me
O'erbear the shores of my mortality,
And drown me with their sweetness. O, come hither,
Thou that beget'st him that did thee beget ;
Thou that wast born at sea, buried at Tharsus,   195
And found at sea again ! O Helicanus,
Down on thy knees, thank the holy gods as loud
As thunder threatens us. This is Marina.
What was thy mother's name ? Tell me but that,
For truth can never be confirm'd enough,   200
Though doubts did ever sleep.

MAR.   First, sir, I pray,
What is your title ?

PER. I am Pericles of Tyre ; but tell me now
My drown'd queen's name, as in the rest you said
Thou hast been godlike perfect,   205
The heir of kingdoms and another life
To Pericles thy father.

MAR. Is it no more to be your daughter than
To say my mother's name was Thaisa ?
Thaisa was my mother, who did end
The minute I began.   210

PER. Now blessing on thee ! Rise ; thou art my child.
Give me fresh garments. Mine own, Helicanus—
She is not dead at Tharsus, as she should have been
By savage Cleon. She shall tell thee all ;
When thou shalt kneel, and justify in knowledge   215
She is thy very princess. Who is this ?

HEL. Sir, 'tis the Governor of Mytilene,
Who, hearing of your melancholy state,
Did come to see you.

PER.   I embrace you.   220

Give me my robes. I am wild in my beholding.
O heavens bless my girl! But hark, what music?
Tell Helicanus, my Marina, tell him
O'er, point by point, for yet he seems to doubt,
How sure you are my daughter. But, what music?   225

HEL. My lord, I hear none.

PER.   None?
The music of the spheres! List, my Marina.

LYS. It is not good to cross him; give him way.

PER. Rarest sounds! Do ye not hear?

LYS. My lord, I hear.   [Music.

PER. Most heavenly music!   231
It nips me unto list'ning, and thick slumber
Hangs upon mine eyes: let me rest.   [Sleeps.

LYS. A pillow for his head.
So, leave him all. Well, my companion-friends,   235
If this but answer to my just belief,
I'll well remember you.   [Exeunt all but PERICLES.

DIANA appears to PERICLES as in a vision.

DIA. My temple stands in Ephesus. Hie thee thither,
And do upon mine altar sacrifice.
There, when my maiden priests are met together,   240
Before the people all,
Reveal how thou at sea didst lose thy wife.
To mourn thy crosses, with thy daughter's, call,
And give them repetition to the life.
Or perform my bidding or thou liv'st in woe;   245
Do it, and happy—by my silver bow!
Awake and tell thy dream.   [Disappears.

PER. Celestial Dian, goddess argentine,
I will obey thee. Helicanus!

Re-enter HELICANUS, LYSIMACHUS, MARINA, &c.

HEL.   Sir?

PER. My purpose was for Tharsus, there to strike   250
The inhospitable Cleon; but I am
For other service first: toward Ephesus
Turn our blown sails; eftsoons I'll tell thee why.
[To LYSIMACHUS.] Shall we refresh us, sir, upon your shore,
And give you gold for such provision   255
As our intents will need?

LYS. Sir,
With all my heart; and when you come ashore
I have another suit.

PER.   You shall prevail,
Were it to woo my daughter; for it seems   260
You have been noble towards her.

LYS. Sir, lend me your arm.

PER. Come, my Marina.   [Exeunt.

SCENE II. *Ephesus. Before the Temple of Diana.*

Enter GOWER.

GOW. Now our sands are almost run ;
   More a little, and then dumb.
   This, my last boon, give me,
   For such kindness must relieve me—
   That you aptly will suppose   5
   What pageantry, what feats, what shows,
   What minstrelsy, and pretty din,
   The regent made in Mytilen
   To greet the King. So he thrived,
   That he is promis'd to be wived   10
   To fair Marina ; but in no wise
   Till he had done his sacrifice,
   As Dian bade ; whereto being bound,
   The interim, pray you, all confound.
   In feather'd briefness sails are fill'd,   15
   And wishes fall out as they're will'd.
   At Ephesus the temple see,
   Our king, and all his company.
   That he can hither come so soon,
   Is by your fancies' thankful boon.   [*Exit*

SCENE III. *Ephesus. The Temple of Diana ;* THAISA *standing near
the altar as High Priestess ; a number of* VIRGINS *on each side ;*
CERIMON *and other* INHABITANTS *of Ephesus attending.*

Enter PERICLES, *with his* TRAIN ; LYSIMACHUS, HELICANUS, MARINA,
and a LADY.

PER. Hail, Dian ! to perform thy just command,
   I here confess myself the King of Tyre ;
   Who, frighted from my country, did wed
   At Pentapolis the fair Thaisa.
   At sea in childbed died she, but brought forth   5
   A maid-child, call'd Marina ; who, O goddess,
   Wears yet thy silver livery. She at Tharsus
   Was nurs'd with Cleon ; who at fourteen years
   He sought to murder ; but her better stars
   Brought her to Mytilene ; 'gainst whose shore   10
   Riding, her fortunes brought the maid aboard us,
   Where, by her own most clear remembrance, she
   Made known herself my daughter.
THAI.   Voice and favour !
   You are, you are—O royal Pericles !   [*Swoons.*
PER. What means the nun ? She dies ! Help, gentlemen !   15
CER. Noble sir,
   If you have told Diana's altar true,
   This is your wife.
PER.   Reverend appearer, no ;
   I threw her o'erboard with these very arms.
CER. Upon this coast, I warrant you.
PER.   'Tis most certain.   20

366

CER. Look to the lady.   O, she's but overjoy'd.
    Early in blustering morn this lady was
    Thrown upon this shore.   I op'd the coffin,
    Found there rich jewels ; recover'd her, and plac'd her
    Here in Diana's temple.
PER.   May we see them ?   25
CER. Great sir, they shall be brought you to my house,
    Whither I invite you.   Look, Thaisa is
    Recovered.
THAI.   O, let me look !
    If he be none of mine, my sanctity   30
    Will to my sense bend no licentious ear,
    But curb it, spite of seeing.   O, my lord,
    Are you not Pericles ?   Like him you spake,
    Like him you are.   Did you not name a tempest,
    A birth and death ?
PER.   The voice of dead Thaisa !   35
THAI. That Thaisa am I, supposed dead
    And drown'd.
PER.   Immortal Dian !
THAI.   Now I know you better.
    When we with tears parted Pentapolis,
    The King my father gave you such a ring   [Shows a ring.
PER. This, this !   No more, you gods ! your present kindness   41
    Makes my past miseries sports.   You shall do well
    That on the touching of her lips I may
    Melt and no more be seen.   O, come, be buried
    A second time within these arms !
MAR.   My heart   45
    Leaps to be gone into my mother's bosom.   [Kneels to THAISA.
PER. Look who kneels here !   Flesh of thy flesh, Thaisa ;
    Thy burden at the sea, and call'd Marina,
    For she was yielded there.
THAI.   Blest and mine own !
HEL. Hail, madam, and my queen !
THAI.   I know you not.   50
PER. You have heard me say, when I did fly from Tyre,
    I left behind an ancient substitute.
    Can you remember what I call'd the man ?
    I have nam'd him oft.
THAI.   'Twas Helicanus then.
PER. Still confirmation.   55
    Embrace him, dear Thaisa ; this is he.
    Now do I long to hear how you were found ;
    How possibly preserv'd ; and who to thank,
    Besides the gods, for this great miracle.
THAI. Lord Cerimon, my lord—this man   60
    Through whom the gods have shown their power—that can
    From first to last resolve you.
PER.   Reverend sir,
    The gods can have no mortal officer
    More like a god than you.   Will you deliver
    How this dead queen re-lives ?
CER.   I will, my lord.   65

Beseech you, first, go with me to my house,
Where shall be shown you all was found with her ;
How she came plac'd here in the temple ;
No needful thing omitted.

PER. Pure Dian, bless thee for thy vision ! I   70
Will offer night-oblations to thee. Thaisa,
This Prince, the fair-betrothed of your daughter,
Shall marry her at Pentapolis. And now,
This ornament
Makes me look dismal will I clip to form ;   75
And what this fourteen years no razor touch'd,
To grace thy marriage-day I'll beautify.

THAI. Lord Cerimon hath letters of good credit, sir,
My father's dead.

PER. Heavens make a star of him ! Yet there, my queen,   80
We'll celebrate their nuptials, and ourselves
Will in that kingdom spend our following days.
Our son and daughter shall in Tyrus reign.
Lord Cerimon, we do our longing stay
To hear the rest untold. Sir, lead's the way. [*Exeunt.*

Enter GOWER.

GOW. In Antiochus and his daughter you have heard
Of monstrous lust the due and just reward :
In Pericles, his queen, and daughter, seen,
Although assail'd with fortune fierce and keen,
Virtue preserv'd from fell destruction's blast,   90
Led on by heaven, and crown'd with joy at last.
In Helicanus may you well descry
A figure of truth, of faith, of loyalty ;
In reverend Cerimon there well appears
The worth that learned charity aye wears.   95
For wicked Cleon and his wife, when fame
Had spread their cursed deed, and honour'd name
Of Pericles, to rage the city turn,
That him and they in his palace burn ;
The gods for murder seemed so content   100
To punish—although not done, but meant.
So, on your patience evermore attending,
New joy wait on you ! Here our play has ending. [*Exit.*

POEMS

VENUS AND ADONIS
THE RAPE OF LUCRECE

Venus and Adonis is Shakespeare's first published work. In his dedication to the Earl of Southampton Shakespeare calls it ' the first heir of my invention '. As we know, from what Greene and Chettle had to say about Shakespeare in 1592, that the dramatist was already well known for ' his facetious grace in writing ', some have argued that Shakespeare must have composed this poem while still at Stratford and before his ventures on the London stage. But references in the poem itself show that it was composed by one already familiar with London and its theatres and the expression ' first heir ' need mean no more than his first published piece. This interpretation not merely squares with the London references in the poem but fits the circumstances in the theatrical world at the time of its composition. A very severe outbreak of plague closed the London theatres from June to December 1592, there being over ten thousand deaths from this cause in the city; in 1593 there was again a break in acting from April to December. These blank periods in the business of the theatre would provide Shakespeare with the opportunity to write his poems, and allow him the leisure to see them through the press, an attention he bestowed only on these two of his publications. This accords with the date of publication of *Lucrece* as well as *Venus and Adonis: Venus and Adonis* was entered in the Stationers' Register on 18 April 1593 and *Lucrece* on 9 May 1594; the quartos that followed these entries are dated 1593 and 1594 respectively.

Shakespeare had also at this time a special incentive to publish compositions of this kind. Greene in his attack on Shakespeare had implied that he was a much overrated playwright, a base player challenging better pens in a business he should leave to Greene and his University friends. *Venus and Adonis* was the complete answer to all such insinuations : at least eight editions were called for in the next ten years, and the claim that Shakespeare made in the modesty of a dead language, for he took his motto from the *Amores* of Ovid,

> Vilia miretur vulgus : mihi flavus Apollo
> Pocula Castalia plena ministret aqua. [1]

was acknowledged by the reading world.

Had there been critics who disapproved of the subject of *Venus and Adonis* and felt it unworthy of a serious poet, *Lucrece*, which followed the next year, would leave no doubts about the poet's standing. As Gabriel Harvey noted, while the younger sort took much delight in *Venus and Adonis* the matter of *Lucrece* could please the wiser sort.

---

[1] In Marlowe's rendering
>   Let base-conceited wits admire vile things,
>   Fair Phœbus lead me to the Muses' springs

Both *Venus and Adonis* and *Lucrece* were printed by Richard Field, a Stratford man, whom Shakespeare must have known as a boy at Stratford.

Shakespeare dedicated both poems to the Earl of Southampton ; the second letter of dedication being framed in terms that show that Southampton must have welcomed Shakespeare's address. South-ampton was in his twentieth year in 1593 ; he had wealth and good looks, but as he was to show later he was not content to enjoy a life of ease ; that he took Essex as his model was in some ways unfortunate, for although Essex was no doubt a model of courage he did not set an example of discretion, and Southampton found himself, after the foolish demonstration in London in 1601, condemned to death with his leader. Only the Queen's clemency saved Southampton from the block. Southampton is the choice of some commentators for the part of the ' fair youth ' of the *Sonnets* ; and the poet is thought to have recorded the release of Southampton from prison by James in the hundred and seventh sonnet :

> Not mine own fears, nor the prophetic soul
> Of the wide world dreaming on things to come
> Can yet the lease of my true love control,
> Suppos'd as forfeit to a confin'd doom.

There is however no agreement on the interpretation of the line that follows :

> The mortal moon hath her eclipse endur'd.

Those who feel Shakespeare is speaking of Southampton's release regard this as a reference to the death of Elizabeth ; while Dr. Hotson dates the sonnet some fifteen years earlier and regards the ' mortal moon ' as referring to the crescent formation of the Armada ; to which some object that only at the full can the moon be eclipsed.

The poems Shakespeare wrote were on the kind of classical themes that were then popular. For *Venus and Adonis* he turned to Ovid, taking the encounter between Venus and Adonis from Book X of the *Metamorphoses*, but drawing details of the manner from the story of the passion of Salmacis for Hermaphroditus in Book IV. A boy from any grammar school would be familiar with some Ovid in the original and there is every reason to regard Shakespeare as well grounded in that author. He was familiar with Golding's translation, as his description of the lines describing the fatal boar make clear, as well as with Brooke's adaptation of the boar passage in his *Romeus and Juliet*, but even here he had Ovid in the original before him. *Lucrece* is a more ambitious blend of classical sources, including Ovid, Livy, and Virgil.

These poems, as Coleridge observed, are sufficient by themselves to dispose of the notion that Shakespeare was a mere child of nature or *automaton* of genius. They are so obviously carefully studied and wrought that the art that has gone to their making is not concealed as in his greatest triumphs ; even therefore to those who cannot fully enjoy their qualities these poems have a special interest for the admirer of the plays.

VENUS AND ADONIS

Vilia miretur vulgus : mihi flavus Apollo
Pocula Castalia plena ministret aqua.

TO THE
RIGHT HONORABLE HENRIE WRIOTHESLEY,
EARLE OF SOUTHAMPTON, AND BARON OF TITCHFIELD.

RIGHT HONOURABLE,

I KNOW not how I shall offend in dedicating my unpolisht lines
to your Lordship, nor how the worlde will censure mee for choosing
so strong a proppe to support so weake a burthen, onelye if your
Honour seeme but pleased, I account my selfe highly praised, and
vowe to take advantage of all idle houres, till I have honoured you
with some graver labour. But if the first heire of my invention
prove deformed, I shall be sorie it had so noble a god-father : and
never after eare so barren a land, for feare it yeeld me still so bad
a harvest, I leave it to your Honourable survey, and your Honor
to your hearts content which I wish may alwaies answere your owne
wish, and the worlds hopefull expectation.

Your Honors in all dutie,
WILLIAM SHAKESPEARE.

EVEN as the sun with purple-colour'd face
Had ta'en his last leave of the weeping morn,
Rose-cheek'd Adonis hied him to the chase ;
Hunting he lov'd, but love he laugh'd to scorn.
 Sick-thoughted Venus makes amain unto him,   5
 And like a bold-fac'd suitor gins to woo him.

' Thrice fairer than myself,' thus she began,
' The field's chief flower, sweet above compare,
Stain to all nymphs, more lovely than a man,
More white and red than doves or roses are ;   10
 Nature that made thee, with herself at strife,
 Saith that the world hath ending with thy life.

' Vouchsafe, thou wonder, to alight thy steed,
And rein his proud head to the saddle-bow ;
If thou wilt deign this favour, for thy meed   15
A thousand honey secrets shalt thou know.
 Here come and sit, where never serpent hisses,
 And being set, I'll smother thee with kisses ;

' And yet not cloy thy lips with loath'd satiety,
But rather famish them amid their plenty,   20
Making them red and pale with fresh variety—
Ten kisses short as one, one long as twenty.
 A summer's day will seem an hour but short,
 Being wasted in such time-beguiling sport.'

373

With this she seizeth on his sweating palm,   25
The precedent of pith and livelihood,
And, trembling in her passion, calls it balm,
Earth's sovereign salve to do a goddess good.
    Being so enrag'd, desire doth lend her force
    Courageously to pluck him from his horse.   30

Over one arm the lusty courser's rein,
Under her other was the tender boy,
Who blush'd and pouted in a dull disdain,
With leaden appetite, unapt to toy ;
    She red and hot as coals of glowing fire,   35
    He red for shame, but frosty in desire.

The studded bridle on a ragged bough
Nimbly she fastens—O, how quick is love !
The steed is stalled up, and even now
To tie the rider she begins to prove :   40
    Backward she push'd him, as she would be thrust,
    And govern'd him in strength, though not in lust.

So soon was she along as he was down,
Each leaning on their elbows and their hips ;
Now doth she stroke his cheek, now doth he frown,   45
And gins to chide, but soon she stops his lips,
    And kissing speaks, with lustful language broken :
    ' If thou wilt chide, thy lips shall never open '.

He burns with bashful shame ; she with her tears
Doth quench the maiden burning of his cheeks ;   50
Then with her windy sighs and golden hairs
To fan and blow them dry again she seeks.
He saith she is immodest, blames her miss ;
    What follows more she murders with a kiss.

Even as an empty eagle, sharp by fast,   55
Tires with her beak on feathers, flesh, and bone,
Shaking her wings, devouring all in haste,
Till either gorge be stuff'd, or prey be gone ;
    Even so she kiss'd his brow, his cheek, his chin,
    And where she ends she doth anew begin.   60

Forc'd to content, but never to obey,
Panting he lies and breatheth in her face ;
She feedeth on the steam as on a prey,
And calls it heavenly moisture, air of grace,
    Wishing her cheeks were gardens full of flowers,   65
    So they were dew'd with such distilling showers.

Look how a bird lies tangled in a net,
So fast'ned in her arms Adonis lies ;
Pure shame and aw'd resistance made him fret,
Which bred more beauty in his angry eyes.   70
    Rain added to a river that is rank
    Perforce will force it overflow the bank.

Still she entreats, and prettily entreats,
For to a pretty ear she tunes her tale ;
Still is he sullen, still he lours and frets,   75
'Twixt crimson shame and anger ashy-pale ;
    Being red, she loves him best ; and being white,
    Her best is better'd with a more delight.

Look how he can, she cannot choose but love ;
And by her fair immortal hand she swears   80
From his soft bosom never to remove
Till he take truce with her contending tears,
    Which long have rain'd, making her cheeks all wet;
    And one sweet kiss shall pay this countless debt.

Upon this promise did he raise his chin,   85
Like a dive-dapper peering through a wave,
Who, being look'd on, ducks as quickly in ;
So offers he to give what she did crave ;
    But when her lips were ready for his pay,
    He winks, and turns his lips another way.   90

Never did passenger in summer's heat
More thirst for drink than she for this good turn :
Her help she sees, but help she cannot get ;
She bathes in water, yet her fire must burn.
    ' O, pity,' gan she cry ' flint-hearted boy !   95
    'Tis but a kiss I beg ; why art thou coy ?

' I have been wooed, as I entreat thee now,
Even by the stern and direful god of war,
Whose sinewy neck in battle ne'er did bow,
Who conquers where he comes in every jar ;   100
    Yet hath he been my captive and my slave,
    And begg'd for that which thou unask'd shalt have.

' Over my altars hath he hung his lance,
His batt'red shield, his uncontrolled crest,
And for my sake hath learn'd to sport and dance,   105
To toy, to wanton, dally, smile, and jest,
    Scorning his churlish drum and ensign red,
    Making my arms his field, his tent my bed.

' Thus he that overrul'd I overswayed,
Leading him prisoner in a red-rose chain ;   110
Strong-temper'd steel his stronger strength obeyed,
Yet was he servile to my coy disdain.
    O, be not proud, nor brag not of thy might,
    For mast'ring her that foil'd the god of fight !

' Touch but my lips with those fair lips of thine ;   115
Though mine be not so fair, yet are they red—
The kiss shall be thine own as well as mine.
What seest thou in the ground ? Hold up thy head ;
    Look in mine eyeballs ; there thy beauty lies.
    Then why not lips on lips, since eyes in eyes ?   120

'Art thou asham'd to kiss? Then wink again,
And I will wink; so shall the day seem night.
Love keeps his revels where there are but twain;
Be bold to play; our sport is not in sight.
   These blue-vein'd violets whereon we lean   125
   Never can blab, nor know not what we mean.

'The tender spring upon thy tempting lip
Shows thee unripe; yet mayst thou well be tasted
Make use of time, let not advantage slip;
Beauty within itself should not be wasted.   130
   Fair flowers that are not gath'red in their prime
   Rot and consume themselves in little time.

'Were I hard-favour'd, foul, or wrinkled-old,
Ill-nurtur'd, crooked, churlish, harsh in voice,
O'er-worn, despised, rheumatic, and cold,   135
Thick-sighted, barren, lean, and lacking juice,
   Then mightst thou pause, for then I were not for thee;
   But having no defects, why dost abhor me?

'Thou canst not see one wrinkle in my brow;
Mine eyes are grey, and bright, and quick in turning;   140
My beauty as the spring doth yearly grow,
My flesh is soft and plump, my marrow burning;
   My smooth moist hand, were it with thy hand felt,
   Would in thy palm dissolve or seem to melt.

'Bid me discourse, I will enchant thine ear,   145
Or, like a fairy, trip upon the green,
Or, like a nymph, with long dishevelled hair,
Dance on the sands, and yet no footing seen.
   Love is a spirit all compact of fire,
   Not gross to sink, but light, and will aspire.   150

'Witness this primrose bank whereon I lie:
These forceless flowers like sturdy trees support me;
Two strengthless doves will draw me through the sky
From morn till night, even where I list to sport me.
   Is love so light, sweet boy, and may it be   155
   That thou should think it heavy unto thee?

'Is thine own heart to thine own face affected?
Can thy right hand seize love upon thy left?
Then woo thyself, be of thyself rejected;
Steal thine own freedom, and complain on theft.   160
   Narcissus so himself himself forsook,
   And died to kiss his shadow in the brook.

'Torches are made to light, jewels to wear,
Dainties to taste, fresh beauty for the use,
Herbs for their smell, and sappy plants to bear: 165
Things growing to themselves are growth's abuse.
   Seeds spring from seeds, and beauty breedeth beauty;
   Thou wast begot—to get it is thy duty.

'Upon the earth's increase why shouldst thou feed,
Unless the earth with thy increase be fed?
By law of nature thou art bound to breed,   170
That thine may live when thou thyself art dead;
    And so in spite of death thou dost survive,
    In that thy likeness still is left alive.'

By this the love-sick queen began to sweat,   175
For where they lay the shadow had forsook them,
And Titan, tired in the mid-day heat,
With burning eye did hotly overlook them;
    Wishing Adonis had his team to guide,
    So he were like him, and by Venus' side.   180

And now Adonis, with a lazy sprite,
And with a heavy, dark, disliking eye,
His louring brows o'erwhelming his fair sight,
Like misty vapours when they blot the sky,
    Souring his cheeks, cries 'Fie, no more of love!   185
    The sun doth burn my face; I must remove'.

'Ay me,' quoth Venus 'young, and so unkind!
What bare excuses mak'st thou to be gone!
I'll sigh celestial breath, whose gentle wind
Shall cool the heat of this descending sun;   190
    I'll make a shadow for thee of my hairs;
    If they burn too, I'll quench them with my tears.

'The sun that shines from heaven shines but warm,
And lo, I lie between that sun and thee;
The heat I have from thence doth little harm;   195
Thine eye darts forth the fire that burneth me;
    And were I not immortal, life were done
    Between this heavenly and earthly sun.

'Art thou obdurate, flinty, hard as steel?
Nay, more than flint, for stone at rain relenteth.   200
Art thou a woman's son, and canst not feel
What 'tis to love? how want of love tormenteth?
    O, had thy mother borne so hard a mind,
    She had not brought forth thee, but died unkind!

'What am I, that thou shouldst contemn me this?   205
Or what great danger dwells upon my suit?
What were thy lips the worse for one poor kiss?
Speak, fair; but speak fair words, or else be mute.
    Give me one kiss; I'll give it thee again,
    And one for int'rest, if thou wilt have twain.   210

'Fie, lifeless picture, cold and senseless stone,
Well-painted idol, image dull and dead,
Statue contenting but the eye alone,
Thing like a man, but of no woman bred!
    Thou art no man, though of a man's complexion,   215
    For men will kiss even by their own direction.'

377

This said, impatience chokes her pleading tongue,
And swelling passion doth provoke a pause ;
Red cheeks and fiery eyes blaze forth her wrong ;
Being judge in love, she cannot right her cause ;　　　　220
    And now she weeps, and now she fain would speak,
    And now her sobs do her intendments break.

Sometime she shakes her head, and then his hand;
Now gazeth she on him, now on the ground ;
Sometime her arms infold him like a band ;　　　　225
She would, he will not in her arms be bound ;
    And when from thence he struggles to be gone,
    She locks her lily fingers one in one.

' Fondling,' she saith ' since I have hemm'd thee here
Within the circuit of this ivory pale,　　　　230
I'll be a park, and thou shalt be my deer ;
Feed where thou wilt, on mountain or in dale ;
    Graze on my lips ; and if those hills be dry,
    Stray lower, where the pleasant fountains lie.

' Within this limit is relief enough,　　　　235
Sweet bottom-grass, and high delightful plain,
Round rising hillocks, brakes obscure and rough,
To shelter thee from tempest and from rain ;
    Then be my deer, since I am such a park ;
    No dog shall rouse thee, though a thousand bark.'　　　　240

At this Adonis smiles as in disdain,
That in each cheek appears a pretty dimple.
Love made those hollows, if himself were slain,
He might be buried in a tomb so simple ;
    Foreknowing well, if there he came to lie,　　　　245
    Why, there Love liv'd and there he could not die.

These lovely caves, these round enchanting pits,
Open'd their mouths to swallow Venus' liking.
Being mad before, how doth she now for wits ?
Struck dead at first, what needs a second striking ?　　　　250
    Poor queen of love, in thine own law forlorn,
    To love a cheek that smiles at thee in scorn !

Now which way shall she turn ?　What shall she say ?
Her words are done, her woes the more increasing ;
The time is spent, her object will away,　　　　255
And from her twining arms doth urge releasing.
    ' Pity ! ' she cries ' Some favour, some remorse ! '
    Away he springs, and hasteth to his horse.

But, lo, from forth a copse that neighbours by,
A breeding jennet, lusty, young, and proud,　　　　260
Adonis' trampling courser doth espy,
And forth she rushes, snorts, and neighs aloud ;
    The strong-neck'd steed, being tied unto a tree,
    Breaketh his rein, and to her straight goes he.

Imperiously he leaps, he neighs, he bounds, 265
And now his woven girths he breaks asunder ;
The bearing earth with his hard hoof he wounds,
Whose hollow womb resounds like heaven's thunder ;
   The iron bit he crusheth 'tween his teeth,
   Controlling what he was controlled with. 270

His ears up-prick'd ; his braided hanging mane
Upon his compass'd crest now stand on end ;
His nostrils drink the air, and forth again,
As from a furnace, vapours doth he send ;
   His eye, which scornfully glisters like fire, 275
   Shows his hot courage and his high desire.

Sometime he trots, as if he told the steps,
With gentle majesty and modest pride ;
Anon he rears upright, curvets, and leaps,
As who should say ' Lo, thus my strength is tried, 280
   And this I do to captivate the eye
   Of the fair breeder that is standing by '.

What recketh he his rider's angry stir,
His flattering ' Holla ' or his ' Stand, I say ' ?
What cares he now for curb, or pricking spur ? 285
For rich caparisons, or trappings gay ?
   He sees his love, and nothing else he sees,
   Nor nothing else with his proud sight agrees.

Look when a painter would surpass the life
In limning out a well-proportioned steed, 290
His art with nature's workmanship at strife,
As if the dead the living should exceed ;
   So did this horse excel a common one
   In shape, in courage, colour, pace, and bone.

Round-hoof'd, short-jointed, fetlocks shag and long, 295
Broad breast, full eye, small head, and nostril wide,
High crest, short ears, straight legs and passing strong,
Thin mane, thick tail, broad buttock, tender hide ;
   Look what a horse should have he did not lack,
   Save a proud rider on so proud a back. 300

Sometime he scuds far off, and there he stares ;
Anon he starts at stirring of a feather ;
To bid the wind a base he now prepares,
And whe'r he run or fly they know not whether ;
   For through his mane and tail the high wind sings, 305
   Fanning the hairs, who wave like feath'red wings.

He looks upon his love and neighs unto her ;
She answers him as if she knew his mind ;
Being proud, as females are, to see him woo her,
She puts on outward strangeness, seems unkind, 310
   Spurns at his love, and scorns the heat he feels,
   Beating his kind embracements with her heels.

Then, like a melancholy malcontent,
He vails his tail, that, like a falling plume,
Cool shadow to his melting buttock lent ;   315
He stamps, and bites the poor flies in his fume.
   His love, perceiving how he was enrag'd,
   Grew kinder, and his fury was assuag'd.

His testy master goeth about to take him,
When, lo, the unback'd breeder, full of fear,   320
Jealous of catching, swiftly doth forsake him,
With her the horse, and left Adonis there.
   As they were mad, unto the wood they hie them,
   Out-stripping crows that strive to overfly them.

All swol'n with chafing, down Adonis sits,   325
Banning his boist'rous and unruly beast ;
And now the happy season once more fits
That love-sick Love by pleading may be blest ;
   For lovers say the heart hath treble wrong,
   When it is barr'd the aidance of the tongue.   330

An oven that is stopp'd, or river stay'd,
Burneth more hotly, swelleth with more rage ;
So of concealed sorrow may be said :
Free vent of words love's fire doth assuage ;
   But when the heart's attorney once is mute,   335
   The client breaks, as desperate in his suit.

He sees her coming, and begins to glow
Even as a dying coal revives with wind,
And with his bonnet hides his angry brow,
Looks on the dull earth with disturbed mind,   340
   Taking no notice that she is so nigh,
   For all askance he holds her in his eye.

O what a sight it was, wistly to view
How she came stealing to the wayward boy !
To note the fighting conflict of her hue !   345
How white and red each other did destroy !
   But now her cheek was pale, and by and by
   It flash'd forth fire, as lightning from the sky.

Now was she just before him as he sat,
And like a lowly lover down she kneels ;   350
With one fair hand she heaveth up his hat,
Her other tender hand his fair cheek feels ;
   His tend'rer cheek receives her soft hand's print
   As apt as new-fall'n snow takes any dint.

O, what a war of looks was then between them,   355
Her eyes, petitioners, to his eyes suing !
His eyes saw her eyes as they had not seen them ;
Her eyes wooed still, his eyes disdain'd the wooing ;
   And all this dumb play had his acts made plain
   With tears which chorus-like her eyes did rain.   360

Full gently now she takes him by the hand,
A lily prison'd in a gaol of snow,
Or ivory in an alabaster band ;
So white a friend engirts so white a foe.
    This beauteous combat, wilful and unwilling, 365
    Showed like two silver doves that sit a-billing.

Once more the engine of her thoughts began :
' O fairest mover on this mortal round,
Would thou wert as I am, and I a man,
My heart all whole as thine, thy heart my wound ! 370
    For one sweet look thy help I would assure thee,
    Though nothing but my body's bane would cure thee '.

' Give me my hand ' saith he. ' Why dost thou feel it ? '
' Give me my heart,' saith she ' and thou shalt have it.
O, give it me, lest thy hard heart do steel it, 375
And being steel'd, soft sighs can never grave it ;
    Then love's deep groans I never shall regard,
    Because Adonis' heart hath made mine hard.'

' For shame,' he cries ' let go, and let me go ;
My day's delight is past, my horse is gone, 380
And 'tis your fault I am bereft him so.
I pray you hence, and leave me here alone ;
    For all my mind, my thought, my busy care,
    Is how to get my palfrey from the mare.'

Thus she replies : ' Thy palfrey, as he should, 385
Welcomes the warm approach of sweet desire.
Affection is a coal that must be cool'd ;
Else, suffer'd, it will set the heart on fire.
    The sea hath bounds, but deep desire hath none,
    Therefore no marvel though thy horse be gone. 390

' How like a jade he stood, tied to the tree,
Servilely master'd with a leathern rein !
But when he saw his love, his youth's fair fee,
He held such petty bondage in disdain,
    Throwing the base thong from his bending crest, 395
    Enfranchising his mouth, his back, his breast.

' Who sees his true-love in her naked bed,
Teaching the sheets a whiter hue than white,
But, when his glutton eye so full hath fed,
His other agents aim at like delight ? 400
    Who is so faint that dares not be so bold
    To touch the fire, the weather being cold ?

' Let me excuse thy courser, gentle boy ;
And learn of him, I heartily beseech thee,
To take advantage on presented joy ; 405
Though I were dumb, yet his proceedings teach thee.
    O, learn to love ! The lesson is but plain,
    And once made perfect never lost again '.

' I know not love,' quoth he ' nor will not know it,
Unless it be a boar, and then I chase it.   410
'Tis much to borrow, and I will not owe it.
My love to love is love but to disgrace it ;
    For I have heard it is a life in death,
    That laughs, and weeps, and all but with a breath.

' Who wears a garment shapeless and unfinish'd ?   415
Who plucks the bud before one leaf put forth ?
If springing things be any jot diminish'd,
They wither in their prime, prove nothing worth.
    The colt that's back'd and burden'd being young
    Loseth his pride and never waxeth strong.   420

' You hurt my hand with wringing ; let us part,
And leave this idle theme, this bootless chat ;
Remove your siege from my unyielding heart ;
To love's alarms it will not ope the gate.
    Dismiss your vows, your feigned tears, your flatt'ry ;
    For where a heart is hard they make no batt'ry.'   425

' What ! canst thou talk ? ' quoth she ' Hast thou a tongue ?
O, would thou hadst not, or I had no hearing !
Thy mermaid's voice hath done me double wrong ;
I had my load before, now press'd with bearing :   430
    Melodious discord, heavenly tune harsh sounding,
    Ear's deep-sweet music, and heart's deep-sore wounding.

' Had I no eyes but ears, my ears would love
That inward beauty and invisible ;
Or were I deaf, thy outward parts would move   435
Each part in me that were but sensible.
    Though neither eyes nor ears, to hear nor see,
    Yet should I be in love by touching thee.

' Say that the sense of feeling were bereft me,
And that I could not see, nor hear, nor touch,   440
And nothing but the very smell were left me,
Yet would my love to thee be still as much ;
    For from the stillitory of thy face excelling
    Comes breath perfum'd, that breedeth love by smelling.

' But, O, what banquet wert thou to the taste,   445
Being nurse and feeder of the other four !
Would they not wish the feast might ever last,
And bid Suspicion double-lock the door,
    Lest Jealousy, that sour unwelcome guest,
    Should by his stealing in disturb the feast ? '   450

Once more the ruby-colour'd portal open'd
Which to his speech did honey passage yield ;
Like a red morn, that ever yet betoken'd
Wreck to the seaman, tempest to the field,
    Sorrow to shepherds, woe unto the birds,   455
    Gusts and foul flaws to herdmen and to herds.

This ill presage advisedly she marketh.
Even as the wind is hush'd before it raineth,
Or as the wolf doth grin before he barketh,
Or as the berry breaks before it staineth,   460
  Or like the deadly bullet of a gun,
  His meaning struck her ere his words begun.

And at his look she flatly falleth down,
For looks kill love, and love by looks reviveth;
A smile recures the wounding of a frown.
But blessed bankrupt that by love so thriveth!   465
  The silly boy, believing she is dead,
  Claps her pale cheek till clapping makes it red;

And all-amaz'd brake off his late intent,
For sharply he did think to reprehend her,
Which cunning love did wittily prevent.   470
Fair fall the wit that can so well defend her!
  For on the grass she lies as she were slain,
  Till his breath breatheth life in her again.

He wrings her nose, he strikes her on the cheeks,   475
He bends her fingers, holds her pulses hard.
He chafes her lips, a thousand ways he seeks
To mend the hurt that his unkindness marr'd;
  He kisses her; and she, by her good will,
  Will never rise, so he will kiss her still.   480

The night of sorrow now is turn'd to day:
Her two blue windows faintly she upheaveth,
Like the fair sun when in his fresh array
He cheers the morn and all the earth relieveth;
  And as the bright sun glorifies the sky,   485
  So is her face illumin'd with her eye;

Whose beams upon his hairless face are fix'd,
As if from thence they borrowed all their shine.
Were never four such lamps together mix'd,
Had not his clouded with his brows' repine;   490
  But hers, which through the crystal tears gave light,
  Shone like the moon in water seen by night.

'O, where am I?' quoth she 'in earth or heaven,
Or in the ocean drench'd, or in the fire?
What hour is this? or morn, or weary even?   495
Do I delight to die, or life desire?
  But now I liv'd, and life was death's annoy;
  But now I died, and death was lively joy.

'O, thou didst kill me! Kill me once again.
Thy eyes' shrewd tutor, that hard heart of thine,   500
Hath taught them scornful tricks, and such disdain
That they have murd'red this poor heart of mine;
  And these mine eyes, true leaders to their queen,
  But for thy piteous lips no more had seen.

' Long may they kiss each other, for this cure !   505
O, never let their crimson liveries wear !
And as they last, their verdure still endure,
To drive infection from the dangerous year !
  That the star-gazers, having writ on death,
  May say the plague is banish'd by thy breath.   510

' Pure lips, sweet seals in my soft lips imprinted,
What bargains may I make, still to be sealing ?
To sell myself I can be well contented,
So thou wilt buy, and pay, and use good dealing ;
  Which purchase if thou make, for fear of slips   515
  Set thy seal manual on my wax-red lips.

' A thousand kisses buys my heart from me ;
And pay them at thy leisure, one by one.
What is ten hundred touches unto thee ?
Are they not quickly told, and quickly gone ?   520
  Say for non-payment that the debt should double,
  Is twenty hundred kisses such a trouble ? '

' Fair queen,' quoth he ' if any love you owe me,
Measure my strangeness with my unripe years ;
Before I know myself, seek not to know me ;   525
No fisher but the ungrown fry forbears.
  The mellow plum doth fall, the green sticks fast,
  Or being early pluck'd is sour to taste.

' Look, the world's comforter, with weary gait,
His day's hot task hath ended in the west ;   530
The owl, night's herald, shrieks ; 'tis very late ;
The sheep are gone to fold, birds to their nest ;
  And coal-black clouds that shadow heaven's light
  Do summon us to part and bid good night.

' Now let me say " good night ", and so say you ;   535
If you will say so, you shall have a kiss.'
' Good night ' quoth she ; and, ere he says ' adieu ',
The honey fee of parting tend'red is :
  Her arms do lend his neck a sweet embrace ;
  Incorporate then they seem ; face grows to face.   540

Till, breathless, he disjoin'd, and backward drew
The heavenly moisture, that sweet coral mouth,
Whose precious taste her thirsty lips well knew,
Whereon they surfeit, yet complain on drouth.
  He with her plenty press'd, she faint with dearth,   545
  Their lips together glued, fall to the earth.

Now quick desire hath caught the yielding prey,
And glutton-like she feeds, yet never filleth ;
Her lips are conquerors, his lips obey,
Paying what ransom the insulter willeth ;   550
  Whose vulture thought doth pitch the price so high
  That she will draw his lips' rich treasure dry.

And having felt the sweetness of the spoil,
With blindfold fury she begins to forage;
Her face doth reek and smoke, her blood doth boil,   555
And careless lust stirs up a desperate courage;
    Planting oblivion, beating reason back,
    Forgetting shame's pure blush, and honour's wrack.

Hot, faint, and weary, with her hard embracing,
Like a wild bird being tam'd with too much handling,   560
Or as the fleet-foot roe that's tir'd with chasing,
Or like the froward infant still'd with dandling,
    He now obeys and now no more resisteth,
    While she takes all she can, not all she listeth.

What wax so frozen but dissolves with temp'ring,   565
And yields at last to every light impression?
Things out of hope are compass'd oft with vent'ring,
Chiefly in love, whose leave exceeds commission.
    Affection faints not like a pale-fac'd coward,
    But then wooes best when most his choice is froward.   570

When he did frown, O, had she then gave over,
Such nectar from his lips she had not suck'd.
Foul words and frowns must not repel a lover;
What though the rose have prickles, yet 'tis pluck'd.
    Were beauty under twenty locks kept fast,   575
    Yet love breaks through and picks them all at last.

For pity now she can no more detain him;
The poor fool prays her that he may depart.
She is resolv'd no longer to restrain him;
Bids him farewell, and look well to her heart,   580
    The which, by Cupid's bow she doth protest,
    He carries thence incaged in his breast.

'Sweet boy,' she says 'this night I'll waste in sorrow,
For my sick heart commands mine eyes to watch.
Tell me, love's master, shall we meet to-morrow?   585
Say, shall we? shall we? wilt thou make the match?'.
    He tells her no; to-morrow he intends
    To hunt the boar with certain of his friends.

'The boar!' quoth she, whereat a sudden pale,
Like lawn being spread upon the blushing rose,   590
Usurps her cheek; she trembles at his tale,
And on his neck her yoking arms she throws;
    She sinketh down, still hanging by his neck,
    He on her belly falls, she on her back.

Now is she in the very lists of love,   595
Her champion mounted for the hot encounter.
All is imaginary she doth prove;
He will not manage her, although he mount her.
    That worse than Tantalus' is her annoy,
    To clip Elysium and to lack her joy.   600

Even so poor birds, deceiv'd with painted grapes,
Do surfeit by the eye and pine the maw;
Even so she languisheth in her mishaps,
As those poor birds that helpless berries saw.
    The warm effects which she in him finds missing   60
    She seeks to kindle with continual kissing.

    But all in vain; good queen, it will not be.
She hath assay'd as much as may be prov'd;
Her pleading hath deserv'd a greater fee;
She's Love, she loves, and yet she is not lov'd.   61
    'Fie, fie,' he says 'you crush me; let me go;
    You have no reason to withhold me so.'

'Thou hadst been gone,' quoth she 'sweet boy, ere this,
But that thou told'st me thou wouldst hunt the boar.
O, be advis'd! Thou know'st not what it is   61
With javelin's point a churlish swine to gore,
    Whose tushes never sheath'd he whetteth still,
    Like to a mortal butcher bent to kill.

'On his bow-back he hath a battle set
Of bristly pikes that ever threat his foes;
His eyes like glow-worms shine when he doth fret;   62
His snout digs sepulchres where'er he goes;
    Being mov'd, he strikes whate'er is in his way,
    And whom he strikes his cruel tushes slay.

'His brawny sides, with hairy bristles armed,
Are better proof than thy spear's point can enter;   62
His short thick neck cannot be easily harmed;
Being ireful, on the lion he will venter.
    The thorny brambles and embracing bushes,
    As fearful of him, part; through whom he rushes.   63

'Alas, he nought esteems that face of thine,
To which Love's eyes pays tributary gazes;
Nor thy soft hands, sweet lips, and crystal eyne,
Whose full perfection all the world amazes;
    But having thee at vantage—wondrous dread!—   63
    Would root these beauties as he roots the mead.

'O, let him keep his loathsome cabin still!
Beauty hath nought to do with such foul fiends.
Come not within his danger by thy will.
They that thrive well take counsel of their friends.   64
    When thou didst name the boar, not to dissemble,
    I fear'd thy fortune, and my joints did tremble.

'Didst thou not mark my face? Was it not white?
Sawest thou not signs of fear lurk in mine eye?
Grew I not faint? And fell I not downright?   6.
Within my bosom, whereon thou dost lie,
    My boding heart pants, beats, and takes no rest,
    But, like an earthquake, shakes thee on my breast.

'For where Love reigns, disturbing Jealousy
Doth call himself Affection's sentinel ;   650
Gives false alarms, suggesteth mutiny,
And in a peaceful hour doth cry " Kill, kill ! "
 Distemp'ring gentle Love in his desire,
 As air and water do abate the fire.

'This sour informer, this bate-breeding spy,   655
This canker that eats up Love's tender spring,
This carry-tale, dissentious Jealousy,
That sometime true news, sometime false doth bring,
 Knocks at my heart, and whispers in mine ear,
 That if I love thee I thy death should fear ;   660

'And, more than so, presenteth to mine eye
The picture of an angry chafing boar,
Under whose sharp fangs on his back doth lie
An image like thyself, all stain'd with gore ;
 Whose blood upon the fresh flowers being shed   665
 Doth make them droop with grief and hang the head.

'What should I do, seeing thee so indeed,
That tremble at th' imagination ?
The thought of it doth make my faint heart bleed,
And fear doth teach it divination :   670
 I prophesy thy death, my living sorrow,
 If thou encounter with the boar to-morrow.

'But if thou needs wilt hunt, be rul'd by me ;
Uncouple at the timorous flying hare,
Or at the fox which lives by subtlety,   675
Or at the roe which no encounter dare.
 Pursue these fearful creatures o'er the downs,
 And on thy well-breath'd horse keep with thy hounds.

'And when thou hast on foot the purblind hare,
Mark the poor wretch, to overshoot his troubles,   680
How he outruns the wind, and with what care
He cranks and crosses with a thousand doubles.
 The many musits through the which he goes
 Are like a labyrinth to amaze his foes.

'Sometime he runs among a flock of sheep,   685
To make the cunning hounds mistake their smell,
And sometime where earth-delving conies keep,
To stop the loud pursuers in their yell ;
 And sometime sorteth with a herd of deer.
 Danger deviseth shifts ; wit waits on fear.   690

For there his smell with others being mingled,
The hot scent-snuffing hounds are driven to doubt,
Ceasing their clamorous cry till they have singled
With much ado the cold fault cleanly out.
 Then do they spend their mouths ; echo replies,   695
 As if another chase were in the skies.

'By this, poor Wat, far off upon a hill,
Stands on his hinder legs with list'ning ear,
To hearken if his foes pursue him still;
Anon their loud alarums he doth hear;
   And now his grief may be compared well
   To one sore sick that hears the passing-bell.

'Then shalt thou see the dew-bedabbled wretch
Turn and return, indenting with the way;
Each envious briar his weary legs do scratch,
Each shadow makes him stop, each murmur stay;
   For misery is trodden on by many,
   And being low never reliev'd by any.

'Lie quietly and hear a little more;
Nay, do not struggle, for thou shalt not rise.
To make thee hate the hunting of the boar,
Unlike myself thou hear'st me moralize,
   Applying this to that, and so to so;
   For love can comment upon every woe.

'Where did I leave?' 'No matter where;' quoth he
'Leave me, and then the story aptly ends.
The night is spent.' 'Why, what of that?' quoth she.
'I am,' quoth he 'expected of my friends;
   And now 'tis dark, and going I shall fall.'
   'In night,' quoth she 'desire sees best of all.'

'But if thou fall, O, then imagine this,
The earth in love with thee thy footing trips,
And all is but to rob thee of a kiss.
Rich preys make true-men thieves; so do thy lips
   Make modest Dian cloudy and forlorn,
   Lest she should steal a kiss, and die forsworn.

'Now of this dark night I perceive the reason:
Cynthia for shame obscures her silver shine,
Till forging Nature be condemn'd of treason
For stealing moulds from heaven that were divine,
   Wherein she fram'd thee in high heaven's despite,
   To shame the sun by day and her by night.

'And therefore hath she brib'd the Destinies
To cross the curious workmanship of Nature,
To mingle beauty with infirmities,
And pure perfection with impure defeature;
   Making it subject to the tyranny
   Of mad mischances and much misery:

'As burning fevers, agues pale and faint,
Life-poisoning pestilence, and frenzies wood,
The marrow-eating sickness whose attaint
Disorder breeds by heating of the blood,
   Surfeits, imposthumes, grief, and damn'd despair,
   Swear Nature's death for framing thee so fair.

' And not the least of all these maladies   745
But in one minute's fight brings beauty under.
Both favour, savour, hue, and qualities,
Whereat th' impartial gazer late did wonder,
    Are on the sudden wasted, thaw'd, and done,
    As mountain snow melts with the midday sun.   750

' Therefore, despite of fruitless chastity,
Love-lacking vestals, and self-loving nuns,
That on the earth would breed a scarcity
And barren dearth of daughters and of sons,
    Be prodigal : the lamp that burns by night   755
    Dries up his oil to lend the world his light.

' What is thy body but a swallowing grave,
Seeming to bury that posterity
Which by the rights of time thou needs must have,
If thou destroy them not in dark obscurity ?   760
    If so, the world will hold thee in disdain,
    Sith in thy pride so fair a hope is slain.

' So in thyself thyself art made away—
A mischief worse than civil home-bred strife,
Or theirs whose desperate hands themselves do slay,   765
Or butcher-sire that reaves his son of life.
    Foul cank'ring rust the hidden treasure frets,
    But gold that's put to use more gold begets.'

' Nay, then,' quoth Adon ' you will fall again
Into your idle over-handled theme ;   770
The kiss I gave you is bestow'd in vain,
And all in vain you strive against the stream ;
    For, by this black-fac'd night, desire's foul nurse,
    Your treatise makes me like you worse and worse.

' If love have lent you twenty thousand tongues,   775
And every tongue more moving than your own,
Bewitching like the wanton mermaid's songs,
Yet from mine ear the tempting tune is blown ;
    For know, my heart stands armed in mine ear,
    And will not let a false sound enter there,   780

' Lest the deceiving harmony should run
Into the quiet closure of my breast ;
And then my little heart were quite undone,
In his bedchamber to be barr'd of rest.
    No, lady, no ; my heart longs not to groan,   785
    But soundly sleeps, while now it sleeps alone.

' What have you urg'd that I cannot reprove ?
The path is smooth that leadeth on to danger ;
I hate not love, but your device in love,
That lends embracements unto every stranger.   790
    You do it for increase !   O strange excuse,
    When reason is the bawd to lust's abuse !

' Call it not love, for Love to heaven is fled,
Since sweating lust on earth usurp'd his name ;
Under whose simple semblance he hath fed   795
Upon fresh beauty, blotting it with blame ;
   Which the hot tyrant stains and soon bereaves,
   As caterpillars do the tender leaves.

' Love comforteth like sunshine after rain,
But Lust's effect is tempest after sun ;   800
Love's gentle spring doth always fresh remain :
Lust's winter comes ere summer half be done.
   Love surfeits not : Lust like a glutton dies.
   Love is all truth : Lust full of forged lies.

' More I could tell, but more I dare not say ;   805
The text is old, the orator too green.
Therefore, in sadness, now I will away ;
My face is full of shame, my heart of teen ;
   Mine ears that to your wanton talk attended
   Do burn themselves for having so offended.'   810

With this he breaketh from the sweet embrace
Of those fair arms which bound him to her breast,
And homeward through the dark laund runs apace ;
Leaves Love upon her back, deeply distress'd.
   Look how a bright star shooteth from the sky,   815
   So glides he in the night from Venus' eye ;

Which after him she darts, as one on shore
Gazing upon a late-embarked friend,
Till the wild waves will have him seen no more,
Whose ridges with the meeting clouds contend ;   820
   So did the merciless and pitchy night
   Fold in the object that did feed her sight.

Whereat amaz'd, as one that unaware
Hath dropp'd a precious jewel in the flood,
Or stonish'd as night-wand'rers often are,   825
Their light blown out in some mistrustful wood ;
   Even so confounded in the dark she lay,
   Having lost the fair discovery of her way.

And now she beats her heart, whereat it groans,
That all the neighbour caves, as seeming troubled,   830
Make verbal repetition of her moans ;
Passion on passion deeply is redoubled :
   ' Ay me ! ' she cries, and twenty times, ' Woe, woe ! '
   And twenty echoes twenty times cry so.

She, marking them, begins a wailing note,   835
And sings extemporally a woeful ditty—
How love makes young men thrall, and old men dote ;
How love is wise in folly, foolish-witty.
   Her heavy anthem still concludes in woe,
   And still the choir of echoes answer so.   840

Her song was tedious, and outwore the night,
For lovers' hours are long, though seeming short ;
If pleas'd themselves, others, they think, delight
In such-like circumstance, with such-like sport.
 Their copious stories, oftentimes begun,   845
 End without audience and are never done.

For who hath she to spend the night withal
But idle sounds resembling parasites,
Like shrill-tongu'd tapsters answering every call,
Soothing the humour of fantastic wits ?   850
 She says ' 'Tis so ' ; they answer all ' 'Tis so ' ;
 And would say after her, if she said ' No '.

Lo, here the gentle lark, weary of rest,
From his moist cabinet mounts up on high,
And wakes the morning, from whose silver breast   855
The sun ariseth in his majesty ;
 Who doth the world so gloriously behold
 That cedar-tops and hills seem burnish'd gold

Venus salutes him with this fair good-morrow :
' O thou clear god, and patron of all light,   860
From whom each lamp and shining star doth borrow
The beauteous influence that makes him bright,
 There lives a son that suck'd an earthly mother
 May lend thee light, as thou dost lend to other '.

This said, she hasteth to a myrtle grove,   865
Musing the morning is so much o'erworn,
And yet she hears no tidings of her love ;
She hearkens for his hounds and for his horn.
 Anon she hears them chant it lustily,
 And all in haste she coasteth to the cry.   870

And as she runs, the bushes in the way
Some catch her by the neck, some kiss her face,
Some twine about her thigh to make her stay ;
She wildly breaketh from their strict embrace,
 Like a milch doe whose swelling dugs do ache   875
 Hasting to feed her fawn hid in some brake.

By this, she hears the hounds are at a bay ;
Whereat she starts, like one that spies an adder
Wreath'd up in fatal folds just in his way,
The fear whereof doth make him shake and shudder ;   880
 Even so the timorous yelping of the hounds
 Appals her senses and her spirit confounds.

For now she knows it is no gentle chase,
But the blunt boar, rough bear, or lion proud,
Because the cry remaineth in one place,   885
Where fearfully the dogs exclaim aloud.
 Finding their enemy to be so curst,
 They all strain court'sy who shall cope him first.

This dismal cry rings sadly in her ear,
Through which it enters to surprise her heart,
Who, overcome by doubt and bloodless fear,
With cold-pale weakness numbs each feeling part ;
    Like soldiers, when their captain once doth yield,
    They basely fly and dare not stay the field.

Thus stands she in a trembling ecstasy ;
Till, cheering up her senses all dismay'd,
She tells them 'tis a causeless fantasy,
And childish error that they are afraid ;
    Bids them leave quaking, bids them fear no more—
    And with that word she spied the hunted boar,

Whose frothy mouth, bepainted all with red,
Like milk and blood being mingled both together,
A second fear through all her sinews spread,
Which madly hurries her she knows not whither :
    This way she runs, and now she will no further
    But back retires to rate the boar for murther.

A thousand spleens bear her a thousand ways ;
She treads the path that she untreads again ;
Her more than haste is mated with delays,
Like the proceedings of a drunken brain,
    Full of respects, yet nought at all respecting,
    In hand with all things, nought at all effecting.

Here kennell'd in a brake she finds a hound,
And asks the weary caitiff for his master ;
And there another licking of his wound,
'Gainst venom'd sores the only sovereign plaster ;
    And here she meets another sadly scowling,
    To whom she speaks, and he replies with howling.

When he hath ceas'd his ill-resounding noise,
Another flap-mouth'd mourner, black and grim,
Against the welkin volleys out his voice ;
Another and another answer him,
    Clapping their proud tails to the ground below,
    Shaking their scratch'd ears, bleeding as they go.

Look how the world's poor people are amazed
At apparitions, signs, and prodigies,
Whereon with fearful eyes they long have gazed,
Infusing them with dreadful prophecies ;
    So she at these sad signs draws up her breath,
    And, sighing it again, exclaims on Death.

' Hard-favour'd tyrant, ugly, meagre, lean,
Hateful divorce of love,'—thus chides she Death—
' Grim-grinning ghost, earth's worm, what dost thou mean
To stifle beauty, and to steal his breath,
    Who when he liv'd, his breath and beauty set
    Gloss on the rose, smell to the violet ?

'If he be dead—O no, it cannot be,
Seeing his beauty, thou shouldst strike at it.
O yes, it may; thou hast no eyes to see,
But hatefully at random dost thou hit.   940
    Thy mark is feeble age; but thy false dart
    Mistakes that aim and cleaves an infant's heart.

'Hadst thou but bid beware, then he had spoke,
And hearing him thy power had lost his power.
The Destinies will curse thee for this stroke: 945
They bid thee crop a weed; thou pluck'st a flower.
    Love's golden arrow at him should have fled,
    And not Death's ebon dart, to strike him dead.

'Dost thou drink tears, that thou provok'st such weeping?
What may a heavy groan advantage thee?   950
Why hast thou cast into eternal sleeping
Those eyes that taught all other eyes to see?
    Now Nature cares not for thy mortal vigour,
    Since her best work is ruin'd with thy rigour.'

Here overcome, as one full of despair,   955
She vail'd her eyelids, who, like sluices, stopp'd
The crystal tide that from her two cheeks fair
In the sweet channel of her bosom dropp'd;
    But through the floodgates breaks the silver rain,
    And with his strong course opens them again.   960

O, how her eyes and tears did lend and borrow!
Her eye seen in the tears, tears in her eye;
Both crystals, where they view'd each other's sorrow—
Sorrow that friendly sighs sought still to dry;
    But like a stormy day, now wind, now rain,   965
    Sighs dry her cheeks, tears make them wet again.

Variable passions throng her constant woe,
As striving who should best become her grief;
All entertain'd, each passion labours so
That every present sorrow seemeth chief,   970
    But none is best. Then join they all together,
    Like many clouds consulting for foul weather.

By this, far off she hears some huntsman hollow;
A nurse's song ne'er pleas'd her babe so well.
The dire imagination she did follow   975
This sound of hope doth labour to expel;
    For now reviving joy bids her rejoice,
    And flatters her it is Adonis' voice.

Whereat her tears began to turn their tide,
Being prison'd in her eye like pearls in glass;   980
Yet sometimes falls an orient drop beside,
Which her cheek melts, as scorning it should pass
    To wash the foul face of the sluttish ground,
    Who is but drunken when she seemeth drown'd.

O hard-believing love, how strange it seems   98
Not to believe, and yet too credulous !
Thy weal and woe are both of them extremes ;
Despair and hope makes thee ridiculous :
    The one doth flatter thee in thoughts unlikely,
    In likely thoughts the other kills thee quickly.   99

Now she unweaves the web that she hath wrought :
Adonis lives, and Death is not to blame ;
It was not she that call'd him all to nought.
Now she adds honours to his hateful name :
    She clepes him king of graves, and grave for kings,   99
    Imperious supreme of all mortal things.

' No, no,' quoth she ' sweet Death, I did but jest ;
Yet pardon me I felt a kind of fear
When as I met the boar, that bloody beast
Which knows no pity but is still severe.   1000
    Then, gentle shadow—truth I must confess—
    I rail'd on thee, fearing my love's decesse.

' 'Tis not my fault ; the boar provok'd my tongue ;
Be wreak'd on him, invisible commander ;
'Tis he, foul creature, that hath done thee wrong ;   100
I did but act ; he's author of thy slander.
    Grief hath two tongues, and never woman yet
    Could rule them both without ten women's wit.'

Thus, hoping that Adonis is alive,
Her rash suspect she doth extenuate ;   1010
And that his beauty may the better thrive,
With Death she humbly doth insinuate ;
    Tells him of trophies, statues, tombs, and stories
    His victories, his triumphs, and his glories.

' O Jove,' quoth she ' how much a fool was I   101
To be of such a weak and silly mind
To wail his death who lives, and must not die
Till mutual overthrow of mortal kind !
    For he being dead, with him is beauty slain,
    And, beauty dead, black chaos comes again.   1020

' Fie, fie, fond love, thou art so full of fear
As one with treasure laden, hemm'd with thieves ;
Trifles, unwitnessed with eye or ear,
Thy coward heart with false bethinking grieves.'
    Even at this word she hears a merry horn,   102
    Whereat she leaps that was but late forlorn.

As falcons to the lure away she flies ;
The grass stoops not, she treads on it so light ;
And in her haste unfortunately spies
The foul boar's conquest on her fair delight ;   1030
    Which seen, her eyes, as murd'red with the view,
    Like stars asham'd of day, themselves withdrew ;

Or as the snail, whose tender horns being hit,
Shrinks backward in his shelly cave with pain,
And there, all smoth'red up, in shade doth sit,   1035
Long after fearing to creep forth again ;
 So at his bloody view her eyes are fled
 Into the deep-dark cabins of her head ;

Where they resign their office and their light
To the disposing of her troubled brain ;   1040
Who bids them still consort with ugly night,
And never wound the heart with looks again ;
 Who, like a king perplexed in his throne,
 By their suggestion gives a deadly groan.

Whereat each tributary subject quakes ;   1045
As when the wind, imprison'd in the ground,
Struggling for passage, earth's foundation shakes,
Which with cold terror doth men's minds confound.
 This mutiny each part doth so surprise
 That from their dark beds once more leap her eyes ; 1050

And, being open'd, threw unwilling light
Upon the wide wound that the boar had trench'd
In his soft flank ; whose wonted lily white
With purple tears that his wound wept was drench'd.
 No flow'r was nigh, no grass, herb, leaf, or weed,   1055
 But stole his blood and seem'd with him to bleed.

This solemn sympathy poor Venus noteth.
Over one shoulder doth she hang her head ;
Dumbly she passions, franticly she doteth ;
She thinks he could not die, he is not dead.   1060
 Her voice is stopp'd, her joints forget to bow ;
 Her eyes are mad that they have wept till now.

Upon his hurt she looks so steadfastly
That her sight dazzling makes the wound seem three ;
And then she reprehends her mangling eye   1065
That makes more gashes where no breach should be.
 His face seems twain, each several limb is doubled ;
 For oft the eye mistakes, the brain being troubled.

' My tongue cannot express my grief for one,
And yet ' quoth she ' behold two Adons dead.   1070
My sighs are blown away, my salt tears gone,
Mine eyes are turn'd to fire, my heart to lead ;
 Heavy heart's lead melt at mine eyes' red fire !
 So shall I die by drops of hot desire.

' Alas, poor world, what treasure hast thou lost !   1075
What face remains alive that's worth the viewing ?
Whose tongue is music now ?   What canst thou boast
Of things long since, or any thing ensuing ?
 The flowers are sweet, their colours fresh and trim ;
 But true-sweet beauty liv'd and died with him.   1080

' Bonnet nor veil henceforth no creature wear ;
Nor sun nor wind will ever strive to kiss you :
Having no fair to lose, you need not fear ;
The sun doth scorn you, and the wind doth hiss you.
 But when Adonis liv'd, sun and sharp air   10
 Lurk'd like two thieves to rob him of his fair ;

' And therefore would be put his bonnet on,
Under whose brim the gaudy sun would peep ;
The wind would blow it off, and, being gone,
Play with his locks. Then would Adonis weep ; 10
 And straight, in pity of his tender years,
 They both would strive who first should dry his tears.

 To see his face the lion walk'd along
Behind some hedge, because he would not fear him.
To recreate himself when he hath song,   10
The tiger would be tame and gently hear him.
 If he had spoke, the wolf would leave his prey,
 And never fright the silly lamb that day.

' When he beheld his shadow in the brook,
The fishes spread on it their golden gills ;   11
When he was by, the birds such pleasure took
That some would sing, some other in their bills
 Would bring him mulberries and ripe-red cherries ;
 He fed them with his sight, they him with berries.

' But this foul, grim, and urchin-snouted boar, 11
Whose downward eye still looketh for a grave,
Ne'er saw the beauteous livery that he wore :
Witness the entertainment that he gave.
 If he did see his face, why then I know
 He thought to kiss him, and hath kill'd him so. 11

' 'Tis true, 'tis true ; thus was Adonis slain :
He ran upon the boar with his sharp spear,
Who did not whet his teeth at him again,
But by a kiss thought to persuade him there ;
 And nuzzling in his flank, the loving swine 11
 Sheath'd unaware the tusk in his soft groin.

' Had I been tooth'd like him, I must confess,
With kissing him I should have kill'd him first ;
But he is dead, and never did he bless
My youth with his ; the more am I accurst.' 11
 With this, she falleth in the place she stood,
 And stains her face with his congealed blood.

She looks upon his lips, and they are pale ;
She takes him by the hand, and that is cold ;
She whispers in his ears a heavy tale,
As if they heard the woeful words she told ; 11
 She lifts the coffer-lids that close his eyes,
 Where, lo, two lamps burnt out in darkness lies ;

Two glasses where herself herself beheld
A thousand times, and now no more reflect,   1130
Their virtue lost wherein they late excell'd,
And every beauty robb'd of his effect.
   ' Wonder of time,' quoth she ' this is my spite,
   That, thou being dead, the day should yet be light.

' Since thou art dead, lo, here I prophesy   1135
Sorrow on love hereafter shall attend :
It shall be waited on with jealousy,
Find sweet beginning but unsavoury end,
   Ne'er settled equally, but high or low,
   That all love's pleasure shall not match his woe.   1140

' It shall be fickle, false, and full of fraud,
Bud and be blasted in a breathing while,
The bottom poison, and the top o'erstraw'd
With sweets that shall the truest sight beguile ;
   The strongest body shall it make most weak,   1145
   Strike the wise dumb, and teach the fool to speak.

' It shall be sparing, and too full of riot,
Teaching decrepit age to tread the measures ;
The staring ruffian shall it keep in quiet,
Pluck down the rich, enrich the poor with treasures ;   1150
   It shall be raging mad, and silly mild,
   Make the young old, the old become a child.

' It shall suspect where is no cause of fear ;
It shall not fear where it should most mistrust ;
It shall be merciful, and too severe,   1155
And most deceiving when it seems most just ;
   Perverse it shall be where it shows most toward,
   Put fear to valour, courage to the coward.

' It shall be cause of war and dire events,
And set dissension 'twixt the son and sire,   1160
Subject and servile to all discontents,
As dry combustious matter is to fire.
   Sith in his prime death doth my love destroy,
   They that love best their loves shall not enjoy.'

By this, the boy that by her side lay kill'd   1165
Was melted like a vapour from her sight,
And in his blood that on the ground lay spill'd
A purple flow'r sprung up, check'red with white,
   Resembling well his pale cheeks, and the blood
   Which in round drops upon their whiteness stood.   1170

She bows her head the new-sprung flow'r to smell,
Comparing it to her Adonis' breath ;
And says within her bosom it shall dwell,
Since he himself is reft from her by death ;
   She crops the stalk, and in the breach appears   1175
   Green dropping sap, which she compares to tears.

' Poor flow'r,' quoth she ' this was thy father's guise—
Sweet issue of a more sweet-smelling sire—
For every little grief to wet his eyes.
To grow unto himself was his desire,   1180
    And so 'tis thine ; but know, it is as good
    To wither in my breast as in his blood.

' Here was thy father's bed, here in my breast ;
Thou art the next of blood, and 'tis thy right.
Lo, in this hollow cradle take thy rest ;   1185
My throbbing heart shall rock thee day and night ;
    There shall not be one minute in an hour
    Wherein I will not kiss my sweet love's flow'r.'

Thus weary of the world, away she hies,
And yokes her silver doves ; by whose swift aid   1190
Their mistress, mounted, through the empty skies
In her light chariot quickly is convey'd,
    Holding their course to Paphos, where their queen
    Means to immure herself, and not be seen.

THE RAPE OF LUCRECE

TO THE

RIGHT HONOURABLE HENRY WRIOTHESLEY,

EARLE OF SOUTHAMPTON, AND BARON OF TITCHFIELD.

THE love I dedicate to your Lordship is without end : whereof this Pamphlet without beginning is but a superfluous Moity. The warrant I have of your Honourable disposition, not the worth of my untutored Lines makes it assured of acceptance. What I have done is yours, what I have to doe is yours, being part in all I have, devoted yours. Were my worth greater my duety would shew greater, meane time, as it is, it is bound to your Lordship ; To whom I wish long life still lengthned with all happinesse.

Your Lordships in all duety.

WILLIAM SHAKESPEARE.

THE ARGUMENT.

LUCIUS TARQUINIUS (for his excessive pride surnamed Superbus), after he had caused his own father-in-law, Servius Tullius, to be cruelly murd'red, and, contrary to the Roman laws and customs, not requiring or staying for the people's suffrages, had possessed himself of the kingdom, went, accompanied with his sons and other noblemen of Rome, to besiege Ardea ; during which siege, the principal men of the army meeting one evening at the tent of Sextus Tarquinius, the King's son, in their discourses after supper every one commended the virtues of his own wife ; amoung whom Collatinus extolled the incomparable chastity of his wife Lucretia. In that pleasant humour they all posted to Rome ; and intending by their secret and sudden arrival to make trial of that which every one had before avouched, only Collatinus finds his wife (though it were late in the night) spinning amongst her maids ; the other ladies were all found dancing and revelling, or in several disports. Whereupon the noblemen yielded Collatinus the victory, and his wife the fame. At that time Sextus Tarquinius, being inflamed with Lucrece' beauty, yet smothering his passions for the present, departed with the rest back to the camp ; from whence he shortly after privily withdrew himself, and was (according to his estate) royally entertained and lodged by Lucrece at Collatium. The same night he treacherously stealeth into her chamber, violently ravish'd her, and early in the morning speedeth way. Lucrece, in this lamentable plight, hastily dispatcheth messengers, one to Rome for her father, another to the camp for Collatine. They came, the one accompanied with Junius Brutus, the other with Publius Valerius ; and, finding Lucrece attired in mourning habit, demanded the cause of her sorrow. She, first taking an oath of them for her revenge, revealed the actor and whole manner of his dealing, and withal suddenly stabbed herself. Which done, with one consent they all vowed to root out the whole hated family of the Tarquins ; and, bearing the dead body to Rome, Brutus acquainted

the people with the doer and manner of the vile deed, with a bitter
invective against the tyranny of the King; wherewith the people
were so moved, that with one consent and a general acclamation the
Tarquins were all exiled, and the state government changed from
kings to consuls.

FROM the besieged Ardea all in post,
Borne by the trustless wings of false desire,
Lust-breathed Tarquin leaves the Roman host,
And to Collatium bears the lightless fire
Which, in pale embers hid, lurks to aspire
    And girdle with embracing flames the waist
    Of Collatine's fair love, Lucrece the chaste.

Haply that name of 'chaste' unhap'ly set
This bateless edge on his keen appetite;
When Collatine unwisely did not let
To praise the clear unmatched red and white
Which triumph'd in that sky of his delight,
    Where mortal stars, as bright as heaven's beauties,
    With pure aspects did him peculiar duties.

For he the night before, in Tarquin's tent,
Unlock'd the treasure of his happy state—
What priceless wealth the heavens had him lent
In the possession of his beauteous mate;
Reck'ning his fortune at such high-proud rate,
    That kings might be espoused to more fame,
    But king nor peer to such a peerless dame.

O happiness enjoy'd but of a few!
And, if possess'd, as soon decay'd and done
As is the morning's silver-melting dew
Against the golden splendour of the sun!
An expir'd date, cancell'd ere well begun:
    Honour and beauty, in the owner's arms,
    Are weakly fortress'd from a world of harms.

Beauty itself doth of itself persuade
The eyes of men without an orator;
What needeth then apologies be made
To set forth that which is so singular?
Or why is Collatine the publisher
    Of that rich jewel he should keep unknown
    From thievish ears, because it is his own?

Perchance his boast of Lucrece' sov'reignty
Suggested this proud issue of a king;
For by our ears our hearts oft tainted be.
Perchance that envy of so rich a thing,
Braving compare, disdainfully did sting
    His high-pitch'd thoughts that meaner men should vaunt
    That golden hap which their superiors want.

But some untimely thought did instigate
His all-too-timeless speed, if none of those.
His honour, his affairs, his friends, his state,   45
Neglected all, with swift intent he goes
To quench the coal which in his liver glows.
   O rash false heat, wrapp'd in repentant cold,
   Thy hasty spring still blasts and ne'er grows old !

When at Collatium this false lord arrived,   50
Well was he welcom'd by the Roman dame,
Within whose face beauty and virtue strived
Which of them both should underprop her fame :
When virtue bragg'd, beauty would blush for shame ;
   When beauty boasted blushes, in despite   55
   Virtue would stain that o'er with silver white.

But beauty, in that white intituled,
From Venus' doves doth challenge that fair field ;
Then virtue claims from beauty beauty's red,
Which virtue gave the golden age to gild   60
Their silver cheeks, and call'd it then their shield ;
   Teaching them thus to use it in the fight,
   When shame assail'd, the red should fence the white.

This heraldry in Lucrece' face was seen,
Argued by beauty's red and virtue's white ;   65
Of either's colour was the other queen,
Proving from world's minority their right ;
Yet their ambition makes them still to fight,
   The sovereignty of either being so great
   That oft they interchange each other's seat.   70

This silent war of lilies and of roses
Which Tarquin view'd in her fair face's field,
In their pure ranks his traitor eye encloses ;
Where, lest between them both it should be kill'd,
The coward captive vanquished doth yield   75
   To those two armies that would let him go
   Rather than triumph in so false a foe.

Now thinks he that her husband's shallow tongue—
The niggard prodigal that prais'd her so—
In that high task hath done her beauty wrong,   80
Which far exceeds his barren skill to show ;
Therefore that praise which Collatine doth owe
   Enchanted Tarquin answers with surmise,
   In silent wonder of still-gazing eyes.

This earthly saint, adored by this devil,   85
Little suspecteth the false worshipper ;
For unstain'd thoughts do seldom dream on evil ;
Birds never lim'd no secret bushes fear.
So guiltless she securely gives good cheer
   And reverend welcome to her princely guest,   90
   Whose inward ill no outward harm express'd ;

For that he colour'd with his high estate,
Hiding base sin in pleats of majesty ;
That nothing in him seem'd inordinate,
Save sometime too much wonder of his eye,　　　95
Which, having all, all could not satisfy ;
　　But, poorly rich, so wanteth in his store
　　That cloy'd with much he pineth still for more.

But she that never cop'd with stranger eyes
Could pick no meaning from their parling looks,　　100
Nor read the subtle-shining secrecies
Writ in the glassy margents of such books.
She touch'd no unknown baits, nor fear'd no hooks ;
　　Nor could she moralize his wanton sight,
　　More than his eyes were open'd to the light.　　105

He stories to her ears her husband's fame,
Won in the fields of fruitful Italy ;
And decks with praises Collatine's high name,
Made glorious by his manly chivalry,
With bruised arms and wreaths of victory.　　110
　　Her joy with heav'd-up hand she doth express,
　　And, wordless, so greets heaven for his success.

Far from the purpose of his coming thither
He makes excuses for his being there.
No cloudy show of stormy blust'ring weather　　115
Doth yet in his fair welkin once appear ;
Till sable Night, mother of Dread and Fear,
　　Upon the world dim darkness doth display,
　　And in her vaulty prison stows the Day.

For then is Tarquin brought unto his bed,　　120
Intending weariness with heavy sprite ;
For, after supper, long he questioned
With modest Lucrece, and wore out the night.
Now leaden slumber with life's strength doth fight ;
　　And every one to rest themselves betake,　　125
　　Save thieves, and cares, and troubled minds that wake.

As one of which doth Tarquin lie revolving
The sundry dangers of his will's obtaining ;
Yet ever to obtain his will resolving,
Though weak-built hopes persuade him to abstaining ;　　130
Despair to gain doth traffic oft for gaining ;
　　And when great treasure is the meed proposed,
　　Though death be adjunct, there's no death supposed.

Those that much covet are with gain so fond
That what they have not, that which they possess　　135
They scatter and unloose it from their bond,
And so, by hoping more, they have but less ;
Or, gaining more, the profit of excess
　　Is but to surfeit, and such griefs sustain
　　That they prove bankrupt in this poor-rich gain.　　140

The aim of all is but to nurse the life
With honour, wealth, and ease in waning age ;
And in this aim there is such thwarting strife
That one for all or all for one we gage :
As life for honour in fell battle's rage ;   145
  Honour for wealth ; and oft that wealth doth cost
  The death of all, and all together lost.

So that in vent'ring ill we leave to be
The things we are for that which we expect ;
And this ambitious foul infirmity,   150
In having much, torments us with defect
Of that we have ; so then we do neglect
  The thing we have and, all for want of wit,
  Make something nothing by augmenting it.

Such hazard now must doting Tarquin make,   155
Pawning his honour to obtain his lust ;
And for himself himself he must forsake—
Then where is truth if there be no self-trust ?
When shall he think to find a stranger just,
  When he himself confounds, betrays   160
  To sland'rous tongues and wretched hateful days ?

Now stole upon the time the dead of night,
When heavy sleep had clos'd up mortal eyes ;
No comfortable star did lend his light,
No noise but owls' and wolves' death-boding cries ;   165
Now serves the season that they may surprise
  The silly lambs.   Pure thoughts are dead and still,
  While lust and murder wake to stain and kill.

And now this lustful lord leap'd from his bed,
Throwing his mantle rudely o'er his arm ;   170
Is madly toss'd between desire and dread ;
Th' one sweetly flatters, th' other feareth harm ;
But honest Fear, bewitch'd with lust's foul charm,
  Doth too too oft betake him to retire,
  Beaten away by brain-sick rude desire.   175

His falchion on a flint he softly smiteth,
That from the cold stone sparks of fire do fly,
Whereat a waxen torch forthwith he lighteth,
Which must be lode-star to his lustful eye ;
And to the flame thus speaks advisedly :   180
  ' As from this cold flint I enforc'd this fire,
  So Lucrece must I force to my desire '.

Here pale with fear he doth premeditate
The dangers of his loathsome enterprise,
And in his inward mind he doth debate   185
What following sorrow may on this arise ;
Then, looking scornfully, he doth despise
  His naked armour of still-slaughtered lust,
  And justly thus controls his thoughts unjust :

' Fair torch, burn out thy light, and lend it not   190
To darken her whose light excelleth thine ;
And die, unhallowed thoughts, before you blot
With your uncleanness that which is divine ;
Offer pure incense to so pure a shrine :
    Let fair humanity abhor the deed   195
    That spots and stains love's modest snow-white weed.

' O shame to knighthood and to shining arms !
O foul dishonour to my household's grave !
O impious act including all foul harms !
A martial man to be soft fancy's slave !   200
True valour still a true respect should have ;
    Then my digression is so vile, so base,
    That it will live engraven in my face.

' Yea, though I die, the scandal will survive
And be an eyesore in my golden coat ;   205
Some loathsome dash the herald will contrive
To cipher me how fondly I did dote ;
That my posterity, sham'd with the note,
    Shall curse my bones, and hold it for no sin
    To wish that I their father had not been.   210

' What win I if I gain the thing I seek ?
A dream, a breath, a froth of fleeting joy.
Who buys a minute's mirth to wail a week ?
Or sells eternity to get a toy ?
For one sweet grape who will the vine destroy ?   215
    Or what fond beggar, but to touch the crown,
    Would with the sceptre straight be strucken down ?

' If Collatinus dream of my intent,
Will he not wake, and in a desp'rate rage
Post hither, this vile purpose to prevent—   220
This siege that hath engirt his marriage,
This blur to youth, this sorrow to the sage,
    This dying virtue, this surviving shame,
    Whose crime will bear an ever-during blame ?

' O, what excuse can my invention make   225
When thou shalt charge me with so black a deed ?
Will not my tongue be mute, my frail joints shake,
Mine eyes forgo their light, my false heart bleed ?
The guilt being great, the fear doth still exceed ;
    And extreme fear can neither fight nor fly,   230
    But coward-like with trembling terror die.

' Had Collatinus kill'd my son or sire,
Or lain in ambush to betray my life,
Or were he not my dear friend, this desire
Might have excuse to work upon his wife,   235
As in revenge or quittal of such strife ;
    But as he is my kinsman, my dear friend,
    The shame and fault finds no excuse nor end.

' Shameful it is—ay, if the fact be known ;
Hateful it is—there is no hate in loving ;　　　　　　240
I'll beg her love—but she is not her own—
The worst is but denial and reproving.
My will is strong, past reason's weak removing—
　　Who fears a sentence or an old man's saw
　　Shall by a painted cloth be kept in awe.'　　　245

Thus, graceless, holds he disputation
'Tween frozen conscience and hot-burning will,
And with good thoughts makes dispensation,
Urging the worser sense for vantage still ;
Which in a moment doth confound and kill　　　250
　　All pure effects, and doth so far proceed
　　That what is vile shows like a virtuous deed.

Quoth he ' She took me kindly by the hand
And gaz'd for tidings in my eager eyes,
Fearing some hard news from the warlike band　　255
Where her beloved Collatinus lies.
O how her fear did make her colour rise !
　　First red as roses that on lawn we lay,
　　Then white as lawn, the roses took away.

' And how her hand in my hand being lock'd　　260
Forc'd it to tremble with her loyal fear !
Which struck her sad, and then it faster rock'd
Until her husband's welfare she did hear ;
Whereat she smiled with so sweet a cheer
　　That had Narcissus seen her as she stood　　265
　　Self-love had never drown'd him in the flood.

' Why hunt I then for colour or excuses ?
All orators are dumb when beauty pleadeth ;
Poor wretches have remorse in poor abuses ;
Love thrives not in the heart that shadows dreadeth ;　　270
Affection is my captain, and he leadeth ;
　　And when his gaudy banner is display'd,
　　The coward fights and will not be dismay'd.

' Then, childish fear avaunt ! debating die !
Respect and reason wait on wrinkled age !　　275
My heart shall never countermand mine eye ;
Sad pause and deep regard beseems the sage ;
My part is youth, and beats these from the stage :
　　Desire my pilot is, beauty my prize ;
　　Then who fears sinking where such treasure lies ? '　　280

As corn o'ergrown by weeds, so heedful fear
Is almost chok'd by unresisted lust.
Away he steals with open list'ning ear,
Full of foul hope, and full of fond mistrust ;
Both which, as servitors to the unjust,　　　285
　　So cross him with their opposite persuasion
　　That now he vows a league, and now invasion.

Within his thought her heavenly image sits,
And in the selfsame seat sits Collatine.
That eye which looks on her confounds his wits;   290
That eye which him beholds, as more divine,
Unto a view so false will not incline;
　　But with a pure appeal seeks to the heart,
　　Which once corrupted takes the worser part;

And therein heartens up his servile powers,   295
Who, flatt'red by their leader's jocund show,
Stuff up his lust, as minutes fill up hours;
And as their captain, so their pride doth grow,
Paying more slavish tribute than they owe.
　　By reprobate desire thus madly led,   300
　　The Roman lord marcheth to Lucrece' bed.

The locks between her chamber and his will,
Each one by him enforc'd, retires his ward;
But, as they open, they all rate his ill,
Which drives the creeping thief to some regard.   305
The threshold grates the door to have him heard;
　　Night-wand'ring weasels shriek to see him there;
　　They fright him, yet he still pursues his fear.

As each unwilling portal yields him way,
Through little vents and crannies of the place   310
The wind wars with his torch, to make him stay,
And blows the smoke of it into his face,
Extinguishing his conduct in this case;
　　But his hot heart, which fond desire doth scorch,
　　Puffs forth another wind that fires the torch;   315

And, being lighted, by the light he spies
Lucretia's glove, wherein her needle sticks;
He takes it from the rushes where it lies,
And griping it, the needle his finger pricks,
As who should say ' This glove to wanton tricks   320
　　Is not inur'd. Return again in haste;
　　Thou seest our mistress' ornaments are chaste '.

But all these poor forbiddings could not stay him;
He in the worst sense consters their denial:
The doors, the wind, the glove that did delay him,   325
He takes for accidental things of trial;
Or as those bars which stop the hourly dial,
　　Who with a ling'ring stay his course doth let,
　　Till every minute pays the hour his debt.

' So, so,' quoth he ' these lets attend the time,   330
Like little frosts that sometime threat the spring,
To add a more rejoicing to the prime,
And give the sneaped birds more cause to sing.
Pain pays the income of each precious thing:
　　Huge rocks, high winds, strong pirates, shelves and sands,   335
　　The merchant fears, ere rich at home he lands.'

Now is he come unto the chamber door
That shuts him from the heaven of his thought,
Which with a yielding latch, and with no more,
Hath barr'd him from the blessed thing he sought.   340
So from himself impiety hath wrought
    That for his prey to pray he doth begin,
    As if the heavens should countenance his sin.

But in the midst of his unfruitful prayer,
Having solicited th' eternal power,   345
That his foul thoughts might compass his fair fair,
And they would stand auspicious to the hour,
Even there he starts—quoth he ' I must deflow'r.
    The powers to whom I pray abhor this fact ;
    How can they then assist me in the act ?   350

' Then Love and Fortune be my gods, my guide !
My will is back'd with resolution.
Thoughts are but dreams till their effects be tried ;
The blackest sin is clear'd with absolution ;
Against love's fire fear's frost hath dissolution.   355
    The eye of heaven is out, and misty night
    Covers the shame that follows sweet delight '.

This said, his guilty hand pluck'd up the latch,
And with his knee the door he opens wide.
The dove sleeps fast that this night-owl will catch.   360
Thus treason works ere traitors be espied.
Who sees the lurking serpent steps aside ;
    But she, sound sleeping, fearing no such thing,
    Lies at the mercy of his mortal sting.

Into the chamber wickedly he stalks,   365
And gazeth on her yet unstained bed.
The curtains being close, about he walks,
Rolling his greedy eyeballs in his head.
By their high treason is his heart misled,
    Which gives the watchword to his hand full soon   370
    To draw the cloud that hides the silver moon.

Look as the fair and fiery-pointed sun,
Rushing from forth a cloud, bereaves our sight ;
Even so, the curtain drawn, his eyes begun
To wink, being blinded with a greater light ;   375
Whether it is that she reflects so bright
    That dazzleth them, or else some shame supposed ;
    But blind they are, and keep themselves enclosed.

O, had they in that darksome prison died,
Then had they seen the period of their ill !   380
Then Collatine again by Lucrece' side
In his clear bed might have reposed still ;
But they must ope, this blessed league to kill ;
    And holy-thoughted Lucrece to their sight
    Must sell her joy, her life, her world's delight.   385

Her lily hand her rosy cheek lies under,
Coz'ning the pillow of a lawful kiss ;
Who, therefore angry, seems to part in sunder,
Swelling on either side to want his bliss ;
Between whose hills her head entombed is ;   390
   Where, like a virtuous monument, she lies,
   To be admir'd of lewd unhallowed eyes.

Without the bed her other fair hand was,
On the green coverlet ; whose perfect white
Show'd like an April daisy on the grass,   395
With pearly sweat, resembling dew of night.
Her eyes, like marigolds, had sheath'd their light,
   And canopied in darkness sweetly lay,
   Till they might open to adorn the day.

Her hair, like golden threads, play'd with her breath—   400
O modest wantons ! wanton modesty !—
Showing life's triumph in the map of death,
And death's dim look in life's mortality.
Each in her sleep themselves so beautify,
   As if between them twain there were no strife,   405
   But that life liv'd in death, and death in life.

Her breasts, like ivory globes circled with blue,
A pair of maiden worlds unconquered,
Save of their lord no bearing yoke they knew,
And him by oath they truly honoured.   410
These worlds in Tarquin new ambition bred,
   Who like a foul usurper went about
   From this fair throne to heave the owner out.

What could he see but mightily he noted ?
What did he note but strongly he desired ?   415
What he beheld, on that he firmly doted,
And in his will his wilful eye he tired.
With more than admiration he admired
   Her azure veins, her alabaster skin,
   Her coral lips, her snow-white dimpled chin.   420

As the grim lion fawneth o'er his prey,
Sharp hunger by the conquest satisfied,
So o'er this sleeping soul doth Tarquin stay,
His rage of lust by gazing qualified ;
Slack'd, not suppress'd ; for standing by her side,   425
   His eye, which late this mutiny restrains,
   Unto a greater uproar tempts his veins ;

And they, like straggling slaves for pillage fighting,
Obdurate vassals, fell exploits effecting,
In bloody death and ravishment delighting,   430
Nor children's tears nor mothers' groans respecting,
Swell in their pride, the onset still expecting,
   Anon his beating heart, alarum striking,
   Gives the hot charge and bids them do their liking.

His drumming heart cheers up his burning eye,   435
His eye commends the leading to his hand;
His hand, as proud of such a dignity,
Smoking with pride, march'd on to make his stand
On her bare breast, the heart of all her land;
    Whose ranks of blue veins, as his hand did scale,   440
    Left their round turrets destitute and pale.

They, must'ring to the quiet cabinet
Where their dear governess and lady lies,
Do tell her she is dreadfully beset,
And fright her with confusion of their cries: 445
She, much amaz'd, breaks ope her lock'd-up eyes,
    Who, peeping forth this tumult to behold,
    Are by his flaming torch dimm'd and controll'd.

Imagine her as one in dead of night
From forth dull sleep by dreadful fancy waking,   450
That thinks she hath beheld some ghastly sprite
Whose grim aspect sets every joint a-shaking—
What terror 'tis! but she, in worser taking,
    From sleep disturbed, heedfully doth view
    The sight which makes supposed terror true.   455

Wrapp'd and confounded in a thousand fears,
Like to a new-kill'd bird she trembling lies;
She dares not look; yet, winking, there appears
Quick-shifting antics, ugly in her eyes.
Such shadows are the weak brain's forgeries,   460
    Who, angry that the eyes fly from their lights,
    In darkness daunts them with more dreadful sights.

His hand, that yet remains upon her breast—
Rude ram, to batter such an ivory wall!—
May feel her heart, poor citizen, distress'd,   465
Wounding itself to death, rise up and fall,
Beating her bulk, that his hand shakes withal.
    This moves in him more rage and lesser pity,
    To make the breach and enter this sweet city.

First like a trumpet doth his tongue begin   470
To sound a parley to his heartless foe,
Who o'er the white sheet peers her whiter chin,
The reason of this rash alarm to know,
Which he by dumb demeanour seeks to show;
    But she with vehement prayers urgeth still   475
    Under what colour he commits this ill.

Thus he replies: 'The colour in thy face,
That even for anger makes the lily pale
And the red rose blush at her own disgrace,
Shall plead for me and tell my loving tale.   480
    Under that colour am I come to scale
    Thy never-conquered fort. The fault is thine,
    For those thine eyes betray thee unto mine.

' Thus I forestall thee, if thou mean to chide :
Thy beauty hath ensnar'd thee to this night,   485
Where thou with patience must my will abide,
My will that marks thee for my earth's delight,
Which I to conquer sought with all my might ;
    But as reproof and reason beat it dead,
    By thy bright beauty was it newly bred.   490

' I see what crosses my attempt will bring ;
I know what thorns the growing rose defends ;
I think the honey guarded with a sting :
All this beforehand counsel comprehends.
But Will is deaf and hears no heedful friends ;   495
    Only he hath an eye to gaze on beauty,
    And dotes on what he looks, 'gainst law or duty.

' I have debated, even in my soul,
What wrong, what shame, what sorrow I shall breed
But nothing can Affection's course control,   500
Or stop the headlong fury of his speed.
I know repentant tears ensue the deed,
    Reproach, disdain, and deadly enmity ;
    Yet strive I to embrace mine infamy '.

This said, he shakes aloft his Roman blade,   505
Which, like a falcon tow'ring in the skies,
Coucheth the fowl below with his wings' shade,
Whose crooked beak threats if he mount he dies.
So under his insulting falchion lies
    Harmless Lucretia, marking what he tells   510
    With trembling fear, as fowl hear falcon's bells.

' Lucrece,' quoth he ' this night I must enjoy thee.
If thou deny, then force must work my way,
For in thy bed I purpose to destroy thee ;
That done, some worthless slave of thine I'll slay,   515
To kill thine honour with thy life's decay ;
    And in thy dead arms do I mean to place him,
    Swearing I slew him, seeing thee embrace him.

' So thy surviving husband shall remain
The scornful mark of every open eye ;   520
Thy kinsmen hang their heads at this disdain,
Thy issue blurr'd with nameless bastardy ;
And thou, the author of their obloquy,
    Shalt have thy trespass cited up in rhymes,
    And sung by children in succeeding times.   525

' But if thou yield, I rest thy secret friend :
The fault unknown is as a thought unacted ;
A little harm done to a great good end
For lawful policy remains enacted.
The poisonous simple sometime is compacted   530
    In a pure compound ; being so applied,
    His venom in effect is purified.

'Then, for thy husband and thy children's sake,
Tender my suit; bequeath not to their lot
The shame that from them no device can take,
The blemish that will never be forgot;   535
Worse than a slavish wipe or birth-hour's blot;
    For marks descried in men's nativity
    Are nature's faults, not their own infamy.'

Here with a cockatrice' dead-killing eye   540
He rouseth up himself, and makes a pause;
While she, the picture of pure piety,
Like a white hind under the grype's sharp claws,
Pleads, in a wilderness where are no laws,
    To the rough beast that knows no gentle right,   545
    Nor aught obeys but his foul appetite.

But when a black-fac'd cloud the world doth threat,
In his dim mist th' aspiring mountains hiding,
From earth's dark womb some gentle gust doth get,
Which blows these pitchy vapours from their biding,   550
Hind'ring their present fall by this dividing;
    So his unhallowed haste her words delays,
    And moody Pluto winks while Orpheus plays.

Yet, foul night-waking cat, he doth but dally,
While in his holdfast foot the weak mouse panteth;   555
Her sad behaviour feeds his vulture folly,
A swallowing gulf that even in plenty wanteth;
His ear her prayers admits, but his heart granteth
    No penetrable entrance to her plaining.
    Tears harden lust, though marble wear with raining. 560

Her pity-pleading eyes are sadly fixed
In the remorseless wrinkles of his face;
Her modest eloquence with sighs is mixed,
Which to her oratory adds more grace.
She puts the period often from his place,   565
    And midst the sentence so her accent breaks
    That twice she doth begin ere once she speaks.

She conjures him by high almighty Jove,
By knighthood, gentry, and sweet friendship's oath,
By her untimely tears, her husband's love,   570
By holy human law, and common troth,
By heaven and earth, and all the power of both,
    That to his borrowed bed he make retire,
    And stoop to honour, not to foul desire.

Quoth she 'Reward not hospitality   575
With such black payment as thou hast pretended;
Mud not the fountain that gave drink to thee;
Mar not the thing that cannot be amended;
End thy ill aim before thy shoot be ended.
    He is no woodman that doth bend his bow   580
    To strike a poor unseasonable doe.

' My husband is thy friend—for his sake spare me ;
Thyself art mighty—for thine own sake leave me ;
Myself a weakling—do not then ensnare me ;
Thou look'st not like deceit—do not deceive me.　　585
My sighs like whirlwinds labour hence to heave thee.
　　If ever man were mov'd with woman's moans,
　　Be moved with my tears, my sighs, my groans ;

' All which together, like a troubled ocean,
Beat at thy rocky and wrack-threat'ning heart ;　　590
To soften it with their continual motion ;
For stones dissolv'd to water do convert.
O, if no harder than a stone thou art,
　　Melt at my tears, and be compassionate !
　　Soft pity enters at an iron gate.　　595

' In Tarquin's likeness I did entertain thee ;
Hast thou put on his shape to do him shame ?
To all the host of heaven I complain me
Thou wrong'st his honour, wound'st his princely name.
Thou art not what thou seem'st ; and if the same,　　600
　　Thou seem'st not what thou art, a god, a king ;
　　For kings like gods should govern everything.

' How will thy shame be seeded in thine age,
When thus thy vices bud before thy spring !
If in thy hope thou dar'st do such outrage,　　605
What dar'st thou not when once thou art a king ?
O, be rememb'red, no outrageous thing
　　From vassal actors can be wip'd away ;
　　Then kings' misdeeds cannot be hid in clay.

' This deed will make thee only lov'd for fear,　　610
But happy monarchs still are fear'd for love ;
With foul offenders thou perforce must bear,
When they in thee the like offences prove.
If but for fear of this, thy will remove ;
　　For princes are the glass, the school, the book,　　615
　　Where subjects' eyes do learn, do read, do look.

' And wilt thou be the school where Lust shall learn ?
Must he in thee read lectures of such shame ?
Wilt thou be glass wherein it shall discern
Authority for sin, warrant for blame,　　620
To privilege dishonour in thy name ?
　　Thou back'st reproach against long-living laud,
　　And mak'st fair reputation but a bawd.

' Hast thou command ?　By him that gave it thee
From a pure heart command thy rebel will ;　　625
Draw not thy sword to guard iniquity,
For it was lent thee all that brood to kill.
Thy princely office how canst thou fulfil,
　　When, pattern'd by thy fault, foul Sin may say
　　He learn'd to sin and thou didst teach the way ?　　630

' Think but how vile a spectacle it were
To view thy present trespass in another.
Men's faults do seldom to themselves appear ;
Their own transgressions partially they smother :
This guilt would seem death-worthy in thy brother.   635
    O, how are they wrapp'd in with infamies
    That from their own misdeeds askance their eyes !

' To thee, to thee, my heav'd-up hands appeal,
Not to seducing lust, thy rash relier ;
I sue for exil'd majesty's repeal ;   640
Let him return and flatt'ring thoughts retire :
His true respect will prison false desire,
    And wipe the dim mist from thy doting eyne,
    That thou shalt see thy state, and pity mine '.

' Have done ; ' quoth he ' my uncontrolled tide   645
Turns not, but swells the higher by this let.
Small lights are soon blown out ; huge fires abide,
And with the wind in greater fury fret.
The petty streams that pay a daily debt
    To their salt sovereign, with their fresh falls' haste,   650
    Add to his flow, but alter not his taste.'

' Thou art ' quoth she ' a sea, a sovereign king ;
And lo, there falls into thy boundless flood
Black lust, dishonour, shame, misgoverning,
Who seek to stain the ocean of thy blood.   655
If all these petty ills shall change thy good,
    Thy sea within a puddle's womb is hearsed,
    And not the puddle in thy sea dispersed.

' So shall these slaves be king, and thou their slave ;
Thou nobly base, they basely dignified ;   660
Thou their fair life, and they thy fouler grave ;
Thou loathed in their shame, they in thy pride.
The lesser thing should not the greater hide ;
    The cedar stoops not to the base shrub's foot,
    But low shrubs wither at the cedar's root.   665

' So let thy thoughts, low vassals to thy state '—
' No more ; ' quoth he ' by heaven, I will not hear thee !
Yield to my love ; if not, enforced hate,
Instead of love's coy touch, shall rudely tear thee ;
That done, despitefully I mean to bear thee   670
    Unto the base bed of some rascal groom,
    To be thy partner in this shameful doom.'

This said, he sets his foot upon the light,
For light and lust are deadly enemies ;
Shame folded up in blind concealing night,   675
When most unseen, then most doth tyrannize.
The wolf hath seiz'd his prey ; the poor lamb cries
    Till with her own white fleece her voice controll'd
    Entombs her outcry in her lips' sweet fold ;

For with the nightly linen that she wears 680
He pens her piteous clamours in her head,
Cooling his hot face in the chastest tears
That ever modest eyes with sorrow shed.
O, that prone lust should stain so pure a bed! 685
   The spots whereof could weeping purify,
   Her tears should drop on them perpetually.

But she hath lost a dearer thing than life,
And he hath won what he would lose again.
This forced league doth force a further strife,
This momentary joy breeds months of pain, 690
This hot desire converts to cold disdain;
   Pure Chastity is rifled of her store,
   And Lust, the thief, far poorer than before.

Look as the full-fed hound or gorged hawk,
Unapt for tender smell or speedy flight, 695
Make slow pursuit, or altogether baulk
The prey wherein by nature they delight;
So surfeit-taking Tarquin fares this night:
   His taste delicious, in digestion souring,
   Devours his will, that liv'd by foul devouring. 700

O, deeper sin than bottomless conceit
Can comprehend in still imagination!
Drunken Desire must vomit his receipt,
Ere he can see his own abomination.
While Lust is in his pride, no exclamation 705
   Can curb his heat or rein his rash desire,
   Till, like a jade, Self-will himself doth tire.

And then with lank and lean discolour'd cheek,
With heavy eye, knit brow, and strengthless pace,
Feeble Desire, all recreant, poor, and meek, 710
Like to a bankrupt beggar wails his case.
The flesh being proud, Desire doth fight with Grace,
   For there it revels; and when that decays,
   The guilty rebel for remission prays.

So fares it with this faultful lord of Rome, 715
Who this accomplishment so hotly chased;
For now against himself he sounds this doom,
That through the length of times he stands disgraced;
Besides, his soul's fair temple is defaced
   To whose weak ruins muster troops of cares, 720
   To ask the spotted princess how she fares.

She says her subjects with foul insurrection
Have batter'd down her consecrated wall,
And by their mortal fault brought in subjection
Her immortality, and made her thrall 725
To living death and pain perpetual;
   Which in her prescience she controlled still,
   But her foresight could not forestall their will.

Ev'n in this thought through the dark night he stealeth,
A captive victor that hath lost in gain ;
Bearing away the wound that nothing healeth,   730
The scar that will despite of cure remain,
Leaving his spoil perplex'd in greater pain.
   She bears the load of lust he left behind,
   And he the burthen of a guilty mind.   735

He like a thievish dog creeps sadly thence,
She like a wearied lamb lies panting there ;
He scowls and hates himself for his offence
She, desperate, with her nails her flesh doth tear.
He faintly flies, sweating with guilty fear ;   740
   She stays, exclaiming on the direful night ;
   He runs, and chides his vanish'd loath'd delight.

He thence departs a heavy convertite,
She there remains a hopeless castaway ;
He in his speed looks for the morning light ;   745
She prays she never may behold the day.
' For day ' quoth she ' night's scapes doth open lay ;
   And my true eyes have never practis'd how
   To cloak offences with a cunning brow.

' They think not but that every eye can see   750
The same disgrace which they themselves behold ;
And therefore would they still in darkness be,
To have their unseen sin remain untold ;
For they their guilt with weeping will unfold,
   And grave, like water that doth eat in steel,   755
   Upon my cheeks what helpless shame I feel.'

Here she exclaims against repose and rest,
And bids her eyes hereafter still be blind.
She wakes her heart by beating on her breast,
And bids it leap from thence, where it may find   760
Some purer chest to close so pure a mind.
   Frantic with grief thus breathes she forth her spite
   Against the unseen secrecy of night :

' O comfort-killing Night, image of hell !
Dim register and notary of shame !   765
Black stage for tragedies and murders fell !
Vast sin-concealing chaos ! nurse of blame !
Blind muffled bawd ! dark harbour for defame !
   Grim cave of death ! whisp'ring conspirator,
   With close-tongu'd treason and the ravisher !   770

' O hateful, vaporous, and foggy night !
Since thou art guilty of my cureless crime,
Muster thy mists to meet the eastern light,
Make war against proportion'd course of time ;
Or if thou wilt permit the sun to climb   775
   His wonted height, yet ere he go to bed,
   Knit poisonous clouds about his golden head.

' With rotten damps ravish the morning air ;
Let their exhal'd unwholesome breaths make sick
The life of purity, the supreme fair,   780
Ere he arrive his weary noontide prick ;
And let thy musty vapours march so thick
   That in their smoky ranks his smoth'red light
   May set at noon and make perpetual night.

' Were Tarquin Night, as he is but Night's child,   785
The silver-shining queen he would distain ;
Her twinkling handmaids too, by him defil'd,
Through Night's black bosom should not peep again ;
So should I have co-partners in my pain ;
   And fellowship in woe doth woe assuage,   790
   As palmers' chat makes short their pilgrimage.

' Where now I have no one to blush with me,
To cross their arms and hang their heads with mine,
To mask their brows and hide their infamy ;
But I alone alone must sit and pine,   795
Seasoning the earth with show'rs of silver brine,
   Mingling my talk with tears, my grief with groans
   Poor wasting monuments of lasting moans.

' O Night, thou furnace of foul reeking smoke,
Let not the jealous Day behold that face   800
Which underneath thy black all-hiding cloak
Immodestly lies martyr'd with disgrace !
Keep still possession of thy gloomy place,
   That all the faults which in thy reign are made
   May likewise be sepulcher'd in thy shade.   805

' Make me not object to the tell-tale Day.
The light will show, character'd in my brow,
The story of sweet chastity's decay,
The impious breach of holy wedlock vow ;
Yea, the illiterate, that know not how   810
   To cipher what is writ in learned books,
   Will quote my loathsome trespass in my looks.

' The nurse, to still her child, will tell my story,
And fright her crying babe with Tarquin's name ;
The orator, to deck his oratory,   815
Will couple my reproach to Tarquin's shame ;
Feast-finding minstrels, tuning my defame,
   Will tie the hearers to attend each line,
   How Tarquin wronged me, I Collatine.

' Let my good name, that senseless reputation,   820
For Collatine's dear love be kept unspotted ;
If that be made a theme for disputation,
The branches of another root are rotted,
And undeserv'd reproach to him allotted
   That is as clear from this attaint of mine   825
   As I ere this was pure to Collatine.

'O unseen shame! invisible disgrace!
O unfelt sore! crest-wounding, private scar!
Reproach is stamp'd in Collatinus' face,
And Tarquin's eye may read the mot afar,   830
How he in peace is wounded, not in war.
   Alas, how many bear such shameful blows,
   Which not themselves but he that gives them knows!

'If, Collatine, thine honour lay in me,
From me by strong assault it is bereft.   835
My honey lost, and I, a drone-like bee,
Have no perfection of my summer left,
But robb'd and ransack'd by injurious theft.
   In thy weak hive a wand'ring wasp hath crept,
   And suck'd the honey which thy chaste bee kept.   840

'Yet am I guilty of thy honour's wrack—
Yet for thy honour did I entertain him;
Coming from thee, I could not put him back,
For it had been dishonour to disdain him;
Besides of weariness he did complain him,   845
   And talk'd of virtue—O unlook'd-for evil,
   When virtue is profan'd in such a devil!

'Why should the worm intrude the maiden bud?
Or hateful cuckoos hatch in sparrows' nests?
Or toads infect fair founts with venom mud?   850
Or tyrant folly lurk in gentle breasts?
Or kings be breakers of their own behests?
   But no perfection is so absolute
   That some impurity doth not pollute.

'The aged man that coffers up his gold   855
Is plagu'd with cramps and gouts and painful fits,
And scarce hath eyes his treasure to behold,
But like still-pining Tantalus he sits,
And useless barns the harvest of his wits,
   Having no other pleasure of his gain   860
   But torment that it cannot cure his pain.

'So then he hath it, when he cannot use it,
And leaves it to be mast'red by his young;
Who in their pride do presently abuse it.
Their father was too weak, and they too strong,   865
To hold their cursed-blessed fortune long.
   The sweets we wish for turn to loathed sours
   Even in the moment that we call them ours.

'Unruly blasts wait on the tender spring;
Unwholesome weeds take root with precious flow'rs;   870
The adder hisses where the sweet birds sing;
What virtue breeds iniquity devours.
We have no good that we can say is ours,
   But ill-annexed Opportunity
   Or kills his life or else his quality.   875

' O Opportunity, thy guilt is great !
'Tis thou that execut'st the traitor's treason ;
Thou sets the wolf where he the lamb may get ;
Whoever plots the sin, thou 'point'st the season ;
'Tis thou that spurn'st at right, at law, at reason ;   880
    And in thy shady cell, where none may spy him,
    Sits Sin, to seize the souls that wander by him.

' Thou makest the vestal violate her oath ;
Thou blowest the fire when temperance is thaw'd ;
Thou smotherest honesty, thou murth'rest troth ;   885
Thou foul abettor ! thou notorious bawd !
Thou plantest scandal and displacest laud.
    Thou ravisher, thou traitor, thou false thief,
    Thy honey turns to gall, thy joy to grief !

' Thy secret pleasure turns to open shame,   890
Thy private feasting to a public fast,
Thy smoothing titles to a ragged name,
Thy sug'red tongue to bitter wormwood taste ;
Thy violent vanities can never last.
    How comes it then, vile Opportunity,   895
    Being so bad, such numbers seek for thee ?

' When wilt thou be the humble suppliant's friend,
And bring him where his suit may be obtained ?
When wilt thou sort an hour great strifes to end ?
Or free that soul which wretchedness hath chained ?   900
Give physic to the sick, ease to the pained ?
    The poor, lame, blind, halt, creep, cry out for thee ;
    But they ne'er meet with Opportunity.

' The patient dies while the physician sleeps ;
The orphan pines while the oppressor feeds ;   905
Justice is feasting while the widow weeps ;
Advice is sporting while infection breeds ;
Thou grant'st no time for charitable deeds ;
    Wrath, envy, treason, rape, and murder's rages,
    Thy heinous hours wait on them as their pages.   910

' When Truth and Virtue have to do with thee,
A thousand crosses keep them from thy aid ;
They buy thy help, but Sin ne'er gives a fee ;
He gratis comes, and thou art well apaid
As well to hear as grant what he hath said.   915
    My Collatine would else have come to me
    When Tarquin did, but he was stay'd by thee.

' Guilty thou art of murder and of theft,
Guilty of perjury and subornation,
Guilty of treason, forgery, and shift,   920
Guilty of incest, that abomination :
An accessary by thine inclination
    To all sins past, and all that are to come,
    From the creation to the general doom.

' Mis-shapen Time, copesmate of ugly Night,   925
Swift subtle post, carrier of grisly care,
Eater of youth, false slave to false delight,
Base watch of woes, sin's packhorse, virtue's snare ;
Thou nursest all, and murd'rest all that are.
   O hear me then, injurious, shifting Time !   930
   Be guilty of my death, since of my crime.

' Why hath thy servant Opportunity
Betray'd the hours thou gav'st me to repose ?
Cancell'd my fortunes and enchained me
To endless date of never-ending woes ?   935
Time's office is to fine the hate of foes,
   To eat up errors by opinion bred,
   Not spend the dowry of a lawful bed.

' Time's glory is to calm contending kings,
To unmask falsehood, and bring truth to light,   940
To stamp the seal of time in aged things,
To wake the morn, and sentinel the night,
To wrong the wronger till he render right
   To ruinate proud buildings with thy hours,
   And smear with dust their glitt'ring golden tow'rs ;   945

' To fill with worm-holes stately monuments,
To feed oblivion with decay of things,
To blot old books and alter their contents,
To pluck the quills from ancient ravens' wings,
To dry the old oak's sap, and cherish springs ;   950
   To spoil antiquities of hammer'd steel,
   And turn the giddy round of Fortune's wheel ;

' To show the beldam daughters of her daughter,
To make the child a man, the man a child,
To slay the tiger that doth live by slaughter,   955
To tame the unicorn and lion wild,
To mock the subtle in themselves beguil'd,
   To cheer the ploughman with increaseful crops,
   And waste huge stones with little water drops.

' Why work'st thou mischief in thy pilgrimage,   960
Unless thou couldst return to make amends ?
One poor retiring minute in an age
Would purchase thee a thousand thousand friends,
Lending him wit that to bad debtors lends.
   O, this dread night, wouldst thou one hour come back,   965
   I could prevent this storm, and shun thy wrack !

' Thou ceaseless lackey to Eternity,
With some mischance cross Tarquin in his flight ;
Devise extremes beyond extremity
To make him curse this cursed crimeful night ;   970
Let ghastly shadows his lewd eyes affright
   And the dire thought of his committed evil
   Shape every bush a hideous shapeless devil.

'Disturb his hours of rest with restless trances,
Afflict him in his bed with bedrid groans;   97
Let there bechance him pitiful mischances
To make him moan, but pity not his moans.
Stone him with hard'ned hearts harder than stones;
 And let mild women to him lose their mildness,
 Wilder to him than tigers in their wildness.   98

'Let him have time to tear his curled hair,
Let him have time against himself to rave,
Let him have time of Time's help to despair,
Let him have time to live a loathed slave,
Let him have time a beggar's orts to crave;   98
 And time to see one that by alms doth live
 Disdain to him disdained scraps to give.

'Let him have time to see his friends his foes,
And merry fools to mock at him resort;
Let him have time to mark how slow time goes   99
In time of sorrow, and how swift and short
His time of folly and his time of sport;
 And ever let his unrecalling crime
 Have time to wail th' abusing of his time.

'O Time, thou tutor both to good and bad,   99
Teach me to curse him that thou taught'st this ill!
At his own shadow let the thief run mad,
Himself himself seek every hour to kill!
Such wretched hands such wretched blood should spill;
 For who so base would such an office have   100
 As sland'rous death's-man to so base a slave?

'The baser is he, coming from a king,
To shame his hope with deeds degenerate.
The mightier man, the mightier is the thing
That makes him honour'd or begets him hate;   100
For greatest scandal waits on greatest state.
 The moon being clouded presently is miss'd,
 But little stars may hide them when they list.

'The crow may bathe his coal black wings in mire
And unperceiv'd fly with the filth away;   101
But if the like the snow-white swan desire,
The stain upon his silver down will stay.
Poor grooms are sightless night, kings glorious day.
 Gnats are unnoted wheresoe'er they fly,
 But eagles gaz'd upon with every eye.   101

'Out, idle words, servants to shallow fools!
Unprofitable sounds, weak arbitrators!
Busy yourselves in skill-contending schools,
Debate where leisure serves with dull debaters;
To trembling clients be you mediators.   102
 For me, I force not argument a straw,
 Since that my case is past the help of law.

'In vain I rail at Opportunity,
At Time, at Tarquin, and uncheerful Night;
In vain I cavil with mine infamy,
In vain I spurn at my confirm'd despite: 1025
This helpless smoke of words doth me no right.
    The remedy indeed to do me good
    Is to let forth my foul defiled blood.

'Poor hand, why quiver'st thou at this decree?   1030
Honour thyself to rid me of this shame;
For if I die my honour lives in thee,
But if I live thou liv'st in my defame.
Since thou couldst not defend thy loyal dame,
    And wast afeard to scratch her wicked foe,   1035
    Kill both thyself and her for yielding so'.

This said, from her betumbled couch she starteth
To find some desp'rate instrument of death,
But this no slaughterhouse no tool imparteth
To make more vent for passage of her breath,   1040
Which thronging through her lips so vanisheth
    As smoke from Ætna, that in air consumes,
    Or that which from discharged cannon fumes.

'In vain,' quoth she 'I live, and seek in vain
Some happy mean to end a hapless life.   1045
I fear'd by Tarquin's falchion to be slain,
Yet for the self-same purpose seek a knife;
But when I fear'd I was a loyal wife;
    So am I now—O no, that cannot be;
    Of that true type hath Tarquin rifled me.   1050

'O, that is gone for which I sought to live,
And therefore now I need not fear to die.
To clear this spot by death, at least I give
A badge of fame to slander's livery;
A dying life to living infamy.   1055
    Poor helpless help, the treasure stol'n away,
    To burn the guiltless casket where it lay!

'Well, well, dear Collatine, thou shalt not know
The stained taste of violated troth;
I will not wrong thy true affection so   1060
To flatter thee with an infringed oath;
This bastard graff shall never come to growth;
    He shall not boast who did thy stock pollute
    That thou art doting father of his fruit.

'Nor shall he smile at thee in secret thought,   1065
Nor laugh with his companions at thy state;
But thou shalt know thy interest was not bought
Basely with gold, but stol'n from forth thy gate.
For me, I am the mistress of my fate,
    And with my trespass never will dispense,   1070
    Till life to death acquit my forc'd offence.

' I will not poison thee with my attaint,
Nor fold my fault in cleanly coin'd excuses ;
My sable ground of sin I will not paint
To hide the truth of this false night's abuses. 1075
My tongue shall utter all ; mine eyes like sluices,
   As from a mountain-spring that feeds a dale,
   Shall gush pure streams to purge my impure tale.'

By this, lamenting Philomel had ended
The well-tun'd warble of her nightly sorrow, 1080
And solemn night with slow-sad gait descended
To ugly hell ; when lo, the blushing morrow
Lends light to all fair eyes that light will borrow ;
   But cloudy Lucrece shames herself to see,
   And therefore still in night would cloist'red be. 1085

Revealing day through every cranny spies,
And seems to point her out where she sits weeping ;
To whom she sobbing speaks : ' O eye of eyes,
Why pry'st thou through my window ? Leave thy peeping ;
Mock with thy tickling beams eyes that are sleeping ; 1090
   Brand not my forehead with thy piercing light,
   For day hath nought to do what's done by night '.

Thus cavils she with every thing she sees.
True grief is fond and testy as a child,
Who wayward once, his mood with nought agrees. 1095
Old woes, not infant sorrows, bear them mild :
Continuance tames the one ; the other wild,
   Like an unpractis'd swimmer plunging still
   With too much labour drowns for want of skill.

So she, deep drenched in a sea of care, 1100
Holds disputation with each thing she views,
And to herself all sorrow doth compare ;
No object but her passion's strength renews,
And as one shifts, another straight ensues.
   Sometime her grief is dumb and hath no words ; 1105
   Sometime 'tis mad and too much talk affords.

The little birds that tune their morning's joy
Make her moans mad with their sweet melody ;
For mirth doth search the bottom of annoy ;
Sad souls are slain in merry company ; 1110
Grief best is pleas'd with grief's society.
   True sorrow then is feelingly suffic'd
   When with like semblance it is sympathiz'd.

'Tis double death to drown in ken of shore ;
He ten times pines that pines beholding food ; 1115
To see the salve doth make the wound ache more ;
Great grief grieves most at that would do it good ;
Deep woes roll forward like a gentle flood,
   Who, being stopp'd, the bounding banks o'erflows ;
   Grief dallied with nor law not limit knows. 1120

' You mocking birds,' quoth she ' your tunes entomb
Within your hollow-swelling feathered breasts,
And in my hearing be you mute and dumb.
My restless discord loves no stops nor rests ;
A woeful hostess brooks not merry guests.   1125
 Relish your nimble notes to pleasing ears ;
 Distress likes dumps when time is kept with tears.

' Come, Philomel, that sing'st of ravishment,
Make thy sad grove in my dishevell'd hair.
As the dank earth weeps at thy languishment,   1130
So I at each sad strain will strain a tear,
And with deep groans the diapason bear ;
 For burthen-wise I'll hum on Tarquin still,
 While thou on Tereus descants better skill.

' And whiles against a thorn thou bear'st thy part   1135
To keep thy sharp woes waking, wretched I,
To imitate thee well, against my heart
Will fix a sharp knife to affright mine eye ;
Who, if it wink, shall thereon fall and die.
 These means, as frets upon an instrument,   1140
 Shall tune our heartstrings to true languishment.

' And for, poor bird, thou sing'st not in the day,
As shaming any eye should thee behold,
Some dark deep desert, seated from the way,
That knows not parching heat nor freezing cold,   1145
Will we find out ; and there we will unfold
 To creatures stern sad tunes, to change their kinds.
 Since men prove beasts, let beasts bear gentle minds.'

As the poor frighted deer, that stands at gaze,
Wildly determining which way to fly,   1150
Or one encompass'd with a winding maze
That cannot tread the way out readily ;
So with herself is she in mutiny,
 To live or die which of the twain were better,
 When life is sham'd, and death reproach's debtor.   1155

' To kill myself,' quoth she ' alack, what were it,
But with my body my poor soul's pollution ?
They that lose half with greater patience bear it
Than they whose whole is swallowed in confusion.
That mother tries a merciless conclusion   1160
 Who, having two sweet babes, when death takes one,
 Will slay the other and be nurse to none.

' My body or my soul, which was the dearer,
When the one pure, the other made divine ?
Whose love of either to myself was nearer,   1165
When both were kept for heaven and Collatine ?
Ay me ! the bark pill'd from the lofty pine,
 His leaves will wither and his sap decay ;
 So must my soul, her bark being pill'd away.

'Her house is sack'd, her quiet interrupted,   117
Her mansion batter'd by the enemy ;
Her sacred temple spotted, spoil'd, corrupted.
Grossly engirt with daring infamy ;
Then let it not be call'd impiety
   If in this blemish'd fort I make some hole   117
   Through which I may convey this troubled soul.

'Yet die I will not till my Collatine
Have heard the cause of my untimely death ;
That he may vow, in that sad hour of mine,
Revenge on him that made me stop my breath.   118
My stained blood to Tarquin I'll bequeath,
   Which by him tainted shall for him be spent,
   And as his due writ in my testament.

'My honour I'll bequeath unto the knife
That wounds my body so dishonoured.   118
'Tis honour to deprive dishonour'd life :
The one will live, the other being dead.
So of shame's ashes shall my fame be bred ;
   For in my death I murther shameful scorn.
   My shame so dead, mine honour is new born.   119

'Dear lord of that dear jewel I have lost,
What legacy shall I bequeath to thee ?
My resolution, love, shall be thy boast,
By whose example thou reveng'd mayst be.
How Tarquin must be us'd, read it in me :   119
   Myself, thy friend, will kill myself, thy foe ;
   And for my sake serve thou false Tarquin so.

'This brief abridgment of my will I make :
My soul and body to the skies and ground ;
My resolution, husband, do thou take ;   120
Mine honour be the knife's that make my wound ;
My shame be his that did my fame confound ;
   And all my fame that lives disbursed be
   To those that live and think no shame of me.

'Thou, Collatine, shalt oversee this will.   120
How was I overseen that thou shalt see it !
My blood shall wash the slander of mine ill ;
My life's foul deed, my life's fair end shall free it.
Faint not, faint heart, but stoutly say " So be it."
   Yield to my hand ; my hand shall conquer thee ;   121
   Thou dead, both die, and both shall victors be.'

This plot of death when sadly she had laid
And wip'd the brinish pearl from her bright eyes,
With untun'd tongue she hoarsely calls her maid,
Whose swift obedience to her mistress hies ;   121
For fleet-wing'd duty with thought's feathers flies.
   Poor Lucrece' cheeks unto her maid seem so
   As winter meads when sun doth melt their snow.

Her mistress she doth give demure good-morrow
With soft-slow tongue, true mark of modesty,   1220
And sorts a sad look to her lady's sorrow,
For why her face wore sorrow's livery ;
But durst not ask of her audaciously
    Why her two suns were cloud-eclipsed so,
    Nor why her fair cheeks over-wash'd with woe.   1225

But as the earth doth weep, the sun being set,
Each flower moist'ned like a melting eye ;
Even so the maid with swelling drops gan wet
Her circled eyne, enforc'd by sympathy
Of those fair suns set in her mistress' sky,   1230
    Who in a salt-wav'd ocean quench their light,
    Which makes the maid weep like the dewy night.

A pretty while these pretty creatures stand,
Like ivory conduits coral cisterns filling :
One justly weeps ; the other taken in hand   1235
No cause but company of her drops spilling.
Their gentle sex to weep are often willing ;
    Grieving themselves to guess at others' smarts,
    And then they drown their eyes, or break their hearts.

For men have marble, women waxen minds,   1240
And therefore are they form'd as marble will ;
The weak oppress'd, th' impression of strange kinds
Is form'd in them by force, by fraud, or skill.
Then call them not the authors of their ill,
    No more than wax shall be accounted evil   1245
    Wherein is stamp'd the semblance of a devil.

Their smoothness, like a goodly champaign plan,
Lays open all the little worms that creep ;
In men, as in a rough-grown grove, remain
Cave-keeping evils that obscurely sleep.   1250
Through crystal walls each little mote will peep.
    Though men can cover crimes with bold stern looks,
    Poor women's faces are their own faults' books.

No man inveigh against the withered flow'r,
But chide rough winter that the flow'r hath kill'd.   1255
Not that devour'd, but that which doth devour,
Is worthy blame. O, let it not be hild
Poor women's faults that they are so fulfill'd
    With men's abuses ! those proud lords to blame
    Make weak-made women tenants to their shame.   1260

The precedent whereof in Lucrece view,
Assail'd by night with circumstances strong
Of present death and shame that might ensue
By that her death, to do her husband wrong.
Such danger to resistance did belong   1265
    That dying fear through all her body spread ;
    And who cannot abuse a body dead ?

By this, mild patience bid fair Lucrece speak
To the poor counterfeit of her complaining.
'My girl,' quoth she 'on what occasion break   1270
Those tears from thee that down thy cheeks are raining?
If thou dost weep for grief of my sustaining,
   Know, gentle wench, it small avails my mood;
   If tears could help, mine own would do me good.

'But tell me, girl, when went '—and there she stay'd   1275
Till after a deep groan—'Tarquin from hence?'
'Madam, ere I was up,' replied the maid
'The more to blame my sluggard negligence.
Yet with the fault I thus far can dispense:
   Myself was stirring ere the break of day,   1280
   And ere I rose was Tarquin gone away.

'But, lady, if your maid may be so bold,
She would request to know your heaviness.'
'O, peace!' quoth Lucrece 'If it should be told,
The repetition cannot make it less,   1285
For more it is than I can well express;
   And that deep torture may be call'd a hell,
   When more is felt than one hath power to tell.

'Go, get me hither paper, ink, and pen—
Yet save that labour, for I have them here.   1290
What should I say?—One of my husband's men
Bid thou be ready, by and by, to bear
A letter to my lord, my love, my dear.
   Bid him with speed prepare to carry it;
   The cause craves haste, and it will soon be writ.'   1295

Her maid is gone, and she prepares to write,
First hovering o'er the paper with her quill.
Conceit and grief an eager combat fight;
What wit sets down is blotted straight with will;
This is too curious-good, this blunt and ill: 1300
   Much like a press of people at a door,
   Throng her inventions, which shall go before.

At last she thus begins: 'Thou worthy lord
Of that unworthy wife that greeteth thee,
Health to thy person! Next vouchsafe t' afford—   1305
If ever, love, thy Lucrece thou wilt see—
Some present speed to come and visit me.
   So I commend me from our house in grief;
   My woes are tedious, though my words are brief'.

Here folds she up the tenour of her woe,   1310
Her certain sorrow writ uncertainly.
By this short schedule Collatine may know
Her grief, but not her grief's true quality;
She dares not thereof make discovery,
   Lest he should hold it her own gross abuse,   1315
   Ere she with blood had stain'd her stain'd excuse.

Besides, the life and feeling of her passion
She hoards, to spend when he is by to hear her;
When sighs and groans and tears may grace the fashion
Of her disgrace, the better so to clear her   1320
From that suspicion which the world might bear her.
    To shun this blot, she would not blot the letter
    With words, till action might become them better.

To see sad sights moves more than hear them told;
For then the eye interprets to the ear   1325
The heavy motion that it doth behold,
When every part a part of woe doth bear.
'Tis but a part of sorrow that we hear:
    Deep sounds make lesser noise than shallow fords,
    And sorrow ebbs, being blown with wind of words.   1330

Her letter now is seal'd, and on it writ
'At Ardea to my lord with more than haste'.
The post attends, and she delivers it
Charging the sour-fac'd groom to hie as fast
As lagging fowls before the northern blast.   1335
    Speed more than speed but dull and slow she deems:
    Extremity still urgeth such extremes.

The homely villain curtsies to her low
And blushing on her, with a steadfast eye
Receives the scroll without or yea or no,   1340
And forth with bashful innocence doth hie.
But they whose guilt within their bosoms lie
    Imagine every eye beholds their blame;
    For Lucrece thought he blush'd to see her shame.

When, silly groom! God wot, it was defect   1345
Of spirit, life, and bold audacity.
Such harmless creatures have a true respect
To talk in deeds, while others saucily
Promise more speed but do it leisurely.
    Even so, this pattern of the worn-out age   1350
    Pawn'd honest looks, but laid no words to gage.

His kindled duty kindled her mistrust,
That two red fires in both their faces blazed;
She thought he blush'd as knowing Tarquin's lust,
And, blushing with him, wistly on him gazed;   1355
Her earnest eye did make him more amazed;
    The more she saw the blood his cheeks replenish
    The more she thought he spied in her some blemish.

But long she thinks till he return again,
And yet the duteous vassal scarce is gone.   1360
The weary time she cannot entertain,
For now 'tis stale to sigh, to weep, and groan,
So woe hath wearied woe, moan tired moan,
    That she her plaints a little while doth stay,
    Pausing for means to mourn some newer way.   1365

At last she calls to mind where hangs a piece
Of skilful painting, made for Priam's Troy;
Before the which is drawn the power of Greece
For Helen's rape the city to destroy,
Threat'ning cloud-kissing Ilion with annoy;   1370
   Which the conceited painter drew so proud,
   As heaven, it seem'd, to kiss the turrets bow'd.

A thousand lamentable objects there,
In scorn of nature, art gave lifeless life
Many a dry drop seem'd a weeping tear   1377
Shed for the slaught'red husband by the wife;
The red blood reek'd to show the painter's strife,
   And dying eyes gleam'd forth their ashy lights,
   Like dying coals burnt out in tedious nights.

There might you see the labouring pioneer   1380
Begrim'd with sweat and smeared all with dust;
And from the towers of Troy there would appear
The very eyes of men through loopholes thrust,
Gazing upon the Greeks with little lust.
   Such sweet observance in this work was had   1383
   That one might see those far-off eyes look sad.

In great commanders grace and majesty
You might behold, triumphing in their faces;
In youth, quick bearing and dexterity;
And here and there the painter interlaces   1390
Pale cowards marching on with trembling paces,
   Which heartless peasants did so well resemble
   That one would swear he saw them quake and tremble.

In Ajax and Ulysses, O what art
Of physiognomy might one behold!   1397
The face of either cipher'd either's heart;
Their face their manners most expressly told:
In Ajax' eyes blunt rage and rigour roll'd;
   But the mild glance that sly Ulysses lent
   Show'd deep regard and smiling government.   1400

There pleading might you see grave Nestor stand,
As 'twere encouraging the Greeks to fight,
Making such sober action with his hand
That it beguil'd attention, charm'd the sight.
In speech, it seem'd, his beard all silver white 1405
   Wagg'd up and down, and from his lips did fly
   Thin winding breath, which purl'd up to the sky.

About him were a press of gaping faces,
Which seem'd to swallow up his sound advice,
All jointly list'ning, but with several graces,   1411
As if some mermaid did their ears entice;
Some high, some low—the painter was so nice—
   The scalps of many, almost hid behind,
   To jump up higher seem'd to mock the mind.

Here one man's hand lean'd on another's head,   1415
His nose being shadowed by his neighbour's ear;
Here one being throng'd bears back, all boll'n and red
Another smother'd seems to pelt and swear;
And in their rage such signs of rage they bear,
    As, but for loss of Nestor's golden words,   1420
    It seem'd they would debate with angry swords.

For much imaginary work was there;
Conceit deceitful, so compact, so kind,
That for Achilles' image stood his spear,
Grip'd in an armed hand; himself, behind   1425
Was left unseen, save to the eye of mind:
    A hand, a foot, a face, a leg, a head,
    Stood for the whole to be imagined.

And from the walls of strong-besieged Troy
When their brave hope, bold Hector, march'd to field,   1430
Stood many Troyan mothers, sharing joy
To see their youthful sons bright weapons wield;
And to their hope they such odd action yield
    That through their light joy seemed to appear,
    Like bright things stain'd, a kind of heavy fear.   1435

And from the strond of Dardan where they fought,
To Simois' reedy banks, the red blood ran,
Whose waves to imitate the battle sought
With swelling ridges; and their ranks began
To break upon the galled shore, and than   1440
    Retire again, till meeting greater ranks
    They join, and shoot their foam at Simois' banks.

To this well-painted piece is Lucrece come,
To find a face where all distress is stell'd.
Many she sees where cares have carved some,   1445
But none where all distress and dolour dwell'd,
Till she despairing Hecuba beheld,
    Staring on Priam's wounds with her old eyes,
    Which bleeding under Pyrrhus' proud foot lies

In her the painter had anatomiz'd   1450
Time's ruin, beauty's wrack, and grim care's reign;
Her cheeks with chaps and wrinkles were disguis'd;
Of what she was no semblance did remain:
Her blue blood chang'd to black in every vein,
    Wanting the spring that those shrunk pipes had fed,   1455
    Show'd life imprison'd in a body dead.

On this sad shadow Lucrece spends her eyes,
And shapes her sorrow to the beldam's woes,
Who nothing wants to answer her but cries,
And bitter words to ban her cruel foes: 1460
The painter was no god to lend her those;
    And therefore Lucrece swears he did her wrong
    To give her so much grief and not a tongue.

'Poor instrument,' quoth she 'without a sound,
I'll tune thy woes with my lamenting tongue,
And drop sweet balm in Priam's painted wound,   1465
And rail on Pyrrhus that hath done him wrong,
And with my tears quench Troy that burns so long;
    And with my knife scratch out the angry eyes
    Of all the Greeks that are thine enemies.   1470

'Show me the strumpet that began this stir,
That with my nails her beauty I may tear.
Thy heat of lust, fond Paris, did incur
This load of wrath that burning Troy doth bear.
Thy eye kindled the fire that burneth here;   1475
    And here in Troy, for trespass of thine eye,
    The sire, the son, the dame, and daughter die.

'Why should the private pleasure of some one
Become the public plague of many moe?
Let sin, alone committed, light alone   1480
Upon his head that hath transgressed so;
Let guiltless souls be freed from guilty woe.
    For one's offence why should so many fall,
    To plague a private sin in general?

'Lo, here weeps Hecuba, here Priam dies,   1485
Here manly Hector faints, here Troilus sounds;
Here friend by friend in bloody channel lies,
And friend to friend gives unadvised wounds,
And one man's lust these many lives confounds.
    Had doting Priam check'd his son's desire,   1490
    Troy had been bright with fame, and not with fire.'

Here feelingly she weeps Troy's painted woes.
For sorrow, like a heavy-hanging bell,
Once set on ringing, with his own weight goes;
Then little strength rings out the doleful knell;   1495
So Lucrece set a-work sad tales doth tell
    To pencill'd pensiveness and colour'd sorrow;
    She lends them words, and she their looks doth borrow.

She throws her eyes about the painting round,
And who she finds forlorn she doth lament.   1500
At last she sees a wretched image bound
That piteous looks to Phrygian shepherds lent;
His face, though full of cares, yet show'd content:
    Onward to Troy with the blunt swains he goes,
    So mild that Patience seem'd to scorn his woes. 1505

In him the painter labour'd with his skill
To hide deceit, and give the harmless show
An humble gait, calm looks, eyes wailing still,
A brow unbent, that seem'd to welcome woe;
Cheeks neither red nor pale, but mingled so   1510
    That blushing red no guilty instance gave,
    Nor ashy pale the fear that false hearts have;

But, like a constant and confirmed devil,
He entertain'd a show so seeming just,
And therein so ensconc'd his secret evil,   1515
That jealousy itself could not mistrust
False-creeping craft and perjury should thrust
  Into so bright a day such black-fac'd storms,
  Or blot with hell-born sin such saint-like forms.

The well-skill'd workman this mild image drew   1520
For perjur'd Sinon, whose enchanting story
The credulous old Priam after slew;
Whose words, like wildfire, burnt the shining glory
Of rich-built Ilion, that the skies were sorry,
  And little stars shot from their fixed places,   1525
  When their glass fell wherein they view'd their faces.

This picture she advisedly perus'd,
And chid the painter for his wondrous skill;
Saying, some shape in Sinon's was abus'd,
So fair a form lodg'd not a mind so ill;   1530
And still on him she gaz'd, and gazing still
  Such signs of truth in his plain face she spied
  That she concludes the picture was belied.

' It cannot be ' quoth she ' that so much guile '
She would have said ' can lurk in such a look '   1535
But Tarquin's shape came in her mind the while,
And from her tongue ' can lurk ' from ' cannot ' took;
' It cannot be ' she in that sense forsook,
  And turn'd it thus : ' It cannot be, I find,
  But such a face should bear a wicked mind;   1540

' For even as subtle Sinon here is painted,
So sober-sad, so weary, and so mild,
As if with grief or travail he had fainted,
To me came Tarquin armed; so beguil'd
With outward honesty, but yet defil'd   1545
  With inward vice. As Priam him did cherish,
  So did I Tarquin; so my Troy did perish.

' Look, look, how list'ning Priam wets his eyes,
To see those borrowed tears that Sinon sheds.
Priam, why art thou old, and yet not wise?   1550
For every tear he falls a Troyan bleeds;
His eye drops fire, no water thence proceeds;
  Those round clear pearls of his that move thy pity
  Are balls of quenchless fire to burn thy city.

' Such devils steal effects from lightless hell;   1555
For Sinon in his fire doth quake with cold,
And in that cold hot burning fire doth dwell;
These contraries such unity do hold
Only to flatter fools, and make them bold;
  So Priam's trust false Sinon's tears doth flatter 1560
  That he finds means to burn his Troy with water.'

Here, all enrag'd, such passion her assails
That patience is quite beaten from her breast.
She tears the senseless Sinon with her nails,
Comparing him to that unhappy guest   1565
Whose deed hath made herself herself detest.
   At last she smilingly with this gives o'er :
   ' Fool ! fool ! ' quoth she ' his wounds will not be sore.'

Thus ebbs and flows the current of her sorrow,
And time doth weary time with her complaining.   1570
She looks for night, and then she longs for morrow,
And both she thinks too long with her remaining.
Short time seems long in sorrow's sharp sustaining ;
   Though woe be heavy, yet it seldom sleeps ;
   And they that watch see time how slow it creeps.   1575

Which all this time hath overslipp'd throught
That she with painted images hath spent,
Being from the feeling of her own grief brought
By deep surmise of others' detriment,
Losing her woes in shows of discontent.   1580
   It easeth some, though none it ever cured,
   To think their dolour others have endured.

But now the mindful messenger, come back,
Brings home his lord and other company ;
Who finds his Lucrece clad in mourning black,   1585
And round about her tear-distained eye
Blue circles stream'd, like rainbows in the sky.
   These water-galls in her dim element
   Foretell new storms to those already spent.

Which when her sad-beholding husband saw,   1590
Amazedly in her sad face he stares :
Her eyes, though sod in tears, look'd red and raw,
Her lively colour kill'd with deadly cares.
He hath no power to ask her how she fares ;
   Both stood like old acquaintance in a trance,   1595
   Met far from home, wond'ring each other's chance.

At last he takes her by the bloodless hand,
And thus begins : ' What uncouth ill event
Hath thee befall'n, that thou dost trembling stand ?
Sweet love, what spite hath thy fair colour spent ?   1600
Why art thou thus attir'd in discontent ?
   Unmask, dear dear, this moody heaviness,
   And tell thy grief, that we may give redress.'

Three times with sighs she gives her sorrow fire
Ere once she can discharge one word of woe ;   1605
At length address'd to answer his desire,
She modestly prepares to let them know
Her honour is ta'en prisoner by the foe ;
   While Collatine and his consorted lords
   With sad attention long to hear her words.   1610

And now this pale swan in her wat'ry nest
Begins the sad dirge of her certain ending.
' Few words ' quoth she ' shall fit the trespass best,
Where no excuse can give the fault amending :
In me moe woes than words are now depending ;   1615
   And my laments would be drawn out too long
   To tell them all with one poor tired tongue.

' Then be this all the task it hath to say :
Dear husband, in the interest of thy bed
A stranger came and on that pillow lay   1620
Where thou wast wont to rest thy weary head ;
And what wrong else may be imagined
   By foul enforcement might be done to me
   From that, alas, thy Lucrece is not free.

' For in the dreadful dead of dark midnight,   1625
With shining falchion in my chamber came
A creeping creature, with a flaming light,
And softly cried " Awake, thou Roman dame,
And entertain my love ; else lasting shame
   On thee and thine this night I will inflict,   1630
   If thou my love's desire do contradict.

' " For some hard-favour'd groom of thine " quoth he,
" Unless thou yoke thy liking to my will,
I'll murder straight, and then I'll slaughter thee,
And swear I found you where you did fulfil   1635
The loathsome act of lust, and so did kill
   The lechers in their deed : this act will be
   My fame, and thy perpetual infamy ".

' With this I did begin to start and cry,
And then against my heart he set his sword,   1640
Swearing, unless I took all patiently,
I should not live to speak another word.
So should my shame still rest upon record,
   And never be forgot in mighty Rome
   Th' adulterate death of Lucrece and her groom.   1645

' Mine enemy was strong, my poor self weak,
And far the weaker with so strong a fear.
My bloody judge forbade my tongue to speak ;
No rightful plea might plead for justice there.
His scarlet lust came evidence to swear   1650
   That my poor beauty had purloin'd his eyes,
   And when the judge is robb'd, the prisoner dies.

' O, teach me how to make mine own excuse !
Or, at the least, this refuge let me find :
Though my gross blood be stain'd with this abuse,   1655
Immaculate and spotless is my mind ;
That was not forc'd ; that never was inclin'd
   To accessary yieldings, but still pure
   Doth in her poison'd closet yet endure.'

Lo, here, the hopeless merchant of this loss,   1660
With head declin'd and voice damm'd up with woe,
With sad-set eyes and wretched arms across,
From lips new-waxen pale begins to blow
The grief away that stops his answer so ;
    But wretched as he is he strives in vain ;   1665
    What he breathes out his breath drinks up again.

As through an arch the violent roaring tide
Outruns the eye that doth behold his haste,
Yet in the eddy boundeth in his pride
Back to the strait that forc'd him on so fast,   1670
In rage sent out, recall'd in rage, being past ;
    Even so his sighs, his sorrows, make a saw,
    To push grief on, and back the same grief draw.

Which speechless woe of his poor she attendeth,
And his untimely frenzy thus awaketh :   1675
'Dear lord, thy sorrow to my sorrow lendeth
Another power no flood by raining slaketh.
My woe too sensible thy passion maketh
    More feeling-painful. Let it then suffice
    To drown one woe one pair of weeping eyes.   1680

'And for my sake, when I might charm thee so,
For she that was thy Lucrece, now attend me :
Be suddenly revenged on my foe,
Thine, mine, his own ; suppose thou dost defend me
From what is past. The help that thou shalt lend me   1685
    Comes all too late, yet let the traitor die ;
    For sparing justice feeds iniquity.

'But ere I name him, you, fair lords,' quoth she,
Speaking to those that came with Collatine,
'Shall plight your honourable faiths to me   1690
With swift pursuit to venge this wrong of mine ;
For 'tis a meritorious fair design
    To chase injustice with revengeful arms :
    Knights, by their oaths, should right poor ladies' harms.'

At this request, with noble disposition   1695
Each present lord began to promise aid,
As bound in knighthood to her imposition,
Longing to hear the hateful foe bewray'd.
But she, that yet her sad task hath not said,
    The protestation stops. 'O speak,' quoth she   1700
    'How may this forced stain be wip'd from me ?

'What is the quality of my offence,
Being constrain'd with dreadful circumstance ?
May my pure mind with the foul act dispense,
My low-declined honour to advance ?   1705
May any terms acquit me from this chance ?
    The poisoned fountain clears itself again ;
    And why not I from this compelled stain ? '

With this, they all at once began to say
Her body's stain her mind untainted clears ;   1710
While with a joyless smile she turns away
The face, that map which deep impression bears
Of hard misfortune, carv'd in it with tears.
  ' No, no,' quoth she, ' no dame hereafter living
  By my excuse shall claim excuse's giving.'   1715

Here with a sigh, as if her heart would break,
She throws forth Tarquin's name : ' He, he,' she says,
But more than he her poor tongue could not speak ;
Till after many accents and delays,
Untimely breathings, sick, and short assays,   1720
  She utters this : ' He, he, fair lords, 'tis he.
  That guides this hand to give this wound to me '.

Even here she sheathed in her harmless breast
A harmful knife, that thence her soul unsheathed.
That blow did bail it from the deep unrest   1725
Of that polluted prison where it breathed.
Her contrite sighs unto the clouds bequeathed
  Her winged sprite, and through her wounds doth fly
  Life's lasting date from cancell'd destiny.

Stone-still, astonish'd with this deadly deed,   1730
Stood Collatine and all his lordly crew ;
Till Lucrece' father, that beholds her bleed,
Himself on her self-slaughter'd body threw,
And from the purple fountain Brutus drew
  The murd'rous knife, and, as it left the place,   1735
  Her blood, in poor revenge, held it in chase ;

And bubbling from her breast, it doth divide
In two slow rivers, that the crimson blood
Circles her body in on every side,
Who like a late-sack'd island vastly stood   1740
Bare and unpeopled in this fearful flood.
  Some of her blood still pure and red remain'd,
  And some look'd black, and that false Tarquin stain'd.

About the mourning and congealed face
Of that black blood a wat'ry rigol goes,   1745
Which seems to weep upon the tainted place
And ever since, as pitying Lucrece' woes,
Corrupted blood some watery token shows ;
  And blood untainted still doth red abide,
  Blushing at that which is so putrified.   1750

'Daughter, dear daughter,' old Lucretius cries,
' That life was mine which thou hast here deprived.
If in the child the father's image lies,
Where shall I live now Lucrece is unlived ?
Thou was not to this end from me derived.   1755
  If children predecease progenitors,
  We are their offspring, and they none of ours.

'Poor broken glass, I often did behold
In thy sweet semblance my old age new born;
But now that fair fresh mirror, dim and old,   1760
Shows me a bare-bon'd death by time outworn;
O, from thy cheeks my image thou hast torn,
    And shiver'd all the beauty of my glass,
    That I no more can see what once I was!

'O time, cease thou thy course and last no longer,   1765
If they surcease to be that should survive.
Shall rotten death make conquest of the stronger,
And leave the falt'ring feeble souls alive?
The old bees die, the young possess their hive.
    Then live, sweet Lucrece, live again, and see   1770
    Thy father die, and not thy father thee.'

By this starts Collatine as from a dream,
And bids Lucretius give his sorrow place;
And then in key-cold Lucrece' bleeding stream
He falls, and bathes the pale fear in his face,   1775
And counterfeits to die with her a space;
    Till manly shame bids him possess his breath,
    And live, to be revenged on her death.

The deep vexation of his inward soul
Hath serv'd a dumb arrest upon his tongue;   1780
Who, mad that sorrow should his use control,
Or keep him from heart-easing words so long,
Begins to talk; but through his lips do throng,
    Weak words, so thick come, in his poor heart's aid,
    That no man could distinguish what he said.   1785

Yet sometime 'Tarquin' was pronounced plain,
But through his teeth, as if the name he tore.
This windy tempest, till it blow up rain,
Held back his sorrow's tide, to make it more;
At last it rains, and busy winds give o'er;   1790
    Then son and father weep with equal strife,
    Who should weep most for daughter or for wife.

The one doth call her his, the other his,
Yet neither may possess the claim they lay.
The father says 'She's mine'. 'O, mine she is!'   1795
Replies her husband. 'Do not take away
My sorrow's interest; let no mourner say
    He weeps for her, for she was only mine,
    And only must be wail'd by Collatine.'

'O,' quoth Lucretius. 'I did give that life   1800
Which she too early and too late hath spill'd.'
'Woe, woe,' quoth Collatine 'she was my wife,
I owed her, and 'tis mine that she hath kill'd.'
'My daughter! and 'My wife!' with clamours fill'd
    The dispers'd air, who, holding Lucrece' life,   1805
    Answer'd their cries, 'My daughter!' and 'My wife!'

Brutus, who pluck'd the knife from Lucrece' side,
Seeing such emulation in their woe,
Began to clothe his wit in state and pride,
Burying in Lucrece' wound his folly's show.   1810
He with the Romans was esteemed so
    As silly jeering idiots are with kings,
    For sportive words and utt'ring foolish things.

But now he throws that shallow habit by
Wherein deep policy did him disguise,   1815
And arm'd his long-hid wits advisedly
To check the tears in Collatinus' eyes.
' Thou wronged lord of Rome,' quoth he ' arise.
    Let my unsounded self, suppos'd a fool,
    Now set thy long-experienc'd wit to school.   1820

' Why, Collatine, is woe the cure for woe ?
Do wounds help wounds, or grief help grievous deeds ?
Is it revenge to give thyself a blow,
For his foul act by whom thy fair wife bleeds ?
Such childish humour from weak minds proceeds.   1825
    Thy wretched wife mistook the matter so,
    To slay herself that should have slain her foe.

' Courageous Roman, do not steep thy heart
In such relenting dew of lamentations,
But kneel with me, and help to bear thy part   1830
To rouse our Roman gods with invocations
That they will suffer these abominations—
    Since Rome herself in them doth stand disgraced—
    By our strong arms from forth her fair streets chased.

' Now by the Capitol that we adore,   1835
And by this chaste blood so unjustly stained,
By heaven's fair sun that breeds the fat earth's store,
By all our country rights in Rome maintained,
And by chaste Lucrece' soul that late complained
    Her wrongs to us, and by this bloody knife,   1840
    We will revenge the death of this true wife.'

This said, he struck his hand upon his breast,
And kiss'd the fatal knife to end his vow :
And to his protestation urg'd the rest
Who wond'ring at him, did his words allow ;   1845
Then jointly to the ground their knees they bow
    And that deep vow which Brutus made before
    He doth again repeat, and that they swore.

When they had sworn to this advised doom,
They did conclude to bear dead Lucrece thence,   1850
To show her bleeding body thorough Rome,
And so to publish Tarquin's foul offence ;
Which being done with speedy diligence,
    The Romans plausibly did give consent
    To Tarquin's everlasting banishment,   1855

THE SONNETS

THE Sonnets fall into two well-marked groups : 1–126 addressed to the fair youth : 127–152 mainly concerned with the dark lady ; in addition are 153–4, two sonnets in which the author tells of going to Bath for a cure but finding no cure for his affections. No. 126 contains only 12 lines in couplets and forms a kind of envoy to the first group ; No. 145 has its lines of eight syllables instead of the standard ten. Following the Sonnets in the original edition came *A Lover's Complaint* also attributed to Shakespeare.

The critical feature of the story told by the Sonnets is the dark lady's betrayal of the poet and her association with the fair friend. This episode must be dated not later than 1599, for in that year William Jaggard included two of the Sonnets in the collection of verse he issued under the title *The Passionate Pilgrim*. These Sonnets are numbered 138 and 144 in the later, and presumably complete, edition. No. 144 begins

> Two Loves I have, of Comfort, and Despaire,
> That like two Spirits, do suggest me still :
> My better Angel is a man (right faire)
> My worser Spirite a Woman (colour'd ill)

The intrigue between the poet's better and worser angel must have been well on the way to consummation when this was written ; indeed the suspicion expressed later in the Sonnet was to prove justified, as other of the Sonnets reveal. From what source Jaggard got his version of these two Sonnets we do not know ; but Meres in 1598 in his *Palladis Tamia* mentions among the works of Shakespeare his ' sugred Sonnets among his private friends '. That two pieces belonging to what was no doubt regarded as the most exciting aspect of the story should escape from the privacy of an intimate circle is not surprising. What does seem remarkable is that no publisher succeeded in getting hold of the others till 1609. In May of that year Thomas Thorpe had the *Sonnets* entered in the Stationers' Register as his copy, and George Eld was the printer of the volume issued in the same year. The title-page emphasized the find by its assertion ' Never before Imprinted '. That the manuscript was a find by Thorpe seems most probable ; yet the number of the items in the series, and the condition of the text, imperfect as it is, indicates that the original owner must have belonged to the private circle indicated by Meres.

Taking it for granted, as nearly every commentator does, that the Sonnets reflect some episodes in Shakespeare's own life, the reader naturally asks who the other actors were taking part in this drama. Unfortunately, he is unlikely, unless he has a private opinion of his own, to be completely satisfied that any answer is possible on the evidence at present available. What may almost be called the classic solution, and one that naturally commends itself in almost every respect, the temperament of the participants, their social standing, and the connection of the man with the life of the theatre, does not accommodate itself to the time scheme suggested by the Sonnets in Jaggard's *Passionate Pilgrim*.

Bernard Shaw in adopting this solution as the ground of his *pièce d'occasion* on behalf of the scheme for a National Theatre, was careful in his *Preface* to *The Dark Lady of the Sonnets* to explain why he did so, although he could not subscribe to its historical accuracy. Among the inducements to assign the part of the dark lady to Mary Fitton and that of the fair friend to the Earl of Pembroke was Shaw's acquaintance with Thomas Tyler who, if not the very first investigator to offer these identifications as meeting the demands of the sonnet story, was the first to show their plausibility and to give them the place they now occupy in what, to borrow a phrase from E. K. Chambers, may be called the Shakespeare mythos. Tyler's suggestions, which Shaw adopted for purely theatrical convenience, Frank Harris incorporated as fact in what he offered to the world as a biographical study of the poet. Harris knew as well as Shaw the difficulty in the way of accepting Tyler's identifications but doubtless felt the story too good not to be true, and of a kind that he felt he could exploit. Shaw was on friendly terms with Harris, and his indulgence stretched so far as to allow him to suggest that Harris's book on Shakespeare was entitled to be styled the best book of its generation on the subject; comments, however, in his *Preface* to *The Dark Lady* on Harris's notions about Shakespeare, provide, in spite of certain whims of his own, a most destructive comment on most of Harris's fantasies.

Two difficulties, among others, confront those who would adopt the Pembroke-Mary Fitton solution : if, as Tyler suggests, Pembroke first saw Shakespeare in the spring of 1598, it is hard to believe that their relations could have progressed so far and so fast as the Sonnets of the *Passionate Pilgrim* indicate. Further *Love's Labour's Lost* published in 1598, but written much earlier, has reference to the dark lady. We should have to suppose that the piece had been re-written for a later performance with insertions pointing to Mary Fitton, were we to accept Tyler's conjectures. Nor do the references in the Sonnets to the dark lady as a married woman agree with Mary Fitton's condition in 1598 as one of the Queen's maids of honour. Finally as Shaw says : ' any tinge lighter than raven black must be fatal to the strongest claim to be the Dark Lady '; and the portrait now identified as that of Mary Fitton has not the complexion demanded by Shakespeare's picture of his mistress.

It may be, as Shaw says, that ' with the plays and sonnets in our hands we know much more about Shakespeare than we know about Dickens and Thackeray '; but this must be by way of imaginative interpretation rather than of those identifications a biographer desires.

SONNETS

THE SONNETS

TO. THE. ONLIE. BEGETTER. OF.
THESE. INSUING. SONNETS.
MR. W. H. ALL. HAPPINESSE.
AND. THAT . ETERNITIE.
PROMISED.
BY.
OUR. EVER-LIVING. POET.
WISHETH.
THE. WELL-WISHING.
ADVENTURER. IN.
SETTING.
FORTH.

T.T.

1

FROM fairest creatures we desire increase,
That thereby beauty's rose might never die,
But as the riper should by time decease,
His tender heir might bear his memory;
But thou, contracted to thine own bright eyes,   5
Feed'st thy light's flame with self-substantial fuel,
Making a famine where abundance lies,
Thyself thy foe, to thy sweet self too cruel.
Thou that art now the world's fresh ornament
And only herald to the gaudy spring,   10
Within thine own bud buriest thy content,
And, tender churl, mak'st waste in niggarding.
   Pity the world, or else this glutton be,
   To eat the world's due, by the grave and thee.

2

When forty winters shall besiege thy brow,
And dig deep trenches in thy beauty's field,
Thy youth's proud livery, so gaz'd on now,
Will be a tatter'd weed of small worth held.
Then being ask'd where all thy beauty lies,   5
Where all the treasure of thy lusty days,
To say within thine own deep-sunken eyes
Were an all-eating shame and thriftless praise.
How much more praise deserv'd thy beauty's use,
If thou couldst answer ' This fair child of mine   10
Shall sum my count, and make my old excuse '
Proving his beauty by succession thine !
   This were to be new made when thou art old,
   And see thy blood warm when thou feel'st it cold.

3

Look in thy glass, and tell the face thou viewest
Now is the time that face should form another ;
Whose fresh repair if now thou not renewest,
Thou dost beguile the world, unbless some mother.
For where is she so fair whose unear'd womb   5
Disdains the tillage of thy husbandry ?
Or who is he so fond will be the tomb
Of his self-love, to stop posterity ?
Thou art thy mother's glass, and she in thee
Calls back the lovely April of her prime ;   10
So thou through windows of thine age shalt see,
Despite of wrinkles, this thy golden time.
　　But if thou live rememb'red not to be,
　　Die single, and thine image dies with thee.

4

Unthrifty loveliness, why dost thou spend
Upon thyself thy beauty's legacy ?
Nature's bequest gives nothing, but doth lend,
And, being frank, she lends to those are free.
Then, beauteous niggard, why dost thou abuse   5
The bounteous largess given thee to give ?
Profitless usurer, why dost thou use
So great a sum of sums, yet canst not live ?
For having traffic with thyself alone,
Thou of thyself thy sweet self dost deceive.   10
Then how when nature calls thee to be gone,
What acceptable audit canst thou leave ?
　　Thy unus'd beauty must be tomb'd with thee,
　　Which, used, lives th' executor to be.

5

Those hours that with gentle work did frame
The lovely gaze where every eye doth dwell
Will play the tyrants to the very same,
And that unfair which fairly doth excel ;
For never-resting time leads summer on   5
To hideous winter, and confounds him there ;
Sap check'd with frost and lusty leaves quite gone,
Beauty o'ersnow'd, and bareness every where.
Then, were not summer's distillation left
A liquid prisoner pent in walls of glass,   10
Beauty's effect with beauty were bereft,
Nor it, nor no remembrance what it was ;
　　But flowers distill'd, though they with winter meet,
　　Leese but their show : their substance still lives sweet.

6

Then let not winter's ragged hand deface
In thee thy summer ere thou be distill'd ;
Make sweet some vial ; treasure thou some place
With beauty's treasure ere it be self-kill'd.
That use is not forbidden usury   5
Which happies those that pay the willing loan—
That's for thyself to breed an other thee,
Or ten times happier, be it ten for one ;
Ten times thy self were happier than thou art,
If ten of thine ten times refigur'd thee.   10
Then what could Death do if thou shouldst depart,
Leaving thee living in posterity ?
    Be not self-will'd, for thou art much too fair
      To be death's conquest and make worms thine heir.

7

Lo, in the orient when the gracious light
Lifts up his burning head, each under eye
Doth homage to his new-appearing sight,
Serving with looks his sacred majesty ;
And having climb'd the steep-up heavenly hill,   5
Resembling strong youth in his middle age,
Yet mortal looks adore his beauty still,
Attending on his golden pilgrimage ;
But when from highmost pitch, with weary car,
Like feeble age he reeleth from the day,   10
The eyes, 'fore duteous, now converted are
From his low tract and look another way ;
    So thou, thyself outgoing in thy noon,
      Unlook'd on diest, unless thou get a son.

8

Music to hear, why hear'st thou music sadly ?
Sweets with sweets war not, joy delights in joy.
Why lov'st thou that which thou receiv'st not gladly,
Or else receiv'st with pleasure thine annoy ?
If the true concord of well-tuned sounds,   5
By unions married, do offend thine ear,
They do but sweetly chide thee, who confounds
In singleness the parts that thou shouldst bear.
Mark how one string, sweet husband to another,
Strikes each in each by mutual ordering ;   10
Resembling sire, and child, and happy mother,
Who, all in one, one pleasing note do sing ;
    Whose speechless song, being many, seeming one,
      Sings this to thee : 'Thou single wilt prove none'.

9

Is it for fear to wet a widow's eye
That thou consum'st thyself in single life ?
Ah ! if thou issueless shalt hap to die,
The world will wail thee like a makeless wife :
The world will be thy widow, and still weep   5
That thou no form of thee hast left behind,
When every private widow well may keep,
By children's eyes, her husband's shape in mind.
Look what an unthrift in the world doth spend
Shifts but his place, for still the world enjoys it ;   10
But beauty's waste hath in the world an end,
And kept unus'd, the user so destroys it.
    No love toward others in that bosom sits
    That on himself such murd'rous shame commits.

10

For shame ! deny that thou bear'st love to any,
Who for thy self art so unprovident.
Grant, if thou wilt, thou art belov'd of many,
But that thou none lov'st is most evident ;
For thou art so possess'd with murd'rous hate   5
That 'gainst thyself thou stick'st not to conspire,
Seeking that beauteous roof to ruinate
Which to repair should be thy chief desire.
O, change thy thought, that I may change my mind !
Shall hate be fairer lodg'd than gentle love ?   10
Be, as thy presence is, gracious and kind,
Or to thy self at least kind-hearted prove ;
    Make thee an other self for love of me,
    That beauty still may live in thine or thee.

11

As fast as thou shalt wane, so fast thou grow'st
In one of thine, from that which thou departest ;
And that fresh blood which youngly thou bestow'st
Thou mayst call thine when thou from youth convertest.
Herein lives wisdom, beauty, and increase ;   5
Without this folly, age, and cold decay.
If all were minded so, the times should cease,
And threescore year would make the world away.
Let those whom Nature hath not made for store,
Harsh, featureless, and rude, barrenly perish.   10
Look whom she best endow'd she gave the more ;
Which bounteous gift thou shouldst in bounty cherish ;
    She carv'd thee for her seal, and meant thereby
    Thou shouldst print more, not let that copy die.

12

When I do count the clock that tells the time,
And see the brave day sunk in hideous night;
When I behold the violet past prime,
And sable curls all silver'd o'er with white;
When lofty trees I see barren of leaves,   5
Which erst from heat did canopy the herd,
And summer's green all girded up in sheaves
Borne on the bier with white and bristly beard;
Then of thy beauty do I question make
That thou among the wastes of time must go,   10
Since sweets and beauties do themselves forsake,
And die as fast as they see others grow;
    And nothing 'gainst Time's scythe can make defence
    Save breed, to brave him when he takes thee hence.

13

O that you were yourself! But, love, you are
No longer yours than you you self here live.
Against this coming end you should prepare,
And your sweet semblance to some other give.
So should that beauty which you hold in lease   5
Find no determination; then you were
Your self again, after your self's decease,
When your sweet issue your sweet form should bear.
Who lets so fair a house fall to decay,
Which husbandry in honour might uphold   10
Against the stormy gusts of winter's day
And barren rage of death's eternal cold?
    O, none but unthrifts! Dear my love, you know
    You had a father: let your son say so.

14

Not from the stars do I my judgment pluck,
And yet methinks I have astronomy;
But not to tell of good or evil luck,
Of plagues, of dearths, or seasons' quality;
Nor can I fortune to brief minutes tell,   5
Pointing to each his thunder, rain, and wind,
Or say with princes if it shall go well
By oft predict that I in heaven find;
But from thine eyes my knowledge I derive,
And, constant stars, in them I read such art   10
As truth and beauty shall together thrive,
If from thy self to store thou wouldst convert.
    Or else of thee this I prognosticate:
    Thy end is truth's and beauty's doom and date.

15

When I consider every thing that grows
Holds in perfection but a little moment,
That this huge stage presenteth nought but shows
Whereon the stars in secret influence comment ;
When I perceive that men as plants increase,   5
Cheered and check'd even by the self-same sky,
Vaunt in their youthful sap, at height decrease,
And wear their brave state out of memory ;
Then the conceit of this inconstant stay
Sets you most rich in youth before my sight,   10
Where wasteful Time debateth with Decay
To change your day of youth to sullied night ;
   And all in war with Time for love of you,
   As he takes from you, I engraft you new.

16

But wherefore do not you a mightier way
Make war upon this bloody tyrant Time ?
And fortify your self in your decay
With means more blessed than my barren rhyme ?
Now stand you on the top of happy hours,   5
And many maiden gardens, yet unset,
With virtuous wish would bear your living flowers,
Much liker than your painted counterfeit ;
So should the lines of life that life repair,
Which this, Time's pencil or my pupil pen,   10
Neither in inward worth, nor outward fair,
Can make you live your self in eyes of men.
   To give away your self keeps your self still ;
   And you must live, drawn by your own sweet skill.

17

Who will believe my verse in time to come,
If it were fill'd with your most high deserts ?
Though yet, heaven knows, it is but as a tomb
Which hides your life and shows not half your parts.
If I could write the beauty of your eyes   5
And in fresh numbers number all your graces,
The age to come would say ' This poet lies ;
Such heavenly touches ne'er touch'd earthly faces.'
So should my papers, yellowed with their age,
Be scorn'd, like old men of less truth than tongue ;   10
And your true rights be term'd a poet's rage,
And stretched metre of an antique song.
   But were some child of yours alive that time,
   You should live twice—in it, and in my rhyme.

18

Shall I compare thee to a summer's day?
Thou art more lovely and more temperate.
Rough winds do shake the darling buds of May,
And summer's lease hath all too short a date:
Sometime too hot the eye of heaven shines,   5
And often is his gold complexion dimm'd;
And every fair from fair some time declines,
By chance, or nature's changing course, untrimm'd;
But thy eternal summer shall not fade
Nor lose possession of that fair thou ow'st;   10
Nor shall Death brag thou wand'rest in his shade,
When in eternal lines to time thou grow'st.
    So long as men can breathe or eyes can see,
    So long lives this, and this gives life to thee.

19

Devouring Time, blunt thou the lion's paws,
And make the earth devour her own sweet brood;
Pluck the keen teeth from the fierce tiger's jaws,
And burn the long-liv'd phœnix in her blood;
Make glad and sorry seasons as thou fleet'st,   5
And do whate'er thou wilt, swift-footed Time,
To the wide world and all her fading sweets;
But I forbid thee one most heinous crime:
O, carve not with thy hours my love's fair brow,
Nor draw no lines there with thine antique pen;   10
Him in thy course untainted do allow
For beauty's pattern to succeeding men.
    Yet, do thy worst, old Time.   Despite thy wrong,
    My love shall in my verse ever live young.

20

A woman's face, with Nature's own hand painted,
Hast thou, the Master Mistress of my passion;
A woman's gentle heart, but not acquainted
With shifting change, as is false woman's fashion;
An eye more bright than theirs, less false in rolling,   5
Gilding the object whereupon it gazeth;
A man in hue all hues in his controlling,
Which steals men's eyes and women's souls amazeth.
And for a woman wert thou first created;
Till Nature, as she wrought thee, fell a-doting,   10
And by addition me of thee defeated
By adding one thing to my purpose nothing.
    But since she prick'd thee out for women's pleasure,
    Mine be thy love, and thy love's use their treasure.

21

So is it not with me as with that Muse,
Stirr'd by a painted beauty to his verse ;
Who heaven itself for ornament doth use,
And every fair with his fair doth rehearse,
Making a couplement of proud compare   5
With sun and moon, with earth and sea's rich gems,
With April's first-born flowers, and all things rare
That heaven's air in this huge rondure hems.
O, let me, true in love, but truly write,
And then believe me, my love is as fair   10
As any mother's child, though not so bright
As those gold candles fix'd in heaven's air.
      Let them say more that like of hearsay well :
      I will not praise that purpose not to sell.

22

My glass shall not persuade me I am old
So long as youth and thou are of one date ;
But when in thee time's furrows I behold,
Then look I death my days should expiate.
For all that beauty that doth cover thee   5
Is but the seemly raiment of my heart,
Which in thy breast doth live, as thine in me ;
How can I then be elder than thou art ?
O, therefore, love, be of thyself so wary,
As I not for myself but for thee will ;   10
Bearing thy heart, which I will keep so chary
As tender nurse her babe from faring ill.
      Presume not on thy heart when mine is slain ;
      Thou gav'st me thine, not to give back again.

23

As an unperfect actor on the stage
Who with his fear is put besides his part,
Or some fierce thing replete with too much rage,
Whose strength's abundance weakens his own heart ;
So I, for fear of trust, forget to say   5
The perfect ceremony of love's rite,
And in mine own love's strength seem to decay,
O'ercharg'd with burthen of mine own love's might.
O, let my looks be then the eloquence
And dumb presagers of my speaking breast ;   10
Who plead for love, and look for recompense,
More than that tongue that more hath more express'd.
      O, learn to read what silent love hath writ !
      To hear with eyes belongs to love's fine wit.

24

Mine eye hath play'd the painter and hath stell'd
Thy beauty's form in table of my heart;
My body is the frame wherein 'tis held,
And perspective it is best painter's art.
For through the painter must you see his skill   5
To find where your true image pictur'd lies,
Which in my bosom's shop is hanging still,
That hath his windows glazed with thine eyes.
Now see what good turns eyes for eyes have done:
Mine eyes have drawn thy shape, and thine for me   10
Are windows to my breast, where through the sun
Delights to peep, to gaze therein on thee;
    Yet eyes this cunning want to grace their art:
    They draw but what they see, know not the heart.

25

Let those who are in favour with their stars
Of public honour and proud titles boast,
Whilst I, whom fortune of such triumph bars,
Unlook'd for joy in that I honour most.
Great princes' favourites their fair leaves spread   5
But as the marigold at the sun's eye;
And in themselves their pride lies buried,
For at a frown they in their glory die.
The painful warrior famoused for fight,
After a thousand victories once foil'd,   10
Is from the book of honour razed quite,
And all the rest forgot for which he toil'd.
    Then happy I, that love and am beloved
    Where I may not remove nor be removed.

26

Lord of my love, to whom in vassalage
Thy merit hath my duty strongly knit,
To thee I send this written embassage,
To witness duty, not to show my wit;
Duty so great, which wit so poor as mine   5
May make seem bare, in wanting words to show it,
But that I hope some good conceit of thine
In thy soul's thought, all naked, will bestow it;
Till whatsoever star that guides my moving
Points on me graciously with fair aspect,   10
And puts apparel on my tattered loving
To show me worthy of thy sweet respect.
    Then may I dare to boast how I do love thee;
    Till then not show my head where thou mayst prove me.

27

Weary with toil, I haste me to my bed,
The dear repose for limbs with travel tired
But then begins a journey in my head
To work my mind when body's work's expired ;
For then my thoughts, from far where I abide,⠀⠀⠀⠀5
Intend a zealous pilgrimage to thee,
And keep my drooping eyelids open wide,
Looking on darkness which the blind do see ;
Save that my soul's imaginary sight
Presents thy shadow to my sightless view,⠀⠀⠀⠀10
Which, like a jewel hung in ghastly night,
Makes black night beauteous and her old face new.
⠀⠀Lo, thus, by day my limbs, by night my mind,
⠀⠀For thee, and for myself, no quiet find.

28

How can I then return in happy plight
That am debarr'd the benefit of rest ?
When day's oppression is not eas'd by night,
But day by night and night by day oppress'd ?
And each, though enemies to either's reign,⠀⠀⠀⠀5
Do in consent shake hands to torture me,
The one by toil, the other to complain
How far I toil, still farther off from thee.
I tell the day, to please him, thou art bright
And dost him grace when clouds do blot the heaven ;⠀⠀⠀⠀10
So flatter I the swart-complexion'd night,
When sparkling stars twire not, thou gild'st the even.
⠀⠀But day doth daily draw my sorrows longer,
⠀⠀And night doth nightly make grief's strength seem stronger.

29

When in disgrace with Fortune and men's eyes,
I all alone beweep my outcast state,
And trouble deaf heaven with my bootless cries,
And look upon myself, and curse my fate,
Wishing me like to one more rich in hope,⠀⠀⠀⠀5
Featur'd like him, like him with friends possess'd,
Desiring this man's art, and that man's scope,
With what I most enjoy contented least ;
Yet in these thoughts myself almost despising,
Haply I think on thee, and then my state,⠀⠀⠀⠀10
Like to the lark at break of day arising
From sullen earth, sings hymns at heaven's gate ;
⠀⠀For thy sweet love rememb'red such wealth brings
⠀⠀That then I scorn to change my state with kings.

30

When to the sessions of sweet silent thought
I summon up remembrance of things past,
I sigh the lack of many a thing I sought,
And with old woes new wail my dear time's waste.
Then can I drown an eye, unus'd to flow,
For precious friends hid in death's dateless night,
And weep afresh love's long since cancell'd woe,
And moan th' expense of many a vanish'd sight.
Then can I grieve at grievances foregone,
And heavily from woe to woe tell o'er   I
The sad account of fore-bemoaned moan,
Which I new pay as if not paid before.
    But if the while I think on thee, dear friend,
    All losses are restor'd, and sorrows end.

31

Thy bosom is endeared with all hearts
Which I by lacking have supposed dead;
And there reigns love and all love's loving parts,
And all those friends which I thought buried.
How many a holy and obsequious tear
Hath dear religious love stol'n from mine eye,
As interest of the dead, which now appear
But things remov'd that hidden in thee lie!
Thou art the grave where buried love doth live,
Hung with the trophies of my lovers gone,   I
Who all their parts of me to thee did give;
That due of many now is thine alone.
    Their images I lov'd I view in thee,
    And thou, all they, hast all the all of me.

32

If thou survive my well-contented day
When that churl Death my bones with dust shall cover,
And shalt by fortune once more re-survey
These poor rude lines of thy deceased lover,
Compare them with the bett'ring of the time,
And though they be outstripp'd by every pen,
Reserve them for my love, not for their rhyme,
Exceeded by the height of happier men.
O, then vouchsafe me but this loving thought:
'Had my friend's Muse grown with this growing age,   I
A dearer birth than this his love had brought,
To march in ranks of better equipage;
    But since he died, and poets better prove,
    Theirs for their style I'll read, his for his love'.

33

Full many a glorious morning have I seen
Flatter the mountain-tops with sovereign eye,
Kissing with golden face the meadows green,
Gilding pale streams with heavenly alchemy;
Anon permit the basest clouds to ride   5
With ugly rack on his celestial face,
And from the forlorn world his visage hide,
Stealing unseen to west with this disgrace.
Even so my sun one early morn did shine
With all triumphant splendour on my brow;   10
But out, alack! he was but one hour mine,
The region cloud hath mask'd him from me now.
   Yet him for this my love no whit disdaineth;
   Suns of the world may stain when heaven's sun staineth.

34

Why didst thou promise such a beauteous day,
And make me travel forth without my cloak,
To let base clouds o'ertake me in my way,
Hiding thy brav'ry in their rotten smoke?
'Tis not enough that through the cloud thou break   5
To dry the rain on my storm-beaten face,
For no man well of such a salve can speak
That heals the wound, and cures not the disgrace.
Nor can thy shame give physic to my grief;
Though thou repent, yet I have still the loss.   10
Th' offender's sorrow lends but weak relief
To him that bears the strong offence's cross.
   Ah! but those tears are pearl which thy love sheds,
   And they are rich, and ransom all ill deeds.

35

No more be griev'd at that which thou hast done:
Roses have thorns, and silver fountains mud;
Clouds and eclipses stain both moon and sun,
And loathsome canker lives in sweetest bud.
All men make faults, and even I in this,   5
Authorizing thy trespass with compare,
Myself corrupting, salving thy amiss,
Excusing thy sins more than thy sins are;
For to thy sensual fault I bring in sense—
Thy adverse party is thy advocate—   10
And 'gainst myself a lawful plea commence;
Such civil war is in my love and hate
   That I an accessary needs must be
   To that sweet thief which sourly robs from me.

36

Let me confess that we two must be twain,
Although our undivided loves are one;
So shall those blots that do with me remain,
Without thy help, by me be borne alone.
In our two loves there is but one respect,   5
Though in our lives a separable spite,
Which though it alter not love's sole effect,
Yet doth it steal sweet hours from love's delight.
I may not evermore acknowledge thee,
Lest my bewailed guilt should do thee shame;   10
Nor thou with public kindness honour me,
Unless thou take that honour from thy name.
    But do not so; I love thee in such sort
    As, thou being mine, mine is thy good report.

37

As a decrepit father takes delight
To see his active child do deeds of youth,
So I, made lame by Fortune's dearest spite,
Take all my comfort of thy worth and truth;
For whether beauty, birth, or wealth, or wit,   5
Or any of these all, or all, or more,
Entitled in thy parts do crowned sit,
I make my love engrafted to this store.
So then I am not lame, poor, nor despis'd,
Whilst that this shadow doth such substance give   10
That I in thy abundance am suffic'd,
And by a part of all thy glory live.
    Look what is best, that best I wish in thee;
    This wish I have; then ten times happy me!

38

How can my Muse want subject to invent,
While thou dost breathe that pour'st into my verse
Thine own sweet argument, too excellent
For every vulgar paper to rehearse?
O, give thyself the thanks if aught in me   5
Worthy perusal stand against thy sight;
For who's so dumb that cannot write to thee,
When thou thy self dost give invention light?
Be thou the tenth Muse, ten times more in worth
Than those old nine which rhymers invocate;   10
And he that calls on thee, let him bring forth
Eternal numbers to outlive long date.
    If my slight Muse do please these curious days,
    The pain be mine, but thine shall be the praise.

39

O, how thy worth with manners may I sing,
When thou art all the better part of me?
What can mine own praise to mine own self bring?
And what is't but mine own, when I praise thee?
Even for this let us divided live,   5
And our dear love lose name of single one,
That by this separation I may give
That due to thee which thou deserv'st alone.
O absence, what a torment wouldst thou prove,
Were it not thy sour leisure gave sweet leave   10
To entertain the time with thoughts of love;
Which time and thoughts so sweetly doth deceive,
    And that thou teachest how to make one twain,
    By praising him here who doth hence remain!

40

Take all my loves, my love, yea, take them all;
What hast thou then more than thou hadst before?
No love, my love, that thou mayst true love call;
All mine was thine before thou hadst this more.
Then if for my love thou my love receivest,   5
I cannot blame thee, for my love thou usest;
But yet be blam'd, if thou thyself deceivest
By wilful taste of what thyself refusest.
I do forgive thy robb'ry, gentle thief,
Although thou steal thee all my poverty;   10
And yet love knows it is a greater grief
To bear love's wrong than hate's known injury.
    Lascivious grace, in whom all ill well shows,
    Kill me with spites; yet we must not be foes.

41

Those pretty wrongs that liberty commits
When I am sometime absent from thy heart,
Thy beauty and thy years full well befits,
For still temptation follows where thou art.
Gentle thou art, and therefore to be won,   5
Beauteous thou art, therefore to be assailed;
And when a woman woos, what woman's son
Will sourly leave her till she have prevailed?
Ay me! but yet thou mightst my seat forbear,
And chide thy beauty and thy straying youth,   10
Who lead thee in their riot even there
Where thou art forc'd to break a twofold truth:
    Hers, by thy beauty tempting her to thee,
    Thine, by thy beauty being false to me.

42

That thou hast her, it is not all my grief,
And yet it may be said I lov'd her dearly;
That she hath thee is of my wailing chief,
A loss in love that touches me more nearly.
Loving offenders, thus I will excuse ye:
Thou dost love her because thou know'st I love her,
And for my sake even so doth she abuse me,
Suff'ring my friend for my sake to approve her.
If I lose thee, my loss is my love's gain,
And, losing her, my friend hath found that loss;
Both find each other, and I lose both twain,
And both for my sake lay on me this cross.
    But here's the joy: my friend and I are one;
    Sweet flattery! then she loves but me alone.

43

When most I wink, then do mine eyes best see,
For all the day they view things unrespected;
But when I sleep, in dreams they look on thee,
And, darkly bright, are bright in dark directed;
Then thou whose shadow shadows doth make bright,
How would thy shadow's form form happy show
To the clear day with thy much clearer light,
When to unseeing eyes thy shade shines so!
How would, I say, mine eyes be blessed made
By looking on thee in the living day,
When in dead night thy fair imperfect shade
Through heavy sleep on sightless eyes doth stay!
    All days are nights to see till I see thee,
    And nights bright days when dreams do show thee me.

44

If the dull substance of my flesh were thought,
Injurious distance should not stop my way;
For then, despite of space, I would be brought
From limits far remote, where thou dost stay.
No matter then, although my foot did stand
Upon the farthest earth remov'd from thee,
For nimble thought can jump both sea and land
As soon as think the place where he would be.
But ah! thought kills me that I am not thought,
To leap large lengths of miles when thou art gone,
But that, so much of earth and water wrought,
I must attend time's leisure with my moan,
    Receiving nought by elements so slow
    But heavy tears, badges of either's woe.

45

The other two, slight air and purging fire,
Are both with thee, wherever I abide ;
The first my thought, the other my desire,
These present-absent with swift motion slide.
For when these quicker elements are gone   5
In tender embassy of love to thee,
My life, being made of four, with two alone
Sinks down to death, oppress'd with melancholy ;
Until life's composition be recured
By those swift messengers return'd from thee,   10
Who even but now come back again, assured
Of thy fair health, recounting it to me.
   This told, I joy ; but then no longer glad,
   I send them back again, and straight grow sad.

46

Mine eye and heart are at a mortal war
How to divide the conquest of thy sight ;
Mine eye my heart thy picture's sight would bar,
My heart mine eye the freedom of that right.
My heart doth plead that thou in him dost lie   5
A closet never pierc'd with crystal eyes ;
But the defendant doth that plea deny,
And says in him thy fair appearance lies.
To 'cide this title is impanelled
A quest of thoughts, all tenants to the heart ;   10
And by their verdict is determined
The clear eye's moiety and the dear heart's part—
   As thus : mine eye's due is thine outward part,
   And my heart's right thine inward love of heart.

47

Betwixt mine eye and heart a league is took,
And each doth good turns now unto the other.
When that mine eye is famish'd for a look,
Or heart in love with sighs himself doth smother ;
With my love's picture then my eye doth feast,   5
And to the painted banquet bids my heart ;
Another time mine eye is my heart's guest,
And in his thoughts of love doth share a part ;
So, either by thy picture or my love,
Thyself away art present still with me ;   10
For thou not farther than my thoughts canst move,
And I am still with them, and they with thee ;
   Or if they sleep, thy picture in my sight
   Awakes my heart to heart's and eye's delight.

48

How careful was I when I took my way,
Each trifle under truest bars to thrust,
That to my use it might unused stay
From hands of falsehood, in sure wards of trust !
But thou, to whom my jewels trifles are,
Most worthy comfort, now my greatest grief,
Thou, best of dearest, and mine only care,
Art left the prey of every vulgar thief.
Thee have I not lock'd up in any chest,
Save where thou art not, though I feel thou art,
Within the gentle closure of my breast,
From whence at pleasure thou mayst come and part ;
   And even thence thou wilt be stol'n, I fear,
   For truth proves thievish for a prize so dear.

49

Against that time, if ever that time come,
When I shall see thee frown on my defects,
When as thy love hath cast his utmost sum,
Call'd to that audit by advis'd respects ;
Against that time when thou shalt strangely pass
And scarcely greet me with that sun, thine eye,
When love, converted from the thing it was,
Shall reasons find of settled gravity—
Against that time do I ensconce me here
Within the knowledge of mine own desert,
And this my hand against myself uprear,
To guard the lawful reasons on thy part :
   To leave poor me thou hast the strength of laws,
   Since why to love I can allege no cause.

50

How heavy do I journey on the way,
When what I seek—my weary travel's end—
Doth teach that ease and that repose to say
' Thus far the miles are measur'd from thy friend ! '
The beast that bears me, tired with my woe,
Plods dully on, to bear that weight in me,
As if by some instinct the wretch did know
His rider lov'd not speed being made from thee.
The bloody spur cannot provoke him on
That sometimes anger thrusts into his hide,
Which heavily he answers with a groan,
More sharp to me than spurring to his side ;
   For that same groan doth put this in my mind :
   My grief lies onward, and my joy behind.

51

Thus can my love excuse the slow offence
Of my dull bearer, when from thee I speed :
From where thou art why should I haste me thence ?
Till I return, of posting is no need.
O, what excuse will my poor beast then find,   5
When swift extremity can seem but slow ?
Then should I spur, though mounted on the wind ;
In winged speed no motion shall I know.
Then can no horse with my desire keep pace ;
Therefore desire, of perfect'st love being made,   10
Shall weigh no dull flesh in his fiery race ;
But love, for love, thus shall excuse my jade :
   Since from thee going he went wilful slow,
   Towards thee I'll run, and give him leave to go.

52

So am I as the rich whose blessed key
Can bring him to his sweet up-locked treasure,
The which he will not ev'ry hour survey,
For blunting the fine point of seldom pleasure.
Therefore are feasts so solemn and so rare,   5
Since seldom coming, in the long year set,
Like stones of worth they thinly placed are,
Or captain jewels in the carcanet.
So is the time that keeps you as my chest,
Or as the wardrobe which the robe doth hide,   10
To make some special instant special blest
By new unfolding his imprison'd pride.
   Blessed are you, whose worthiness gives scope,
   Being had, to triumph, being lack'd, to hope.

53

What is your substance, whereof are you made,
That millions of strange shadows on you tend ?
Since every one hath, every one, one shade,
And you, but one, can every shadow lend.
Describe Adonis, and the counterfeit   5
Is poorly imitated after you ;
On Helen's cheek all art of beauty set,
And you in Grecian tires are painted new.
Speak of the spring and foison of the year :
The one doth shadow of your beauty show,   10
The other as your bounty doth appear,
And you in every blessed shape we know.
   In all external grace you have some part,
   But you like none, none you, for constant heart.

54

O, how much more doth beauty beauteous seem
By that sweet ornament which truth doth give !
The rose looks fair, but fairer we it deem
For that sweet odour which doth in it live.
The canker-blooms have full as deep a dye
As the perfumed tincture of the roses,
Hang on such thorns, and play as wantonly
When summer's breath their masked buds discloses ;
But for their virtue only is their show,
They live unwoo'd, and unrespected fade ;
Die to themselves.   Sweet roses do not so ;
Of their sweet deaths are sweetest odours made.
   And so of you, beauteous and lovely youth,
   When that shall vade, by verse distills your truth.

55

Not marble nor the gilded monuments
Of princes shall outlive this pow'rful rhyme ;
But you shall shine more bright in these contents
Than unswept stone, besmear'd with sluttish time.
When wasteful war shall statues overturn,
And broils root out the work of masonry,
Nor Mars his sword nor war's quick fire shall burn
The living record of your memory.
'Gainst death and all-oblivious enmity
Shall you pace forth ; your praise shall still find room,
Even in the eyes of all posterity
That wear this world out to the ending doom.
   So, till the judgment that yourself arise,
   You live in this, and dwell in lovers' eyes.

56

Sweet love, renew thy force ; be it not said
Thy edge should blunter be than appetite,
Which but to-day by feeding is allay'd,
To-morrow sharp'ned in his former might.
So, love, be thou ; although to-day thou fill
Thy hungry eyes, even till they wink with fulness,
To-morrow see again, and do not kill
The spirit of love with a perpetual dulness.
Let this sad int'rim like the ocean be
Which parts the shore where two contracted new
Come daily to the banks, that, when they see
Return of love, more blest may be the view ;
   Or call it winter, which, being full of care,
   Makes summer's welcome thrice more wish'd, more rare.

57

Being your slave, what should I do but tend
Upon the hours and times of your desire ?
I have no precious time at all to spend,
Nor services to do, till you require.
Nor dare I chide the world-without-end hour,   5
Whilst I, my sovereign, watch the clock for you,
Nor think the bitterness of absence sour,
When you have bid your servant once adieu ;
Nor dare I question with my jealous thought
Where you may be, or your affairs suppose,   10
But, like a sad slave, stay and think of nought
Save where you are how happy you make those.
    So true a fool is love that in your will,
    Though you do anything, he thinks no ill.

58

That god forbid that made me first your slave
I should in thought control your times of pleasure,
Or at your hand th' account of hours to crave,
Being your vassal bound to stay your leisure !
O, let me suffer, being at your beck,   5
Th' imprison'd absence of your liberty,
And patience, tame to sufferance, bide each check
Without accusing you of injury
Be where you list ; your charter is so strong
That you yourself may privilege your time   10
To what you will ; to you it doth belong
Your self to pardon of self-doing crime.
    I am to wait, though waiting so be hell ;
    Not blame your pleasure, be it ill or well.

59

If there be nothing new, but that which is
Hath been before, how are our brains beguil'd,
Which labouring for invention bear amiss
The second burthen of a former child !
O, that record could with a backward look,   5
Even of five hundred courses of the sun,
Show me your image in some antique book,
Since mind at first in character was done !
That I might see what the old world could say
To this composed wonder of your frame ;   10
Whether we are mended, or whe'er better they,
Or whether revolution be the same.
    O, sure I am, the wits of former days
    To subjects worse have given admiring praise.

60

Like as the waves make towards the pebbled shore,
So do our minutes hasten to their end ;
Each changing place with that which goes before,
In sequent toil all forwards do contend.
Nativity, once in the main of light, 5
Crawls to maturity, wherewith being crown'd,
Crooked eclipses 'gainst his glory fight,
And Time that gave doth now his gift confound.
Time doth transfix the flourish set on youth,
And delves the parallels in beauty's brow, 10
Feeds on the rarities of nature's truth,
And nothing stands but for his scythe to mow.
      And yet to times in hope my verse shall stand,
      Praising thy worth, despite his cruel hand.

61

Is it thy will thy image should keep open
My heavy eyelids to the weary night ?
Dost thou desire my slumbers should be broken,
While shadows like to thee do mock my sight ?
Is it thy spirit that thou send'st from thee 5
So far from home into my deeds to pry,
To find out shames and idle hours in me,
The scope and tenour of thy jealousy ?
O no ! thy love, though much, is not so great :
It is my love that keeps mine eye awake ; 10
Mine own true love that doth my rest defeat
To play the watchman ever for thy sake.
      For thee watch I, whilst thou dost wake elsewhere,
      From me far off, with others all too near.

62

Sin of self-love possesseth all mine eye,
And all my soul, and all my every part ;
And for this sin there is no remedy,
It is so grounded inward in my heart.
Methinks no face so gracious is as mine, 5
No shape so true, no truth of such account,
And for myself mine own worth do define
As I all other in all worths surmount.
But when my glass shows me myself indeed,
Beated and chopt with tann'd antiquity, 10
Mine own self-love quite contrary I read ;
Self so self-loving were iniquity.
      'Tis thee, my self, that for myself I praise,
      Painting my age with beauty of thy days.

63

Against my love shall be as I am now,
With Time's injurious hand crush'd and o'erworn ;
When hours have drain'd his blood, and fill'd his brow
With lines and wrinkles ; when his youthful morn
Hath travell'd on to age's steepy night ;   5
And all those beauties whereof now he's king
Are vanishing or vanish'd out of sight,
Stealing away the treasure of his spring—
For such a time do I now fortify
Against confounding age's cruel knife,   10
That he shall never cut from memory
My sweet love's beauty, though my lover's life.
  His beauty shall in these black lines be seen,
    And they shall live, and he in them still green.

64

When I have seen by Time's fell hand defaced
The rich proud cost of outworn buried age ;
When sometime lofty towers I see down-rased,
And brass eternal slave to mortal rage ;
When I have seen the hungry ocean gain   5
Advantage on the kingdom of the shore,
And the firm soil win of the wat'ry main,
Increasing store with loss, and loss with store ;
When I have seen such interchange of state,
Or state itself confounded to decay ;   10
Ruin hath taught me thus to ruminate—
That Time will come and take my love away.
  This thought is as a death, which cannot choose
    But weep to have that which it fears to lose.

65

Since brass, nor stone, nor earth, nor boundless sea,
But sad mortality o'ersways their power,
How with this rage shall beauty hold a plea,
Whose action is no stronger than a flower ?
O, how shall summer's honey breath hold out   5
Against the wrackful siege of batt'ring days,
When rocks impregnable are not so stout,
Nor gates of steel so strong, but Time decays ?
O fearful meditation ! Where alack,
Shall Time's best jewel from Time's chest lie hid ?   10
Or what strong hand can hold his swift foot back ?
Or who his spoil of beauty can forbid ?
  O, none, unless this miracle have might,
    That in black ink my love may still shine bright.

66

Tir'd with all these, for restful death I cry:
As, to behold desert a beggar born,
And needy nothing trimm'd in jollity,
And purest faith unhappily forsworn,
And gilded honour shamefully misplac'd,   5
And maiden virtue rudely strumpeted,
And right perfection wrongfully disgrac'd,
And strength by limping sway disabled,
And art made tongue-tied by authority,
And folly, doctor-like, controlling skill,   10
And simple truth miscall'd simplicity,
And captive good attending captain ill—
 Tir'd with all these, from these would I be gone,
 Save that, to die, I leave my love alone.

67

Ah! wherefore with infection should he live
And with his presence grace impiety,
That sin by him advantage should achieve,
And lace itself with his society?
Why should false painting imitate his cheek,   5
And steal dead seeming of his living hue?
Why should poor beauty indirectly seek
Roses of shadow, since his rose is true?
Why should he live now Nature bankrupt is,
Beggar'd of blood to blush through lively veins? 10
For she hath no exchequer now but his,
And, proud of many, lives upon his gains.
 O, him she stores, to show what wealth she had
 In days long since, before these last so bad.

68

Thus is his cheek the map of days outworn,
When beauty liv'd and died as flowers do now,
Before these bastard signs of fair were born,
Or durst inhabit on a living brow;
Before the golden tresses of the dead,   5
The right of sepulchres, were shorn away
To live a second life on second head,
Ere beauty's dead fleece made another gay.
In him those holy antique hours are seen,
Without all ornament, itself and true,   10
Making no summer of another's green,
Robbing no old to dress his beauty new;
 And him as for a map doth Nature store,
 To show false Art what beauty was of yore.

69

Those parts of thee that the world's eye doth view
Want nothing that the thought of hearts can mend.
All tongues, the voice of souls, give thee that due,
Utt'ring bare truth, even so as foes commend.
Thine outward thus with outward praise is crown'd ;   5
But those same tongues that give thee so thine own
In other accents do this praise confound
By seeing farther than the eye hath shown.
They look into the beauty of thy mind,
And that, in guess, they measure by thy deeds ;   10
Then, churls, their thoughts, although their eyes were kind,
To thy fair flower add the rank smell of weeds.
   But why thy odour matcheth not thy show,
    The soil is this—that thou dost common grow.

70

That thou art blam'd shall not be thy defect,
For slander's mark was ever yet the fair ;
The ornament of beauty is suspect,
A crow that flies in heaven's sweetest air.
So thou be good, slander doth but approve   5
Thy worth the greater, being woo'd of time ;
For canker vice the sweetest buds doth love,
And thou present'st a pure unstained prime.
Thou hast pass'd by the ambush of young days,
Either not assail'd, or victor being charg'd ;   10
Yet this thy praise cannot be so thy praise
To tie up envy, evermore enlarg'd.
   If some suspect of ill mask'd not thy show,
    Then thou alone kingdoms of hearts shouldst owe.

71

No longer mourn for me when I am dead
Than you shall hear the surly sullen bell
Give warning to the world that I am fled
From this vile world, with vilest worms to dwell.
Nay, if you read this line, remember not   5
The hand that writ it ; for I love you so,
That I in your sweet thoughts would be forgot,
If thinking on me then should make you woe.
O, if, I say, you look upon this verse,
When I perhaps compounded am with clay,   10
Do not so much as my poor name rehearse,
But let your love even with my life decay ;
   Lest the wise world should look into your moan,
    And mock you with me after I am gone.

72

O, lest the world should task you to recite
What merit liv'd in me, that you should love
After my death, dear love, forget me quite,
For you in me can nothing worthy prove ;
Unless you would devise some virtuous lie,   5
To do more for me than mine own desert,
And hang more praise upon deceased I
Than niggard truth would willingly impart.
O, lest your true love may seem false in this,
That you for love speak well of me untrue,   10
My name be buried where my body is,
And live no more to shame nor me nor you !
   For I am sham'd by that which I bring forth,
   And so should you, to love things nothing worth.

73

That time of year thou mayst in me behold
When yellow leaves, or none, or few, do hang
Upon those boughs which shake against the cold,
Bare ruin'd choirs where late the sweet birds sang.
In me thou seest the twilight of such day   5
As after sunset fadeth in the west,
Which by and by black night doth take away,
Death's second self, that seals up all in rest.
In me thou seest the glowing of such fire
That on the ashes of his youth doth lie,   10
As the death-bed whereon it must expire,
Consum'd with that which it was nourish'd by.
   This thou perceiv'st which makes thy love more strong,
   To love that well which thou must leave ere long.

74

But be contented. When that fell arrest
Without all bail shall carry me away,
My life hath in this line some interest,
Which for memorial still with thee shall stay.
When thou reviewest this, thou dost review   5
The very part was consecrate to thee.
The earth can have but earth, which is his due ;
My spirit is thine, the better part of me.
So then thou hast but lost the dregs of life,
The prey of worms, my body being dead ;   10
The coward conquest of a wretch's knife,
Too base of thee to be remembered.
   The worth of that is that which it contains,
   And that is this, and this with thee remains.

75

So are you to my thoughts as food to life,
Or as sweet-season'd showers are to the ground ;
And for the peace of you I hold such strife
As 'twixt a miser and his wealth is found :
Now proud as an enjoyer, and anon   5
Doubting the filching age will steal his treasure ;
Now counting best to be with you alone,
Then better'd that the world may see my pleasure ;
Sometime all full with feasting on your sight,
And by and by clean starved for a look ;   10
Possessing or pursuing no delight
Save that is had or must from you be took.
　　Thus do I pine and surfeit day by day,
　　Or gluttoning on all, or all away.

76

Why is my verse so barren of new pride ?
So far from variation or quick change ?
Why, with the time, do I not glance aside
To new-found methods and to compounds strange ?
Why write I still all one, ever the same,   5
And keep invention in a noted weed,
That every word doth almost tell my name,
Showing their birth, and where they did proceed ?
O, know, sweet love, I always write of you,
And you and love are still my argument ;   10
So all my best is dressing old words new,
Spending again what is already spent ;
　　For as the sun is daily new and old,
　　So is my love still telling what is told.

77

Thy glass will show thee how thy beauties wear,
Thy dial how thy precious minutes waste ;
The vacant leaves thy mind's imprint will bear,
And of this book this learning mayst thou taste.
The wrinkles which thy glass will truly show   5
Of mouthed graves will give thee memory ;
Thou by thy dial's shady stealth mayst know
Time's thievish progress to eternity.
Look what thy memory cannot contain
Commit to these waste blanks, and thou shalt find   10
Those children nurs'd, deliver'd from thy brain,
To take a new acquaintance of thy mind.
　　These offices, so oft as thou wilt look,
　　Shall profit thee, and much enrich thy book.

78

So oft have I invok'd thee for my Muse,
And found such fair assistance in my verse,
As every alien pen hath got my use,
And under thee their poesy disperse.
Thine eyes, that taught the dumb on high to sing   5
And heavy ignorance aloft to fly,
Have added feathers to the learned's wing
And given grace a double majesty.
Yet be most proud of that which I compile,
Whose influence is thine, and born of thee :   10
In others' works thou dost but mend the style,
And arts with thy sweet graces graced be ;
  But thou art all my art, and dost advance
  As high as learning my rude ignorance.

79

Whilst I alone did call upon thy aid,
My verse alone had all thy gentle grace ;
But now my gracious numbers are decay'd,
And my sick Muse doth give another place.
I grant, sweet love, thy lovely argument   5
Deserves the travail of a worthier pen ;
Yet what of thee thy poet doth invent
He robs thee of, and pays it thee again.
He lends thee virtue, and he stole that word
From thy behaviour ; beauty doth he give,   10
And found it in thy cheek ; he can afford
No praise to thee but what in thee doth live.
  Then thank him not for that which he doth say,
  Since what he owes thee thou thyself dost pay.

80

O, how I faint when I of you do write,
Knowing a better spirit doth use your name
And in the praise thereof spends all his might
To make me tongue-tied, speaking of your fame !
But since your worth, wide as the ocean is,   5
The humble as the proudest sail doth bear,
My saucy bark, inferior far to his,
On your broad main doth wilfully appear.
Your shallowest help will hold me up afloat,
Whilst he upon your soundless deep doth ride ;   10
Or, being wreck'd, I am a worthless boat,
He of tall building and of goodly pride.
  Then if he thrive, and I be cast away,
  The worst was this : my love was my decay.

81

Or I shall live your epitaph to make,
Or you survive when I in earth am rotten ;
From hence your memory death cannot take,
Although in me each part will be forgotten.
Your name from hence immortal life shall have,   5
Though I, once gone, to all the world must die ;
The earth can yield me but a common grave,
When you entombed in men's eyes shall lie.
Your monument shall be my gentle verse,
Which eyes not yet created shall o'er-read ;   10
And tongues to be your being shall rehearse,
When all the breathers of this world are dead.
    You still shall live, such virtue hath my pen,
    Where breath most breathes, even in the mouths of men.

82

I grant thou wert not married to my Muse,
And therefore mayst without attaint o'erlook
The dedicated words which writers use
Of their fair subject, blessing every book.
Thou art as fair in knowledge as in hue,   5
Finding thy worth a limit past my praise
And therefore art enforc'd to seek anew
Some fresher stamp of the time-bettering days.
And do so, love ; yet when they have devis'd
What strained touches rhetoric can lend,   10
Thou truly fair wert truly sympathiz'd
In true plain words by thy true-telling friend ;
    And their gross painting might be better us'd
    Where cheeks need blood ; in thee it is abus'd.

83

I never saw that you did painting need,
And therefore to your fair no painting set ;
I found, or thought I found, you did exceed
The barren tender of a poet's debt ;
And therefore have I slept in your report,   5
That you yourself, being extant, well might show
How far a modern quill doth come too short,
Speaking of worth, what worth in you doth grow.
This silence for my sin you did impute,
Which shall be most my glory, being dumb ;   10
For I impair not beauty, being mute,
When others would give life, and bring a tomb.
    There lives more life in one of your fair eyes
    Than both your poets can in praise devise.

84

Who is it that says most which can say more
Than this rich praise—that you alone are you?
In whose confine immured is the store
Which should example where your equal grew?
Lean penury within that pen doth dwell   5
That to his subject lends not some small glory;
But he that writes of you, if he can tell
That you are you, so dignifies his story.
Let him but copy what in you is writ,
Not making worse what nature made so clear,   10
And such a counterpart shall fame his wit,
Making his style admired every where.
   You to your beauteous blessings add a curse,
    Being fond on praise, which makes your praises worse.

85

My tongue-tied Muse in manners holds her still,
While comments of your praise, richly compil'd,
Reserve their character with golden quill
And precious phrase by all the Muses fil'd.
I think good thoughts, whilst other write good words,   5
And, like unlettered clerk, still cry ' Amen '
To every hymn that able-spirit affords
In polish'd form of well-refined pen.
Hearing you prais'd, I say, ' 'Tis so, 'tis true ',
And to the most of praise add something more;   10
But that is in my thought, whose love to you,
Though words come hindmost, holds his rank before.
   Then others for the breath of words respect,
    Me for my dumb thoughts, speaking in effect.

86

Was it the proud full sail of his great verse,
Bound for the prize of all-too-precious you,
That did my ripe thoughts in my brain inhearse,
Making their tomb the womb wherein they grew?
Was it his spirit, by spirits taught to write   5
Above a mortal pitch, that struck me dead?
No, neither he, nor his compeers by night
Giving him aid, my verse astonished.
He nor that affable familiar ghost
Which nightly gulls him with intelligence,   10
As victors, of my silence cannot boast:
I was not sick of any fear from thence.
   But when your countenance fill'd up his line,
    Then lack'd I matter; that enfeebled mine.

87

Farewell! thou art too dear for my possessing,
And like enough thou know'st thy estimate.
The charter of thy worth gives thee releasing;
My bonds in thee are all determinate.
For how do I hold thee but by thy granting? 5
And for that riches where is my deserving?
The cause of this fair gift in me is wanting,
And so my patent back again is swerving.
Thy self thou gav'st, thy own worth then not hnowing,
Or me, to whom thou gav'st it, else mistaking; 10
So thy great gift, upon misprision growing,
Comes home again, on better judgment making.
    Thus have I had thee, as a dream doth flatter:
    In sleep a king, but waking no such matter.

88

When thou shalt be dispos'd to set me light,
And place my merit in the eye of scorn,
Upon thy side against myself I'll fight,
And prove thee virtuous, though thou art forsworn.
With mine own weakness being best acquainted, 5
Upon thy part I can set down a story
Of faults conceal'd, wherein I am attainted;
That thou, in losing me, shall win much glory.
And I by this will be a gainer too;
For bending all my loving thoughts on thee, 10
The injuries that to myself I do,
Doing thee vantage, double vantage me.
    Such is my love, to thee I so belong,
    That for thy right myself will bear all wrong.

89

Say that thou didst forsake me for some fault,
And I will comment upon that offence;
Speak of my lameness, and I straight will halt;
Against thy reasons making no defence.
Thou canst not, love, disgrace me half so ill, 5
To set a form upon desired change,
As I'll myself disgrace, knowing thy will.
I will acquaintance strangle and look strange,
Be absent from thy walks, and in my tongue
Thy sweet beloved name no more shall dwell, 10
Lest I, too much profane, should do it wrong,
And haply of our old acquaintance tell.
    For thee, against myself I'll vow debate,
    For I must ne'er love him whom thou dost hate.

90

Then hate me when thou wilt ; if ever, now ;
Now while the world is bent my deeds to cross,
Join with the spite of fortune, make me bow,
And do not drop in for an after-loss.
Ah, do not, when my heart hath scap'd this sorrow,   5
Come in the rearward of a conquer'd woe ;
Give not a windy night a rainy morrow,
To linger out a purpos'd overthrow.
If thou wilt leave me, do not leave me last,
When other petty griefs have done their spite,   10
But in the onset come ; so shall I taste
At first the very worst of fortune's might ;
 And other strains of woe, which now seem woe,
 Compar'd with loss of thee will not seem so.

91

Some glory in their birth, some in their skill,
Some in their wealth, some in their body's force ;
Some in their garments, though new-fangled ill ;
Some in their hawks and hounds, some in their horse ;
And every humour hath his adjunct pleasure,   5
Wherein it finds a joy above the rest ;
But these particulars are not my measure :
All these I better in one general best.
Thy love is better than high birth to me,
Richer than wealth, prouder than garments' cost,   10
Of more delight than hawks and horses be ;
And, having thee, of all men's pride I boast—
 Wretched in this alone, that thou mayst take
 All this away, and me most wretched make.

92

But do thy worst to steal thy self away,
For term of life thou art assured mine ;
And life no longer than thy love will stay,
For it depends upon that love of thine.
Then need I not to fear the worst of wrongs,   5
When in the least of them my life hath end.
I see a better state to me belongs
Than that which on thy humour doth depend.
Thou canst not vex me with inconstant mind,
Since that my life on thy revolt doth lie.   10
O what a happy title do I find,
Happy to have thy love, happy to die !
 But what's so blessed-fair that fears no blot ?
 Thou mayst be false, and yet I know it not.

93

So shall I live, supposing thou art true,
Like a deceived husband ; so love's face
May still seem love to me, though alter'd new—
Thy looks with me, thy heart in other place.
For there can live no hatred in thine eye ;   5
Therefore in that I cannot know thy change.
In many looks the false heart's history
Is writ in moods and frowns and wrinkles strange ;
But heaven in thy creation did decree
That in thy face sweet love should ever dwell ;   10
Whate'er thy thoughts or thy heart's workings be,
Thy looks should nothing thence but sweetness tell.
    How like Eve's apple doth thy beauty grow,
    If thy sweet virtue answer not thy show !

94

They that have power to hurt and will do none,
That do not do the thing they most do show,
Who, moving others, are themselves as stone,
Unmoved, cold, and to temptation slow—
They rightly do inherit Heaven's graces,   5
And husband nature's riches from expense ;
They are the lords and owners of their faces,
Others but stewards of their excellence.
The summer's flow'r is to the summer sweet
Though to itself it only live and die ;   10
But if that flow'r with base infection meet,
The basest weed outbraves his dignity.
    For sweetest things turn sourest by their deeds :
    Lilies that fester smell far worse than weeds.

95

How sweet and lovely dost thou make the shame
Which, like a canker in the fragrant rose,
Doth spot the beauty of thy budding name !
O, in what sweets dost thou thy sins enclose !
That tongue that tells the story of thy days,   5
Making lascivious comments on thy sport,
Cannot dispraise but in a kind of praise :
Naming thy name blesses an ill report.
O, what a mansion have those vices got
Which for their habitation chose out thee,   10
Where beauty's veil doth cover every blot,
And all things turns to fair that eyes can see !
    Take heed, dear heart, of this large privilege;
    The hardest knife ill-us'd doth lose his edge.

96

Some say thy fault is youth, some wantonness ;
Some say thy grace is youth and gentle sport ;
Both grace and faults are lov'd of more and less :
Thou mak'st faults graces that to thee resort.
As on the finger of a throned queen 5
The basest jewel will be well esteem'd ;
So are those errors that in thee are seen
To truths translated and for true things deem'd.
How many lambs might the stern wolf betray,
If like a lamb he could his looks translate ! 10
How many gazers mightst thou lead away,
If thou wouldst use the strength of all thy state !
    But do not so ; I love thee in such sort,
    As, thou being mine, mine is thy good report.

97

How like a winter hath my absence been
From thee, the pleasure of the fleeting year !
What freezings have I felt, what dark days seen !
What old December's bareness everywhere !
And yet this time remov'd was summer's time, 5
The teeming autumn, big with rich increase,
Bearing the wanton burden of the prime,
Like widowed wombs after their lord's decease ;
Yet this abundant issue seem'd to me
But hope of orphans, and unfathered fruit ; 10
For summer and his pleasures wait on thee,
And, thou away, the very birds are mute ;
    Or, if they sing, 'tis with so dull a cheer
    That leaves look pale, dreading the winter's near.

98

From you have I been absent in the spring,
When proud-pied April, dress'd in all his trim,
Hath put a spirit of youth in every thing,
That heavy Saturn laugh'd and leap'd with him.
Yet nor the lays of birds, nor the sweet smell 5
Of different flowers in odour and in hue,
Could make me any summer's story tell,
Or from their proud lap pluck them where they grew ;
Nor did I wonder at the lily's white,
Nor praise the deep vermilion in the rose : 10
They were but sweet, but figures of delight,
Drawn after you, you pattern of all those.
    Yet seem'd it winter still, and, you away,
    As with your shadow I with these did play.

99

The forward violet thus did I chide :
Sweet thief, whence didst thou steal thy sweet that smells,
If not from my love's breath ?   The purple pride
Which on thy soft cheek for complexion dwells
In my love's veins thou hast too grossly dy'd.   5
The lily I condemned for thy hand,
And buds of marjoram had stol'n thy hair ;
The roses fearfully on thorns did stand,
One blushing shame, another white despair ;
A third, nor red nor white, had stol'n of both,   10
And to his robb'ry had annex'd thy breath ;
But, for his theft, in pride of all his growth
A vengeful canker eat him up to death.
  More flowers I noted, yet I none could see
  But sweet or colour it had stol'n from thee.

100

Where art thou, Muse, that thou forget'st so long
To speak of that which gives thee all thy might ?
Spend'st thou thy fury on some worthless song,
Dark'ning thy power to lend base subjects light ?
Return, forgetful Muse, and straight redeem   5
In gentle numbers time so idly spent ;
Sing to the ear that doth thy lays esteem
And gives thy pen both skill and argument.
Rise, resty Muse, my love's sweet face survey,
If Time have any wrinkle graven there ;   10
If any, be a satire to decay,
And make Time's spoils despised everywhere.
  Give my love fame faster than Time wastes life ;
  So thou prevent'st his scythe and crooked knife.

101

O truant Muse, what shall be thy amends
For thy neglect of truth in beauty dy'd ?
Both truth and beauty on my love depends ;
So dost thou too, and therein dignified.
Make answer, Muse.   Wilt thou not haply say   5
' Truth needs no colour with his colour fix'd ;
Beauty no pencil, beauty's truth to lay ;
But best is best, if never intermix'd ' ?
Because he needs no praise, wilt thou be dumb ?
Excuse not silence so ; for't lies in thee   10
To make him much outlive a gilded tomb,
And to be prais'd of ages yet to be.
  Then do thy office, Muse.   I teach thee how
  To make him seem long hence as he shows now.

102

My love is strength'ned, though more weak in seeming;
I love not less, though less the show appear;
That love is merchandiz'd whose rich esteeming
The owner's tongue doth publish every where.
Our love was new, and then but in the spring,   5
When I was wont to greet it with my lays;
As Philomel in summer's front doth sing,
And stops her pipe in growth of riper days.
Not that the summer is less pleasant now
Than when her mournful hymns did hush the night,   10
But that wild music burthens every bough,
And sweets grown common lose their dear delight.
    Therefore, like her, I sometime hold my tongue,
    Because I would not dull you with my song.

103

Alack, what poverty my Muse brings forth,
That, having such a scope to show her pride,
The argument all bare is of more worth
Than when it hath my added praise beside!
O blame me not, if I no more can write!   5
Look in your glass, and there appears a face
That over-goes my blunt invention quite,
Dulling my lines, and doing me disgrace.
Were it not sinful then, striving to mend,
To mar the subject that before was well?   10
For to no other pass my verses tend
Than of your graces and your gifts to tell;
    And more, much more, than in my verse can sit
    Your own glass shows you, when you look in it.

104

To me, fair friend, you never can be old,
For as you were when first your eye I ey'd,
Such seems your beauty still.   Three winters cold
Have from the forests shook three summers' pride,
Three beauteous springs to yellow autumn turn'd   5
In process of the seasons have I seen,
Three April perfumes in three hot Junes burn'd,
Since first I saw you fresh, which yet are green.
Ah, yet doth beauty, like a dial-hand,
Steal from his figure, and no pace perceiv'd;   10
So your sweet hue, which methinks still doth stand,
Hath motion, and mine eye may be deceiv'd.
    For fear of which, hear this, thou age unbred:
    Ere you were born was beauty's summer dead.

105

Let not my love be call'd idolatry,
Nor my beloved as an idol show,
Since all alike my songs and praises be
To one, of one, still such, and ever so.
Kind is my love to-day, to-morrow kind,   5
Still constant in a wondrous excellence;
Therefore my verse, to constancy confin'd,
One thing expressing, leaves out difference.
' Fair, kind, and true ' is all my argument,
' Fair, kind, and true ' varying to other words;   10
And in this change is my invention spent,
Three themes in one, which wondrous scope affords.
    Fair, kind, and true, have often liv'd alone,
    Which three, till now, never kept seat in one.

106

When in the chronicle of wasted time
I see descriptions of the fairest wights,
And beauty making beautiful old rhyme
In praise of ladies dead and lovely knights,
Then, in the blazon of sweet beauty's best,   5
Of hand, of foot, of lip, of eye, of brow,
I see their antique pen would have express'd
Even such a beauty as you master now.
So all their praises are but prophecies
Of this our time, all you prefiguring;   10
And, for they look'd but with divining eyes,
They had not skill enough to sing your worth to sing;
    For we, which now behold these present days,
    Have eyes to wonder, but lack tongues to praise.

107

Not mine own fears, nor the prophetic soul
Of the wide world dreaming on things to come,
Can yet the lease of my true love control,
Suppos'd as forfeit to a confin'd doom.
The mortal moon hath her eclipse endur'd,   5
And the sad augurs mock their own presage;
Incertainties now crown themselves assur'd,
And peace proclaims olives of endless age.
Now with the drops of this most balmy time
My love looks fresh, and Death to me subscribes,   10
Since spite of him I'll live in this poor rhyme,
While he insults o'er dull and speechless tribes.
    And thou in this shalt find thy monument,
    When tyrants' crests and tombs of brass are spent.

108

What's in the brain that ink may character
Which hath not figur'd to thee my true spirit?
What's new to speak, what new to register,
That may express my love or thy dear merit?
Nothing, sweet boy; but yet, like prayers divine   5
I must each day say o'er the very same;
Counting no old thing old, thou mine, I thine,
Even as when first I hallowed thy fair name.
So that eternal love in love's fresh case
Weighs not the dust and injury of age,   10
Nor gives to necessary wrinkles place,
But makes antiquity for aye his page;
    Finding the first conceit of love there bred,
    Where time and outward form would show it dead.

109

O, never say that I was false of heart,
Though absence seem'd my flame to qualify!
As easy might I from my self depart
As from my soul, which in thy breast doth lie:
That is my home of love. If I have rang'd,   5
Like him that travels, I return again,
Just to the time, not with the time exchang'd,
So that my self bring water for my stain.
Never believe, though in my nature reign'd
All frailties that besiege all kinds of blood,   10
That it could so preposterously be stain'd
To leave for nothing all thy sum of good;
    For nothing this wide universe I call
    Save thou, my rose; in it thou art my all.

110

Alas, 'tis true I have gone here and there
And made myself a motley to the view,
Gor'd mine own thoughts, sold cheap what is most dear,
Made old offences of affections new.
Most true it is that I have look'd on truth   5
Askance and strangely; but, by all above,
These blenches gave my heart another youth,
And worse essays prov'd thee my best of love.
Now all is done, have what shall have no end;
Mine appetite I never more will grind   10
On newer proof, to try an older friend,
A god in love, to whom I am confin'd.
    Then give me welcome, next my heaven the best,
    Even to thy pure and most most loving breast.

III

O, for my sake do you with Fortune chide,
The guilty goddess of my harmful deeds,
That did not better for my life provide
Than public means which public manners breeds.   5
Thence comes it that my name receives a brand,
And almost thence my nature is subdu'd
To what it works in, like the dyer's hand.
Pity me then, and wish I were renew'd ;
Whilst, like a willing patient, I will drink
Potions of eisel, 'gainst my strong infection ;   10
No bitterness that I will bitter think,
No double penance, to correct correction.
    Pity me then, dear friend, and I assure ye,
    Even that your pity is enough to cure me.

112

Your love and pity doth th' impression fill
Which vulgar scandal stamp'd upon my brow ;
For what care I who calls me well or ill,
So you o'ergreen my bad, my good allow ?
You are my all the world, and I must strive   5
To know my shames and praises from your tongue ;
None else to me, nor I to none alive,
That my steel'd sense or changes right or wrong.
In so profound abysm I throw all care
Of others' voices that my adder's sense   10
To critic and to flatterer stopped are.
Mark how with my neglect I do dispense :
    You are so strongly in my purpose bred
    That all the world besides methinks are dead.

113

Since I left you, mine eye is in my mind ;
And that which governs me to go about
Doth part his function, and is partly blind,
Seems seeing, but effectually is out ;
For it no form delivers to the heart   5
Of bird, of flow'r, or shape, which it doth latch ;
Of his quick objects hath the mind no part,
Nor his own vision holds what it doth catch ;
For if it see the rud'st or gentlest sight,
The most sweet favour of deformed'st creature,   10
The mountain or the sea, the day or night,
The crow or dove, it shapes them to your feature.
    Incapable of more, replete with you,
    My most true mind thus mak'th mine eye untrue.

114

Or whether doth my mind, being crown'd with you,
Drink up the monarch's plague, this flattery ?
Or whether shall I say mine eye saith true,
And that your love taught it this alchemy
To make of monsters and things indigest   5
Such cherubins as your sweet self resemble,
Creating every bad a perfect best
As fast as objects to his beams assemble ?
O, 'tis the first ; 'tis flatt'ry in my seeing,
And my great mind most kingly drinks it up.   10
Mine eye well knows what with his gust is 'greeing,
And to his palate doth prepare the cup.
  If it be poison'd, 'tis the lesser sin
  That mine eye loves it, and doth first begin.

115

Those lines that I before have writ do lie ;
Even those that said I could not love you dearer ;
Yet then my judgment knew no reason why
My most full flame should afterwards burn clearer.
But reckoning Time, whose million'd accidents   5
Creep in 'twixt vows and change decrees of kings,
Tan sacred beauty, blunt the sharp'st intents,
Divert strong minds to th' course of alt'ring things—
Alas, why, fearing of Time's tyranny,
Might I not then say ' Now I love you best '   10
When I was certain o'er incertainty,
Crowning the present, doubting of the rest ?
  Love is a babe ; then might I not say so,
  To give full growth to that which still doth grow ?

116

Let me not to the marriage of true minds
Admit impediments.   Love is not love
Which alters when it alteration finds,
Or bends with the remover to remove.
O, no ! it is an ever-fixed mark,   5
That looks on tempests and is never shaken ;
It is the star to every wand'ring bark,
Whose worth's unknown, although his height be taken.
Love's not Time's fool, though rosy lips and cheeks
Within his bending sickle's compass come ;   10
Love alters not with his brief hours and weeks,
But bears it out even to the edge of doom.
  If this be error, and upon me prov'd,
  I never writ, nor no man ever lov'd.

117

Accuse me thus : that I have scanted all
Wherein I should your great deserts repay ;
Forgot upon your dearest love to call,
Whereto all bonds do tie me day by day ;
That I have frequent been with unknown minds,   5
And given to time your own dear-purchas'd right ;
That I have hoisted sail to all the winds
Which should transport me farthest from your sight.
Book both my wilfulness and errors down,
And on just proof surmise accumulate ;   10
Bring me within the level of your frown,
But shoot not at me in your wakened hate ;
    Since my appeal says I did strive to prove
    The constancy and virtue of your love.

118

Like as to make our appetites more keen
With eager compounds we our palate urge,
As to prevent our maladies unseen
We sicken to shun sickness when we purge ;
Even so, being full of your ne'er-cloying sweetness,   5
To bitter sauces did I frame my feeding,
And, sick of welfare, found a kind of meetness
To be diseas'd ere that there was true needing.
Thus policy in love, t' anticipate
The ills that were not, grew to faults assured,   10
And brought to medicine a healthful state,
Which, rank of goodness, would by ill be cured.
    But thence I learn, and find the lesson true,
    Drugs poison him that so fell sick of you.

119

What potions have I drunk of Siren tears,
Distill'd from limbecks foul as hell within,
Applying fears to hopes, and hopes to fears,
Still losing when I saw my self to win !
What wretched errors hath my heart committed,   5
Whilst it hath thought it self so blessed never !
How have mine eyes out of their spheres been fitted
In the distraction of this madding fever !
O benefit of ill !   Now I find true
That better is by evil still made better ;   10
And ruin'd love, when it is built anew,
Grows fairer than at first, more strong, far greater.
    So I return rebuk'd to my content,
    And gain by ill thrice more than I have spent.

120

That you were once unkind befriends me now,
And for that sorrow which I then did feel
Needs must I under my transgression bow,
Unless my nerves were brass or hammered steel.
For if you were by my unkindness shaken,   5
As I by yours, y'have pass'd a hell of time;
And I, a tyrant, have no leisure taken
To weigh how once I suffered in your crime.
O that our night of woe might have rememb'red
My deepest sense how hard true sorrow hits,   10
And soon to you, as you to me, then tend'red
The humble salve which wounded bosoms fits!
    But that your trespass now becomes a fee;
    Mine ransoms yours, and yours must ransom me.

121

'Tis better to be vile than vile esteemed,
When not to be receives reproach of being,
And the just pleasure lost, which is so deemed
Not by our feeling, but by others' seeing.
For why should others' false adulterate eyes   5
Give salutation to my sportive blood?
Or on my frailties why are frailer spies,
Which in their wills count bad what I think good?
No; I am that I am; and they that level
At my abuses reckon up their own.   10
I may be straight though they themselves be bevel;
By their rank thoughts my deeds must not be shown
    Unless this general evil they maintain:
    All men are bad, and in their badness reign.

122

Thy gift, thy tables, are within my brain
Full character'd with lasting memory,
Which shall above that idle rank remain
Beyond all date, even to eternity;
Or at the least so long as brain and heart   5
Have faculty by nature to subsist;
Till each to raz'd oblivion yield his part
Of thee, thy record never can be miss'd.
That poor retention could not so much hold,
Nor need I tallies thy dear love to score;   10
Therefore to give them from me was I bold,
To trust those tables that receive thee more.
    To keep an adjunct to remember thee
    Were to import forgetfulness in me.

123

No, Time, thou shalt not boast that I do change.
Thy pyramids built up with newer might
To me are nothing novel, nothing strange ;
They are but dressings of a former sight.
Our dates are brief, and therefore we admire   5
What thou dost foist upon us that is old,
And rather make them born to our desire
Than think that we before have heard them told.
Thy registers and thee I both defy,
Not wond'ring at the present nor the past,   10
For thy records and what we see doth lie,
Made more or less by thy continual haste.
    This I do vow, and this shall ever be :
    I will be true, despite thy scythe and thee.

124

If my dear love were but the child of state,
It might for Fortune's bastard be unfather'd,
As subject to Time's love or to Time's hate,
Weeds among weeds, or flowers with flowers gather'd.
No, it was builded far from accident ;   5
It suffers not in smiling pomp, nor falls
Under the blow of thralled discontent,
Whereto th' inviting time or fashion calls.
It fears not Policy, that heretic,
Which works on leases of short-numb'red hours,   10
But all alone stands hugely politic,
That it nor grows with heat nor drowns with show'rs.
    To this I witness call the fools of time,
    Which die for goodness, who have liv'd for crime.

125

Were't aught to me I bore the canopy,
With my extern the outward honouring,
Or laid great bases for eternity,
Which proves more short than waste or ruining ?
Have I not seen dwellers on form and favour   5
Lose all, and more, by paying too much rent,
For compound sweet forgoing simple savour—
Pitiful thrivers, in their gazing spent ?
No, let me be obsequious in thy heart,
And take thou my oblation, poor but free,   10
Which is not mix'd with seconds, knows no art
But mutual render, only me for thee.
    Hence, thou suborn'd informer !   A true soul,
    When most impeach'd, stands least in thy control.

126

O thou, my lovely boy, who in thy power
Dost hold Time's fickle glass, his sickle hour;
Who hast by waning grown, and therein show'st
Thy lovers withering as thy sweet self grow'st;
If Nature, sovereign mistress over wrack,
As thou goest onwards, still will pluck thee back,
She keeps thee to this purpose, that her skill
May time disgrace, and wretched minutes kill.
Yet fear her, O thou minion of her pleasure!
She may detain, but not still keep, her treasure;
 Her audit, though delay'd, answer'd must be,
 And her quietus is to render thee.

127

In the old age black was not counted fair,
Or if it were, it bore not beauty's name;
But now is black beauty's successive heir,
And beauty slander'd with a bastard shame;
For since each hand hath put on nature's power,
Fairing the foul with art's false borrow'd face,
Sweet beauty hath no name, no holy bower,
But is profan'd, if not lives in disgrace.
Therefore my mistress' brows are raven black,
Her eyes so suited, and they mourners seem
At such who, not born fair, no beauty lack,
Sland'ring creation with a false esteem.
 Yet so they mourn, becoming of their woe,
 That every tongue says beauty should look so.

128

How oft, when thou, my music, music play'st
Upon that blessed wood whose motion sounds
With thy sweet fingers, when thou gently sway'st
The wiry concord that mine ear confounds,
Do I envy those jacks that nimble leap
To kiss the tender inward of thy hand,
Whilst my poor lips, which should that harvest reap,
At the wood's boldness by thee blushing stand!
To be so tickled, they would change their state
And situation with those dancing chips
O'er whom thy fingers walk with gentle gait,
Making dead wood more blest than living lips.
 Since saucy jacks so happy are in this,
 Give them thy fingers, me thy lips to kiss.

129

Th' expense of spirit in a waste of shame
Is lust in action ; and till action, lust
Is perjur'd, murd'rous, bloody, full of blame,
Savage, extreme, rude, cruel, not to trust ;
Enjoy'd no sooner but despised straight ;   5
Past reason hunted, and, no sooner had,
Past reason hated, as a swallowed bait,
On purpose laid to make the taker mad—
Mad in pursuit, and in possession so ;
Had, having, and in quest to have, extreme ;   10
A bliss in proof, and prov'd, a very woe ;
Before, a joy propos'd ; behind, a dream.
    All this the world well knows ; yet none knows well
    To shun the heaven that leads men to this hell.

130

My mistress' eyes are nothing like the sun ;
Coral is far more red than her lips' red ;
If snow be white, why then her breasts are dun ;
If hairs be wires, black wires grow on her head.
I have seen roses damask'd, red and white,   5
But no such roses see I in her cheeks ;
And in some perfumes is there more delight
Than in the breath that from my mistress reeks.
I love to hear her speak, yet well I know
That music hath a far more pleasing sound ;   10
I grant I never saw a goddess go—
My mistress when she walks treads on the ground.
    And yet, by heaven, I think my love as rare
    As any she belied with false compare.

131

Thou art as tyrannous, so as thou art,
As those whose beauties proudly make them cruel ;
For well thou know'st to my dear doting heart
Thou art the fairest and most precious jewel.
Yet, in good faith, some say that thee behold   5
Thy face hath not the power to make love groan,
To say they err I dare not be so bold,
Although I swear it to myself alone.
And, to be sure that is not false I swear,
A thousand groans, but thinking on thy face,   10
One on another's neck, do witness bear
Thy black is fairest in my judgment's place.
    In nothing art thou black save in thy deeds,
    And thence this slander, as I think, proceeds.

132

Thine eyes I love, and they, as pitying me,
Knowing thy heart torments me with disdain,
Have put on black, and loving mourners be,
Looking with pretty ruth upon my pain.
And truly not the morning sun of heaven   5
Better becomes the grey cheeks of the east,
Nor that full star that ushers in the even
Doth half that glory to the sober west,
As those two mourning eyes become thy face.
O, let it then as well beseem thy heart   10
To mourn for me, since mourning doth thee grace,
And suit thy pity like in every part.
    Then will I swear beauty herself is black,
    And all they foul that thy complexion lack.

133

Beshrew that heart that makes my heart to groan
For that deep wound it gives my friend and me !
Is't not enough to torture me alone,
But slave to slavery my sweet'st friend must be ?
Me from my self thy cruel eye hath taken,   5
And my next self thou harder hast engrossed ;
Of him, my self, and thee, I am forsaken ;
A torment thrice three-fold thus to be crossed.
Prison my heart in thy steel bosom's ward,
But then my friend's heart let my poor heart bail ;   10
Whoe'er keeps me, let my heart be his guard ;
Thou canst not then use rigour in my gaol.
    And yet thou wilt ; for I, being spent in thee,
    Perforce am thine, and all that is in me.

134

So now I have confess'd that he is thine,
And I myself am mortgag'd to thy will ;
My self I'll forfeit, so that other mine
Thou wilt restore to be my comfort still.
But thou wilt not, nor he will not be free,   5
For thou art covetous, and he is kind ;
He learn'd but surety-like to write for me
Under that bond that him as fast doth bind.
The statute of thy beauty thou wilt take,
Thou usurer that put'st forth all to use,   10
And sue a friend came debtor for my sake ;
So him I lose through my unkind abuse.
    Him have I lost ; thou hast both him and me ;
    He pays the whole, and yet am I not free.

135

Whoever hath her wish, thou hast thy Will,
And Will to boot, and Will in over-plus ;
More than enough am I that vex thee still,
To thy sweet will making addition thus.
Wilt thou, whose will is large and spacious,   5
Not once vouchsafe to hide my will in thine ?
Shall will in others seem right gracious,
And in my will no fair acceptance shine ?
The sea, all water, yet receives rain still,
And in abundance addeth to his store ;   10
So thou, being rich in Will, add to thy Will
One will of mine, to make thy large Will more.
    Let no unkind, no fair beseechers kill ;
    Think all but one, and me in that one Will.

136

If thy soul check thee that I come so near,
Swear to thy blind soul that I was thy Will,
And will, thy soul knows, is admitted there ;
Thus far for love my love-suit, sweet, fulfil.
Will will fulfil the treasure of thy love,   5
Ay, fill it full with wills, and my will one.
In things of great receipt with ease we prove
Among a number one is reckon'd none.
Then in the number let me pass untold,
Though in thy store's account I one must be ;   10
For nothing hold me, so it please thee hold
That nothing me, a something sweet to thee ;
    Make but my name thy love, and love that still,
    And then thou lov'st me, for my name is Will.

137

Thou blind fool, Love, what dost thou to mine eyes
That they behold, and see not what they see ?
They know what beauty is, see where it lies,
Yet what the best is take the worst to be.
If eyes, corrupt by over-partial looks,   5
Be anchor'd in the bay where all men ride,
Why of eyes' falsehood hast thou forged hooks,
Whereto the judgment of my heart is tied ?
Why should my heart think that a several plot,
Which my heart knows the wide world's common place ?   10
Or mine eyes, seeing this, say this is not,
To put fair truth upon so foul a face ?
    In things right true my heart and eyes have erred,
    And to this false plague are they now transferred.

485

138

When my love swears that she is made of truth,
I do believe her, though I know she lies,
That she might think me some untutor'd youth,
Unlearned in the world's false subtleties.
Thus vainly thinking that she thinks me young,
Although she knows my days are past the best,
Simply I credit her false-speaking tongue ;
On both sides thus is simple truth suppress'd.
But wherefore says she not she is unjust ?
And wherefore say not I that I am old ?
O, love's best habit is in seeming trust,
And age in love loves not to have years told.
   Therefore I lie with her, and she with me,
   And in our faults by lies we flattered be.

139

O, call not me to justify the wrong
That thy unkindness lays upon my heart ;
Wound me not with thine eye, but with thy tongue ;
Use power with power, and slay me not by art.
Tell me thou lov'st elsewhere ; but in my sight,
Dear heart, forbear to glance thine eye aside.
What need'st thou wound with cunning, when thy might
Is more than my o'erpress'd defence can bide ?
Let me excuse thee : ah ! my love well knows
Her pretty looks have been mine enemies ;
And therefore from my face she turns my foes,
That they elsewhere might dart their injuries.
   Yet do not so ; but since I am near slain,
   Kill me outright with looks and rid my pain.

140

Be wise as thou art cruel ; do not press
My tongue-tied patience with too much disdain ;
Lest sorrow lend me words, and words express
The manner of my pity-wanting pain.
If I might teach thee wit, better it were,
Though not to love, yet, love, to tell me so ;
As testy sick men, when their deaths be near,
No news but health from their physicians know.
For, if I should despair, I should grow mad,
And in my madness might speak ill of thee.
Now this ill-wresting world is grown so bad
Mad slanderers by mad ears believed be.
   That I may not be so, nor thou belied,
   Bear thine eyes straight, though thy proud heart go wide.

141

In faith, I do not love thee with mine eyes,
For they in thee a thousand errors note ;
But 'tis my heart that loves what they despise,
Who in despite of view is pleas'd to dote.
Nor are mine ears with thy tongue's tune delighted ;   5
Nor tender feeling to base touches prone,
Nor taste nor smell desire to be invited
To any sensual feast with thee alone ;
But my five wits nor my five senses can
Dissuade one foolish heart from serving thee,   10
Who leaves unsway'd the likeness of a man,
Thy proud heart's slave and vassal wretch to be.
    Only my plague thus far I count my gain,
    That she that makes me sin awards me pain.

142

Love is my sin, and thy dear virtue hate,
Hate of my sin, grounded on sinful loving.
O, but with mine compare thou thine own state,
And thou shalt find it merits not reproving ;
Or, if it do, not from those lips of thine,   5
That have profan'd their scarlet ornaments,
And seal'd false bonds of love as oft as mine ;
Robb'd others' beds' revenues of their rents.
Be it lawful I love thee as thou lov'st those
Whom thine eyes woo as mine importune thee.   10
Root pity in thy heart, that, when it grows,
Thy pity may deserve to pitied be.
    If thou dost seek to have what thou dost hide,
    By self-example mayst thou be denied !

143

Lo as a careful huswife runs to catch
One of her feathered creatures broke away,
Sets down her babe, and makes all swift dispatch
In pursuit of the thing she would have stay ;
Whilst her neglected child holds her in chase,   5
Cries to catch her whose busy care is bent
To follow that which flies before her face,
Not prizing her poor infant's discontent ;
So run'st thou after that which flies from thee,
Whilst I thy babe chase thee afar behind ;   10
But if thou catch thy hope, turn back to me,
And play the mother's part, kiss me, be kind.
    So will I pray that thou mayst have thy Will,
    If thou turn back and my loud crying still.

144

Two loves I have, of comfort and despair,
Which like two spirits do suggest me still ;
The better angel is a man right fair,
The worser spirit a woman colour'd ill.
To win me soon to hell, my female evil
Tempteth my better angel from my side,
And would corrupt my saint to be a devil,
Wooing his purity with her foul pride.
And whether that my angel be turn'd fiend,
Suspect I may, yet not directly tell ;
But being both from me, both to each friend,
I guess one angel in another's hell.
    Yet this shall I ne'er know, but live in doubt,
    Till my bad angel fire my good one out.

145

Those lips that Love's own hand did make
Breath'd forth the sound that said ' I hate '
To me that languish'd for her sake ;
But when she saw my woeful state,
Straight in her heart did mercy come,
Chiding that tongue that ever sweet
Was us'd in giving gentle doom ;
And taught it thus anew to greet :
' I hate ' she alter'd with an end
That follow'd it as gentle day
Doth follow night, who like a fiend
From heaven to hell is flown away :
    ' I hate ' from hate away she threw,
    And sav'd my life, saying ' not you '.

146

Poor soul, the centre of my sinful earth,
[My sinful earth] these rebel pow'rs that thee array,
Why dost thou pine within and suffer dearth,
Painting thy outward walls so costly gay ?
Why so large cost, having so short a lease,
Dost thou upon thy fading mansion spend ?
Shall worms, inheritors of this excess,
Eat up thy charge ?   Is this thy body's end ?
Then, soul, live thou upon thy servant's loss,
And let that pine to aggravate thy store ;
Buy terms divine in selling hours of dross ;
Within be fed, without be rich no more.
    So shalt thou feed on Death, that feeds on men,
    And, Death once dead, there's no more dying then.

147

My love is as a fever, longing still
For that which longer nurseth the disease;
Feeding on that which doth preserve the ill,
Th' uncertain sickly appetite to please.
My Reason, the physician to my Love,   5
Angry that his prescriptions are not kept,
Hath left me, and I desperate now approve
Desire is death, which physic did except.
Past cure I am, now reason is past care,
And frantic mad with evermore unrest;   10
My thoughts and my discourse as mad men's are,
At random from the truth vainly express'd;
    For I have sworn thee fair, and thought thee bright,
    Who art as black as hell, as dark as night.

148

O me, what eyes hath Love put in my head,
Which have no correspondence with true sight!
Or, if they have, where is my judgment fled,
That censures falsely what they see aright?
If that be fair whereon my false eyes dote,   5
What means the world to say it is not so?
If it be not, then love doth well denote
Love's eye is not so true as all men's—no,
How can it? O, how can Love's eye be true,
That is so vex'd with watching and with tears?   10
No marvel then though I mistake my view:
The sun itself sees not till heaven clears.
    O cunning Love! with tears thou keep'st me blind,
    Lest eyes well seeing thy foul faults should find.

149

Canst thou, O cruel! say I love thee not,
When I against myself with thee partake?
Do I not think on thee when I forgot
Am of myself, all tyrant, for thy sake?
Who hateth thee that I do call my friend?   5
On whom frown'st thou that I do fawn upon?
Nay, if thou lour'st on me, do I not spend
Revenge upon myself with present moan?
What merit do I in myself respect
That is so proud thy service to despise,   10
When all my best doth worship thy defect,
Commanded by the motion of thine eyes?
    But, love, hate on, for now I know thy mind:
    Those that can see thou lov'st, and I am blind.

150

O, from what pow'r hast thou this pow'rful might
With insufficiency my heart to sway?
To make me give the lie to my true sight,
And swear that brightness doth not grace the day?
Whence hast thou this becoming of things ill,
That in the very refuse of thy deeds
There is such strength and warrantise of skill
That in my mind thy worst all best exceeds?
Who taught thee how to make me love thee more,
The more I hear and see just cause of hate?
O, though I love what others do abhor,
With others thou shouldst not abhor my state;
    If thy unworthiness rais'd love in me,
    More worthy I to be belov'd of thee.

151

Love is too young to know what conscience is;
Yet who knows not conscience is born of love?
Then, gentle cheater, urge not my amiss,
Lest guilty of my faults thy sweet self prove.
For thou betraying me, I do betray
My nobler part to my gross body's treason;
My soul doth tell my body that he may
Triumph in love; flesh stays no farther reason,
But, rising at thy name, doth point out thee
As his triumphant prize. Proud of this pride,
He is contented thy poor drudge to be,
To stand in thy affairs, fall by thy side.
    No want of conscience hold it that I call
    Her ' love ' for whose dear love I rise and fall.

152

In loving thee thou know'st I am forsworn,
But thou art twice forsworn, to me love swearing;
In act thy bed-vow broke, and new faith torn
In vowing new hate after new love bearing.
But why of two oaths' breach do I accuse thee,
When I break twenty? I am perjur'd most;
For all my vows are oaths but to misuse thee,
And all my honest faith in thee is lost,
For I have sworn deep oaths of thy deep kindness,
Oaths of thy love, thy truth, thy constancy;
And, to enlighten thee, gave eyes to blindness,
Or made them swear against the thing they see;
    For I have sworn thee fair—more perjur'd I,
    To swear against the truth so foul a lie!

153

Cupid laid by his brand, and fell asleep.
A maid of Dian's this advantage found,
And his love-kindling fire did quickly steep
In a cold valley-fountain of that ground ;
Which borrow'd from this holy fire of Love   5
A dateless lively heat, still to endure,
And grew a seething bath, which yet men prove
Against strange maladies a sovereign cure.
But at my mistress' eye Love's brand new-fired,
The boy for trial needs would touch my breast ;   10
I, sick withal, the help of bath desired,
And thither hied, a sad distemper'd guest,
   But found no cure.   The bath for my help lies
   Where Cupid got new fire—my mistress' eyes.

154

The little love-god, lying once asleep,
Laid by his side his heart-inflaming brand,
Whilst many nymphs that vow'd chaste life to keep
Came tripping by ; but in her maiden hand
The fairest votary took up that fire   5
Which many legions of true hearts had warm'd ;
And so the general of hot desire
Was sleeping by a virgin hand disarm'd.
This brand she quenched in a cool well by,
Which from Love's fire took heat perpetual,   10
Growing a bath and healthful remedy
For men diseas'd ; but I, my mistress' thrall,
   Came there for cure, and this by that I prove :
   Love's fire heats water, water cools not love.

A LOVER'S COMPLAINT

FROM off a hill whose concave womb reworded
A plaintful story from a sist'ring vale,
My spirits t' attend this double voice accorded,
And down I laid to list the sad-tun'd tale ;
Ere long espied a fickle maid full pale,   5
Tearing of papers, breaking rings a-twain,
Storming her world with sorrow's wind and rain.

Upon her head a platted hive of straw,
Which fortified her visage from the sun,
Whereon the thought might think sometime it saw   10
The carcase of a beauty spent and done.
Time had not scythed all that youth begun,
Nor youth all quit ; but, spite of heaven's fell rage,
Some beauty peep'd through lattice of sear'd age.

Oft did she heave her napkin to her eyne,   15
Which on it had conceited characters,
Laund'ring the silken figures in the brine
That seasoned woe had pelleted in tears,
And often reading what contents it bears
As often shrieking undistinguish'd woe,   20
In clamours of all size, both high and low.

Sometimes her levell'd eyes their carriage ride,
As they did batt'ry to the spheres intend ;
Sometime diverted their poor balls are tied
To th' orbed earth ; sometimes they do extend   25
Their view right on ; anon their gazes lend
To every place at once, and nowhere fix'd,
The mind and sight distractedly commix'd.

Her hair, nor loose nor tied in formal plat,
Proclaim'd in her a careless hand of pride ;   30
For some, untuck'd, descended her sheav'd hat,
Hanging her pale and pined cheek beside ;
Some in her threaden fillet still did bide,
And, true to bondage, would not break from thence,
Though slackly braided in loose negligence.   35

A thousand favours from a maund she drew
Of amber, crystal, and of beaded jet,
Which one by one she in a river threw,
Upon whose weeping margent she was set ;
Like usury, applying wet to wet,   40
Or monarch's hands that lets not bounty fall
Where want cries some but where excess begs all.

Of folded schedules had she many a one,
Which she perus'd, sigh'd, tore, and gave the flood ;
Crack'd many a ring of posied gold and bone,   45
Bidding them find their sepulchres in mud ;
Found yet moe letters sadly penn'd in blood,
With sleided silk feat and affectedly
Enswath'd and seal'd to curious secrecy.

These often bath'd she in her fluxive eyes,   50
And often kiss'd, and often gan to tear ;
Cried ' O false blood, thou register of lies,
What unapproved witness dost thou bear !
Ink would have seem'd more black and damned here ! '.
This said, in top of rage the lines she rents,   55
Big discontent so breaking their contents.

A reverend man that graz'd his cattle nigh,
Sometime a blusterer that the ruffle knew
Of court, of city, and had let go by
The swiftest hours observed as they flew,   60
Towards this afflicted fancy fastly drew,
And, privileg'd by age, desires to know
In brief the grounds and motives of her woe.

So slides he down upon his grained bat,
And comely distant sits he by her side ;   65
When he again desires her, being sat,
Her grievance with his hearing to divide.
If that from him there may be aught applied
Which may her suffering ecstasy assuage,
'Tis promis'd in the charity of age.   70

' Father,' she says ' though in me you behold
The injury of many a blasting hour,
Let it not tell your judgment I am old :
Not age, but sorrow, over me hath power.
I might as yet have been a spreading flower,   75
Fresh to myself, if I had self-applied
Love to myself, and to no love beside.

' But woe is me ! too early I attended
A youthful suit—it was to gain my grace—
O ! one by nature's outwards so commended   80
That maidens' eyes stuck over all his face.
Love lack'd a dwelling and made him her place ;
And when in his fair parts she did abide,
She was new lodg'd and newly deified.

' His browny locks did hang in crooked curls ;   85
And every light occasion of the wind
Upon his lips their silken parcels hurls.
What's sweet to do, to do will aptly find :
Each eye that saw him did enchant the mind ;
For on his visage was in little drawn   90
What largeness thinks in Paradise was sawn.

' Small show of man was yet upon his chin ;
His phœnix down began but to appear,
Like unshorn velvet, on that termless skin,
Whose bare out-bragg'd the web it seem'd to wear   9⁵
Yet show'd his visage by that cost more dear ;
And nice affections wavering stood in doubt
If best were as it was, or best without.

' His qualities were beauteous as his form,
For maiden-tongu'd he was, and thereof free ;   10⁰
Yet, if men mov'd him, was he such a storm
As oft 'twixt May and April is to see,
When winds breathe sweet, unruly though they be.
His rudeness so with his authoriz'd youth
Did livery falseness in a pride of truth.   10⁵

' Well could he ride, and often men would say
" That horse his mettle from his rider takes :
Proud of subjection, noble by the sway,
What rounds, what bounds, what course, what stop he makes ! "
And controversy hence a question takes,   11⁰
Whether the horse by him became his deed,
Or he his manage by th' well-doing steed.

' But quickly on this side the verdict went :
His real habitude gave life and grace
To appertainings and to ornament,   11⁵
Accomplish'd in himself, not in his case.
All aids, themselves made fairer by their place,
Came for additions ; yet their purpos'd trim
Piec'd not his grace, but were all grac'd by him.

' So on the tip of his subduing tongue   12⁰
All kind of arguments and question deep,
All replication prompt, and reason strong,
For his advantage still did wake and sleep.
To make the weeper laugh, the laugher weep,
He had the dialect and different skill,   12⁵
Catching all passions in his craft of will ;

' That he did in the general bosom reign
Of young, of old, and sexes both enchanted,
To dwell with him in thoughts, or to remain
In personal duty, following where he haunted.   13⁰
Consents bewitch'd, ere he desire, have granted,
And dialogu'd for him what he would say,
Ask'd their own wills, and made their wills obey.

' Many there were that did his picture get,
To serve their eyes and in it put their mind ;   13⁵
Like fools that in th' imagination set
The goodly objects which abroad they find
Of lands and mansions, theirs in thought assign'd ;
And labouring in moe pleasures to bestow them
Than the true gouty landlord which doth owe them.   14⁰

494

' So many have, that never touch'd his hand,
Sweetly suppos'd them mistress of his heart.
My woeful self, that did in freedom stand,
And was my own fee-simple, not in part,
What with his art in youth, and youth in art,   145
Threw my affections in his charmed power,
Reserv'd the stalk and gave him all my flower.

' Yet did I not, as some my equals did,
Demand of him, nor being desired yielded ;
Finding myself in honour so forbid,   150
With safest distance I mine honour shielded.
Experience for me many bulwarks builded
Of proofs new-bleeding, which remain'd the foil
Of this false jewel, and his amorous spoil.

' But ah ! who ever shunn'd by precedent   155
The destin'd ill she must herself assay ?
Or forc'd examples, 'gainst her own content,
To put the by-past perils in her way ?
Counsel may stop awhile what will not stay ;
For when we rage, advice is often seen   160
By blunting us to make our wits more keen.

'Nor gives it satisfaction to our blood
That we must curb it upon others' proof,
To be forbod the sweets that seem so good
For fear of harms that preach in our behoof.   165
O appetite, from judgment stand aloof !
The one a palate hath that needs will taste,
Though Reason weep, and cry " It is thy last ".

' For further I could say " This man's untrue ",
And knew the patterns of his foul beguiling ;   170
Heard where his plants in others' orchards grew ;
Saw how deceits were gilded in his smiling ;
Knew vows were ever brokers to defiling ;
Thought characters and words merely but art,
And bastards of his foul adulterate heart.   175

' And long upon these terms I held my city,
Till thus he gan besiege me : " Gentle maid,
Have of my suffering youth some feeling pity,
And be not of my holy vows afraid,
That's to ye sworn to none was ever said ;   180
For feasts of love I have been call'd unto,
Till now did ne'er invite nor never woo.

' All my offences that abroad you see
Are errors of the blood, none of the mind ;
Love made them not ; with acture they may be,   185
Where neither party is nor true nor kind.
They sought their shame that so their shame did find ;
And so much less of shame in me remains
By how much of me their reproach contains.

   ' " Among the many that mine eyes have seen,   190
Not one whose flame my heart so much as warmed,
Or my affection put to th' smallest teen,
Or any of my leisures ever charmed.
Harm have I done to them, but ne'er was harmed ;
Kept hearts in liveries, but mine own was free,   195
And reign'd commanding in his monarchy.

   ' " Look here what tributes wounded fancies sent me,
Of pallid pearls and rubies red as blood ;
Figuring that they their passions likewise lent me
Of grief and blushes, aptly understood   200
In bloodless white and the encrimson'd mood—
Effects of terror and dear modesty,
Encamp'd in hearts, but fighting outwardly.

   ' " And, lo, behold these talents of their hair,
With twisted metal amorously empleach'd,   205
I have receiv'd from many a several fair,
Their kind acceptance weepingly beseech'd,
With the annexions of fair gems enrich'd,
And deep-brain'd sonnets that did amplify
Each stone's dear nature, worth, and quality.   210

   ' " The diamond—why, 'twas beautiful and hard,
Whereto his invis'd properties did tend ;
The deep-green em'rald, in whose fresh regard
Weak sights their sickly radiance do amend ;
The heaven-hu'd sapphire and the opal blend   215
With objects manifold ; each several stone,
With wit well blazon'd, smil'd, or made some moan.

   ' " Lo, all these trophies of affections hot,
Of pensiv'd and subdu'd desires the tender,
Nature hath charg'd me that I hoard them not,   220
But yield them up where I myself must render—
That is, to you, my origin and ender ;
For these, of force, must your oblations be,
Since I their altar, you enpatron me.

   ' " O, then, advance of yours that phraseless hand   225
Whose white weighs down the airy scale of praise :
Take all these similes to your own command,
Hallowed with sighs that burning lungs did raise ;
What me, your minister, for you obeys,
Works under you ; and to your audit comes   230
Their distract parcels in combined sums.

   ' " Lo, this device was sent me from a nun,
Or sister sanctified, of holiest note,
Which late her noble suit in court did shun,
Whose rarest havings made the blossoms dote ;   235
For she was sought by spirits of richest coat,
But kept cold distance, and did thence remove
To spend her living in eternal love.

' " But, O my sweet, what labour is't to leave
The things we have not, mast'ring what not strives,   240
Paling the place which did no form receive,
Playing patient sports in unconstrained gyves !
She that her fame so to herself contrives,
The scars of battle scapeth by the flight,
And makes her absence valiant, not her might.   245

' " O, pardon me, in that my boast is true !
The accident which brought me to her eye
Upon the moment did her force subdue,
And now she would the caged cloister fly.
Religious love put out religion's eye.   250
Not to be tempted, would she be immur'd,
And now, to tempt all, liberty procur'd.

' " How mighty then you are, O, hear me tell !
The broken bosoms that to me belong
Have emptied all their fountains in my well,   255
And mine I pour your ocean all among.
I strong o'er them, and you o'er me being strong,
Must for your victory us all congest,
As compound love to physic your cold breast.

' " My parts had pow'r to charm a sacred nun,   260
Who, disciplin'd, ay, dieted in grace,
Believ'd her eyes when they t' assail begun,
All vows and consecrations giving place.
O most potential love ! vow, bond, nor space,
In thee hath neither sting, knot, nor confine,   265
For thou art all, and all things else are thine.

' " When thou impressest, what are precepts worth
Of stale example ? When thou wilt inflame,
How coldly those impediments stand forth,
Of wealth, of filial fear, law, kindred, fame !   270
Love's arms are peace, 'gainst rule, 'gainst sense, 'gainst shame,
And sweetens, in the suff'ring pangs it bears,
The aloes of all forces, shocks, and fears.

' " Now all these hearts that do on mine depend,
Feeling it break, with bleeding groans they pine,   275
And supplicant their sighs to you extend,
To leave the batt'ry that you make 'gainst mine,
Lending soft audience to my sweet design,
And credent soul to that strong-bonded oath,
That shall prefer and undertake my troth ".   280

' This said, his wat'ry eyes he did dismount,
Whose sights till then were levell'd on my face ;
Each cheek a river running from a fount
With brinish current downward flow'd apace.
O, how the channel to the stream gave grace !   285
Who glaz'd with crystal gate the glowing roses
That flame through water which their hue encloses.

' O father, what a hell of witchcraft lies
In the small orb of one particular tear !
But with the inundation of the eyes   290
What rocky heart to water will not wear ?
What breast so cold that is not warmed here ?
O cleft effect ! cold modesty, hot wrath,
Both fire from hence and chill extincture hath.

' For lo, his passion, but an art of craft,   295
Even there resolv'd my reason into tears ;
There my white stole of chastity I daff'd,
Shook off my sober guards and civil fears ;
Appear to him as he to me appears
All melting ; though our drops this diff'rence bore: 300
His poison'd me, and mine did him restore.

' In him a plenitude of subtle matter,
Applied to cautels, all strange forms receives,
Of burning blushes or of weeping water,
Or swooning paleness ; and he takes and leaves, 305
In either's aptness, as it best deceives,
To blush at speeches rank, to weep at woes,
Or to turn white and swoon at tragic shows ;

' That not a heart which in his level came
Could scape the hail of his all-hurting aim,   310
Showing fair nature is both kind and tame ;
And, veil'd in them, did win whom he would maim.
Against the thing he sought he would exclaim ;
When he most burn'd in heart-wish'd luxury,
He preach'd pure maid and prais'd cold chastity. 315

' Thus merely with the garment of a Grace
The naked and concealed fiend he cover'd,
That th' unexperient gave the tempter place,
Which, like a cherubin, above them hover'd.
Who, young and simple, would not be so lover'd ? 320
Ay me ! I fell ; and yet do question make
What I should do again for such a sake.

' O, that infected moisture of his eye,
O, that false fire which in his cheek so glowed,
O, that forc'd thunder from his heart did fly,   325
O, that sad breath his spongy lungs bestowed,
O, all that borrowed motion, seeming owed,
Would yet again betray the fore-betray'd,
And new pervert a reconciled maid ! '

THE PASSIONATE PILGRIM
THE PHŒNIX AND TURTLE

The Passionate Pilgrim is one of the earliest ventures of William Jaggard as a publisher, as *The First Folio* edition of Shakespeare's plays was his last and greatest achievement as a publisher and printer. Jaggard, although he put Shakespeare's name on the collection of short pieces he issued in 1599 under the familiar title of *The Passionate Pilgrim*, was taking a liberty with the dramatist's reputation, for only a few of the poems included were by Shakespeare, a fact that Jaggard himself must have known, and the items by Shakespeare were no doubt there without any sanction from the poet. Indeed, some years later, Jaggard in his zeal to make a later edition even more popular and to increase its bulk added to the collection two poems by Thomas Heywood; these poems, which were in the form of Ovid's love-epistles and represented themselves as epistles of Paris to Helen and of Helen to Paris, were printed and published by Jaggard himself in 1609 in circumstances that throw serious doubt on the propriety of Jaggard's dealings in this particular venture. Jaggard did not hesitate in 1612 in issuing his third edition of *The Passionate Pilgrim* not only to transfer to it from the *Troia Britanica* of 1609 these two poems but to add to his title page the statement he knew to be a deliberate falsehood : ' newly corrected and augmented by W. Shakespeare '.

This piece of effrontery did not escape the notice of Shakespeare and Heywood, and we are fortunate in having in an epistle that Heywood inserted in his *Apology for Actors* (1612) an account not only of Heywood's own feelings about the business but also of Shakespeare's reaction. Heywood's words, with the explanatory parentheses added by Sidney Lee in his introduction to the Oxford facsimile of Jaggard's publication, are as follows :

> Here, likewise, I must necessarily insert a manifest injury done me in that worke [i.e. *Troia Britanica*] by taking the two epistles of Paris to Helen, and Helen to Paris, and printing them in a lesse volume (i.e. *The Passionate Pilgrim* of 1612) under the name of another [i.e. Shakespeare], which may put the world in opinion I might steale them from him, and hee, to doe himselfe right, hath since published them in his owne name : but, as I must acknowledge my lines not worth his [i.e. Shakespeare's] patronage under whom he [i.e. Jaggard] hath publisht them, so the author, I know, much offended with M. Jaggard that altogether unknowne to him presumed to make so bold with his name.

Shakespeare and Heywood must have made their displeasure sufficiently clear to disturb even Jaggard, for he cancelled the title page with the untruthful and offensive reference to Shakespeare and substituted another without any author's name.

As early as 1599 Jaggard had a firm faith in the market value of Shakespeare's name, and this faith was strong enough to bring to him in his last years by however devious a path the collected plays of the master.

The only real interest for the student of Shakespeare in the items contained in the collection lies in the first two Sonnets. These were to appear in Thorpe's 1609 edition of the *Sonnets* as numbers 138 and 144, and their publication by Jaggard in 1599 fixes a definite *terminus ad quem* for certain episodes in the Sonnet story. Numbers 3, 5 16, are from *Love's Labour's Lost*. These five pieces are the only items that are certainly by Shakespeare.

Numbers 8 and 20, are, as Jaggard knew, by Richard Barnfield, for Jaggard's brother John had published them in 1598 as Barnfield's. Number 17 is found in Thomas Weelkes's *Madrigals* (1597) and may be by Barnfield. Bartholomew Griffin published a version of number 11 in his *Fidessa* (1596). Number 19 is the famous poem by Marlowe, with Love's answer by Raleigh. There are fuller versions in *England's Helicon* and Walton's *Compleat Angler*. The authorship of the remainder is doubtful or unknown.

Before number 15 Jaggard inserted another title page headed *Sonnets, to sundry notes of Musicke*, ' sonnets ' here meaning songs, as ' passionate ' in the main title page means amorous.

The Phœnix and Turtle Shakespeare contributed to a publication of 1601. In that year Robert Chester, a member of the household of the wealthy Sir John Salisbury of Denbigh in Wales, published a volume entitled *Love's Martyr: or Rosalin's Complaint. Allegorically shadowing the truth of Love, in the constant Fate of the Phœnix and Turtle*. Sir John Salisbury was a very acceptable figure at Court, and as the Queen had just knighted him in June 1601 the volume Chester published was another tribute, this time by a local poet, to Sir John's virtues. The opening tribute celebrates the faithful loves of Salisbury, who is the Turtle, and his wife Ursula Stanley, the Phœnix. Sir John, to give the volume some ballast, invited several of the leading dramatists to contribute verses. As Salisbury was a generous patron of the theatre the dramatists responded no doubt readily, and after Chester's contribution comes a title page : ' Hereafter Follow Diverse Poeticall Essaies on the Former Subject ; viz. The Turtle and Phœnix, Done by the Best and Chiefest of our Moderne Writers, with their Names Subscribed to their Particular Works : Never before Extant. And (now first) Consecrated by them all Generally to the Love and Merite of the True-Noble Knight, Sir John Salisburie.' The contributors included Shakespeare, Marston, Chapman, and Jonson.

Shakespeare does not seem to have studied Chester's allegory of the Phœnix and the Turtle with any care ; at least, if he subjected it to a close reading, he decided to go his own way and contributed the metaphysical invention that illustrates so perfectly one vein in his genius.

1

When my love swears that she is made of truth,
I do believe her, though I know she lies,
That she might think me some untutor'd youth,
Unskilful in the world's false forgeries.
Thus vainly thinking that she thinks me young,   5
Although I know my years be past the best,
I smiling credit her false-speaking tongue,
Outfacing faults in love with love's ill rest.
But wherefore says my love that she is young?
And wherefore say not I that I am old?   10
O, love's best habit is a soothing tongue,
And age in love love's not to have years told.
    Therefore I'll lie with love, and love with me,
    Since that out faults in love thus smother'd be.

2

Two loves I have, of comfort and despair,
That like two spirits do suggest me still;
My better angel is a man right fair,
My worser spirit a woman colour'd ill.
To win me soon to hell, my female evil   5
Tempteth my better angel from my side,
And would corrupt my saint to be a devil,
Wooing his purity with her fair pride.
And whether that my angel be turn'd fiend,
Suspect I may, yet not directly tell;   10
For being both to me, both to each friend,
I guess one angel in another's hell.
    The truth I shall not know, but live in doubt,
    Till my bad angel fire my good one out.

3

Did not the heavenly rhetoric of thine eye,
'Gainst whom the world could not hold argument,
Persuade my heart to this false perjury?
Vows for thee broke deserve not punishment.
A woman I forswore; but I will prove,   5
Thou being a goddess, I forswore not thee:
My vow was earthly, thou a heavenly love;
Thy grace being gain'd cures all disgrace in me.
My vow was breath, and breath a vapour is;
Then, thou fair sun, that on this earth doth shine,   10
Exhale this vapour vow; in thee it is:
If broken, then it is no fault of mine.
    If by me broke, what fool is not so wise
    To break an oath, to win a paradise?

4

Sweet Cytherea, sitting by a brook
With young Adonis, lovely, fresh, and green,
Did court the lad with many a lovely look,
Such looks as none could look but beauty's queen.
She told him stories to delight his ear ;   5
She show'd him favours to allure his eye ;
To win his heart she touch'd him here and there :
Touches so soft still conquer chastity.
But whether unripe years did want conceit,
Or he refus'd to take her figured proffer,   10
The tender nibbler would not touch the bait,
But smile and jest at every gentle offer.
    Then fell she on her back, fair queen, and toward :
    He rose and ran away ; ah, fool too froward !

5

If love make me forsworn, how shall I swear to love ?
O never faith could hold, if not to beauty vowed ;
Though to myself forsworn, to thee I'll constant prove ;
Those thoughts, to me like oaks, to thee like osiers bowed.
Study his bias leaves and makes his book thine eyes,   5
Where all those pleasures live that art can comprehend.
If knowledge be the mark, to know thee shall suffice ;
Well learned is that tongue that well can thee commend ;
All ignorant that soul that sees thee without wonder ;
Which is to me some praise, that I thy parts admire.   10
Thine eye Jove's lightning seems, thy voice his dreadful thunder.
Which, not to anger bent, is music and sweet fire.
    Celestial as thou art, O, do not love that wrong,
    To sing heaven's praise with such an earthly tongue.

6

Scarce had the sun dried up the dewy morn,
And scarce the herd gone to the hedge for shade,
When Cytherea, all in love forlorn,
A longing tarriance for Adonis made
Under an osier growing by a brook,   5
A brook where Adon us'd to cool his spleen.
Hot was the day ; she hotter that did look
For his approach that often there had been.
Anon he comes, and throws his mantle by,
And stood stark naked on the brook's green brim.   10
The sun look'd on the world with glorious eye,
Yet not so wistly as this queen on him.
    He, spying her, bounc'd in whereas he stood ;
    ' O Jove,' quoth she ' why was not I a flood ? '

7

Fair is my love, but not so fair as fickle ;
Mild as a dove, but neither true nor trusty ;
Brighter than glass, and yet, as glass is, brittle ;
Softer than wax, and yet, as iron, rusty ;
   A lily pale, with damask dye to grace her ;   5
   None fairer, nor none falser to deface her.

Her lips to mine how often hath she joined,
Between each kiss her oaths of true love swearing !
How many tales to please me hath she coined,
Dreading my love, the loss whereof still fearing !   10
   Yet, in the midst of all her pure protestings,
   Her faith, her oaths, her tears, and all, were jestings.

She burn'd with love, as straw with fire flameth,
She burn'd out love, as soon as straw outburneth ;
She fram'd the love, and yet she foil'd the framing,   15
She bade love last, and yet she fell a-turning.
   Was this a lover, or a lecher whether ?
   Bad in the best, though excellent in neither.

8

If music and sweet poetry agree,
As they must needs, the sister and the brother,
Then must the love be great 'twixt thee and me,
Because thou lov'st the one, and I the other.
Dowland to thee is dear, whose heavenly touch   5
Upon the lute doth ravish human sense ;
Spenser to me, whose deep conceit is such
As, passing all conceit, needs no defence.
Thou lov'st to hear the sweet melodious sound
That Phœbus' lute, the queen of music, makes ;   10
And I in deep delight am chiefly drown'd
Whenas himself to singing he betakes.
   One god is god of both, as poets feign ;
   One knight loves both, and both in thee remain.

9

Fair was the morn, when the fair queen of love,
*   *   *   *   *   *   *   *
Paler for sorrow than her milk-white dove,
For Adon's sake, a youngster proud and wild,
Her stand she takes upon a steep-up hill.   5
Anon Adonis comes with horns and hounds ;
She, silly queen, with more than love's good will,
Forbade the boy he should not pass those grounds.

'Once' quoth she 'did I see a fair sweet youth
Here in these brakes deep-wounded with a boar,   10
Deep in the thigh, a spectacle of ruth!
See in my thigh,' quoth she 'here was the sore.'
    She showed hers; he saw more wounds than one,
    And blushing fled, and left her all alone.

10

Sweet rose, fair flower, untimely pluck'd, soon vaded,
Pluck'd in the bud, and vaded in the spring!
Bright orient pearl, alack, too timely shaded!
Fair creature, kill'd too soon by death's sharp sting!
Like a green plum that hangs upon a tree,   5
And fals, through wind, before the fall should be.

I weep for thee, and yet no cause I have;
For why thou lefts me nothing in thy will.
And yet thou lefts me more than I did crave;
For why I craved nothing of thee still.   10
    O yes, dear friend, I pardon crave of thee!
    Thy discontent thou didst bequeath to me.

11

Venus, with Adonis sitting by her
Under a myrtle shade, began to woo him.
She told the youngling how god Mars did try her,
And as he fell to her, she fell to him.
'Even thus' quoth she 'the warlike god embrac'd me.'   5
And then she clipp'd Adonis in her arms.
'Even thus' quoth she 'the warlike god unlac'd me'
As if the boy should use like loving charms.
'Even thus' quoth she 'he seized on my lips'
And with her lips on his did act the seizure;   10
And as she fetched breath, away he skips,
And would not take her meaning nor her pleasure.
    Ah! that I had my lady at this bay,
    To kiss and clip me till I run away!

12

Crabbed age and youth cannot live together:
Youth is full of pleasance, age is full of care;
Youth like summer morn, age like winter weather;
Youth like summer brave, age like winter bare.
Youth is full of sport, age's breath is short;   5
Youth is nimble, age is lame;
Youth is hot and bold, age is weak and cold;
Youth is wild, and age is tame.

Age, I do abhor thee ; youth, I do adore thee.
O, my love, my love is young !   10
Age, I do defy thee.
O sweet shepherd, hie thee,
For methinks thou stays too long.

13

Beauty is but a vain and doubtful good,
A shining gloss that vadeth suddenly ;
A flower that dies when first it gins to bud ;
A brittle glass that's broken presently ;
   A doubtful good, a gloss, a glass, a flower,   5
   Lost, vaded, broken, dead within an hour.

And as goods lost are seld or never found,
As vaded gloss no rubbing will refresh,
As flowers dead lie withered on the ground,
As broken glass no cement can redress ;   10
   So beauty, blemish'd once, for ever lost,
   In spite of physic, painting, pain, and cost.

14

Good night, good rest.   Ah, neither be my share !
She bade good night that kept my rest away,
And daff'd me to a cabin hang'd with care,
To descant on the doubts of my decay.
   'Farewell,' quoth she 'and come again to-morrow.'
   Fare well I could not, for I supp'd with sorrow.   5

Yet at my parting sweetly did she smile,
In scorn or friendship, nill I construe whether :
'T may be she joy'd to jest at my exile ;
'T may be again to make me wander thither—   10
   'Wander', a word for shadows like myself
   As take the pain but cannot pluck the pelf.

Lord, how mine eyes throw gazes to the east !
My heart doth charge the watch ; the morning rise
Doth cite each moving sense from idle rest,
Not daring trust the office of mine eyes.   15
   While Philomela sits and sings, I sit and mark,
   And wish her lays were tuned like the lark ;

For she doth welcome daylight with her ditty,
And drives away dark dreaming night.   20
The night so pack'd, I post unto my pretty ;
Heart hath his hope, and eyes their wished sight ;
   Sorrow chang'd to solace, and solace mix'd with sorrow ;
   For why she sigh'd, and bade me come to-morrow.

Were I with her, the night would post too soon ;   25
But now are minutes added to the hours ;
To spite me now, each minute seems a moon ;
Yet not for me, shine sun to succour flowers !
    Pack night, peep day ; good day, of night now borrow ;
    Short, night, to-night, and length thyself to-morrow.   30

15

It was a lording's daughter, the fairest one of three,
That liked of her master as well as well might be,
Till looking on an Englishman, the fairest that eye could see,
    Her fancy fell a-turning.
Long was the combat doubtful that love with love did fight,   5
To leave the master loveless, or kill the gallant knight ;
To put in practice either, alas, it was a spite
    Unto the silly damsel !
But one must be refused ; more mickle was the pain
That nothing could be used to turn them both to gain,   10
For of the two the trusty knight was wounded with disdain,
    Alas, she could not help it !
Thus art with arms contending was victor of the day,
Which by a gift of learning did bear the maid away.
Then, lullaby, the learned man hath got the lady gay ;   15
    For now my song is ended.

16

On a day, alack the day !
Love, whose month was ever May,
Spied a blossom passing fair,
Playing in the wanton air.
Through the velvet leaves the wind,   5
All unseen, gan passage find ;
That the lover, sick to death,
Wish'd himself the heaven's breath.
'Air,' quoth he ' thy cheeks may blow ;
Air, would I might triumph so !   10
But, alas, my hand hath sworn
Ne'er to pluck thee from thy thorn ;
Vow, alack, for youth unmeet,
Youth, so apt to pluck a sweet.
Thou for whom Jove would swear   15
Juno but an Ethiope were ;
And deny himself for Jove,
Turning mortal for thy love.'

17

My flocks feed not,
My ewes breed not,
My rams speed not,
    All is amiss ;
Love is dying,   5
Faith's defying,
Heart's denying,
    Causer of this.

All my merry jigs are quite forgot,
All my lady's love is lost, God wot.   10
Where her faith was firmly fix'd in love,
There a nay is plac'd without remove.
One silly cross
Wrought all my loss.
  O frowning Fortune, cursed fickle dame!   15
For now I see
Inconstancy
  More in women than in men remain.

In black mourn I,
All fears scorn I,   20
Love hath forlorn me,
  Living in thrall;
Heart is bleeding,
All help needing,
O cruel speeding,   25
  Fraughted with gall!
My shepherd's pipe can sound no deal;
My wether's bell rings doleful knell;
My curtail dog, that wont to have play'd,
Plays not at all, but seems afraid.   30
With sighs so deep,
Procures to weep,
  In howling wise, to see my doleful plight.
How sighs resound
Through heartless ground,   35
  Like a thousand vanquish'd men in bloody fight!

Clear wells spring not,
Sweet birds sing not,
Green plants bring not
  Forth their dye.   40
Herds stand weeping,
Flocks all sleeping,
Nymphs back peeping
  Fearfully.
All our pleasure known to us poor swains,   45
All our merry meetings on the plains,
All our evening sport from us is fled,
All our love is lost, for Love is dead.
Farewell, sweet lass;
Thy like ne'er was   50
  For a sweet content, the cause of all my moan.
Poor Corydon
Must live alone;
  Other help for him I see that there is none.

18

When as thine eye hath chose the dame,
And stall'd the deer that thou shouldst strike,
Let reason rule things worthy blame,
As well as fancy, partial wight;

Take counsel of some wiser head, 5
Neither too young nor yet unwed.

And when thou com'st thy tale to tell,
Smooth not thy tongue with filed talk,
Lest she some subtle practice smell—
A cripple soon can find a halt; 10
   But plainly say thou lov'st her well,
   And set her person forth to sell.

And to her will frame all thy ways;
Spare not to spend, and chiefly there
Where thy desert may merit praise 15
By ringing in thy lady's ear.
   The strongest castle, tower, and town,
   The golden bullet beats it down.

Serve always with assured trust,
And in thy suit be humble-true; 20
Unless thy lady prove unjust,
Press never thou to choose a new.
   When time shall serve, be thou not slack
   To proffer, though she put thee back.

What though her frowning brows be bent, 25
Her cloudy looks will calm ere night;
And then too late she will repent
That thus dissembled her delight;
   And twice desire, ere it be day,
   That which with scorn she put away. 30

What though she strive to try her strength,
And ban and brawl and say thee nay?
Her feeble force will yield at length,
When craft hath taught her thus to say:
   ' Had women been so strong as men, 35
   In faith, you had not had it then '.

The wiles and guiles that women work,
Dissembled with an outward show,
The tricks and toys that in them lurk,
The cock that treads them shall not know. 40
   Have you not heard it said full oft,
   A woman's nay doth stand for nought?

Think women still to strive with men
To sin, and never for to saint;
There is no heaven—be holy then— 45
When time with age shall them attaint.
   Were kisses all the joys in bed,
   One woman would another wed.

But soft ; enough—too much I fear ;
Lest that my mistress hear my song ;
She will not stick to round me on th' ear,
To teach my tongue to be so long.   50
   Yet will she blush, here be it said,
   To hear her secrets so bewray'd.

19

Live with me, and be my love,
And we will all the pleasures prove
That hills and valleys, dales and fields,
And all the craggy mountains yields.

There will we sit upon the rocks,   5
And see the shepherds feed their flocks,
By shallow rivers, by whose falls
Melodious birds sing madrigals.

There will I make thee a bed of roses,
With a thousand fragrant posies,
A cap of flowers, and a kirtle   10
Embroidered all with leaves of myrtle ;

A belt of straw and ivy buds,
With coral clasps and amber studs.
And if these pleasures may thee move,   15
Then live with me and be my love.

LOVE'S ANSWER

If that the world and love were young,
And truth in every shepherd's tongue,
These pretty pleasures might me move,
To live with thee and be thy love.   20

20

As it fell upon a day,
In the merry month of May,
Sitting in a pleasant shade
Which a grove of myrtles made,
Beasts did leap and birds did sing,   5
Trees did grow and plants did spring ;
Every thing did banish moan,
Save the nightingale alone.
She, poor bird, as all forlorn,
Lean'd her breast up-till a thorn,   10
And there sung the dolefull'st ditty,
That to hear it was great pity.
' Fie, fie, fie ! ' now would she cry ;
' Teru, Teru ! ' by and by ;

That to hear her so complain 15
Scarce I could from tears refrain;
For her griefs, so lively shown,
Made me think upon mine own.
Ah, thought I, thou mourn'st in vain;
None takes pity on thy pain: 20
Senseless trees, they cannot hear thee;
Ruthless bears, they will not cheer thee.
King Pandion, he is dead;
All thy friends are lapp'd in lead;
All thy fellow birds do sing, 25
Careless of thy sorrowing.
Even so, poor bird, like thee,
None alive will pity me.
Whilst as fickle Fortune smil'd,
Thou and I were both beguil'd. 30
Every one that flatters thee
Is no friend in misery.
Words are easy, like the wind;
Faithful friends are hard to find.
Every man will be thy friend 35
Whilst thou hast wherewith to spend;
But if store of crowns be scant,
No man will supply thy want.
If that one be prodigal,
Bountiful they will him call, 40
And with such-like flattering,
'Pity but he were a king'.
If he be addict to vice,
Quickly him they will entice;
If to women he be bent, 45
They have at commandement;
But if Fortune once do frown,
Then farewell his great renown.
They that fawn'd on him before
Use his company no more. 50
He that is thy friend indeed, ;
He will help thee in thy need
If thou sorrow, he will weep;
If thou wake, he cannot sleep.
Thus of every grief in heart 55
He with thee doth bear a part.
These are certain signs to know
Faithful friend from flatt'ring foe.

THE PHŒNIX AND TURTLE

LET the bird of loudest lay,
On the sole Arabian tree,
Herald sad and trumpet be,
To whose sound chaste wings obey.

But thou shrieking harbinger,   5
Foul precurrer of the fiend,
Augur of the fever's end,
To this troop come thou not near.

From this session interdict
Every fowl of tyrant wing,   10
Save the eagle, feath'red king :
Keep the obsequy so strict.

Let the priest in surplice white,
That defunctive music can,
Be the death-divining swan,   15
Lest the requiem lack his right.

And thou treble-dated crow,
That thy sable gender mak'st
With the breath thou giv'st and tak'st
'Mongst our mourners shalt thou go.   20

Here the anthem doth commence :
Love and constancy is dead ;
Phœnix and the turtle fled
In a mutual flame from hence.

So they lov'd as love in twain   25
Had the essence but in one ;
Two distincts, division none :
Number there in love was slain.

Hearts remote, yet not asunder ;
Distance, and no space was seen   30
'Twixt this turtle and his queen ;
But in them it were a wonder.

So between them love did shine
That the turtle saw his right
Flaming in the phœnix' sight :   35
Either was the other's mine.

Property was thus appalled,
That the self was not the same ;
Single nature's double name
Neither two nor one was called.   40

Reason, in itself confounded,
Saw division grow together,
To themselves yet either neither,
Simple were so well compounded,

That it cried ' How true a twain   45
Seemeth this concordant one !
Love hath reason, reason none,
If what parts can so remain '.

Whereupon it made this threne
To the phœnix and the dove,   50
Co-supremes and stars of love,
As chorus to their tragic scene.

THRENOS

Beauty, truth, and rarity,
Grace in all simplicity,
Here enclos'd in cinders lie.   55

Death is now the phœnix' nest ;
And the turtle's loyal breast
To eternity doth rest,

Leaving no posterity—
'Twas not their infirmity,   60
It was married chastity.

Truth may seem, but cannot be ;
Beauty brag, but 'tis not she :
Truth and beauty buried be.

To this urn let those repair   65
That are either true or fair ;
For these dead birds sigh a prayer.

GLOSSARY

'A, weak form of he, *e.g. Ant. and Cleo.,* 2.vii.89 and 132.

ABATE, deprive, *Lear,* 2.iv.157 ; *abate her nothing,* in no way lower my estimate of her, *Cym.,* 1.iv.64.

ABATEMENT, reduced condition, *Cym.,* 5.iv.21.

ABHOR, *it does abhor me,* horrify and disgust, *Oth.,* 4.ii.163.

ABHORRING, *blow me into abhorring,* reduce to object of loathing, *Ant. and Cleo.,* 5.ii.60.

ABIDE, *abide it,* face consequences of, *Cym.,* 3.iv.182.

ABILITY, *abilities,* means of defence, *Oth.,* 1.iii.25.

ABJURE, solemnly renounce, *Lear,* 2.iv.207.

ABLE, *be able,* be of strength in resources, *Ant. and Cleo.,* 1.iv.78 ; talented, *Son.,* 85,7 ; *verb,* to answer for, *Lear,* 4.vi.168.

ABODE, *desire my man's abode,* my servant's remaining, *Cym.,* 1.vi.52.

ABOMINATION, revolting nature, *Lucrece,* 704 ; inhuman act, *Ant. and Cleo.,* 3.vi.94.

ABOUT, *about it,* set about it, *Oth.,* 4.ii.241.

ABRIDGEMENT, summary, short account, *Cym.,* 5.v.382.

ABSENT, *lovers' absent hours,* hours when they are apart, *Oth.,* 3.iv.175.

ABSOLUTE, *absolute queen,* in no way vassal to Rome, *Ant. and Cleo.,* 3.vi.11 ; *absolute hope,* a feeling of certainty, *Ant. and Cleo.,* 4.iii.10 ; *absolute soldiership,* superiority in generalship, *Ant. and Cleo.,* 3.vii.42 ; used humorously at *Ant. and Cleo.,* 1.ii.2.

ABSOLUTION, remission of sin, *Lucrece,* 354.

ABSTRACT, *abstract of all faults,* as if he had picked out the faults of men and compressed them into his own way of life, *Ant. and Cleo.,* 1.iv.9.

ABUSE, *verb,* misapply, *Son.,* 82,14 ; misrepresent, *Oth.,* 2.i.300 ; insult, *Cym.,* 2.iii.149 ; deceive, *Cym.,* 4.ii.352, *Oth.,* 1.iii.389 ; *noun,* crime, *Lucrece,* 269.

ACCENT, *accents and delays,* stresses and pauses, *Lucrece,* 1719 ; tone of voice, *Oth.,* 1.i.76 ; expression, *Lear,* 2.ii.106.

ACCEPTABLE, that can be received with satisfaction, *Son.,* 4,12.

ACCEPTANCE, quality that induces favourable reception, *Son.,* 135,8.

ACCESSARY, *noun,* accomplice, *Son.,* 35,13 ; *adj.,* sharing in guilt, *Lucrece,* 1658.

ACCESSIBLE, clearly approachable, *Cym.,* 3.ii.81.

ACCIDENT, unexpected happening, *Oth.,* 4.ii.225 ; *moving accident,* exciting happening, *Oth.,* 1.iii.135.

ACCOMMODATE, dress up, *Lear,* 4.vi.81 ; *unaccommodated man,* man naked or deprived of the clothing of civilization, *Lear,* 3.iv.106.

ACCOMPLISHMENT, achievement, *Lucrece,* 716.

ACCOUNTANT, liable to answer for, *Oth.,* 2.i.287.

ACE, single spot on dice (with pun on ' ass '), *Cym.,* 2.iii.2.

ACERBE, bitter, *Oth.,* 1.iii.347.

ACKNOWN, *be not acknown on't,* don't admit knowledge of this, *Oth.,* 3.iii.323.

ACQUIT, pay for, *Lucrece,* 1071.

ACQUITTANCE, discharge of a debt, *Cym.,* 5.iv.169.

ACT, *native act,* habitual action, *Oth.,* 1.i.63 ; action, *Cym.,* 5.iii.29 ; *Ven. and Ad.,* 359.

ACTION-TAKING, seeking redress in law rather than by his own hand, *Lear,* 2.ii.16.

ACTUAL, *actual deed,* physical act, *Oth.,* 4.ii.154.

ACTURE, action, performance, *Lov. Comp.,* 185.

ADDICTION, natural inclination, *Oth.,* 2.ii.5.

ADDITION, description or title acquired by habits or service ; dignities that go with a title or office, *Lear,* 1.i.135.

ADDRESS, *address'd,* clothed, *Per.,* 2.iii.95 ; make ready, *Lucrece,* 1606.

ADJUNCT, connected with, consequent on, *Lucrece,* 133 ; *an adjunct,* an added help to memory, *Son.,* 122,13.

ADMIRAL, flagship, *Ant. and Cleo.,* 3.x.2.

ADMIRATION, assumption of doubt and wonder, *Lear,* 1.iv.236 ; wonder and delight, *Lucrece,* 418.

ADOPTION, *the adoption of the crown,* being chosen as the king's heir, *Cym.,* 5.v.56.

ADULTERATE, unchaste, *Son.,* 121,5.

ADVICE, consideration, *Cym.,* 1.i.156.

ADVISED, *advised doom,* deeply-determined pronouncement (against criminal), *Lucrece,* 1849.

AERIAL, *th' aerial blue,* the blue of the sky, *Oth.,* 2.i.39.

AFFECT, incline to, *Oth.,* 3.iii.233 ; *feat and affectedly,* with loving art, *Lov.Comp.,* 48.

AFFECTION, desire, *Ven. and Ad.,* 387.

AFFIANCE, trust, *Cym.,* 1.vi.162.

AFFIN'D, *partially affin'd,* so akin to him as to misrepresent things in his favour, *Oth.,* 2.iii.210.

AFFINITY, *of great affinity,* with powerful family connection, *Oth.,* 3.i.46.

AFFIRMATION, *of bloody affirmation*, to support an assertion with one's blood (as in a duel), *Cym.*, 1.iv.55.

AFFRONT, meet as in battle, *Cym.*, 4.iii.29.

AFRAID, distrustful, *Lov.Comp.*, 179.

AGGRAVATE, increase, *Son.*, 146,10.

AGNIZE, admit, acknowledge, *Oth.*, 1.iii.231.

AIM, conjecture, *Oth.*, 1.iii.6.

ALCIDES, Hercules, *Ant. and Cleo.*, 4.xii.44.

ALL, *all myself*, only myself, *Lear*, 4.vi.195 ; *all distress*, nothing but distress, *Lucrece*, 1444.

ALLAY, weaken, detract from, *Ant. and Cleo.*, 2.v.50 ; *allayment*, antidote, *Cym.*, 1.v.22.

ALLOW, sanction, prescribe, *Lear*, 2.iv.190 ; *of very expert and approved allowance*, of acknowledged competence, *Oth.*, 2.i.49.

ALMANAC, calendar, but such compilations contained prognostications of various sorts, *Ant. and Cleo.*, 1.ii.145.

ALMS, *at fortune's alms*, as an act of charity, *Lear*, 1.i.278 ; *to fortune's alms*, taking what fortune chooses to give, *Oth.*, 3.iv.123.

AMAZE, confuse, *Ven. and Ad.*, 684 ; astonishes with delight, *Ven. and Ad.*, 634 ; *amazement*, astonishment that paralyses, *Per.*, 1.ii.26.

ANCIENT, (corrupt form of ' ensign') standard-bearer, *Oth.*, 1.i.33.

ANDIRON, fire-dog, *Cym.*, 2.iv.88.

ANNEXIONS, additions, accompaniments, *Lov.Comp.*, 208.

ANNOY, injure, *Cym.*, 4.iii.34.

ANTHROPOPHAGI, cannibals, *Oth.*, 1.iii.144.

ANTIC, *antick'd us all*, turned us all into fools, *Ant. and Cleo.*, 2.vii.123.

ANTIQUITIES, relics of past ages, *Lucrece*, 951.

ANTRE, cave, *Oth.*, 1.iii.140.

APPETITE, desire, caprice, *Oth.*, 2.iii.336.

APPLIANCE, remedy (from medicine), *Per.*, 3.ii.91.

APPOINTMENT, armament, dispositions for battles, *Ant. and Cleo.*, 4.x.8.

APPROOF, *on thy approof*, your conduct will provide the proof of my praise, *Ant. and Cleo.*, 3.ii.27.

ARABIAN, *Arabian bird*, the phoenix, so the sole specimen of his kind, *Ant. and Cleo.*, 3.ii.12 ; *Cym.*, 1.vi.17 ; *Arabian tree*, tree of the phoenix, *Phoenix*, 2.

ARCH, *arch and patron*, chief, first in rank, *Lear*, 2.i.59 ; *arch-mock*, most spiteful jest, *Oth.*, 4.i.70.

ARGENTINE, shining like silver, *Per.*, 5.i.248.

ARGUE, set forth in the contention of red and white, *Lucrece*, 65.

ARGUMENT, evidence, *Ant. and Cleo.*, 3.xii.3.

ARM-GAUNT, *arm-gaunt steed*, of doubtful meaning, sometimes explained as horse lean with service in armour, *Ant. and Cleo.*, 1.v.48.

AROINT, *aroint thee*, begone, *Lear*, 3.iv.122.

ARRAIGNING, *arraigning his unkindness* charging him with unkindness, *Oth.*, 3.iv.153.

ARRANT, out-and-out, complete, *Lear*, 2.iv.51.

ARREARAGES, the arrears of tribute *Cym.*, 2.iv.13.

ARTS, training in manners and knowledge, *Cym.*, 5.v.338.

ARTIFICIAL, *artificial feat*, the operation of your art (skill), *Per.*, 5.i.71.

ARTIST, a skilful practitioner in arms, *Per.*, 2.iii.15.

ASHAM'D, disgraced, *Oth.*, 2.iii.155.

ASKANCE, *askance their eyes*, turn aside their eyes, *Lucrece*, 637.

ASPECT, *anchor his aspect*, fix his gaze *Ant. and Cleo.*, 1.v.33 ; the favourable or unfavourable way a star looks on a man, used of eyes at *Lucrece*, 14 ; satirically at *Lear*, 2.ii.101.

ASPIC, the deadly asp, *Ant. and Cleo.*, 5.ii.291 ; *aspics' tongues*, the stings of snakes, *Oth.*, 3.iii.454.

ASPIRE, ascend, *Lucrece*, 548.

ASSAIL, woo, *Cym.*, 2.iii.39.

ASSAULT, *strong assault*, violation, *Lucrece*, 835.

ASSAY, to try, *Oth.*, 2.iii.199 ; discover from experience, *Lov.Comp.*, 156 ; *noun*, test, *Oth.*, 1.iii.18 ; attempt, *Lucrece*, 1720.

ASSIGN, allot, *Lov.Comp.*, 138 ; entrust *Oth.*, 1.iii.285.

ASSUME, *assume the lists*, take up the challenge of the riddle, like a champion entering to fight at a tournament, *Per.*, 1.i.61.

ASSURANCE, security, certainty of victory, *Ant. and Cleo.*, 3.vii.46.

ASTONISH, to strike dumb, *Son.*, 86,8 ; to stun, *Lucrece*, 1730.

ASTRONOMER, astrologer, *Cym.*, 3.ii.27 ; *sectary astronomical*, a devotee of astrology, *Lear*, 1.ii.143 ; *astronomy*, used with reference to astrological motions, *Son.*, 14,2.

ATHWART, across, *Cym.*, 5.iii.18.

ATONE, to bring together in friendship, *Oth.*, 4.i.227 ; *Ant. and Cleo.*, 2.ii.106.

ATTACH, arrest, *Oth.*, 1.ii.77.

ATTAINT, *attainted*, charged with or guilty of wrongdoing ; *in thine attaint*, as a partner in the treason, *Lear*, 5.iii.84 ; dishonour, *Lucrece*, 1072.

ATTEMPT, *for him attempting who was self-subdued*, for attacking a man who was down by accident, *Lear*, 2.ii.117 ; *an attempt of ease and gain*, an enterprise easy and sure of success, *Oth.*, 1.iii.29.

ATTEMPTABLE, *less attemptable than any*, more armed against seduction, *Cym.*, 1.iv.57.

ATTEND, give heed to, *Cym.*, 1.vi.141 ; be present at as participant, *Ant. and Cleo.*, 5.ii.46 ; to dance attendance, *Cym.*, 3.iii.22.

ATTENT, attentive, *Per.*, 3.*Prol*.11.

ATTORNEY, advocate; *the heart's attorney*, the tongue, *Ven. and Ad.*, 335.

ATTRIBUTE, *for an honest attribute*, to get credit for honesty, *Per.*, 4.iii.18.

AUDIENCE, *gibe my missive out of audience*, mocked my messenger out of a hearing, *Ant. and Cleo.*, 2.ii.78.

AUDIT, reckoning, *Cym.*, 5.iv.27.

AUGUR, *my auguring hope*, my hope that divines the future, *Ant. and Cleo.*, 2.i.10; diviner, *Son.*, 107,6; *Phoenix*, 7.

AULD, old, *Oth.*, 2.iii.89.

AURICULAR, *auricular assurance*, satisfaction by hearing for yourself, *Lear*, 1.ii.88.

AUSPICIOUS, favourable, helping, *Lear*, 2.i.40.

AUTHORITY, *authorities*, writings of the masters of medicine, *Per.*, 3.ii.33; *authorized youth*, youth as justifying or excusing certain conduct, *Lov.Comp.*, 104.

AVAUNT, begone, *Ant. and Cleo.*, 4.xii.30.

AVOID, to depart, *Ant. and Cleo.*, 5.ii.241.

AVOUCH, assert, *Lear*, 5.i.44.

AWARD, give as a judgement, *Son.*, 141,14.

AWFUL, commanding fear and respect, *Per.*, 2.Prol.4.

AWKWARD, *awkward casualties*, thwarting accidents, *Per.*, 5.i.92.

BACCHANAL, dance, *Ant. and Cleo.*, 2.vii.102, in honour of the wine-god, Bacchus, *Ant. and Cleo.*, 2.viii.112.

BACK, to support, *Lucrece*, 352.

BACKSIDE, the unfrequented side, such as a debtor anxious to escape arrest might use, *Cym.*, 1.ii.12.

BADGE, retainers wore a badge to indicate the lord they served, *Lucrece*, 1054.

BAGGAGE, wench, *Per.*, 4.ii.22.

BAIL, *arrest without all bail*, arrest from which no person or payment can release one, death, *Son.*, 74,2; *Son.*, 133,10.

BALK, miss completely, *Lucrece*, 696.

BALLASTING, *more equal ballasting*, more equal in rank, *Cym.*, 3.vi.77.

BALLOW, cudgel, *Lear*, 4.vi.243.

BALMY, *this most balmy time*, favourable, comforting, *Son.*, 107,9; fragrant, *Oth.*, 5.ii.16.

BANDY, to exchange (as a ball is hit to and fro), *Lear*, 1.iv.83.

BANE, *body's bane*, what destroys the body (like poison), *Ven. and Ad.*, 372.

BANNING, *banning shore*, prohibiting the advance of the sea, *Oth.*, 2.i.11.

BANNS, official notice of marriage, *Lear*, 5.iii.88.

BAR, shut out, ward off, *Per.*, 2.iv.15; deny, *Ven. and Ad.*, 784.

BARBER-MONGER, one always at the barber, so conceited, effeminate, *Lear*, 2.ii.30.

BARE, bare skin, *Lov.Comp.*, 95; *bare excuses*, poor, unfounded excuses, *Ven. and Ad.*, 188.

BARN, to store as in a barn, *Lucrece*, 859

BASAN, a land noted for its cattle (Psalm xxii.12) and hills, *Ant. and Cleo.*, 3.xiii.127.

BASE, course, as at game of prisoners' base, *Cym.*, 5.iii.20.

BASES, cloth extensions to knee, worn by mounted knights, *Per.*, 2.i.159.

BASILISK, the fabled cockatrice that kills with its look, *Cym.*, 2.iv.108.

BATE, *be bated*, be reduced (in price), *Per.*, 4.ii.50.

BATE-BREEDING, provoking strife, *Ven. and Ad.*, 655.

BATELESS, *bateless edge*, not to be blunted, *Lucrece*, 9.

BAUBLE, the fool's staff, so something trifling, not to be taken seriously, *Oth.*, 4.i.133; used of ships worthless in stormy seas, *Cym.*, 3.i.27.

BAY, reddish-brown (horse), *Lear*, 3.iv.55.

BAY, bark, *Cym.*, 5.v.223; *at a bay*, the hunted animal having turned on its pursuers, the dogs close in barking, *Ven. and Ad.*, 877.

BEACON, *beacon to this under globe*, the moon, *Lear*, 2.ii.158.

BEAR, *the burning bear*, the constellation of the Great Bear, *Oth.*, 2.i.14.

BEAR, obtain, win, *Oth.*, 1.iii.23; *bear in hand*, pretend, *Cym.*, 5.v.43.

BEARING, *quick bearing*, appearance of alacrity, *Lucrece*, 1389.

BECK, summoning gesture, *Ant. and Cleo.*, 3.xi.60; verb at *Ant. and Cleo.*, 4.xii.26.

BECOME, adorns, harmonizes with, *Son.*, 132,6; *becomes his flow*, conducts himself in his misfortune, *Ant. and Cleo.*, 3.xii.34; *Cym.*, 5.v.406.

BECOMING, *becoming of things ill*, snatching a grace even from misdeeds, *Son.*, 150,5; *becomings*, graces, *Ant. and Cleo.*, 1.iii.96.

BEDLAM, the asylum in London was the hospital of Saint Mary of Bethlehem, shortened to *Bedlam*, which could be used of the institution or those afflicted with madness; *Tom o' Bedlam*, the name of a *Bedlam beggar*, a vagrant half-wit, *Lear*, 1.ii.129 and 2.iii.14.

BEFOREHAND, *beforehand counsel*, thought before the event, *Lucrece*, 494.

BEGET, produce, *Ven. and Ad.*, 768.

BEGGAR, *beggar'd all description*, left one's powers of description without resource, *Ant. and Cleo.*, 2.ii.202; *Son.*, 67,10.

BEGGARY, *beggary of his change*, the lowness of his new life, *Cym.*, 1.vi.114.

BEGUILE, deceive and entice, *Ven. and Ad.*, 1144; charm and attract, *Lucrece*, 1404; *beguile the thing I am*, disguise or direct my anxiety by an assumption of mirth, *Oth.*, 2.i.122; disguise, *Lucrece*, 1544.

BEHALF, *sands that run i' the clock's behalf*, in an hour-glass that serves as a clock, *Cym.*, 3.ii.72; *on his behalf*, in his interest, *Oth.*, 3.iv.17.

515

BEHAVIOUR, *light behaviour*, jesting manner, *Oth.*, 4.i.102; so *sad behaviour*, *Lucrece*, 556; conduct, *Lear*, 1.ii.115.

BEHEST, command, *Cym.*, 5.iv.122.

BEHOLD, look, *Ant. and Cleo.*, 3.x.1; *wild in my beholding*, disordered in my appearance, *Per.*, 5.i.221; *beholding to you*, indebted to you, *Per.*, 2.v.25.

BEHOOF, advantage, welfare, *Lov.Comp.*, 165.

BELDAM, grandmother, *Lucrece*, 953.

BE-LEE'D, cut off from the wind, so held up (in my progress to promotion), *Oth.*, 1.i.30.

BELIE, fill with lies, *Cym.*, 3.iv.34; misrepresent, *Lucrece*, 1533; slander, *Oth.*, 4.i.36.

BELIKE, probably, *Lear*, 4.v.20.

BELL, *falcon's bells*, attached to the bird's legs, *Lucrece*, 511.

BE-MONSTER, to assume an inhuman shape or appearance, *Lear*, 4.ii.63.

BEND, *made their bends adornings*, added a beauty to the tableau by their graceful service, *Ant. and Cleo.*, 2.ii.212.

BEND, to direct, *Lear*, 2.i.46.

BENEDICTION, blessing, *Lear*, 2.ii.156.

BENEFICIAL, *beneficial news*, good news, *Oth.*, 2.ii.6.

BENISON, blessing, *Lear*, 1.i.265.

BENT, *to the bent of*, according to the humour or inclination of, *Cym.*, 1.i.13; *bent with sin*, determined on evil, *Per.*, 2. Prol., 23.

BEREAVE, to deprive or injure, *Lear*, 4.iv.9; *Ven. and Ad.*, 797.

BESEEMING, appearance, *Cym.*, 5.v.409.

BESHREW, used as an imprecation, plague on someone or something, *Oth.*, 4.ii.129.

BESIDE, *spare no blood beside*, spare no one else, *Cym.*, 5.v.92.

BESIDES, *actor . . . put besides his part*, so put out that he can't act his part, *Son.*, 23,2; *Cym.*, 2.iv.149.

BESORT, *may besort your age*, may be like you in age and gravity, *Lear*, 1.iv.250; *noun, accommodation and besort*, suitable provision, *Oth.*, 1.iii.238.

BESPOKE, engaged to be married (used ironically as her husband is speaking), *Lear*, 5.iii.90.

BEST, *at the best*, make the best of what may seem an unfortunate event, *Oth.*, 1.iii.173; *to the best*, for the best, *Lear*, 1.ii.163.

BESTOW, to place, *Oth.*, 3.i.54; lodge, accommodate, *Lear*, 2.iv.288; expend, *Lov.Comp.*, 139; dispose of, *Ant. and Cleo.*, 5.ii.181; give, *Lear*, 2.i.126.

BETHINK, *bethink yourself*, call to mind, *Oth.*, 5.ii.27; *Lear*, 1.ii.151; *am bethought to*, purpose to, have a plan to, *Lear*, 2.iii.6.

BETIDE, *betid to*, happened to, *Cym.*, 4.iii.40.

BETIME, early, *Ant. and Cleo.*, 4.iv.20.

BETOKEN, foretell, *Ven. and Ad.*, 453.

BETRAY, deceive, *Oth.*, 5.ii.6; *betray my life*, kill, *Lucrece*, 233; *Son.*, 96,9;

reveal, *Ant. and Cleo.*, 2.vii.77; *women's traitors*, deceivers of women, *Cym.*, 3.iv.52.

BETTER, *better thee*, have the advantage of you, *Per.*, 4.vi.160; *better phrase*, more educated idiom, *Lear*, 4.vi.8; *bettering of the time*, the improved forms that come later, *Son.*, 32,5.

BEVEL, not on the square, oblique, dishonest, *Son.*, 121,11.

BEWRAY, reveal, discover, *Lucrece*, 1698; *Lear*, 2.i.107.

BEYOND, *beyond beyond*, infinite, *Cym.*, 3.ii.55.

BIAS, the curved course given by the shape of the bowl, so *bias of nature*, the conduct prescribed by our humanity, *Lear*, 1.ii.106.

BIDING, resting place, *Lucrece*, 550; dwelling, refuge, *Lear*, 4.vi.226.

BIG, pregnant, *Son.*, 97,6; *a heart as big*, proud and courageous, *Cym.*, 4.ii.78 (here and in the next line several uses of *big* are seen), so *bigger*, more boastful; *the big wars*, the pride, pomp and circumstance of battle, *Oth.*, 3.iii.353; *big in clamour*, loud in lamentation, *Lear*, 5.iii.208 (or perhaps filled with lament).

BILL, a weapon like a pole-axe; *the brown bills*, the regiment so armed, the weapon being browned against rust, *Lear*, 4.vi.91.

BIRTH-CHILD, *Thetis' birth-child*, Marina having been born at sea, the element of Thetis, *Per.*, 4.iv.41.

BITUMED, *caulk'd and bitumed*, the seams made tight with oakum and melted pitch, *Per.*, 3.i.71.

BLACK, *black stage for tragedies*, the stage had black hangings for tragedies, *Lucrece*, 766 (see 1 *Henry VI*, 1.i.1).

BLAME, ill-report, *Ven. and Ad.*, 796; *his own blame*, fault, *Lear*, 2.iv.289; wickedness, *Lucrece*, 620; *full of blame*, faults, *Son.*, 129,3.

BLANK, *waste blanks*, empty pages, *Son.*, 77,10; white spot in centre of target, so target of any sort, *Lear*, 1.i.158; *within the blank of his displeasure*, in the line of fire, directly exposed to his anger, *Oth.*, 3.iv.129.

BLAST, *half blasted*, partly withered, not young, *Ant. and Cleo.*, 3.xiii.105; *blasting hour*, destructive hour, *Lov.Comp.*, 72; *Lucrece*, 49; to split with noise, *Ant. and Cleo.*, 4.vii.36.

BLAZON, *blazon of sweet beauty's best*, description (from description of coat of arms), *Son.*, 106,5; *blazoning pens*, writers attempting to describe perfection, *Oth.*, 2.i.63; *thyself thou blazon'st*, reveal yourself, *Cym.*, 4.ii.171; well described, *Lov.Comp.*, 217.

BLEEDING, *bleeding stream*, blood, *Lucrece*, 1774.

BLENCH, swerving, inconstancy, *Son.*, 110,7.

BLEST, *blest infusions*, with healing power, *Per.*, 3.ii.35.

BLOCK, wood on which hats were

moulded, so *This's a good block*, this is a well-fashioned hat, *Lear*, 4.vi.18.4.

BLOOD, passion, feeling, *Lear*, 4.ii.64 ; *the blood and baseness of our natures*, its carnal tendencies, *Oth.*, 1.iii.328 ; *Son.*, 109,10 ; *Lov.Comp.*, 162 ; temperament, nature generally, *Cym.*, 1.i.1.

BLOSSOM, *made the blossoms dote*, her youthful rivals, *Lov.Comp.*, 235 ; *blossoming Caesar*, coming to the height of prosperity and success, *Ant. and Cleo.* 4.xii.23.

BLOWN, *blown ambition*, puffed-up, swollen, *Lear*, 4.iv.27 ; *blown sails*, swollen by the winds, *Per.*, 5.i.253 ; *blows my heart*, bursts it with shame, *Ant. and Cleo.*, 4.vi.34 ; *that quicken even with blowing*, fly-blown meat being fouled by eggs and maggots of flies, *Oth.*, 4.ii.68.

BLUNT, brusque, rude, *Cym.*, 5.v.325 ; *without affectation*, *Lear*, 1.iv.34 ; devoid of courtesy, *Lear*, 2.ii.91.

BLUR, *blurr'd those lines of favour*, made his features unrecognizable, *Cym.*, 4.ii.105.

BLURT, *blurt at*, make mouths at, show contempt for, *Per.*, 4.iii.34.

BLUSTEROUS, *blusterous birth*, being born in a storm, *Per.*, 3.i.28.

BOAST, make a display of, *Lucrece*, 55.

BOB, swindle, *Oth.*, 5.i.16.

BODE, to foretell (generally evil), *Ven. and Ad.*, 647 ; *boding to all*, ominous, *Oth.*, 4.i.22.

BODY, *the common body*, the populace, *Per.*, 3.iii.21.

BOGGLER, a disloyal capricious wanton, *Ant. and Cleo.* 3.xiii.110.

BOIL, *boil'd stuff*, diseased flesh (venereal disease was treated by sweating the patient in a tub), *Cym.*, 1.vi.124.

BOLD, *bold cure*, confident of cure, *Oth.*, 2.i.51 ; confident, *Cym.*, 2.iv.2 ; verb, as France *invades our land not bolds the king*, not because France comforts the king but because France invades our land, *Lear*, 5.i.25.

BOLIN, bowline, rope from sail to bow, *Per.*, 3.i.43.

BOLL'N, swollen, *Lucrece*, 1417.

BOLT, to fetter, *Ant. and Cleo.*, 5.ii.6.

BOMBAST, cotton stuffing for garments, so inflated language ; *a bombast circumstance*, inflated and roundabout speech, *Oth.*, 1.i.13.

BOND, obligation, duty, *Ant. and Cleo.* 1.iv.84 ; *bonds*, ties (the idea comes from deeds or documents binding one to payments or service), *Son.*, 142,7.

BONE, *her young bones*, her child, *Lear*, 2.iv.161.

BONDAGE, firm attachment, loyalty, *Cym.*, 2.iv.111 ; *bound like a malefactor*, *Cym.*, 5.v.306.

BONNET, man's hat, *Ven. and Ad.*, 339.

BOOK, a written document, *Cym.*, 5.iv.133 ; account, history, *Per.*, 1.i.94.

BOOT, *make boot of*, take advantage of, *Ant. and Cleo.*, 4.i.9 ; verb, to add by way of an extra, *Ant. and Cleo.*, 2.v.71 ; *nor boots it me*, it profits me not, *Per.*, 1.ii.20 ; *very bootless*, utterly useless, *Lear*, 5.iii.294.

BORDER, *border'd certain*, surely confined within the bounds of humane conduct, *Lear*, 4.ii.33.

BORE, *bores of hearing*, the ears, *Cym.*, 3.ii.56.

BORROW, *borrow'd tears*, false tears, *Lucrece*, 1549 ; *borrow'd motion*, false show of feeling, *Lov.Comp.*, 327 ; *Per.*, 4.iv.24.

BOSOM, *common bosom*, affections of the people, *Lear*, 5.iii.50 ; *of her bosom*, in her confidence, *Lear*, 4.v.26 ; thoughts, mind, *Oth.*, 3.i.55 ; *Lear*, 2.i.126 ; verb, *bosom'd with*, most intimate with, *Lear*, 5.i.13.

BOTS, a disease of horses ; used as an oath, *Per.*, 2.i.116.

BOTTOM-GRASS, pasture in valley, *Ven. and Ad.*, 236.

BOUND, *are bound to the like*, also intend to do so, *Lear*, 3.vii.10.

BOURN, brook, *Lear*, 3.vi.25 ; boundary, *Ant. and Cleo.*, 1.i.16 ; *this chalky bourn*, the cliffs of Dover, *Lear*, 4.vi.57.

BOW, to bend, *Per.*, 4.ii.87 ; *Ant. and Cleo.*, 2.iii.3.

BOY, *boy my greatness*, act the part of Queen (boys taking the female parts in the Elizabethan and Jacobean theatre), *Ant. and Cleo.*, 5.ii.219.

BRACE, (i) a pair, *Oth.*, 2.iii.28 ; (ii) armour for the arms, usually, but the whole suit at *Per.*, 2.i.125 ; *stands not in such warlike brace*, so armed for war, *Oth.*, 1.iii.24.

BRACH, a bitch hound, *Lear*, 1.iv.111.

BRAG, *brags his service*, boasts of his actions, *Cym.*, 5.iii.93.

BRAID, upbraid, censure, *Per.*, 1.i.93.

BRAIN, *tongue and brain not*, utter without understanding, *Cym.*, 5.iv.145 ; *brainsick*, mad, *Lucrece*, 175.

BRAKE, thicket, *Ven. and Ad.*, 237.

BRAN, husks of grain ; *meal and bran*, the flour and the husks, so the qualities of men, *Cym.*, 4.ii.27.

BRANCH, *branches of another root*, descendants of a particular family, *Lucrece*, 823 ; *branchless*, stripped of honour, *Ant. and Cleo.*, 3.iv.24 ; *circumstantial branches*, detailed parts, *Cym.*, 5.v.383.

BRAND, torch, *Son.*, 153,1 ; *depending on their brands*, Cupids leaning on their torches, *Cym.*, 2.iv.91 ; mark of disgrace, stigma, *Son.*, 111,5.

BRASS, used to describe objects whose enduring qualities seem to defy time, *Son.*, 107,14 ; *nerves of brass*, utterly unfeeling, *Son.*, 120,4.

BRAVE, pleasant, splendid, *Son.*, 12,2 ; *brave night*, fine night (used ironically), *Lear*, 3.ii.79 ; verb, provoke, threaten, *Oth.*, 5.ii.329 ; defy, *Ant. and Cleo.*, 4.iv.5 ; *a piece of work so bravely done*, so splendidly wrought, *Cym.*, 2.iv.73.

BRAVERY, bravado, *Oth.*, 1.i.101 ; *natural bravery of the isle*, defiant or challenging features and position, *Cym.*, 3.i.18.

BRAWN, *the brawns of Hercules*, arms like Hercules, *Cym.*, 4.ii.312.

BRAZE, *brazed to it*, hardened to it, indifferent, *Lear*, 1.i.10 ; *brazen-faced*, shameless, *Lear*, 2.ii.25.

BREACH, gap in the defences, *Lucrece*, 469 ; *deadly breach*, where fighting would be most fierce, *Oth.*, 1.iii.136 ; a gap in friendship, *Oth.*, 4.i.220 ; *nuptial breaches*, divorces, *Lear*, 1.ii.142.

BREADTH, extent, *Per.*, 4.i.38.

BREAK, interrupt, *Ant. and Cleo.*, 4.xiv.31 ; communicate, disclose, *Ant. and Cleo.*, 1.iii.171 ; *break themselves*, perjure themselves (that is the speaker), *Ant. and Cleo.*, 1.iii.31 ; *broken debtors*, bankrupts, *Cym.*, 5.iv.19 ; *broken bosoms*, broken hearts, *Lov.Comp.*, 254.

BREATHING, exercise, *Per.*, 2.iii.101 ; express in words, *Ant. and Cleo.*, 1.iii.14 ; *untimely breathings*, pauses, *Lucrece*, 1720.

BREATH'D, fit physically, *Ant. and Cleo.*, 3.xiii.178.

BREATHER, *breathers of this world*, men of the present day, *Son.*, 81,12 ; a human being, *Ant. and Cleo.*, 3.iii.23.

BREED, *breed of greatness*, noble strain, race, *Cym.*, 4.ii.25 ; children, descendants, *Son.*, 12,14 ; *verb*, maintained, *Lear*, 4.ii.73 ; *bred of alms*, brought up on charity, *Cym.*, 2.iii.114.

BREEZE, gadfly, *Ant. and Cleo.*, 3.x.14.

BRIEF, mortal, *Cym.*, 5.v.165 ; *noun*, inventory, *Ant. and Cleo.*, 5.ii.137.

BRIEFLY, quickly, *Cym.*, 5.v.106 ; *Ant. and Cleo.*, 4.iv.10 ; *briefness*, speed, *Lear*, 2.i.18.

BROACH, *the business she hath broached*, the trouble she has started, *Ant. and Cleo.*, 1.ii.165.

BROGUE, rustic shoe, *Cym.*, 4.ii.215.

BROKER, agent, procurer, *Lov.Comp.*, 173.

BROOCH, *be brooch'd*, adorned (in his triumph), *Ant. and Cleo.*, 4.xv.25.

BUG, *the mortal bugs*, the deadly terrors, *Cym.*, 5.iii.51.

BUILDING, place, *Per.*, 2.i.154 ; *tall building*, of large construction, *Son.*, 80,12.

BULK, wooden projection (of a shop), *Oth.*, 5.i.1.

BURDEN-WISE, as an undersong, *Lucrece*, 1133.

BURGONET, helmet, *Ant. and Cleo.*, 1.v.24.

BUTT, target at archery, so aim, goal, *Oth.*, 5.ii.270.

BUXOM, comely, *Per.*, 1.Prol.23.

BUY, *does buy my injuries*, pays for them like benefits, *Cym.*, 1.i.105.

BY-DEPENDANCES, accompanying detail, *Cym.*, 5.v.390.

CABINET, a small place of habitation ;

a nest, *Ven. and Ad.*, 854 ; the heart Lucrece, 442.

CABLE, *give him cable*, give him rope o scope, *Oth.*, 1.ii.17.

CADENT, falling, *Lear*, 1.iv.285.

CAITIFF, villain, *Oth.*, 5.ii.321 ; wretch (in a pitiful sense), *Oth.*, 4.i.108.

CALL, *call on him*, call him to account *Ant. and Cleo.*, 3.xiii.90.

CALLET, a trull, *Oth.*, 4.ii.122.

CAN, (i) have skill in, *Phoenix*, 14 know, *Cym.*, 4.ii.395 ; (ii) = gan began, *Per.*, 3.Prol.36.

CANCEL, terminate, have done with *Cym.*, 5.iv.28 ; *life's lasting date from cancell'd destiny*, her immortal sou from her dead body, *Lucrece*, 1729 *noun*, destruction, *Per.*, 1.i.113.

CANDLE, star, *Son.*, 21,12.

CANKER, canker-worm, *Son.*, 35,4 *canker-bit*, eaten into by the worm *Lear*, 5.iii.122 ; *canker-bloom*, dog rose, *Son.*, 54,5.

CANOPY, a state-covering carried i processions, *Son.*, 125,1 ; *verb*, cover shade, *Son.*, 12,6 ; *Cym.*, 2.ii.21.

CANTLE, a segment cut from a sphere *Ant. and Cleo.*, 3.x.6.

CANVAS-CLIMBER, sailor aloft to trin sails, *Per.*, 4.i.63.

CAP, *gain the cap*, get a respectfu salutation, *Cym.*, 3.iii.25 ; *held m cap oft to thy fortunes*, served yo loyally, *Ant. and Cleo.*, 2.vii.56 *wore gloves in my cap*, a lady's glov as a love-token, *Lear*, 3.iv.85.

CAPABLE, capacious, *Oth.*, 3.iii.463 able to inherit, *Lear*, 2.i.85.

CAPARISON, horse-cloth, *Ven. and Ad* 286.

CAPITOL, the fortress and sanctuary o Rome, *Lucrece*, 1835.

CAR, chariot, *Ant. and Cleo.*, 4.viii.29 *Cym.*, 5.v.191.

CARBONADO, score across like piece c meat for broiling, *Lear*, 2.ii.35.

CARBUNCLE, tumour, *Lear*, 2.iv.223 precious stone of red colou *Cym.*, 5.v.189 ; *carbuncled*, decorate with carbuncles, *Ant. and Cleo* 4.viii.28.

CARCANET, necklace set with jewels *Son.*, 52,8.

CARE, *my peculiar care*, for myself, *Cym* 5.v.83 ; *verb*, feel other than in different, *Lear*, 2.ii.9.

CARL, churl, *Cym.*, 5.ii.4.

CARRACK, a galleon, *Oth.*, 1.ii.50 (wher marriage to an heiress is likene to the capture of a ship with ric cargo).

CARRIAGE, conveyance, *Cym.*, 3.iv.186 gun-carriage, but used figurative *her eyes their carriage ride*, are s directed, *Lov.Comp.*, 22 ; *the carriag of his chafe*, his deportment in anger *Ant. and Cleo.*, 1.iii.85.

CARRY, *if he can carry't thus*, if h succeeds in spite of the oppositior *Oth.*, 1.i.68 ; *carry it so*, execute th deed thus, *Lear*, 5.iii.37 ; endure *Lear*, 3.ii.48 ; *carry out my side* execute my plan, *Lear*, 5.i.61; *Lear*, I.iv.3.

CARVE, *carve for his own rage*, satisfy his desire to attack his enemy, *Oth.*, 2.iii.165.

CASE, the external features in which or through which he manifested his skill, *Lov.Comp.*, 116; *case of favour*, choice between two faces, *Cym.*, I.vi.41; the circumstances in which he needs an advocate, *Cym.*, 2.iii.75.

CASHIER, dismiss, *Oth.*, 1.i.48; bring about the dismissal, *Oth.*, 2.iii.363.

CAST, remove him from command, *Oth.*, I.i.150; *cast in his mood*, dismissed in a burst of displeasure, *Oth.*, 2.iii.264; *cast on*, directed against, *Ant. and Cleo.*, 2.vi.23; reckon, *Ant. and Cleo.*, 3.ii.17.

CASTIGATION, self-discipline, *Oth.*, 3.iv.38.

CASUAL, subject to accident, *Cym.*, I.iv.87; casually, *Oth.*, 2.ii.141.

CASUALTY, *foreign casualties*, the chances of life in a strange country, *Lear*, 4.iii.44; *awkward casualties*, adverse chances, *Per.*, 5.i.92.

CAT, the civet-cat, *Lear*, 3.iv.104.

CATASTROPHE, *like the catastrophe of the old comedy*, like the concluding event that however improbably rounds off the plays of long ago, *Lear*, I.ii.128.

CAULK, to make seams (of ship, barrel) water-tight, *Per.*, 3.i.71.

CAUSE, the affair, *Oth.*, 3.iii.415; charge, *Lear*, 4.vi.109; her interest (as if in a law-suit), *Ven. and Ad.*, 220; *it is the cause*, the nature of the charge, the peculiar form of guilt, *Oth.*, 5.ii I.

CAUSELESS, no material foundation, merely imaginary, *Ven. and Ad.*, 897.

CAUTELS, deceit, *Lov.Comp.*, 303.

CAVE-KEEPING, secret, *Lucrece*, 1250.

CAVIL, quarrel, *Lucrece*, 1025.

CEASELESS, perpetual, *Lucrece*, 967.

CELEBRATE, make a ceremony of, *Ant. and Cleo.*, 2.vii.103.

CENSURE, *mouths of wisest censure*, men of soundest judgement, *Oth.*, 2.iii.185; condemnation, *Oth.*, 5.ii.371; blame, *Lear*, 1.iv.229; reproof, *Cym.*, 3.iii.55; *verb*, judge, *Son.*, 148,4; pronounce sentence, *Lear*, 5.iii.3.

CENTURY, a company of a hundred soldiers, *Lear*, 4.iv.6.

CHAFE, anger, *Ant. and Cleo.*, I.iii.85.

CHAFFLESS, without chaff, so without worthless elements of character, *Cym.*, I.iv.177.

CHAIR, throne, *Ant. and Cleo.*, 3.vi.4; sedan-chair, *Oth.*, 5.i.82.

CHALICE, cup, so *chalic'd flowers*, shaped like cups, *Cym.*, 2.iii.22.

CHALLENGE, claim deservedly, *Oth.*, 2.i.209; deserve, *Lear*, 1.i.52; claim (as a challenger at a tournament), *Lucrece*, 58.

CHAMBERER, a frequenter of ladies' chambers rather than the field of battle, *Oth.*, 3.iii.269.

CHAMBER-HANGING, tapestry, *Cym.*, 5.v.204.

CHAMPAIN, open country, *Lear*, I.i.63; *Lucrece*, 1247.

CHANCE, *from chance to chance*, from one event to another, *Cym.*, 5.v.391; so *disastrous chances*, *Oth.*, I.iii.134; *what a chance*, what an opportunity for advancement, *Cym.*, I.v.68; fortune, *Cym.*, 5.iv.132; luck, *Ant. and Cleo.*, 2.iii.36; *each other's chance*, the accident that brought the other there, *Lucrece*, 1596; *verb*, *how chance?* how comes it about? *Lear*, 2.iv.62.

CHANGE, capricious change of mind, *Lear*, I.i.288; political change, *Ant. and Cleo.*, I.iii.54; change of affection, *Cym.*, I.vi.114; change in music or tone of verse, *Son.*, 76,2; *verb*, exchange, *Oth.*, I.iii.316; change of countenance, blush, *Cym.*, I.vi.11.

CHAOS, *chaos is come again*, the end of the world will have come, *Oth.*, 3.iii.93.

CHAPS, jaws, *Ant. and Cleo.*, 3.v.13.

CHARACTER, handwriting, *Lear*, I.ii.59; writing, *Per.*, 3.ii.72; *Son.*, 59,8; *verb*, express in writing, *Son.*, 108,1.

CHARE, chore, routine tasks about house, *Ant. and Cleo.*, 4.xv.75.

CHARGE, outlay, expense, *Son.*, 146,8; military command, *Ant. and Cleo.*, 4.iv.19; *verb*, *if sleep charge nature*, weigh down, overcome, *Cym.*, 3.iv.40.

CHARM, to silence, *Oth.*, 5.ii.186; *his charmed power*, powerful because of its magic charm, *Lov.Comp.*, 146; *my charm*, witch who has beguiled him, *Ant. and Cleo.*, 4.xii.16; *charmer*, sorceress, *Oth.*, 3.iv.57.

CHARTER, an acknowledged right or privilege, *Son.*, 58,9; *a charter in your voice*, your support of the right I now plead for, *Oth.*, I.iii.245.

CHARY, carefully, *Son.*, 22,11.

CHASE, hunt, *Oth.*, 2.iii.352; *tired with chasing*, with being hunted, *Ven. and Ad.*, 561.

CHAT, friendly converse, *Lucrece*, 791.

CHE, *che* = I, *che vor ye*, I warrant you, *Lear*, 4.vi.242. Shakespeare here used a Somerset dialect adapted for stage purposes, where *chill* = I will, *chud* = I would, and where initial *f* and *s* are voiced to *v* and *z*, as in *vortnight* and *zir*.

CHEAPEN, *cheapen a kiss*, bargain for a kiss, *Per.*, 4.vi.9.

CHEATER, office of the Exchequer, then of a swindler generally, *Son.*, 151,3.

CHECK, hold back, *Oth.*, 2.iii.321; reprove, *Lear*, 2.ii.137.

CHEER, mood, *Son.*, 97,13; hospitable welcome, *Lucrece*, 89.

CHEQUIN, gold coin, Italian or Turkish, *Per.*, 4.ii.25.

CHERISH, to entertain with kindness, *Lucrece*, 1546.

CHEST, *Time's chest*, the grave, *Son.*, 65,10; breast, *Lucrece*, 761.

CHIDE, rebuke, *Son.*, 111,1 ; quarrel, *Cym.*, 5.iv.32 ; *as chiding a nativity*, as stormy a birth, *Per.*, 3.i.32.

CHILD, daughter, *Lear*, 4.vii.70 ; candidate for knighthood, *Child Rowland*, *Lear*, 3.iv.178 ; *childed*, having children, *Lear*, 3.vi.110 ; *child-changed*, reduced to misery by his children's treatment, *Lear*, 4.vii.17.

CHIMNEY, fire-place, *Cym.*, 2.iv.80.

CHIP, *those dancing chips*, the keys of the instrument, *Son.*, 128,10.

CHIVALRY, bravery, *Lucrece*, 109.

CHOICE, excellent, *Lear*, 1.iv.263 ; *most choice forsaken*, specially worthy of being chosen, *Lear*, 1.i.251.

CHOIR, east end of church reserved for choir, *Son.*, 73,4 ; *choir of echoes*, like company of singers, *Ven. and Ad.*, 840.

CHOLERIC, easily angered, *Lear*, 1.i.298.

CHOOSE, *when I cannot choose*, have no alternative, *Lear*, 1.iv.17.

CHORUS, commentator, *Phoenix*, 52 ; *chorus-like*, like the character in a play that explains the dumb-show, *Ven. and Ad.*, 360.

CHOUGH, jackdaw, *Lear*, 4.vi.13.

CHRYSOLITE, precious stone of green colour, *Oth.*, 5.ii.148.

CHURL, niggard, *Son.*, 1,12 ; *churlish*, rude, rough, *Ven. and Ad.*, 134.

'CIDE, decide, *Son.*, 46,9.

CINQUE-SPOTTED, with five spots, *Cym.*, 2.ii.38.

CIPHER, decipher, *Lucrece*, 811 ; express, *Lucrece*, 207 and 1396.

CIRCLE, *the wheel is come full circle*, the wheel of Fortune has completed its turn, *Lear*, 5.iii.174 ; crown, *Ant. and Cleo.*, 3.xii.18.

CIRCUMSTANCE, the conditions in which an action takes place, *Lucrece*, 1703 ; *breed itself so out of circumstance*, continue because of new conditions, *Oth.*, 3.iii.16 ; *strong circumstances*, strong circumstantial evidence, *Oth.*, 3.iii.410 ; *pride, pomp and circumstance*, ceremony, trappings, *Oth.*, 3.iii.358 ; *bombast circumstance*, made much of some detail and so long-winded roundabout story, *Oth.*, 1.i.13.

CIRCUMSTANCED, submit to the conditions of the occasion, *Oth.*, 3.iv.202.

CIRCUMSTANTIAL, *circumstantial branches*, detail of time, place, etc., that emerges from the story, *Cym.*, 5.v.383.

CITE, quoted as an example, *Lucrece*, 524.

CITIZEN, *so citizen a wanton*, so effeminate because of city-breeding, *Cym.*, 4.ii.8.

CIVET, a musky perfume from civet-cat, *Lear*, 4.vi.30.

CIVIL, *civil streets*, the ways of orderly society, *Ant. and Cleo.*, 5.i.16 ; civilized and with the appropriate feelings, *Cym.*, 3.vi.23 ; *civil swords*, used in civil war, *Ant. and Cleo.*, 1.iii.45 ; polite, *Oth.*, 2.i.235.

CIVILITY, humane manners, *Cym.*, 4.ii.180.

CLAP, applause, *Per.*, 3. Prol. 36 ; *at clap*, at a blow, *Lear*, 1.iv.294.

CLASP, hold shut, *Cym.*, 3.ii.3 ; embrace, *Oth.*, 1.i.127.

CLAY, often used to convey idea of mortality, *as kingdoms are clay*, *Ant. and Cleo.*, 1.i.35 ; *Cym.*, 4.ii.4, where the differences in living creatures are contrasted with the uniformity of their dust.

CLEAN, *cleanly-coin'd excuses*, cleverly devised excuses, *Lucrece*, 1073.

CLEAR, *clearest*, glorious, *Lear*, 4.vi.73, without fault or blemish, *Ant. and Cleo.*, 5.ii.121 ; free from reproach, apparently innocent, *Per.*, 1.i.141, forgive, *Lucrece*, 354.

CLEAVE, split, *Ant. and Cleo.*, 3.v.31 and 4.xiv.39 ; *cleft effect*, twofold, *Lov.Comp.*, 293.

CLERK, scholar, *Per.*, 5.Prol.5.

CLIMATE, region, *Oth.*, 1.i.71.

CLIMB, reach, *Lucrece*, 775.

CLIP, to cut, omit, *Lear*, 4.vii.6 ; embrace, hold, *Ant. and Cleo.*, 5.ii.356 ; *Oth.*, 3.iii.468.

CLOAK-BAG, portmanteau, *Cym.*, 3.iv.168.

CLOCK, *'twixt clock and clock*, between the striking of one hour and the next, *Cym.*, 3.iv.40.

CLOG, *to hang clogs on them*, to impose restrictions (as one restricts an animal's movements by fastening some weight to it), *Oth.*, 1.iii.198.

CLOSE, shut fast, *Lucrece*, 367 ; prison, *Oth.*, 5.ii.338 ; secret, *Cym.*, 1.vi.138 ; inward and involuntary, *Oth.*, 3.iii.127.

CLOSET, private room, press or lock-up in a room, so *a closet lock and key of villainous secrets*, one who keeps the secrets she knows undivulged, *Oth.*, 4.ii.22.

CLOSURE, an enclosure, *Ven. and Ad.*, 782.

CLOTH, *by a painted cloth be kept in awe*, a hanging for a room made of canvas on which were painted figures and moral sentences (a substitute for tapestry), *Lucrece*, 245 ; *a squire's cloth*, a livery suitable for a squire, *Cym.*, 2.iii.123.

CLOTHIER, *draw me a clothier's yard*, draw the arrow, which was a clothier's yard in length, to the head, *Lear*, 4.vi.88.

CLOUD, *cloud in's face*, darkened as with a cloud of grief, then turned by Enobarbus into the term as used of horses, a dark spot on the face, *Ant. and Cleo.*, 3.ii.50.

CLOUT, the centre of the target, *Lear*, 4.vi.92.

CLOUTED, *clouted brogues*, shoes studded with nails, *Cym.*, 4.ii.215.

CLOY, (i) to claw, *Cym.*, 5.iv.118 ; (ii) fill to overflowing, *Cym.*, 4.iv.19 ; *cloyless*, that prevents satiety, *Ant. and Cleo.*, 2.i.25.

CLYSTER-PIPE, syringe, *Oth.*, 2.i.175.

COAT, suit of armour, *Per.*, 2.i.134

spirits of richest coat, men of most aristocratic connection (coat = armorial bearings), *Lov.Comp.*, 236 ; *lined their coats*, made a substantial fortune, *Oth.*, 1.i.53.

COCK, the weather-cock on the steeple, *Lear*, 3.ii.3.

COCKATRICE, the deadly basilisk, the fabled serpent that kills with a glance, *Lucrece*, 540.

COCKNEY, indicates stupidty or inefficiency in some way, here perhaps a city woman unaccustomed to eel-pie, *Lear*, 2.iv.120.

COG, to cheat, *Oth.*, 4.ii.133.

COGNIZANCE, badge worn by retainers to indicate the lord they served, so token in *the cognizance of her incontinency*, the bracelet, *Cym.*, 2.iv.127.

COIGN, corner-stone, *Per.*, 3.Prol.17.

COISTREL, low knave, *Per.*, 4.vi.164.

COLD, cool, phlegmatic, *Cym.*, 2.iii.2, and, in following line, gloomy, disappointed ; chaste, *Lov.Comp.*, 293 ; chilling, *Lear*, 1.i.254 ; *the cold fault*, a break in the pursuit of the game owing to faintness of scent, *Ven. and Ad.*, 694.

COLDNESS, lack of zeal, *Oth.*, 2.iii.376.

COLLECTION, *no collection of it*, no interpretation of it, *Cym.*, 5.v.432.

COLLIED, darkened, *Oth.*, 2.iii.198.

COLOQUINTIDA, colocynth, a bitter purge, *Oth.*, 1.iii.347.

COLOUR, *under her colours*, those who take her side in the trouble, *Cym.*, 1.iv.18 ; *against all colour*, without any show of justice, *Cym.*, 3.i.49 ; *a fellow of the self-same colour*, a rascal of the same sort as, *Lear*, 2.ii.133 ; *seek no colour*, offer no excuse, *Ant. and Cleo.*, 1.iii.32 ; *verb*, to dye, *Cym.*, 5.i.2 ; *colour'd with his high estate*, apparently noble because of his rank, *Lucrece*, 92 ; *a woman colour'd ill*, dark in complexion and character, *Son.*, 144,4.

COME, *lack humanity so much as this fact comes to*, so inhuman as to be capable of this deed, *Cym.*, 3.ii.17 ; *come forth*, appear (as on the stage of the world), *Ant. and Cleo.*, 5.ii.46.

COMELY, *comely-distant*, at a modest distance, *Lov.Comp.*, 65.

COMFORT, aid, assistance, *Lear*, 4.i.16 ; encouragement, *Oth.*, 4.ii.190 ; *verb*, to bring relief to, *Lear*, 3.v.19.

COMFORTABLE, one who will aid and comfort, *Lear*, 1.iv.306 ; *of good comfort*, in good spirits, *Per.*, 1.ii.36.

COMFORTLESS, providing no help, *Lear*, 3.vii.84.

COMMEND, commendation, *Per.*, 2.ii.49 ; *verb*, deliver, *Lear*, 2.iv.27 ; mention as worthy, *Ant. and Cleo.*, 4.viii.12.

COMMENT, comment like the audience on a play, or explain it like a chorus, *Son.*, 15.4.

COMMISSION, mandate, *Oth.*, 4.ii.219 ; warrant, *Ant. and Cleo.*, 2.iii.42 ; *bore the commission of my place and person*, had warrant to act as if he were

of my rank and my very self, *Lear*, 5.iii.65 ; *o' the commission*, one of those entrusted with a task, *Lear*, 3.vi.38.

COMMIT, commit adultery, *Lear*, 3.iv.80 ; so *committed* at *Oth.*, 4.ii.73 and 81.

COMMODITY, profitable quality, advantage, *Lear*, 4.i.22 ; merchandise, *Per.*, 4.ii.29, and profit at *Per.*, 4.ii.30.

COMMONER, prostitute, *Oth.*, 4.ii.74.

COMMON-KISSING, kissing everyone, *Cym.*, 3.iv.162.

COMPACT, (i) *all compact of*, all made up of, *Ven. and Ad.*, 149 ; *is compacted*, compounded with, *Lucrece*, 530 ; *well compact*, well made, *Lear*, 1.ii.7 ; (ii) *compact and flattering his displeasure*, leagued with him, having an understanding with, *Lear*, 2.ii.113.

COMPANION, fellow (used contemptuously), *Oth.*, 4.ii.142 ; *companion me with my mistress*, make me the equal in rank, *Ant. and Cleo.*, 1.ii.29.

COMPARATIVE, *made comparative for your virtues*, made a measure of your respective merits, *Cym.*, 2.iii.129.

COMPARE, *there would be something failing in him that should compare*, some lack of judgement in the man who thought he had found the equal of Posthumus, *Cym.*, 1.i.22.

COMPARISON, *his gay comparison*, what makes him compare so advantageously in external resources (some editors read *caparisons*), *Ant. and Cleo.*, 3.xiii.26.

COMPASS, yearly circuit, *Oth.*, 3.iv.71 ; scope, reach, *Oth.*, 3.iv.18 ; *within reason and compass*, reasonably possible, *Oth.*, 4.ii.217 ; *verb*, to obtain, *Ven. and Ad.*, 346 ; embracing, winning, *Oth.*, 1.iii.357.

COMPEER, to equal, *Lear*, 5.iii.70 ; associate, *Son.*, 86.7.

COMPELLED, involuntary, *Lucrece*, 1708.

COMPETITOR, associate, *Ant. and Cleo.*, 1.iv.3, 2.vii.69 and 5.i.42.

COMPLAIN, to lament, *Lucrece*, 1269 and 1839 ; *Cym.*, 4.ii.376 ; *complaint*, a lament as in *A Lover's Complaint* ; the idea of accusation is often included, *Lear*, 1.iv.326.

COMPLIMENT, *in compliment extern*, in outward behaviour, *Oth.*, 1.i.64 ; ceremony, *Lear*, 1.i.301 ; *mechanic compliment*, vulgar show, *Ant. and Cleo.*, 4.iv.32.

COMPLETE, *complete knave*, fully equipped for knavery, *Oth.*, 2.i.243.

COMPLEXION, temperament, nature, which was supposed to be determined by the proportions in which the four humours were mixed in the individual, *Per.*, 4.ii.79 ; so appearance, *Ven. and Ad.*, 214.

COMPLY, *to comply with*, satisfy, *Oth.*, 1.iii.263.

COMPOSE, to come to terms, make a treaty, *Ant. and Cleo.*, 2.ii.15.

COMPOSITION, treaty, *Ant. and Cleo.*, 2.vi.58 ; *life's composition*, compounded of the four elements (as indicated in the sonnet), *Son.*, 45,9 ; *Lear*, 2.ii.19 ; *no composition in these news*, no consistency in the reports, *Oth.*, 1.iii.1.

COMPOSURE, nature, temperament, *Ant. and Cleo.*, 1.iv.22.

COMPOUND, drug (compounded of simples), *the poisonous simple sometime is compacted in a pure compound*, *Lucrece*, 531 ; *Cym.*, 1.v.8 ; *compound love*, one love in which many had been mixed, *Lov.Comp.*, 259.

COMPT, the reckoning, so Day of Judgement, *Oth.*, 5.ii.276.

CONCAVE, hollow, *Lov.Comp.*, 1.

CONCEIT, *the conceit of this inconstant stay*, the idea, *Son.*, 15,9 ; *Oth.*, 3.iii.119 ; the faculty of mind, *Per.*, 3.i.16 ; *verb, the conceited painter*, the painter imaginatively inspired, *Lucrece*, 1371 ; *conceited characters*, ingenious designs, *Lov.Comp.*, 16.

CONCEIVE, form in the mind and in the womb, *Lear*, 1.i.11 and 12.

CONCEPTION, belief, *Oth.*, 5.ii.58.

CONCLUSION, experiment, *Ant. and Cleo.*, 5.ii.352 ; *Cym.*, 1.v.18 ; *still conclusion*, quiet judgement, *Ant. and Cleo.*, 4.xv.28 ; riddle, *Per.*, 1.i.56.

CONDEMN, *condemning shadows*, as things inferior to the reality, *Ant. and Cleo.*, 5.ii.100 ; sentence, *Lear*, 1.i.v.5 ; *the lily I condemned for thy hand*, for stealing its whiteness from thy hand, *Son.*, 99,6.

CONDITION, *imperfections of long-engraffed condition*, faults long associated with his nature, *Lear*, 1.i.296 ; *full of most blest condition*, a nature entirely virtuous, *Oth.*, 2.i.246.

CONDOLEMENT, a solatium, payment in compensation, *Per.*, 2.i.148.

CONDUCT, guide, escort, *Cym.*, 3.v.8 ; *extinguishing his conduct*, his torch, *Lucrece*, 313 ; guidance, *Lear*, 3.vi.97 ; command, leadership, *Cym.*, 4.ii.341.

CONDUIT, pipe for water, often incorporated in a figure over a fountain, *Lucrece*, 1234.

CONFECTION, drug, so at times poison, *Cym.*, 1.v.15 and 5.v.246.

CONFEDERACY, league, alliance, *Lear*, 3.vii.43 ; *confederate*, associated with, *Cym.*, 3.iii.68.

CONFIDENT, trustful, *Cym.*, 5.v.187 ; *three thousand confident*, as determined as if they were three thousand, *Cym.*, 5.iii.29.

CONFINE, prison, *Ant. and Cleo.*, 3.v.12 ; limit, *Lov.Comp.*, 265 ; *the very verge of her confine*, on the boundary of the land of the living, *Lear*, 2.iv.146 ; *verb*, *Cym.*, 5.iv.110 ; *confiner*, inhabitant, *Cym.*, 4.ii.338.

CONFOUND, to mingle and make indistinguishable, *Son.*, 8,7 ; destroy, *Ant. and Cleo.*, 3.ii.58 ; waste, *Ant. and Cleo.*, 1.i.45.

CONGEST, press together, *Lov.Comp.*, 258.

CONJUNCT, intimately associated, *Lear*, 2.ii.12 ; *conjunctive*, closely united, *Oth.*, 1.iii.364.

CONJURATION, incantation, *Oth.*, 1.iii.92 ; *verb*, call on with magic spells, *Lear*, 2.i.39 ; *conjured to this effect*, rendered efficacious by magic, *Oth.*, 1.iii.105.

CONSCIENCE, knowledge, inmost thoughts, *Cym.*, 1.vi.115 ; regard for right and wrong, *Oth.*, 3.iii.207 ; *conscionable*, conscientious, *Oth.*, 2.i.235.

CONSENT, agreement, *Son.*, 28,6 ; assent, *Lov.Comp.*, 131 ; *verb, consent in*, together plan, *Oth.*, 5.ii.300.

CONSEQUENCE, the sequel, what follows, *Oth.*, 2.iii.58 ; *the consequence of the crown*, the royal succession, *Cym.*, 2.iii.121.

CONSERVE, to prepare (of a drug), *Oth.*, 3.iv.75.

CONSIDER, reward, *Cym.*, 2.iii.28 ; *considerate*, thoughtful, *Ant. and Cleo.*, 2.ii.114 ; *consideration*, speculation, *Ant. and Cleo.*, 4.ii.45.

CONSIGN, to subscribe to, to accept the same terms as, *Cym.*, 4.ii.276.

CONSORT, company, used in depreciatory sense, *Lear*, 2.i.97 ; *his consorted lords*, the lords accompanying him, *Lucrece*, 1609.

CONSTANTLY, faithfully, *Cym.*, 3.v.119.

CONSTRAIN, *constrains the garb from his nature*, forces his manner of address to assume a form very different from his true nature, *Lear*, 2.ii.92.

CONSUMMATION, death, *Cym.*, 4.ii.281.

CONTAINING, contents, *Cym.*, 5.v.430.

CONTENT, to reward, *Oth.*, 3.i.1 ; to be content, *Ven. and Ad.*, 61.

CONTINENT, what contains something, so breast or body at *Ant. and Cleo.*, 4.xiv.40 ; *Lear*, 3.ii.58 ; *adj.*, restraining, *Lear*, 1.ii.157.

CONTINUATE, *more continuate time*, less interrupted, *Oth.*, 3.iv.179.

CONTRACT, *contracted to them both*, to both given contract of marriage, *Lear*, 5.iii.228.

CONTRIVE, *contriving friends*, friends involved in the political plots, *Ant. and Cleo.*, 1.ii.176.

CONTROL, to master, *Oth.*, 5.ii.268 ; overcome, silence, *Lucrece*, 678 ; hinder, prevent, *Lear*, 3.vii.26.

CONVENIENCE, favourable circumstances, *Lear*, 3.vi.99 ; *required conveniences*, necessary aids, *Oth.*, 2.i.228 ; *conveniency*, opportunity, *Oth.*, 4.ii.178 ; *convenient*, suitable, fitting, *Lear*, 4.v.31 ; *convenient seeming*, appearance of decency, *Lear*, 3.ii.56.

CONVERSANT, experienced, *Cym.*, 4.i.12.

CONVERSATION, deportment, *Oth.*, 3.iii.268 ; *Ant. and Cleo.*, *Cym.*, 1.iv.119.

CONVERSE, associate, *Lear*, 1.iv.15.

CONVEY, manage secretly, *Lear*, 1.i.97 ; *so convey'd*, stolen away, *Cym.*, 1.i.63.

CONVINCE, overcome, *Oth.*, 4.i.28 ; *Cym.*, 1.iv.91.

COPE, sky, *Per.* 4.vi.22.

COPE, to encounter, *Lear*, 5.iii.124; have to do with, *Lucrece*, 99.

COPESMATE, companion, *Lucrece*, 925.

COPP'D, *copp'd hills*, peaked, *Per.*, 1.i.101

COPY, the original, from which copies are taken, *Son.*, 11,14.

CORDIAL, comforting, reviving, *Cym.*, 4.ii.328.

CORPORAL, bodily, *Cym.*, 2.iv.119.

CORRIGIBLE, *the corrigible authority*, with power to correct, *Oth.*, 1.iii.325; submissive to correction, *Ant. and Cleo.*, 4.xiv.74.

COSTARD, large apple, so the head, *Lear*, 4.vi.243.

CO-SUPREMES, equals in their eminence, *Phoenix*, 51.

COUCH, remain in its den, *Lear*, 3.i.12; to cause to lie hid, *Lucrece*, 507.

COUNTENANCE, patronage, approval, *Son.*, 86,13; authority, *Lear*, 5.i.63; demeanour, *Lear*, 1.ii.149.

COUNTER-CASTER, arithmetician (used scoffingly), *Oth.*, 1.i.31.

COUNTERCHANGE, *the counterchange is severally in all*, all have exchanged looks, individually and collectively, *Cym.*, 5.v.397.

COUNTERFEIT, false coin, so a bastard, *Cym.*, 2.v.5; portrait, *Son.*, 16,8; mere deceit, *Oth.*, 5.i.43; verb, forge, *Oth.*, 2.i.239.

COUNTERVAIL, to equal, *Per.*, 2.iii.56.

COURSE, routine, *by monthly course*, every month alternately, *Lear*, 1.i.131; *the old course of death*, habits, *Oth.*, 3.vii.100; 4.i.276; career, way of life, *Oth.*, 3.iv.122; *your journal course*, your daily routine, *Cym.*, 5.ii.10; the attack (as of dogs at bear-baiting), *Lear*, 3.vii.53; verb, run, *Oth.*, 3.iv.71; hunt, *Lear*, 3.iv.56.

COURSER, *the courser's hair*, a horse's hair placed in water was supposed to become a living creature, *Ant. and Cleo.*, 1.ii.187.

COURTESY, *the courtesy your cradle promised*, the rank and kind of life natural in the station of life in which you were born, *Cym.*, 4.iv.28.

COURT HOLY WATER, flattery, soothing but empty words, *Lear*, 3.ii.10.

COURTSHIP, manners acceptable at a court, *Oth.*, 2.i.169.

COVERT, secret, *Lear*, 3.ii.56.

COXCOMB, fool's cap, *Lear*, 1.iv.103; head, *Lear*, 2.iv.122.

COZEN, *cozening*, cheating, *Lucrece*, 387; *cozening slave*, *Oth.*, 4.ii.133; *cozener*, cheat, *Lear*, 4.vi.163.

CRAB, crab apple, *Lear*, 1.v.14.

CRACK, change of voice between youth and manhood, *Cym.*, 4.ii.237; verb, give out in boasting voice, *Cym.*, 5.v.177.

CRANK, to zigzag, *Ven. and Ad.*, 682.

CRARE, a small trading vessel, *Cym.*, 4.ii.206.

CRAZE, damage, crack, *Lear*, 3.iv.166.

CREATURE, *your creatures*, those who owe their lives to your skill, *Per.*, 3.ii.45.

CREDENT, credulous, *Lov.Comp.*, 279.

CREDIT, *my credit*, your faith in me, *Lear* 3.i.35; *gives them credit*, makes them credible, *Oth.*, 1.iii.1.

CRESCENT, growing, *Ant. and Cleo.*, 2.i.10.

CREST, helmet (with plume), *Ven. and Ad.*, 104; *his rear'd arm crested the world*, was raised above (like the arm that formed a crest to some heraldic coats), *Ant. and Cleo.*, 5.ii.83; *crest-wounding*, dishonouring the family name (like a blot on the escutcheon), *Lucrece*, 828.

CROW-KEEPER, boy stationed to scare crows from field, *Lear*, 4.vi.88.

CRUEL, *cruel garters* (with pun on a crewel = worsted), *Lear*, 2.iv.7.

CRUSADE, Portuguese coin, stamped with a cross, *Oth.*, 3.iv.23.

CRY, *fill up the cry*, just one of the pack (used of hounds), *Oth.*, 2.iii.353; report, rumour, *Oth.*, 4.i.123.

CUNNING, skill, *Ant. and Cleo.*, 2.iii.35; *in cunning*, deliberately, knowingly, *Oth.*, 3.iii.50; learning, knowledge, *Per.*, 3.ii.27.

CURIOSITY, minute examination, *Lear*, 1.i.6; *curiosity of nations*, the scruples nations show in the laws about bastards, *Lear*, 1.ii.4.

CURIOUS, anxious, particular, *Cym.*, 1.vi.190; *curious days*, fastidious, critical, *Son.*, 38,13; *Ant. and Cleo.*, 3.ii.35; *curious mantle*, skilfully made, *Cym.*, 5.v.361; so *curious workmanship*, *Ven. and Ad.*, 734.

DAFF, to put off, *Lov.Comp.*, 297; *Ant. and Cleo.*, 4.iv.13; to thrust aside, *Oth.*, 4.ii.176.

DALLY, delay, trifle the time away, *Lear*, 3.vi.93.

DAMASK'D, *roses damask'd*, red and white, with colours intermingled, like the figuration on Damascus work; often damask refers to the blush-red colour of the rose named from Damascus, *Son.*, 130,5.

DAMN, condemn, *Ant. and Cleo.*, 1.i.24.

DAMP, mist drawn from the ground, *Lucrece*, 778; *Ant. and Cleo.*, 4.ix.13.

DANGER, the range of an enemy's weapon or power to harm, *Ven. and Ad.*, 639; verb, to endanger, *Ant. and Cleo.*, 1.ii.186.

DANGEROUS, *the dangerous year*, the time that threatens danger, with a reference to the years that bring age and death, *Ven. and Ad.*, 508.

DANK, humid, *Lucrece*, 1130.

DARE, *given the dare*, defied, *Ant. and Cleo.*, 1.ii.178; *I durst to*, I venture to, *Oth.*, 4.ii.12.

DARK, *our darker purpose*, our more secret intention, *Lear*, 1.i.35; verb, to obscure, *Per.*, 4.Prol.35.

DARKEN, *gain which darkens him*, success which brings envy and detraction, *Ant. and Cleo.*, 3.i.24; to bring to shame, *Lucrece*, 191.

DARKLING, in the dark, *Ant. and Cleo.*, 4.xv.10; *Lear*, 1.iv.216.

DARKNESS, realm of darkness, death, *Cym.*, 5.iii.25 ; *act of darkness*, fornication, *Lear*, 3.iv.86.

DARNEL, a weed, tares, *Lear*, 4.iv.5.

DARTING, *darting Parthia* (the Parthian cavalry's favourite manoeuvre was to retreat discharging their arrows on the advancing enemy), *Ant. and Cleo.*, 3.i.1.

DASH, mark of shame, *Lucrece*, 206 ; *verb*, to depress, *Oth.*, 3.iii.218.

DATE, end of a prescribed period, *Son.*, 14,14 ; allowed period, *Son.*, 123,5 ; *dateless night*, without ending, eternity, *Son.*, 30,6.

DAUB, cover, plaster, *Lear*, 2.ii.61 ; cover with a disguise, *Lear*, 4.i.53.

DAW, jackdaw (regarded as a foolish bird, so used of fools), *Oth.*, 1.i.66.

DAY, *time of day*, greeting, *Per.*, 4.iii.35 ; *the duty of the day*, morning salutation, *Cym.*, 3.v.32 ; light, so *day o' the world*, *Ant. and Cleo.*, 4.viii.13.

DAZZLE, *her sight dazzling*, losing clear vision, *Ven. and Ad.*, 1064.

DEAD, pale as death, *Oth.*, 2.iii.169 ; *deadly*, fatal, *Lucrece*, 1730 ; like death, *Lear*, 5.iii.290.

DEAL, *deal of man*, show of manhood, *Lear*, 2.ii.115 ; *dealt on lieutenantry*, acted through his officers, *Ant. and Cleo.*, 3.xi.39.

DEAR, (i) expensive, *Cym.*, 2.iii.79 ; precious, *Son.*, 30,4 ; *Son.*, 110,3 ; important, *Lear*, 3.i.19 ; *your dear*, your lover, *Oth.*, 5.i.33 ; (ii) *dear absence*, grievous, *Oth.*, 1.iii.259 ; *dearest spite*, worst spite, *Son.*, 37,3.

DEARLY, richly, finely, *Cym.*, 2.ii.18 ; lovingly, *Cym.*, 1.vi.13.

DEATH-PRACTISED, *the death-practised duke*, the duke against whose life a plot was made, *Lear*, 4.vi.277.

DEBATE, quarrel, *Son.*, 89,13 ; *Cym.*, 1.iv.153 ; *verb*, dispute, quarrel, *Lucrece*, 1421 ; *Ant. and Cleo.*, 2.ii.20.

DEBITOR, *debitor and creditor*, accountant, *Cym.*, 5.iv.166 ; *Oth.*, 1.i.31.

DEBOSH'D, debauched, *Lear*, 1.iv.241.

DECAY, death, *Lucrece*, 516 ; loss, ruin, *Son.*, 80,14 ; *verb*, to destroy, *Cym.*, 1.v.56 ; perish, *Ant. and Cleo.*, 2.i.4.

DECEITFUL, *conceit deceitful*, beguiling invention, *Lucrece*, 1423.

DECLARE, interpret, make clear, *Cym.*, 5.v.434.

DECLINE, *fathers declin'd*, enfeebled by age, *Lear*, 1.ii.70 ; *Oth.*, 3.iii.270 ; fallen in fortune, *Ant. and Cleo.*, 3.xiii.27.

DECREE, decision, *Lucrece*, 1030.

DEDICATE, to commit oneself to, *Cym.*, 5.i.29 ; *dedicated words*, the language of the dedicatory epistle before a work (naturally complimenting the patron), *Son.*, 82,3.

DEED, *my very deed of love*, my love as it indeed is, *Lear*, 1.i.70.

DEEM, judge, *Cym.*, 5.iv.57.

DEEP, *as deep with me*, as inward or heartfelt, *Cym.*, 2.iii.91 ; *deep vow*, grave, serious, *Lucrece*, 1847 ; *deep*

clerks, learned scholars, *Per.*, 5. Prol. 5 ; *deep brain'd sonnets*, ingenious, *Lov.Comp.*, 209.

DEER, beasts, *Lear*, 3.iv.135.

DEFAME, *harbour of defame*, shelter of infamy, *Lucrece*, 768.

DEFEAT, ruin, destroy, *Son.*, 61,11 ; *Oth.*, 4.ii.161 ; disappoint, *Ant. and Cleo.*, 4.xiv, 68 ; *defeat thy favour*, do away with your unsoldierly looks, *Oth.*, 1.iii.339.

DEFEATURE, disfigurement, *Ven. and Ad.*, 736.

DEFECT, faultiness, *Son.*, 149,11.

DEFECTIVE, wanting, lacking, *Oth.*, 2.i.227.

DEFENCE, *defences*, armour, equipment, *Ant. and Cleo.*, 4.iv.10 ; *Isis else defend*, Isis forbid that it should be otherwise! *Ant. and Cleo.*, 3.iii.42 ; *Oth.*, 1.iii.266.

DEFICIENT, *the deficient sight*, vision failing, *Lear*, 4.vi.23.

DEFINITE, without hesitation, *Cym.*, 1.vi.42.

DEFUNCT, *the defunct*, the dead, *Cym.*, 4.ii.359 ; *defunctive music*, music fitting for the service for the dead, *Phoenix*, 14.

DEFUSE, confuse others about my identity, disguise, *Lear*, 1.iv.2.

DEFY, challenge, *Ant. and Cleo.*, 2.ii.162 ; set at defiance, *Lear*, 3.iv.96 ; *Cym.*, 3.i.66.

DEGREE, *stands so eminent in the degree of this fortune*, so high on that steps that lead to this good fortune, *Oth.*, 2.i.233 ; *low degree*, low in social rank, *Oth.*, 2.iii.87.

DEIGN, not disdain to eat, *Ant. and Cleo.*, 1.iv.63.

DELATION, *close delations*, secret and instinctive accusations, *Oth.*, 3.iii.127.

DELICATE, delightful, *Ant. and Cleo.*, 2.vii.106 ; exquisite, *Cym.*, 2.iv.136 ; skilful, *Oth.*, 4.i.183 ; ingenious, *Lear*, 4.vi.185.

DELIGHTED, *delighted beauty*, giving delight, *Oth.*, 1.iii.289 ; delightful, *Cym.*, 5.iv.102.

DELIVERED, brought forward, *Oth.*, 1.iii.367.

DEMAND, question, *Lear*, 1.v.3.

DEMERIT, desert, whether good or bad, *Oth.*, 1.ii.22.

DEMESNE, region, *Cym.*, 3.iii.70.

DEMI-ATLAS, Atlas carried the earth on his shoulders ; Antony now shared the task, so Cleopatra suggests, with Augustus, *Ant. and Cleo.*, 1.v.23.

DEMON, guardian spirit, genius, *Ant and Cleo.*, 2.iii.20.

DEMONSTRABLE, apparent, *Oth.*, 3.iv.143.

DENOTE, indicate, *Oth.*, 3.iii.432.

DEPART, to separate, *Cym.*, 1.i.108.

DEPEND, to lean, *Cym.*, 2.iv.91 ; remain as dependants, retainers, *Lear*, 1.iv.249 ; impend, *Lucrece*, 1615 ; *Cym.*, 4.iii.23.

DEPENDENCY, responsibility in social world, *Cym.*, 2.iii.118.

DEPRIVE, disinherit, *Lear*, 1.ii.4.

DEPUTATION, *in deputation*, through his deputy, *Ant. and Cleo.*, 3.xiii.74.

DEPUTE, appoint as representative, *Oth.*, 4.i.233.

DERN, wild, dark, *Lear*, 3.vii.62 ; *Per.*, 3. *Prol*.15.

DEROGATE, to lose dignity, *Cym.*, 2.i.43 (at l.46 the meaning is shifted to 'degenerate') ; degenerate, *Lear*, 1.iv.280.

DESCANT, a term from music indicating the upper or treble part elaborated above the plain song or basic melody, *Lucrece*, 1134.

DESCENDING, *good descending*, noble parentage, *Per.*, 5.i.127.

DESCRY, *the main descry stands on the hourly thought*, the main body may be reported as in sight almost immediately, *Lear*, 4.vi.215.

DESERT, *to this desert*, to this act that deserves well, *Cym.*, 1.v.73.

DESERVING, *a fair deserving*, a good chance to seem entitled to reward, *Lear*, 3.iii.23 ; *lost without deserving*, through no fault, *Oth.*, 2.iii.262.

DESIGN, scheme, enterprise, *Ant. and Cleo.*, 2.ii.153 ; *in top of all design*, in the greatest enterprises, *Ant. and Cleo.*, 5.i.43.

DESIGNMENT, enterprise, *Oth.*, 2.i.22.

DESIRE, entreat, *Lov. Comp.*, 66 ; bid, instruct, *Cym.*, 1.v.52 ; *well desired*, warmly welcome, *Oth.*, 2.i.202.

DESPERATE, hopeless, *Ven. and Ad.*, 336 ; *Oth.*, 2.iii.321 ; reckless, *Oth.*, 5.ii.210 ; *Ant. and Cleo.*, 1.iii.54 ; *desperately*, hopeless and reckless, *Lear*, 5.iii.292.

DESPISED, *despised time*, my old age now made hateful to me, *Oth.*, 1.i.162.

DESPITE, *in high heaven's despite*, in defiance of heaven, *Ven. and Ad.*, 731 ; *in your despite*, in contempt of you, *Cym.*, 1.vi.134 ; scorn, *Oth.*, 4.ii.117 ; *in despite*, spitefully, *Oth.*, 4.iii.89.

DESPITEFUL, malicious and ungrateful, *Ant. and Cleo.*, 2.vi.22 ; *despitefully*, maliciously, *Lucrece*, 670.

DESTINED, inevitable, *Lov. Comp.*, 156.

DESTINIES, the three Fates, goddesses who spin and cut the thread of life, *Ven. and Ad.*, 733 ; *Per.*, 1.ii.108.

DETECT, regard as evil, *Per.*, 2.i.51 ; *detector*, the revealer, the informer, *Lear*, 3.v.12.

DETERMINATE, expired, *Son.*, 88,4 ; final, decisive, *Oth.*, 4.iii.226.

DEVICE, *device in love*, attitude to love, *Ven. and Ad.*, 789 ; design, *Cym.*, 1.vi.188 ; the emblem or motto on a shield, *Per.*, 2.ii.15 ; ingenious piece of workmanship, *Lov. Comp.*, 232.

DEVISE, imagine, *Ant. and Cleo.*, 2.ii.193.

DIAL, clock, watch, *Lucrece*, 327 ; *dial-hand*, *Son.*, 104,9.

DIALOGUE, imagined his expressing the requests they were anxious to answer, *Lov. Comp.*, 132.

DIAPASON, accompaniment in the bass, an octave lower than the strain, *Lucrece*, 1132.

DIDO, queen of Carthage, in love with Æneas. In Virgil she rejects his advances when he visits the underworld ; *Ant. and Cleo.*, 4.xiv.53.

DIET, sustenance, *Oth.*, 3.iii.15 (as if prescribed for an invalid) ; *dieted in grace*, the course prescribed for a nun, *Lov. Comp.*, 261.

DIETER, one administering a prescribed diet, *Cym.*, 4.ii.52.

DIFFERENCE, *leaves out difference*, remains the same kind throughout, *Son.*, 105,8 ; disagreement, *Cym.*, 1.iv.48 ; change of condition, *Lear*, 5.iii.288.

DIFFERING, *that nothing-gift of differing multitudes*, the worthless approval of the changeable many, *Cym.*, 3.vi.85.

DIFFICULT, *difficult weight*, difficult to estimate, or handle, *Oth.*, 3.iii.83.

DIFFIDENCE, mistrust among groups, *Lear*, 1.ii.141.

DIGEST, arrange, settle, *Ant. and Cleo.*, 2.ii.180 ; incorporate, *Lear*, 1.i.127.

DIGNITY, worth, *Cym.*, 5.iv.57.

DIGRESSION, transgression, *Lucrece*, 202.

DILATE, narrate in full, *Oth.*, 1.iii.153.

DILIGENT, *diligent discovery*, active reconnaissance, *Lear*, 5.i.52.

DIMENSION, *my dimensions*, bodily shape, *Lear*, 1.ii.7.

DIMINISH, injure the active principle, *Ven. and Ad.*, 418.

DIMINUTIVES, *for poor'st diminutives, for doits*, for paltry payments (*doits* most editors read for Folio *dolts* ; those who retain *dolts* read *fore* (before) in place of *for*, and interpret: before the poorest sort and dolts) ; *Ant. and Cleo.*, 4.xii.37.

DINT, impression, *Ven. and Ad.*, 354.

DIRECTION, the disposition of affairs or soldiers, *Oth.*, 1.iii.299, and 2.iii.115 ; *by their own direction*, of their own volition, *Ven. and Ad.*, 216.

DIRECTLY, by evidence leading straight to the conclusion, *Cym.*, 1.iv.152.

DISASTER, unlucky, harmful circumstances (*disaster* signifying the unfavourable influence of some star), *Lear*, 1.i.174 ; verb (used with terms of astronomy), ruin, *Ant. and Cleo.*, 2.vii.16.

DISCANDY, lose firmness, *Ant. and Cleo.*, 4.xii.22.

DISCERNINGS, power of discerning, *Lear*, 1.iv.227.

DISCHARGE, payment, *Cym.*, 5.iv.168.

DISCLAIM, *disclaims in*, disowns, *Lear*, 2.ii.50.

DISCONTENTS, malcontents, those who feel hostile to the established order, *Ant. and Cleo.*, 1.iv.38.

DISCOURSE, *discourse of thought*, in meditation, *Oth.*, 4.ii.154 ; tell over, *Per.*, 1.iv.19.

DISCOVER, expose, *Lear*, 2.i.66 ; spy, *Cym.*, 4.ii.131.

DISCOVERY, means of discovering, *Ven.*

525

and Ad., 828 ; reconnaissance, *Lear*, 5.i.52.

DISGUISE, intoxication, *Ant. and Cleo.*, 2.vii.122.

DISHONOUR'D, dishonourable, *Lear*, 1.i.228.

DISLIKE, dissension, *Lear*, 1.iv.326 ; *verb*, displease, *Oth.*, 2.iii.43.

DISLIMN, *the rack dislimns*, the cloud loses the shape fancy gives it, *Ant. and Cleo.*, 4.xiv.10.

DISMAL, sinister, *Ven. and Ad.*, 889.

DISMISSION, rejection, *Cym.*, 2.iii.52.

DISNATURED, unnatural, *Lear*, 1.iv.283.

DISORDER'D, disorderly, *Lear*, 1.iv.241.

DISPATCH, *attend dispatch*, ready waiting to be sent with messages, *Lear*, 2.i.125 ; the verb often means 'to hasten' and when added to 'post', which can mean the same, forms the expression *post-post-haste dispatch*, with the utmost haste, *Oth.*, 1.iii.46 ; to settle business with, *Ant. and Cleo.*, 3.ii.2 ; to settle with life, kill oneself, *Ant. and Cleo.*, 5.ii.229 ; kill, *Lear*, 2.i.58 ; *well dispatch'd*, happily parted with, *Per.*, 2.v.15.

DISPENSE, *dispense with*, pardon, excuse, *Lucrece*, 1070 ; *Son.*, 112,12.

DISPOSE, *a smooth dispose*, an agreeable manner of address, *Oth.*, 1.iii.391 ; *dispose myself*, order my proceedings, *Per.*, 1.ii.117 ; *disposed with*, come to terms with, *Ant. and Cleo.*, 4.xiv.123 ; *dispose you*, arrange for you, *Ant. and Cleo.*, 5.ii.185.

DISPOSITION, arrangements, *Oth.*, 1.iii.236 ; *dispositions*, humours, caprice, *Lear*, 1.ii.303.

DISPROPORTION'D, inconsistent, contradictory, *Oth.*, 1.iii.2.

DISSIPATION, *dissipation of cohorts*, the disbanding of regiments, *Lear*, 1.ii.142.

DISSOLUTION, liquefaction, *Lucrece*, 355 ; destruction, *Lear*, 1.ii.139.

DISSOLVE, destroy, *Lear*, 4.iv.19.

DISTAIN, sully, overshadow, *Per.*, 4.iii.31.

DISTANCE, *with safest distance I mine honour shielded*, proper reserve, *Lov.Comp.*, 151 ; *that hold their honours in a wary distance*, like fencers they keep dishonour at a proper distance ready to deal with a false move, *Oth.*, 2.iii.52.

DISTASTE, be unpalatable, *Oth.*, 3.iii.331 ; dislike, *Lear*, 1.iii.15.

DISTEMPER, *distempering draughts*, excess of drink, *Oth.*, 1.i.100.

DISTEMPERATURE, disturbance of mind, *Per.*, 5.i.27.

DISTINCTLY, explicitly, directly, *Oth.*, 3.iii.239.

DISTRACT, *distract parcels*, separate items, *Lov.Comp.*, 231 ; *verb*, *distract your army*, divide (perhaps 'confuse'), *Ant. and Cleo.*, 3.vii.43 ; divide, parcel it out, *Oth.*, 1.iii.323.

DISTRACTEDLY, in confusion, *Lov. Comp.*, 28.

DISTRACTION, *distractions*, detachments, divisions, *Ant. and Cleo.*, 3.vii.76 ; confusion, *Ant. and Cleo.*, 4.i.9.

DIVISION, *the division of a battle*, the right division of his troops, *Oth.*, 1.i.23.

DOCTRINE, lesson, *Ant. and Cleo.*, 5.ii.31.

DOIT, a Dutch coin of small value, *Ant. and Cleo.*, 4.xii.37.

DOLE, grief, *Per.*, 3.Prol.42.

DOLOURS, sorrows (with play on 'dollars'), *Lear*, 2.iv.53.

DOMESTIC, *domestic powers*, forces of the same country, *Ant. and Cleo.*, 1.iii.47 ; *domestic-door particulars*, family quarrels, *Lear*, 5.i.30.

DOOM, decision, *Lucrece*, 1849 ; *the general doom*, Day of Judgement, *Lucrece*, 924 ; *verb*, to judge, *Cym.*, 5.v.420.

DOOMSDAY, Day of Judgement, *Ant. and Cleo.*, 5.ii.231.

DOOR, *speak within door*, speak quietly (don't be heard in the street), *Oth.*, 4.ii.145.

DOTE, to act or speak foolishly or frantically, *Ven. and Ad.*, 1059 ; to be foolishly fond, *Ven. and Ad.*, 837 ; *Lucrece*, 1064 ; *Lear*, 1.iv.38.

DOUBLE, *doubles*, zig-zag movements, *Ven. and Ad.*, 682.

DOUBLET, a man's coat, *Cym.*, 3.iv.168.

DOUBT, fear, *Oth.*, 3.iii.19 and 3.iii.174.

DOUBTFUL, *I am doubtful*, I suspect, *Lear*, 5.i.12.

DRAGON, *the dragon's tail*, the moon's descending node, where it cuts the plane of the ecliptic ; astrologers, when they had to allow for it in any horoscope, regarded its effects as specially malignant, *Lear*, 1.ii.123.

DRAM, eighth of an ounce apothecaries' weight, *Cym.*, 1.iv.130 ; potion, *Oth.*, 1.iii.105.

DRAW, *draw me*, win for me (as in a lottery), *Lear*, 3.iii.23.

DREADFUL, *dreadful bell*, alarm bell, so spreading fear, *Oth.*, 2.iii.167.

DRINK, carousing, *Ant. and Cleo.*, 2.vii.103 ; *verb*, *I drunk him to his bed*, I was still sober while he, drinking equally with me, was so drunk that he was put to bed, *Ant. and Cleo.*, 2.v.21.

DROPPING, *dropping industry*, dripping wet as they work, *Per.*, 4.i.64.

DROUTH, thirst, *Per.*, 3.Prol.8.

DRUG, poison, harmful potion, *Oth.*, 1.ii.74 ; *drug-damn'd Italy*, detested for the use there of poison, *Cym.*, 3.iv.15.

DUCAT, gold coin, value about ten shillings, *Cym.*, 1.iv.122.

DUMB, *verb*, strikes dumb, *Per.*, 5.Prol.5.

DUMP, melancholy tune, *Lucrece*, 1127.

DUTEOUS, attentive, respectful, *Son.*, 7,11 ; servile, *Oth.*, 1.i.45.

DUTY, obedience, *Lear*, 4.v.18.

DWELLERS, *dwellers on form and favour*, those who unduly prize ceremony and the countenance of the great, *Son.*, 125,5.

EACH, *ten masts at each*, one above the other, *Lear*, 4.vi.53.

GLOSSARY

EAGER, sharp, poignant, *Son.*, 118,2; vehement, *Lucrece*, 1298.

EAGLE, *Jove's bird, the Roman eagle,* the eagle was the most important standard of a Roman legion; the bird an emblem of Jove, *Cym.*, 4.ii.349 and 5.v.471.

EAN, to give birth to, *Per.*, 3.iv.6.

EAR, to plough, *Ant. and Cleo.*, 1.iv.49; *ear-bussing arguments,* the lips kissing the listener's ear, so whispered news, *Lear*, 2.i.8.

EARN, *earn our chronicle,* deserve our place in story, *Ant. and Cleo.*, 3.xiii.175.

EARNEST, *my earnest,* the token payment to confirm a bargain (in this instance to have an option), *Per.*, 4.ii.44; *Lear*, 1.iv.93.

EARTH, *my sinful earth,* my body, *Son.*, 146,1; *earth-delving,* burrowing, *Ven. and Ad.*, 687.

EASILY, in comfort, *Oth.*, 5.i.83.

EASY, *an easy battery might lay flat,* which criticism would find an easy target, *Cym.*, 1.iv.20; compliant, *Cym.*, 2.iv.47; *easy-borrowed pride,* not native pride but vanity that comes easily to one in such employment, *Lear*, 2.iv.184.

EAT, *eat in,* rust, *Lucrece*, 755; *eats the sword,* turns it against itself, *Ant. and Cleo.*, 3.xiii.200.

EBB, *the ebb'd man,* from whom success has withdrawn, *Ant. and Cleo.*, 1.iv.43; *ne'er feels retiring ebb,* the current runs one way only, *Oth.*, 3.iii.459.

EBON, black, *Ven. and Ad.*, 948.

ECHE, to piece out, *Per.*, 3.Prol.13.

ECSTASY, swoon, *Oth.*, 4.i.79; state of being beside oneself, *Ven. and Ad.*, 895; frenzy, *Lov.Comp.*, 69.

EDGE, keenness, *Son.*, 56,2.

EDIFY, to instruct, *Oth.*, 3.iv.13.

EFFECT, *warm effects,* realization of desire, *Ven. and Ad.*, 605; *thy thoughts touch their effects,* your fears are realized, *Ant. and Cleo.*, 5.ii.328; *to effect,* to the purpose, *Lear*, 3.i.52; *Oth.*, 1.iii.105; *the large effects,* the pomp and circumstance, *Lear*, 1.i.130.

EFFECTLESS, vain, *Per.*, 5.i.52.

EFFECTUALLY, in reality, *Son.*, 113,4.

EFTSOONS, soon, *Per.*, 5.i.253.

EGREGIOUS, *egregious murderer,* out of the ordinary, monstrous, *Cym.*, 5.v.211; *egregiously,* to an unusual degree, *Oth.*, 2.i.303.

EISEL, vinegar, *Son.*, 111,10.

ELECTED, *the elected deer,* the victim singled out, *Cym.*, 3.iv.108.

ELEMENT, the four elements were earth, air, fire and water, from which everything was supposed to be compounded; *receiving nought by elements so slow,* earth and water, *Son.*, 44,13; *these quicker elements,* air and fire, *Son.*, 45,5; *I am fire and air; my other elements I give to baser life, Ant. and Cleo.*, 5.ii.287; *you elements,* as manifested in storm, etc., *Lear,*

3.ii.16; the conditions in which some being or essence finds its natural habitation, *Ant. and Cleo.*, 5.ii.90; *Lear*, 2.iv.57.

ELF, tangle, *Lear*, 2.iii.10.

EMBASSAGE, message, *Son.*, 26,3; so *embassy, Son.*, 45,6.

EMBATTLE, form line of battle, *Ant. and Cleo.*, 4.ix.3.

EMBAY'D, anchored in some safe bay, *Oth.*, 2.i.18.

EMBER-EVES, the evenings before ember-days, *Per.*, 1.Prol.6.

EMBOSS, to foam at the mouth as from exertion, *Ant. and Cleo.*, 4.xiii.3; raised like a boss on a shield, *Lear*, 2.iv.223.

EMBRACE, welcome as a retainer, *Cym.*, 3.iv.175; cherish, maintain, *Lear*, 504; submit to, endure, *Lear*, 4.i.7; *embrace your offer,* accept with gratitude, *Per.*, 3.iii.37.

EMINENT, *not so eminent,* not even of that rank, *Cym.*, 2.iii.124.

EMPERY, *fasten'd to an empery,* married to one who ruled an empire, *Cym.*, 1.vi.119.

EMPHASIS, *such another emphasis,* strong expression of admiration, *Ant. and Cleo.*, 1.v.68.

EMPLOY, to use one's services, *Cym.*, 2.iii.63.

EMPTY-HEARTED, hollow, lacking feelings, *Lear*, 1.i.152.

EMULATION, *emulation in their woe,* sorrow that rivalled, equalled, his own, *Lucrece*, 1808.

ENACT, *for lawful policy remains enacted,* is considered as an act of discretion, *Lucrece*, 529.

ENCAVE, conceal, *Oth.*, 4.i.81.

ENCHAFED, *enchafed flood,* the furious sea, *Oth.*, 2.i.17; angered, roused, *Cym.*, 4.ii.175.

ENCHANTING, bewitching, as having more than natural powers, *Ant. and Cleo.*, 1.ii.125.

ENCLOG, to hinder, *Oth.*, 2.i.70.

ENCOUNTER, meeting with hostile intent, *Ven. and Ad.*, 676; with amatory intent, *Ven. and Ad.*, 596; *Cym.*, 2.v.19; verb, to befall, *Cym.*, 1.vi.111; to meet, *Cym.*, 1.ii.132.

END, *hath . . . an end,* no further existence, *Son.*, 9,11; *the promis'd end,* the end of the world, *Lear*, 5.iii.263; verb, to kill, *Ant. and Cleo.*, 4.xiv.22.

ENDEAR, *endeared with all hearts,* made more precious by representing all the poet has loved, *Son.*, 31,1.

ENDER, *my origin and ender,* my first and last love, *Lov.Comp.*, 222.

ENDOW, to bestow, *Lear*, 2.iv.180; to furnish, *Cym.*, 1.i.24.

ENDUE, to infect, *Oth.*, 3.iv.147.

ENDURANCE, suffering, *Per.*, 5.i.135.

ENDURE, to continue, *Lucrece*, 1659.

ENFORCE, *enforced obedience,* involuntary submission, *Lear*, 1.ii.119; obtain by force, *Lucrece*, 181; *thy mistress enforced,* ravished, *Cym.*, 4.i.17;

enforce their charity, importune, *Lear*, 2.iii.20.

ENFORCEMENT, constraint, *Lucrece*, 1623.

ENFRANCHED, freed from bondage, *Ant. and Cleo.*, 3.xiii.149.

ENFRANCHISE, to free from subjection, *Ant. and Cleo.*, 1.i.23.

ENGAGE, to pledge, *Oth.*, 3.iii.466; *engaged ourselves too far*, ventured too far, *Ant. and Cleo.*, 4.vi.1.

ENGINE, *engines for my life*, schemes against my life, *Oth.*, 4.ii.216; *the engine of her thought*, her tongue, *Ven. and Ad.*, 367; some mechanical contrivance, *Lear*, 1.iv.268.

ENGIRT, beset, *Lucrece*, 1173.

ENGLUT, swallow, *Oth.*, 1.iii.57.

ENGRAFFED, *imperfections of long-engraffed condition*, faults of character deeply rooted, *Lear*, 1.i.296; *engraft infirmity*, habitual weakness, *Oth.*, 2.iii.132; rooted in, attached to, *Son.*, 37,8.

ENGROSS, to take over completely, *Son.*, 133,6; to collect, *Ant. and Cleo.*, 3.vii.36.

ENJOY, *enjoy thy plainness*, still possess your blunt speech, *Ant. and Cleo.*, 2.vi.78; *Cym.*, 1.iv.75.

ENJOYER, possessor, *Son.*, 75,5.

ENKINDLE, *enkindle all the sparks of nature*, act as becomes a son, *Lear*, 3.vii.85.

ENLARGE, *enlarge his confine*, set him free, *Ant. and Cleo.*, 3.v.12.

ENLARGEMENT, freedom of choice, *Cym.*, 2.iii.120.

ENORMOUS, abnormal, monstrous, *Lear*, 2.ii.164.

ENOW, enough, *Ant. and Cleo.*, 1.iv.11.

ENPATRON, *you enpatron me*, you are as my patron saint, *Lov.Comp.*, 224.

ENSCONC'D, to place as in a sconce, or fortification, conceal, *Lucrece*, 1515.

ENSTEEP'D, under the water, *Oth.*, 2.i.70.

ENSUE, follow as a consequence, *Lucrece*, 502; following, *Ven. and Ad.*, 1078; *Per.*, 2.i.7.

ENTER, *enter me with him*, gain me favourable reception by, *Ant. and Cleo.*, 4.xiv.113.

ENTERTAIN, to receive hospitably, *Lucrece*, 596; to treat, to attend to, *Lear*, 1.iv.57; *I entertain you for one of my hundred*, take into my service, *Lear*, 3.vi.78; to accept a suggestion, *Ant. and Cleo.*, 2.vii.62; to maintain, *Lucrece*, 1514.

ENTERTAINMENT, reception, treatment, *Ven. and Ad.*, 1108; *your commendation for my more free entertainment*, your letter of introduction that will ensure a cordial reception, *Cym.*, 1.iv.149; employment in someone's service, *Ant. and Cleo.*, 4.vi.17.

ENTIRE, aloof from the entire point, missing the whole point, *Lear*, 1.i.240; *of one entire and perfect chrysolite*, wholly of flawless chrysolite, *Oth.*, 5.ii.148; entirely, completely, *Ant. and Cleo.*, 4.xiv.25.

ENTITLED, *entitled in thy parts* (the metaphor is from heraldry), displayed, blazoned (*parts* referring to places on a shield as well as to personal qualities), *Son.*, 37,7.

ENTRANC'D, unconscious, *Per.*, 3.ii.99.

ENTREASUR'D, stored as if in a treasure-house, *Per.*, 3.ii.70.

ENVY, malice, *Ant. and Cleo.*, 5.ii.163; *verb*, to grudge but in honourable way, *Cym.*, 4.ii.159.

ENWHEEL, encompass, *Oth.*, 2.i.87.

EPICURE, hardened toper, *Ant. and Cleo.*, 2.vii.51; *epicurean cooks*, cooks fit to serve a sybarite, *Ant. and Cleo.*, 2.i.24; *epicurism*, riotous living, *Lear*, 1.iv.243.

EPILEPSY, falling sickness, *Oth.*, 4.i.50; *epileptic visage*, grinning countenance (for Oswald is trying to put a smiling face on it), *Lear*, 2.ii.76.

EPITHETS, *epithets of war*, martial expressions, *Oth.*, 1.i.14.

EQUALITY, *equalities are so weigh'd*, the shares are so equally balanced, *Lear*, 1.i.5; *equality of two domestic powers*, two factions in the state of equal strength, *Ant. and Cleo.*, 1.iii.47; *equalness*, partnership, *Ant. and Cleo.*, 5.i.48.

EQUINOX, equal length of day and night, *Oth.*, 2.iii.116.

EQUIPAGE, *in ranks of better equipage*, in verse more splendidly appointed, *Son.*, 32,12.

EQUIVALENT, equal in power and dignity, *Per.*, 5.i.90.

EQUIVOCAL, ambiguous, *Oth.*, 1.iii.217.

ERRING, wandering, *Oth.*, 1.iii.353.

ERROR, *error of the moon*, deviation from normal course, *Oth.*, 5.ii.112.

ERST, formerly, *Per.*, 1.i.49.

ESCAPE, escapade, *Oth.*, 1.iii.197.

ESPERANCE, hope, *Lear*, 4.i.4.

ESPOUSE, *espoused to more fame*, married to, enjoying, *Lucrece*, 20.

ESSAY, trial, *Lear*, 1.ii.44; *Son.*, 110,8.

ESSENCE, life, principle of being, *Phoenix*, 26; quality, characteristic, *Oth.*, 4.i.16.

ESSENTIAL, *the essential vesture of creation*, the actual endowments devised for her by her Creator, *Oth.*, 2.i.64.

ESTATE, condition, *Lear*, 5.iii.209; unhappy position, *Cym.*, 5.v.74; rank, *Lucrece*, 92; fortune, *Per.*, 4.ii.32.

ESTEEM, value, *Cym.*, 5.v.253; *verb*, to value, *Cym.*, 1.iv.74; *esteeming*, worth, *Son.*, 102,3.

ESTIMATE, value, *Son.*, 87,2.

ESTIMATION, *your brace of unprizeable estimations*, these two things that you regard as beyond all price, *Cym.*, 1.iv.86; reputation, *Oth.*, 1.iii.274.

ESTRIDGE, ostrich, *Ant. and Cleo.*, 3.xiii.197.

ETERNAL, *would be eternal*, would make ever memorable, *Ant. and Cleo.*, 5.i.66; *eternal villain* (used intensively), *Oth.*, 4.ii.131.

EVEN, *to make him even o'er*, to make him clear about, *Lear*, 4.vii.80 ; *we'll even all*, to be equal to all, *Cym.*, 3.iv.180 ; *even'd with him*, to be quits with him, *Oth.*, 2.i.293 ; *to go even*, act in accord with, *Cym.*, 1.iv.41.

EVENT, *the event*, the sequel, what's to come (will decide between us), *Lear*, 1.iv.349 ; *the event is yet to name the winner*, the issue, *Cym.*, 3.v.15.

EVERMORE, *not evermore*, nevermore, *Son.*, 36,9.

EVIDENCE, *their evidence*, the evidence against them, *Lear*, 3.vi.35 ; as a witness, *Lucrece*, 1650.

EVIDENT, acceptable as proof, *Cym.*, 2.iv.120.

EVIL, misfortune, *Oth.*, 1.i.161 ; wickedness, *Lucrece*, 846 ; sin, *Lucrece*, 972.

EVIL-EY'D, maliciously disposed, *Cym.*, 1.i.72.

EXACT, *in the most exact regard*, with the strictest attention, *Lear*, 1.iv.265 ; *exactly wrought*, so true to nature, *Cym.*, 2.iv.75.

EXALT, *exalt himself*, achieve rank and status, *Lear*, 5.iii.68.

EXAMPLE, excel, *Per.*, 2.iii.16 ; *to be greater*, *Lucrece*, 229 ; *exceeding*, outstanding, *Oth.*, 3.iii.262.

EXCELLENT, *excellent falsehood*, *Ant. and Cleo.*, 1.i.40 ; *excellent foppery*, *Lear*, 1.ii.113 ; used to emphasize the extent of the folly or untruth.

EXCEPT, to oppose, *Son.*, 147,8.

EXCEPTION, disapproval, *Oth.*, 4.ii.207.

EXCESS, surfeit, *Lov.Comp.*, 42 ; profusion, superfluity, *Son.*, 146,7.

EXCHANGE, the acceptance given to the challenge, *Lear*, 5.iii.98 ; *not with the time exchanged*, *Son.*, 109,7.

EXCLAIM, *exclaim against*, denounce, *Oth.*, 2.iii.300 ; *exclaim on*, accuse, *Ven. and Ad.*, 930.

EXCUSE, justification, pardon, *Lucrece*, 1715 ; *my old excuse*, excuse for my age, *Son.*, 2,11.

EXECUTE, *to execute upon him*, to attack him, *Oth.*, 2.iii.220.

EXECUTION, administration, *Lear*, 1.i.136 ; *the execution of his wit*, what his mind can do, *Oth.*, 3.iii.470.

EXERCISE, bodily act, *Oth.*, 2.i.257 ; religious act, *Oth.*, 3.iv.38 ; verb, perform, inflict, *Cym.*, 5.iv.82.

EXHALE, to draw out, *Lucrece*, 779.

EXHIBITION, cash allowance, *Oth.*, 1.iii.237 ; *confined to exhibition*, depending entirely on an allowance, *Lear*, 1.ii.25 ; *Cym.*, 1.vi.121.

EXIGENT, emergency, fatal moment, *Ant. and Cleo.*, 4.xiv.63.

EXORCISER, one who calls up spirits, *Cym.*, 4.ii.277.

EXPECT, await, *Ant. and Cleo.*, 4.iv.23 ; *Per.*, 1.iv.94.

EXPECTANCY, expectation, *Oth.*, 2.i.41.

EXPECTATION, readiness, *Lear*, 4.iv.23.

EXPEDIENCE, hasty enterprise, *Ant. and Cleo.*, 1.ii.173.

EXPENSE, squandering, *Lear*, 2.i.100

Son., 94,6 and 129,1 ; loss, *Son.*, 30,8.

EXPIATE, to end, *Son.*, 22,4.

EXPOSTULATE, argue, *Oth.*, 4.i.201.

EXPRESS, manifest, *Lear*, 4.iii.17 ; *expressly*, distinctly, *Lucrece*, 1397.

EXSUFFLICATE, *exsufflicate and blown* (perhaps) puffy and fly-blown, *Oth.*, 3.iii.186.

EXTEND, *extend him within himself*, enlarge on his merits only within the bounds of truth, *Cym.*, 1.i.25 ; *to magnify his virtues*, *Cym.*, 1.iv.19 ; take possession of (legal metaphor), *Ant. and Cleo.*, 1.ii.98 ; display, *Oth.*, 2.i.98.

EXTERN, *compliment extern*, outward deportment, *Oth.*, 1.i.64 ; *my extern the outward honouring*, observing the formalities of ceremony, *Son.*, 125,2.

EXTRAVAGANT, wandering, *Oth.*, 1.i.137.

EXTREMITY, deadliness, *Cym.*, 3.iv.17.

EYE, *eye well to you*, appear good in your eyes, *Ant. and Cleo.*, 1.iii.97.

EYE-SORE, blemish, *Lucrece*, 205.

FABLE, a fiction, *Oth.*, 5.ii.289.

FACE, *that great face of war*, its dangerous look, *Ant. and Cleo.*, 3.xiii.5 ; *so face of peril*, *Cym.*, 5.i.28 ; *so of open recognition or avowal*, *Lear*, 3.i.20.

FACT, evil deed, *Lucrece*, 349 ; *to lack humanity so much as this fact comes to*, to be inhuman enough to commit such a crime, *Cym.*, 3.ii.17.

FACTION, party strife ; *equality of two domestic powers breed scrupulous faction*, with opposite parties in the state equal they quarrel over trifles, *Ant. and Cleo.*, 1.iii.48.

FACTOR, substitute, deputy, *Ant. and Cleo.*, 2.vi.10 ; agent, *Cym.*, 1.vi.187.

FACULTY, *have faculty by nature to subsist*, retain their natural powers, *Son.*, 122,6.

FAIL, failure in truth and honesty, *Cym.*, 3.iv.62 ; verb, omit, come short in, *Lear*, 2.iv.140 ; *Cym.*, 3.iv.177.

FAIN, glad ; but often willing only because there was no other resource, *Lear*, 4.vii.38 ; adv., gladly, *Oth.*, 4.i.163.

FAINT, *a most faint neglect*, lack of active and ready service, *Lear*, 1.iv.67 ; verb, *faint not*, *faint heart*, do not lack resolution, *Lucrece*, 1209 ; lose heart, *Ven. and Ad.*, 569 ; *Son.*, 80,1.

FAINTLY, (of a description) only hinting at the truth, *Lear*, 1.ii.166 ; without conviction, *Oth.*, 4.i.112.

FAIR, beauty, *Ven. and Ad.*, 1083 ; *Son.*, 68,3 ; *the supreme fair*, the sun, *Lucrece*, 780 ; a beautiful person, *his fair fair*, *Lucrece*, 346 ; verb, to beautify, *Son.*, 127,6.

FAIRLY, with proper respect, *Per.*, 5.i.10 ; auspiciously, *Ant. and Cleo.*, 2.ii.149 ; *and that unfair which fairly doth excel*, detract from what now excels in beauty, *Son.*, 5,4.

GLOSSARY

FAIRNESS, beauty, *Cym.*, 5.v.168; *Oth.*, 2.i.129.

FAIRY, enchantress, *Ant. and Cleo.*, 4.viii.12.

FAITH, fidelity, *Son.*, 66,4; faithfulness in love, *Son.*, 152,3; honourable faiths, word of honour, *Lucrece*, 1690.

FAITH'D, credited, *Lear*, 2.i.70.

FAITHFULNESS, true love, *Per.*, 1.i.63.

FALCHION, sword, *Lucrece*, 176; *Lear*, 5.iii.276.

FALCON, female hawk, *Ven. and Ad.*, 1027.

FALL, befall, *Ant. and Cleo.*, 3.vii.39; fall away, desert, *Ant. and Cleo.*, 4.vi.17; drop, *Lucrece*, 1551.

FALL'N-OFF, fall'n-off Britons, revolted Britons, *Cym.*, 3.vii.6.

FALSE, verb, to turn traitor, false themselves, *Cym.*, 2.iii.69; adv., perfidiously, false struck, *Cym.*, 3.iv.113; adj., false with, commit adultery with, allure false hearts, and be false with them, *Cym.*, 2.iv.34.

FALSEHOOD, excellent falsehood, deceit, *Ant. and Cleo.*, 1.i.40; eyes' falsehood, *Son.*, 137,7.

FALSELY, wrongly, *Oth.*, 5.ii.120.

FALSENESS, untruth, *Per.*, 5.i.119; perfidy, *Lov.Comp.*, 105.

FAME, rumour, report, *Ant. and Cleo.*, 2.ii.167; *Per.*, 5.iii.96; reputation, good name, *Lucrece*, 1202; the fame, the prize, *Ant. and Cleo.*, 2.vi.64; renown, *Cym.*, 3.iii.51; verb, make famous, *Son.*, 84,11.

FAMILIAR, good wine is a good familiar creature, homely, serviceable, *Oth.*, 2.iii.299; known, *Cym.*, 5.v.93; acquainted, *Cym.*, 1.iv.97; the affable familiar ghost, a familiar spirit being a demon attached to some individual and obeying his commands, *Son.*, 86,9.

FAMINE, starvation, *Cym.*, 3.vi.19.

FAMISH'D, hungry, *Son.*, 47,3.

FAMOUS, famous pirates, notorious, *Ant. and Cleo.*, 1.iv.48.

FAMOUSED, famoused for fight, renowned as a soldier, *Son.*, 25,9.

FAN, test (from the winnowing-fan that removes the chaff), *Cym.*, 1.vi.176.

FANCY, after new fancies, after new loves, *Oth.*, 3.iv.63; this afflicted fancy, this lady afflicted with love, *Lov.Comp.*, 61; so wounded fancies, *Lov.Comp.*, 197; imagination, *Ant. and Cleo.*, 2.ii.205.

FANE, temple, *Cym.*, 4.ii.243.

FANGLED, our fangled world, given over to show and appearance, *Cym.*, 5.iv.134.

FANTASTICAL, prodigious, *Oth.*, 2.i.200.

FANTASY, whim, *Oth.*, 3.iii.303.

FAR, you speak him far, you praise him highly, *Cym.*, 1.i.24.

FARE, both meanings, feed and be in luck, at, *Cym.*, 3.i.80.

FASHION, manner, *Lucrece*, 1319; out of fashion, unbecomingly, *Oth.*, 2.i.204; of all fashions, of all kinds, *Per.*, 4.ii.78; verb, arrange, *Oth.*,

4.iii.235; fashion fit, contrive to my own advantage, *Lear*, 1.ii.175.

FAST, firm, fixed, *Lear*, 1.i.37; unwavering as a support, *Oth.*, 1.iii.359.

FASTEN, fasten upon, thrust upon, pass off upon, *Oth.*, 2.iii.44; fasten'd villain, confirmed, hardened villain, *Lear*, 2.i.77.

FAT, vat, *Ant. and Cleo.*, 2.vii.113.

FATE, oppose his fate, bar the path on which fate leads him, *Ant. and Cleo.*, 3.xiii.169; the Fates, the Goddesses of Destiny, *Per.*, 4.iii.14; verb, hang fated o'er men's faults, are the inevitable punishment of faults, *Lear*, 3.iv.67; predestined, *Oth.*, 3.iii.280.

FATHOM, another of his fathom, grasp (the original meaning of fathom being the embrace of the two arms), *Oth.*, 1.i.153.

FAULT, break in scent in hunting, *Ven. and Ad.*, 694; misfortune, *Per.*, 4.ii.73; faultaful, culpable, *Lucrece*, 715.

FAVOUR, pardon, mercy, *Ant. and Cleo.*, 3.xiii.113; *Ven. and Ad.*, 257; appearance, charm, *Cym.*, 1.vi.41; my hospitable favours, the features of your host, *Lear*, 3.vii.39; *Son.*, 113,10; verb, to express approval, *Ant. and Cleo.*, 4.viii.23.

FAVOURABLY, advantageously, *Oth.*, 2.i.264.

FAWN, young deer, *Ven. and Ad.*, 876; verb, to express satisfaction (as of animals wagging their tails), *Lucrece*, 421.

FEALTY, loyalty, *Cym.*, 5.iv.73.

FEAR, various meanings illustrated at *Ven. and Ad.*, 1153–58: distrust, dread; for fear of trust, fearing to trust my own powers, *Son.*, 23,5; put thyself into a haviour of less fear, do not behave in a manner that so gives cause for fear, *Cym.*, 3.iv.9; verb, fears me, gives me cause for apprehension, *Lear*, 3.v.3; frighten, *Ant. and Cleo.*, 2.vi.24; as fear not but you shall, as you certainly will, *Lear*, 3.i.47; fear'd hopes, hopes not free from fear, *Cym.*, 2.iv.6.

FEARFUL, dreadful, cause of fear, *Lucrece*, 1741; so fearful to be granted, *Oth.*, 3.iii.84; grow fearful, filled with fear, *Lear*, 1.iv.204.

FEARFULLY, looks fearfully, looks menacingly, *Lear*, 4.ii.75.

FEAST, verb, keep holiday, *Per.*, 1.iv.107; so feasting, *Oth.*, 2.ii.9; feast-finding minstrels, performing at banquets, *Lucrece*, 817.

FEATS, feats, exhibitions of various skills, *Per.*, 5.ii.6; exploits, *Ant. and Cleo.*, 4.viii.9; a glass that feated them, a mirror, an example, by which they could see how to improve their fashion and form, *Cym.*, 1.i.49; adj., dexterous, neat, *Cym.*, 5.v.88; adv., feat and affectedly, neatly and lovingly, *Cym.*, 48.

FEATHER, with thought's feathers, wings, *Lucrece*, 1216; the best feather of our *wing*, chief among us, *Cym.*, 1.vi.185 ; *feather'd Cupid*, *Oth.*, 1.iii.269 ; *in feather'd briefness*, winged, *Per.*, 5.ii.15.

FEATURE, form, *Lear*, 4.ii.63 ; appearance generally, *Ant. and Cleo.*, 2.v.112 ; *Cym.*, 5.v.163 ; so *featur'd*, *Son.*, 29,6 ; *featureless*, shapeless, ugly, *Son.*, 11,10.

FEDARY, accomplice, *Cym.*, 3.ii.21.

FEE, prize, *Ven. and Ad.*, 538 ; reward, *Ven. and Ad.*, 609 ; remuneration, *Lear*, 1.i.163 ; *fee-simple*, land held by the owner in absolute possession, so *did in freedom stand, and was my own fee-simple, not in part*, her own mistress, fancy free, *Lov. Comp.*, 144.

FEEDER, servant, *Ant. and Cleo.*, 3.xiii.109.

FEEDING, diet, *Son.*, 188 6.

FEEL, to test, *Lear*, 1.ii.83 ; *to the felt absence now I feel a cause*, I now understand the cause of your absence which has so affected me, *Oth.*, 3.iv.183 ; *feeling sorrows*, heartfelt, *Lear*, 4.vi.224.

FEELER, *the feeler's soul*, the soul of the person affected by the touch, *Cym.*, 1.vi.100.

FEELINGLY, *true sorrow then is feelingly sufficed*, sorrow is properly assuaged, *Lucrece*, 1112 ; *I see it feelingly*, I understand it not by my senses but by my inward sorrow, *Lear*, 4.vi.149.

FELICITATE, made happy, *Lear*, 1.i.74.

FELL, skin, *Lear*, 5.iii.74.

FELL, cruel, *Oth.*, 5.ii.365 ; deadly, *Cym.*, 4.ii.110 ; *verb*, strike down, *Lear*, 4.ii.76.

FELLOW, *princely fellows*, her equals in rank, *Cym.*, 3.iv.89 ; fellow-servant, *Lear*, 1.iii.14 ; *these great fellows*, the triumvirs and allies, *Ant. and Cleo.*, 2.vii.131.

FELLOWSHIP, *a name in great men's fellowship*, to associate with the great without the qualification of greatness, *Ant. and Cleo.*, 2.vii.12 ; used of a convoy of ships, *Oth.*, 2.i.93 ; *fellowship in woe*, partnership in distress, *Lucrece*, 790.

FEN-SUCK'D, *fen-suck'd fogs*, fogs drawn up from the marshes, *Lear*, 2.iv.165.

FERE, spouse, *Per.*, 1.Prol.21.

FERVENCY, eagerness, *Ant. and Cleo.*, 2.v.18.

FESTINATE, speedy, *Lear*, 3.vii.10.

FETCH, *fetches*, tricks, pretexts, *Lear*, 2 iv.87.

FETCH, *verb*, fetch my life and being, am descended from, *Oth.*, 1.ii.21 ; *fetch a turn*, walk a little, *Cym.*, 1.i.81 ; *fetch in*, to capture, *Ant. and Cleo.*, 4.i.14 ; *fetch thee with a wanion*, deal you a blow, *Per.*, 2.i.17.

FEVER, to put in a fever, *Ant. and Cleo.*, 3.xiii.138.

FIELD, field of battle, *Ven. and Ad.*, 108 ; *challenge that fair field*, the surface that carries armorial bearings as on a shield, *Lucrece*, 58, with play on battlefield ; so *Lucrece*, 72.

FIERCE, *fierce abridgement*, impetuous summary, *Cym.*, 5.v.382 ; fiery, *Lear*, 1.ii.112.

FIGURE, figure on dial of clock, *Oth.*, 4.ii.55 ; *in as like a figure*, as if acting a similar part, *Cym.*, 3.iv.96 ; embroidered pattern, *Lov.Comp.*, 17 ; carven images, *Cym.*, 2.iv.82 ; *figure of truth*, embodiment of truth, *Per.*, 5.iii.93 ; *figure of my heart*, character, *Oth.*, 1.i.63 ; physical features (with play on figure on dial), *Son.*, 104,10 ; figure of speech, *Ant. and Cleo.*, 3.ii.16.

FILE, effective strength of a fighting-force, *Cym.*, 5.iii.30 ; ranks, *Ant. and Cleo.*, 1.i.3.

FILE, to perfect, polish, *Son.*, 85,4.

FILL, *fills up the cry*, like a hound that merely runs with the pack, *Oth.*, 2.iii.353.

FILLET, band for the head, *Lov.Comp.*, 33.

FIND, *the woman hath found him already*, has seen his true nature, *Oth.*, 2.i.244 ; *find me to*, discover (from a study of my hand) that, *Ant. and Cleo.*, 1.ii.28 ; *how you find her*, in what mood or condition she is, *Ant. and Cleo.*, 5.i.68.

FINE, *in fine*, finally, *Lear*, 2.i.48 ; *a fine fool*, an egregious ass, *Oth.*, 4.i.148 ; *verb*, *Time's office is to fine the hate of foes*, to end, *Lucrece*, 936.

FINELESS, *riches fineless*, endless wealth, *Oth.*, 3.iii.177.

FINGER, to play on an instrument, *Cym.*, 2.iii.14 ; *Per.*, 1.i.82.

FINISH, to die, *Ant. and Cleo.*, 5.ii.192 ; *Cym.*, 5.v.412.

FIRE, *fire us hence like foxes*, as foxes are smoked out of their holes, *Lear*, 5.iii.23 ; *Son.*, 144,14 ; *noun*, *stand on fire*, burn with impatience, *Cym.*, 5.v.168 ; *gives her sorrow fire*, from the idea of a gunner putting the match to his powder, *Lucrece*, 1604.

FIRE-NEW, *fire-new fortune*, brand-new honours, *Lear*, 5.iii.132.

FIRM, constant, *Ant. and Cleo.*, 1.v.43.

FIRST, *familiar at first*, intimate at our first meeting, *Cym.*, 1.iv.98 ; *since at first*, since the time when man first (attempted some task), *Son.*, 59,8.

FISTING, abuse, rough usage, *Per.*, 4.vi.165.

FIT, well-fitting (of garments), *Cym.*, 4.i.2 ; *I have already fit*, ready, *Cym.*, 3.iv.167 ; *all with me's meet that I can fashion fit*, all is fair to me that I can turn to my own advantage, *Lear*, 1.ii.175 ; *must make content with his fortunes fit*, find his content in whatever fortune does for him, *Lear*, 3.ii.76.

FIT, *how have mine eyes out of their spheres been fitted*, afflicted by fits, driven by recurring attacks of delirium, *Son.*, 119,7 ; *if it be a day fits you*, if your fit of lunacy recurs on a particular day, *Per.*, 2.i.54.

FITCHEW, polecat, *Lear*, 4.vi.122; wench, *Oth.*, 4.i.144.

FITLY, *may fitly like your grace*, may please your grace sufficiently, *Lear*, 1.i.200; *I will fitly bring you to hear*, at a suitable moment, *Lear*, 1.ii.160.

FITMENT, '*twas a fitment for the purpose I then follow'd*, equipment, designed for my purpose, *Cym.*, 5.v.409; *do her fitment*, what is appropriate, proper in the circumstances, *Per.*, 4.vi.6.

FITNESS, *a woman's fitness comes by fits*, a woman's inclination is variable, *Cym.*, 4.i.6; *were't my fitness to*, did my humanity permit, *Lear*, 4.ii.63.

FIX, *truth needs no colour, with his colour fix'd*, truth is so surely dyed in his beauty that it needs no further attempts at improvement, *Son.*, 101,6.

FLAKE, lock of hair, *Lear*, 4.vii.30.

FLAPJACK, pancake, *Per.*, 2.i.82.

FLATTER, to provoke with false hope, *Ven. and Ad.*, 978.

FLATTERY, *sweet flattery*, pleasing delusion, *Son.*, 42,14; *Oth.*, 4.i.129.

FLAW, break in fortunes, *Ant. and Cleo.*, 3.xii.34.

FLEECE, hair, *Son.*, 68,8.

FLEER, sneer, *Oth.*, 4.i.82.

FLEET, to be afloat, *Ant. and Cleo.*, 3.xiii.171; *the fleeting moon*, inconstant, *Ant. and Cleo.*, 5.ii.239.

FLESH, *he means in flesh*, in physical attractions (then taken up as meaning in complexion), *Ant. and Cleo.*, 1.ii.17; *eat strange flesh*, from animals normally unacceptable to man, *Ant. and Cleo.*, 1.iv.67; *the flesh being proud, Desire doth fight with Grace*, man's carnal nature, *Lucrece*, 712; *Son.*, 151,8; *verb, I'll flesh you*, to give him his first taste of fighting (the adaptation of a term from hunting), with the further suggestion of giving him a taste of the sword, *Lear*, 2.ii.42.

FLESHMENT, *in the fleshment of this dread exploit*, in the eagerness for combat provoked by this earlier initiation, *Lear*, 2.ii.118.

FLIBBERTIGIBBET, one of the devils in Harsnett's *Declaration of Egregious Popish Impostures* (1603), *Lear*, 3.iv.113 and 4.i.62. From the name *Declaration* Shakespeare took Smulkin, Modo, Mahu, Obidicut and Hobbididence.

FLOOD-GATE, impetuous (like water pouring through a sluice), *Oth.*, 1.iii.56.

FLOURISH, *transfix the flourish set on youth*, remove the embellishments peculiar to youth, *Son.*, 60,9.

FLOW, fulness, *Lucrece*, 561; *the flow o' the Nile*, height of the river, *Ant. and Cleo.*, 2.vii.17; *verb*, to come by descent, *Per.*, 4.iii.27; *ebb and flow*, to fall and rise as the tide, *Lear*, 5.iii.19.

FLOWER, beauty, *Per.*, 3.ii.101.

FLUSH, lusty, *Ant. and Cleo.*, 1.iv.52.

FLUSTER, to heat with wine, *Oth.*, 2.iii.54

FLUXIVE, *fluxive eyes*, flowing with tears, *Lov.Comp.*, 50.

FLY, *flying off*, desertion, *Lear*, 2.iv.88; *fly off*, to separate, *Ant. and Cleo.*, 2.ii.157.

FOB, *fopt in it*, duped in this matter, *Oth.*, 4.ii.195.

FOIL, (i) setting for a jewel, *Lov.Comp.*, 153; (ii) disgrace, *Ant. and Cleo.*, 1.iv.24.

FOIL, to defeat, to overcome, *Ven. and Ad.*, 114; *Son.*, 25,10.

FOIN, thrust in fencing, *Lear*, 4.vi.247.

FOISON, good harvest, *Ant. and Cleo.*, 2.vii.20.

FOIST, *foist upon us that is old*, deceiving us into thinking it new, *Son.*, 123,6.

FOLLOW, pursue in hostile manner, *Ant. and Cleo.*, 5.i.36; *following her affairs*, attending to, in performance of her business, *Lear*, 2.ii.145; *follows but for form*, serves only in show, *Lear*, 2.iv.77.

FOLLY, wantonness, *Oth.*, 2.i.137; lust, *Lucrece*, 556.

FOND, *fond bondage*, endured only by the foolish, *Lear*, 1.ii.47; doting, *Oth.*, 4.i.193; *with gain so fond*, so eager for gain, *Lucrece*, 134; silly, *Oth.*, 2.i.138; desirous, *Cym.*, 1.i.37.

FOOL, *to fool their preparation*, to make ridiculous, *Ant. and Cleo.*, 5.ii.224; to make foolish, *Lear*, 2.iv.274.

FOOLISH-WITTY, *love is wise in folly, foolish-witty*, foolish in its wisdom, *Ven. and Ad.*, 838.

FOOT, *at whose foot*, immediately after which, *Ant. and Cleo.*, 1.v.44; *on foot*, on the move, *Ven. and Ad.*, 679; unit of verse, *Per.*, 4.Prol.48; *verb*, to seize with talons, *Cym.*, 5.iv.116; *a power already footed*, a force already landed, *Lear*, 3.iii.13.

FOOTING, step, *Ven. and Ad.*, 722; *whose footing here*, whose landing here, *Oth.*, 2.i.76; foot-print, *Ven. and Ad.*, 148.

FOPT, see fob.

FOPPERY, folly, *Lear*, 1.ii.113.

FOPPISH, foolish, *Lear*, 1.iv.165.

FOR, *I forgive thee for a witch*, being as you are a witch, sorcerer, *Ant. and Cleo.*, 1.ii.38; *stands up for the main soldier*, has claims to be the chief soldier of the age, *Ant. and Cleo.*, 1.ii.185; *the lily I condemned for thy hand*, because of (its theft from) your hand, *Son.*, 99,6; *advise thee to desist for going on death's net*, for fear of going, *Per.*, 1.i.40.

FORAGE, to prey on greedily, *Ven. and Ad.*, 554.

FORBEAR, *forbear his presence*, avoid meeting with him, *Lear*, 1.ii.152; *forbear me*, withdraw, *Ant. and Cleo.*, 1.ii.118 and 5.ii.174; *no fisher but the ungrown fry forbears*, leaves alone, *Ven. and Ad.*, 526; *Cym.*, 4.ii.279; *forbear him*, leave uninjured, *Oth.*, 1.ii.10; withdraw, *Per.*, 2.iv.41; endure, *Per.*, 2.iv.46.

FORBEARANCE, restraint, *Cym.*, 2.iii.98.

FORBID, deny, *Son.*, 65,12 ; *the heavens forbid but that our loves and comfort should increase*, may the heavens avert that they should not, *Oth.*, 2.i.191 ; *to be forbod the sweets*, forbidden, *Lov.Comp.*, 164.

FORBIDDINGS, obstacle, *Lucrece*, 323.

FORCE, *forces*, operative power, *Cym.*, I.v.18 ; *verb*, compel, *Lear*, 3.iii.66 ; *indirect and forced courses*, dishonest and violent (as with poison) means, *Oth.*, 1.iii.111 ; to violate, *Lucrece*, 1657 ; urge, *Lov.Comp.*, 157 ; value, *Lucrece*, 1021.

FORDO, to kill, *Lear*, 5.iii.255 ; to ruin, *Oth.*, 5.i.129.

FORE, before (of place), *Per.*, 3.Prol.6 ; (of time) *Son.*, 7,11 ; (of rank or estimation) *Cym.*, 1.iv.61.

FORE-BEMOANED, previously lamented, *Son.*, 30,11.

FORE-BETRAY'D, already betrayed, *Lov.Comp.*, 328.

FORE-END, earlier part, *Cym.*, 3.iii.73.

FOREGONE, past, *Son.*, 30,9 ; *a foregone conclusion*, a previous act (of which the dream was an echo), *Oth.*, 3.iii.432 (the expression bears a different sense in modern usage).

FOREIGN, not of the household ; *with more than foreign heart*, not like a stranger, *Per.*, 4.i.35 ; so *foreign laps*, *Oth.*, 4.iii.86.

FORESAY, decree, predetermine, *Cym.*, 4.ii.147.

FORESPENT, formerly bestowed, *Cym.*, 2.iii.59.

FORESTALL, *this night forestall him of the coming day*, rid himself of the anger we should expect tomorrow, *Cym.*, 3.v.70.

FORFEIT, what is lost by some failure of duty, *Cym.*, 5.v.208 ; *verb*, *forfeit to a confin'd doom*, subject to, *Son.*, 107,4.

FORFEITERS, those failing to keep some bond, *Cym.*, 3.ii.38.

FORFEND, to avert, forbid, *Oth.*, 5.ii.33 ; *forfended*, forbidden, *Lear*, 5.i.10.

FORGET, to forget oneself, *Oth.*, 2.iii.233.

FORGETFUL, neglectful, *Son.*, 100,5.

FORK, arrow head, *Lear*, 1.i.143.

FORLORN, lost, *Cym.*, 5.v.405 ; outcast, *Lear*, 4.vii.39.

FORM, likeness, *Son.*, 9,6.

FORMAL, normal, *Ant. and Cleo.*, 2.v.41 ; precise, *Lov.Comp.*, 29.

FORSAKE, refuse, *Oth.*, 4.ii.126 ; reject, *Lucrece*, 1538.

FORSOOTH, in truth, *Lear*, i.iv.193 ; ironically at *Oth.*, 1.i.19.

FORSWEAR, to swear to renounce ; so *comfort forswear me*, *Oth.*, 4.ii.160.

FORTH, *did make my way long forth*, my excursion seem long, *Cym.*, 4.ii.150 ; elsewhere, at sea, *Ant. and Cleo.*, 4.xi.3.

FORTIFY, to protect, *Lov.Comp.*, 9.

FORTITUDE, strength (offensive or defensive), *Oth.*, 1.iii.222.

FORTUNE, the goddess with her wheel, *Lucrece*, 952 ; *Ant. and Cleo.*, 4.xv.44 ; *to prey at fortune*, at random, at whatever chance offers, *Oth.*, 3.iii.267 ; success, *Lear*, 5.iii.165 ; *fortunes*, possessions, *Oth.*, 5.ii.369 ; *verb*, to arrange someone's future career, *Ant. and Cleo.*, 1.ii.69.

FORWARD, stirring, early at the task, *Cym.*, 3.v.29.

FOSTER, to feed, *Cym.*, 2.iii.114.

FOUL, ugly, ill-favoured, *Oth.*, 2.i.140 ; *Ant. and Cleo.*, 1.ii.67 ; stormy, *Oth.*, 2.i.34 ; evil, *Son.*, 144,8.

FOULNESS, wickedness, *Lear*, 1.i.227.

FOUND, to build on, *Oth.*, 3.iv.95.

FOUNDATIONS, plays on the meanings : a place like a town fixed on its foundations, and a charitable establishment, *Cym.*, 3.vi.7.

FRAGMENT, *a fragment of Cneius Pompey's*, what is left after his enjoyment of her, *Ant. and Cleo.*, 3.xiii.117 ; *fragments in hard voyages*, at first despised then of consequence, *Cym.*, 5.iii.44.

FRAME, body, person, *Son.*, 59,10 ; *frame of nature*, the fabric of my being, *Lear*, 1.iv.268 ; *verb*, to perform, *Ant. and Cleo.*, 1.iii.215 ; *frame my feeding*, order my diet, *Son.*, 118,6 ; *thither frame*, direct their steps there, *Per.*, 1.Prol.32.

FRANCHISE, *whose repair and franchise* (of laws), renewal and free use, *Cym.*, 3.i.55.

FRANK, generous, *Lear*, 3.iv.20 ; honest, free, *Oth.*, 3.iv.41.

FRANKLIN, a freeholder, but not of aristocratic family, *Cym.*, 3.ii.76.

FRANKLY, without restraint or reservation, *Oth.*, 2.iii.288.

FRAUGHT, *noun*, *Oth.*, 3.iii.454 ; *verb*, to burden, *Cym.*, 1.i.126 ; stored, *Lear*, 1.iv.220.

FREE, honourable, *Oth.*, 3.iii.203 ; *free duty*, devoted in service, *Oth.*, 1.iii.41 ; innocent, *Oth.*, 3.iii.259 ; cheerful, *Lear*, 4.vi.80 ; *Oth.*, 3.iii.344 ; *verb*, expiate, *Lucrece*, 1208 ; remove, *Cym.*, 3.v.79.

FREEDOM, privilege, *Son.*, 46,4.

FREELY, in freedom, *Ant. and Cleo.*, 4.vi.7.

FREENESS, generosity, *Cym.*, 5.v.421.

FREQUENT, *adj.*, familiar, *Son.*, 117,5.

FRESH, *fresh regard*, refreshing sight, *Lov.Comp.*, 213 ; *Cym.*, 5.iii.71 ; *fresh-new*, inexperienced, *Per.*, 3.i.41.

FRET, bars on an instrument, like guitar (with further meaning of annoyance, infliction), *Lucrece*, 1140.

FRET, (i) *verb*, to wear away. *Ven. and Ad.*, 767 ; (ii) to adorn a ceiling with patterns or figures, *Cym.*, 2.iv.88 ; *fretted fortunes*, combines both meanings, chequered and decayed, *Ant. and Cleo.*, 4.xii.8.

FRIEND, paramour, *Oth.*, 4.i.3 ; *though I profess myself her adorer, not her friend*, speaking not merely as her lover (who might exaggerate) but her adorer, *Cym.*, 1.iv.65 ; *verb*, to assist, *Cym.*, 2.iii.47.

FRIENDSHIP, service, *Lear*, 3.ii.62.

FRIEZE, coarse woollen cloth, *Oth.*, 2.i.126.

FROM, *from the present*, beside the matter at issue, *Ant. and Cleo.*, 2.vi.30.

FRONT, forehead, forelock, *Oth.*, 3.i.49; *Ant. and Cleo.*, 1.i.6; *front of war*, front rank, *Ant. and Cleo.*, 5.i.44; *summer's front*, spring, early summer, *Son.*, 102,7; *verb*, oppose, *Ant. and Cleo.*, 2.ii.65.

FRONTLET, a band round forehead, and so used of frown at *Lear*, 1.iv.187.

FRUIT, offspring, *Lucrece*, 1064; consequence, *Oth.*, 5.i.116.

FRUITFUL, *fruitful as the free elements*, a generosity like the elements at the disposal of all, *Oth.*, 2.iii.331; *fruitful prognostication*, sign of fertility, *Ant. and Cleo.*, 1.ii.48.

FRUITFULLY, abundantly, *Lear*, 4.vi.266.

FRUSTRATE, ineffectual, *Ant. and Cleo.*, 5.i.2.

FULFIL, perform, *Lucrece*, 1635.

FULL, complete, *Oth.*, 2.i.36; *fullest man*, exceeding others in qualities of man, *Ant. and Cleo.*, 3.xiii.87; *adv.*, emphatic use common, *full suddenly*, instantly, *Lear*, 2.i.56.

FULL-ACORN'D, full of acorns, *Cym.*, 2.v.16.

FULL-FLOWING, *full-flowing stomach*, the full tide of anger, *Lear*, 5.iii.75.

FULNESS, prosperity, wealth, *Cym.*, 3.vi.12.

FULSOME, disgusting, *Oth.*, 4.i.37.

FUME, *fuming*, fuddled with wine, *Ant. and Cleo.*, 2.i.24.

FUNCTION, power of body and mind, *Oth.*, 2.iii.335.

FURNACE, *verb*, to give off as a furnace does, *Cym.*, 1.vi.65.

FURNISH, to supply, *Ant. and Cleo.*, 1.iv.77.

FURNISHINGS, what shows outward, *Lear*, 3.i.29.

FURTHER, *hark further*, listen longer, *Ant. and Cleo.*, 4.ix.11; in addition, *Lov.Comp.*, 169; *adj.*, *tomorrow or at further space*, tomorrow or some time later, *Lear*, 5.iii.54; *verb*, to help forward, *Ant. and Cleo.*, 2.ii.151; *furtherance*, help, *Per.*, 2.i.152.

FURY, *Fury crown'd with snakes*, a goddess of vengeance, *Ant. and Cleo.*, 2.v.40; *prophetic fury*, inspired rapture, *Oth.*, 3.iv.72; poetic rage, *Son.*, 100,3.

FUSTIAN, rubbish (*fustian* being a coarse cloth), *Oth.*, 2.iii.271.

GAD, a sharp-pointed iron instrument; *upon the gad*, on the spur of the moment, *Lear*, 1.ii.26.

GAGE, *to gage*, as security of his innocence, *Lucrece*, 1351; *verb*, to stake, risk, *Lucrece*, 144.

GAIN, wealth, *Lucrece*, 860; *Son.*, 67,12; *verb*, to profit, *Lucrece*, 131; to acquire, *Per.*, 4.Prol.8; *gain the cap*, obtain the respectful salutation, *Cym.*, 3.iii.25; to restore, *Cym.*,

4.ii.168; *gains or loses your sword or mine*, the result of one or other proving victor in the duel, *Cym.*, 2.iv.59.

GAIT, *go your gait*, go your own way, *Lear*, 4.vi.239; *what majesty is in her gait?* her deportment generally, *Ant. and Cleo.*, 3.iii.17; style of fingering the keyboard, *Son.*, 128,11.

GALL, gall, it was thought, provided the impulses that issue in resentment and anger, *Oth.*, 4.iii.90; *verb*, injuring by friction, *Per.*, 4.i.55; *the galled shore*, fretted by the waves, *Lucrece*, 1440.

GALLIA, France, *Cym.*, 1.vi.200; *Gallian*, French, *Cym.*, 1.vi.65.

GALLOW, to terrify, *Lear*, 3.ii.44.

GAME, amorous play, *Oth.*, 2.iii.19.

GAMESTER, prostitute, *Per.*, 4.vi.74.

GARB, manner (not dress); *doth affect a saucy roughness, and constrains the garb quite from his nature*, pretending to be blunt he is merely impertinent, so distorting the real nature of the manner he assumes, *Lear*, 2.ii.92; *abuse him in the rank garb*, slander him in a vile way, *Oth.*, 2.i.300.

GARBOILS, disturbances, troubles, *Ant. and Cleo.*, 1.iii.61.

GARLAND, *the garland of the war*, the first of soldiers, *Ant. and Cleo.*, 4.xv.64.

GASTED, frightened, *Lear*, 2.i.55.

GASTNESS, look of fear, *Oth.*, 5.i.106.

GATHER, *you may gather more*, form a conclusion from the hints given, *Lear*, 4.v.32.

GAUDY, festive, *Ant. and Cleo.*, 3.xiii.183.

GAZE, object that attracts men's eyes, *Son.*, 5,2; *stands at gaze*, looking about in distraction, *Lucrece*, 1149.

GECK, gull, fool, *Cym.*, 5.iv.67.

GENDER, race, kind, *Oth.*, 1.iii.323; *thy sable gender mak'st with the breath thou giv'st and tak'st*, crows were supposed to breed by interchange of breath, *gender* here being offspring, *Phoenix*, 18; *verb*, to beget, *Oth.*, 4.ii.62.

GENERAL, *general warranty*, the permission given to all, *Oth.*, 5.ii.63; *the general dependants*, the servants as a body, *Lear*, 1.iv.60; *the general camp*, the whole camp, *Oth.*, 3.iii.349; *general graces*, all-over merit, *Ant. and Cleo.*, 2.ii.134; *general services*, engagements in which armies take part, *Cym.*, 4.i.12; *noun*, *to plague a private sin in general*, to visit an individual's sin on the people as a whole, *Lucrece*, 1484; *most wise in general*, in all respects, *Per.*, 5.i.182.

GENERATION, *makes his generation messes*, eats his offspring, *Lear*, 1.i.116.

GENEROUS, well-born; *the generous islanders*, men of rank in the island, *Oth.*, 3.iii.284.

GENNET, horse of Spanish breed, *Oth.*, 1.i.114.

GENTLE, well-born, *Cym.*, 4.ii.39; *of a gentle kind*, of a good family, *Per.*, 5.i.57.

GENTRY, birth, rank, *Lucrece*, 569; men of rank, *Cym.*, 3.vii.7.

GERMANS, close kin, *Oth.*, 1.i.114.

GERMENS, seeds of life, *Lear*, 3.ii.8.

GESTS, deeds, achievements, *Ant. and Cleo.*, 4.viii.2.

GET, to make money, *Per.*, 4.ii.28; to beget children, *Ven. and Ad.*, 168.

GHOST, spectre, *Ven. and Ad.*, 933; *verb*, to haunt, *Ant. and Cleo.*, 2.vi.13.

GIGLOT, strumpet, *Cym.*, 3.i.31.

GILD, to make like gold, *Ant. and Cleo.*, 1.v.37.

GIN, to begin to, *Cym.*, 2.iii.20; *gan*, began, *Cym*, 5.v.197.

GIPSY, the gipsies were supposed to come from Egypt; Cleopatra is given their dark complexion, *Ant. and Cleo.*, 1.i.10.

GIVE, represent, report, *Ant. and Cleo.*, 1.iv.40; surrender (*gave eyes to blindness*), *Son.*, 152,11.

GIVING OUT, report, *Oth.*, 4.i.127.

GLAD, *to give him glad*, good luck, gladness, *Per.*, 2.Prol.38.

GLASS, hour-glass, *Son.*, 126,2; *fair glass of light*, reflection of beauty, *Per.*, 1.i.76.

GLASS EYES, spectacles, *Lear*, 4.vi.170.

GLASS-GAZING, vain, *Lear*, 2.ii.16.

GLORIOUS, *the desire that's glorious*, set on fame or excellence, *Cym.*, 1.vi.7; *Per.*, 1.Prol.9.

GLOW, to flush, *Ant. and Cleo.*, 2.ii.208; to shine, *Ant. and Cleo.*, 1.i.4.

GLOZE, to talk beside the point, speciously, *Per.*, 1.i.110.

GO, to walk, *Lear*, 1.iv.120; to accord, *Lear*, 1.i.105; *went about to*, set himself to, *Lucrece*, 412; *to go even with what I heard*, to give what I heard the weight my own judgement indicated, *Cym.*, 1.iv.41; *gone through for*, made a bargain for, *Per.*, 4.ii.42.

GOAL, *get goal for goal of youth*, prove a match for, *Ant. and Cleo.*, 4.viii.22.

GOATISH, lustful, *Lear*, 1.ii.122.

GOD, *the gods yield you for't*, repay you, *Ant. and Cleo.*, 4.iii.33.

GODLIKE, *godlike perfect*, divinely, *Per.*, 5.i.205.

GOLDEN, *Love's golden arrow*, Cupid's best arrow that causes love (cf. *Mid.N.Dr.*, 1.i.170), *Ven. and Ad.*, 947; *golden coat*, royal escutcheon, *Lucrece*, 205; *golden lads and girls*, fortunate and fair, *Cym.*, 4.ii.263.

GOOD, *as good as*, not better than, *Per.*, 4.ii.8; *our potency made good*, our authority asserted, maintained, *Lear*, 1.i.172; to confirm, *Ant. and Cleo.*, 2.ii.147; *noun*, cherished possession, *Lucrece*, 873.

GOOD-CONCEITED, ingeniously conceived, *Cym.*, 2.iii.17.

GOODMAN, *goodman boy*, expressing contempt, *Lear*, 2.ii.41.

GOOD YEAR, *the good years shall devour them* (cf. *Mer. Wives Win.*, 1.iv.110 where it is used as an exclamation), used here to denote some undefined malefic power, *Lear*, 5.iii.25.

GORDIAN KNOT, Gordius, elected king of Phrygia, tied the yoke of his chariot which he dedicated to Zeus with a knot so intricate that it was believed that the man who could untie it would become ruler of the East. Alexander entered the Acropolis at Gordium and cut it, *Cym.*, 2.ii.34.

GORGE, what has been swallowed, so *heave the gorge*, vomit, reject, at *Oth.*, 2.i.229; crop of bird of prey, *Ven. and Ad.*, 58; *verb*, to glut, *Lear*, 1.i.117; *Lucrece*, 694.

GORGON, one of three fabulous women with snakes for hair; Medusa the mortal one of the trio turned beholders to stone, *Ant. and Cleo.*, 2.v.116.

GOVERN, prevail, *Ant. and Cleo.*, 2.ii.152; master, *Ven. and Ad.*, 42; direct, *Son.*, 113,2.

GOVERNMENT, discretion, *Lucrece*, 1400; *Oth.*, 3.iii.260; command, *Oth.*, 4.i.233.

GRACE, *mourning doth thee grace*, becomes you, *Son.*, 132,11; *a Grace*, one of the beautiful daughters of Zeus, *Lov.Comp.*, 316; *Per.*, 1.i.12; mercy, *Lear*, 3.ii.59; blessedness, happiness, *Cym.*, 1.i.137; virtue, the prompting of heaven, *Lucrece*, 712; *verb*, to add distinction or beauty to, *Lov.Comp.*, 119; *a graced palace*, dignified, honourable, *Lear*, 1.iv.245.

GRACEFUL, favourable, *Ant. and Cleo.*, 2.ii.64.

GRACIOUS, attractive, *Son.*, 62,5; kind, *Lear*, 4.ii.41.

GRACIOUSLY, virtuously, charitably, *Per.*, 4.vi.59.

GRADATION, *by the old gradation*, the former system of promotion, *Oth.*, 1.i.37.

GRAFF, shoot, *Per.*, 5.i.59; graft, scion, *Lucrece*, 1062.

GRAINED, pronged, *Lov.Comp.*, 64.

GRAND, principal, chief, *Ant. and Cleo.*, 3.i.9; *grand sea*, ocean, *Ant. and Cleo.*, 3.xii.10.

GRANGE, house in the country, so isolated, *Oth.*, 1.i.107.

GRANT, *a fool granted*, an allowed fool, *Cym.*, 2.i.45; to allow, *Ant. and Cleo.*, 3.i.29.

GRATE, to annoy, *Ant. and Cleo.*, 1.i.18.

GRATIFY, reward, *Oth.*, 5.ii.216; *Cym.*, 2.iv.7.

GRAVE, to cut into, *Ven. and Ad.*, 376; *Son.*, 100,10.

GRAVE, *this grave charm*, deadly, *Ant. and Cleo.*, 4.xii.25.

GREAT, *great morning*, broad day, *Cym.*, 4.ii.62.

'GREE, to agree, *Ant. and Cleo.*, 2.vi.37; *what with his gust is 'greeing*, what is acceptable to its taste, *Son.*, 114,11.

GREEN SICKNESS, form of anaemia associated with love-lorn girls, *Ant. and Cleo.*, 3.ii.6; *Per.*, 4.vi.13.

GREET, meet as friends, *Ant. and Cleo.*, 2.i.39; to gratify, *Per.*, 4.iii.38;

greet the time, at once meet the danger of the moment, *Lear*, 5.i.54.

GRIEF, grievance, *Ant. and Cleo.*, 2.ii.104 ; *Per.*, 2.iv.25 ; pain, suffering, *Lucrece*, 139.

GRIEVANCE, annoyance, distress, *Oth.*, 1.ii.15 ; trouble, suffering, *Son.*, 30,9.

GRIEVE, be a grievance, *Per.*, 2.iv.19 ; to regret, *Lear*, 4.iii.53.

GRIEVOUSLY, distressfully, *Oth.*, 5.i.53.

GRIPE, (i) grasp, *Cym.*, 1.vi.105 ; (ii) a vulture, *Lucrece*, 543.

GRIPE, *verb*, grasp, *Cym.*, 3.i.39 ; grasp, *Per.*, 1.i.49.

GRISE, degree, step, *Oth.*, 1.iii.200.

GRIZZLED, greyish, *Ant. and Cleo.*, 3.xiii.17 ; snowy, *Per.*, 3.Prol.47.

GROSS, *gross in sense*, obvious to the intelligence, *Oth.*, 1.ii.72 ; dull, heavy, *Ven. and Ad.*, 150.

GROSSLY, stupidly, dully, *Oth.*, 3.iii.399 ; shamefully, *Ant. and Cleo.*, 3.x.9 ; evidently, *Lear*, 1.i.291 ; *Son.*, 99,5.

GROUND, earth, *Cym.*, 5.v.146 ; *get ground of*, secure an advantage over, *Cym.*, 1.iv.100 ; reason, *Lov.Comp.*, 63 ; the under-painting over which the painter in oils worked, *Lucrece*, 1074 ; *verb*, to fix, *Son.*, 62,4 ; to have as a base or reason, *Son.*, 142,2.

GROW, to increase, *Lear*, 5.iii.106 ; *nor curstness grow to the matter*, do not allow bad feeling to become incorporated with the business, *Ant. and Cleo.*, 2.ii.25 ; *his whole action grows not in the power on't*, his plan doesn't spring from its strength to ensure victory, *Ant. and Cleo.*, 3.vii.68.

GUARD, *to my guard*, into my custody, *Ant. and Cleo.*, 5.ii.67 ; *the guards of th' ever-fixed pole*, the two stars of Ursa Minor which protect the pole-star from the Great Bear (Ursa Major), *Oth.*, 2.i.15 ; *sober guards*, discretion (*guards* also means trimmings), *Lov.Comp.*, 298.

GUARDAGE, protected condition, *Oth.*, 1.ii.70.

GUILTY, *guilty instance*, sign of guilt, *Lucrece*, 1511.

GUISE, *the guise o' the world*, the custom of the world, *Cym.*, 5.i.32 ; *thy father's guise*, way, habit, *Ven. and Ad.*, 1177.

GULF, crop, gullet, *Lucrece*, 557.

GUST, taste, *Son.*, 114,11.

GUTTER'D, *gutter'd rocks*, channelled by the sea, *Oth.*, 2.i.69.

GYVE, to fetter, to entangle, *Oth.*, 2.i.169 ; *gyves*, fetters, shackles, *Lov. Comp.*, 242.

HABILIMENTS, dress, *Ant. and Cleo.*, 3.vi.17.

HABITS, *these thin habits*, flimsy dressing for your suspicions, *Oth.*, 1.iii.108 ; appearance, *Per.*, 2.ii.57.

HABITUDE, *his real habitude*, his own nature, *Lov.Comp.*, 114.

HAGGARD, wild hawk, so applied to unchaste woman, *Oth.*, 3.iii.264.

HAIR, *the courser's hair*, horsehair

placed in water was supposed to become an eel, *Ant. and Cleo.*, 1.ii.187.

HALCYON, kingfisher ; *turn their halcyon beaks with every gale*, a dead kingfisher when hung up was supposed to act as a weather-cock, *Lear*, 2.ii.73.

HALF-BLOODED, *half-blooded fellow*, a bastard, of good blood only on one side, *Lear*, 5.iii.81.

HALT, *no further halting*, hesitation, faltering, *Cym.*, 3.v.93.

HAM, crook of the knee, *Per.*, 4.ii.106.

HAND, *in hands with*, engaged with, *Ven. and Ad.*, 912 ; *whom she bore in hand to love*, merely professed to love, *Cym.*, 5.v.43 ; *done unto thy hand*, already done, *Ant. and Cleo.*, 4.xiv.29 ; *on whom plenty held full hand*, where plenty reigned, *Per.*, 1.iv.22.

HAND-FAST, marriage-bond, *Cym.*, 1.v.78.

HAND-IN-HAND, *a kind of hand-in-hand comparison*, the objects compared being treated as equal, *Cym.*, 1.iv.66.

HANDY-DANDY, which hand will you take ?—formula in choosing-game, *Lear*, 4.vi.153.

HANGINGS, the fruit, the honours already mentioned, *Cym.*, 3.iii.63.

HAP, *the golden hap*, rich fortune, *Lucrece*, 42.

HAPLY, HAPPILY, *happily repent*, perhaps rue her bargain, *Oth.*, 3.iii.242 ; *and haply of our old acquaintance tell*, perchance speak of our former friendship, *Son.*, 89,12.

HAPPINESS, used as a greeting at parting, *Cym.*, 3.v.17.

HAPPY, favourable, convenient, *Lear*, 2.iii.2 ; fortunate, *Lear*, 4.vi.228 ; convenient, *Lucrece*, 1045 ; gifted, accomplished, *Cym.*, 3.iv.173.

HARBOUR, shelter, hiding-place, *Lucrece*, 768.

HARD, hardened, confirmed, *Ant. and Cleo.*, 3.xiii.111 ; *hard point*, critical situation, *Cym.*, 3.iv.16 ; *adv.*, *hard at hand*, almost immediately, *Oth.*, 2.i.56 ; *full hard forbear him*, with great difficulty refrain from attacking him, *Oth.*, 1.ii.10 ; *hard-favour'd*, ugly, *Ven. and Ad.*, 133.

HARDIMENT, brave service, bold exploit, *Cym.*, 5.iv.75.

HARDINESS, courage, *Cym.*, 3.vi.22.

HARDLY, *how hardly*, with what difficulty, *Ant. and Cleo.*, 5.i.74 ; unfeelingly, *Cym.*, 3.iii.8.

HARDNESS, *so from sense in hardness*, so difficult to make sense of, *Cym.*, 5.v.431 ; hardship, *Oth.*, 1.iii.233 ; *Cym.*, 3.vi.21.

HARDOCKS, some variety of dock-weed, *Lear*, 4.iv.4.

HARLOTRY, harlot, *Oth.*, 4.iii.232.

HARMS, wrongs, injuries, *Lucrece*, 1694.

HARMONY, music, *Per.*, 5.i.44.

HARNESS, *through proof of harness*, through the armour's proved strength, *Ant. and Cleo.*, 4.viii.15.

HARP, to keep coming over, *Ant. and Cleo.*, 3.xiii.142.

HARPY. fabulous vulture with face and breasts of a woman, *Per.*, 4.iii.46.

HART, male deer, *Cym.*, 2.iv.27.

HASTE, *put it to the haste*, do it quickly, *Ant. and Cleo.*, 5.ii.195.

HATCH, half-door, *Lear*, 3.vi.72 ; *beneath the hatches*, in the hold, *Per.*, 3.i.70.

HATCHED, *our door hatched*, closed, *Per.*, 4.ii.32.

HAUNT, *all the haunt be ours*, the throng will follow us, *Ant. and Cleo.*, 4.xiv.54.

HAVE, *have at it*, I shall begin, *Cym.*, 5.v.315 ; *have with you*, lead the way, *Oth.*, 1.ii.53.

HAVING, *rarest havings*, fine gifts, accomplishments, *Lov.Comp.*, 235 ; possession, *Per.*, 2.i.137 ; allowance, *Oth.*, 4.iii.89.

HAVIOUR, bearing, *Cym.*, 3.iv.9.

HAZARD, risk, peril, *Per.*, 1.i.5 ; *Cym.*, 4.iv.46 ; *verb, hazard such a place with one of*, take a chance about the efficiency of the appointment in selecting such a man, *Oth.*, 2.iii.131 ; *the circle of the Ptolemies now hazarded to thy grace*, the disposal of the crown of Egypt lost by us to you in the chance of war depends on your favour and generosity, *Ant. and Cleo.*, 3.xii.19.

HEAD, *drawn to head*, mobilized, *Cym.*, 3.v.25 ; *the very head and front of my offending hath this extent*, bring together and set out all the ways I have offended and the total will come to no more than this, *Oth.*, 1.iii.80 ; *heave to head*, to eat, *Cym.*, 5.v.157.

HEAR, *I heard no letter from my master*, received no word, *Cym.*, 4.iii.36 ; *hear these tears*, be moved by such miseries, *Per.*, 1.iv.54.

HEARSED, buried, *Lucrece*, 657.

HEART, *the very heart of loss*, loss beyond all hope of recovery, *Ant. and Cleo.*, 4.xii.29.

HEARTED, *I hate the Moor ; my cause is hearted*, planted deep in my heart, *Oth.*, 1.iii.363 ; *hearted throne*, throne in the heart, *Oth.*, 3.iii.452.

HEARTLESS, disheartened, *Lucrece*, 471.

HEART-STRUCK, inflicted on the heart, *Lear*, 3.i.17.

HEART-WISH'D, ardently desired, *Lov.Comp.*, 314.

HEARTY, kind-hearted, *Ant. and Cleo.*, 4.ii.38.

HEAT, *i' th' heat*, immediately, *Lear*, 1.i.306 ; *business of some heat*, urgent matter, *Oth.*, 1.ii.39 ; *verb, heat my blood*, anger me, *Ant. and Cleo.*, 1.iii.80.

HEAVE, *heave the gorge*, sicken with disgust, *Oth.*, 2.i.229.

HEAVILY, sorrowfully, *Son*, 30.10.

HEAVINESS, oppression, *Cym.*, 5.ii.1.

HEAVY, *discourse is heavy, fasting*, talk is tedious and irksome to the hungry man, *Cym.*, 3.vi.90 ; *heavy terms*, abusive names, *Oth.*, 4.ii.117 ; *heavy causes*, just and good reason, *Lear*, 5.i.27 ; *heavy anthem*, sorrowful song, *Ven. and Ad.*, 839 ; *heavy ignorance*

aloft to fly, dullness, stupidity, *Son.*, 78,6 ; *Oth.*, 2.i.143 ; dark, *Oth.*, 5.i.42.

HECATE, goddess in classical times associated with ghost world, *Lear*, 1.i.109.

HEEDFULLY, consciously, with waking eyes, *Lucrece*, 454.

HEEL, *out at heels*, depressed, out of luck, *Lear*, 2.ii.152 ; *took heel*, ran away, *Cym.*, 5.iii.67.

HEIGHT, *the star . . . whose worth's unknown, although his height be taken*, ' a very mystical assertion that, as the unknown worth and occult influence of a star is in excess of the practical service it affords to mariners, so has Love an eternal value immeasurably superior to the accidents of Time ' (Wyndham quoted by Fort), *Son.*, 116,8 ; skill, excellence, *Son.*, 32,8 ; maturity, *Son.*, 15,7 ; *the fight in height*, at its most critical phase, *Ant. and Cleo.*, 3.x.21.

HEINOUS, wicked, *Lear*, 5.iii.92.

HELL-HATED, as hateful as hell, *Lear*, 5.iii.147.

HELP, *helps*, helpers, *Per.*, 1.i.22 ; *helpless help*, unavailing remedy, *Lucrece*, 1056 ; *help of Bath*, the cure at Bath, *Son.*, 153,11 ; *verb*, cure, *Lucrece*, 1822 ; *Lear*, 4.iv.10.

HELPLESS, *helpless berries*, berries that provide no sustenance, being merely painted ones, *Ven. and Ad.*, 604 ; incurable (or perhaps ' unavailing '), *Lucrece*, 756.

HENCE, *long hence*, in after times, *Son.*, 101,14 ; *messengers from hence*, messengers to go from this place, *Lear*, 2.i.125.

HER, represents at times old form of possessive pronoun 3rd person plural (modern ' their ') ; as *the wars must make examples out of her best*, at *Oth.*, 3.iii.67.

HERALD, an officer concerned with the ceremonies proper to chivalry, intercourse between belligerents, order of precedence, armorial bearings, conduct of funerals, proclamations, state occasions ; *some loathsome dash the herald will contrive*, for her coat-of-arms and that of her descendants, *Lucrece*, 206 ; *let but the herald cry*, at *Lear*, 5.i.48 ; forerunner, announcer, *Son.*, 1,10 ; *herald sad and trumpet be*, the announcer of the obsequies, *Phoenix*, 3 ; *verb*, to usher, *Per.*, 3.i.34.

HERALDRY, the code administered by the heralds, especially concerning the right to armorial bearings, formalities of individual combat, state ceremonies ; *our new heraldry*, our new code (here of conduct), *Oth.*, 3.iv.44 ; *this heraldry in Lucrece' face*, virtue and beauty showed on Lucrece's face as the dignities of a family show in their coat-of-arms, *Lucrece*, 64.

HERE, used as noun ; *thou losest here*, the life you lead here, this particular set, *Lear*, 1.i.261 ; *stranger of here and everywhere*, of no fixed abode, *Oth.*, 1.1.137.

HEROD, *Herod of Jewry*, the suggestion here is that even such a tyrant (his character in the miracle plays) couldn't face Cleopatra in her rage, *Ant. and Cleo.*, 3.iii.3.

HESPERIDES, three nymphs who with an unsleeping dragon guarded the golden apples in their far western garden; used of the daughter of Antiochus to indicate the danger attending her wooing, *Per.*, 1.i.27.

HEWGH, to imitate the sound of an arrow, *Lear*, 4.vi.92.

HIDE, protect, *Cym.*, 4.ii.391 ; *till the cup be hid*, brimming, *Ant. and Cleo.*, 2.vii.86.

HIDEOUS, revolting, *Lear*, 1.i.150.

HIE, hasten, *Ven. and Ad.*, 1189.

HIGH, *high supper-time*, more than time for supper, *Oth.*, 4.ii.240 ; *high order*, special arrangements, *Ant. and Cleo.*, 5.ii.363.

HIGH-BATTLED, in high command, *Ant. and Cleo.*, 3.xiii.29.

HIGH-ENGENDER'D, begun in the heavens, *Lear*, 3.ii.23.

HIGH-JUDGING, judging in heaven, supreme judge, *Lear*, 2.iv.227.

HIGH-PITCH'D, high flown, proud, *Lucrece*, 41.

HIGHT, called, named, *Per.*, 4.Prol.18.

HILD, held, *Lucrece*, 1257.

HILDING, menial, *Cym.*, 2.iii.123.

HIND, the most ordinary man, *Cym.*, 5.iii.77.

HINT, occasion, *it was my hint to speak*, I had occasion to relate, *Oth.*, 1.iii.142 ; *upon this hint I spake* (*hint* does not mean as today ' suggestion '; Othello is not informing the senate that Desdemona made him an overt invitation), I took advantage of this opportunity, *Oth.*, 1.iii.166 ; *when the best hint was given him*, when the occasion was most favourable, *Ant. and Cleo.*, 3.iv.9.

HIP, *on the hip*, at a disadvantage (term from wrestling), *Oth.*, 2.i.299.

HIS, used as possessive case of ' it ', the modern form ' its ' being found only very rarely in the First Folio, some ten times ; and not at all in early Quartos ; so *this dumb play had his acts made plain*, at *Ven. and Ad.*, 359.

HISTORY, story, *Oth.*, 1.iii.139 ; account, *Cym.*, 3.v.100 ; *Lear*, 1.i.236.

HIT, *let's hit together*, agree to act together, *Lear*, 1.i.302.

HIVE, hat of straw, *Lov.Comp.*, 8.

HOBBIDIDENCE, see *Flibbertigibbet*.

HOBBY-HORSE, trull, *Oth.*, 4.i.152.

HOLD, *take hold of me*, arrest my attention, *Oth.*, 1.iii.55 ; fastness, *Cym.*, 3.vi.18 ; verb, *holds idleness your subject*, makes trifling serve you as a subject might, *Ant. and Cleo.*, 1.iii.92 ; *I hold it*, I am convinced now as always, *Per.*, 3.ii.26 ; *hold there still*, continue to affirm something, *Ant. and Cleo.*, 2.v.92.

HOLDING, burden of a song, *Ant. and Cleo.*, 2.vii.109.

HOLLOWNESS, *reverbs no hollowness*, does not sound as empty vessels do, loud with insincerity, *Lear*, 1.i.153.

HOLY-ALES (suggestion for holy dayes (Q₁), to rhyme with festivals), church-ales or festivals, *Per.*, 1.Prol.6.

HOLY-WATER, *court holy water*, flattery, specious promises, *Lear*, 3.ii.10.

HOMAGER, vassal, *Ant. and Cleo.*, 1.i.31.

HOME, *charges home*, attempts a fatal thrust, *Lear*, 2.i.51 ; *revenged home*, thoroughly repaid, in full measure, *Lear*, 3.iii.12 ; *he speaks home*, home truths, bluntly, *Oth.*, 2.i.164 ; *take her home*, where she may learn, *Per.*, 4.ii.124.

HONEST, truthful, *Oth.*, 3.iii.382 ; chaste, *Oth.*, 3.iii.388.

HONESTY, *why should honour outlive honesty ?* why should the respect and formal honour men showed me survive my loss of honourable character ? *Oth.*, 5.ii.248 ; proper in a subordinate, *Oth.*, 4.i.274 ; chastity, *Lucrece*, 885 ; *Ant. and Cleo.*, 5.ii.252.

HONOURABLE, dignified, *Oth.*, 4.iii.233 ; *an honourable trial*, the trial of its honourable nature, *Ant. and Cleo.*, 1.iii.75.

HONOURED, *honour'd finger*, that of a gentleman, *Cym.*, 5.v.184 ; *an honour'd triumph*, a royal entertainment, *Per.*, 2.ii.53 ; honourable, *Ant. and Cleo.*, 4.viii.11 ; *Lear*, 5.i.9.

HOODWINK'D, blindfolded, *Cym.*, 5.ii.16.

HOPE, *in thy hope*, in your youth when men expect well of you, *Lucrece*, 605 ; *Lucrece*, 1003 ; *their brave hope*, on whom they relied, *Lucrece*, 1430 ; *the worst, which late on hopes depended*, the misfortune which hitherto could be estimated only by your fears (*hope* being expectation of any kind, even fear), *Oth.*, 1.iii.203 ; verb, to expect, suppose, *Ant. and Cleo.*, 2.i.38.

HORN, the horn carried by beggars sounded to attract the charitable and used to hold what was given them to drink, *Lear*, 3.vi.74 ; *his horns*, which he will get by marrying one who will cuckold him, *Ant. and Cleo.*, 1.ii.4.

HOROLOGE, clock, *Oth.*, 2.iii.122.

HORSEHAIRS, for the fiddle-bow, *Cym.* 2.iii.30.

HOSE, doublet and hose were articles of male dress, hose covering the legs, *Cym.*, 3.iv.168.

HOT, impetuous, *Ant. and Cleo.*, 1.iv.50 ; hotly, urgently, *Oth.*, 1.ii.44.

HOURLY, marking the hours, *Lucrece*, 327.

HOUSE, *becomes the house*, does credit to a well-governed family, *Lear*, 2.iv.151 ; *not to keep house*, not to stay indoors, *Cym.*, 3.iii.1 and 3.vi.36, where *keep'st thyself* means that he thought it empty.

HOW, *how say you ?* what do you make

of ? *Oth.*, 1.iii.17 ; what price ? *Per.*, 4.vi.19 ; *look how he can*, however he looks, *Ven. and Ad.*, 79.

HOWBEIT, *howbeit that*, although, *Oth.*, 2.i.282.

HOWEVER, HOWE'ER, *however else*, in whatever manner in other respects, *Lear*, 2.i.117 ; notwithstanding, *Lear*, 4.ii.66 ; although, *Cym.*, 4.ii.47.

HOWSOEVER, HOWSOE'ER, *howsoe'er 'tis strange*, notwithstanding the remarkable nature of the fact, *Cym.*, 1.i.65 ; whatever the event, *Cym.*, 4.ii.147.

HUE, colour, form ; *a man in hue, all hues in his controlling*, a man whose hue captivates men and women, *Son.*, 20,7.

HUMAN, HUMANE (always *humane* in early texts), *human law*, characteristic of mankind, *Lucrece*, 571 ; *civil and humane seeming*, good breeding, *Oth.*, 2.i.236.

HUMANITY, human qualities, *Oth.*, 1.iii.316 ; *Ant. and Cleo.*, 5.i.32.

HUMBLE, *humble salve*, sympathy, *Son.*, 120,12 ; *humbled*, contrite, *Oth.*, 3.iii.53.

HUMOUR, *his humour was nothing but mutation*, his outstanding characteristic was desire for constant novelty, change of interest, *Cym.*, 4.ii.133 ; *the sun drew all such humours from him*, follies such as jealousy ; *humours* being caused by the excess of one or other of the fluids (blood, phlegm, choler, melancholy) in the system, *Oth.*, 3.iv.28.

HUNT, the game, *Cym.*, 3.vi.89.

HURRICANO, waterspout, *Lear*, 3.ii.2.

HUSBAND, manage economically, *Son.*, 94,6 ; marry, *Lear*, 5.iii.71.

HUSBANDRY, good management ; *husbandry in honour*, also refers to honourable marriage, *Son.*, 13,10 ; diligence as shown by early rising, *Per.*, 3.ii.20.

HYDRA, many-headed monster in form of a snake, killed by Hercules, *Oth.*, 2.iii.295.

HYMEN, invoked at Greek marriages, so taken for god of marriage, *Per.*, 3.Prol.9.

HYSTERICA PASSIO, hysteria, *Lear*, 2.iv.56.

ICE-BROOK, *the ice-brook's temper*, tempered in ice-cold water, the blades of Toledo being famous for their quality, *Oth.*, 5.ii.256.

IDIOT, professional fool, *Lucrece*, 1812.

IDLE, trifling, *Oth.*, 1.ii.95 ; useless, *Lear*, 4.iv.5 ; barren, lifeless, *Oth.*, 1.iii.140.

IDLENESS, frivolity, *Ant. and Cleo.*, 1.iii.92 and 93.

IGNORANT, *ignorant in what I am commanded*, unskilled in the business, *Cym.*, 3.ii.23 ; *ignorant sin*, fault committed in ignorance, *Oth.*, 4.ii.71.

ILION, the citadel of Troy, *Lucrece*, 1370.

ILL, misfortune, *Lov.Comp.*, 156 ; wickedness, *Lucrece*, 91 ; sin, *Cym.*, 5.i.14 ; adj., wicked, *Lucrece*, 579.

ILL-ANNEXED, *ill-annexed opportunity*, the unfortunate addition of evil chance, *Lucrece*, 874.

ILLUSTRIOUS, famous, *Lear*, 5.iii.135 ; lacking lustre, *Cym.*, 1.vi.108.

ILL-WRESTING, *this ill-wresting world*, ready to make the worst of report, *Son.*, 140.11.

IMAGE, likeness, *Son.*, 3,14 ; *the images of revolt*, the signs of, *Lear*, 2.iv.88 ; *image of hell*, applied to night, *Lucrece*, 764 ; type, *Lear*, 4.vi.158.

IMAGINARY, *imaginary work*, in which images are used to suggest to the imagination related figures, *Lucrece*, 1422 ; *all is imaginary*, in the mind only, without corresponding reality, *Ven. and Ad.*, 597.

IMAGINATION, *wrong imaginations*, delusions, *Lear*, 4.vi.283.

IMITATE, to represent, depict, *Son.*, 53.6.

IMMEDIACY, *the which immediacy*, as my direct representative, *Lear*, 5.iii.66.

IMMEDIATE, *the immediate jewel of their souls*, next their very heart, *Oth.*, 3.iii.160 ; *the immediate author*, the direct cause, *Ant. and Cleo.*, 2.vi.125.

IMMOMENT, of no importance, *Ant. and Cleo.*, 5.ii.165.

IMMURE, to withdraw from the world, as if shut off by walls, *Ven. and Ad.*, 1195 ; *Lov. Comp.*, 251 ; *Son.*, 84,3.

IMPAIR, injure, *Son.*, 83,11.

IMPANNEL, enrol as jury, *Son.*, 46,9.

IMPART, to provide, *Lucrece*, 1039.

IMPARTIAL, *the impartial gazer*, equally delighted by various aspects, *Ven. and Ad.*, 748.

IMPERCEIVERANT, lacking in discernment, *Cym.*, 4.i.13.

IMPERIOUS, *imperious supreme*, imperial ruler, *Ven. and Ad.*, 996 ; *imperious show*, the emperor's triumph, *Ant. and Cleo.*, 4.xv.23.

IMPERTINENCY, *matter and impertinency*, sense and incoherence, *Lear*, 4.vi.175.

IMPLEACH'D, intertwined, *Lov.Comp.*, 205.

IMPLY, *imply her*, have as a consequence for her, *Per.*, 4.i.83.

IMPORT, importance, *Oth.*, 3.iii.320 ; verb, to involve, *Lear*, 4.iii.4 ; to carry as a consequence, *Ant. and Cleo.*, 2.ii.137 ; signify, *Oth.*, 4.i.136 ; have as purport, *Oth.*, 5.ii.313 ; *as doth import you*, to be important for your business, *Oth.*, 1.iii.283 ; *Ant. and Cleo.*, 1.iii.118.

IMPORTANCE, *importance of so slight and trivial a nature*, a matter of no importance, *Cym.*, 1.iv.38.

IMPORTANCY, value, *Oth.*, 1.iii.20.

IMPORTANTLY, with urgent business, *Cym.*, 4.iv.19.

IMPORTUNE, beg a respite, *Ant. and Cleo.*, 4.xv.19 ; to ask, *Oth.*, 4.i.113.

IMPORTUN'D, importunate, *Lear*, 4.iv.26.

IMPOSITION, behest, *Lucrece*, 1697 ; *an idle and most false imposition*, the public imposing on or giving a man his reputation thoughtlessly, *Oth.*, 2.iii.261.

IMPOSTHUME, abscess, swelling, *Ven. and Ad.*, 743.

IMPRESS, compulsory recruitment, *Ant. and Cleo.*, 3.vii.36 ; *verb*, to compel into service, *Lov.Comp.*, 267 ; *our impress'd lances*, those enlisted in our forces, *Lear*, 5.iii.51.

IMPRISON, *the imprison'd absence of your liberty*, the sense of imprisonment which your absence, whenever you choose, leaves with me, *Son.*, 58,6.

IMPUTATION, *imputation and strong circumstance*, probability founded on circumstantial evidence, *Oth.*, 3.iii.410.

IMPUTE, to reckon, *Son.*, 83,9.

IN, *to be in*, drunk, *Ant. and Cleo.*, 2.vii.31.

IN-A-DOOR, at home, within doors, *Lear*, 1.iv.124.

INCAPABLE, *incapable of more*, full to capacity, *Son.*, 113,13.

INCENSE, to incite, *Lear*, 2.iv.305.

INCIVIL, rude, *Cym.*, 5.v.292.

INCLINATION, temper, character, *Ant. and Cleo.*, 2.v.113.

INCLINE, *the inclining Desdemona*, sympathetic, *Oth.*, 2.iii.329 ; to side with *Lear*, 3.iii.13 ; bend her ear, *Oth.*, 1.iii.146 ; to have a disposition towards, *Cym.*, 1.vi.61 ; to yield, *Lucrece*, 1658.

INCLINING, *you of my inclining*, my party, *Oth.*, 1.ii.82.

INCLIPS, embraces, *Ant. and Cleo.*, 2.vii.67.

INCOME, gain, *Lucrece*, 334.

INCONTINENT, at once, *Oth.*, 4.iii.11.

INCONTINENTLY, immediately, *Oth.*, 1.iii.305.

INCORPORATE, made one body, *Ven. and Ad.*, 540 ; *Oth.*, 2.i.257.

INCREASE, offspring, *Son.*, 1,1.

INCREASEFUL, fruitful, *Lucrece*, 958.

INDENT, *indenting with the way*, running a zigzag course, *Ven. and Ad.*, 704.

INDENTURE, agreement, *Per.*, 1.iii.8.

INDEX, table of contents to book, so indication of what is to follow, *Oth.*, 2.i.252.

INDICT, to accuse, *Oth.*, 3.iv.155.

INDIGEST, formless, ill-shaped, *Son.*, 114,5.

INDIGN, disgraceful, *Oth.*, 1.iii.273.

INDIRECT, unlawful, *Oth.*, 1.iii.111.

INDIRECTLY, by artificial devices, *Son.*, 67,7.

INFECTED, false, assumed, *Lov.Comp.*, 323 ; *the infected house*, plague-stricken, *Oth.*, 4.i.21.

INFERENCE, train of thought, *Oth.*, 3.iii.187.

INFIRMITY, human weakness, fault, *Per.*, 2.i.49 ; ill-health, *Lear*, 2.iv.104 ; impotence, *Phoenix*, 60.

INFLUENCE, the power supposed to flow from the stars, *Lear*, 1.ii.120 and 2.ii.102 ; *Ven. and Ad.*, 862.

INFORM, instruct, *Ant. and Cleo.*,

3.ii.48 ; *Cym.*, 1.i.79 ; *inform against* to denounce, *Lear*, 4.ii.92.

INFUSE, *infusing them with*, inspiring them to, *Ven. and Ad.*, 928.

INFUSIONS, medicinal qualities, *Per.*, 3.ii.35.

INGENER, inventor, *Oth.*, 2.i.65.

INGENIOUS, *ingenious feeling*, full consciousness, *Lear*, 4.vi.280.

INGRAFT, firmly implanted, *Oth.*, 2.iii.132.

INGREDIENCE, ingredient, *Oth.*, 2.iii.298.

INHEARSE, to coffin, *Son.*, 86,3.

INHERIT, possess, govern, *Lear*, 4.vi.126 ; *Cym.*, 3.ii.60.

INHIBITED, prohibited, *Oth.*, 1.ii.79.

INHOOP'D, in the small circular arena confining the fighting birds, *Ant. and Cleo.*, 2.iii.59.

INJOINT, to combine, *Oth.*, 1.iii.35.

INJURIOUS, insulting, *Cym.*, 4.ii.87 ; malicious, *Ant. and Cleo.*, 4.xv.76.

INKLE, tape, or linen yarn from which it is made, *Per.*, 5.Prol.8.

INNOCENT, fool, *Lear*, 3.vi.7 ; *Per.*, 4.iii.17.

INNOVATION, disturbance, *Oth.*, 2.iii.36.

INQUIRE, search, *Per.*, 3.Prol.22 ; *inquire him out*, ask where he stays, *Oth.*, 3.iv.13.

INSINUATE, to wheedle, *Oth.*, 4.ii.133 ; *insinuate with*, ingratiate herself with, *Ven. and Ad.*, 1012.

INSTANCE, *guilty instance*, evidence of guilt, *Lucrece*, 1511.

INSTRUCT, to inform, *Cym.*, 4.ii.361.

INSTRUCTION, *without some instruction*, without there being good grounds for it, *Oth.*, 4.i.41.

INSTRUMENT, agent, *Oth.*, 4.ii.46 ; document, *Oth.*, 4.i.213.

INSULT, triumph over, *Lear*, 2.ii.114 ; *Son.*, 107,12.

INSULTER, triumphing victor, *Ven. and Ad.*, 550.

INSULTMENT, *speech of insultment*, expression of victor's triumph and contempt, *Cym.*, 3.v.141.

INTELLIGENCE, secret, inspired communication, *Son.*, 86,10 ; *Cym.*, 4.ii.348.

INTELLIGENT, *intelligent of our state*, conveying information about our government, *Lear*, 3.i.25 ; informative, *Lear*, 3.vii.11.

INTEND, *intend my travel*, propose to travel, *Per.*, 1.ii.116 ; *Son.*, 27,6 ; to pretend, *Lucrece*, 121 ; *how intend you—practis'd ?* what do you imply by 'practis'd' ? *Ant. and Cleo.*, 2.ii.44.

INTENDMENTS, intentions, purposes, *Ven. and Ad.*, 222.

INTENT, meaning, *Ant. and Cleo.*, 2.ii.45.

INTENTIVELY, with complete attention, *Oth.*, 1.iii.155.

INTERDICT, to exclude, *Phoenix*, 9.

INTERRESS'D, entitled, *Lear*, 1.i.84.

INTEREST, *interest of territory*, possession and rule of territory, *Lear*, 1.i.49 ; *in the interest*, to usurp the rightful possession, *Lucrece*, 1619.

INTERROGATORIES, questions, *Cym.*, 5.v.392.

INTERLUDE, a kind of brief play, usually comic ; so applied to farcical episode, *Lear*, 5.iii.90.

INTERMISSION, *spite of intermission*, though it meant delay in other business, *Lear*, 2.iv.32.

INTO, towards, *Cym.*, 1.vi.166.

INTRINSE, intricate, *Lear*, 2.ii.70 ; *this knot intrinsicate*, *Ant. and Cleo.*, 5.ii.302.

INVENTION, new ideas, *Son.*, 59,3.

INVIS'D, invisible, *Lov.Comp.*, 212.

INVISIBLE, pervasive, *Ant. and Cleo.*, 2.ii.216 ; hidden, *Cym.*, 4.ii.178.

IRREGULOUS, lawless, *Cym.*, 4.ii.316.

ISIS, national Egyptian deity, wife of Osiris and mother of Horus, *Ant. and Cleo.*, 1.ii.60.

ISSUE, act, *Cym.*, 2.i.46 ; *better issue*, better fortune, *Ant. and Cleo.*, 1.ii.90 ; consequence, *Oth.*, 3.iii.223.

IT, ' his ' is the usual genitive of ' it ', the later form being ' its ' ; so, *it had it head bit off*, *Lear*, 1.iv.215.

ITERANCE, repetition, *Oth.*, 5.ii.153.

IWIS, certainly, in truth, *Per.*, 2. Prol. 2.

JACK, *this Jack of Caesar's*, menial, *Ant. and Cleo.*, 3.xiii.103 ; *Jack-slave*, common fellow, *Cym.*, 2.i.20 ; *Jacks*, part of percussion mechanism in virginals, used of the keys, *Son.*, 128,5 ; used in bowls as aiming-mark, *Cym.*, 2.i.2.

JACKANAPES, ape, but used of interfering fellow, *Cym.*, 2.i.3.

JADE, to drive to exhaustion, reduce to sorry condition, *Ant. and Cleo.*, 3.i.34.

JAKES, a privy, *Lear*, 2.ii.61.

JANUS, represented with two faces, one looking forward, the other backward ; used at *Oth.*, 1.ii.33, because Iago comes to a conclusion quite opposed to his earlier opinion.

JAY, showy female, *Cym.*, 3.iv.47.

JEALOUS, suspicious, *Oth.*, 3.iv.186 ; apprehensive, *Lear*, 5.i.56.

JEALOUSY, suspicion, *Lucrece*, 1516 ; mistrust, *Son.*, 61,8.

JENNET, small Spanish horse, *Ven. and Ad.*, 260 ; *Oth.*, 1.i.114.

JESSES, fastenings on legs of hawks, *Oth.*, 3.iii.265.

JET, to swagger, *Cym.*, 3.iii.5.

JOINT-RING, ring with two separable halves, *Oth.*, 4.iii.71.

JOINT-STOOL, carefully made stool, *Lear*, 3.vi.51.

JOLLITY, *needy nothing trimm'd in jollity*, worthlessness dressed in finery, *Son.*, 66,3.

JOURNAL, daily, *Cym.*, 4.ii.10.

JOVIAL, those born under Jupiter (Jove) were supposed to have temperament and features characteristic of the god, *Cym.*, 4.ii.312 and 5.iv.105.

JUDICIOUS, fitting the crime, *Lear*, 3.iv.73.

JUG, Joan, *Lear*, 1.iv.224.

JUMP, venture, *Ant. and Cleo.*, 3.viii.6 ; *adv.*, exactly, *Oth.*, 2.iii.374 ; *verb*, to risk, *Cym.*, 5.iv.181.

JUST, honest, faithful, *Lucrece*, 159 ; *in thy just proof*, on the evidence of your honesty, innocence, *Lear*, 3.vi.113 ; *just report*, true report, *Lear*, 3.i.37 ; *a just equinox*, when night and day are exactly equal ; so vice and virtue balance exactly, *Oth.*, 2.iii.116 ; *just to the time*, punctual, *Son.*, 109,7.

JUSTICE, *do you justice*, keep level with you in drinking, *Oth.*, 2.iii.80.

JUSTICER, judge, *Lear*, 3.vi.21 ; *Cym.*, 5.v.214.

JUSTIFY, *justify in knowledge*, acknowledge, *Per.*, 5.i.215.

KEEP, to dwell, gather, *Ven. and Ad.*, 687 ; *thy spirit which keeps thee*, dwells with thee as guardian, *Ant. and Cleo.*, 2.iii.20 ; *it kept where I kept*, remained always with me, *Per.*, 2.i.128.

KEN, *within a ken*, within sight (a ken being reckoned at 20 miles or so), *Cym.*, 3.vi.6 ; *in ken of shore*, in sight of land, *Lucrece*, 1114.

KIBE, chilblain, often in the heel, *Lear*, 1.v.8.

KILLEN, old form of infinitive of ' kill ', *Per.*, 2.Prol.20.

KIND, natural, *Lucrece*, 1423 ; human, *Son.*, 10,11 ; *noun*, nature, *Lucrece*, 1147 ; *the worm will do its kind*, the serpent will act according to its nature, *Ant. and Cleo.*, 5.ii.261 ; *in that kind*, in the very manner, *Lear*, 4.vi.162.

KINDLY, *kindly creatures*, the kind of harmless useful creatures supported by the land, *Ant. and Cleo.*, 2.v.78 ; *adv.*, *use thee kindly*, after their nature, *i.e.*, heartlessly, *Lear*, 1.v.14.

KISS, *kissed the jack*, touched the jack at bowls, *Cym.*, 2.i.2.

KITE, foul bird of prey, used of person, *Lear*, 1.iv.262.

KNAP, to rap, hit, *Lear*, 2.iv.121.

KNAVE, young fellow, *Lear*, 1.i.20 ; a servant, *Lear*, 1.iv.42 ; *Ant. and Cleo.*, 5.ii.3.

KNEE, *here's my knee*, that is, he kneels, *Cym.*, 5.v.325 ; *knee-crooking knave*, obsequious fellow, *Oth.*, 1.i.45 ; *verb*, to kneel before, *Lear*, 2.iv.213.

KNIT, to unite, *Per.*, 1.i.11 and 2.iv.58.

KNOT, intertwine, *Oth.*, 4.ii.63.

KNOW, *know of*, learn from, *Lear*, 5.i.1 ; recognize, *Ant. and Cleo.*, 2.vi.71 ; acknowledge, *Cym.*, 5.i.29.

KNOWING, breeding, *Cym.*, 1.iv.26 and 2.iii.97 ; *adj.*, intelligent, *Ant. and Cleo.*, 3.iii.23.

KNOWINGLY, by experience, *Cym.*, 3.iii.46.

KNOWLEDGE, *mine own knowledge*, knowledge of myself, sense of responsibility, *Ant. and Cleo.*, 2.ii.95.

LABEL, a document, *Cym.*, 5.v.430.

LABOUR, pain and distress, *Lov.Comp.*, 239 ; *verb*, to exert oneself, *Lear*, 4.vi.2 ; suffer pangs of childbirth, *Oth.*, 2.i.127 ; *labour'd scholar*, on whom much labour has been bestowed, so highly finished, *Per.*, 2.iii.17.

LABOURSOME, elaborate, so demanding much attention, *Cym.*, 3.iv.163.

LACE, to ornament, *Son.*, 67,4.

LACK, to miss, *Oth.*, 3.iii.322; *Son.*, 31,2; *by being lack'd*, when his absence becomes felt, *Ant. and Cleo.*, 1.iv.44.

LACKEY, to follow in servile fashion, *Ant. and Cleo.*, 1.iv.46.

LADY, mistress, *Lear*, 1.i.65.

LAG, *lag of*, later than, *Lear*, 1.ii.6.

LAME, to make rivals appear lame and imperfect, *Cym.*, 5.v.163.

LANGUISH, lingering disease, *Ant. and Cleo.*, 5.ii.42.

LANK, to become shrunken, *Ant. and Cleo.*, 1.iv.71.

LAP, to wrap, *Cym.*, 5.v.360.

LAPSE, *to lapse in fulness*, to sin or lie when prosperous (and so not constrained by poverty), *Cym.*, 3.vi.12.

LARGE, *largest bounty*, most valuable, *Lear*, 1.i.51; *large speeches*, great in promise and protestation, *Lear*, 1.i.184; *most large in his abominations*, unrestrained in his immoral acts, *Ant. and Cleo.*, 3.vi.94.

LAST, *at the last*, at the very end, *Ant. and Cleo.*, 5.ii.332.

LATCH, to catch, *Lear*, 2.i.52; *Son.*, 113,6.

LATE, recent, *Lear*, 4.v.24; *Cym.*, 3.v.125; *of late*, till a short time ago, *Ant. and Cleo.*, 3.xii.8; adv., recently, *Son.*, 73,4; *late-sack'd*, recently plundered, *Lucrece*, 1740.

LATED, belated, *Ant. and Cleo.*, 3.xi.3.

LATTICE, wrinkles, like lattice-work of window, *Lov.Comp.*, 14.

LAUD, praise, reputation, *Lucrece*, 622; verb, praise, *Cym.*, 5.v.474.

LAUND, glade, *Ven. and Ad.*, 813.

LAW-DAY, a meeting of a court, *Oth.*, 3.iii.144.

LAY, stake, wager, *Oth.*, 2.iii.313; *no lay*, no wager, *Cym.*, 1.iv.142; verb, *laid no words*, pledged no words (mere promises), *Lucrece*, 1351; *Cym.*, 4.ii.234; *and down I laid*, I lay down, *Lov.Comp.*, 4; *lay up*, expend, *Cym.*, 2.iii.87.

LEAD, in invitations to withdraw, so *will you lead* at *Ant. and Cleo.*, 2.vi.81; *Cym.*, 4.iv.53.

LEADEN, sluggish, *Ven. and Ad.*, 34.

LEADING, direction, *Lucrece*, 436.

LEAGUE, friendship, partnership, *Son.*, 47,1.

LEAGU'D, folded, *Ant.*, 4.ii.214; *leagu'd in office*, because of professional loyalty, *Oth.*, 2.iii.210.

LEAN, *a leaner action*, a less important matter, *Ant. and Cleo.*, 2.ii.19.

LEAN, to incline, submit, *Cym.*, 1.i.78; to be on point of collapse, *Cym.*, 1.v.58.

LEARN, to teach, *Oth.*, 1.iii.183; *Cym.*, 1.v.12.

LEARNED, experienced, *Oth.*, 3.iii.263.

LEARNING, instruction, *Cym.*, 1.i.43; information, *Ant. and Cleo.*, 2.ii.51.

LEAST, *in the least*, at the lowest, *Lear*, 1.i.191.

LEAVE, to desist, to drop the subject, *Cym.*, 1.iv.95; leave off, *Cym.*, 2.ii.4; *Ven. and Ad.*, 715.

LECTURES, instruction, *Lucrece*, 618.

LEESE, to lose, *Son.*, 5,14.

LEET, court held by a lord of a manor, *Oth.*, 3.iii.144.

LEIGER, ambassador, representative, agent, *Cym.*, 1.v.80.

LEISURE, *leisures*, times of pleasure, *Lov.Comp.*, 193; *leisurely*, with no promptness, *Lucrece*, 1349.

LEND, to bestow on, *Lear*, 4.iii.54; *Lucrece*, 1399.

LENDINGS, clothes (provided by art not nature), *Lear*, 3.iv.107.

LENGTH, *all length*, any further extension of life, *Ant. and Cleo.*, 4.xiv.46.

LENGTHEN, *lengthening my return*, postponing the date of my return, *Cym.*, 1.vi.200.

LESS (sometimes used in negative or virtual negative expressions where meaning is 'more'), *Cym.*, 1.iv.21.

LET, (i) hindrance, *Lucrece*, 330; verb, to hinder, *Lucrece*, 328; *let their ears hear their faults hid*, prevent their ears hearing their faults, *Per.*, 1.ii.62; (ii) *did not let to praise*, did not forbear to praise, *Lucrece*, 10.

LET-ALONE, *the let-alone*, the prohibition, *Lear*, 5.iii.80.

LETHARGIED, dulled, *Lear*, 1.iv.228.

LETHARGY, unconscious fit, *Oth.*, 4.i.53.

LETHE, the waters of Lethe produced forgetfulness, so wine relieves the mind of care and substitutes a happy oblivion, *Ant. and Cleo.*, 2.vii.106; so *Lethe'd dulness* at *Ant. and Cleo.*, 2.i.27.

LETTER, *I heard no letter*, not a jot, *Cym.*, 4.iii.36; *by letter*, by influence (as in letters of recommendation), *Oth.*, 1.i.36; *the letter of the law*, *Oth.*, 1.iii.68; *the letter of the oracle*, the literal meaning, *Cym.*, 5.v.448; *letters*, learning, *Per.*, 4.Prol.8.

LEVEL, aim, *Son.*, 117,11; *Lov.Comp.*, 309; verb, guess, *Ant. and Cleo.*, 5.ii.333; *levels with her breeding*, to be adequate for one of her station, *Oth.*, 1.iii.239.

LEVY, *levy offence* (as in 'levy war'), to bring together for offensive action, *Per.*, 2.v.51.

LEWD, lustful, *Lucrece*, 392; *Oth.*, 3.iii.479.

LIABLE, subject, exposed to, *Per.*, 4.vi.166.

LIBERAL, adv., freely, *Oth.*, 5.ii.223; adj., licentious, *Oth.*, 2.i.162; full and grateful, *Ant. and Cleo.*, 2.vi.47.

LIBERTIES, royal rights, domains, *Per.*, 1.ii.112.

LICENCE, permission, *Ant. and Cleo.*, 1.ii.105.

LICTORS, officers attending on Roman magistrates, *Ant. and Cleo.*, 5.ii.213.

LIE, lodge, *Oth.*, 3.iv.1; to rest, *Per.*, 3.i.48.

LIEF, *I had as lief*, I should as willingly, *Ant. and Cleo.*, 2.vii.12.

LIEUTENANTRY, *dealt on lieutenantry*, directed but did not participate in the fighting, *Ant. and Cleo.*, 3.xi.39.

LIFE, *the life*, our earthly existence, *Lucrece*, 141; *a life*, an animated being, *Ant. and Cleo.*, 3.iii.20; *the true life on't*, its fidelity to nature, *Cym.*, 2.iv.76; *to the life*, in accordance with the facts, *Per.*, 5.i.244.

LIGHT, *light of ear*, a ready ear for wickedness, *Lear*, 3.iv.91; venial, *Oth.*, 2.iii.240; cheap, *Oth.*, 2.iii.166; frivolous, *Oth.*, 4.i.102; *Ant. and Cleo.*, 1.ii.170; light-headed, *Cym.*, 5.iv.163.

LIGHT, to descend, *Oth.*, 1.iii.178; *you are light into my hands*, you have fallen into my keeping, *Per.*, 4.ii.71.

LIKE, *lads more like to*, lads whom one might have expected to, *Cym.*, 5.iii.19; *adv.*, like in every part, equally, *Son.*, 132,12; *Cym.*, 3.iii.41; *most like*, probably, *Ant. and Cleo.*; 1.i.25; *Cym.*, 5.v.259; *conj.* as, *Per.*, 1.i.164.

LIKE, please, *Lear*, 1.i.200; in ceremonious forms of address, as *so like you, sir*, may you be pleased to see, *Cym.*, 2.iii.54.

LIKELIHOODS, *poor likelihoods of modern seeming*, weak grounds of proof from common misrepresentations, *Oth.*, 1.iii.108; probability, *Oth.*, 4.ii.139.

LIKELY, *likely thoughts*, thoughts about what is indeed probable, *Ven. and Ad.*, 990.

LILY-LIVER'D, cowardly, *Lear*, 2.ii.15.

LIMBECKS, alembics, stills, *Son.*, 119,2.

LIMB-MEAL, limb from limb, *Cym.*, 2.iv.147.

LIMED, to be caught with bird-lime, *Ven. and Ad.*, 88.

LIMIT, region, *Ven. and Ad.*, 235; *Son.*, 44,4.

LIMN, to draw, paint, *Ven. and Ad.*, 290.

LINE, *lines of favour*, the contours of his face, *Cym.*, 4.ii.105; *lines of life*, the features of your living descendants, *Son.*, 16,9.

LINE, *lined their coats*, enriched themselves, *Oth.*, 1.i.53; *Per.*, 4.vi.57.

LINGER, to delay, *Oth.*, 4.ii.224; to postpone, *Son.*, 90,8; *lingering by inches*, operating imperceptibly, *Cym.*, 5.v.51.

LIST, (1) boundary; *in a patient list*, within the limits of self-control, *Oth.*, 4.i.75; *lists*, the area enclosed for combat, *Ven. and Ad.*, 595; *Per.*, 1.i.61; (2) muster-roll, *Ant. and Cleo.*, 3.vi.76.

LIST, (1) inclination, *Oth.*, 2.i.104; *verb*, to desire, *Ven. and Ad.*, 564; *Oth.*, 2.iii.335; (2) to listen, hearken, *Lear*, 5.iii.181.

LITIGIOUS, *a litigious peace*, a precarious peace, *Per.*, 3.iii.3.

LITTLE, *in little*, in miniature *Lov.Comp.*, 90.

LIVELIHOOD, animation, life, *Ven. and Ad.*, 26.

LIVELY, *lively joy*, joy of life, *Ven. and Ad.*, 498; life-like, *Lucrece*, 1593.

LIVER, a live person, *Cym.*, 3.iv.139.

LIVER, the organ associated with passion, love and courage, *Lucrece*, 47.

LIVERY, the uniform of a retainer, *Lucrece*, 1054; *verb*, to dress up, *Lov.Comp.*, 105.

LIVING, lifetime, *Lov.Comp.*, 238; possession, means of livelihood, *Lear*, 1.iv.106.

LOAD, reward, *Cym.*, 1.v.74.

LOATHLY, in abhorrence, *Oth.*, 3.iv.62; *loathly opposite*, utterly opposed, *Lear*, 2.i.49.

LOATHNESS, reluctance, *Ant. and Cleo.*, 3.xi.18; *Cym.*, 1.i.108.

LOCUSTS, suggested perhaps by the biblical diet (Matthew 3,4) of locusts and wild honey; some take it as the fruit of the carob tree, *Oth.*, 1.iii.346.

LODE-STAR, guiding star, *Lucrece*, 179.

LODGING, apartment, *Lear*, 1.ii.159; *Per.*, 2.iii.110; *shameful lodging*, the stocks, *Lear*, 2.ii.167.

LONG, (1) *long she thinks till*, she thinks the time long till, *Lucrece*, 1359; (2) *long of her*, because of her, *Cym.*, 5.v.271.

LONGS, *this longs the text*, belongs to the play, not to Gower, *Per.*, 2.Prol.40.

LONG-ENGRAFFED, firmly embedded, *Lear*, 1.i.296.

LOOF'D, a technical term from sailing, but at *Ant. and Cleo.*, 3.x.18, means moved away from the battle (the term being borrowed from North).

LOOK, *look it be done*, see that it is done, *Oth.*, 4.iii.8; prefixed to *who*, *what*; *when*, etc., to form indefinite relatives, *look what thy memory cannot contain*, whatever you cannot remember, *Son.*, 77,9; search for, *Lear*, 3.iii.14; expect, *Son.*, 22,4.

LOOP, hook, *Oth.*, 3.iii.369.

LOOP'D, full of holes, *Lear*, 3.iv.31.

LOOSE, undisciplined, *Oth.*, 3.iii.420; wanton, *Oth.*, 2.i.237; separate, *Lear*, 5.i.19.

LOOSE-WIVED, married to a wanton, *Ant. and Cleo.*, 1.ii.67.

LOSE, *lose thee nothing*, prove not unprofitable to you, *Lear*, 1.ii.110; *lost me in your liking*, deprived me of, *Lear*, 1.i.233; *loses your sword*, leaves it without a master, *Cym.*, 2.iv.59; *a lost fear*, needless, *Oth.*, 5.ii.272; forgotten, *Ven. and Ad.*, 408.

LOSS, destruction, *Lear*, 3.vi.95; *the heart of loss*, complete ruin, *Ant. and Cleo.*, 4.xii.29.

LOTTERY, prize, *Ant. and Cleo.*, 2.ii.247.

LOUD, emphatic, *Oth.*, 1.i.151.

LOUSE, become lousy, *Lear*, 3.ii.29.

LOVE, *of all loves*, form of entreaty, *Oth.*, 3.i.12.

LOVER'D, *so lover'd*, made love to by such a wooer, *Lov.Comp.*, 320.

Low, base, *Cym.*, 3.v.77; humbler, *Cym.*, 3.iii.85.

Lown, rascal, *Oth.*, 2.iii.85; *lord and lown*, high and low, *Per.*, 4.vi.17.

Lowness, degradation, *Lear*, 3.iv.70; *Ant. and Cleo.*, 3.xi.63.

Lucre, gain, greed of, *Cym.*, 4.ii.325.

Lud's town, London (the name of the mythical king Lud is preserved in Ludgate), *Cym.*, 3.i.32.

Lure, the imitation bird used to lure the falcon back, *Ven. and Ad.*, 1027.

Lust, pleasure, *Lucrece*, 1384.

Lust-breathed, inflamed by lust, *Lucrece*, 3.

Lust-dieted, surfeited, *Lear*, 4.i.68.

Lute, stringed instrument like a guitar, *Per.*, 4.Prol.25.

Luxuriously, lasciviously, *Ant. and Cleo.*, 3.xiii.120.

Luxury, lust, *Lov.Comp.*, 314.

Lym, bloodhound, *Lear*, 3.vi.68.

Magnifico, title given to Venetian grandees, *Oth.*, 1.ii.12.

Mahu, a devil, *Lear*, 3.iv.140.

Main, sea, *Oth.*, 2.i.3; the mainland, *Lear*, 3.i.6; *the main soldier*, the most distinguished, *Ant. and Cleo.*, 1.ii.185.

Mainly, mainly ignorant, absolutely ignorant, *Lear*, 4.vii.65.

Maintain, assert, *Lear*, 1.ii.69.

Make, mate and make, husband and wife, *Lear*, 4.iii.34.

Makeless, *a makeless wife*, a widow, *Son.*, 9,4.

Make, *make good time with*, prove successful against, *Cym.*, 4.ii.109; *makes me*, brings me success, *Oth.*, 5.i.129 and 1.ii.51; *what make you from home?* what business takes you from home? *Oth.*, 3.iv.170; *makes not up*, makes not its choice, *Lear*, 1.i.206; *from your love make such a stray*, wander from the way to your love, *Cym.*, 1.i.209.

Maliciously, without remorse, *Ant. and Cleo.*, 3.xiii.179.

Malign, regard with envy, *Per.*, 5.i.88.

Malignant, evilly-disposed, *Oth.*, 5.ii.356.

Malkin, kitchen-wench, *Per.*, 4.iii.34.

Mammering, hesitating, *Oth.*, 3.iii.71.

Man, *man but a rush against*, direct, manage (as a weapon) a bulrush against, *Oth.*, 5.ii.273.

Manage, training and handling of horses, *Lov.Comp.*, 112; direction, *Per.*, 4.vi.63; *verb*, exercise, *Lear*, 1.iii.18; conduct, carry on, *Oth.*, 2.iii.207.

Mandragora, mandrake, a narcotic was made from the plant, *Oth.*, 3.iii.334; *Ant. and Cleo.*, 1.v.4.

Manifest, show plainly, *Oth.*, 1.ii.32.

Manner'd, educated in deportment, *Per.*, 3.iii.17.

Mantle, scum, *Lear*, 3.iv.131.

Many, *many our contriving friends*, many friends plotting on our behalf, *Ant. and Cleo.*, 1.ii.176; *many looks*, the looks of many, *Son.*, 93,7.

Map, *the map of death*, the image of death, suggested by the sleeping figure, *Lucrece*, 402; *Son.*, 58,1.

Marble, *marble heaven*, bright and variegated like marble (or eternal), *Oth.*, 3.iii.464; *marble-hearted*, hard hearted, *Lear*, 1.iv.251; *marble-constant*, firm of purpose, *Ant. and Cleo.*, 5.ii.239.

Margent, bank of river, *Lov.Comp.*, 39; margin of book in which commentary on the text stood, *Lucrece*, 102.

Mark, *God bless the mark!* sometimes used to avert evil omen when the topic was unhappy, sometimes scornfully as at *Oth.*, 1.i.33; *beyond the mark of*, beyond the reach of, *Ant. and Cleo.*, 3.vi.87; sea-mark, beacon, *Son.*, 116,5; notice, *Oth.*, 2.iii.307.

Marry, from Mary, in asseverations, to express surprise, etc.; indeed, to be sure, *Cym.*, 1.i.76; scornfully, at *Lear*, 4.ii.68.

Mart, to traffic, *Cym.*, 1.vi.150; *noun*, market-gathering, *Per.*, 4.ii.21.

Martial, *Martial thigh*, like that of Mars, the god of war, *Cym.*, 4.ii.311.

Martyr, to disfigure, *Lucrece*, 802.

Marvel, astonishment, *Cym.*, 3.i.10.

Mary-buds, buds of marigold, *Cym.*, 2.iii.23.

Master, *adj.*, same as 'main' in *master and main*, *Oth.*, 2.i.257; *Per.*, 4.vi.8; *verb*, to own, *Lucrece*, 863; *Son.*, 106,8.

Match, wager, *Cym.*, 1.iv.140; bargain, *Cym.*, 3.vi.30; *verb*, to meet in combat, *Cym.*, 2.i.21.

Mate, to baffle, *Ven. and Ad.*, 909.

Material, important, *Cym.*, 1.vi.206; *material sap*, the sap that provides the growth and substance, *Lear*, 4.ii.35.

Matter, sense, *matter and impertinency mix'd*, *Lear*, 4.vi.175; *matter in't*, the business is serious, *Oth.*, 3.iv.140.

Maugre, in spite of, *Lear*, 5.iii.131.

Maund, wicker basket, *Lov.Comp.*, 36.

Mazard, head, *Oth.*, 2.iii.146.

Mean, *this mean*, this that stands between us as a link, *Ant. and Cleo.*, 3.ii.32; opportunity, *Oth.*, 3.i.36; *what means do you make?* what efforts do you make to placate the king? *Cym.*, 2.iv.3; instrument, device, *Ant. and Cleo.*, 4.vi.3.

Measure, *not my measure*, do not fill my capacity, or satisfy my sense of glory, *Son.*, 91,7; glass, health, *Oth.*, 2.iii.28; dance, *Ven. and Ad.*, 1148; *verb*, *measure your lubber's length*, lie stretched on the ground, *Lear*, 1.iv.89; compare, judge, *Ven. and Ad.*, 524.

Mechanic, engaged in manual work, *Ant. and Cleo.*, 5.ii.208; vulgar, *Ant. and Cleo.*, 4.iv.32.

Mediator, one who pleads for another, *Lucrece*, 1020; *Oth.*, 1.i.16.

Med'cinable, healing, *Oth.*, 5.ii.354; having a medicinal effect (figuratively), *Cym.*, 3.ii.33.

GLOSSARY

MEDICINE, poison, *Lear*, 5.iii.97; slander (as if a poison), *Oth.*, 4.i.45; love-philtre, *Oth.*, 1.iii.61; *that great medicine*, the elixir of the alchemist that would turn common objects to gold, *Ant. and Cleo.*, 1.v.36; *verb*, to restore, *Oth.*, 3.iii.336; cure, *Cym.*, 4.ii.244.

MEED, reward, *Ven. and Ad.*, 15; *Cym.*, 2.v.162.

MEEK, without spirit, *Lucrece*, 710.

MEETLY, not bad, *Ant. and Cleo.*, 1.iii.81.

MEETNESS, fitness, *Son.*, 118,7.

MEINY, household retainers, *Lear*, 2.iv.34.

MELTING, *the melting mood*, tearfulness, *Oth.*, 5.ii.352.

MEMBER, *a member of his love*, a person loved by him, *Oth.*, 3.iv.113.

MEMORIES, reminders, *Lear*, 4.vii.7; *memory of my womb*, children, *Ant. and Cleo.*, 3.xiii.163.

MEND, to make more valuable, to atone for its imperfection, *Ant. and Cleo.*, 1.v.45; to put right again, *Oth.*, 2.iii.292; adjust, *Ant. and Cleo.*, 5.ii.316; *people such that mend upon the world*, grow better with time, *Cym.*, 2.iv.26; *Heaven mend all!* expression of pious resignation, *Cym.*, 5.v.68.

MERCURIAL, *his foot Mercurial*, swift, like that of Mercury, the messenger of the Gods, *Cym.*, 4.ii.311.

MERCY, *cry you mercy*, jocular apology, *Lear*, 3.vi.51; *in mercy*, at his mercy, *Lear*, 1.iv.328.

MERE, *mere perdition*, complete destruction, *Oth.*, 2.ii.3; *Cym.*, 4.ii.93; *your pleasure was my mere offence*, my only offence was your caprice, *Cym.*, 5.v.334; *mere fetches*, nothing but pretexts, *Lear*, 2.iv.87; *merely*, completely, *Ant. and Cleo.*, 3.vii.8.

MERED, *he being the mered question*, he alone being on trial (not Cleopatra), *Ant. and Cleo.*, 3.xiii.10.

MERIT, *others' merits*, others' deservings, good or bad, *Ant. and Cleo.*, 5.ii.177; *a provoking merit*, a lack of merit prompting hostile reaction, *Lear*, 3.v.6; *for the sake of merit*, because of my faithful service, *Ant. and Cleo.*, 2.vii.54.

MESS, *makes his generation messes*, makes his children his food, *Lear*, 1.i.116; portions, as if of food, *Oth.*, 4.i.196.

METTLE, spirit, *Lov.Comp.*, 107; *Oth.*, 4.ii.204.

METRE, *stretched metre*, the bombastic verse, *Son.*, 17,12.

MIGHT, validity, *Son.*, 65,13; power, *Son.*, 90,12.

MILD, *her mild companion*, companion of her mildness, serenity, *Per.*, 1.i.18; serene, *Per.*, 3.i.27.

MILK-LIVER'D, cowardly, without spirit, *Lear*, 4.ii.50.

MILKY, ineffective, soft-hearted, *Lear*, iv.342.

MILLION'D, *million'd accidents*, innumerable, *Son.*, 115,5.

MINCE, make light of, *Oth.*, 2.iii.239; *Ant. and Cleo.*, 1.ii.102; *minces virtue*, to pose as virtuous in affected manner, *Lear*, 4.vi.120.

MIND, *unknown minds*, persons not only unknown to his friend but of a different social or intellectual standing, *Son.*, 117,5.

MIND, *not minding*, not caring, *Per.*, 2.v.20; *minded*, inclined, *Lear*, 3.i.2.

MINERAL, love-philtre, *Oth.*, 1.ii.74; poison, *Oth.*, 2.i.291; *Cym.*, 5.v.50.

MINGLE, mixture, *Ant. and Cleo.*, 1.v.59; *verb*, *mingle eyes*, exchange friendly and knowing looks, *Ant. and Cleo.*, 3.xiii.156; to subscribe together, *Cym.*, 1.vi.185.

MINIKIN, *thy minikin mouth*, delicate, youthful, *Lear*, 3.vi.43.

MINION, shameless woman, *Oth.*, 5.i.33.

MINISTER, agent of vengeance, *Ant. and Cleo.*, 3.vi.88; servant, *Oth.*, 5.ii.8; *verb*, serve, *Cym.*, 3.iii.76; impart, *Cym.*, 1.i.45; administer (of a drug), *Per.*, 3.ii.8.

MINORITY, *from world's minority their right*, from earliest times, so a title or right of long-standing, *Lucrece*, 67.

MIRACLE, *doth miracle itself*, be incomprehensible, *Cym.*, 4.ii.29.

MIRTH, a jest, *Ant. and Cleo.*, 1.iv.18.

MISCARRY, to come to harm, *Lear*, 5.i.5.

MISCHIEF, misfortune, *Oth.*, 1.iii.204; harm, *Lear*, 1.ii.155.

MISDOUBT, mistrust, *Ant. and Cleo.*, 3.vii.62.

MISDREAD, fear of evil, *Per.*, 1.ii.12.

MISERY, *noble misery*, shameful state for one of rank, *Cym.*, 5.iii.64.

MISGIVE, to have suspicions, *Oth.*, 3.iv.90.

MISPRISION, misunderstanding, *Son.*, 87,11.

MISS, offence, *Ven. and Ad.*, 53.

MISSIVE, messenger, *Ant. and Cleo.*, 2.ii.78.

MISTAKE, *mistake their scent*, go on false scent, *Ven. and Ad.*, 686; to err, *Lucrece*, 1826; *thy place mistook*, failed to honour your office as king's messenger, *Lear*, 2.iv.11; misunderstand, misrepresent, *Ant. and Cleo.*, 2.ii.49.

MISTHOUGHT, are thought ill of, *Ant. and Cleo.*, 5.ii.175.

MISTRUST, *fond mistrust*, doubt mingled with folly of desire, *Lucrece*, 284.

MISTRUSTFUL, *mistrustful wood*, a wood inspiring doubts and fear, *Ven. and Ad.*, 826.

MISUSE, to misrepresent, *Son.*, 152,7.

MOE, *a million moe*, a million more, *Ant. and Cleo.*, 4.xiv.18.

MOAN, *fore-bemoaned moan*, grief already the subject of lamentation, *Son.*, 30,11; *finished joy and moan*, joy and sorrow, *Per.*, 4.iii.274.

MOCK, *he mocks the pauses that he makes*, his delay in surrendering is ridiculous,

Ant. and Cleo., 5.i.2 ; to cheat, *Cym.*, 4.ii.64.

MODERN, *likelihoods of modern seeming*, grounds of probability that are no more than everyday happenings without significance, *Oth.*, 1.iii.108 ; *modern friends*, mere acquaintances, *Ant. and Cleo.*, 5.ii.166.

MODEST, *the modest truth*, the very opposite of exaggeration, *Lear*, 4.vii.5 ; *modest haste*, briefly, yet keeping to the facts, *Lear*, 2.iv.24.

MOIETY, *a moiety of the world*, half the world, *Ant. and Cleo.*, 5.i.19 ; share, *Lear*, 1.i.6.

MOLESTATION, turmoil, *Oth.*, 2.i.16.

MOMENT, *upon the moment*, instantly, at first sight, *Lov.Comp.*, 248 ; *upon far poorer moment*, for a much less important cause, *Ant. and Cleo.*, 1.ii.138.

MONSTER, *that monsters it*, that makes it seem so unnatural and huge, *Lear*, 1.i.220.

MONSTROUS, unnatural, *Per.*, 5.iii.8.

MONUMENT, Cleopatra's tomb, *Ant. and Cleo.*, 4.xiii.3 ; *Per.*, 4.iii.42 ; effigy, *Cym.*, 2.ii.3.

MONUMENTAL, *monumental alabaster*, alabaster being favourite material for effigies on tomb, *Oth.*, 5.ii.5.

MOOD, anger, displeasure, *Oth.*, 2.iii.265 ; *the encrimson'd mood*, rubies, *Lov.Comp.*, 201.

MOON, *till now some nine moons wasted*, until some nine months ago, *Oth.*, 1.iii.84.

MOONSHINE, *twelve or fourteen moonshines lag of a brother*, twelve or so months younger than my brother, *Lear*, 1.ii.5 ; *a sop o' the moonshine*, let the moonshine into him with his sword, *Lear*, 2.ii.29.

MOP, grimace, *mopping and mowing*, making faces, like the waiting-women moved by the devil Flibbertigibbet, *Lear*, 4.i.62.

MORAL, *a moral fool*, a moralizing fool, *Lear*, 4.ii.58.

MORALER, one who expounds moral principles, *Oth.*, 2.iii.289.

MORALIZE, *moralize his wanton sight*, realize the meaning of his lascivious looks, *Lucrece*, 104.

MORTAL, *mortal rage*, decay, death, *Son.*, 64,4 ; *more than a mortal seeming*, more than the air of a mere human being, *Cym.*, 1.vi.170.

MORTALITY, death, *Lear*, 4.vi.133 ; *in life's mortality*, in life itself, *Lucrece*, 403 ; *the shores of my mortality*, the bounds of my life, *Per.*, 5.i.192.

MORTALLY, *mortally brought forth*, of human parents, *Per.*, 5.i.103 ; in deadly fashion, *Per.*, 3.iii.6.

MORTIFY, to numb, to render insensible, *Lear*, 2.iii.15.

MORTISE, *hold the mortise*, hold together at the joints, *Oth.*, 2.i.9.

MOT, motto, device, *Lucrece*, 830.

MOTH, a parasite, *Oth.*, 1.iii.256.

MOTHER, hysteria, *Lear*, 2.iv.55 ; *whose mother was her painting*, a creature of rouge and paint, *Cym.*, 3.iv.48.

MOTION, the action of the virginal, *Son.*, 128,2 ; *Cym.*, 4.ii.189 ; desire, *Oth.*, 1.iii.330 ; sense, intelligence, *Oth.*, 1.ii.75 ; mental sight, intuition, *Ant. and Cleo.*, 2.iii.14 ; *the heavy motion*, the sad spectacle, *Lucrece*, 1326.

MOTIVE, the cause, *Ant. and Cleo.*, 2.ii.100 ; *Oth.*, 4.ii.44.

MOTLEY, the long coat worn by professional fools, woven of green and yellow threads, *Lear*, 1.iv.145 ; *made myself a motley to the view*, played the fool in public, wrote for and acted on the stage, *Son.*, 110,2.

MOULD, pattern, *Ven. and Ad.*, 730.

MOUTH, of the barking of dogs, *Ven. and Ad.*, 695 ; *mouths of wisest censure*, the judgements of the wise, *Oth.*, 2.iii.185 ; *mouth-made vows*, promise without performance, *Ant. and Cleo.*, 1.iii.30 ; *mouthed*, gaping, *Son.*, 77,6.

MOVE, *moved*, angered, *Ven. and Ad.*, 623 ; *moved my lord*, made representations to my lord, *Oth.*, 3.iv.17 ; *move your suit*, plead your case, *Oth.*, 3.iv.167 ; *moving accidents*, exciting events, *Oth.*, 1.iii.135.

MOVER, cause, *Cym.*, 1.v.9 ; active creature, *Ven. and Ad.*, 368.

MOW, a grimace, *Cym.*, 1.vi.40 ; verb, to make faces, *Lear*, 4.i.62.

MUCH, *'tis much to*, it is a serious matter to, *Ven. and Ad.*, 411 ; *'tis very much*, serious indeed, *Oth.*, 4.i.239 ; very, *Oth.*, 1.i.1.

MUMMY, a preparation from dead bodies for magical purposes, *Oth.*, 3.iv.74.

MUSIC, company of musicians, *Cym.*, 2.iii.11.

MUSIT, opening in hedge or thicket through which hare regularly passes, *Ven. and Ad.*, 683.

MUSS, a scramble for articles thrown to a group, *Ant. and Cleo.*, 3.xiii.91.

MUTATION, change, *Lear*, 4.i.11 ; capricious change, *Cym.*, 4.ii.134.

MUTE, dumb servant, *Cym.*, 3.v.153.

MUTINY, contention, *Ven. and Ad.*, 426 ; verb, to break into strife, *Oth.*, 2.i.269 ; quarrel, *Ant. and Cleo.*, 3.xi.13.

MUTUAL, *mutual cunning*, cunning on both sides, each deceiving the other, *Lear*, 3.i.21 ; *a mutual pair*, united in feeling, each an echo to other's love, *Ant. and Cleo.*, 1.i.37 ; common, *Ven. and Ad.*, 1018.

MUTUALITIES, exchange of intimacies between pair, *Oth.*, 2.i.256.

MYSTERY, trade, *Oth.*, 4.ii.30 ; *the mysteries of Hecat*, the secret rites of the queen of Hades, and goddess of magic, *Lear*, 1.i.109.

NAG, *ribaudred nag*, lewd jade, *Ant. and Cleo.*, 3.x.10.

NAKED, unarmed, *Oth.*, 5.ii.261 ; *her*

naked bed, sleeping naked, as was the custom, in bed, *Ven. and Ad.*, 397.

NAME, character, *Lucrece*, 820; honourable reputation, *Cym.*, 1.iv.3.

NAPKIN, handkerchief, *Oth.*, 3.iii.291; *Lov.Comp.*, 15.

NAPLES, associated at the time with venereal disease, *Oth.*, 3.i.4.

NARCISSUS, destroyed by self-love, *Ven. and Ad.*, 161; used as a type of beauty, *Ant. and Cleo.*, 2.v.96.

NARROW, *narrow measure*, grudging praise, *Ant. and Cleo.*, 3.iv.8; *narrowly*, thoroughly, *Per.*, 4.i.3.

NATIVE, natural, normal, *Oth.*, 2.i.214; characteristic of my true nature, *Oth.*, 1.i.63.

NATIVITY, birth, with reference to the circumstances, planetary, etc., affecting the child's destiny, *Lear*, 1.ii.124; *Per.*, 3.i.32.

NATURAL, *natural father*, real father, *Cym.*, 3.iii.107; *natural boy*, though illegitimate he seems to behave like a true son, *Lear*, 2.i.84; not artificial, *Per.*, 5.Prol.7.

NATURE, *the wisdom of nature*, scientific explanation, *Lear*, 1.ii.100; *falls from the bias of nature*, acts contrary to humane feeling, *Lear*, 1.ii.107; *where nature doth with merit challenge*, where the claim of merit is added to that of nature (she being his child), *Lear*, 1.i.52.

NAUGHT, ruin, *Ant. and Cleo.*, 3.x.1; worthless, wicked, *Lear*, 2.iv.132.

NAUGHTY, wicked, *Lear*, 3.vii.36; bad, *Lear*, 3.iv.109.

NE, nor, *Per.*, 2.Prol.36.

NEAR, *so near*, as in my honour as a soldier, that being nearest my heart, *Oth.*, 2.iii.212.

NEARLY, with certain reserves, *Ant. and Cleo.*, 2.ii.95; intimately, *Lear*, 1.i.284.

NEAT, *you neat slave*, you dandified rascal, *Lear*, 2.ii.37.

NEAT-HERD, cowherd, *Cym.*, 1.i.149.

NECESSARY, inevitable, *Son.*, 108,11.

NECESSITY, poverty, *Lear*, 2.iv.210; *the art of our necessities is strange*, our poverty and distress have a strange power of making precious what seems common to the well-off, *Lear*, 3.ii.70.

NECK, *one on another's neck*, one immediately after the other, *Son.*, 31,11; *on your neck*, to your charge, *Oth.*, 5.ii.173.

NEEDS, *what needs this iterance?* what necessity is there for this repetition? *Oth.*, 5.ii.153; *Ant. and Cleo.*, 2.vii.123.

NEEDY, *your needy bread*, the bread necessary for your sustenance, *Per.*, 1.iv.95.

NEGLECTION, neglect, *Per.*, 3.iii.20.

NEGLIGENT, *and we in negligent danger*, in danger if we neglected to take action, *Ant. and Cleo.*, 3.vi.81.

NEIGHBOUR'D, friendly and familiar, *Lear*, 1.i.118.

NEPHEW, grandson, *Oth.*, 1.i.113.

NEPTUNE, god of the sea, so often the sea itself; *the mask'd Neptune*, calm seas, *Per.*, 3.iii.36.

NEREIDES, daughters of Nereus, sea-nymphs, fifty in number, *Ant. and Cleo.*, 2.ii.210.

NERVE, sinew, *Ant. and Cleo.*, 4.viii.21; *Cym.*, 3.iii.94.

NESSUS, the centaur killed by Hercules; a shirt dipped in the centaur's blood, given to the hero's wife Deianira as a love-charm and given by her in good faith to retain her husband's love, that burnt into the flesh of Hercules and drove him to death, *Ant. and Cleo.*, 4.xii.43.

NETHER, *nether crimes*, done here below, *Lear*, 4.ii.79.

NEW, *adv.*, so as to restore to former state, *Son.*, 15,14; *shall make your lord that which he is new o'er*, shall now go back from my false description to give a true account of him as he is, *Cym.*, 1.vi.164.

NICE, *mine hours were nice and lucky*, so permitting the gratification of caprice, *Ant. and Cleo.*, 3.xiii.180; *nice affections*, delicately poised admiration and love, *Lov.Comp.*, 97; *the painter was so nice*, skilful, *Lucrece*, 1412; *nice longings*, capricious, discontented, *Cym.*, 2.v.26; *nice and waterish diet*, unsubstantial, *Oth.*, 3.iii.15.

NICELY, gracefully, *Cym.*, 2.iv.90; punctiliously, *Lear*, 2.ii.99 and 5.iii.144.

NICENESS, demure, reserved, *Cym.*, 3.iv.154.

NICK, *in the nick*, at the critical moment, *Oth.*, 5.ii.320.

NIGGARD, to hoard, to grudge to spend, *Son.*, 1,12.

NIGHT-BIRD, nightingale, *Per.*, 4.Prol.26.

NIGHTED, *his nighted life*, darkened by blindness and misery, *Lear*, 4.v.13.

NIGHT-GOWN, dressing-gown, *Oth.*, 4.iii.33.

NIGHTLY, *the nightly linen*, used by night, *Lucrece*, 680.

NILL, will not, *Per.*, 3.Prol.55.

NINE-FOLD, the nine foals that go with the night-mare, *Lear*, 3.iv.119.

NIP, to grip the attention, *Per.*, 5.i.232.

NOBLENESS, high rank, aristocratic birth, *Per.*, 3.ii.28; *nobly base*, low character in man of high rank, *Lucrece*, 660.

NOISE, music, *Ant. and Cleo.*, 4.iii.12; verb, *noises it against us*, raises disturbance against us, *Ant. and Cleo.*, 3.vi.96.

NONE, *none our parts*, none of our features, *Ant. and Cleo.*, 1.iii.36.

NONPAREIL, one with no equal, *Ant. and Cleo.*, 3.ii.11; *Cym.*, 2.v.8.

NONSUIT, to dismiss, *Oth.*, 1.i.16.

NORTH, *the north*, the north wind, *Oth.*, 5.ii.223.

NOT, not only, *Per.*, 3.ii.46.

NOTARY, clerk authorized to record contracts, etc., *Lucrece*, 765.

NOTE, mark, *Cym.*, 2.ii.28; stigma, *Lucrece*, 208 character, reputation,

Lov.Comp., 233 ; *make better note*, observe more accurately, *Ant. and Cleo.*, 3.iii.23 ; *warrant of my note*, my confidence that comes from my knowledge of you, *Lear*, 3.i.18 ; *even to the note o' the king*, so that the king shall have knowledge of it, *Cym.*, 4.iii.44.

NOTHING-GIFT, worthless gift, *Cym.*, 3.vi.85.

NOTICE, information, *Oth.*, 3.iii.154.

NOTION, understanding, *Lear*, 1.iv.227.

NOUZLE, rear, *Per.*, 1.iv.42.

NUMBER, to put into verse, *Ant. and Cleo.*, 3.ii.17.

NUNCLE, from 'mine uncle'; customary address of a fool to his master, *Lear*, 1.iv.116.

NURSERY, care, *Lear*, 1.i.123.

O, *an O without a figure*, nothing, *Lear*, 1.iv.191 ; the earth, *Ant. and Cleo.*, 5.ii.81.

O', for *on* or *of*.

OBJECT, *object to the tell-tale Day*, something visible, *Lucrece*, 806 ; *her object*, her beloved, *Ven. and Ad.*, 255 ; what the mind is directed at, *Oth.*, 3.iv.146 ; *Lear*, 1.i.214.

OBLOQUY, ill-report, *Lucrece*, 523.

OBSCURE, *obscure prologue*, indicating the sequel, though not explicitly, *Oth.*, 2.i.252 ; verb, *obscured course*, disguised, *Lear*, 2.ii.163.

OBSEQUIOUS, dutiful, *Son.*, 125,9 ; *obsequious bondage*, used cynically by Iago who regards dutiful service as folly, *Oth.*, 1.i.46 ; proper respect for the dead, *Son.*, 31,5.

OBSEQUY, funeral ceremony, *Phoenix*, 12.

OBSERVANCE, perception, *Ant. and Cleo.*, 3.ii:.22 ; truthful rendering, *Lucrece*, 1385.

OBSERVANCY, care and attention, *Oth.*, 3.iv.150.

OBSERVANT, flunkey, *Lear*, 2.ii.98.

OBSERVATION, experience, *Lear*, 1.i.289.

OBSTRUCT, hindrance, *Ant. and Cleo.*, 3.vi.61.

OCCASION, *occasions*, needs, *Cym.*, 5.v.87 ; *he married but his occasion*, for political convenience, *Ant. and Cleo.*, 2.vi.127 ; cause, circumstance, *Lear*, 2.i.120.

OCCUPATION, *royal occupation*, soldiering, *Ant. and Cleo.*, 4.iv.17.

OD, used in oaths for God ; *Od's pittikins*, God's pity, *Cym.*, 4.iv.17.

ODD, *odd action*, gestures in which two emotions were at strife, *Lucrece*, 1433.

ODD-EVEN, of night, between midnight and one, but perhaps later, *Oth.*, 1.i.124.

ODDS, *'gainst the odds*, contrary to expectation, *Ant. and Cleo.*, 2.iii.28 ; the probability, *Cym.*, 5.iii.9 ; contention, *Oth.*, 2.iii.177.

OEILLADES, amorous looks, *Lear*, 4.v.25.

O'ERGREEN, to put a good interpretation on, *Son.*, 112,4.

O'ERGROWN, advanced in years, *Cym.*, 4.iv.33.

O'ERSKIP, disregard, *Lear*, 3.vi.106.

O'ERSWAY, to prevail over, *Son.*, 65.2.

OFFENCE, injury, *Oth.*, 2.iii.214 ; displeasure, *Ant. and Cleo.*, 3.i.26 ; *Cym.*, 1.iv.107 ; *the slow offence*, the displeasing slowness, *Son.*, 51,1.

OFFEND, to afflict, *Oth.*, 3.iv.48 ; *Cym.*, 5.iv.94 ; to wrong, *Oth.*, 5.ii.62 ; *offended reputation*, wounded my honour, *Ant. and Cleo.* 3.xi.49 ; *offended in*, displeased by, *Ant. and Cleo.*, 3.ii.33.

OFFICE, function, *Son.*, 101,13 ; *Lucrece* 936 ; *the office and devotion*, devoted attention, *Ant. and Cleo.*, 1.i.5 ; *office of my heart*, devotion, *Oth.*, 3.iv.114 ; *all offices are open*, buttery, kitchen, etc., where feasting was possible, *Oth.*, 2.ii.8.

OFFIC'D, having special function or duty ; *my speculative and offic'd instruments*, eyes, mental as well as of body, *Oth.*, 1.iii.270.

OFFICER, agent, *Per.*, 5.iii.63 ; hangman, *Cym.*, 5.iv.174.

OFT, frequent, *Son.*, 14,8.

'OLD, wold, moor land, *Lear*, 3.iv.118.

OLD, *my old excuse*, apology for my old age, *Son.*, 2,11 ; *old course*, his aged steps, *Lear*, 1.i.187 ; *old course of death*, customary, *Lear*, 3.vii.100 ; as expression of loving familiarity, *old Nile*, *Ant. and Cleo.*, 1.v.25 ; adv., in olden days, *Per.*, 1.Prol.1.

OMIT, forgo, *Oth.*, 2.i.71.

ON, sometimes used for *of*, *Cym.*, 4.ii.199.

ONCE, once for all, *Oth.*, 3.iii.184 ; at any time, *Ant. and Cleo.*, 5.ii.50.

ONE-TRUNK-INHERITING, possessing no more than the goods that would fill only a chest, *Lear*, 2.ii.17.

OPEN, *the open night*, night in the open, out of doors, *Lear*, 3.iv.2 ; *open banner*, their allegiance openly declared, *Lear*, 3.i.34 ; generous, unsuspecting, *Oth.*, 1.iii.393 ; verb, *in opening it*, in revealing it, *Cym.*, 5.v.42 ; *Per.*, 4.iii.23.

OPERATION, effect, potency, *Ant. and Cleo.*, 4.xv.26.

OPERATIVE, effective, *Lear*, 4.iv.14.

OPINION, self-confidence, *Ant. and Cleo.*, 2.i.36 ; unfavourable judgement, *Oth.*, 4.ii.110.

OPPOSE, *oppos'd against*, exposed to, *Lear*, 4.vii.32 ; *oppose the bolt against*, to bar the door against, *Lear*, 2.iv.175.

OPPOSITE, enemy, *Lear*, 5.iii.43 ; adj., opposed to, *Oth.*, 1.ii.67.

OPPOSITION, *single oppositions*, duels, single combats, *Cym.*, 4.i.13.

OPPRESS, to suppress, *Per.*, 3.Prol.29 ; distress, *Lear*, 5.iii.5.

OPPRESSION, distress of body or mind, *Son.*, 28,3.

OR, before, *Cym.*, 2.iv.14.

ORB, sphere, *Ant. and Cleo.*, 3.xiii.146 ; *Cym.*, 5.v.371 ; sphere of action, *Per.*, 1.ii.122 ; the earth, *Ant. and Cleo.*, 5.ii.85 ; *operation of the orbs*, influence of the planets, *Lear*, 1.i.110 ; adj., spherical, *Lov.Comp.*, 25.

548

ORDAIN, institute, *Cym.*, 3.i.54.

ORDER, *order of law*, in a legitimate way, *Lear*, 1.i.18; due ceremony, *Ant. and Cleo.*, 5.ii.363; *take order for*, arrange for, *Oth.*, 5.ii.76; *verb, more order'd than when*, more disciplined than when, *Cym.*, 2.iv.21.

ORDINANCE, *that slaves your ordinance*, who converts to his own selfish desires the mercies God provides for man, *Lear*, 4.i.69; the dispensation of the gods, *Cym.*, 4.ii.146.

ORDINARY, meal to be had at a recognized price in a tavern or inn; applied ironically at *Ant. and Cleo.*, 2.ii.229.

ORIENT, *orient pearl*, as the finest pearls came from the East, Ceylon, etc., *Ant. and Cleo.*, 1.v.41; so of tears, *Ven. and Ad.*, 981.

ORISON, prayer, *Cym.*, 1.iii.32.

ORT, fragment left over, *Lucrece*, 985.

OSTENT, display, *Per.*, 1.ii.25.

OSTENTATION, manifestation, *Ant. and Cleo.*, 3.vi.52.

OTHER, sometimes used as plural, *Lear*, i.iv.200; *Cym.*, 4.ii.180; *adv.*, otherwise, *Oth.*, 4.ii.13.

OTTOMITE, Turk, *Oth.*, 1.iii.33.

OUT, abroad, on service, *Lear*, 1.i.31; out of favour, office, *Lear*, 5.iii.15; *out at heels*, signifies state of penury, ill-fortune, *Lear*, 2.ii.152.

OUT-BRAG, to surpass in appearance, *Lov.Comp.*, 95.

OUTBRAVE, to surpass in beauty, *Son.*, 94,12.

OUT-CRAFTY, to defeat by guile, treachery, *Cym.*, 3.iv.15.

OUTFACE, to defy, *Lear*, 2.iii.11.

OUT-GO, out-run, exhaust, *Ant. and Cleo.*, 3.ii.61.

OUT-PARAMOUR, *out-paramour'd the Turk*, more mistresses than the Turk wives and concubines, *Lear*, 3.iv.90.

OUT-PEER, to surpass, *Cym.*, 3.vi.86.

OUTSTAND, overstay, *Cym.*, 1.vi.206.

OUTSTRIKE, strike more forcibly than, *Ant. and Cleo.*, 4.vi.36.

OUT-SWEETEN, to surpass in fragrance, *Cym.*, 4.ii.225.

OUT-WALL, exterior, *Lear*, 3.i.45.

OVERBUY, outweigh in worth, *Cym.*, 1.i.146.

OVERSEE, to supervise the execution of a will, *Lucrece*, 1205; *overseen*, betrayed, *Lucrece*, 1206.

OVERSHOT, to escape, *Ven. and Ad.*, 680.

OVERSLIP, pass unobserved, *Lucrece*, 1576.

OVERT, objective, verifiable, *Oth.*, 1.iii.107.

OVERTURE, disclosure, *Lear*, 3.vii.88.

OWE, to possess, own, *Lucrece*, 1803; *Oth.*, 1.i.67; *Lov.Comp.*, 327.

PACE, control, as in horsemanship, *Ant. and Cleo.*, 2.ii.68; to train, *Per.*, 4.vi.62.

PACK, a gang, conspiring to some end, *Lear*, 5.iii.18.

PACKING, plotting, *Lear*, 3.i.26.

PAGEANT, (the wagon on which a scene in the Miracle plays was staged at the various stations appointed for performance), so of show of spectacle, sometimes with idea of unreality or deception, *Ant. and Cleo.*, 4.xiv.8; *Oth.*, 1.iii.18.

PAIN, punishment, *Son.*, 141,14; toil, *Cym.*, 3.iii.50.

PAINFUL, *the painful warrior*, undergoing toil, *Son.*, 25,9; *by many a painful perch*, laborious journey (see ' perch '), *Per.*, 3.Prol.15.

PAINTED, *a painted beauty*, imitation of beauty, false, *Son.*, 21,2; *painted cloth*, canvas hangings painted with figures and moral sentences were a cheap substitute for figured tapestries, *Lucrece*, 245.

PALATE, to taste, *Ant. and Cleo.*, 5.ii.7.

PALE, an enclosure, a fenced park, *Ven. and Ad.*, 230; *verb*, to enclose, *Ant. and Cleo.*, 2.vii.67; *Cym.*, 3.i.19.

PALL, *pall'd fortunes*, drooping fortunes, *Ant. and Cleo.*, 2.vii.81.

PALTER, to dodge, cheat, *Ant. and Cleo.*, 3.xi.63.

PANG, *pang'd by*, tormented by, *Cym.*, 3.iv.94.

PARADOX, *old fond paradoxes*, views contrary to received opinion, inspired by drink rather than wisdom, *Oth.*, 2.i.138.

PARAGON, to compare with an ideal, *Ant. and Cleo.*, 1.v.71; to provide a model for, *Oth.*, 2.i.62.

PARALLEL, *the parallels*, furrows on brow, like trenches in siege, *Son.*, 60,10; *adj.*, running in the same direction, *Oth.*, 2.iii.338.

PARCEL, *distract parcels*, individual items, *Lov.Comp.*, 231; *Oth.*, 1.iii.154; *a parcel of their fortunes*, merely a part of their fortunes, *Ant. and Cleo.*, 3.xiii.32; *verb*, to add to the items, *Ant. and Cleo.*, 5.ii.162.

PARDON, permission, *Ant. and Cleo.*, 3.vi.60; *verb, pardon that man's life*, remit the death-penalty, *Lear*, 4.vi.109.

PAREL, apparel, *Lear*, 4.i.50.

PARLE, *parling looks*, glances that spoke his mind, *Lucrece*, 100.

PARLEY, *sound a parley*, to give sign of willingness to come together, *Oth.*, 2.iii.22.

PART, *parts*, features, natural endowments, *Lov.Comp.*, 260; *entitled in thy parts do crowned sit*, a play on *parts* as a man's gifts and graces and the places on a shield on which armorial devices are borne, *crowned*, indicating that the coat of arms is that of a peer, as indicated by the coronet. As devices are blazoned on a shield, so are beauty, birth, etc., displayed in your person, *Son.*, 37,7.

PARTAKE, to impart, *Per.*, 1.i.153; *against myself with thee partake*, to take sides with against, *Son.*, 149,2.

PARTIALLY, *their own transgressions partially they smother*, regarding their own sins in a favourable light, *Lucrece*, 634; *partially affined*, constrained by undue favour (owing to friendship, etc.), *Oth.*, 2.iii.210.

PARTICULAR, *my particular fear*, my own cause for apprehension, *Lear*, 1.iv.338 ; *my particular grief*, private, personal, *Oth.*, 1.iii.55 ; *something particular*, an individual exploit, *Ant. and Cleo.*, 3.xiii.22 ; *noun, for his particular*, for him as an individual, *Lear*, 2.iv.291 ; *my more particular*, my own especial reason, *Ant. and Cleo.*, 1.iii.54 ; *forgive me in thine own particular*, for your part, as the individual I have wronged, *Ant. and Cleo.*, 4.ix.20.

PARTISAN, long-handled spear and axe, *Ant. and Cleo.*, 2.vii.13.

PARTY, cause, interest ; *upon his party*, on his side, *Lear*, 2.i.26 ; *an intelligent party*, a confederate of the enemy, giving them information, *Lear*, 3.v.10.

PASS, to undergo, experience, *Oth.*, 1.iii.167 ; *pass upon*, pass sentence on, *Lear*, 3.vii.23.

PASSABLE, affording free passage, *Cym.*, 1.ii.8.

PASSAGE, *no passage ?* are there no passers-by ? *Oth.*, 5.i.37 ; occurrence, *Cym.*, 3.iv.90.

PASSING, exceedingly, *Oth.*, 1.iii.160.

PASSION, suffering, unhappiness, *Ant. and Cleo.*, 5.i.63 ; violent sorrow and its expression, *Ven. and Ad.*, 832 ; emotion, *Lear*, 5.iii.198.

PATCH, *patch a quarrel*, find excuse of any kind for a quarrel, *Ant. and Cleo.*, 2.ii.56.

PATENT, privilege, *Oth.*, 4.i.194.

PATIENCE, *by your patience*, by your leave, *Lear*, 5.iii.60.

PAUSE, reflection, hesitation, *Lucrece*, 277.

PAVEMENT, the sky, the floor of heaven (the trapdoor of the ' heavens '), *Cym.*, 5.iv.120.

PAVILION, awning, *Ant. and Cleo.*, 2.ii.203.

PAWN, to forfeit, *Ant. and Cleo.*, 1.iv.32 ; to wager, *Cym.*, 1.iv.104 ; *noun*, a pledge, *Lear*, 1.i.154.

PECULIAR, private, reserved for an individual, *Oth.*, 4.i.69 ; *my peculiar care*, my concern for myself, *Cym.*, 5.v.83.

PELICAN, supposed to feed its young with its own blood, so *pelican daughters*, living on their parent's blood, *Lear*, 3.iv.74.

PELLET, to form into pellets, *Lov.Comp.*, 18 ; *Ant. and Cleo.*, 3.xiii.165.

PELT, to curse, *Lucrece*, 1418.

PELTING, paltry, *Lear*, 2.iii.18.

PENCIL, *pencill'd pensiveness*, the painted image of sorrow, *Lucrece*, 1497.

PENDULOUS, overhanging, *Lear*, 3.iv.66.

PENETRATIVE, *penetrative shame*, deepest shame, *Ant. and Cleo.*, 4.xiv.75.

PERCH, measure of length, *Per.*, 3.*Prol.*15.

PERDITION, ruin, destruction, *Oth.*, 3.iv.67.

PERDU, a soldier on a post or task of special danger, so as good as lost, *Lear*, 4.vii.35.

PERDURABLE, lasting, *Oth.*, 1.iii.337.

PERDY, ' by God!', certainly, for sure, *Lear*, 2.iv.83.

PEREMPTORY, resolved, determined, *Per.*, 2.v.72.

PERFECT. fully informed, sure, *Cym.*, 3.i.71 ; *perfect age*, manhood, *Lear*, 1.ii.69 ; *perfect soul*, clear conscience, *Oth.*, 1.ii.31 ; *verb*, to instruct, *Per.*, 3.ii.72.

PERFECTION, achievement, what i excellent, *Lucrece*, 837.

PERFORCE, forcibly, involuntarily, *Lear*, 1.iv.298.

PERIOD, conclusion, end of sentence, *Oth.*, 5.ii.360 ; pause marking meaning, *Lucrece*, 565.

PERJURE, to corrupt, *Ant. and Cleo.*, 3.xii.30.

PERSIAN, rich and ornate, *Lear*, 3.vi.79.

PERSISTED, persisted in, steadily pur sued, *Ant. and Cleo.*, 5.i.30.

PERSON, *he hath a person*, a handsome exterior, *Oth.*, 1.iii.391.

PERSONAL, *in personal duty*, serving in person, *Lov.Comp.*, 130 ; *Oth.*, 1.i.9

PERSONATE, to represent, stand for, *Cym.*, 5.v.452.

PERSPECTIVE, the art that makes the kin of picture that appears coherent an intelligible only from one particula point of view, the poet's eye providin this unity, *Son.*, 24,4.

PERSUADE, *false persuaded*, wrongl convinced, *Lear*, 1.iv.232 ; *Son* 22,1 ; *Oth.*, 4.i.12.

PERSUASION, opinion, *Cym.*, 1.iv.109.

PERUSE, inspect, *Cym.*, 1.iv.6.

PERVERT, to turn aside, divert, *Cym.*, 2.iv.151.

PEW, balcony (outside window perhaps) *Lear*, 3.iv.54.

PHILIPPAN, *his sword Philippan*, th sword he carried at Philippi, *Ant. an Cleo.*, 2.v.23.

PHILOMEL, the nightingale, *Lucrece* 1079 ; daughter of Pandion, ravishe by Tereus and changed to a nightin gale, *Lucrece*, 1128.

PHOENIX, *phoenix down*, matchless *Lov.Comp.*, 93 ; fabulous Arabia bird ; only one existed at a time, th new phoenix springing from th ashes of its predecessor, *Son.*, 19,4.

PHRASELESS, beyond description *Lov.Comp.*, 225.

PHYSIC, keep in health, vigour, *Cym.* 3.ii.34.

PHYSIOGNOMY, the art of portrayin character by the artist, *Lucrece*, 1395

PIECE, to complete by addition, *Ant. an Cleo.*, 1.v.45.

PIGHT, fixed, determined, *Lear*, 2.i.65

PILL, to strip, peel, *Lucrece*, 1167.

PIN, *the web and the pin*, the eye condi tion known as cataract, *Lear*, 3.iv.115

PINION, feather, *Ant. and Cleo.*, 3.xii.4

PITCH, height, *Son.*, 7,9.

PITIFULLY, contemptibly, *Ant. an Cleo.*, 2.vii.16.

PITTIKINS, 'Ods pittikins, corruption of 'God's pity', Cym., 4.ii.294.

PLACE, residence, Lov.Comp., 82; accommodation, Oth., 1.iii.237.

PLACKET, petticoat, Lear, 3.iv.95.

PLAGUE, plague of custom, the disabilities the common law imposes on me, Lear, 1.ii.3.

PLAIN, (i) to explain, Per., 3.Prol.14; (ii) to complain, Lear, 3.i.39.

PLANETARY, planetary influence, the force that was supposed to flow down from the planets and affect human affairs, Lear, 1.ii.119.

PLANT, sole of the foot, also vegetable, Ant. and Cleo., 2.vii.1.

PLATE, plates, coins, Ant. and Cleo., 5.ii.92; verb, plate sin with gold, cover sin with armour of gold, Lear, 4.vi.165; plated Mars, Mars in armour, Ant. and Cleo., 1.i.4.

PLAUSIBLY, with acclamation, Lucrece, 1854.

PLEACH'D, folded, Ant. and Cleo., 4.xiv.73.

PLEASANCE, pleasure, Oth., 2.iii.282.

PLEASANT, mirthful, Cym., 1.vi.58.

PLEASING, pleasing ears, ears that hear with pleasure, Lucrece, 1126.

PLEDGE, to drink a health to, or in answer to a toast, Ant. and Cleo., 2.vii.84.

PLIANT, suitable, Oth., 1.iii.151.

PLIGHTED, concealed in the folds of hypocrisy, Lear, 1.i.280.

PLUCK, to pull down, Lear, 4.ii.85.

PLUME, plume up my will, add another feather to my cap, Oth., 1.iii.387.

PLUNGE, struggle ineffectively, Lucrece, 1098.

POINT, his points, laces attaching hose to doublet, Ant. and Cleo., 3.xiii.157; at point, in readiness, Lear, 1.iv.325; just about to, Lear, 3.i.33.

POINT, to appoint, to assign to, Son., 14.6.

POISE, weight, importance, Lear, 2.i.120; verb, to counterbalance, Oth., 1.iii.327.

POISON, to cause to sicken, Oth., 5.ii.367.

POLE, Pole Star, Oth., 2.i.15.

POLICY, established regime, Lear, 1.ii.45; expediency, Lucrece, 529; device, stratagem, Lucrece, 1815.

POLITIC, hugely politic, firm in the wisdom that truly understands the moral conduct of life, contrasted with policy that is a form of mere expediency, Son., 24,11; a politic distance, a reserve made necessary by the state of public feeling, Oth., 3.iii.13.

POLITICIAN, time-server and self-seeker, Lear, 4.vi.171.

PONTIC, Pontic sea, Black Sea, Oth., 3.iii.457.

POOP, to cause to founder, Per., 4.ii.23.

POPULOUS, numerous, Ant. and Cleo., 3.vi.50.

PORRIDGE, pottage, soup, Lear, 3.iv.54.

PORT, (i) city gate, Ant. and Cleo., 4.iv.23; (ii) demeanour, bearing, Ant. and Cleo., 4.xiv.52.

PORTABLE, endurable, Lear, 3.vi.108.

PORTAGE, the profit the sailor could make on what he was permitted to trade on his own, apart from the owner's cargo; so the loss the child has sustained by her mother's death is greater than any gain her subsequent voyage through life will produce, Per., 3.i.35.

PORTANCE, conduct, Oth., 1.iii.139.

PORTLY, a portly sail of ship, an imposing fleet, Per., 1.iv.61.

POSIED, with posy or motto inscribed in the ring, Lov.Comp., 45.

POSITION, in position, in the assertion I now make, Oth., 3.iii.238.

POSSESS, I will possess you, I will give you, Ant. and Cleo., 3.xi.21; where folly now possesses, where folly now rules (like an evil spirit), Cym., 1.v.48.

POST, messenger, Lear, 2.iv.29; all in post, with all speed, Lucrece, 1; post speedily, Per., 4.Prol.48; post-posthaste, Oth., 1.iii.46; verb, to carry with speed, Cym., 2.iv.27.

POTENTIAL, influential, Oth., 1.ii.13.

POTTING, drinking, boozing, Oth., 2.iii.72.

POTTLE, a large (two quart) tankard, Oth., 2.iii.78.

POWER, army, Lucrece, 1368.

PRACTICE, trickery, Lear, 5.iii.151; my practices, my treacherous designs, Lear, 1.ii.173.

PRACTISE, practise on, to employ foul trickery on, Oth., 1.ii.73; so practiser, Oth., 1.ii.78.

PRAISE, praise which makes your praises worse, commendation which misrepresents your merits, Son., 84,14; book of praises, virtues, Per., 1.i.15; that praise, that praiseworthy being, Lucrece, 82; verb, praised, prized, valued, Per., 3.ii.107.

PRAY, pray in aid, legal expression for asking help from someone with interest in one's case; so treat you as an ally not as conquered enemy, Ant. and Cleo., 5.ii.27.

PRECEDENCE, the good precedence, what was said before, Ant. and Cleo., 2.v.51.

PRECEDENT, (i) done before, Ant. and Cleo., 4.xiv.83; (ii) noun, token, Ven. and Ad., 26; example, Lov.Comp., 155.

PRECIOUS, spectacles so precious, eyes so sensitive, Cym., 1.vi.36; ironically, at Oth., 5.ii.238.

PRECIPITATING, falling headlong, Lear, 4.vi.50.

PRECURSOR, forerunner, Phoenix, 6.

PREDICT, prediction, Son., 14,8.

PREDOMINANCE, spherical predominance, the compulsion exercised by some ruling planet or planets, Lear, 1.ii.118.

PREFER, that doth prefer himself, present himself, Per., 2.ii.17; prefer him to a better place, offer him a more hospitable home, Lear, 1.i.274; to introduce, recommend, Cym., 2.iii.46; to further, promote, Oth., 2.i.272.

PREGNANT, ready, Lear, 2.i.76; manifest

Oth., 2.i.232 ; *Were't not that . . . 'Twere pregnant they should,* reasonable to suppose that they would, *Ant. and Cleo.,* 2.i.45.

PREPARATION, armament, *Oth.,* 1.iii.14.

PRESAGE, sign, omen, *Ven. and Ad.* 457 ; interpretation of the omens, *Son.,* 107,6 ; *presagers,* interpreters, means of expressing, *Son.,* 23,10.

PRESCIENCE, *his prescience,* a mock title for the soothsayer (on the model of ' his reverence '), *Ant. and Cleo.,* 1.ii.20.

PRESCRIPT, the instructions, orders, *Ant. and Cleo.,* 3.viii.5.

PRESENCE, company, conference, *Ant. and Cleo.,* 2.ii.113.

PRESENT, immediate, *Lucrece,* 551 ; urgent, *Oth.,* 1.ii.90 ; *noun, from the present,* away from the point, not relevant to the matter in hand, *Ant. and Cleo.,* 2.vi.30 ; *verb,* relate, *Oth.,* 1.iii.124.

PRESENTLY, immediately, *Lucrece,* 864.

PRESS-MONEY, paid to the recruit as an earnest of his enlistment, *Lear,* 4.vi.87.

PREST, ready, *Per.,* 4.Prol.45.

PRETENCE, intention, design, *Lear,* 1.ii.84.

PRICK, point against the hour on dial of clock, *Lucrece,* 781.

PRIDE, lust, *Son.,* 144,8.

PRINCIPAL, main rafter, *Per.,* 3.ii.16.

PRIZE, value, *Cym.,* 3.vi.76.

PROBAL, such as commends itself to thought, *Oth.,* 2.iii.327.

PROBATION, proof, *Oth.,* 3.iii.369.

PROCEED, to come from, be caused, *Cym.,* 3.v.59.

PROCESS, summons, command, *Ant. and Cleo.,* 1.i.28 ; the sequence of adventures (or, the manner of wooing), *Oth.,* 1.iii.142.

PROCURE, to cause, *Lear,* 2.iv.302.

PRODIGY, omen, what seems out of nature's normal course, *Ven. and Ad.,* 926.

PRODUCTED, produced, *Oth.,* 1.i.147.

PROFESS, *What dost thou profess ?* What is your trade or skill ? *Lear,* 1.iv.11 ; to avow one's code of duty (the sense into which Kent turns Lear's question), *Lear,* 1.iv.13 ; *professed bosoms,* full of protestations, *Lear,* 1.i.272.

PROFIT, lesson, instruction, *Oth.,* 3.ii.383.

PROGNOSTICATE, foretell, *Son.,* 14, 13.

PROGNOSTICATION, *a fruitful prognostication,* a sure sign of fertility, *Ant. and Cleo.,* 1.ii.48.

PROJECT, to set forth, state, *Ant. and Cleo.,* 5.ii.120.

PROMETHEAN, *Promethean heat,* the fire from heaven (the demigod Prometheus stole fire from the gods to give to men), *Oth.,* 5.ii.12.

PROMISE, *I promise you,* I assure you, *Lear,* 1.ii.137.

PROMPT, ready, *Ant. and Cleo.,* 3.xiii.75.

PROMULGATE, publish to the world, *Oth.,* 1.ii.21.

PRONE, ready and eager, *Cym.* 5.iv.198 ; *Lucrece,* 684.

PROOF, *targes of proof,* strong shields *Cym.,* 5.v.5 ; *in thy just proof,* proof that you are honest, *Lear,* 3.vi.113 ; experience, *Cym.,* 1.vi.69 ; *others proof,* experience of others, *Lov.Comp.,* 163.

PROPER, *our proper son,* our own son, *Oth.,* 1.iii.69 ; *proper deformity . . . in* the fiend, naturally associated with the devil, *Lear,* 4.ii.60 ; *a proper man,* handsome man, *Oth.,* 1.iii.386.

PROPERTIED, had the quality, *Ant. and Cleo.,* 5.ii.83.

PROPERTY, individuality, *Phoenix,* 37 ; *great property,* characteristic magnanimity, *Ant. and Cleo.,* 1.i.58 ; *property of blood,* identity of blood, consanguinity, *Lear,* 1.i.113.

PROPONTIC, Sea of Marmora, *Oth.,* 3.iii.460.

PROPORTION, portion, fortune, *Per.,* 4.ii.26.

PROPORTION'D, *proportion'd course of time,* the established rhythm of time, *Lucrece,* 774.

PROPOSE, to discourse, *Oth.,* 1.i.25.

PROPRIETY, the condition proper to a community, *Oth.,* 2.iii.168.

PROROGUE, *prorogue his honour,* to delay the action demanded by honour, *Ant. and Cleo.,* 2.i.26 ; to protract, *Per.,* 5.i.26.

PROSECUTION, *the inevitable prosecution,* the pursuit one cannot escape, *Ant. and Cleo.,* 4.xiv.65.

PROSPECT, *to that prospect,* to that revelation of their conduct, *Oth.,* 3.iii.402.

PROTEST, to assert, *Oth.,* 4.ii.202.

PROTRACT, to postpone, *Cym.,* 4.ii.233.

PROVE, to experience, *Ant. and Cleo.,* 1.ii.32.

PROVIDE, *provide your going,* make the necessary preparations for your journey, *Ant. and Cleo.,* 3.iv.36.

PROVOKE, impel, *Son.,* 50,9 ; produce, *Lear,* 4.iv.13.

PRUNE, *prunes the immortal wing,* preens its heavenly plumage, *Cym.,* 5.iv.118.

PUBLISH, *publish'd,* proclaimed, *Lear,* 4.vi.234.

PUBLISHER, the declarer, *Lucrece,* 33.

PUDDER, commotion, *Lear,* 3.ii.50.

PUDENCY, modesty, *Cym.,* 2.v.11.

PUISSANT, powerful, *Lear,* 5.iii.216.

PURBLIND, dim of sight, *Ven. and Ad.,* 679.

PURCHASE, the profit, *Per.,* 1.Prol.9 ; *verb, faults . . . hereditary rather than purchas'd,* inherited not deliberately adopted, *Ant. and Cleo.,* 1.iv.4.

PURL UP, curl upward like smoke, *Lucrece,* 1407.

PURPOSE, proposal, *Ant. and Cleo.,* 2.vi.4 ; *this war's purpose,* the campaign, *Cym.,* 4.ii.346.

PUT, to compel, *Cym.,* 2.iii.105 ; *put back,* to repulse, *Lucrece,* 843 ; *put by,* desist from, *Oth.,* 2.iii.164 ; *put on* to stake, *Cym.*, I.iv.118; *to put on*, incite, urge, *Lear*, 2.i.99; *put me to't*, drive me to a task (of plain speaking), *Oth.*, 2.i.118.

PUTTOCK, inferior bird of prey, kite, *Cym.*, I.i.140.

QUAIL, to terrify, *Ant. and Cleo.*, 5.ii.85.

QUAINTLY, *quaintly eche*, eke out imaginatively the brief doings on the stage, *Per.*, 3.Prol.13.

QUALIFICATION, *whose qualification*, whose disturbed condition (the peace of mind of the islanders having been qualified by threats of violence), *Oth.*, 2.i.269.

QUALIFY, *one cup . . . craftily qualified*, the spirit diluted, skilfully mixed to neutralize intoxicant, *Oth.*, 2.iii.36; mollify, *Lear*, I.ii.153.

QUALITY, *qualities*, attractions, *Per.*, 4.ii.45; rank, *Cym.*, I.iv.27; profession, *Oth.*, I.iii.251; nature, character, *Lear*, 2.iv.135.

QUARREL, occasion of fighting, *Lear*, 5.iii.57; pugnacity, *Oth.*, 2.iii.46.

QUARRELOUS, quarrelsome, *Cym.*, 3.iv.158.

QUARTER, the area over which the guard extends, *Ant. and Cleo.*, 4.iii.24; *their quarter'd fires*, the camp-fires in the area occupied by the enemy, *Cym.*, 4.iv.18; *in quarter*, in good comradeship, *Oth.*, 2.iii.172.

QUAT, pimple, *Oth.*, 5.i.11.

QUEASY, disgusted with, *Ant. and Cleo.*, 3.vi.20; *of a queasy question*, of a hazardous kind, *Lear*, 2.i.17.

QUENCH, to slacken in ardour, *Cym.*, I.v.47.

QUEST, a jury, those holding an enquiry, *Son.*, 46,10; search-party, *Oth.*, I.ii.46.

QUESTION, discussion, *Lear*, I.ii.14; consideration, *Son.*, 12,9; *this gentleman in question*, the gentleman we are discussing, *Cym.*, I.i.34; *made she no verbal question?* did she not speak? *Lear*, 4.iii.24; conversation, *Oth.*, I.iii.113; *with more facile question bear it*, capture it in an easier encounter, *Oth.*, I.iii.23; *no question*, without doubt, *Oth.*, 4.iii.61; *verb*, *to question farther*, to fight a duel over the business, *Cym.*, 2.iv.52.

QUESTRISTS, seekers, *Lear*, 3.vii.16.

QUICK, fresh, caller, *Per.*, 4.i.28; *quick of ear*, quick in appreciation, so can interpret even a short prayer, *Per.*, 4.i.76.

QUICK-ANSWER'D, sharp in reply, *Cym.*, 3.iv.157.

QUICKEN, to revive, *Ant. and Cleo.*, 4.xv.39.

QUIETUS, final settlement of an account; Nature will have to make her settlement with Time by surrendering her favourite at last, *Son.*, 126,14.

QUILLETS, *keep up thy quillets*, spare your quibbles, *Oth.*, 3.i.23.

QUIRE, place for singers, *Cym.*, 3.iii.43.

QUIRK, *quirks*, caprices, *Per.*, 4.vi.7;

ingenious turns of expression, *Oth.*, 2.i.63.

QUIT, to leave, *Lov.Comp.*, 13; *Cym.*, I.i.38; free, *Cym.*, 5.iv.165; avenge, requite, *Lear*, 3.vii.86; repay, *Per.*, 3.i.35; to conduct oneself, *Lear*, 2.i.30.

QUITTAL, requital, *Lucrece*, 236.

QUOTE, observe, *Lucrece*, 812.

QUOTH-A, said he (in repeating some remark, with ironic or jesting intention), *Per.*, 2.i.78.

RACE, *a race of heaven*, of heavenly kind, *Ant. and Cleo.*, I.iii.37.

RACK, driven clouds in upper air, *Ant. and Cleo.*, 4.xiv.10.

RAGE, frenzy, *Lear*, 4.vii.78; *a poet's rage*, poetic exaggeration, *Son.*, 17,11; *verb*, *raging motions*, vehement impulses, *Oth.*, I.iii.330; to act madly, *Ant. and Cleo.*, 4.i.7.

RAMP, a wanton, *Cym.*, I.vi.133.

RANGE, *whose several ranges*, whose respective ranks, *Ant. and Cleo.*, 3.xiii.5.

RANGER, *Diana's rangers*, the virgins who made up Diana's troup of hunters, *Cym.*, 2.iii.69.

RANK, foul-smelling (with pun on 'social position'), *Cym.*, 2.i.15; *Ant. and Cleo.*, 5.ii.211; swollen, *Ven. and Ad.*, 71; unchaste, *Cym.*, 2.v.24; *in the rank garb*, in lascivious style, or as one lascivious in manner, *Oth.*, 2.i.300; *rank of goodness*, suffering from exuberance of happiness, *Son.*, 118,12; gross, coarse, *Lov.Comp.*, 307.

RANSOM, atonement, *Cym.*, 5.iii.80; *verb*, to atone for, *Son.*, 120,14.

RAP, *what thus raps you?* puts you beside yourself, *Cym.*, I.vi.50.

RAPTURE, robbery, *Per.*, 2.i.153.

RARITY, excellence, *Phoenix*, 53.

RASH, sudden, *Lucrece*, 473.

RASH, stick, *Lear*, 3.vii.57.

RATE, to assign (a share), *Ant. and Cleo.*, 3.vi.25; to equal in value, *Ant. and Cleo.*, 3.xi.69.

RAVEN, to devour, *Cym.*, I.vi.48.

RAVISH, to tear away, *Lear*, 3.vii.37; to pollute, *Lucrece*, 778.

RAW, untaught, unskilled, *Per.*, 4.ii.54.

RAZE, to obliterate, *Son.*, 25,11; *raz'd oblivion*, the razure of oblivion, blotting out from memory, *Son.*, 122,7.

REACH, *the hand of death hath raught him*, taken hold of him, *Ant. and Cleo.*, 4.ix.29.

READY, dressed, her toilet completed, *Cym.*, 2.iii.81.

REARWARD, *in the rearward*, as if following up with another blow, *Son.*, 90,6.

REASON, discourse, argument, *Son.*, 151,8; equity, *Phoenix*, 47; reasonable conjecture, *Cym.*, 4.ii.132; *verb*, to discourse, *Cym.*, 4.ii.14; to argue, *Lear*, 2.iv.263.

553

REAVE, to deprive, *Ven. and Ad.*, 766; *Cym.*, 3.iii.103.

REBOUND, *by the rebound of yours*, echoing yours, *Ant. and Cleo.*, 5.ii.104.

REBUKE, to check, *Per.*, 3.i.1.

RECEIPT, capacity, *Son.*, 136,7; what is received, *Lucrece*, 703.

RECEIVE, to hear, *Per.*, 1.i.1.

RECK, to care for, *Cym.*, 4.ii.155.

RECOGNIZANCE, a legal bond, so a pledge, token, *Oth.*, 5.ii.219.

RECOIL, to degenerate, show yourself unworthy, *Cym.*, 1.vi.127.

RECOLLECT, observe in the specimens they catch, *Per.*, 2.i.50.

RECOMMEND, to inform, *Oth.*, 1.iii.41.

RECONCILE, to recall to favour, *Lear*, 3.vi.113.

RECONCILIATION, *his present reconciliation take*, be reconciled with him now, *Oth.*, 3.iii.48.

RECORD, *upon record*, chronicled, *Lucrece*, 1643; *Ant. and Cleo.*, 4.xiv.99; *verb*, to put in writing, *Cym.*, 1.iv.161; to sing, to relate in song, *Per.*, 4.Prol.27.

RECOVER, to reconcile, *Oth.*, 2.iii.264.

RECREANT, traitor, *Lear*, 1.i.166.

RECREATE, to disport, refresh, *Ven. and Ad.*, 1095.

RECURE, to restore, heal, *Ven. and Ad.*, 465.

REDEEM, to repay for, *Lear*, 5.iii.266.

REEL, to reel the streets, to stagger in drunken fashion through the streets, *Ant. and Cleo.*, 1.iv.20; *noun*, reels, revelry, *Ant. and Cleo.*, 2.vii.92.

REFER, *I'll refer me*, to appeal to, *Oth.*, 1.ii.64; *hath referr'd herself*, married, *Cym.*, 1.i.6.

REFERENCE, appointment, *Oth.*, 1.iii.237; *make your full reference to*, entrust yourself completely to, *Ant. and Cleo.*, 5.ii.23.

REFIGURE, to resemble, *Son.*, 6,10.

REFLECT, *reflect upon him*, regard him, *Cym.*, 1.vi.23.

REFLECTION, shining, brightness, *Cym.*, 1.ii.30.

REFUGE, extenuation, *Lucrece*, 1654.

REFUSE, reject, *Oth.*, 3.i.47; declining to encounter, *Ant. and Cleo.*, 3.vii.39.

REGARD, view, *Lov.Comp.*, 213; *an indistinct regard*, a prospect in which sky and sea are indistinguishably blended, *Oth.*, 2.i.40; *exact regard*, special care, *Lear*, 1.iv.265; thought, *Lucrece*, 277; *regards*, considerations, *Lear*, 1.i.239; *in which regard*, by reason of this, *Oth.*, 1.i.154.

REGIMENT, rule, sway, *Ant. and Cleo.*, 3.vi.95.

REGION, *the region clouds*, the clouds in the sky, *Son.*, 33,12; *region low*, the lowest of the strata of the atmosphere, its inhabitants' low rank, *Cym.*, 5.iv.93.

REGISTER, *in register*, in the chronicle of actions, *Ant. and Cleo.*, 4.ix.21.

REHEARSE, repeat, *Son.*, 81,11.

REIN, *the hard rein*, the severe treatment, *Lear*, 3.i.27.

REJOICE, to feel joy at, *Cym.*, 5.v.370; *rejoicing fires*, bonfires, *Cym.*, 3.i.32.

RELENT, to soften, *Ven. and Ad.*, 200; *relenting dew*, tears of emotion, *Lucrece*, 1829.

RELIEF, sport, pastime, *Ven. and Ad.*, 235.

RELIER, *thy rash relier*, on whose heedless advice you rely, *Lucrece*, 639.

RELIGION, feeling for the truth, respect, *Cym.*, 1.iv.131; a supreme form of devotion, *Ant. and Cleo.*, 5.ii.198.

RELIGIOUS, *religious love*, piety, *Son.*, 31,6; *religious love put out Religion's eye*, passionate devotion, *Lov.Comp.*, 250.

RELISH, (i) *never relish'd of*, never tainted with, *Per.*, 2.v.59; (ii) to sing, *Lucrece*, 1126.

RELUME, to rekindle, *Oth.*, 5.ii.13.

REMAIN, *the remain*, what is left to do, *Cym.*, 3.i.84; *verb*, keep the same position or relation, *Phoenix*, 48; *for lawful policy remains enacted*, is once enacted regarded as right and proper, *Lucrece*, 529; *let her remain*, leave her alone, *Cym.*, 2.iii.15; to dwell, *Cym.*, 4.iii.14.

REMAINDER, those who remain, *Cym.*, 1.i.129.

REMEDIATE, remedial, *Lear*, 4.iv.17.

REMEMBER, *briefly thyself remember*, recall and repent your sins quickly, *Lear*, 4.vi.231; to remind, *Lear*, 1.iv.66; *be remember'd*, do not forget, be warned, *Lucrece*, 607.

REMEMBRANCE, reputation, *Ant. and Cleo.*, 2.i.16; memory, *Cym.*, 2.iv.93; token of love, *Oth.*, 3.iii.295.

REMEMBRANCER, one whose presence keeps one in mind of some duty or obligation, *Cym.*, 1.v.77.

REMORSE, pity, *Lear*, 4.ii.73; *shall be in me remorse*, the deed, however bloody, will seem to me like a compassionate act, *Oth.*, 3.iii.472.

REMOTION, removal, journeying, *Lear*, 2.iv.112.

REMOVE, to kill, *Oth.*, 4.iii.226; *this time remov'd*, time of absence, separation, *Son.*, 97,5.

REMOVER, one who changes his place, or mind, *Son.*, 116,4.

RENDER, admission, statement, *Cym.*, 4.iv.11; the rendering of an account, *Cym.*, 5.iv.17; *verb*, to describe, *Cym.*, 3.iv.149.

RENEGE, to deny, *Lear*, 2.ii.73; to renounce, *Ant. and Cleo.*, 1.i.8.

RENEW, to revive, *Lucrece*, 1103.

RENOWN, reputation, *Cym.*, 5.v.202; *Per.*, 4.vi.38.

REPAIR, renew, *Cym.*, 2.ii.12.

REPEAL, to recall to favour, *Oth.*, 2.iii.346; to recall the sentence of banishment, *Lear*, 3.vi.113.

REPENT, to regret, *Cym.*, 5.v.59.

REPETITION, recital, *Per.*, 5.i.244.

REPINE, discontent, *Ven. and Ad.*, 490.

REPLICATION, repartee, *Lov.Comp.*, 122.

REPORT, rumour, *Ant. and Cleo.*, 2.ii.189; *your report*, my account of you, *Son.*, 83,5; hearsay, *Lear*, 4.vi.141; *true reports*, trustworthy witnesses, *Ant. and Cleo.*, 2.ii.51; verb, *to report themselves*, to speak for themselves, *Cym.*, 2.iv.83; *where the aim reports*, where the purpose makes itself clear, *Oth.*, 1.iii.6.

REPORTER, informant, *Ant. and Cleo.*, 2.ii.192.

REPOSURE, reposal, *Lear*, 2.i.68.

REPROACH, disgrace, *Lucrece*, 824.

REPROBANCE, damnation, *Oth.*, 5.ii.212.

REPROOF, *your reproof were well deserved of rashness*, you would deserve the reproach of rashness, *Ant. and Cleo.*, 2.ii.125.

REPROVE, to disprove, *Ven. and Ad.*, 787.

REQUIRE, to request, *Ant. and Cleo.*, 3.xii.12.

RESCUE, deliverance, *Ant. and Cleo.*, 3.xi.48.

RESERVE, to preserve, to keep in one's own possession, *Lear*, 1.i.148; *Son.*, 32,7; to guard carefully, *Cym.*, 4.iv.49; *always reserved my holy duty*, so far as I may say it without breach of duty, *Cym.*, 1.i.87.

RESIST, prove distasteful to, repel, *Per.*, 2.iii.29.

RESOLUTION, certainty about the matter, *Lear*, 1.ii.96.

RESOLVE, to dissolve, *Lov.Comp.*, 296; solve a riddle, *Per.*, 1.i.71; to explain to, *Lear*, 2.iv.24.

RESORTERS, frequenters, customers, *Per.*, 4.vi.23.

RESPECT, *in my respect*, in my eyes, *Cym.*, 2.iii.135; *Per.*, 3.iii.33; *respects of fortune*, considerations of money and rank, *Lear*, 1.i.248; rank, *Oth.*, 1.iii.282; thought, *Ven. and Ad.*, 911; *upon respect*, on the king's messenger entitled to privilege and respect, *Lear*, 2.iv.23; verb, to regard, heed, *Ven. and Ad.*, 911; to esteem, *Son.*, 149,9; *Per.*, 2.ii.13.

REST, (i) *above the rest*, above all, *Son.*, 91,6; *to set up one's rest*, was an expression from game at prinero, *rest* signifying how much the player ventured on his hand; here *rest* means repose, but the form of the expression is that from cards, *Lear*, 1.i.122; (ii) abode, stay, *Per.*, 2.*Prol.*26; pause in music, *Lucrece*, 1124.

RESTEM, to sail back again, *Oth.*, 1.iii.37.

RESTY, sluggish, *Son.*, 100,9; *resty sloth*, indolence, *Cym.*, 3.vi.34.

RETENTION, *that poor retention*, that inadequate means of preserving impressions (the table-book), *Son.*, 122,9; detention, *Lear*, 5.iii.48.

RETIRE, to return, *Ven. and Ad.*, 906.

REVERB, to reverberate, *Lear*, 1.i.153.

REVERENCE, *saving reverence*, apologetic phrase, introducing indecent suggestions at *Cym.*, 4.i.5.

REVIEW, to read again, *Son.*, 74,5.

REVOLT, rebel, *Cym.*, 4.iv.6; desertion,

Ant. and Cleo., 4.ix.19; disobedient act, *Oth.*, 1.i.135.

REVOLUTION, *whether revolution be the same*, whether history repeats itself, *Son.*, 59,12; *by revolution*, in course of time, *Ant. and Cleo.*, 1.ii.122.

REWARD, punishment, *Per.*, 5.iii.87.

RHEUM, watering at the eyes, *Ant. and Cleo.*, 3.ii.57.

RIBAUDRED, wanton, *Ant. and Cleo.*, 3.x.10.

RICH, *your rich opinion*, the good character people have of you, *Oth.*, 2.iii.187; *richly*, splendidly, *Cym.*, 5.v.3; verb, enriched, *Lear*, 1.i.63.

RID, to remove, *Son.*, 139,14.

RIGGISH, wanton, *Ant. and Cleo.*, 2.ii.244.

RIGHT, *gentle right*, humanity, *Lucrece*, 545; just description, *Son.*, 17,11; reparation, amend, *Lucrece*, 1027.

RIGOL, ring, circle, *Lucrece*, 1745.

RIOTOUS, full of drunkards, *Lear*, 1.iv.243; unrestrained, *Ant. and Cleo.*, 1.iii.29.

RIPELY, at once, the time being ripe, *Cym.*, 3.v.22.

RIPENESS, *ripeness is all* (cf. *Ham.*, 5.ii.214, 'the readiness is all'), *Lear*, 5.ii.11.

RIVALITY, partnership, equality, *Ant. and Cleo.*, 3.v.8.

RIVE, to split, *Lear*, 3.ii.58; to rend, *Ant. and Cleo.*, 4.xiii.5.

RIVET, *riveted trim*, armour, *Ant. and Cleo.*, 4.iv.22.

ROGUE, vagrant, *Lear*, 4.vii.39; term of affection, *Oth.*, 4.i.111.

ROGUING, roaming, *Per.*, 4.i.98; *his roguish madness*, being a half-wit and a vagrant, *Lear*, 3.vii.103.

RONDURE, circle, sphere, *Son.*, 21,8.

ROOM, a place, *Son.*, 55,10.

ROSE, *roses of shadow*, artificial colourings, painting; *since his rose is true*, his youthful beauty and complexion is natural, *Son.*, 67,8.

ROUND, honest, straightforward, *Oth.*, 1.iii.90; *in the roundest manner*, in the plainest way, without observing ceremony, *Lear*, 1.iv.53; *round and safe*, unblemished and trustworthy, *Per.*, 1.ii.122; noun, *this mortal round*, the earth, *Ven. and Ad.*, 368.

ROUSE, a bumper, *Oth.*, 2.iii.60.

ROUT, the whole company, *Per.*, 3.*Prol.*1; confusion, tumult, *Oth.*, 2.iii.202.

ROYAL, *royal peril*, war being for Antony 'a royal occupation', fit for kings and heroes, *Ant. and Cleo.*, 4.viii.35.

ROYALTY, princely bearing and behaviour, *Cym.*, 4.ii.179.

RUB, *will not be rubb'd nor stopp'd*, diverted by any opposition, *Lear*, 2.ii.149.

RUDDOCK, robin, *Cym.*, 4.ii.225.

RUDE, unpolished, *Son.*, 32,4; untaught, *Son.*, 78,14; *rudely*, violently, without thought of appearance, *Lucrece*, 170.

RUDENESS, rusticity, clumsiness, *Cym.*, 4.ii.215; forcefulness, violence, *Lov. Comp.*, 104.

RUFFLE, the swank, *Lov.Comp.*, 58; *verb*, bluster, *Lear*, 2.iv.300.

RUINATE, to destroy, *Lucrece*, 944.

RULE, precept, law, *Lov.Comp.*, 271.

RUNAGATES, fugitives, *Cym.*, 4.ii.63.

RUSH, rushes were spread as a covering for the floor, *Cym.*, 2.ii.13; emblem of a harmless weapon, *Oth.*, 5.ii.273.

SABLE, black, *Lucrece*, 117; dark, *Son.*, 12,4; *thy sable gender*, thy black kind, offspring, fledglings, *Phoenix*, 18.

SACRED, of royal persons, so *sacred breast*, royal breast, *Per.*, 1.ii.34.

SAD, serious, *Lucrece*, 277.

SADNESS, *in sadness*, in earnestness, *Ven. and Ad.*, 807.

SAFE, sane; *the safer sense*, a sound mind, *Lear*, 4.vi.81; *Oth.*, 4.i.266; *verb*, to provide safe-conduct, *Ant. and Cleo.*, 4.vii.26; to render safe, *Ant. and Cleo.*, 1.iii.55.

SAFETY, *is in safety*, is well, *Cym.*, 1.vi.12.

SAGITTARY, the Centaur, the sign of a house, *Cym.*, 1.i.159.

SAKE, *for such a sake*, on a similar provocation, *Lov.Comp.*, 322.

SALAD, *my salad days*, my early, green, inexperienced years, *Ant. and Cleo.*, 1.v.73.

SALT, *a man of salt*, reduced to tears, *Lear*, 4.vi.196; *adj.*, lewd, *Oth.*, 2.i.237; lascivious, *Ant. and Cleo.*, 2.i.21; *salt-waved ocean*, of tears, *Lucrece*, 1231.

SALUTATION, *false adulterate eyes give salutation to*, they attribute to my blood their own falseness; they hail me as their fellow, *Son.*, 121,6.

SAMPHIRE, sea-fennel, for which Dover cliffs were famous, *Lear*, 4.vi.15.

SAMPLE, an example, *Cym.*, 1.i.48.

SANCTIMONY, *sanctimony and a frail vow*, (in the circumstances) an outward show of piety and faith, *Oth.*, 1.iii.353.

SAND, of the hour-glass, *Cym.*, 3.ii.71.

SANGUINE, red, *Cym.*, 5.v.364.

SANS, without, *Oth.*, 1.iii.64.

SARUM, *Sarum plain*, Salisbury plain, *Lear*, 2.ii.78.

SATIRE, *satire to*, satirist of, *Son.*, 100,11

SATURN, *old Saturn*, regarded as the image of the cold and morose temperament, *Cym.*, 2.v.12.

SAUCY, lascivious, *Cym.*, 1.vi.150.

SAVE, *save thee*, a greeting, God save thee, *Lear*, 2.i.1; to deliver from the law, *Cym.*, 2.iii.71; *conj.*, save that, were it not that, *Son.*, 66,14.

SAVOUR, to smell, *Per.*, 4.vi.109; *filths savour but themselves*, the wicked have a taste only for their own kind of vileness, *Lear*, 4.ii.39.

SAWN, seen, *Lov.Comp.*, 91.

SAY, flavour, touch, *Lear*, 5.ii.144; *verb*, to assay, attempt, *Per.*, 1.i.59.

SAY, *say you?* what do you say? *Oth.*, 3.iv.82; *you've said*, you speak truly,

Ant. and Cleo., 2.vi.104; *say they are*, suppose they are, *Oth.*, 3.iii.140.

'SBLOOD, God's blood, *Oth.*, 1.i.4.

SCALE, *scales*, scaled markings, *Ant. and Cleo.*, 2.vii.18.

SCANDAL, to bring scandal on, *Cym.*, 3.iv.58.

SCANT, *scant my sizes*, reduce my allowances, *Lear*, 2.iv.174; withhold, *Lear*, 1.i.278; *scantly*, grudgingly, depreciatingly, *Ant. and Cleo.*, 3.iv.6.

'SCAPE, escapade, transgression, *Lucrece*, 747; escape, *Oth.*, 1.iii.136.

SCATTER, *this scatter'd kingdom*, disunited realm, *Lear*, 3.i.31; *scattering*, random, *Oth.*, 3.iii.155.

SCHEDULE, document, letter, *Lucrece*, 1312.

SCION, twig, for grafting, *Oth.*, 1.iii.331.

SCORE, to notch (with swords), *Ant. and Cleo.*, 4.vii.12; to score up against, score off a person, *Oth.*, 4.i.126.

SCORN, a scoff, *Oth.*, 4.i.82; object of derision, *Cym.*, 1.vi.53.

SCORNFUL, provoking contempt, *Lucrece*, 520.

SCOTCH, cut, wound, *Ant. and Cleo.*, 4.vii.10.

SCRIPTURES, writings, *Cym.*, 3.iv.79.

SCRUPLE, *made scruple of*, to doubt, question, *Cym.*, 5.v 182; *scrupulous faction*, bickering about trifles, *Ant. and Cleo.*, 1.iii.48.

SEAL, to finish, complete (like putting a seal to a document), *Ant. and Cleo.*, 4.xiv.49; to confirm, to sanction, *Cym.*, 3.vi.84.

SEAR, *sear-up*, render lifeless, to wrap as in death, *Cym.*, 1.i.116; withered, *Lov.Comp.*, 14.

SEARCH, search-party, *Oth.*, 1.i.159; *verb*, to test, probe, *Lucrece*, 1109.

SEASON, *of such a season*, of about your own age, *Cym.*, 3.iv.171; *verb*, *seasons comfort*, brings out the full flavour of happiness, *Cym.*, 1.vi.9; *season'd woe*, woe salted with tears, *Lov.Comp.*, 18.

SEAT, abode, *Cym.*, 5.iv.60; *verb*, situated, *Lucrece*, 1144.

SECOND, supporter, *Lear*, 4.vi.195; *seconds*, flour of second quality, so inferior elements, *Son.*, 125,11; *verb*, to follow up, *Cym.*, 5.i.14.

SECT, (i) party, *Lear*, 5.iii.18; (ii) a cutting, twig for grafting, *Oth.*, 1.iii.331.

SECTARY, *sectary astronomical*, a devotee of astrology, *Lear*, 1.ii.143.

SECURE, free from suspicion or fear, *Oth.*, 4.i.71; *verb*, to render careless, to deprive of circumspection, *Lear*, 4.i.21; to make safe, *Cym.*, 4.iv.8.

SEE, to meet, to see each other, *Cym.*, 1.i.124; to see to, to arrange, *Ant. and Cleo.*, 5.ii.362.

SEED, *seeded*, full grown, mature, prolific, *Lucrece*, 603.

SEEING, appearance, *Son.*, 67,6.

SEEK, to reclaim, *Cym.*, 3.i.70.

SEEL, to close up, *Oth.*, 3.iii.214; *Ant. and Cleo.*, 3.xiii.112.

SEEMING, hypocrisy, disguise, *Lear*, 3.ii.56; *modern seeming*, commonplace, everyday appearances, *Oth.*, 1.iii.109; deceptive bearing, *Oth.*, 3.iii.213; *this hath some seeming*, probability, *Cym.*, 5.v.450; *adj.*, a *seeming mermaid*, in the guise of a mermaid, *Ant. and Cleo.*, 2.ii.213; *seeming owed*, *Lov. Comp.*, 327.

SEETHE, sod, seethed, *Lucrece*, 1592; *sodden*, diseased, *Per.*, 4.ii.19.

SEGREGATION, dispersal, *Oth.*, 2.i.10.

SELF, *one self mate and make*, the very same husband and wife, *Lear*, 4.iii.34; *that self exhibition*, that very money, *Cym.*, 1.vi.121; *self-bounty*, your own generosity, *Oth.*, 3.iii.204; *self-explication*, the ability to express one's condition, *Cym.*, 3.iv.8; *self-kill'd*, allowed to die by one's own neglect, *Son.*, 6,4; *self-cover'd*, covered with deformity of your own choice, *Lear*, 4.ii.62.

SEMBLABLE, similar, *Ant. and Cleo.*, 3.iv.3.

SEMBLANCE, outward attraction, *Cym.*, 2.iv.109.

SEND, *I send him the greatness he has got*, I acknowledge by my message his sovereignty, *Ant. and Cleo.*, 5.ii.29.

SE'NNIGHT, a week, *Oth.*, 3.i.77.

SENSE, reason, *Son.*, 35,9; vital powers, *Cym.*, 2.ii.11; sensual being, *Per.*, 5.iii.31; *to the sense*, to the quick, limit of endurance, *Oth.*, 5.i.11.

SENSELESS, not perceived by the senses, *Lucrece*, 820; deaf, *Cym.*, 2.iii.53; without meaning, *Cym.*, 5.iv.146.

SENSIBLE, deeply felt, *Lucrece*, 1678; reasonable, *Oth.*, 2.iii.296.

SENSUAL, of the senses, *Son.*, 141,8.

SENTENCE, proverb, maxim, *Lucrece*, 244.

SEPARABLE, *a separable spite*, malevolent fortune decrees our separation, *Son.*, 36,6.

SEQUENT, *sequent effects*, what follows, *Lear*, 1.ii.102.

SEQUESTER, separation, *Oth.*, 3.iv.37.

SEQUESTRATION, separation, parting, *Oth.*, 1.iii.343.

SERVICEABLE, *a serviceable villain*, a useful tool in crime, *Lear*, 4.vi.254.

SESSA, an interjection expressing complacency, *Lear*, 3.iv.99.

SESSION, meeting of court of law or official business, judicial proceedings, *Son.*, 30,1; *Phoenix*, 9.

SET, the group of the twelve figures on the clock, *Oth.*, 2.iii.122; *verb*, sit, *Lov.Comp.*, 39; stake, *Lear*, 1.iv.122; to esteem, value, *Son.*, 88,1; *set down the pegs*, slacken the strings, untune, *Oth.*, 2.i.198; *set my rest* (*see* ' rest '), *Lear*, 1.i.122.

SETTLING, *till further settling*, till his mind is more composed, *Lear*, 4.vii.82.

SEVERAL, *a several plot*, private, belonging to some individual, as opposed to ground held in common, *Son.*, 137,9; *severally in all*, all rejoice, each in his own particular way, *Cym.*, 5.v.397.

SHADE, dream image, *Son.*, 43,8; shadow, *Son.*, 53,3.

SHADOW, departed spirits, *Cym.*, 4.v.97; picture, portrait, *Lucrece*, 1457; *gentle shadow*, Death, *Ven. and Ad.*, 1001.

SHADOWING, *shadowing passion*, like an eclipse (this time of the mind), portending something, *Oth.*, 4.i.40.

SHADY, *thy dial's shady stealth*, the shadow stealing away the hours, *Son.*, 77,7.

SHAG, hairy, *Ven. and Ad.*, 295.

SHARD, *the sharded beetle*, the winged beetle, though *shards* are the case of the wings, *Cym.*, 3.iii.20; wings, *Ant. and Cleo.*, 3.ii.20.

SHARP, hungry, keen, *Ven. and Ad.*, 55; *verb*, excite, *Ant. and Cleo.*, 2.i.25.

SHE, woman, *Cym.*, 1.iii.29.

SHEAL'D, shelled, *sheal'd peascod*, empty, the peas having been extracted, *Lear*, 1.iv.198.

SHEAV'D, *sheav'd hat*, hat made of straw, *Lov.Comp.*, 31.

SHEET, to cover as with a sheet, *Ant. and Cleo.*, 1.iv.65.

SHIFT, ruse, *Ven. and Ad.*, 690; trick, *Lucrece*, 920; *verb*, to exchange, *Ant. and Cleo.*, 5.ii.151; to change (of clothing), *Cym.*, 1.ii.1; to move, *Oth.*, 4.i.78.

SHORE, (i) *the varying shore o' th' world*, where fortune ebbs and flows as on the sea-shore, *Ant. and Cleo.*, 4.xv.11; (ii) *common shores*, drains, *Per.*, 4.vi.173.

SHORT, *come too short*, to prove inadequate, *Son.*, 83,7; *verb*, *short my word*, fail to keep my promise, *Cym.*, 1.vi.199.

SHORTEN, *shortens my made intent*, would anticipate and spoil my plan, *Lear*, 4.vii.9.

SHOT, the reckoning, *Cym.*, 5.iv.155.

SHREW, *shrew me*, beshrew me, blame on me, *Cym.*, 2.iii.142.

SHREWD, vexatious, *Ant. and Cleo.*, 4.ix.5; malicious, *Ven. and Ad.*, 500.

SHRIFT, confessional, or penance demanded for absolution, *Oth.*, 3.iii.24.

SHRILL-GORG'D, *shrill gorg'd lark*, shrill-throated, *Lear*, 4.vi.58.

SHRINE, *the shrine of Venus*, the image of Venus, *Cym.*, 5.v.164.

SHROUD, protection, *Ant. and Cleo.*, 3.xiii.71.

SHUT, *shut myself up in*, confine myself to, *Oth.*, 3.iv.122.

SIBYL, name given to certain prophetic females, *Oth.*, 3.iv.70.

SICK, disordered, *Ant. and Cleo.*, 1.iii.53; *sickly*, weakly, with little force, *Ant. and Cleo.*, 3.iv.7.

SICK-THOUGHTED, troubled with desire, *Ven. and Ad.*, 5.

SIDE-PIERCING, harrowing, heart-rending, *Lear*, 4.vi.85.

SIEGE, seat, chair, *men of royal siege*, men of kingly rank, *Oth.*, I.ii.22.

SIGHTLESS, unseeing, *Son.*, 43,12.

SIGN, *signs of fair*, imitations of beauty, *Son.*, 68,3; outward appearance, *Cym.*, I.ii.29; *verb*, to signify, to bode, *Ant. and Cleo.*, 4.iii.14.

SIGNIORY, the governing body of Venice, *Oth.*, I.ii.18.

SILLY, helpless, *Ven. and Ad.*, 1098; simple, *Lucrece*, 1345; *in a silly habit*, poorly, humbly dressed, *Cym.*, 5.iii.86.

SIMPLE, a single ingredient in a compound, so of a plant yielding such an ingredient, *Lucrece*, 530; *Lear*, 4.iv.14; *adj.*, pure, unadulterated, *Son.*, 66,11; *simple-answer'd*, truthful, without evasions, *Lear*, 3.vii.142.

SIMPLENESS, innocent of the arts of persuasion; plain integrity of purpose, *Oth.*, I.iii.246.

SIMPLICITY, folly, *Son.*, 66,11.

SIMULAR, *simular man of virtue*, hypocrite, *Lear*, 3.ii.54; *simular proof*, fabricated evidence, *Cym.*, 5.v.200.

SINEW, nerve, *Lear*, 3.vi.98.

SINGLE, individual, *Lear*, 5.iii.104; *a single doom*, the fall of one man only, *Ant. and Cleo.*, 5.i.18.

SINON, the Greek whose tearful lies moved the Trojans to admit the fatal horse, *Cym.*, 3.iv.57.

SIR, *sole sir*, sovereign, *Ant. and Cleo.*, 5.ii.119; gentleman, *Cym.*, I.vi.159.

SIRE, to beget, *Cym.*, 4.ii.26.

SISTER, to be akin to, *Per.*, 5.Prol.7; *sistering*, neighbouring, *Lov. Comp.*, 2.

SIT, to sit discussing, *Per.*, 2.iii.93; *sits down*, to besiege, *Ant. and Cleo.*, 5.xiii.168.

SITH, since, *Ven. and Ad.*, 762.

SIZE, *sizes*, allowances, *Lear*, 2.iv.174; *our size of sorrow*, share, dimension, *Ant. and Cleo.*, 4.xv.4.

SKILL, mind, memory, *Lear*, 4.vii.66; cunning, policy, *Cym.*, 2.v.33.

SKILLET, saucepan, *Oth.*, I.iii.272.

SLACK, *come slack of*, fail to come up to the standard of, *Lear*, I.iii.10; *verb*, to neglect, *Lear*, 2.iv.244.

SLAKE, to abate, *Lucrece*, 1677.

SLANDER, to discredit, *Cym.*, 3.v.77; *Son.*, 127,12; *noun*, the insult, *Ven. and Ad.*, 1006; *no slander, that's true*, *Ant. and Cleo.*, 2.vi.99.

SLANDEROUS, *slanderous deathsman*, the disgraceful office of executioner, *Lucrece*, 1001.

SLAVE, *slaves your ordinance*, misuses the dispensations of God, *Lear*, 4.ii.69.

SLEIDED, *sleided silk*, raw silk, *Per.*, 4.Prol.21; *Lov.Comp.*, 48.

SLIGHT, irresponsible, *Oth.*, 2.iii.269; *too slight in sufferance*, too patient, forbearing, *Cym.*, 3.v.35.

SLIP, a counterfeit coin, with quibble on 'slip' = fault, *Ven. and Ad.*, 515; *verb*, to free, *Cym.*, 4.iii.22.

SLIPPER, slippery, cunning, *Oth.*, 2.i.238.

SLIPPERY, fickle, inconstant, *Ant. and Cleo.*, I.ii.179.

SLIPSHOD, in slippers, *Lear*, I.v.11.

SLIVER, to tear off, *Lear*, 4.ii.34.

SLUBBER, to spoil, sully, *Oth.*, I.iii.226.

SMALL, *small beer*, weak beer, so the trivialities of daily life, *Oth.*, 2.i.159; slender, *Per.*, 4.Prol.22.

SMILE, *smile you my speeches*, to mock at my remarks, *Lear*, 2.ii.77.

SMOOTH, to flatter, speak in friendly way, *Per.*, I.ii.78; to humour, *Lear*, 2.ii.70.

SMUG, spruce, *Lear*, 4.vi.200.

SMULKIN, a fiend, taken from Harsnet's *Declaration*, *Lear*, 3.iv.137.

SNATCH, *snatches in his voice*, staccato style of utterance, *Cym.*, 4.ii.106.

SNEAPED, pinched with cold, *Lucrece*, 333.

SNIPE, fool, *Oth.*, I.iii.379.

SNUFF, (i) charred wick, so of some worn out or inferior person, *Cym.*, I.vi.86; *my snuff*, the useless end of my life, *Lear*, 4.vi.39; (ii) huff, offence-taking, *Per.*, I.i.26.

SOD, see 'seethe'.

SOFT, stop, *Ant. and Cleo.*, 2.ii.87.

SOIL, (i) solution, *Son.*, 69,14; (ii) *soiled horse*, stall-fed with green food, *Lear*, 4.vi.122.

SOLACE, to enjoy oneself, *Cym.*, I.vi.85.

SOLE, unique, *Phoenix*, 2.

SOLEMNITY, ceremony, *Ant. and Cleo.*, 5.ii.363.

SOLICIT, to pray to heaven, *Oth.*, 5.ii.29; *orderly soliciting*, business-like wooing, *Cym.*, 2.iii.47.

SOLICITATION, illicit courtship, *Oth.*, 4.ii.199.

SOMETIME, formerly, *Cym.*, 5.v.333; from time to time, *Lucrece*, 95; *adj.*, former, *Lear*, I.i.119.

SONNET, poem in praise of person or quality, *Lov.Comp.*, 209.

SOON, *soon at night*, towards evening, *Oth.*, 3.iv.199; *soonest*, quickest, *Ant. and Cleo.*, 3.v.27.

SOOTH, flattery; personified, *Signior Sooth*, *Per.*, I.ii.44.

SOOTHE, to humour, *Ven. and Ad.*, 850.

SOOTHSAYER, diviner, foreteller of the future, *Ant. and Cleo.*, I.ii.2; *verb*, to foretell, *Ant. and Cleo.*, I.ii.47.

SOP, *sop o' th' moonshine of you*, steep you in moonshine by stabbing you in many places and so letting it in, *Lear*, 2.ii.29.

SOPHISTICATED, not 'the thing itself', contaminated, disguised by clothes, *Lear*, 3.iv.105.

SORRY, troublesome, *Oth.*, 3.iv.48.

SORT, kind, *Per.*, 4.ii.98; *verb*, to associate with, consort, *Ven. and Ad.*, 689; to ordain, *Lucrece*, 899; to adopt, to assume (as in harmony with something), *Lucrece*, 1221.

SOUND, to swoon, *Lucrece*, 1486.

SOUR, *souring his cheeks*, giving them an unfriendly appearance, *Ven. and Ad.*, 185.

SOUR-FAC'D, with worn, harsh, features, *Lucrece*, 1334.

SOVEREIGN, *opinion, a sovereign mistress of effects,* confidence is the supreme agent in securing success, *Oth.,* I.iii.225 ; potent, *Son.,* 153,8.

SOVEREIGNTY, supreme excellence, *Lucrece,* 36.

SPACE, interval of time, *Lear,* 5.iii.54.

SPANIEL, to follow, fawn, *Ant. and Cleo.,* 4.xii.21.

SPARE, *spare me,* save me having to speak my mind, *Lear,* 2.iii.95.

SPARTAN, *Spartan dog,* fierce, relentless, *Oth.,* 5.ii.364.

SPEAK, *speak him far,* praise him highly, *Cym.,* I.i.24 ; *speak with thee at sea,* fight you on the sea, *Ant. and Cleo.,* 2.vi.25 ; to reveal, *Ant. and Cleo.,* 3.xii.35 ; to indicate, *Cym.,* 4.ii.355 ; *Per.,* I.iii.13 ; *speak parrot,* utter words without sense, *Oth.,* 2.iii.270.

SPECTACLES, glasses, *Lear,* I.ii.35 ; eyes, *Cym.,* I.vi.36.

SPECULATIONS, scouts, *Lear,* 3.i.24.

SPECULATIVE, with power of vision, *Oth.,* I.iii.270.

SPEECHLESS, *speechless song,* song without words, *Son.,* 8,13.

SPEED, *a se'nnight's speed,* a week before they were expected, *Oth.,* 2.i.77 ; fortune, success (with quibble on ' speed ' = swiftness), *Cym.,* 3.v.161 ; *verb,* fare for good or ill, *Cym.,* 5.iv.182 ; succeed, *Lear,* I.ii.19.

SPEKEN (archaic form), to speak, *Per.,* 2.*Prol.*12.

SPEND, *spend their mouths,* to bark, bay, *Ven. and Ad.,* 695 ; *spent,* destroyed, forgotten, *Son.,* 107,14 ; to forfeit, exchange, *Oth.,* 2.iii.187.

SPHERE, in the Ptolemaic system the sun, moon and planets were carried by hollow crystalline spheres concentric with the earth, *Ant. and Cleo.,* 4.xv.10 ; *Lov.Comp.,* 23 ; *the tuned spheres,* the spheres were thought to give out a heavenly music as they revolved, *Ant. and Cleo.,* 5.ii.84 ; *the music of the spheres* at *Per.,* 5.i.228 ; so of worldly place and duty, *Ant. and Cleo.,* 2.vii.14.

SPHERICAL, *spherical predominance,* the influence of the planets, *Lear,* I.ii.118.

SPILL, to destroy, *Lear,* 3.i.8.

SPINSTER, one who spins yarn, *Oth.,* I.i.24.

SPIRIT, soul, *Son.,* 129,1 ; life, *Ant. and Cleo.,* 4.xv.58 ; courage, *Cym.,* 5.iii.35 ; inclination, *Cym.,* I.v.34 ; genius, *Son.,* 86,5 ; power, *Oth.,* 2.iii.272 ; the immortal part, *Son.,* 74,8 ; *spirits of richest coat,* men of noblest rank, *Lov.Comp.,* 236.

SPITE, injury, vexation, *Lucrece,* 1600 ; *in spite of,* in contempt of, regardless of, *Oth.,* I.iii.96 ; insult, *Oth.,* 4.i.70.

SPLEEN, regarded as the seat of passion and emotion ; *child of spleen,* of disobedient temper, *Lear,* I.iv.282 ; of ungovernable passion, *Oth.,* 4.i.88 ;

conflicting emotions, *Ven. and Ad.,* 907.

SPLINTER, to join with splints, to mend, *Oth.,* 2.iii.313.

SPLIT, to mangle, stutter, *Ant. and Cleo.,* 2.vii.122.

SPOIL, booty, prey, *Ven. and Ad.,* 553 ; plundering, *Lov.Comp.,* 154 ; victim, *Lucrece,* 733 ; *verb,* plunder, vanquish, *Ant. and Cleo.,* 3.vi.25 ; to mar, undo, *Lear,* 5.iii.278.

SPONGY, *the spongy South,* the moist, wet South, *Cym.,* 4.ii.350.

SPORT, amorous play, *Oth.,* 2.i.224 ; *sportive,* amorous, *Son.,* 121,6.

SPOT, disgrace, *Ant. and Cleo.,* 4.xii.35 ; *verb,* spotted with, having as a pattern, *Oth.,* 3.iii.439.

SPRIGHT, mood, spirit, *Ven. and Ad.,* 181.

SPRING, a young shoot, bud, *Lucrece,* 950.

SPRITE, ghost, soul, *Lucrece,* 1728 ; *verb, I am sprited with,* haunted, disturbed by, *Cym.,* 2.iii.139.

SPRITELY, ghostly, *Cym.,* 5.v.428.

SQUARE, *not kept my square,* not observed the proper limit of conduct, *Ant. and Cleo.,* 2.iii.6 ; *the most precious square of sense,* the utmost sensibility, *Lear,* I.i.73 ; *in the brave squares of war,* among the front-line formations, *Ant. and Cleo.,* 3.xi.40 ; *adj.,* square brows, high forehead, *Per.,* 5.i.109 ; *if report be square to her,* accurate in its report of her, *Ant. and Cleo.,* 2.ii.189 ; *verb,* to quarrel, *Ant. and Cleo.,* 2.i.45.

SQUENE, to squint, *Lear,* 3.iv.115.

SQUINY, to squint, look askance, *Lear,* 4.vi.137.

SQUIRE-LIKE, like one of the attendants, *Lear,* 2.iv.213.

STABLISHMENT, the possession, rule, *Ant. and Cleo.,* 3.vi.9.

STAGE, to exhibit in public, *Ant. and Cleo.,* 3.xiii.30 ; to present a play about persons and scenes, *Ant. and Cleo.,* 5.ii.216.

STAGGER, perplexity, giddiness, *Cym.,* 5.v.233.

STAIN, *stain to all nymphs,* his beauty surpassing theirs, overwhelming them, *Ven. and Ad.,* 9 ; *verb,* to eclipse, *Ant. and Cleo.,* 3.v.27.

STALL, *stall together,* rest at peace with one another, *Ant. and Cleo.,* 5.i.39.

STAMP, a coin, with effigy stamped on it, *Cym.,* 5.iv.24 ; *verb,* to coin, to turn to advantage, *Oth.,* 2.i.239.

STANCH, firm, watertight, *Ant. and Cleo.,* 2.ii.119.

STAND, the butt past which the deer is driven within range of the hunter, *Cym.,* 2.ii.70 ; *verb, stands our lives upon to,* it is a matter of life and death to us to, *Ant. and Cleo.,* 2.i.50 ; *the main descry stands on the hourly thought,* the appearance of the main body is expected hourly, *Lear,* 4.vi.216.

STAR, *our Jovial star,* those born under Jupiter were supposed to be fortunate and happy, *Cym.*, 5.iv.105 ; lode star, guide, *Son.*, 116,7 ; *the seven stars*, the Pleiades, *Lear*, 1.v.34.

STAR-BLASTING, blighted by the influence of a malignant star (*e.g.* lunatic under the influence of the moon), *Lear*, 3.iv.58.

START, caprice, *Lear*, 1.i.299 ; *by starts*, now and then for no good reason, *Ant. and Cleo.*, 4.xii.7 ; *startingly*, abruptly, wildly, *Oth.*, 3.iv.79.

STATE, *my state*, my place among the factions, *Lear*, 5.i.68 ; his place, rank, *Lucrece*, 45 ; *child of state*, born of considerations of rank or material gain, *Son.*, 124,1 ; *states*, persons of rank, nobles, *Cym.*, 3.iv.35.

STATION, manner of standing, *Ant. and Cleo.*, 3.iii.19.

STATIST, statesman, *Cym.*, 2.iv.16.

STATUTE, *the statute of thy beauty*, the bond entitling you to seize the surety's body and possessions, *Son.*, 134,9.

STAY, *this inconstant stay*, this fleeting moment of perfection, *Son.*, 15,9 ; *verb*, *stay the field*, remain to fight, *Ven. and Ad.*, 894.

STEAD, to help, profit, *Oth.*, 1.iii.337.

STEEPY, precipitous, *Son.*, 63,5.

STEERAGE, course steered by ship, *Per.*, 4.*Prol.*79.

STEW, brothel, *Cym.*, 1.vi.151.

STILL, continually, *Oth.*, 1.iii.147 ; *still-soliciting*, always looking for advantage to self, *Lear*, 1.i.231 ; *still-gazing*, continually gazing, *Lucrece*, 84.

STILLITORY, alembic, still, *Ven. and Ad.*, 443.

STINT, to cease, *Per.*, 4.iv.42.

STOCK, to put in the stocks, *Lear*, 2.ii.127 ; *stock-punished*, by being put in the stocks, *Lear*, 3.iv.132.

STOLE, a long robe, *Lov.Comp.*, 297.

STOMACH, seat of emotions ; anger, *Lear*, 5.iii.75 ; *verb*, *stomach not all*, do not take offence at everything, *Ant. and Cleo.*, 3.iv.12 ; *private stomaching*, personal quarrels, *Ant. and Cleo.*, 2.ii.9.

STOMACHER, ornamental covering of the breast, worn by women, *Cym.*, 3.iv.82.

STONE, used of dumbness ; *your considerate stone*, dumb though thoughtful, *Ant. and Cleo.*, 2.ii.114 ; polished crystal as mirror, *Lear*, 5.iii.262 ; *verb*, to harden, *Oth.*, 5.ii.66.

STONISH'D, bewildered, *Ven. and Ad.*, 825.

STOOP, in falconry, to swoop on the prey, used of the eagle, *Cym.*, 5.iv.116.

STOP, check, *Cym.*, 5.iii.40.

STORE, for procreation, *Son.*, 11,9 ; fertility, *Lucrece*, 1837 ; *what store*, what kind of process, type of thought *cf.* ' a generation of still-breeding thoughts ', *Rich. II*, 5.iii.8), *Lear*, 3.vi.53 ; *verb*, to people, *Oth.*, 4.iii.83.

STORM, to raise a storm, *Lov.Comp.*, 7.

STORY, the history of noble actions, *Ant.*

and *Cleo.*, 3.xiii.46 ; *verb*, to praise, commend, *Cym.*, 1.iv.31.

STOUP, a tankard, *Oth.*, 2.iii.27.

STOUT, strong, *Son.*, 65,7 ; *adv.*, strongly, *Oth.*, 2.i.48.

STRAIGHT, immediately, *Ant. and Cleo.*, 4.xii.3.

STRAIGHT-PIGHT, erect, *Cym.*, 5.v.164.

STRAIN, (i) race, descent, *Lear*, 5.iii.41 ; *Cym.*, 4.ii.24 ; character, quality, *Cym.*, 3.iv.91 ; (ii) tune, *Lucrece*, 1131 ; *verb*, to stretch, *Oth.*, 3.iii.222 ; *strain his entertainment*, exert herself unduly for his restoration to office, *Oth.*, 3.iii.254 ; *strain courtesy*, give place to others, *Ven. and Ad.*, 888.

STRAIT, narrow passage, *Lucrece*, 1670 ; *adj.*, narrow, *Cym.*, 5.iii.7.

STRANGE, foreign, unfamiliar with the customs of the country, *Cym.*, 1.vi.53 ; unacquainted, *Son.*, 89,8 ; unusual, out of the ordinary, *Ant. and Cleo.*, 2.ii.159.

STRANGENESS, reserve, distant demeanour, *Ven. and Ad.*, 310 ; *Oth.*, 3.iii.12 ; *verb*, *stranger'd with our oath*, disowned as a daughter by my vow, *Lear*, 1.i.204.

STRANGLE, *I will acquaintance strangle*, choke, suppress, *Son.*, 89,8.

STRAY, lapse, turning aside, *Lear*, 1.i.209.

STRENGTH, force, army, *Ant. and Cleo.*, 2.i.17 ; authority, *Lear*, 2.i.112.

STRETCH, *stretch their duties*, to perform in an officious manner, *Lear*, 1.ii.99.

STRICT, close, *Ven. and Ad.*, 874 ; rigorous, *Cym.*, 5.iv.17 ; inexorable, *Per.*, 3.iii.8.

STRIDE, *stride a limit*, pass beyond a restricted area, *Cym.*, 3.iii.35.

STRIKE, to blast, infect, *Lear*, 2.iv.161 ; *strike the vessels*, broach the casks of wine, *Ant. and Cleo.*, 2.vii.95.

STUBBORN, harsh, *Oth.*, 1.iii.227.

STUDIED, *well studied for*, thoroughly prepared, *Ant. and Cleo.*, 2.vi.47.

SUB-CONTRACTED, a sub-contract is consequent on a contract and affects some part of the whole ; the lady's liaison is here treated ironically as affecting a detail in the contract of marriage, *Lear*, 5.iii.87.

SUBJECT, *a subject of this war*, one under authority, *Lear*, 5.iii.61 ; the people as a body owing obedience to a rule or ruler ; *the finny subject of the sea*, fishes, *Per.*, 2.i.48.

SUBSCRIBE, to put one's signature to a document, *Ant. and Cleo.*, 4.vi.14 ; *all cruels else subscribe*, let all other cruelties pass as forgivable, *Lear*, 3.vii.64 ; yields, *Son.*, 107,10.

SUBSCRIPTION, submission, obedience, *Lear*, 3.ii.18.

SUBTLETY, stratagem, *Per.*, 2.v.44.

SUCCEED, to follow, *Lear*, 1.ii.137 ; *Per.*, 1.iv.104 ; to devolve on, pass legally to, *Oth.*, 5.ii.370.

SUCCESS, the outcome, result, *Ant. and Cleo.*, 3.v.6.

SUCCESSION, *his succession*, those who

followed him on the throne, his heirs *Cym.*, 3.i.8.

SUCCESSIVE, hereditary, *Son.*, 127,3.

SUDDEN, immediate, *Oth.*, 4.ii.190; hasty, *Oth.*, 2.i.266.

SUDDENLY, immediately, *Lucrece*, 1683.

SUFFER, to endure, *Per.*, 5.i.136; submit, *Oth.*, 5.ii.259; to deteriorate, *Ant. and Cleo.*, 3.xiii.34; *discerning thine honour from thy suffering*, distinguishing what honour must reject from what should be endured, *Lear*, 4.ii.53.

SUFFERANCE, forbearance, *Cym.*, 3.v.35; distress, *Lear*, 3.vi.106; damage, *Oth.*, 2.i.23.

SUFFICIENT, fit, able, *Oth.*, 3.iv.91.

SUGGEST, to prompt, *Son.*, 144,2; to tempt, *Oth.*, 2.iii.341.

SUGGESTION, prompting, temptation, *Lear*, 2.i.73.

SUIT, attendance, *Lov.Comp.*, 234; courtship, *Lov.Comp.*, 79; *verb*, to dress, *Lear*, 4.vii.6.

SULLEN, dark, *Son.*, 29,12.

SULLIED, tarnished, *Son.*, 15,12.

SULPHUR, *stones of sulphur*, thunderbolt, ball of lightning, *Cym.*, 5.v.240.

SULPHUROUS, of lightning, *Lear*, 3.ii.4; of hell-fire, *Lear*, 4.vi.128.

SUM, *the sum*, the import, what it adds up to, *Ant. and Cleo.*, 1.i.18.

SUMMONER, officer of ecclesiastical court who summons offenders, *Lear*, 3.ii.59.

SUPERFLUOUS, *superfluous kings*, a superfluity of kings, *Ant. and Cleo.*, 3.xii.5; beyond mere necessity, *Lear*, 2.iv.264; *Lear*, 4.i.68; *superfluous riots*, revelling in luxury, *Per.*, 1.iv.54.

SUPERFLUX, superfluity, *Lear*, 3.iv.35.

SUPERSERVICEABLE, over-officious, *Lear*, 2.ii.16.

SUPERVISOR, spectator, *Oth.*, 3.iii.399.

SUPPLY, reinforcement, *Cym.*, 5.ii.16; to gratify, *Oth.*, 4.i.28; *my place supplied*, filled, *Oth.*, 3.iii.17.

SUPPLYANT, auxiliary, *Cym.*, 3.vii.14.

SUPPLYMENT, continuance of supply, *Cym.*, 3.iv.178.

SUPPOSING, imagination, *Per.*, 5.Prol.21; *supposed*, pretended, *Lear*, 5.iii.112.

SUR-ADDITION, additional name, in honour of his valour, *Cym.*, 1.i.33.

SURCEASE, to cease, *Lucrece*, 1766.

SURE, *make him sure enough*, kill him, *Per.*, 1.i.170; infallible, *Cym.*, 5.iv.7.

SURETY, *do as if for surety*, act as if it were true, *Oth.*, 1.iii.384.

SURETY-LIKE, as one going bail for another, *Son.*, 137,7.

SURMISE, suspicion, *Son.*, 117,10; *Oth.*, 3.iii.186; *Cym.*, 3.iv.23.

SURPRISE, *surpriz'd*, captured, *Ant. and Cleo.*, 5.ii.35; to confound, *Ven. and Ad.*, 890.

SUSPECT, suspicion, *Ven. and Ad.*, 1010; *verb*, to mistrust, *Ven. and Ad.*, 1153.

SUSPICION, *his suspicion*, the suspicion entertained about him, *Lear*, 3.v.20.

SUSTAIN, *sustaining corn*, nourishing, *Lear*, 4.iv.6.

SWART-COMPLEXION'D, dark, *Son.*, 28,11.

SWATHING, *swathing clothes*, bands wrapped round infants, *Cym.*, 1.i.59.

SWAY, *limping sway*, ill-directed control, *Son.*, 66,8; rule, *Lear*, 1.i.136; *verb*, to control, *Son.*, 128,3.

SWEAR, *swear thy gods*, to invoke, *Lear*, 1.i.160.

SWELL, to billow with the wind, *Ant. and Cleo.*, 2.ii.214.

SWERVING, turning aside from duty, *Ant. and Cleo.*, 3.xi.50.

SWITHOLD, Saint Vitalis, invoked as a protection against nightmare, *Lear*, 3.iv.118.

SWORDER, gladiator, *Ant. and Cleo.*, 3.xiii.31.

SYMPATHIZE, *is sympathized*, is matched, is echoed, *Lucrece*, 1113; *truly sympathiz'd*, faithfully realized, *Son.*, 82,11.

SYMPATHY, harmony, *Oth.*, 2.i.226; *for sympathy*, because of the correspondence, *Cym.*, 5.iv.149.

TABLE, board on which picture is painted, *Son.*, 24,2; *Cupid's tables*, love-letters, *Cym.*, 3.ii.39; *tables*, note-book, *Son.*, 122,1; *tabled*, set down in writing, *Cym.*, 1.iv.5.

TABOURINE, side-drum, *Ant. and Cleo.*, 4.viii.37.

TAINT, fault, *Ant. and Cleo.*, 5.i.30; *fall'n into taint*, become corrupted, *Lear*, 1.i.221; *verb*, to injure, *Oth.*, 1.iii.271; to infect, *Cym.*, 3.iv.25; to disparage, *Oth.*, 2.i.262; *tainting*, corruption, *Cym.*, 1.iv.131.

TAKE, to have recourse to, *Per.*, 4.iv.3; *the witch take me*, cast evil spell on me, *Ant. and Cleo.*, 4.ii.37; *taking airs*, infectious, harmful, *Lear*, 2.iv.162; *taking off*, murder, *Lear*, 5.i.65; *take upon's*, to assume some knowledge or power, to pretend to, *Lear*, 5.iii.16; *I'll have the work ta'en out*, I shall have the pattern copied, *Oth.*, 3.iii.300; to learn, *Lear*, 4.vi.141; *take me up for*, to rebuke, *Cym.*, 2.i.4.

TAKING, *in worser taking*, in worse plight (for the cause of fear was not imaginary), *Lucrece*, 453.

TALENT, *these talents of their hair*, precious treasures, *Lov.Comp.*, 204; *beyond all talents*, beyond price, *Cym.*, 1.vi.79.

TALL, of ship, large, *Lear*, 4.vi.18; *tall youth*, good fighting-men, *Ant. and Cleo.*, 2.vi.7.

TALLY, stick, notched to keep a reckoning, and split in two, both debtor and creditor having a part, *Son.*, 122,10.

TANLING, one so exposed as to be tanned by the sun, *Cym.*, 4.iv.29.

TANTALUS, a king, condemned in the underworld to stand in water that always withdrew as he tried to drink; over his head hung fruit that also evaded his grasp, *Ven. and Ad.*, 599; *Lucrece*, 858.

TAPER, candle, *Oth.*, 1.i.142.

TARGE, shield, *Cym.*, 5.v.5.

TARGET, shield, *Ant. and Cleo.*, 1.iii.82.

TART, unpleasant, *Lear*, 4.ii.87; sour-looking, *Ant. and Cleo.*, 2.v.38.

TASTE, *whose qualification shall come into no true taste again*, the mutinous spirit will not be qualified or diluted to something that has a taste agreeable with health and peace, *Oth.*, 2.i.269; *verb*, to experience, to test, *Lear*, 2.iv.290.

TAX, teen, woe, *Ven. and Ad.*, 808.

TELAMON, Ajax, son of Telamon, was competitor with Ulysses for the arms of Achilles; he lost his reason when they were given to Ulysses, *Ant. and Cleo.*, 4.xiii.2.

TELL, to count, *Ven. and Ad.*, 277; *Oth.*, 3.iii.173; to solve a riddle, *Per.*, 1.Prol.38.

TELLUS, Tellus was an earth-goddess, so the earth, *Per.*, 4.i.14.

TEMPER, *in temper*, in equable state of mind, *Lear*, 1.v.44; *verb*, to compound, *Cym.*, 5.v.250; to moisten to workable condition, *Lear*, 1.iv.304; to soften, *Ven. and Ad.*, 565.

TEMPERANCE, normal condition, sanity, *Lear*, 4.vii.24; chastity, *Ant. and Cleo.*, 3.xiii.121.

TEND, to wait upon, serve, *Ant. and Cleo.*, 2.ii.211; *Lear*, 2.i.95.

TENDANCE, care, attention, *Cym.*, 5.v.53.

TENDER, (i) regard, care, *Lear*, 1.iv.209; (ii) offer, *Son.*, 83,4; *verb*, (i) to regard, *Lucrece*, 534; (ii) to offer, *Cym.*, 3.v.154.

TENDER-HEFTED (sensitive (though the exact meaning is doubtful), *Lear*, 2.iv.170.

TENOUR, summary, indication of nature, *Lucrece*, 1310.

TENT, a probe for a wound, *Cym.*, 3.iv.114.

TEREUS, Thracian king, married to Procne, daughter of Pandion, king of Athens; ravished and mutilated his wife's sister Philomela, *Cym.*, 2.ii.45.

TERMLESS, *that termless skin*, its charm beyond description, *Lov.Comp.*, 94.

TERRENE, earthly, *Ant. and Cleo.*, 3.xiii.153.

TEST, evidence, *Oth.*, 1.iii.107.

THAN, then, *Lucrece*, 1440.

THANKFUL, worthy of thanks, *Per.*, 5.ii.20.

THEME, subject, question at issue, *Ant. and Cleo.*, 2.ii.48.

THEORIC, theory, *Oth.*, 1.i.24.

THERE, *are you there with me?* is that your meaning? *Lear*, 4.vi.145; so, *are you thereabouts? Ant. and Cleo.*, 3.x.30.

THERETO, in addition, *Cym.*, 4.iv.33; so *thereunto*, *Oth.*, 2.i.141.

THESSALY, *the boar of Thessaly*, the boar sent by Artemis to ravage Thessaly, killed in the Calydonian hunt by Meleager, *Ant. and Cleo.*, 4.xiii.2.

THETIS, for Tethys, wife of Oceanus; Thetis was a sea-nymph and mother of Achilles; used of Cleopatra as

partner of Antony who hoped to rule the sea, *Ant. and Cleo.*, 3.vii.60; *Per.*, 4.iv.41.

THICK, *speak thick*, fast, *Cym.*, 3.ii.55; *thicken*, to grow dim, *Ant. and Cleo.*, 2.iii.28.

THICK-SIGHTED, dim-sighted, *Ven. and Ad.*, 136.

THINK, to brood, meditate, *Ant. and Cleo.*, 3.xiii.1; *thinks*, methinks, *Lov.Comp.*, 91.

THIS, sometimes for 'this is', *Lear*, 4.vi.184; thus, *Ven. and Ad.*, 205.

THOROUGH, through, *Per.*, 4.iii.35; *prep.*, *Lucrece*, 1851.

THOUGHTEN, *be you thoughten*, think, *Per.*, 4.vi.107.

THOUGHT-EXECUTING, rapid as thought, *Lear*, 3.ii.4.

THREE-NOOK'D, three-cornered, *Ant. and Cleo.*, 4.vi.6.

THREE-SUITED, a servant's allowance of livery, *Lear*, 2.ii.14.

THRENE, dirge, *Phoenix*, 49.

THRIFT, gain, prosperity, *Cym.*, 5.i.15.

THRIFTLESS, unprofitable, *Son.*, 2,8.

THRONG'D, oppressed, *Per.*, 1.i.101.

THROUGH, thoroughly (so as to find the opponent), *Cym.*, 4.ii.161; *throughly*, thoroughly, *Cym.*, 3.vi.36.

THUNDER-BEARER, Jove, *Lear*, 2.iv.226.

THUNDERER, Jove, *Cym.*, 5.iv.95.

THUNDER-STONE, thunderbolt, *Cym.*, 4.ii.272.

THWART, perverse, *Lear*, 1.iv.283; *verb*, *thwarting the wayward seas*, crossing, *Per.*, 4.iv.10.

TIB, slang term for woman, *Per.*, 4.vi.164.

TIGHT, deft, *Ant. and Cleo.*, 4.iv.15.

TIKE, cur, *Lear*, 3.vi.69.

TIME, *his time*, his time of life, age, *Cym.*, 1.i.43; lifetime, *Lear*, 1.i.294; life, *Oth.*, 1.i.162; the present state of things, *Ant. and Cleo.*, 3.vi.82; the future, *Son.*, 18,12; *the rights of time*, the claim of society, *Ven. and Ad.*, 759; *time of scorn*, scornful world, *Oth.*, 4.ii.55.

TIME-BETTERING, *the time-bettering days*, these progressive, innovating times, *Son.*, 82,8.

TIMELESS, untimely; so *all-too-timeless*, *Lucrece*, 44.

TIMELIER, earlier, *Ant. and Cleo.*, 2.vi.51.

TINCT, colour, *Cym.*, 2.ii.23; the grand elixir of the alchemists that was to turn base metal into gold; so used of the value conferred on Antony's messenger, *An. and Cleo.*, 1.v.37.

TIRE, *rich tire about you*, living in opulence, *Per.*, 3.ii.22; head-dress, *Ant. and Cleo.*, 2.v.22; *verb*, dressed, *Ven. and Ad.*, 177.

TIRE, (from falconry) to devour, *Ven. and Ad.*, 56; to embrace lustfully, *Cym.*, 3.iv.93; to devour with the eye, *Lucrece*, 417.

TISSUE, fabric woven of gold thread and silk, *Ant. and Cleo.*, 2.ii.203.

GLOSSARY

TITAN, the god of the sun, *Ven. and Ad.*, 177.

TITHING, a locality (originally containing some ten families, or the tenth of a hundred), *Lear*, 3.iv.132.

TOAD-SPOTTED, the toad was regarded as venomous; so *toad-spotted traitor*, as marked all over by infamy as the toad is covered by its venomous spots, *Lear*, 5.iii.138.

TO-BLESS, bless entirely, *Per.*, 4.vi.20.

TOGED, gowned, *Oth.*, 1.i.25.

TOKEN'D, *token'd pestilence*, the spots that marked the plague-stricken were called the 'Lord's tokens', *Ant. and Cleo.*, 3.x.9; *Lucrece*, 1748.

TONGUE, to utter, *Cym.*, 5.iv.145.

TOUCH, *a touch*, a feeling, *Cym.*, 1.i.135; occasion, incentive, *Ant. and Cleo.*, 1.ii.174; the artist's brushwork or the poet's phrasing, *Son.*, 17,8; *Son.*, 82,10; *verb*, to try as with a touchstone, *Oth.*, 3.iii.82; *thy thoughts touch their effects in this*, your fears are realized in this event, *Ant. and Cleo.*, 5.ii.328.

TOWARD, willing, accommodating, *Ven. and Ad.*, 1157; *adv.*, in preparation, *Lear*, 2.i.10.

TOWER, of falcon, to circle up above prey, *Lucrece*, 506.

TOY, whim, *Oth.*, 3.iv.157; a trifle, *Cym.*, 4.ii.194.

TRACT, course, path, *Son.*, 7,12.

TRANC'D, in a swoon, *Lear* 5.iii.218.

TRANSFIX, to remove, *Son.*, 80,9

TRANSLATE, *if like a lamb he could his looks translate*, if he could change his appearance so as to look like a lamb, *Son.*, 96,10.

TRASH, poor quality material, poor specimen, *Oth.*, 2.i.297.

TRASH, to weight a dog's collar to keep him from outrunning the pack, *Oth.*, 2.i.297.

TRAVAIL, labour, *Son.*, 79,6.

TRAVERSE, military command: march! *Oth.*, 1.iii.367.

TREACHER, traitor, *Lear*, 1.ii.118.

TREASURE, treasury, *Son.*, 136,5; *verb*, to enrich, *Son.*, 6,3.

TREATISE, discourse, talk, *Ven. and Ad.*, 774.

TREATY, *humble treaties*, proposals, *Ant. and Cleo.*, 3.xi.62.

TREBLE-DATED, *treble-dated crow*, living thrice as long as man, *Phoenix*, 17.

TRENCHES, wrinkles, *Son.*, 2,2.

TRENCHER, wooden plate, *Ant. and Cleo.*, 3.xiii.117.

TRESPASS, *did trespasses to*, offended against, *Ant. and Cleo.*, 2.i.40.

TRICK, characteristic reaction, *Ant. and Cleo.*, 5.ii.75; peculiarity, *Lear*, 4.vi.106; caprice, *Oth.*, 4.ii.130.

TRIPLE, *the triple pillar*, one of three, *Ant. and Cleo.*, 1.i.12.

TRIPLE-TURN'D, three times faithless, *Ant. and Cleo.*, 4.xii.13.

TRIUMPH, procession of victorious general and his troops on return to Rome, *Ant. and Cleo.*, 5.ii.109;

trump-card, *Ant. and Cleo.*, 4.xiv.20.

TRIUMPHANT, splendid, *Ant. and Cleo.*, 2.ii.188.

TROTH, truth, *Cym.*, 5.v.274; faith, *Lucrece*, 571; *Cym.*, 1.i.96.

TROW, to believe, *Lear*, 1.iv.121; *what is the matter, trow?* I wonder, *Cym.*, 1.vi.46.

TRUCE, *take truce with*, to make peace with, *Ven. and Ad.*, 82.

TRUE, *truest bars*, reliable, *Son.*, 48,2; well-proportioned, *Lear*, 1.ii.8; *truest manner'd*, honestly and kindly disposed, *Cym.*, 1.vi.165.

TRUMPET, trumpeter, *Phoenix*, 3.

TRUNDLE-TAIL, dog with long curling tail, *Lear*, 3.vi.69.

TRUST, *for fear of trust*, for lack of self-possession, *Son.*, 23,5; *of trust*, reliable, *Son.*, 48,4.

TRUTH, loyalty, *Cym.*, 5.v.107.

TRIED, proved, *Ven. and Ad.*, 280.

TUB, *that tub both fill'd and running*, like the leaky jar the Danaides were condemned in Hades to fill, *Cym.*, 1.vi.47.

TURK, *the Turk*, the Sultan of Turkey, *Lear*, 3.iv.91.

TURLYGOD, apparently a name for a bedlam-beggar, *Lear*, 2.iii.20.

TURN, to return, to be false to one's promise, to turn to men, *Oth.*, 4.i.249-251.

TURTLE, turtle-dove, *Phoenix*, 23.

TUSHES, tusks, *Ven. and Ad.*, 617.

TWAIN, *we two must be twain*, separated, *Son.*, 36,1; pair, *Ant. and Cleo.*, 1.i.38.

TWIGGEN, *twiggen bottle*, bottle cased in wicker-work, *Oth.*, 2.iii.140.

TWIN, *twin with*, imitate perfectly, resemble completely, *Per.*, 5.Prol.8; *twinn'd stones*, resembling each other, *Cym.*, 1.vi.34.

TWIRE, to twinkle, *Son.*, 28,12.

TYPE, title, *Lucrece*, 1050.

TYRANNOUS, cruel, *Lear*, 3.iv.147.

TYRANT, cruel individual, *Cym.*, 1.i.84.

UNACCOMMODATED, *unaccommodated man*, man without the clothing, implements, etc., he has devised for his convenience, *Lear*, 3.iv.106.

UNADVISED, *unadvised wounds*, inflicted unintentionally, in ignorance, *Lucrece*, 1488.

UNAPPROVED, without proof, unconfirmed, *Lov.Comp.*, 53.

UNBEND, *to be unbent*, to be unprepared to strike the final blow (as if discharging an arrow), *Cym.*, 3.iv.107; *a brow unbent*, without frowning, not aggressive, *Lucrece*, 1509.

UNBITTED, unbridled, *Oth.*, 1.iii.330.

UNBLESS, to deprive of happiness, *Son.*, 3,4; *unblest*, wretched, *Oth.*, 5.i.34.

UNBOLTED, unsifted, coarse, *Lear*, 2.ii.61.

UNBONNETED, without cover on his head, *Lear*, 3.i.14; *speak unbonneted*, speak without removing the cap, or showing any sign of inequality (*cf. bonneted into their estimation,* by addressing them, his cap off, as superiors, *Cor.,* 2.ii.25), *Oth.,* 1.ii.23.

UNBOOKISH, ignorant, *Oth.,* 4.i.101.

UNBRED, unborn, *Son.,* 104,13.

UNCAPABLE, unfit, *Oth.,* 4.iii.228.

UNCONSTRAINED, that are not felt as a constraint, *Lov.Comp.,* 242.

UNCONTROLLED, unconquered, *Ven. and Ad.,* 104; not to be restrained, *Lucrece,* 645.

UNCOUTH, strange, disturbing, *Lucrece,* 1598.

UNCROSS'D, *his book uncross'd,* the account unpaid, not scored out as paid, *Cym.,* 3.iii.26.

UNDER, *each under eye,* earthly, *Son.,* 7.2 ; *this under globe,* the earth, *Lear,* 2.ii.158.

UNDERGO, to take upon oneself, *Cym.,* 1.iv.136.

UNDERTAKE, *undertake every companion,* have to do with, answer the challenge of, *Cym.,* 2.i.25 ; to enter, *Per.,* 2.v.3 ; *undertake my troth,* guarantee my truth and loyalty, *Lov.Comp.,* 280 ; *to undertake for me,* to act on my behalf, *Oth.,* 2.iii.320 ; to take action, *Lear,* 4.ii.13.

UNDERTAKER, *his undertaker,* see to him (by murdering him), *Oth.,* 4.i.206.

UNDISTINGUISH'D, the detail indistinguishable, *Lov.Comp.,* 20.

UNDO, to solve a riddle, *Per.,* 1.i.117 ; to prevent, be a bar to, *Per.,* 4.vi.4.

UNEAR'D, untilled, *Son.,* 3.5.

UNEQUAL, unjust, *Ant. and Cleo.,* 2.v.101.

UNEXPERIENT, inexperienced, *Lov. Comp.,* 318.

UNFATHER'D, *unfather'd fruit,* unnatural, out of course of nature, *Son.,* 97,10.

UNFELT, *unfelt sore,* not a matter of sensation, *Lucrece,* 828.

UNFOLD, to reveal, *Cym.,* 1.i.26 ; *Oth.,* 4.ii.142 ; *unfolded,* exposed, *Ant. and Cleo.,* 5.ii.169 ; *my unfolding,* my proposal, *Oth.,* 1.iii.244.

UNHANDSOME, unfair, failing to take the rough with the smooth in the soldier's life, *Oth.,* 3.iv.152.

UNHAPPILY, *unhap'ly,* evilly, *Lucrece,* 8 ; miserably, *Son.,* 66,4.

UNHAPPY, evil, injurious, *Lucrece,* 1565 ; of evil omen, *Cym.,* 5.v.153.

UNHOUSED, free from domestic cares, *Oth.,* 1.ii.26.

UNIVERSAL, *universal landlord,* of the whole earth, *Ant. and Cleo.,* 3.xiii.72.

UNJUST, lawless, faithless, *Lucrece,* 189 ; faithless, *Son.,* 138,9 ; *unjustly,* perfidiously, *Lucrece,* 1836.

UNKIND, lacking humanity, *Lear,* 3.iv.70 ; in opposition to natural instinct, childless, *Ven. and Ad.,* 204.

UNKNOWN, *unknown minds,* persons not to be named, *Son.,* 117,5 ; incalculable, *Son.,* 116,8.

UNLACE, *unlace your reputation,* divest yourself of your good name, *Oth.,* 2.iii.186.

UNLAID, *ghost unlaid,* active, not exorcised, *Cym.,* 4.ii.279 ; *unlaid ope,* concealed, *Per.,* 1.iii.89.

UNLAWFUL, illegitimate, *Ant. and Cleo.,* 3.vi.7.

UNLESS, except, *Oth.,* 1.i.24.

UNLIKE, *more unlike than,* even more wonderful than, *Cym.,* 5.v.354.

UNLIVED, deprived of life, *Lucrece,* 1754.

UNLOOKED, *unlooked for,* undistinguished, unheeded, *Son.,* 25,2.

UNMOVED, sang-froid, *Son.,* 94.4.

UNMOVING, always pointed at the victim, *Oth.,* 4.ii.56.

UNNATURALNESS, lack of human affection and its consequences, *Lear,* 1.ii.138.

UNNUMBER'D, innumerable, *Lear,* 4.vi.21.

UNPARAGON'D, matchless, *Cym.,* 1.iv.76.

UNPAVED, castrated, without stones, *Cym.,* 2.iii.31.

UNPOLICIED, devoid of sense for life, *Ant. and Cleo.,* 5.ii.306.

UNPOSSESSING, without rights of inheritance, *Lear,* 2.i.67.

UNPRIZABLE, beyond reckoning, *Cym.,* 1.iv.86.

UNPRIZ'D, *unpriz'd precious,* not valued by her family but precious to me, *Lear,* 1.i.259.

UNPROPER, *unproper beds,* beds that are not confined as they should be to their owner, *Oth.,* 4.i.68.

UNPROVIDE, shake his resolution, disarm, *Oth.,* 4.i.201 ; *unprovided,* unarmed, *Lear,* 2.i.52.

UNQUALIFIED, deprived of resolution, sense of responsibility, *Ant. and Cleo.,* 3.xi.44.

UNRECALLING, beyond recall, *Lucrece,* 993.

UNRESISTED, irresistible, *Lucrece,* 282.

UNRESPECTED, unregarded, *Son.,* 43,2 ; *Son.,* 54,10.

UNSANCTIFIED, wicked, *Lear,* 4.vi.274.

UNSEASONABLE, outwith the season in which the animal is suitable for hunting, *Lucrece,* 581.

UNSEMINAR'D, castrated, *Ant. and Cleo.,* 1.v.11.

UNSET, unplanted, *Son.,* 16,6.

UNSPEAKING, wanting adequate powers of description, *Cym.,* 5.v.178.

UNSTATE, *I would unstate myself,* to divest myself of rank and possessions, *Lear,* 1.ii.95 ; *unstate his happiness,* surrender the advantage of his fortune, *Ant. and Cleo.,* 3.xiii.30.

UNSWAY'D, ungoverned by reason, *Son.,* 141,11.

UNTAINTED, unspoiled, not defaced, *Son.,* 19,11.

UNTENTED, *untented woundings,* wounds too deep to be cleansed by a tent (roll of lint), *Lear,* 1.iv.300.

UNTHRIFT, spendthrift, *Son.,* 9.9.

UNTIE, to interpret, explain, *Cym.,* 5.iv.147 ; *untied my virgin knot,* in the classical sense of keeping the virgin zone untied, *Per.,* 4.ii.148.

UNTOLD, uncounted, *Son.,* 136,9.

UNTRUE, faithless, *Lov.Comp.,* 169 ; *adv.,* untruly, *Son.,* 72,10.

UNTUTOR'D, uninstructed, simple, *Per.*, 1.iv.74.

UNWIT, to deprive of reason, *Oth.*, 2.iii.174.

UP, in confinement, *Ant. and Cleo.*, 3.v.12.

UP-CAST, a shot at bowls, *Cym.*, 2.i.2.

UPWARD, *extremest upward*, top, *Lear*, 5.iii.135.

URCHIN-SNOUTED, with a snout like a hedgehog's, *Ven. and Ad.*, 1105.

URGE, *urge me in this act*, to put forward my name as cover or excuse for the war, *Ant. and Cleo.*, 2.ii.50.

USE, habit, *Oth.*, 4.iii.271; conduct, *Oth.*, 4.iii.102; *in use*, in trust, *Ant. and Cleo.*, 1.iii.44; a loan at interest, *Son.*, 6,5; *Ven. and Ad.*, 768; *verb*, to make a habit of, to adopt as a practice, *Lear*, 1.iv.170; to lend at interest, *Son.*, 4,7; *my so used a guest*, my habitual companion, *Per.*, 1.ii.3.

USURP, to encroach on, *Per.*, 3.ii.87; *Ven. and Ad.*, 591; *an usurp'd beard*, a beard you take upon yourself to wear, as if a soldier, *Oth.*, 1.iii.339.

UTTERANCE, *to keep at utterance*, to keep even at the peril of death, *Cym.*, 3.i.71.

VACANCY, the vacuum nature abhors, *Ant. and Cleo.*, 2.ii.220; the periods between duty and business, leisure, *Ant. and Cleo.*, 1.iv.26.

VAIL, to let fall, *Ven. and Ad.*, 314; to bow in respect, *Per.*, 2.iii.42; do homage, *Per.*, 4.Prol.29.

VAILS, perquisites, gratuities, *Per.*, 2.i.148.

VAIN-GLORY, vanity, *Cym.*, 4.i.7.

VALIDITY, value, *Lear*, 1.i.80.

VANITY, *Vanity the puppet*, Lady Vanity was a character in the morality plays, *Lear*, 2.ii.33.

VANTAGE, *doing thee vantage*, being to your profit or in your favour, *Son.*, 88,12; *urging the worser sense for vantage still*, always representing it to best advantage, in most favourable light, *Lucrece*, 249; *having thee at vantage*, having you at his mercy, at a disadvantage, *Ven. and Ad.*, 635; *for my vantage*, for my gain, *Cym.*, 5.v.198; *to the vantage*, in addition, *Oth.*, 4.iii.82; *with his next vantage*, at his earliest opportunity, *Cym.*, 1.iii.24.

VARIANCE, quarrel, *Ant. and Cleo.*, 2.vi.125.

VARLETRY, rabble, *Ant. and Cleo.*, 5.ii.56.

VARY, change of mood, *Lear*, 2.ii.74; *varying*, with the ebb and flow of fortune, *Ant. and Cleo.*, 4.xv.11.

VASSALAGE, fealty, *Son.*, 26,1.

VASTLY, *vastly stood bare*, desolate through its whole extent, *Lucrece*, 1740.

VAULTY, arched, *Lucrece*, 119.

VAUNT-COURIER, forerunner, *Lear*, 3.ii.5.

VEGETIVES, plants, *Per.*, 3.ii.36.

VEINS, *the Trojan horse stuff'd with bloody veins*, the 'bloody veins' being the soldiers concealed within and intent on slaughter, *Per.*, 1.iv.94.

VENGEANCE, used at times in curses, *Lear*, 2.iv.93.

VENOM, harmful principle, *Lucrece*, 532; *adj.*, poisonous, *Lucrece*, 850.

VENOMOUSLY, spitefully, *Per.*, 3.i.7.

VENT, *vent of blood*, discharge of blood, *Ant. and Cleo.*, 5.ii.346; utterance, *Ven. and Ad.*, 334; *verb*, to emit, *Cym.*, 1.ii.4; *Lear*, 1.i.165.

VENTURES, those whose trade exposes them to the risk of disease, *Cym.*, 1.vi.122.

VERBAL, *made she no verbal question?* did she not speak? *Lear*, 4.iii.24; *so verbal*, so insistent in your address, *Cym.*, 2.iii.106.

VERONESA, *a Veronesa*, a ship chartered from Verona, *Oth.*, 2.i.26.

VERY, *'twas very Cloten*, Cloten beyond all doubt, *Cym.*, 4.ii.108; *a very pretence*, a deliberate intention, *Lear*, 1.iv.69; *verier knaves*, more complete rascals, *Cym.*, 5.iv.199; *adv.*, *very now*, at this instant, *Oth.*, 1.i.89.

VESPER, evening, *Ant. and Cleo.*, 4.xiv.8.

VESSEL, used, as in the Bible, of the human body, *Oth.*, 4.ii.84.

VESTAL, a priestess of Vesta, vowed to chastity, *Per.*, 4.v.7.

VESTURE, *the essential vesture of creation*, that is in form, moving, action, apprehension, *Oth.*, 2.i.64.

VEX, *the vex'd sea*, in commotion, *Lear*, 4.iv.2; to afflict, *Lear*, 3.iv.59.

VEXATION, anguish of mind, *Lucrece*, 1779.

VICIOUS, mistaken, at fault, *Oth.*, 3.iii.149.

VIE, to compete with; *nature wants stuff to vie strange forms with fancy*, nature cannot compete with fancy in the creation of strange forms, *Ant. and Cleo.*, 5.ii.98; *Per.*, 4.Prol.33.

VIEW, *to my sister's view*, to see my sister, *Ant. and Cleo.*, 2.ii.171; *their view*, their glance, *Lov.Comp.*, 26.

VILLAIN, servant, *Lucrece*, 1338.

VIRTUE, *O infinite virtue*, bravest of the brave, *Ant. and Cleo.*, 4.viii.17; *thy single virtue*, your individual courage, *Lear*, 5.iii.104; *virtues*, accomplishments, *Per.*, 4.vi.182; *not in my virtue to*, not in my power to, *Oth.*, 1.iii.318.

VIRTUOUS, *by your virtuous means*, by your powerful help, *Oth.*, 3.iv.112.

VOICE, support, vote, *Cym.*, 3.v.115; judgement, opinion, *Son.*, 112,10; authority, *Oth.*, 1.ii.13.

VOLLEY, *volley out*, to discharge, bark, *Ven. and Ad.*, 921; to bellow, *Ant. and Cleo.*, 2.vii.110.

VOLUNTARY, willing, *Cym.*, 3.v.153.

VOTARESS, woman vowed to the service of, *Per.*, 4.Prol.4.

VOTARIST, one vowed to chastity, *Oth.*, 4.iii.188.

VOTARY, one vowed to chastity, *Son.*, 154,5.

VOUCH, testimony, *Oth.*, 2.i.146 ; *verb*, to bear witness, *Oth.*, 1.iii.261 ; to maintain, *Oth.*, 1.iii.103.

VOUCHER, proof, *Cym.*, 2.ii.39.

VOUCHSAFE, to condescend, *Ven. and Ad.*, 13 ; to be pleased to grant, *Cym.*, 2.iii.39.

VULGAR, *vulgar scandal*, public defamation, *Son.*, 112,2 ; common knowledge, *Lear*, 4.vi.212.

WAGE, to stake, *Lear*, 1.i.155 ; to take the risk of, *Oth.*, 1.iii.30 ; to put to the test, to try, *Ant. and Cleo.*, 3.vii.31 ; to contend, *Lear*, 2.iv.208 ; *the commodity wages not with the danger*, the profit does not equal the risk, *Per.*, 4.ii.30 ; *his taints and honours waged equal with him*, his virtues and vices were equally matched in him, *Ant. and Cleo.*, 5.i.31.

WAGGISH, sporting, frolicsome, *Cym.*, 3.iv.156.

WAIT, to attend, *Ant. and Cleo.*, 5.ii.53 ; to go with, *Lucrece*, 1006.

WAKE, festival on anniversary of a church dedication ; such celebrations began the evening before, by all-night feasts, *Lear*, 3.vi.73 ; *verb*, to give the night to revelry, *Son.*, 61,13.

WALL-NEWT, *the wall-newt and the water*, the wall-newt and the water-newt, *Lear*, 3.iv.128.

WAN'D, *thy wan'd lip*, ageing, withered, *Ant. and Cleo.*, 2.i.21.

WANION, *with a wanion*, with a vengeance, *Per.*, 2.i.17.

WANTON, *wanton modesty*, sportive modesty, *Lucrece*, 401 ; lascivious, *Ven. and Ad.*, 777 ; *noun*, playful person, *Lucrece*, 401 ; *so citizen a wanton*, so pampered a person by my city life, *Cym.*, 4.ii.8 ; an adulteress, *Oth.*, 4.i.71.

WANTONNESS, lasciviousness, *Son.*, 96,1.

WARD, one under the care of another, *Lear*, 1.ii.70 ; prison, *Son.*, 133,9 ; bolt, *Lucrece*, 303.

WARRANT, assurance, *Oth.*, 3.iii.20 ; *the warrant of my note*, the assurance of your fidelity my knowledge of you gives me, *Lear*, 3.i.18 ; *out of warrant*, forbidden by law, *Oth.*, 1.ii.79 ; in asseverations, *Oth.*, 2.iii.19.

WARRANTISE, guarantee, *Son.*, 150,7.

WARRANTY, *with such general warranty*, in the way heaven permits all of us to love, *Oth.*, 5.ii.63.

WASSAIL, carousing, *Ant. and Cleo.*, 1.iv.56.

WASTE, empty ; *these waste blanks*, unused pages, *Son.*, 77,10 ; *noun*, *the wastes of time*, what time has ruined, *Son.*, 12,10 ; the expenditure on so extravagant a scale, *Ant. and Cleo.*, 4.i.16 ; *verb*, to destroy, *Cym.*, 5.v.52 ; annihilate, *Per.*, 4.iv.1 ; *the chronicle of wasted time*, the story of past times, *Son.*, 106,1 ; *till now some nine moons wasted*, till the last nine months, *Oth.*, 1.iii.84 ; to expend, *Per.*, 1.Prol.16.

WAT, name for the hare, *Ven. and Ad.*, 697.

WATCH, sleeplessness, *Cym.*, 3.iv.39 ; guard, group of soldiers on such duty, *Oth.*, 2.iii.152 ; *watch o' th' night*, period of time, generally associated with periods of duty, *Oth.*, 1.i.124 ; *time base watch of woes*, the sentinel who neglects to warn against mishaps, *Lucrece*, 928 ; *verb*, to lie awake, *Lucrece*, 1575 ; *watch him tame*, tame him, as hawks are tamed by being kept awake, *Oth.*, 3.iii.23.

WATER, *water that doth eat in steel*, aqua fortis, nitric acid, *Lucrece*, 755 ; tears, *Lov.Comp.*, 304 ; lustre of a diamond, *Per.*, 3.ii.107 ; water-newt, *Lear*, 3.iv.128.

WATER-GALL, a secondary rainbow, *Lucrece*, 1588.

WAY, *give him way*, yield to his fancy, do not contradict him, *Per.*, 5.i.229.

WE, 'us' for 'we' ; *where shall's lay him ? Cym.*, 4.ii.234 ; 'we' for 'us', *Cym.*, 5.iii.72.

WEAL, *a wholesome weal*, a well-ordered commonwealth, *Lear*, 1.iv.209.

WEARY, *weary of all*, *shall want some*, shall want again what he has in his disgust discarded, *Lear*, 1.iv.197.

WEATHER, storm, *Cym.*, 3.iii.64.

WEB, *the web and the pin*, the eye trouble now called cataract, *Lear*, 3.iv.115.

WEED, dress, style, *Son.*, 76,6.

WEET, to know, *Ant. and Cleo.*, 1.i.39.

WEIGH, to consider, *Son.*, 120,8.

WELFARE, health, *Son.*, 118,7.

WELL, at rest (of the dead), *Ant. and Cleo.*, 2.v.33.

WELL-A-NEAR, alas ! *Per.*, 3.Prol.51.

WELL-BREATH'D, in good condition, *Ven. and Ad.*, 678.

WELL-CONTENTED, *well contented day*, the day in which I shall be well (at rest), *Son.*, 32.1.

WENCH, in affectionate talk to a servant, *Lucrece*, 1273.

WENCHLESS, without girls, *Per.*, 4.ii.5.

WENCH-LIKE, effeminate, *Cym.*, 4.ii.231.

WHARF, bank of a river, *Ant. and Cleo.*, 2.ii.217.

WHAT, why, *Ant. and Cleo.*, 5.ii.311 ; whatever, *Lear*, 3.vi.114 ; whoever, *Lear*, 5.iii.98.

WHEEL, of Fortune, *Lear*, 5.iii.174 ; *Ant. and Cleo.*, 4.xv.44 ; *go on wheels*, go smoothly, *Ant. and Cleo.*, 2.vii.91.

WHEELING, *wheeling stranger*, wandering, *Oth.*, 1 i.137.

WHELK'D, in ridges, as on the shell of the whelk, *Lear*, 4.vi.71.

WHERE, whereas, *Lucrece*, 792.

WHEREAS, where, *Per.*, 1.iv.70.

WHILST, *the whilst*, during which time, *Cym.*, 4.ii.255.

WHIPSTER, whippersnapper, *Oth.*, 5.ii.247.

WHIPSTOCK, *practis'd the whipstock*, been a carter, *Per.*, 2.ii.51.

WHISTLE, with reference to the proverb, ' It is a poor dog that is not worth the whistling', *Lear*, 4.ii.29 ; *whistle her off* *and let her down the wind*, like a falconer getting rid of an unsatisfactory hawk, *Oth.*, 3.iii.266.

WHITE, *white herring*, fresh herring, *Lear*, 3.vi.31.

WHO, whom, *Oth.*, 4.ii.100; *Oth.*, 2.iii.15.

WHOLESOME, well ordered, *Lear*, 1.iv.209; *in wholesome wisdom*, out of prudent considerations, *Oth.*, 3.i.46.

WHORESON, bastard, *Lear*, 1.i.22.

WHY, *for why*, because, *Lucrece*, 1222; *for why*, for which, *Oth.*, 1.iii.257.

WIDOW, *widow them all*, outlive them all, be the widow of each in turn, *Ant. and Cleo.*, 1.ii.26.

WIGHT, person, *Oth.*, 2.i.157.

WILDNESS, madness, *Cym.*, 3.iv.9.

WILFUL, eager, *Ven. and Ad.*, 365; *wilfully*, in spite of everything, *Son.*, 80,8.

WILL, carnal desire, *Lucrece*, 243; *verb*, *would she be*, she wished to be, *Lov.Comp.*, 251; *it will not be*, all is in vain, *Ven. and Ad.*, 607.

WILLOW, emblem of disappointed love, *Oth.*, 4.iii.27.

WIN, to gain on, *Son.*, 64,7; *win two days*, be ahead by two days, *Ant. and Cleo.*, 2.iv.9; to overcome by charm, *Lov.Comp.*, 312.

WIND, *sits in the wind against me*, has the stronger position, has the windward position in naval fighting, *Ant. and Cleo.*, 3.x.37.

WINDOWS, eyelids, *Ant. and Cleo.*, 5.ii.314.

WINDOW'D, looking from a window, *Ant. and Cleo.*, 4.xiv.72; *window'd raggedness*, full of holes, *Lear*, 3.iv.31.

WINK, *winking Cupids*, with closed eyes, *Cym.*, 2.iv.89; *Cym.*, 2.iii.23; to close the eyes in sleep, *Son.*, 43,1.

WINTER-GROUND, to protect from effects of winter, *Cym.*, 4.ii.230.

WIPE, stigma, like brand on slave, *Lucrece*, 537.

WIRY, *wiry concord*, the strings of the well-tuned instrument, *Son.*, 128,4.

WISDOM, *the wisdom of nature*, science, *Lear*, 1.ii.100.

WISE, *in no wise*, not at all, *Per.*, 5.ii.11.

WISTLY, *wistly to view*, attentively, *Ven. and Ad.*, 343.

WIT, *thy five wits*, mental powers listed like the five senses, *Lear*, 3.iv.57; *with wit well blazon'd*, their quality cleverly expressed in verse or motto, *Lov.Comp.*, 217; cunning, *Lear*, 1.ii.175; *fantastic wits*, capricious minded drinkers, *Ven. and Ad.*, 850.

WIT, to know, *Per.*, 4.iv.31.

WITCH, sorcerer, male as well as female, *Ant. and Cleo.*, 1.ii.38; *a holy witch*, a man whose goodness enchants men's hearts, *Cym.*, 1.vi.165.

WITH, by, *Ant. and Cleo.*, 5.ii.170; *are you there with me?* is that your meaning, *Lear*, 4.vi.145.

WITHAL, with this, *Son.*, 153,11.

WITHIN, *speak within door*, less loudly, vehemently, *Oth.*, 4.ii.145.

WITTY, clever, *Oth.*, 2.i.131.

WONDER, *but in them it were a wonder*, except in them it were miraculous, *Phoenix*, 32; *Oth.*, 3.iv.102; admiration, *Lucrece*, 84; *verb*, to admire, *Son.*, 106,14.

WOOD, mad, *Ven. and Ad.*, 740.

WOODMAN, hunter, *Cym.*, 3.vi.28.

WOO'T, wilt thou, *Ant. and Cleo.*, 4.xv.59.

WORD, *the word*, the motto, *Per.*, 2.ii 21; *verb*, to express, *Ant. and Cleo.*, 4.xiii.9; to recite (instead of singing), *Cym.*, 4.ii.241; to persuade, cajole, *Ant. and Cleo.*, 5.ii.190; *words him*, gives him a reputation, *Cym.*, 1.iv.14.

WORK, *the works*, the fortifications, *Oth.*, 3.ii.3.

WORK, *to work upon*, to injure, *Lucrece*, 235; *he wrought upon her*, he bewitched her, *Oth.*, 1.iii.106; to become agitated, tempestuous, *Per.*, 3.i.48; *being wrought*, having his passions roused, *Oth.*, 5.ii.348.

WORLD, *her world's delight*, her whole happiness in life, *Lucrece*, 385; mankind, *Per.*, 3.ii.108; *his little world of man*, man regarded as the microcosm, a complete universe in miniature, *Lear*, 3.i.10; *storming her world*, her little world, *Lov.Comp.*, 7; the present age, *Son.*, 81,12.

WORLDLY, *worldly task*, your task in this life, *Cym.*, 4.ii.261; *an hour of love of worldly matter*, the private hour to be snatched from his duties as soldier, *Oth.*, 1.iii.299 (*of meaning from*).

WORM, serpent, *Ant. and Cleo.*, 5.ii.242.

WORN-OUT, *worn-out age*, a time that with its loyalties has passed away, *Lucrece*, 1350.

WORSHIP, dignity, authority, *Ant. and Cleo.*, 4.xiv.86; *the worship of their name*, their honourable reputation, *Lear*, 1.iv.266.

WORSTED-STOCKING, *worsted-stocking knave*, the better class wearing silk, *Lear*, 2.ii.15.

WORTH, service of value, *Cym.*, 5.v.307; *adj.*, deserving (in bad sense), *Lear*, 1.i.279; *Lear*, 2.iv.43.

WORTHY, *worthier pen*, better poet, *Son.*, 79,6; *worthy cause*, justifiable reason, *Oth.*, 3.iii.258; *subdue my worthiest self*, since to live would be dishonourable, it is the honourable part that he will kill; honour calls for death, *Ant. and Cleo.*, 4.xii.47; *verb*, *that worthied him*, gained him credit, *Lear*, 2.ii.116.

WOT, *God wot*, God knows, *Lucrece*, 1345.

WRACK, ruin, *Per.*, 4.Prol.12; *Lucrece*, 558.

WRACKFUL, destructive, *Son.*, 65,6.

WREAK, to revenge, *Ven. and Ad.*, 1004.

WRETCH, as term of endearment, *Oth.*, 3.iii.91.

WRING, to suffer in mind, *Cym.*, 3.vi.78.

WRIT, *holy writ*, the Scriptures, *Oth.*, 3.iii.328 ; *thinks all is writ he speken can*, all is as true as the ' gospel ', *Per.*, 2.*Prol.*12 ; order, *Lear*, 5.iii.245.

WRITE, *write happy*, count yourself fortunate, *Lear*, 5.iii.36 ; to denounce, *Cym.*, 2.v.32 ; *to write for me*, to sign as a surety for me, *Son.*, 134,7.

WRONG, *wrong this presence*, offend by your behaviour this company, *Ant. and Cleo.*, 2.ii.113 ; *to wrong the wronger*, to give measure for measure, *Lucrece*, 943.

WRY, to err, *Cym.*, 5.i.5.

YARD, *a clothier's yard*, the length of the arrow for the long-bow, *Lear*, 4.vi.88.

YARE, dexterous, quick, *Ant. and Cleo.*, 3.xiii.131 ; *yarely*, skilfully, *Ant. and Cleo.*, 2.ii.215.

YAWN, as in an earthquake, open in terror, *Oth.*, 5.ii.104.

YEOMAN, freeholder, *Lear*, 3.v.12.

YERK, to stab, *Oth.*, 1.i.5.

YIELD, to report of, *Ant. and Cleo.*, 2.v.28 ; *the gods yield you*, reward you, *Ant. and Cleo.*, 4.ii.33.

YOKE, *yoked*, married, *Oth.*, 4.i.66 ; to partner, associate oneself, *Cym.*, 4.ii.19.

YOKE-FELLOW, colleague, *Lear*, 3.vi.37.

YOND, yon, *Lear*, 4.vi.18.

YORE, olden times, *Son.*, 68,14.

YOUNGER, *two summers younger*, two summers ago, *Per.*, 1.iv.39.

YOUNGLY, in youth, *Son.*, 11,3.

YOUR, often used of what is common and familiar, with no personal reference, so *your crocodile* at *Ant. and Cleo.*, 2.vii.27.

YOUTHFUL, *a youthful suit*, the love-making of a youth, *Lov.Comp.*, 79.

Y-RAVISHED, delighted, *Per.*, 3. *Prol.* 35

YSLAKED, overcome, relaxed. *Per.* 3.*Prol.*1.

ZED, described as unnecessary, since ' s ' often takes its place, *Lear*, 2.ii.59.

ZOUNDS, by God's wounds, *Oth.*, 1.i.87

INDEX OF CHARACTERS
IN SHAKESPEARE'S PLAYS

BEDFORD, DUKE OF, Regent of Fr., 1 *Hen. VI.*
BELARIUS, Banished Lord, *Cym.*
BELCH, SIR TOBY, Uncle of Olivia, *Tw. Night.*
BENEDICK, Young Lord, *Much Ado.*
BENVOLIO, Friend of Romeo, *Rom. and Jul.*
BERKELEY, EARL, *Rich. II.*
BERNARDO, Officer, *Ham.*
BERTRAM, Count of Rousillon, *All's Well.*
BEVIS, GEORGE, Follower of Cade, 2 *Hen. VI.*
BIANCA, Mistress of Cassio, *Oth.*
BIANCA, Sister of Kath., *Tam Shrew.*
BIGOT, Earl of Norfolk, *John.*
BIONDELLO, Servant of Lucentio, *Tam. Shrew.*
BEROWNE, Lord Attend. on K. of Navarre, *L. Lab. Lost.*
BLANCH OF SPAIN, Niece of K. John, *John.*
BLOUNT, SIR JAMES, *Rich III.*
BLUNT, SIR WALTER, Friend of Henry IV., 1, 2 *Hen. IV.*
BOLINGBROKE, Afterwards Henry IV., *Rich. II.*
BOLINGBROKE, ROGER, Conjuror, 2 *Hen. VI.*
BONA, Sister of Fr. Queen, 3 *Hen. VI.*
BORACHIO, Follower of Don John, *Much Ado.*
BOTTOM, Weaver, *Mid. N. Dr.*
BOULT, Servant, *Per.*
BOURBON, DUKE OF, *Hen. V.*
BOURCHIER, CARDINAL, Arch. of Canterbury, *Rich. III.*
BOYET, Lord attend. Princess of Fr., *L. Lab. Lost.*
BRABANTIO, Senator, Father of Desdemona, *Oth.*
BRAKENBURY, SIR ROBERT, Lieut. of Tower, *Rich. III.*
BRANDON, *Hen. VIII.*
BRUTUS, DECIUS, Conspirator, *Jul. Cæs.*
BRUTUS, JUNIUS, Tribune, *Cor.*
BRUTUS, MARCUS, Rom. Conspirator, *Jul. Cæs.*
BUCKINGHAM, DUKE OF, *Rich. III.*
BUCKINGHAM, DUKE OF, Of King's Party, 2 *Hen. VI.*
BUCKINGHAM, DUKE OF, *Hen. VIII.*
BULLCALF, Recruit, 2 *Hen. IV.*
BURGUNDY, DUKE OF, *Hen. V.*
BURGUNDY, DUKE OF, 1 *Hen. VI.*
BURGUNDY, DUKE OF, *Lear.*
BUSHY, ' Creature ' of Rich. II., *Rich II.*
BUTTS, DR., Physician, *Hen. VIII.*

CADE, JACK, Rebel, 2 *Hen. VI.*
CADWAL, Arviragus in Disguise, *Cym.*
CÆSAR, JULIUS, *Jul. Cæs.*
CÆSAR, OCTAVIUS, *Ant. and Cleo.*, *Jul. Cæs.*
CAITHNESS, Scot. Nobleman, *Mac.*
CAIUS, DR., Fr. Physician, *Mer. Wives Win.*
CAIUS, LIGARIUS, Conspirator, *Jul. Cæs.*
CALCHAS, Trojan Priest, supporter of Greeks, *Troil. and Cres.*
CALIBAN, Deformed Slave, *Tem.*

CALPHURNIA, Wife of Cæsar, *Jul. Cæs.*
CAMBRIDGE, EARL OF, Conspirator *Hen. V.*
CAMILLO, Sicilian Lord, *Win. Tale.*
CAMPEIUS, CARDINAL, *Hen. VIII.*
CANIDIUS, Lieut.-Gen. of Antony. *Ant. and Cleo.*
CANTERBURY, ARCHBISHOP OF, *Hen. V.*
CANTERBURY, ARCHBISHOP OF, Cardinal Bourchier, *Rich. III.*
CANTERBURY, ARCHBISHOP OF, Cranmer, *Hen. VIII.*
CAPHIS, Servant, *Timon.*
CAPUCIUS, Ambassador from Charles V., *Hen. VIII.*
CAPULET, Father of Juliet, At variance with Montague, *Rom. and Jul.*
CAPULET, LADY, Wife of Capulet, *Rom. and Jul.*
CARLISLE, BISHOP OF, *Rich. II.*
CASCA, Rom. Conspirator, *Jul. Cæs.*
CASSANDRA, Prophetess, *d.* of Priam, *Troil. and Cres.*
CASSIO, Lieut. to Othello. *Oth.*
CASSIUS, Rom. Conspirator, *Jul. Cæs.*
CATESBY, SIR WILLIAM, *Rich. III.*
CATO, YOUNG, Friend of Brutus, *Jul. Cæs.*
CELIA, *d.* of Frederick, *As You Like.*
CERES, Spirit, *Tem.*
CERIMON, A Lord of Ephesus, *Per.*
CHARLES, The Dauphin, 1 *Hen. VI.*
CHARLES, Wrestler, *As You Like.*
CHARLES VI., K. of Fr., *Hen. V.*
CHARMIAN, Attendant on Cleopatra, *Ant. and Cleo.*
CHATILLON, Ambassador from Fr., *John.*
CHIRON, *s.* of Tamora, *Titus.*
CHRISTOPHER SLY, Tinker, *Tam. Shrew.*
CHRISTOPHER URSWICK, Priest, *Rich. III.*
CICERO, Rom. Senator, *Jul. Cæs.*
CIMBER, METELLUS, Conspirator, *Jul. Cæs.*
CINNA, Poet, *Jul. Cæs.*
CINNA, Rom. Conspirator, *Jul. Cæs.*
CLARENCE, GEORGE, DUKE OF, Brother of Edward IV., *Rich. III.*
CLARENCE, THOMAS, DUKE OF, *s.* of Henry IV., 2 *Hen. IV.*
CLAUDIO, Young Lord, *Much Ado.*
CLAUDIO, Young Gentleman, *M. Meas.*
CLAUDIUS, K. of Denmark, Uncle of Hamlet, *Ham.*
CLAUDIUS, Servant of Brutus, *Jul. Cæs.*
CLEOMENES, Sicilian Lord, *Win. Tale.*
CLEON, Gov. of Tharsus, *Per.*
CLEOPATRA, Queen of Egypt, *Ant. and Cleo.*
CLIFFORD, LORD, Of King's Party, 2, 3 *Hen. VI.*
CLIFFORD, YOUNG, *s.* of Lord Clifford, 2 *Hen. VI.*
CLITUS, Servant of Brutus, *Jul. Cæs.*
CLOTEN, *s.* of Queen, *Cym.*
COBWEB, Fairy, *Mid. N. Dr.*
COLVILLE, SIR JOHN, Enemy to King, 2 *Hen. IV.*
COMINIUS, Gen. against Volscians, *Cor.*
CONRADE, Follower of Don John, *Much Ado.*
CONSTABLE OF FRANCE, *Hen. V.*
CONSTANCE, Mother of Arthur, *John.*
CORDELIA, Daughter of Lear, *Lear.*

573

INDEX OF CHARACTERS

POPILIUS LENA, Rom. Senator, *Jul. Cæs.*

PORTIA, Rich Heiress, *Mer. Ven.*

PORTIA, Wife of Brutus, *Jul. Cæs.*

POSTHUMUS LEONATUS, Husband of Imogen, *Cym.*

PRIAM, K. of Troy, *Troil. and Cres.*

PRINCE HENRY, s. of K. John, *John.*

PRINCE HUMPHREY OF GLOUCESTER, s. of K. Henry IV., *2 Hen. IV.*

PRINCE JOHN OF LANCASTER, s. of K. Henry IV., 1, *2 Hen. IV, Hen. V, 1 Hen. VI.*

PRINCE OF ARRAGON, Suitor of Portia, *Mer. Ven.*

PRINCE OF MOROCCO, Suitor of Portia, *Mer. Ven.*

PRINCE OF WALES, s. of K. Edward IV., *Rich. III.*

PRINCE OF WALES, HENRY, Afterwards K. Henry V., 1, *2 Hen. IV.*

PRINCESS KATHARINE, d. of K. Charles VI., *Hen. V.*

PRINCESS OF FRANCE, *L. Lab. Lost.*

PROCULEIUS, Friend of Cæsar, *Ant. and Cleo.*

PROSPERO, Rightful Duke of Milan, *Tem.*

PROTEUS, Gentleman of Verona, *Two Gent. Ver.*

PROVOST, *M. Meas.*

PUBLIUS, Rom. Senator, *Jul. Cæs.*

PUBLIUS, s. of Marcus, *Titus.*

PUCELLE, JOAN LA, Joan of Arc, *1 Hen. VI.*

PUCK, Fairy, *Mid. N. Dr.*

PYRAMUS, Character in Interlude, *Mid. N. Dr.*

QUEEN, Wife of Cymbeline, *Cym.*

QUEEN ELIZABETH, Queen of K. Edward IV., *Rich. III.*

QUEEN KATHARINE, Wife of K. Henry VIII., *Hen. VIII.*

QUEEN MARGARET, Wife of K. Henry VI., 1, 2, *3 Hen. VI, Rich. III.*

QUEEN OF KING RICHARD II., *Rich. II.*

QUICKLY, MISTRESS, Hostess of Tavern, 1, *2 Hen. IV.*, Wife of Pistol, *Hen. V., Mer. Wives Win.*

QUINCE, Carpenter, *Mid. N. Dr.*

QUINTUS, s. of Titus, *Titus.*

RAMBURES, Fr. Lord, *Hen. V.*

RATCLIFF, SIR RICHARD, *Rich. III.*

REGAN, d. of K. Lear, *Lear.*

REIGNIER, Duke of Anjou, *1 Hen. VI.*

REYNALDO, Servant of Polonius, *Ham.*

RICHARD, s. of Plantagenet, Afterwards Duke of Gloucester, 2, *3 Hen. VI.*

RICHARD, DUKE OF GLOUCESTER, Afterwards K. Rich. III.. *Rich. III.*

RICHARD, DUKE OF YORK, s. of K. Edward IV., *Rich. III.*

RICHARD PLANTAGENET, Duke of York, 1, 2, *3 Hen. VI.*

RICHMOND, EARL OF, Afterwards K. Henry VII., *Rich. III.*

RIVERS, EARL, Brother of Lady Grey, *3 Hen. VI ; Rich. III.*

ROBIN, Page to Falstaff, *Mer. Wives Win.*

ROBIN GOODFELLOW, see PUCK.

RODERIGO, A Venetian Gentleman, *Oth.*

ROGERO, A Sicilian Gentleman, *Win. Tale.*

ROMEO, s. of Montague, *Rom. and Jul.*

ROSALIND, d. of Banished Duke, *As You Like.*

ROSALINE, Lady attend. on Princess of Fr. *L. Lab. Lost.*

ROSENCRANTZ, Courtier, *Ham.*

ROSS, Scot. Nobleman, *Mac.*

ROSS, LORD, *Rich. II.*

ROTHERHAM, THOMAS, Arch. of York, *Rich. III.*

ROUSILLON, BERTRAM, COUNT OF, *All's Well.*

ROUSILLON, COUNTESS OF, Mother of Bertram, *All's Well.*

RUGBY, Servant of Dr. Caius, *Mer. Wives Win.*

RUMOUR, As a Prologue, *2 Hen. IV.*

RUTLAND, EDMUND, EARL OF, *3 Hen. VI.*

SALERIO, Friend of Antonio, *Mer. Ven.*

SALISBURY, EARL OF, *John.*

SALISBURY, EARL OF, *Hen. V ; 1 Hen. VI.*

SALISBURY, EARL OF, *2 Hen. VI., Rich. II.*

SALISBURY, EARL OF, Of the York Faction, *2 Hen. VI.*

SAMPSON, Servant of Capulet, *Rom. and Jul.*

SANDYS, LORD, *Hen. VIII.*

SATURNINUS, Emperor of Rome, *Titus.*

SAY, LORD, *2 Hen. VI.*

SCALES, LORD, Gov. of Tower, *2 Hen. VI.*

SCARUS, Friend of Antony, *Ant. and Cleo.*

SCROOP, Arch. of York, 1, *2 Hen. IV.*

SCROOP, LORD, Conspirator, *Hen. V.*

SCROOP, SIR STEPHEN, *Rich. II.*

SEBASTIAN, Brother of K. of Naples, *Tem.*

SEBASTIAN, Brother of Viola, *Tw. Night.*

SELEUCUS, Attend. on Cleopatra, *Ant. and Cleo.*

SEMPRONIUS, A Lord, *Timon.*

SERVILIUS, Servant of Timon, *Timon.*

SEYTON, Officer attend. on Macbeth, *Mac.*

SHADOW, Recruit, *2 Hen. IV.*

SHALLOW, Country Justice, *2 Hen. IV ; Mer. Wives Win.*

SHYLOCK, Jew, *Mer. Ven.*

SICINIUS VELUTUS, Tribune, *Cor.*

SILENCE, Country Justice, *2 Hen. IV.*

SILIUS, Officer of Ventidius's Army, *Ant. and Cleo.*

SILVIA, d. of Duke of Milan, *Two Gent. Ver.*

SILVIUS, Shepherd, *As You Like.*

SIMONIDES, K. of Pentapolis, *Per.*

SIMPCOX, Impostor, *2 Hen. VI.*

SIMPLE, Servant of Slender, *Mer. Wives Win.*

SIWARD, Earl of Northumberland, *Mac.*

SIWARD, YOUNG, s. of Siward, *Mac.*

SLENDER, Cousin of Justice Shallow, *Mer. Wives Win.*

SMITH THE WEAVER, *2 Hen. VI.*

SNARE, Sheriff's Officer, *2 Hen. IV.*

SNOUT, Tinker, *Mid. N. Dr.*

SNUG, Joiner, *Mid. N. Dr.*

SOLANIO, Friend of Antonio and Bassanio, *Mer. Ven.*

SOLINUS, Duke of Ephesus, *Com. Err.*

SOMERSET, DUKE OF, Of King's Party, 2, 3 *Hen. VI.*
SOMERVILLE, SIR JOHN, 3 *Hen. VI.*
SOUTHWELL, Priest, 2 *Hen. VI.*
SPEED, Clownish Servant, *Two Gent. Ver.*
STAFFORD, LORD, Of Duke's Party, 3 *Hen. VI.*
STAFFORD, SIR HUMPHREY, 2 *Hen. VI.*
STAFFORD, WILLIAM, Brother of Sir Humphrey, 2 *Hen. VI.*
STANLEY, LORD, *Rich. III.*
STANLEY, SIR JOHN, 2 *Hen. VI.*
STANLEY, SIR WILLIAM, 3 *Hen. VI.*
STARVELING, Tailor, *Mid. N. Dr.*
STEPHANO, Drunken Butler, *Tem.*
STEPHANO, Servant of Portia, *Mer. Ven.*
STRATO, Servant of Brutus, *Jul. Cæs.*
SUFFOLK, DUKE OF, *Hen. VIII.*
SUFFOLK, DUKE OF, Of King's Party, 2 *Hen. VI.*
SUFFOLK, EARL OF, 1 *Hen. VI.*
SURREY, DUKE OF, *Rich. II.*
SURREY, EARL OF, *Hen. VIII.*
SURREY, EARL OF, s. of Duke of Norfolk, *Rich. III.*

TALBOT, JOHN, s. of Lord Talbot, 1 *Hen. VI.*
TALBOT, LORD, Afterwards Earl of Shrewsbury, 1 *Hen. VI.*
TAMORA, Queen of Goths, *Titus.*
TAURUS, Lieut.-Gen. of Cæsar, *Ant. and Cleo.*
TEARSHEET, DOLL, A Bawd, 2 *Hen. IV.*
THAISA, d. of Simonides, *Per.*
THALIARD, A Lord of Antioch, *Per.*
THERSITES, Deformed Greek, *Troil. and Cres.*
THESEUS, Duke of Athens, *Mid. N. Dr.*
THISBE, Character in Interlude, *Mid. N. Dr.*
THURIO, Rival of Valentine, *Two Gent. Ver.*
THYREUS, Friend of Cæsar, *Ant. and Cleo.*
TIMANDRA, Mistress of Alcibiades, *Timon.*
TIME, As Chorus, *Win. Tale.*
TIMON, Noble Athenian, *Timon.*
TITANIA, Queen of Fairies, *Mid. N. Dr.*
TITINIUS, Friend of Brutus and Cassius, *Jul. Cæs.*
TITUS, Servant, *Timon.*
TITUS ANDRONICUS, Rom. Gen. against Goths. *Titus.*
TOUCHSTONE, Clown, *As You Like.*
TRANIO, Servant of Lucentio, *Tam. Shrew.*
TRAVERS, Servant of Northumberland, 2 *Hen. IV.*
TREBONIUS, Rom. Conspirator, *Jul. Cæs.*
TRINCULO, Jester, *Tem.*
TROILUS, s. of Priam, *Troil. and Cres.*
TUBAL, Jew, Friend of Shylock, *Mer. Ven.*
TYBALT, Nephew of Capulet, *Rom. and Jul.*
TYRREL, SIR JAMES, *Rich. III.*

ULYSSES, Greek Commander, *Troil. and Cres.*

URSULA, Attend. on Hero, *Much Ado.*

VALENTINE, Attend. on Duke of Illyria, *Tw. Night.*
VALENTINE, Gentleman of Verona, *Two Gent. Ver.*
VALERIA, Friend of Virgilia, *Cor.*
VARRIUS, Friend of Pompey, *Ant. and Cleo.*
VARRIUS, Servant of Duke of Vienna, *M. Meas.*
VARRO, Servant, *Timon.*
VARRO, Servant of Brutus, *Jul. Cæs.*
VAUGHAN, SIR THOMAS, *Rich. III.*
VAUX, 2 *Hen. VI.*
VAUX, SIR NICHOLAS, *Hen. VIII.*
VENICE, DUKE OF, *Oth.*
VENICE, DUKE OF, *Mer. Ven.*
VENTIDIUS, False Friend, *Timon.*
VENTIDIUS, Friend of Antony, *Ant. and Cleo.*
VERGES, Foolish Officer, *Much Ado.*
VERNON, Of White-Rose Faction, 1 *Hen. VI.*
VERNON, SIR RICHARD, 1 *Hen. IV.*
VINCENTIO, Duke of Vienna, *M. Meas.*
VINCENTIO, Old Gentleman of Pisa, *Tam. Shrew.*
VIOLA, In love with Duke of Illyria, *Tw. Night.*
VIOLENTA, Neighbour to Widow of Florence, *All's Well.*
VIRGILIA, Wife of Coriolanus, *Cor.*
VOLTIMAND, Courtier, *Ham.*
VOLUMNIA, Mother of Coriolanus, *Cor.*
VOLUMNIUS, Friend of Brutus, *Jul. Cæs.*

WART, Recruit, 2 *Hen. IV.*
WARWICK, EARL OF, Of King's Party, 2 *Hen. IV.*, 1 *Hen. VI.*
WARWICK, EARL OF, Of York Faction, 2, 3 *Hen. VI.*
WESTMINSTER, ABBOT OF, *Rich. II.*
WESTMORELAND, EARLS OF, 1, 2 *Hen. IV.; Hen. V*; 3 *Hen. VI.*
WHITMORE, WALTER, 2 *Hen. VI.*
WILLIAM, Country Fellow, *As You Like.*
WILLIAMS, Soldier in King's Army, *Hen. V.*
WILLOUGHBY, LORD, *Rich. II.*
WINCHESTER, BISHOP OF, Gardiner, *Hen. VIII.*
WOLSEY, CARDINAL, *Hen. VIII.*
WOODVILLE, Lieut. of Tower, 1 *Hen. VI*
WORCESTER, EARL OF, Thomas Percy, 1 *Hen. IV.*
YORK, ARCHBISHOP OF, Scroop, 1, 2 *Hen. IV.*
YORK, ARCHBISHOP OF, Thomas Rotherham, *Rich. III.*
YORK, DUCHESS OF, *Rich. II.*
YORK, DUCHESS OF, Mother of K. Edward IV., *Rich. III.*
YORK, DUKE OF, Cousin of King, *Hen. V.*
YORK, DUKE OF, Edmund of Langley, Uncle of K. Rich. II., *Rich. II.*
YORK, DUKE OF, s. of K. Edward IV., *Rich. III.*